Professional Prepress, Printing, and Publishing

ISBN 0-13-099744-7

9 780130 997449

90000

Other PH PTR books by Frank J. Romano:

Encyclopedia of Graphic Communications by Frank J. Romano and Richard M. Romano (ISBN: 0-13-096422-0)

On-Demand Printing: The Revolution in Digital and Customized Printing, 2nd Edition by Howard M. Fenton and Frank J. Romano (ISBN: 0-13-096424-7)

PDF Printing and Workflow by Frank J. Romano (ISBN 0-13-020837-X)

QuarkXPress 4 Only by Eike Lumma and Frank Romano (ISBN: 0-13-099770-6)

Professional Prepress, Printing, and Publishing

Frank J. Romano

with

Barry Lee
Agostinho Rodrigues
Sankarshanan

Prentice Hall PTR
Upper Saddle River, NJ 07458
http://www.phptr.com

Library of Congress Cataloging-in-Publication Data

```
Professional prepress, printing, and publishing / Frank J. Romano ...
   [et al.].
      p.    cm.
   Includes index.
   ISBN 0-13-099744-7 (alk. paper)
   1. Printing. 2. Electronic publishing.  I. Romano, Frank J.
 Z244.5.P8765  1998
 070.5--dc201                                    98-50144
                                                   CIP
```

Editorial/Production Supervision: Craig Little
Acquisitions Editor: Tim Moore
Manufacturing Manager: Alexis R. Heydt
Marketing Manager: Kaylie Smith
Cover Design Director: Jerry Votta
Cover Design: Talar Agasyan

The publisher offers discounts on this book when ordered in bulk quantities.
For more information, contact: Corporate Sales Department at 800-382-3419, fax: 201-236-7141,
email: corpsales@prenhall.com or write

> Corporate Sales Department
> Prentice Hall PTR
> One Lake Street
> Upper Saddle River, NJ 07458

Printed in the United States of America
  10 9 8 7 6 5 4 3 2 1

ISBN 0-13-099770-6

Prentice-Hall International (UK) Limited, *London*
Prentice-Hall of Australia Pty. Limited, *Sydney*
Prentice-Hall Canada Inc., *Toronto*
Prentice-Hall Hispanoamericana, S.A., *Mexico*
Prentice-Hall of India Private Limited, *New Delhi*
Prentice-Hall of Japan, Inc., *Tokyo*
Simon & Schuster Asia Pte. Ltd., *Singapore*
Editora Prentice-Hall do Brasil, Ltda., *Rio de Janeiro*

ACKNOWLEDGEMENTS

It takes an army of people to assemble a book of this magnitude.

First, Dennis Kamp.

Then, David Broudy, Charles Herrick, Althea Keough, Jens Kjaergaard, Erich Lehman, Heather Shaub, Matt Schmitt, Voraphot Vacheravothan, Kevin Willi, and Nathaniel Withers.

Plus Peter Muir, Eric Kenly, and Dave Moysey.

And, of course, Truly Donovan, the copy editor who made us all sound coherent and whose marginal notations may become another book someday.

Certainly, Robert Romano who created all the line art illustrations.

Lastly, Craig Little who juggled the schedule and this book into existence.

Thanks everybody.

Frank Romano
January, 1999

INTELLECTUAL PROPERTY

There are many product and company names used throughout this book.

To try to list all of them, or to put the trademark symbol in the text, would be an overwhelming task.

Therefore, all proper names, almost always spelled with a capital letter, are someone's intellectual property.

Please respect the rights of the owners of such trademarks.

INTRODUCTION

A president of R.R. Donnelley once said "In a corner of a printing plant in Illinois, there stands a giant printing press that once ran night and day, producing sets of encyclopedias that would line the walls of American homes. Today, it stands silently. It will never run again on a regular basis."

Overnight, the preferred medium for encyclopedias switched from print to CD-ROM. People used to pay more than $2,000 for a printed set of encyclopedias. Now they can buy a CD-ROM encyclopedia for $40—or get it free with the purchase of almost any home computer.

The advantages over print are obvious. You can search and retrieve information faster and hyperlink to related subjects. There are pictures and sound and even video. With print, a high schooler would copy the text and in the process perhaps actually learn something. Today's cut and paste does not help a student at all. If fact, the encyclopedia is moving beyond the recorded disk. Britannica is on line. All 44 million words—and it is up to date. Multimedia gives you virtually unlimited access to information.

Multimedia or digital media or interactive media or electronic publishing or digital publishing — call it what you will — has changed the way in which we present and communicate information. Much of what I see is multi-mediocrity. But the potential is enormous. When it is good, it is mindboggling. When it is bad, it is the norm. We are still in the incunabula period of multimedia.

My world is publishing ink-on-paper products. Today printing companies maintain databases, printers stamp CD-ROMs, printers produce multimedia. And by the way, they also put ink on paper or board or plastic or foil. What then is a printer? What then is the printing industry? It does not only print books. There are also magazines and newspapers and journals and catalogs and direct mail and wallpaper and packaging. 80% of what printers print is because someone wants to sell something to someone else. And 70% of what it prints ultimately winds up in a landfill.

The pundits and consultants opine that print must die in order that electronic approaches must thrive. This may not be so. Digital media does absorb some volume of the material that might have made it into print. The Adobe web site is the equivalent of over 1 million pages. But much of it is programs and information that might not have made it into print in any case. Those who say print is dead do so in newsletters. The *Wall Street Journal* described printing as a "sunset industry" a while back. They had to say it in print as well.

The key is not to doggedly defend an indefensible position in paper publishing but to look at the entire publishing marketplace and search for an opportunity to change the rules. Book publishers often miss the market by printing too many copies or too few. The frontend costs of printing were so high that a publisher could not afford to print a few and come back later to print a few more if the demand warranted it. Only 2% of the 51,000 plus new book titles printed each year ever make it to a second printing. Like my books. 50% of the magazines you see at the newsstand are thrown away.

So my industry developed a concept for taking a publisher's content in digital form and using digital processes to print only as many copies as the publisher needed in the short term. It is called on-demand printing. No inventory. No warehouse. Just-in-time manufacturing. We use ink and toner and inkjet with conventional presses and new printers. There is no neutrality in the Digital Revolution. You must become a digital revolutionary.

So, welcome to the new world of prepress, printing and publishing.

TABLE OF CONTENTS

1. Quick History of Communication..1

Jurassic Quark...1

Creative cavemen...2

Signs and symbols "pictographs" 2

Early civilization..2

Horses to holograms..3

Pictures are worth a thousand words 3

The early canvas...3

Brushes and ink..4

The woodcutters...5

Pretty money, pretty hard to fake 5

Paper trail...5

Scrolls become books...6

Movable type 8

Gutenberg and printing..8

Spread of printing 11

Letterpress problems 12

The invention of lithography..12

Return to metal 13

Printing color 14

Photography: the birth and the death of painting 14

The halftone screen 14

Automating type 16

Hot metal composition 16

Linotype 17

Monotype..17

Phototypesetting 18

Commercial success of phototypesetting..18

The arrival of Apple 19

The dawn of the Macintosh 20

The onset of laser printing 20

The print industry today 21

2. Prepress and Preparation Basics 29

What is prepress? 29
Digital defined 30
Prepress 31
Art and image origination 32
Text origination 33
Conversion of text, images, and art 34
Scanners 35
Digital cameras 36
Photo CDs and stock photography 37
Layout—designing and producing pages 37
Image editing 39
Prepress for real 41
Page assembly 41
Trapping 42
Color separation 43
Imposition 43
Output 44
PostScript RIPs 44
Image recorders 46
Digital recorders 47
The RIP 48
RIP evolution 49
PostScript printer description files 50
PostScript interpreters and RIPS 51
Output media 51
Photomedia development and processing 52
Photographic processing 53
Computer-to-plate (platesetters) 53
Direct to press 54
Concepts of proofing 55
Critical issues in proofing 57
Digital proofing 58
Bits are the building blocks of digital imaging 60
Pixels are picture elements 61
Gray levels 61
Making sense of the digital ga-ga 62
Contone means continuous tone 62
Halftones are dots of varying sizes 63

Dots refer to halftone dots...65
Halftone dot size 65
Halftone dot shape..65
Screen angle..71
Screen frequency 73
Spots are there or not there 74
Pixels are picture elements...74
Halftone dots revisited..75
Halftone dots and the imagesetter grid...77
AM versus FM screening..78
Stochastic screening 79
File management, storage, and transfer 80
Keep file sizes small...80
Storage...82
File transfers 83
Concepts of pre-flight check 84
Imaging issues 84
Dot gain, linearization, and densitometry 85
Densitometry...86
The big picture 87

3. Printing Processes...89

Relief printing—Letterpress..89
Flexography..90
Planographic printing—Offset lithography 92
Plate, blanket and impression cylinders...93
Image transfer 94
Types of offset presses...94
Printing unit 95
Dampening system...95
Dampening types..95
Perfecting 96
Inking system..96
Image transfer 97
What does offset mean?...97
Waterless offset 98
Exposure and development 99
Waterless press...99
Direct imaging technology 101
Digital Front End (DFE)...102

Direct imaging 102
Register control..103
Recess printing—Gravure...104
Press construction 104
Doctor blade..104
Stencil printing—Screen printing......................................106
Printing capability...107
Other printing processes 108
Dot matrix...109
Electrostatic 109
Laser printing..109
Thermal printing 110
Dye diffusion printers..111
Thermal wax printing...111
Inkjet printing 112
Drop-on-demand inkjet printing 113
Phase-change inkjet printing 113
Bubble-jet printers...114
Slide or film recorders 114
Ink..115
Ink drying 118
Inkjet ink 120
Toner 125
Digital presses 132
Variable data 132
Variable printing..134
Packaging..137
Traditional printing processes 138
Gravure packaging 139
Flexographic packaging..140
Anilox cells 142
Plate cylinders and repeat length 143
Multicolor capabilities...144
Reverse-side printing 145
Flexographic plates..145
Molded rubber plates...146
Laser-ablated plates and design rolls..................................147
Photopolymer plates 148
Platemounting systems...148
Mounting tapes 149

Cylinder preparation...149
Substrate and substrate influence on flexographic printing 150
Color 151
Whiteness/brightness 151
Opacity 152
Smoothness...152
Absorption...153
Gloss 153
Caliper 154
Flexographic design considerations 154
Trapping..154
Typography 155
Plate distortion and elongation 157
Halftones and screening 159
Dot gain..160
Highlights 161
Vignettes...161
Screen ruling and substrate...162
Screen angles...162
Stochastic screening..162
Step & repeat..163
Die-cutting & converting...164
Prepress output...165
Proofing..166
Packaging conclusions 168
Paper issues in reproduction..171
Runnability...171
Basis weight 172
Basic paper sizes...172
Paper grain direction...173
Why grain long?..173
Finishing & bindery..174
Dimensional stability..174
Conditioning and trimming paper 175
Cleanliness..175
Strength 175
Print quality..175
Whiteness..176
Brightness 176
Opacity 176

Smoothness 177
Formation 177
Ink mileage 178
Set-off 178
Blocking 178
Spray powder 178
Racking or traying 179
Chalking 179
Blistering 179
The digital movement 180
Digital images 180
Digital type 181
Graphical data 182
Direct to print 184
Distribute and print 186
Fast turnaround 186
Personalization 186

4. Desktop Publishing 187

Photographers 189
Tools of photographers 189
Responsibilities of photographers 190
Illustrators 190
Tools of illustrators 191
Responsibilities of illustrators 191
Copywriters 192
Responsibilities of copywriters 192
Designers 192
Tools of designers 193
Responsibilities of designers 193
Platforms 196
Macintosh 196
PC/Windows 197
Windows 197
UNIX 198
Inside your computer system 199
Computer hardware 199
CPU 200
Clock speeds 200
Expansion 201

Bus..201
Memory chips..201
RAM..202
Memory...203
VRAM..207
Cache..208
RAM extenders...208
Operating systems...208
System software...209
The operating environment...210
Windows...211
Windows NT...212
Mac System 8...212
Monitors and accelerators..212
Resolution..213
Color depth...213
Refresh rates..214
Screen size..215
Display accelerators...215
Input..215
Storage technologies..216
Data storage...217
Fixed disks..218
Removable disks...218
RAID (Redundant Arrays of Inexpensive Disks)........................219
Magneto-optical disks...219
CD-ROM...220
Digital audio tape...221
Data cartridges..222
Ablative recording..222
Phase change recording...222
Bubble forming recording..223
Dye polymer recording...223
WORMS...223
Digital Video Disks...224
Input/output technologies...225
Pen-based systems..225
Digitizing tablets..225
Output devices..225
FPDs..226

HDTV 226
File formats...227
Bitmapped file 228
Vector graphics 229
TIFF..230
PICT..235
PostScript..236
EPS 238
DCS...239
PDF 240
JPEG..240
Compression 241
File extensions..243
Discussion of file formats 245
Content creation (art and design)..249
Tending the creative flame 249
Digital graphic design and prepress 249
Creating images...250
Other ways 251
Creating and importing text 252
Computer-ready art...253
Designing and layout: combining images and text 253
Illustration programs..254
Image editing 255
Page layout...256

5. The Mystery and Magic of Color 259

Basic color reproduction theory 263
Basic addition and subtraction...263
Color imaging system 266
Great gamuts 268
What is a "gamut" anyhow? 268
Spaces, solids, models, and systems 268
Munsell and the desert island 268
RGB...271
CMYK...272
CIELAB 273
Color matching systems (Pantone, etc.) 274
Viewing 277
Standard lighting...277

High Fidelity color..278
Famous color conversions: Living on the wild side.......................279
Gray balance 279
Tone reproduction..280
Tone compression...282
Color correction..282
Image sharpness...284
Memory colors..285
UCR and GCR & UCA...287
Digital proofs 288
Pre-proofs and proofs..290
Advantages of digital proofing 290
Proofing before film output 291
Remote proofing sites..291
Registration 291
Printing conditions 292
Disadvantages of digital proofing 292
Acceptance of digital contract proofs 293
Consideration for four-process color printing 294
Influences on image quality 294
Printer maintenance 294
Viewing conditions 295
The viewing booth 296
The human factor...296
Influence of artwork borders...297
Adjustment to the light source..297
Color summary 297
Digital terminology and tips..297
Color is black magic 302
To be or RGB 303
Way back when 304

6. Image Capture **305**
Digitizing process...312
Digitizing 312
What makes a scanner?...314
High-end scanners (aka drum scanners) 316
Analyzing unit...316
Color computer 317
Recording unit 317

Desktop scanners (aka flatbed scanners) 317
Advantages of high end and desktop scanning systems 319
Midrange scanners..321
Hybrid scanners 321
Drum scanners...322
Flatbed scanners..323
How scanners work..323
PMT scanners...324
CCD scanners 325
Let's start a scan 326
Essentials for scanning..327
Finer aspects of image capture..328
What is a highlight area?...328
Using a step wedge 328
Highlight placement...329
Color casts 330
Shadow placement...330
Midtones 331
Fingerprinting the press 331
Keyness of the original..332
Color correction...332
Printing inks and hue error...333
Scanner controls for color correction...334
General color correction...334
Selective color correction 334
Detail enhancement...335
O'Brien effect...336
Under color removal (UCR)...337
Gray component replacement (GCR) 337
Digital photography...338
Static array CCD..339
Scanning array CCD..339
Resolution..340
Photo memory 340
Back to the desktop...341
A filmless world 341
Digital cameras and scanners...341

7. Finishing 343
Finishing and binding...343

Imposition...343
Imposition nomenclature 344
Register and alignment...344
Gripper edge 344
Side guide 345
Types of imposition 345
Work-and-turn..346
Sheetwise (also known as work-and-back) 345
Work-and-tumble..346
Signature imposition 347
Multiple image imposition..347
Ganged image imposition 348
Folding 348
Folding layout...348
Implications of paper grain...349
Folder types...349
Tape/knife folders 350
Buckle folders 350
Binding 350
Sewing..350
Side sewing 350
Smyth sewing 351
Perfect binding..351
Covers...352
Paper grain and perfect binding 352
Will the publication stay open?..352
Otabind and RepKover..353
Do solvents migrate?...353
Perfect binding allowances 354
Saddle stitching 354
Creep...355
Perfect binding versus saddle stitching..355
Advantages of perfect binding...356
Disadvantages of perfect binding..356
Advantages of saddle stitching..356
Disadvantages of saddle stitching...356
Inserting 357
Tipping 357
Hard cover bookbinding...357
Casemaking..357

Casing-in 358
Binding on-demand for digital printing 358
In-line and off-line finishing 359
In-line stapling 359
Hole drilling 360
Mechanical binding 360
Comb binding 360
Wire coil binding 360
Channel binding 361
In-line perfect binding 361
Press sheet sizes 362
The signature 362
Folding the job—part two 363
Types of imposition 364
2-up layouts 364
4-up layouts 365
8-up layouts 366
Imposition marks 367
Color bars 367
Crop and fold marks 367
Registration marks 368
Job information 368
Some simple folds 368
Paper 370
End-use requirements 372
Paper grades 377
Paper and printing problems and defects 377
Runnability issues—milking 379
Runnability issues 379
Print quality issues—mottle 379
Runnability factors—ink 380

8. Workflow 381
Component files 382
Consolidated files 382
Embedded elements 382
Editability 383
Embedded elements 383
Islands of automation 383
Why workflow automation? 384

Workflow design 385
Typical tasks in a print production environment 385
Preflighting 385
Color management 385
PostScript file creation 386
PDF file creation 386
Imposition 386
RIP 387
Proofing 387
Remote proofing 387
Corrections 388
Plate output 388
Blueline proof 388
Printing 389
Storage 389
Variable data printing 390
The RIP 392
RIP evolution 392
Hardware and software RIPs 394
PostScript 3 394
Extreme neé Supra and the future of RIPs 395
Working with PostScript 396
Trapping 386
Outputting PostScript 397
PostScript conclusions 398
Telecommunications 400
Data signals 401
Modems 401
Lines and connections 402
Wireless connections 405
Networking 406
Topology 407
Networking Macintosh computers 409
Networking Windows computers 410
Security 410
Servers 411
Choosing a server 411
Dedicated servers 412
Proprietary servers 412
Queue management 413

Multiple print queues...414
Network infrastructure 415
Network implementation 416
Server and client computers 417
Open Prepress Interface (OPI) servers.....................................417
Open Prepress Interface (OPI)..418
DCS and OPI...419
Document management 420
Digital ads...421
Differences between PostScript and PDF...............................422
Creating a PDF file...423
Prepress issues 424
Output 424
Workflow models...425
Color Management Systems...428
Networks and communications..428
Server evolution and integration 432
Hot folders..436
Scanning folders 437
Changing workflows..437
Print production work flow 438
The job process 444
CIP3...445

9. Publishing 455
Intellectual property 463
CCC beginning 465
Digital organizational trends in publishing...........................469
On-demand approaches 475
Magazines..476
Types of magazines..477
Size of the magazine industry 478
Behind the magazine..479
Subscriptions and newsstands 480
Advertising revenue...480
Association/custom publishing..480
Cost savings 481
The future 483
The World Wide Web 483
CD-ROM and DVD 484

10. New Media..485

Diverse kinds of information..486
Digital video..487
The changing nature of information 487
Expanding communication opportunities.....................................487
Digital libraries 487
CD-ROM and online publishing (Internet) 488
CD-ROM...488
Acceptance in the market..488
Online publishing (Internet) 490
The ability of the Internet..490
Impact of the Internet on publishing 492
Internet for business 492
Advantages of the Internet 493
Disadvantages of the Internet...494
Trends of Internet...495
Digital becomes the universal standard 496
Multimedia...498
Physical media...505
DVD: itís called a medium because it's not well done....................506
DVD technology...506
DVD-ROM..507
Re-writable DVD-R..507
DVD-R/W 507
DVD-RAM..508
DVD-RW 508
Inside the DVD...508
Codes 512
The future of DVDs 513
DVD issues 513
CD-ROM and DVD 513
Digital environment 514
The CD-ROM..514
SGML and HTML...516
The largest document...519
Reasons for interest..520
Data structure 521
Data formats..522
Text-only users...522

Other web issues 522
HTML programming 523
Style issues 523
Inline versus external images 524
External images 525
Sound 525
Video 526
HTTP 527
Data size 529
Basic structure of an HTML document 530
Creating a basic HTML document 531
What are headings? 532
Controlling text spacing 533
Paragraph tags 533
Line break tag 533
Horizontal rule 534
Creating an HTML document 534
Character emphasis 535
Logical styles 535
Physical styles 537
Other formatting markup tags 538
Preformatted text 538
Block quote 539
Lists 540
Hotlinks 543
Hotlinks concepts 543
Hotlinks in practice 544
Absolute vs. relative URLs 544
Creating links 545
Graphics 546
Inline images 547
GIF 547
JPEG 548
Placing inline images in documents 548
Image alternatives 550
Performance 551
Images as links 552
External objects (video & sound) 552
Formats 553
Size and format indicators 553

In conclusion 554
The confluence of communications systems 555
The new information developer 556
Romano's 21 rules for interactive media...557

11. Challenges 559
On-demand printing 559
Defining digital printing..559
Defining variable printing..560
Typical lengths..560
On-demand printing and publishing 560
Future on-demand 561
What is a portable document?..561
The portable document enters the market..563
The ultimate portability 563
Towards the ideal digital document 564
Design richness...564
Portability 565
Editability 566
Searchability 566
Predictability 566
Repurposability 567
Traditional methods for variable-data printing 568
Page-to-page variability...569
First-generation VDP solutions 570
Xeikon Technology: master page and variable fields 570
Adobe's PostScript forms 571
The Scitex approach...572
Scitex VPS: Variable Print Specification..575

12. Advanced Imaging 577
Raster file and bitmap file 577
Wide-format printing and processes 581
Electrostatic printing 582
Inkjet 583
Piezo drop-on demand inkjet 583
Thermal inkjet...584
Phase change...584
Inkjet ink for wide-format printers 585
Inkjet ink and substrates..586

Choosing your media...587
Quality and speed developments..591
Superwide...592
Ink-jet..593
Thermography...594
How does xerography work?..594
Dry toner/liquid toner...598
The Xeikon digital press and Indigo E-Print 1000 598
Problems of digital machines 599
Limits of toner-based technology 599
The polygon 600

13. Typography and Design 601

Design elements 604
Font issues 606

14. The Future of Communications..607

The never-ending cycle of change 607
Technology is running rampant...608
The seven pillars of new technology 608
World's tiniest transistor, or nanotransistor 610
Clock outputs up to 160 MHz..610
Superfast wonder chips 610
1000 MHz microprocessor 611
IBM disk drive technology 611
Paper-thin LCD 612
High-resolution color flat panel display 613
New TVs 613
Plastic TV 614
New 8-Bit column diver expands color depth........................614
New blue laser technique...615
Modems that handle up to 56,000 bits of data per second.............615
1Mbps digital modem technology goes beyond K56flex modems 616
Faster Internet...617
Private networks 619
The other Internet 620
The CPU advances...621

Index 623

Chapter 1

QUICK HISTORY
OF COMMUNICATION

Many of us in printing and publishing today have seen the giant leaps that the industry has taken over the past few decades. The advent of computers and digital technology has revolutionized the printing and publishing worlds and every year the industry has undergone rapid changes of immense magnitude. One is left to wonder how long the technology that we know today will last. In fact the question would be, how soon would the technology change. We live today in a world of absolute uncertainty as far technological changes are concerned.

Printing as we know it today is less of a craft and more of a science. A trip through the history of printing leads us to understand and appreciate better how printing has evolved from being a craft and emerged into a science. Of course, publishing may or may not involve printing as we enter a new electronic age.

Jurassic Quark

Okay, okay, who cares about prehistoric printing? Well, some of us grew up during those times. There really was no prehistoric printing. There was no Jurrasic Quark. The history of publishing is the fascinating story of the evolution of human communication, through drawing, writing, and pictures. It is nothing short of the combined history of art, science, and literature. In essence, it is the history of human civilization. Therefore, maybe we should start with the origins of the earth and "the big bang." But don't worry, we won't go that far. However, the suggestion that we start with the cosmos is not entirely wild. The stars and the natural human connection to time were the real beginnings of publishing and humanity's need to communicate.

To "publish" means "to make known" or to "go public." At some point in prehistoric time, people gazed into the sky and marveled at what they saw. They may have tried to show their"vision" to others, possibly by drawing marks or a picture. They probably wanted it delivered "yesterday."

Creative cave dwellers

The marks were crude. The tools for scratching or drawing were crude. Almost like MacDraw. Art was being created and "published" in 45000–25000 BC on the surface of bones, teeth, ivory, and on the walls of caves. This surprisingly sophisticated imagery was the first art movement. Right after that, art critics were born.

Signs and symbols "pictographs"

It would seem logical that the moon and similar signs would be the first type to be recorded (or published). Ironically, this is not the case. The first known published marks are combinations of: — • « and left- and right-handed spirals. Yes, the em dash was among the first. Symbols which represented God or some unseen power were used. Later, signs which look like hands and feet, the sun and moon, rain, a bird, plants, and the heart were "published." And, of course, pre-historic authors used real quotes, not inch marks.

Early civilization

In the area now around Baghdad, Iraq, the first known cities formed around 4000–5000 BC. In the same place, several thousand years earlier there is evidence of agriculture. But how does this relate to publishing? We have no idea.

The cities are where there are lots of people and they are known to work, create, sing, pray, and play, among many other things. This means more counting, more art, music, language, money, games, and inventions. People need to "go public"—to communicate their thoughts and ideas and work to others. People ultimately need to publish, orally or otherwise. The rural community comes to the city to do business, to play, and to connect and communicate. They bring food and stuff. Cities breed publishers. They do lunch.

Horses to holograms

At the end of the last ice age, the oldest known art was created. This doesn't mean that no art was created earlier. There were "wounded Bison" with surprising elements of sophisticated shading and artistic merit discovered in caves in Altimira, Spain, which were estimated at 15000–10000 BC. Around the same time, a black bull was painted on a cave wall in Lascaux, France. The oldest known carving in ivory (mammoth tusk), that of an animal, was found near Vogelherd, Germany (c. 30000 BC). The problem was running down to Kinko's and getting a few thousand run off.

Pictures are worth a thousand words

Some of us are "visual" thinkers. We picture things in our mind and are lost without pencil and paper to make a sketch. Others think on the left side of the brain. Numbers and words are the preferred way to organize thoughts. Still others are predominantly oral, and communicate by talking or story telling. Some are artists, some are technical, and all of us are in between from time to time. Sort of "middle of the brainers." This modern trichotomy has probably existed in some form in humans back to ancient times. Documents and books, even the oldest ones, often have both images and text. Pictures are worth a thousand words. Back then, accounting for inflation, pictures may have been worth a million words . . . or grunts.

The history of alphabet and language development also reflects this co-dependence of images with symbols and sound. The inter-woven history of images and words supports their mutual interdependence and co-development, as well as our inability to choose one over the other. This fascinating aspect of human nature will be a recurring theme as you read on, or stop now and remain ignorant.

The early canvas

All images must have a background on which they appear. Today we have ubiquitous paper, which we will talk more about later. Other "canvases" before paper were clay, wood, bark, leaves, animal skin, cloth, and other vegetable "forerunners" like papyrus and rice pith. We wonder if they had high gloss rice pith.

Stone—that is, the earth itself was certainly the first canvas. If you think about this philosophically, it still remains the only canvas. The next "advance" beyond stone was clay. The first evidence of movable re-usable "type" was clay. The first evidence of painting and color art was on clay and pottery. Getting a pot in an envelope was not easy.

Papyrus was made by removing the stringy fibers from the pith of the plant stalks. This was laid side by side in strips and pounded flat. Then another layer was laid across perpendicular to the first, and again pounded. The resulting "sheet" of crossed fibers was often smoothed further with a stone, bone or shell. This is the origin of "paper," and civilization (and this book) would be totally different without it. This book is pithy enough.

Cloth and animal skins also play important historical roles in printing history. The concept and use of the "screen" pattern formed by the crossed fibers is especially important. This effect is still in use today in the screen printing process. The screening effect of cloth was again used in early photography experiments. Animal skin or leather became the canvas of choice in many parts of the world. But first you had to get it off the animal. Paper finally came to be used in Europe in the 15th century, just before the invention of the printing press. "Parchment" or "vellum" was used for about 1500 years up until then. Thus the history of sheep was important . . . but we'll stop here.

Brushes and ink

Oil lamps were in use in by Sumerians in Babylon (now Iraq) by 2500 BC. Soot and "lamp black" were eventually widely used as black pigment for ink on woodblock printing in China. Brush and ink painting were known in China by 900 BC, but lacquers had been used even earlier. Oil itself was to be used in paint and ink, and was to become a prime basis for the printing processes. The connections between printing and cloth and "text"-iles is subtle. The relation to "ink" and art is the fact that textiles embody both the figure and the background for some of the most beautiful early imagery. This intricate patterned art has influenced the evolution of painting, photography, literature, and Calvin Klein.

The woodcutters

"Show me the money" may be timeless. The origin of money is of course trade and bartering. Early physical representations of money as we know it were shells and tokens. The Chinese were also the first to use paper money, which arose because of counterfeit coinage (counterfeiting is as old as currency). Around 100 BC, foot square currency with patterns impressed on special rare "white stag" hide were issued. These were big bucks. Later, in 800 AD, money was printed with wooden blocks. About 400 years later, records show that a chinese printer was put to death for counterfeiting. Rest assured that from that time on, the quality of images that were produced on paper money were probably some of the best possible. Also, they probably utilized the most sophisticated and "difficult to duplicate" printing technologies of the time. Early Chinese paper money was called "flying money" because it could be blown away. At the pub.

Pretty money, pretty hard to fake

Another piece of the puzzle in the history of fine image reproduction is that of playing cards. Again the Chinese are responsible. The power of human need to "play" and its influence on the evolution of civilization could easily be proven in the study of the history of playing cards. The woodblock was the primary means of card production, and fine artists were employed in the design of card faces and backs. The popularity of the game(s) perpetuated the production of cards and advanced many of the elements necessary for the development of printing. From found cards, it is believed that they spread to the Islamic world, and that this was the link to Europe and the west and also the link which brought paper to the West.

Paper trail

The evolution of printing can be traced back to the year 105AD with the invention of paper. Printing and paper go hand in hand. In 1931, Swedish archaeologist Folke Bergman discovered in China an example of a piece of paper dated from 105AD. The invention of paper was reported to the Emperor of China by Ts'ai Lun. This paper was made from the barks of trees, rags, hemp, and fish nets . . . a little soy sauce and a delightful duck paté.

Although paper was known in civilized Europe two centuries earlier, it was not until the beginnings of the fifteenth century that it was produced in sufficient quantity and with acceptable quality. Most historians accept that early European papermaking techniques were derived from technologies developed in Asia, although the country of origin is not so clear—China, Persia, or India. There is evidence of the use of a certain material somewhat related to paper in the fifth century when the production of papyrus was declining and the material was known as carta gossypina, and was made out of cotton. This material was more like a paper board—thick, coarse, yellow, and fragile. Copyists generally neglected it due to its inferiority compared to papyrus or parchment.

Linen paper was later used in Europe by the year 1270. Others, however, affirm that it was introduced by Arabs in the eighth century. There is also some evidence that the Moors operated a cotton-paper mill at Toledo; it passed into the hands of Christians in 1085. Spaniards improved the papermaking process to preserve the long fibers. Longer fibers gave paper much more strength. Moors also introduced paper in Sicily, Italy, and in other cities of Spain. In the year of 114 AD the first form of type originated in the form of inscriptions at the base of Trajan's column in Rome. Considered to be a fine example of Roman lettering style, it has been a great source of inspiration for type designers and letter cutters. Trajan never lived to see it.

Scrolls become books

In the period between 200 and 700 AD, many of the concepts of printing became known in China. Unlike the fame of Gutenberg, no one person or date is known. The Chinese had silk and paper, ink, and many clay and stone objects with three-dimensional relief surfaces. Eventually they found a way to combine them. There were the texts of Buddhist ideas and pictures carved on religious seals. In India, in 670 AD, images of the Buddha were created via impressed imagery. A Chinese monk visited India and saw this. It was a tour. By 700 AD in China, the objects were used with ink to transfer images and text to paper and silk. There is some debate on this point in that the Koreans take credit for putting it all together and inventing printing.

A hundred years later, the objects used for relief printing became wooden blocks which were hand carved to create the necessary relief patterns. The oldest known "works of print" have been dated to between 764 and 868 AD. Buddhist prayers were found in Japan, a scroll was found in Korea dated 768, and the most famous was the "Diamond Sutra" in China (868 AD), which is usually cited as the first book. (The scroll may be an earlier example of a "book.")

The "Diamond Sutra" bears on it the inscriptions of the date it was printed—May 11, 868. This book was found in 1907 by Sir Aurel Stein in a roll form that was sixteen feet long, one foot wide, and made up of seven sheets pasted together. This book was produced from wooden blocks, and from the quality of craftsmanship, it appeared that such a form of printing may have existed in China long before.

Use of paper was not common in Europe before the end of the fourteenth century, with the exception of Spain, Italy, and the south of France. Books at this time were seen more as a luxury object than a knowledge tool. Copyists considered vellum the only material fit for writing, and disregarded paper because it was coarse, knotty, and therefore not fitted for ornamental characters or for the use of illumination.

From the sixth to the thirteenth century in Europe, only Catholic ecclesiastics wrote books. They also controlled the libraries and taught the schools. Nearly every book was written in Latin and the predominant subject was theology. Monks played an important role on the bookmaking of this period. They worked cheap. During the fourteenth and fifteenth century, paper became more accepted. "Men of letters" began to use rough handmade paper for books and correspondence. This shows not only a change in the fashion of bookmaking, but also a change in the taste for literature. In this period, books about love, bravery, and gallantry constituted the greater portion of the non-religious literature of Europe. These changes called for new copyists, away from the ecclesiastic world, who could perform with the elegance, lightness and delicacy required for this new field of literature. The stage was set for someone to invent printing.

Movable type

Pi Sheng of the Northern Sung dynasty had invented type between the periods 1040 and 1048 AD. These were movable types that were made of clay, and hardened by baking them. Since the written Chinese language was ideographic, this form did not take off well. Had Chinese been alphabetic at that time, this invention of movable type could have written the history of printing differently. Traces of the first use of metal type dating from 1403 have been found in Korea. A set of 100,000 copper types was cast under the command of the King, and was used for printing of books.

Gutenberg and printing

Widely believed to be the inventor of the printing process, Johann Gutenberg was born in Mainz, Germany. The exact date of his birth is not known, though it is believed that he must have been born between 1399 and 1406. Gutenberg's original name was Johann Gensfleisch zur Laden.

He was practicing the art of printing in Strausberg where he had settled in 1428 after leaving Mainz. A lot of information about Gutenberg is hearsay or found mostly from depictions of him involved in some legal matter or other. In 1438, he went into a partnership with Hans Riffe, Andreas Dritzehn, and Andreas Heilmann, involving the practice of a secret art. When Andreas Dritzhen died in 1439, his brothers wanted to join the partnership, which was refused by Gutenberg. The matter went to court and the case went in favor of Gutenberg. It is from the trial of this case from that we know the craft that was secretly practiced by Gutenberg. A key witness in the case was a goldsmith, Hans Dünne who told the court that Gutenberg had borrowed large sums of money from him as early as 1436 for "that which appertains to printing." He was probably also investigated by a special prosecutor for the Justice Department.

Historians tell us that Gutenberg had a knowledge of three different arts. The first one was the polishing of stones or gems. The second was the making of mirrors. It is assumed that the first press that Gutenberg built was for pressing molding for the frames of mirrors, and the lead was therefore for this purpose. The third one, and it is not clear, was probably printing. These arts combined to provide the necessary infrastructure for developing the printing process.

The first known document printed from movable type was a 30-line Indulgence by Pope Nicolaus V, produced in 1454. This was a document that recorded the names of donors who contributed money to fight the Turks who had captured Constantinople in 1433. The document was printed for sale in two issues during 1454 and 1455. This document attributes its origin from the press of Gutenberg, Fust, and Schoeffer. It was around the same time that the great Bible was printed on the Gutenberg press. Some of the early Bible type was used in the Turkencalender, a piece of propaganda literature that was used against the Turks about 1454.

Less than one hundred copies of the Bible were printed. It is interesting to note that the majority of those Bibles that have survived the times are now in the United States. Edward Lazare in his book "Die Gutenberg—Ein Census" lists 46 known copies of this Bible, 12 on vellum and 34 on paper. The actual number of complete copies is 40 on vellum and 17 on paper. Some historians however, state that a 36-line bible was printed before the 42-line Bible, based on similarities to earlier printed works. Actually it was produced later from an early version of the font which a Gutenberg worker took to another city.

The problem with identifying the exact date of these books is that each edition was published without a date and without the name of the printer. The Bible was printed in three different font sizes—36, 41 or 42 lines to a page. In the font that gave 41 lines to a page, the ascenders and descenders were too close and it caused a breakage. The 36 lines-to-a-page version was not economical, in that the Bible needed more pages to be printed. So the 42 lines-to-a-page font became the Bible font. This version had two columns and all lines were justified. If you wondered how they managed this, they simply broke the line where the line ended, anywhere in the word. There was no such thing as Medieval hyphenation, just like some early versions of desktop publishing programs.

The 42-line Bible, often called the "Gutenberg Bible," was probably printed in Mainz around 1455. The printing of the Bible may have commenced in 1453 and been completed in 1455. The reason why there is some certainty as to the period of completion, if not the exact date, is because it was certainly finished before August 15th, 1456. That is the rubricator's date from the Mazarin Bible found as part of Cardinal Mazarin's library.

In 1455 Gutenberg was again on trial. Fust, a money lender from whom Gutenberg had borrowed large sums of money, filed a suit against Gutenberg on November 6, 1455, claiming return of the money that Gutenberg owed. A sum of 2,026 gulden, which was borrowed in two loans of 800 gulden each in 1455, plus the interest, was due from Gutenberg. Gutenberg had relied on the production and sale of the Bible as the way of paying back the money borrowed. In the lawsuit, the case was decided in favor of Fust and Gutenberg was obliged to repay the money. The ownership of the press and the equipment moved to the possession of Fust.

Fust took possession of all materials made by Gutenberg. With the materials (types, presses and books) went also the skilled workmen with Peter Shoeffer as their head. Peter Shoeffer was a very talented man who had been employed in the Gutenberg's printing office, where he learned the art of printing. It is clear that Fust would not have broken with Gutenberg if he had not a competent successor. Shoeffer had also demonstrated excellent managerial skills, and he was hopping to win the hand of Fust's daughter Christina, to whom he was married afterwards. Later, they both went on the Jerry Springer show. It is accepted that the three conspired in favor of the withdrawal of Gutenberg from the printing office and the consequent promotion of Shoeffer. Although Gutenberg was deprived of his printing office, it is not true that he was left in utter impoverishment. Due to his friendships with people with influence he could find help to open a new printing office by the year 1456. Important documents were printed in this new office, like the letter of indulgence of 1461 by Pope Pius II and the Catholicon of 1460. Most of what we know about Gutenberg is secondhand.

In 1466 due to a war between two Archbishops for the control of Mainz that ended up with the partial destruction of the city, his printing office had moved to Eltvill, a village not far from Mainz. In 1465 Gutenberg was made one of the gentleman of Adolph II's court. Nothing is known about the circumstances of his death. Gutenberg was laid to rest in the church of Mainz Franciscans. Although his merit as an original inventor was not fully recognized during his lifetime, it was never denied. The merit of Gutenberg's invention may be inferred from its permanency. His type mold was the only practical mechanism for making type for more than four hundred years.

Spread of printing

One can attribute the spreading of this craft of printing outside of Mainz to two contending and rival Archbishops of the city of Mainz. They were Adolph von Nassau and Diether von Isenberg. On October 27, 1462, they put a ban on the printing trade for the next two years. Since no more printing was done in the city of Mainz, the craftsmen were left with no income to support themselves and were forced to move to other towns. When they left Mainz, they also took with them the equipment and tools needed to print. Which is a reason why one would encounter German names in some of the earliest printed books in other countries of Europe.

After this, printing spread rapidly to other parts of Europe and books were printed in several different places. William Caxton of England went to Cologne to understand the craft of printing better, so that he could eventually set up his own printing press in London, by which time printing had spread to Nuremberg, Venice, Verona, Milan, and Belgium. Printing was no more the domain of Mainz.

William Caxton printed the *Dictes or Sayengis of the Philosophers*, the first book that was printed in England. Though originally printed in French, the works were translated to English by Earl Rivers, a friend and patron of Caxton. This was in 1477. In the fifteenth century the first known advertisement in print was printed from Caxton's press. Only two copies of this print advertisement have survived the times and they can be found in Oxford and Manchester, England.

Letterpress problems

Letterpress had been used for printing type for centuries, but little was done to improve the illustration methods. Illustrations were made by engraving either wood or copper. Engraving was a tedious procedure and required a great amount of effort to obtain good detail. With copper, the artists could achieve better quality but the printing process from these plates was very slow because the ink had to be removed from the non-image area by hand before it could actually print. Another disadvantage was that the engraving had to be done by the artist, which means that the person needed to have the ability to create the piece of art, and also to engrave on copper or wood. Printing musical symbols was another issue for the musicians and printers of that period.

The invention of lithography

During this period there were other experiments that were taking place to improve the current form of printing from movable types. One such experiment by a Bavarian named Alois Senefelder in Munich, led to the invention of lithography in 1798. Because he had to struggle to have his works printed, Alois Senefelder, a Bavarian actor, artist, and musician, was well aware of the problem of printing musical symbols. Since a great part of the revenues from the pieces he wrote went to the printer's bill, he was very motivated to find a cheaper and more effective way of printing.

Lithography was a planographic process, unlike printing from a raised surface. His invention was based on the simple chemical principle that grease and water did not mix. And both were materials that could be absorbed. Grease when applied to a stone would repel water and subsequently when ink was applied to the greasy area in the stone it adhered well to it, whereas the same ink was repelled by the other areas that had water over them. Here was a situation where the printing image areas and the non-printing areas were all in the same plane. Which is why the lithographic process is also referred to as the "planographic" process, though Alois Senefelder termed it as "polyautography." This form of printing was patented by him first in Munich and later in London (1800) and Paris (1801).

He started his experiments by engraving on copper, writing directly on the metal plate and writing in reverse. Copper was still too expensive even for his experiments. Therefore he searched for another material to replace it. He began to experiment with Bavarian limestone. He developed a retouching ink made of wax, soap and ashes to correct the many errors he made when writing in reverse.

The story goes that one day while he was polishing his stones, his mother asked him to write down a list of items to be washed. Not having a piece of paper handy, he took one of these sticks and wrote down the list upon the nearest limestone. As an experiment he etched the stone's surface with aquafortis without washing off the greasy ink from the stick. He found that the acid etched all the surface of the stone with the exception of the part covered with his writing. After several other experiments, he observed that when he dipped a gummed sheet of paper into a vessel containing water and a small amount of oil, the oil would distribute itself evenly over the parts of the writing, while the remaining parts of this paper would take no oil. He had discovered by simple observation that the moist surface of the paper repelled the oil and the greasy writing of his ink attracted it.

He now was able to print just by placing a sheet of paper over the stone and exerting pressure, without the inconvenience of etching. The image was produced from the transfer of the excess ink retained by the greasy writing on the stone.

Return to metal

Senefelder also discovered that zinc metal plates behaved much like the stones he was studying. The best lithostones were a fine grain limestone which had come from a quarry in Solnhofen, Germany. That quarry is now exhausted and lithography is now most often practiced using specially manufactured aluminum, and it still works quite well. The use of zinc and aluminum has enabled the lithographic printing surface to be curved and wrapped around a cylinder. This simple modification was a tremendous advance in efficiency, speed, and even quality of reproduction via lithography.

Lithography is a derivation from two Latin words "litho" which means "stone" and "graphos" which meant "writing." The two words together meant writing with stone. Today, lithography is the dominant printing process.

Printing color

In 1719, a painter by the name of Jacques Le Blond applied for an interesting patent in England. It describes a four-color process of printing which includes four separate printing plates, one for each color. The paper receives the ink from each one in turn. A fine grid was used for engraving the plates in order to adjust the relative strength of each color. The description of this process has many of the elements used in color lithography today; yet it predates the invention of photography, photolithography, and halftone screens, which are key to modern practical use.

Photography: the birth and the death of painting

The concept of capturing images of nature on a special canvas was prophetically described in fiction by de la Roche nearly 100 years before the actual invention. The first real photo picture was made in 1826 by Joseph Niepce, and the exposure time was 8 hours. He was attempting to develop a way to easily put images on litho stone, so he could print on tin, in order to be able to more easily engrave a metal cylinder. Printing was on his mind. Many of the early developers of photography were also working on its application to reproduction.

Later, in 1839, Neipce's partner Daguerre sold the rights a new process called Daguerreotype to the French government. The time to capture and see an image had dropped to under an hour. As is often the case, definite "firsts" are rare. Another key inventor was Fox Talbot, who made the first "negative" in 1835. This was to lead to the reproduction of photo images as we now know it, and to their practical use in printing. By the end of the 18th century, the exposure time was in seconds, flexible film was perfected by George Eastman, and the reproduction of images from nature and from artists were being "published" as never before.

The halftone screen

In one of Talbot's experiments in 1852, he was attempting to photograph a leaf. Between the leaf and the photosensitive surface he inserted a "tulle." A tulle is an open mesh woven fabric with square holes formed from the crossed threads. He noticed that the leaf image became broken up into tiny islands. The size of the islands was related to the leaf patterns and the amount of exposure in the light and dark areas. This was the beginning of something extremely important to printing: the screen.

A few decades later, two pieces of glass with many parallel lines were placed together such that the lines crossed to form a similar fine grid of square holes. This was used like the tulle to render photo images into many tiny islands of various size which related to the exposure. The result fools the eye and recreates the soft tone variations we see in nature. The screening process is essential to creating fine images with most printing processes, because usually, the processes are on (ink is printed), or they are off (that is, no ink). For example, the litho stone can have areas that like water, or areas that are "greased" and like oil or ink. There is no "inbetween." The screening concept is central to the advancement of image reproduction even to this day. The patent was issued in 1886.

The world's first book illustrated with photographs was published in 1844. (Photography is just another form of "publication.") The first photo-produced halftone screen image printed in a periodical appeared in the New York Daily Graphic in 1880. This thinking was behind predictions of the "death of painting and art" which were common in response to the invention of photography. No longer was there as much demand for realistic "copies" of nature to be put onto canvas with paint. Photography not only provided another wonderful medium for creative interpretation of nature but it did even more for the artist. The artist is now much more free to imagine and compose and execute any image in any media of choice. All compositions and subject matter now stand on their own without compulsory relative comparison to "photographic realism." The illusion of the "threat" of mass publication of art via printing (or other media) is similarly empty. The true value of works of art lies in the intangibles of the creative imagination and skills of draftsmanship. It is not diminished by duplication, only enhanced. One might even go so far as to say that "good art" is art that can be published without any fear of loss of value. Art not "published" is still in your head.

Automating type

The printers of the time were also looking at ways of composing faster. One of the notable inventions of those times and which still has relevance is the typewriter. Henry Mill wanted to create a machine that would impress letters one after the other like in handwriting, but would have all the neatness and legibility of print. It was more of an idea than a design. Although he had this patented in 1714, there is no evidence that suggests a machine like this was invented at that time.

But it was a revolutionary idea, and was picked up by many others. Notable among those who took this idea and developed a machine that came close to actually working were W. A. Burt of Detroit in 1829 and X. Progin of Marseilles in 1833. It took an American printer, Christopher Latham Scholes, to develop the "Universal" arrangement in the keyboard that we use today in the machine used to compose. Christopher is considered the father of the modern typewriter.

The commercialization of the typewriter was initiated by Christopher's associate, James Densmore, who submitted a model to the firm of E. Remington & Sons. So the first reliable typewriter was put on the market by Remington in America in 1874. Thereafter, several different models of typewriters with improvements in styles of letters, letterwidths, and one-time ribbons came about, especially after to the advent of electrical power.

Hot metal composition

The other major development in the production of type was the mechanization of the casting and setting of hot metal type. By the end of the nineteenth century, most of the setting and casting of type was mechanized. Until this period, type had been cast by hand by pouring molten lead in a letter mould. The output was something like 400–500 pieces of book-size type per hour. This was quite a small number for the foundries and they were looking at faster and more efficient ways of casting types. However the foundries themselves were a little apprehensive of any development for they suspected a threat to their livelihood and did whatever they could to sabotage the onset of mechanization.

The first mechanized typecasting machine produced 6,000 pieces of type and was the invention of David Bruce of New York in 1838. Though his machine was taken up well in America and in Europe it was not until 1849 the machine was introduced in England. This was because of the opposition of the founders (owners of type foundries). The greater need to speed up the typecasting mechanism came from the newspaper industry.

At the end of the nineteenth century newer machines were built that had the capability to control individual letter matrices, which enabled type to be cast and set simultaneously. The machine that could cast single pieces of type on the punch of a keyboard was tried out by Charles Wescott of New Jersey in 1872.

Linotype

At around this time, a young German emigrant to America named Ottmar Mergenthaler had designed a type-composing machine that could cast an entire line in the form of a slug. He called it the Linotype machine due to its ability to cast an entire line of type. Though the Linotype lacked the refinements of hand setting, it was well accepted in the industry. The first models of the Linotype machines were installed in England at the Newcastle *Chronicle* in 1889 and in Leeds *Mercury* in 1890. They became so popular that more than 450 machines were in operation in less than four years in the provinces alone.

Monotype

The other type of hotmetal composition in use at this time was the Monotype machine. It was invented by Tolbert Lanston between

1885 and 1897. This machine cast type from two separate units. It had a keyboard where the types were punched into a perforated paper tape. This perforated paper tape is then fed into a casting machine, which takes instructions from the perforated tape and moves the appropriate matrix to cast the type from a mould and a jet of hot metal. Though the idea of setting type from data on a perforated paper tape was not new (Alexander Mackie dreamed it up in 1867), Monotype's machine was the first to commercialize the idea.

Phototypesetting

The next and the final development that took place in the area of type setting was the attempt to replace hot metal type. The initiative was taken by E. Porzholt in 1896 when he attempted to project individual letters from the keyboard to a sensitized plate by using light. Though several attempts were made to improvise this technique of using light to replace hot metal, it was only after the Second World War that the phototypesetting machine became a commercial reality. Roto-photo was the first British commercial phototypesetting machine, which worked in conjunction with a Monotype keyboard and was invented by George Westover in 1948. Harris Intertype Fotosetter was the first to make an impact in phototypesetting and had its first installations in Washington at the Government Printing office in 1946. The other phototypesetting machines entering the market were Monophoto, Linofilm, and Photon-Lumitype.

Commercial success of phototypesetting

The technology of phototypesetting by itself was not embraced by the printing industry, because the economic viability of switching over from hot metal type to photocomposition was not anything much for the printer. The advantages of phototypesetting did not lie in the composition of the type itself, as phototypesetting by itself was an expensive proposition. The dominant printing process was letter-press and that was about to be challenged.

The real break for phototypesetting came with the needs of the lithographic printers. They had already been able to develop their images from plates which were created by photographic process. For their text composition, they were taking photographs of proofs that were manually composed using hot metal type. Phototypesetting these texts made their jobs a lot simpler and faster. Besides, another advantage came in the additional saving that the printers got in terms of space. The vast amounts of storage space that the hot metal types demanded were reduced drastically with the onset of photo-typesetting. Also, the phototypeset matter could be stored in the form of films that were convenient and easily reused later, unlike their hot metal counterparts.

The arrival of Apple

It is a big jump from phtotypesetting to Apple, but what the heck. One machine that has practically revolutionized the printing indus-try is the Macintosh computer. The seeds for the development of this remarkable machine were sown way back in 1976. The company which made the Macintosh computer, Apple Computer, was found-ed by two former schoolmates, Steven Jobs and Steven Wozniak. They dropped out of school and were pursuing their career in the computer industry in Silicon Valley. Wozniak designed the comput-er which came to be called the Apple I computer, and thus on April 1, 1976, Apple computer was born.

The Apple computer was an outright success. The company grew rapidly and had in 1980 a few thousand employees. Apple was being built as a company with shareholders, managers, and the parapher-nalia that goes with building an organization. However, things were not fine with Apple in the beginning of 1981. There was a saturation in the computer market which affected Apple as well.

A crucial turn of events came when Steve Jobs paid a visit to Palo Alto Research Center (PARC), a research division of Xerox, in 1979. It was here that the visions of bringing to the commercial market the powers of the Graphical User Interface (GUI) and the ability of the mouse as an input device dawned on him. On coming back he and a few other engineers worked on developing "Lisa," a project that was to redefine the power of personal computing and evolve into the Macintosh.

The dawn of the Macintosh

"Lisa" was not successful so Steve Jobs began working on the next generation. And in January 1984 the Macintosh was launched to the world. It was the first personal computer to have a GUI. Up to that point users had to type in long strings of commands to get the computer to perform a function. The GUIs were pictorial depictions of a function that told the user what operation that GUI could perform.

The mouse was another revolutionary device that came with the Macintosh. The mouse looked similar to a rodent in some ways (which is from where it got its name) and it acted as the easy way to interface to the computer. The combination of the mouse and the GUI made personal computing almost like a child's play. No more did users have to remember those complicated commands. It was just clicking on the icon using the mouse, which interfaced with the computer to execute the operation the user wanted.

The Mac (as it came to be popularly called) came with text editing programs that featured many typefaces and graphics functionality. It had the ability to interchange graphics and typefaces between files. It was not that such a capability didn't exist, but certainly not in the personal computing arena. This made Macintosh the low cost computer that performed many an operation which facilitated publishing. Soon it became the center of attention of the publishing world where it still dominates.

The onset of laser printers

With the ease of computation and graphics, publishing became relatively easier. However the publishers of the Macintosh soon encountered a newer problem. The fine graphics that they could create and see on their computer monitors could in no way look similar when printed. For the only way they could get a hard copy of their work was from dot matrix printers. These printers created text or image by aligning several dots together. Though it was a well-accepted device as far as word processing was concerned, it did not satisfy the expectations of the graphic users to give them the quality that they demanded.

Keeping up with the needs of the market, Apple introduced the LaserWriter printer in 1986. This printer operated like a copier. Some of the underlying principles on which the copier and the laser printer worked were pretty much the same, though of course for the laser printer a microcomputer acted as its front end. And in this case, the front end microcomputer was the Macintosh. The computer sent the digital data that it contained in the page to the printer. The data from the computer was charged to a drum using the principles of laser technology. The imaged (charged) drum functioned the same way as a copier did, and transferred the image to paper. The quality of the image that the laser printer provided was far superior to that of the dot matrix printer. The LaserWriter was the prime factor which made desktop publishing a reality and a big success.

The print industry today

According to research data compiled by RIT:

- In 1996 the American print industry included 52,097 establishments with 1,013,234 employees producing $132.1 billion at a total payroll of $41.5 billion
- From 1995 to 1996, printing shipments increased by 8.9% and industry employment increased by 5000
- 5% of all manufacturing employees are print industry employees
- The printing industry is the most geographically diverse manufacturing industry in the U.S.

(Note: these figures do not include inplant and corporate printing divisions and departments)

The prepress market has traditionally been composed of typesetters (typographers) and trade shops (engravers and color separators)—and some printers who provide prepress services. After 1985, enter the service bureau, a little bit of both typesetter and trade shop. The changing role of each — as well as a certain functional overlap — has created confusion as to who they are and what they do. A little history is helpful. Back in the halcyon days of handset type, every printer had to set their own type to have the metal from which to print. The first such firm came into being at the turn of the century to set type for ads that would appear in newspapers.

For illustrations, an engraver created a metal etching that was integrated with the raised metal type to produce a printable page. After the invention of the linecaster, printers were overwhelmed when the number of typefaces reached 100 (!). They divested themselves of the typesetting operation and a new entrepreneurial service was born: the trade typesetter. "Trade" meant that the service set type for printers or others in the printing trade. They actually delivered the chases of metal type pages to the printer.

At the same time, illustrations underwent their own revolution as the photoengraving process developed. A group of entrepreneurs created a service out of the beginnings of technology: the engraver or trade shop. They handled pictures, artwork, and color separations, each resulting in the form of raised metal images mounted on wood blocks. The surface was at the same height as the metal type so all images would print evenly. For those of you who have forgotten this magic number, the height to paper was .918".

The printing world was composed of printers who printed, trade typesetters who set type, and trade engravers who made color separations. Offset lithography came into use in the 1950s and no longer required a raised type or image surface for letterpress printing. What the eye could see could be photographed to negative film which was needed to make offset printing plates. However, for almost 20 years, type was set in hot metal and an inked proof was made as camera ready copy.

The trade typesetter started doing less and less work for printers and more and more work for ad agencies and art studios and businesses with art departments. Trade typesetters, in some cases, renamed themselves "typographers." Typographic services converted to film production. A few new firms were started that did camera work for printers and others and a few more made offset plates for printers.

Enter technology. The hot metal linecaster initially was used to provide the metal type to the printer. With offset lithography, a proof was "pulled" from the metal and used as "art" for the camera. The linecaster was replaced after 1970 by the phototypesetter. It had the ability to set type directly on film, eliminating the need for camera operations. Companies like AM Varityper, Autologic, Compugraphic, Photo, Mergenthaler Linotype, Star, and others supplied photographic typesetters. These machines hastened the introduction of offset lithographic printing. Once again, almost all were installed by typesetting services—and, moreover, new services were born as phototypesetting provided smaller investments than hot metal.

In 1920 there were 550 typesetting services in the United States. In 1960 there were 1,800. In 1980 there were 6,000.

The camera was also used for color separation of photographs and it was attacked by the electronic color scanner which produced film directly. Cameras were still used for art or illustration, giving rise to the term "camera ready art" or "camera ready copy." Engraving services were the first to install scanners, and shortly thereafter new services were born which bypassed any camera approach and installed scanners for all work.

In 1920 there were 380 engraving services in the United States. In 1960 there were 550 engraving/camera services. In 1980 there were 900 color separators.

All three kinds of film came together at the stripping stage to produce the flats (signatures) needed to make plates. Printers did stripping, but so did typographers, trade shops and a new service that stripped film and/or made plates for printers. The prepress market was now formed and it was based on film. Printers printed, typographers set type on film, trade shops were renamed color separators and produced color separations on film, and they and miscellaneous services did camera work. All was right with the world.

In the late 1970s the raster-based photographic imagesetter was born. "Raster" meant that it defined a page by addressing every possible dot position that could be placed on that page with a laser or other imaging system. Those dots did not care whether they created type or illustration or pictures. But this technology needed a method to convert the data from the front end system that made the page to the imagesetter that exposed the dots. That method was, and still is, called Raster Image Processing and the device or function that does it is called a "RIP."

After 1985 the page description language that became common to laser printers as well as laser imagesetters was PostScript. It demonstrated that the same file could be sent to the laser printer for proofing on plain paper at low resolution and/or to the laser imagesetter for film output at high resolution. The imagesetter was an expensive device and was initially installed by entrepreneurs who saw a new developing market. Art and design professionals who used desktop systems could create and produce pages with type and illustrations and then proof them on their office laser printer. When finalized, they could be sent to one of the new "service bureaus" that had laser imagesetters. These firms were also called imaging services or PostScript services or even output services.

They were based on the simple premise that you produced and proofed your pages and just brought them files for output at high resolution. It was a cash-and-carry business. At the beginning, with few services and few files the page rate was $10 each. As the number of firms and the volume of page files increased, competition brought the price down to $5 and $4.

As more and more page creators employed desktop systems, more and more of them set their own type, negating the need for some of the re-keying done by typesetting services. Thus, the volume of typesetting as done by prepress services was reduced and these firms either survived, merged, disappeared or became service bureaus. The net result was that the number of firms was reduced from 6,000 to under 500 in the period 1985 to 1992. Today only 230 companies have the word "typesetter" or "typographer" in their name.

It is ironic that the Standard Industrial Classification (SIC) for typesetting services—2791—is now used by service bureaus and desktop publishing services. Thus it appears that the number of typesetting services actually grew in the last decade, when in fact a new breed of service essentially replaced them. The 1991 census reported 2,513 firms and 1996 data reported 3,372. The 1992 number represented a drop of 31% from the 1987 census. After 1992 other firms were categorized in SIC 2791 and thus comparison with the past becomes difficult. There are about 26,000 employees in this category as of today, with about 300 having 20 employees or more.

Most of the surviving typesetting services installed imagesetters and became service bureaus, but the service bureau part of the business was not as profitable as traditional typesetting. Some typesetters offered other services, such as electronic art and design, screen printing, and color proofing. They sought new technology that would allow them to provide value-added services.

Nor were the color separators immune from the relentless march of technology. Their expensive color scanners eventually had competitive counterparts on the desktop. Over a decade, scanners dropped from $500,000 to $250,000 to $85,000 to $41,000 to about $20,000. Desktop scanners with excellent quality are under $1,000. The volume of color separations was divided up between the high-end scanners with sophisticated color systems and the desktop level scanners and systems. As the desktop scanners increased in capability, the percentage scanning volume for the desktop increased.

Color separators are also struggling to keep pace with digital photography, which negates the need for a scanner. Kodak's PhotoCD tried to make color labs into color separators. With digital photography growing at a rapid rate and with evolving developments, there are new threats to the traditional color separator. Today there are about 800 color separation services. SIC 2796 is called "Platemaking Services" and it includes an agglomeration of color separators, film services and platemakers to the trade. The total number of firms dropped from 1,678 to 1,206. About 600 firms have 20 or more employees. Today, there are about 5,500 prepress services. This is half of what it was a decade ago.

Service bureaus began to install desktop scanners to compete for a part of the color separation market. To remain competitive, the color separators added high-end color makeup systems and linked RIPs to the film recorders attached to their scanners or installed high-quality imagesetters. Thus, the difference between firms in SIC 2791 and in 2796 is almost none.

Buyers of imaging services or color separation services also installed color printers so that they could proof their pages in color prior to sending them to the service bureau or color separator for output. They were already using desktop drawing and painting programs to create electronic artwork—computer-ready art instead of camera-ready art. They added low-end scanners to do comps and dummies.

To complicate matters even more, these customers of the service bureaus and color separators installed better scanners and printers and imagesetters and even higher-capacity digital color printers. These firms included art and design services, inhouse departments, publishers, and even printers. They acquired the devices and systems to scan their own color and output their own film. Then some of them started taking files from other companies, effectively competing with true prepress services.

Today, some prepress services are offering art and design services to compete with art and design services that are offering prepress services. To summarize:
- most service bureaus are doing color separation work
- most color separators are doing service bureau work
- many printers are doing some of each
- some prepress services are doing printing, especially digital printing
- many art and design services are doing prepress
- everybody is doing some art and design

Enter technology, yet again. A laser imagesetter that outputs a large sheet of film with all pages imposed in the correct orientation and order is called an "imposetter." It eliminates the stripping process.

The first of these machines were installed in commercial book printers because they were limited to black and white work. Now they are all oriented for color output. By 1994 imposetters had evolved into computer-to-plate systems. Where will these devices be installed? It is predicted that they will go to the printer as we go full circle—back to prepress and press functions within the same organization. With digital proofing, such devices could be installed in customer offices for remote proofing.

For every platesetter that is installed, one or more imagesetters are not being installed. Although film use is high, mostly because of these reasons, it will over time decline:

1. More color printing has increased the number of pieces of film required for platemaking.
2. Large-format and drum-based imagesetters have slightly more waste than capstan-based imagesetters.
3. The economy over the last three years has increased printing volumes.

It may take a decade, but computer-to-plate, on or off press, and digital printing will reduce film volume. Will there still be prepress services? Of course. Not every printer will install their own prepress, so there will still be the need for trade services. Creative services will still want to deal with a prepress organization independent of a printing company.

Enter technology, ad nauseum. A digital printer, like the Agfa Chromapress, takes PostScript files directly, images pages of type, pictures, illustration, and color, prints them on paper, and, with proper peripherals, outputs completed units. It negates the need for film and plates. It is designed for short run, on-demand printing. Who will use it? Quick printers are printers who have a retail, while-you-wait orientation. They were the first to apply copiers, black and white and, after 1988, color. They would seem to be natural adopters of digital printers, although the first of the breed are expensive, perhaps forcing the technology into the printing establishments. Most of the buyers of digital printing have been prepress services.

What happens when a prepress service installs a digital printing press? Are they then a printer? Is a printer who installs prepress, a prepress service? This is happening and it is blurring the lines between traditional definitions within our industry.

As more and more of the creators and producers of pages adopt desktop computers, the pool of pages in standardized electronic form will increase, forcing all services within the printing and publishing industries to deal with those files. Today over 80% of all pages are in digital form.

We are now seeing the technology for scanning bring prices down and bring quality up, coupled with digital photography. Color pictures will be more accessible to more people in electronic form for print and non-print requirements. As new forms of information dissemination in non-print form evolve, from on-line services to CD-ROM to DVD-ROM to the World Wide Web, some volume of printing may be affected. Digital printing may have an effect as well.

All of these developments and more will continue to change who we are as an industry and what we do for customers. Eventually, it will come down to the very name for our industry. Are we still going to be printers or is there a better word or words for what we will do in the future? Prepress, you see, is only the tip of the iceberg called change. And our industry could be like a great ocean liner, propelled through the cold, dark sea for an inevitable collision with the future.

Chapter 2

PREPRESS AND PREPARATION BASICS

Those who have read the history of printing in chapter one, congratulations. For all of you who skipped (more or less) forward to here, welcome. We'll try hard to keep this chapter as simple as possible. However, the cruel fact remains that good successful prepress and print reproduction are not always simple. Usually, both can be explained without having to resort to rocket science but there is good deal of technical information to absorb.

What is prepress?

Any work done prior to a printing job, printed on a press or a printer, is technically called prepress. This means anything from artist's thumbnail sketches, to photo transparencies (chromes), to the imaging of the printing plates. This is the conventional meaning of the word. A more comprehensive modern definition would need to include work which may never reach a conventional printing press. It might be printed on a direct digital printer, or used to create an interactive CD, or it might go into cyberspace as a web site. The term "prepublishing" has been used for any of the work leading up to any form of reproduction or information dissemination. So has the term "preparation." But, prepress has been around for a long time and the term is still used more than any other. Just think of a press as any form of information dissemination.

This chapter will introduce you to a number of technical prepress topics that will be dealt with in more detail later. This means that we will be discussing science, and even some math. So hang on, and try to refrain from returning the book to the store. We promise we'll stay away from rocket science.

We believe that people usually get lost in printing and publishing due to lack of understanding of the new technology, and there is an overwhelming amount of it. We have absolutely no doubt that if you have experienced this "lost" feeling, you were not alone. The industry is full of frequent far flung flinging of fancy terminology, with precious little in the way of explanation.

Digital defined

Today, most images are produced or enhanced "digitally" using computers. In the past, all text and images were created using photographic and mechanical production methods. With the advent of computers in the printing industry, the creation of text and images also became "digital." A digit is just a number (like counting on your fingers). Digits are the fundamental basis for digital imaging. At its most basic level, a computer uses binary digits. It *understands* every input given to it in terms of "Yes" or "No" using the binary digits "0" and "1."

Digital has two other aspects that pertain to this new world:

- Almost all material destined for reproduction or dissemination now must be in digital form—that is, in the form of a digital file.
- Almost all material reproduced or disseminated is done via spots, dots, and pixels, whether that material is output on paper or viewed on a computer monitor from recorded media or over the Internet.

In the early days of painting, artists needed to know many of the details about the chemicals, pigments, paint formulas, and other technical aspects of their craft. This is not as true for the artists of today. Art supply specialists make their careers engineering supplies for artists; and now artists are more free to just be creative. The inks and colors of today's digital art images are essentially numbers or digits. They work behind the scene as you use the mouse to pick and choose functions and effects. But overall, the computer is simply another tool, just a more complicated one. Eventually, the computer will be as friendly a tool to an artist as a paint brush.

Prepress takes place after the creative process and before the "press." Today the press can mean any form of reproduction or any method of information dissemination. All require that the information is prepared in some manner for dissemination to an audience.

CREATE

Over time, and especially with the introduction of desktop publishing in 1985, the creative and preparation phases are merging.

PREPARE

If print is the dissemination method, some form of proof will be required to verify fidelity to what was created when it is finally printed.

PROOF/PRINT

DISSEMINATE

Dissemination can be anything from mail to the World Wide Web.

Prepress

Prepress is not one process; it is several processes. Prepress encompasses these major phases:

The creative phase
- art origination
- text origination
- design and layout of pages/documents

The preparation phase
- conversion of text, images, and art to digital formats
- placement of visual elements into pages/documents

The dissemination phase
- output to film or plate for ink-on-paper print
- output to toner or inkjet printing or other digital printing
- conversion to electronic publishing for dissemination

Each phase is made up of many steps but ultimately any of the information you want to disseminate to some audience must pass through at least a few of these phases. You can combine some of the phases, especially some of the creative and preparation tasks.

Art and image origination

Art (or all information) may be created in one of two forms:
- Analog
- Digital

Analog art creation involves pen and ink, watercolor, oil, or other methods that use phyical media to render art or images. All analog art must be converted into digital form for prepress and production use. Although a few printers still use graphic arts cameras and film, the overwhelming trend is digital. Art, illustration, or images may be created digitally or converted from analog form. Digital art creation involves:
- drawing programs, which are vector- or line-based
- paint programs, which are pixel- or bitmap-based
- imaging programs, which are pixel- or bitmap-based

Drawing programs are vector-based, which means that the computer artist is using lines and strokes to create a line art illustration on the screen. Those lines and strokes are like little electronic rubber bands, which allows the drawing to be sized, skewed, or manipulated without a loss in quality during output at different resolutions. The most common programs are:
- Adobe Illustrator
- Macromedia FreeHand
- ClarisDraw
- CorelDraw
- Deneba Canvas

Many are derived from the concepts in MacDraw back in 1984. Imaging programs, on the other hand, are pixel-based, and provide a method more like painting with brushes and color. Programs are:
- Adobe Photoshop
- Corel Photo-Paint
- Fractal Design Painter
- Live Picture
- Macromedia xRes
- Micrografx Picture Publisher

Eventually both kinds of art become spots, dots and pixels, but vector art can be sized (made smaller or larger) without any affect on quality, where pixel-based images are usually created for a fixed resolution. Think of vector art as created with lots of little elastic strokes defining the lines. They can stretch or contract but still keep the clean edges and curves. Think of pixel (or bitmap) art as bathroom tiles. Once down you cannot make the image area bigger for a bigger bathroom without tearing them up.

The term "graphics" encompasses art, image, illustration, tint, and other visual elements, but not type, although type could be a graphic element as well. Art and images may be created on screen or they may be captured from reflective or transmissive physical originals and then manipulated on screen. The capturing is done via scanners or digital cameras. In either case, the result is an electronic file which is then imported into the page layout program.

Text origination

You have two options for acquiring text for your jobs:
- entering text in a word processing application and converting or importing it to your page assembly program
- copying text from other electronic files
- using an OCR scanner to capture text that is in hard copy form (an old book, for instance that does not have a digital file)

The word processing application is used to enter, edit, and partially format text. Most word processors have basic type control. Because a word processor doesn't have all the page layout and typographic control features, you usually can type faster. Formatting text can really slow you down. The most important feature of a word processor is that it can save documents in a format that can be read and imported into a page layout application. Most word processors allow you to format text directly or create tags to define formatting, and some even let you create tables of contents or index tags. If the page layout application can import the file with formatting and tags included, you can save time. Most word processing applications now support the following:

- text input and formatting
- page layout
- document layout
- graphics conversion and placement
- editing of text
- file management
- collaboration among authors (on some)
- compatibility with your page layout application

Microsoft Word and Corel WordPerfect are commonly used word processors. Some users even type right into their page layout program, such as QuarkXPress or PageMaker.

This is a good place to tell you that the word processor should be used as a word processor, not a layout program. We realize that for text-only documents, or those with minimal images, the word processors are pretty good. But high-end page layout programs have more tools for document assembly and layout control and they have much better typographic functionality. As word processors evolve, they will probably acquire more sophisticated typographic tools.

Conversion of text, images, and art

In this phase of the prepress or preparation process, you need to gather the building blocks of your page and document—text, graphics, and images—and put them into digital form. To acquire images you can use one or more of the following:

- scanners
- digital cameras
- PhotoCD
- stock photography

This step is required when the art or image is not already in digital form and must be converted into the zeroes and ones. As more digital photography is applied, there will be less reliance on this step. However, even if everyone on earth used a digital camera, there is still a very large archive of analog photos and images that will still need conversion to digital form.

The text and graphics then get combined at the design and layout stage of the prepress process.

Scanners

A scanner takes an image—photographic print, 35mm slide, 4x5 chrome or transparency, or black-and-white line art—and using a light source to illuminate every possible spot on the image, electronically records the amount of light reflected and converts that information into binary data to store the image data in a computer as a set of numbers. The type of scanner you need depends on the types of originals to be scanned. Depending on your originals, you can use a drum, transparency, or flatbed scanner, or a combination of them, since drum scanners handle all reflection and transmission materials, and fladbeds have adaptors for transmission materials.

Flatbed scanner

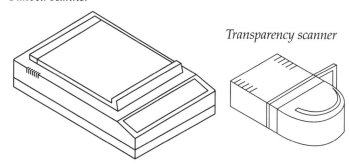

Transparency scanner

Drum scanner

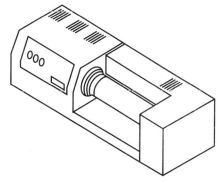

Drum scanners are the most versatile and scan both refective and transmissive originals. Reflective means print; transmissive means slide or chrome or even film negative. Scanners come with control software, and some have sophisticated color editing and manipulation tools. Some are controlled by plug-ins which run with image manipulation software.

Scanners use two types of image capture technology:
- PMT (photomultiplier tube)
- CCD (charge-coupled device)

For both technologies, the scanner divides the original image into a square grid of millions of very small cells. Each cell in the grid represents a spot on the original and is assigned a number, based on the main color in that cell reflected off or through the original, using red, green, and blue light values (or gray values for black and white images). The result of this scan is called a bitmap, which has a value for every spot on the image. This value represents the amount of the color for that spot.

Digital cameras

Digital cameras combine cameras and scanners into one device. Instead of taking a photograph as we know it, developing it, and scanning the print or slide to electronically record a bitmap of the image, digital cameras capture and store the bitmap directly in memory. The captured image may be immediately stored on a disk or memory system of some sort for later transfer to a computer, or the camera may be directly connected to a computer and transfer the image as the picture is taken. All digital cameras are of two styles:
- integrated digital camera—all in one unit
- scanning back on existing analog camera

Digital camera with scanning back

The digital camera captures and stores images digitally. Scanning backs connect to standard film cameras and replace the film exposure area. The camera takes the photo; the scanning back converts the visual image into electronic format. Scanning backs are designed to be connected to specific cameras from selected manufacturers. There are low-end and high-end digital cameras based on quality. For reproduction in print, high-end cameras are required in order to provide enough data for quality photo reproduction on press.

Photo CDs and stock photography

Kodak initially introduced PhotoCD as a consumer product to let you view pictures on your computer or television. You took photos on film but when the film was developed, it was scanned for you and the images were stored on a compact disk. It was not successful for home use but has seen application in prepress. A single CD can contain up to 100 photographs in YCC (a color system based on hue, saturation, and brightness with the color information for best viewing on a computer monitor or TV screen). Graphics applications, including Adobe PhotoShop and QuarkXPress, read the PhotoCD image format and import images directly. PhotoCD images are composed of five or more quality levels of the same image and users select the specific quality they need.

The advent of digital imaging has seen an explosion in stock photography images. The Internet is now a catalog of pictures that may be ordered electronicaly and downloaded immediately in the format you select for inclusion in either your print or electronic page and document. This is a growing area.

Layout—designing and producing pages

All information must be designed in order to be presented in a cohesive and understandable form to an audience. Sometimes, this step is called informtion formatting. This step starts just as images and text are being completed, but not always. Graphic designers usually sketch a rough version first. There are two or three of these rough versions and the following levels of visual presentation for review and approval:

- thumbnail—pre-creative stage
- comprehensive (or comp)—creative stage
- pre-proof—production stage
- proof—color or imposition—production stange
- contract proof—reproduction stage

A thumbnail is usually a small black-and-white rendition, drawn by pencil or pen, perhaps even by computer, but always showing the general orientation of the piece, the position of graphics, and perhaps display type, key images, and the company logo. At this stage the designer tests their concept and may indicate alternative approaches. During this stage, the creative professional is seeking a design concept, unifying visual theme, or graphic approach. The thumbnails are usually only for the designer and are rarely shown to the client.

A comprehensive is the next step and it is a more detailed version showing color, images, and type. At this stage the designer has finalized the creative stage and presents the piece to the client. They may have immediate feedback for changes or the comp is left with the client and the designer awaits approval or changes from the client, which is why they made a comp. Most comps are output from the layout program. This allows changes to be made much faster.

A pre-proof is the final version before the job goes to the prepress service or printer. It is output from a color printer and usually pasted together to look more or less like the final version. It is the final version for approval and sign-off by the client. There may still be some changes at this stage.

A proof is made by the prepress service or printer from film or digital file. It is a close approximation of what the color and trim and other aspects will be when the piece is printed. Changes are possible but charges apply. There are two kinds:
- color proof
- imposition proof

A color proof must show fidelity to the final output process. An imposition proof, sometimes called a blue line or salt print, shows the orientation of all pages and is usually folded and cut into a facsimile of the final piece. It may be output on a desktop inkjet printer or higher-end color printers using electrophotography or dye sublimation.

A contract proof is prepared by the printer as an expectation of what the final printed version will look like. Changes at this stage are extremely expensive and often delay the job.

Image editing

After capturing an image by scanning or digital photography, you need to prepare the digital image for use in the layout. Very rarely can you use a scanned or digitally shot photo without editing. To prepare the image for use, you may need to do one or, most often, several of these tasks:

- sizing and cropping
- clean up artifacts in the image
- curves adjustment
- resampling
- tone compression
- cast removal
- unsharp masking
- UCR/GCR
- digital retouching

You perform these tasks using a photoediting application, such as Adobe PhotoShop, Live Picture, or others. Key functions include:

Sizing and cropping. After scanning an image, you need to crop the image and resize it as required. By getting rid of unneeded areas of the image, you save disk space and processing time because the application can save and make color separations faster, and the workstation does not need to transmit unused data. You can crop and resize the graphic either when you scan it or afterward in photoediting applications. We do not recommend resizing in the layout program, although it is done. Make the image size just a hair larger than the box in which it will be placed.

Resampling. Original scans performed at a resolution two times the line screen may result in more data than is necessary to reproduce the image on a printing press or digital printer. Excess data means more storage space and longer processing times for everything from workstation response to RIP performance. You can resample the image to bring the size down while retaining the quality desired. Generally, a 1.5-to-1 resampling ratio produces very good results under most offset lithographic printing conditions.

Tone compression. Density range, the difference between the highlight point (light area) and shadow point (dark area) of the original image, is measured with a densitometer on a scale of 0.0 to 4.0—white to black. A transparency that measures 0.4 at the highlight point and 2.8 at the shadow point has a density range of 2.4, the difference between the two values. The density range of good quality desktop scanners is about 3.9, so you can usually scan the image and retain the density range. The best offset presses have a maximum density range of about 1.8. You need to compress the tonal range to conform to the density of the printing press, or you will not accurately reproduce the image. Photoediting applications lets you create a custom tone curve to compress the tonal range as necessary for reproduction.

Cast removal. Color casts occur in original prints, slides, and transparencies for a variety of reasons because certain films from certain film manufacturers have certain overall casts, and duplicate slides made from those originals could produce a yellow or other cast, indoor film shot outdoors could produce a blue cast, outdoor film shot indoors could produce an orange cast, and fluorescent light could produce a green cast. These casts have to be removed in order for the image to reproduce successfully. Most color or photo editing programs allow you to make adjustments to individual colors as well as equally to all colors or colors in an area.

UCR/GCR. Undercolor removal (UCR) and gray component replacement (GCR) are two methods used in the prepress process to replace the gray components of an image that are cyan, magenta and yellow, with black ink. The largest concentration of gray components in an image is usually found in the shadow (dark) areas. UCR removes the under colors—cyan, magenta, and yellow—in the neutral shadows and replaces them with black. GCR, on the other hand, replaces gray components with black throughout the whole image, in both the neutral areas and the desaturated colors. By replacing the process color inks with black, you use more black ink or toner, rather than colored inks or toners, and reduce the overall amount of ink applied to paper, and thus reduce drying and ink trapping problems on the press or even on the printer.

Unsharp masking. When an image is transferred from the original print or transparency through the reproduction process, the overall sharpness is often reduced and a correction known as unsharp masking is performed. Unsharp masking is the enhancement of the differences between light and dark areas of an image which results in a sharpening of the edges. The eye picks up these differing tones and reads them as sharp edges. The term is not helpful in that the function actually sharpens the image.

Digital retouching. Images frequently need to be retouched to clean up certain visual problems or to achieve special effects. You may want to remove a blemish in the original image or you may want to change the color of a model's eyes to match their dress.

Prepress for real

Once you have all the text and graphics, you need to combine them into the final pages, then prepare that document for output to a proofer, film imagesetter, digital printer, or platesetting system. In this phase of the prepress process, you will perform these functions:

- page assembly
- trapping
- color separation
- imposition

Some applications can perform more than one of these tasks.

Page assembly

You use a page layout application to define how the job should look: page size, image area, folio (page number) placement, column widths, typographic styles, and more. For some jobs, you can design a template that defines these items, then you import the text, created by a word processing program, and flow it into the template. The template or master document layout allows you to reuse standard formats so you don't need to recreate them for each job that has a similiar layout. For ads and other types of one-of-a-kind jobs, you can create new layouts for each job. Style sheets allow you to store repetitive typographic formats for reuse.

You also import (some applications say *place*) graphics, whether they're halftones or line art illustrations. Once all the elements have been placed, you make typographic refinements to make everything fit and look the way you want it, then proof the layout on a printer. The two most popular page layout programs are Adobe PageMaker and QuarkXPress. Both page layout applications initially ran on Macs, and are now available for PCs, where for years Ventura Publisher (now Corel Ventura) was the dominant layout program. Adobe FrameMaker is another layout application that incorporates word processing, illustration, and page layout tools in one application. FrameMaker runs on PC, Macintosh, and UNIX platforms and has made its mark as a tool for producing long technical documentation.

Trapping

In color printing and prepress, trapping is the adjusting of overlapping color areas to account for misregistration on the press. Typically light colors are slightly spread or choked in relation to darker colors. For example, when printing light yellow letters on a dark blue background, you spread the yellow into the blue; the blue background maintains the sharp edge of the letter. However, when printing dark blue letters on a light yellow background, you choke the yellow background into the blue; the blue of the letter maintains the edge.

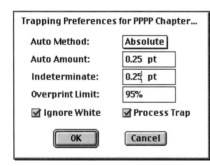

Application-level trapping preferences setup

To set your own traps, you can work within the application program or you can use a dedicated trapping program. If you trap within the application, do it as early in the process as possible. QuarkXPress, Adobe Illustrator, and Macromedia Freehand offer tools for trapping, but you need to understand how the tools work and how the applications interact. For instance, if you import an Illustrator drawing into your Quark file, you cannot use the Quark tools to trap objects in the drawing. You must perform the trapping within the original Illustrator file.

You can avoid applications-level trapping with a dedicated trapping program such as Luminous TrapWise or DK&A Trapper (formerly Island Trapper). These programs interpret color data in the job file and automatically apply chokes and spreads. Automated trapping produces professional results more easily and with fewer pitfalls than manual trapping within the application program.

Color separation

After image editing, page layout, and trapping is done, the document must be separated into its cyan, magenta, yellow, and black components. From QuarkXPress or Adobe PageMaker, you can simply select a checkbox in the *Print* dialog to output color separations. You can also use a stand-alone application.

Imposition

Imposition means the arrangement of pages on a large press sheet so that when folded the pages read consecutively. How you arrange the pages on the sheet depends on the sizes of the press sheet and the pages, and how the job will be folded and bound. For presses that don't print both sides of the paper in one pass (simplex rather than duplex or perfecting), the printer needs to refeed the printed paper through the press to print the flip side. The pages on the plate need to be arranged in the correct order so that when the paper is flipped, the correct back pages print on the back of the front pages (that is, page 3 prints on the back of page 4 and not on the back of page 1).

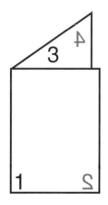

A 4-page imposition at left

An 8-page imposition below

Two Identical Units

Output

The output phase of production includes plain-paper proofing for layout, digital color proofing of images and layout, photographic output of film negatives, and analog or off-press color proofing of the film negatives. Specialized devices have been developed for these tasks: black-and-white laser and inkjet printers for layout and typographic proofing; color printers for digital color comps and proofs; high-resolution, high-accuracy film recorders for film negatives, and press-accurate color proofing systems for proofing color separations.

- PostScript RIP (Raster Image Processors)
- film imagesetter
- screening
- platesetter
- proofing
- photomedia processor

Today, there are two steps: RIP the file and output to an imager.

RIP

IMAGING ENGINE

Every imaging device today must have a Raster Image Processor to produce the page bitmap which drives the imaging engine to actually make marks on the film, plate or paper.

PostScript RIPs

A RIP (Raster Image Processor) works with PostScript code. The PostScript page description language communicates the appearance of text, graphical shapes, and bitmapped images to output devices with a PostScript interpreter. PostScript has become a dominant factor in the printing industry because of its device and resolution independence. Device independence means that the image (the page to print or display) is defined without reference to any specific device features (printer resolution, page size, etc.). A single page description can be used on any PostScript-compatible printer—from a 600 dpi laser printer to a 3,000+ dpi imagesetter or platesetting system or even a high-speed digital printer.

Most applications that can print to a PostScript printer also let you print to a file. Printing to a file means that the application (or the computer running the application, with the help of a PostScript driver) converts the job data to PostScript commands and saves it as a file instead of transmitting the code to a printer. With a PostScript file, you can download that file to any PostScript printer to print the file.

Printer

Destination: ✓ **File**

Downloading is different from printing in that no data conversion (from job data to PostScript) takes place, the file is merely sent to the printer. Most computer platforms have a variety of PostScript downloaders. The PostScript code contains all data, fonts, and images.

RIPs may be built around an Adobe core RIP capability, like CPSI, or a different PostScript interpreter. All RIPs supposedly will support the standard PostScript commands but this should be verified if possible. RIPs are configured for many common platforms, such as Macintosh, Power Macintosh, Windows NT, DEC Alpha NT, and Sun SPARCstations. Each RIP vendor has its own user interface and output device drivers. The user interface is how you tell the RIP how you want your jobs output: you want to use 3,000+ dpi, produce a negative image, emulsion down, have pages automatically color-separated, and have the image recorder punch each page.

The end result of RIPping is a bitmap—a grid of spots represented as numbers for everything on the page. For color work, there are two or more bitmaps for each page. The bitmap is what is sent to the recording engine to make film, plates, or to print digitally.

The RIP uses the device driver to communicate with the actual output device. Communication involves more than just transmitting the raster data; it also includes transmitting instructions such as changing the resolution or specifying another function and receiving status information back from the recorder.

Image recorders

An image recorder records marks; it puts marks on a substrate, whether film, or plate, or paper. Marks make up images which can be text, line art, or halftones. Most recorders use a laser beam to make a mark on photographic or other media. An imagesetting system includes an image recorder and a RIP. Most people use the terms "imagesetter" and "image recorder" as synonyms, but they're not the same thing. An imagesetter usually includes the functions of an image recorder and a RIP. An image recorder is any marking engine.

To output a job, the RIP converts a digital document, which may contain text, line art, and digital images, into a series of spots. The image recorder exposes the spot sequence onto the media with a laser. Imaged film is developed in an online or offline processor. Some films are dry and do not require processing with chemistry. Some plates may require a processor, but many are now dry.

Film image recorders are of three types:
- capstan
- internal drum
- external drum

An image recorder may use drum or capstan technology. Drum and capstan recorders used to deliver different levels of quality. Capstan recorders worked for general-purpose type- and imagesetting, and drum recorders were used for proprietary high-end color systems. A capstan recorder feeds media from a roll in a supply cassette, over or under the laser, and into a takeup cassette or directly into an online processor. To transport the media, sets of rubber or other rollers are used to pull or push the media from the supply cassette, maintain accurate positioning during image exposure, and feed the media into the takeup cassette.

In an internal drum recorder, the film or plate is mounted to the inside surface of a cylindrical drum. While the drum and film remain stationary, the laser (or optics controlling the laser beam) spins around the axis of the drum to image the film or plate.

In an external drum recorder, film or plate is mounted to the outside surface of a cylindrical drum. A laser is mounted so that its beam aims at the media wrapped around the drum. In this type of recorder, the laser remains stationary while the drum spins around its axis, exposing the media with the laser beam. For this type of device, media must be sheetfed or cut off of a roll and mounted as a sheet.

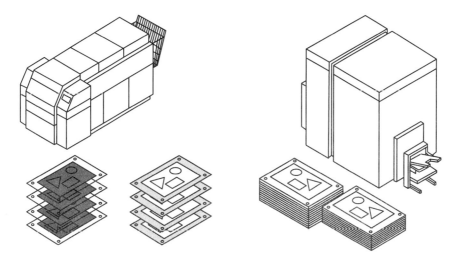

Film recorders (left) output a negative or positive piece of film for each color. Plate recorders (right) output a negative or positive plate for each color.

Digital recorders

Image recorders can also image directly to paper or other substrates using toner or inkjet systems. Many of these devices output to a re-imageable drum or belt and then transfer toner to paper. Inkjet systems bypass any form of image carrier and image directly to the paper or substrate. Digital printers may be as simple as a desktop laser printer, or a color copier with a RIP, or a high-speed digital color press. All take digital data and produce images in monochrome or color on paper or some other material.

An image recorder can image to an image carrier and then transfer the image to paper, or image directly to paper. Inkjet is the most common direct-to-paper technology.

We say *record*, or *image*, or *expose*, and even *burn* with essentially the same meaning. An imaging system includes an image recorder that images film, plate or paper and a RIP (Raster Image Processor). To image a job, the RIP converts an original document, which may contain text, line art, and digital images, into a series of spots. The image recorder images the spot sequence onto an image carrier or directly to a substrate.

The RIP

In a sense, the RIP, or raster image processor, is really the PostScript programming language compiler. It interprets the file and "executes" its commands which are to draw objects on a page, whether those objects are type characters, or artwork, or other images. A RIP is the essential element in any form of raster-based imaging which includes computer-to-paper, film, plate, cloth, plastic, metal, and perhaps epidermis. The end result of ripping is a bitmap for the entire image that tells the output engine where to place spots. The RIP performs three functions:

1. Interpretation of the PostScript page description language from the application program.
2. Display list generation. This is a list of every object on the page and serves as an intermediate file before rasterization. PDF is very close to this object list.
3. Rasterizing (screening, color transforms and making the page bitmap).

Almost every imaging device available today is a raster imager—using spots to build text, lines, pictures, etc. Thus, every imager must, out of necessity, have a RIP, whether it is a lowly desktop printer or a giant computer-to-plate (CTP) system. And every RIP is just a little bit different. Many are based on Adobe's design, with some additional features, and some are legally derived from public information on the PostScript language. These have been called PostScript clones. Most of the small or home office market is dominated by Hewlett-Packard's PCL printer language, a PostScript wannabe. Differences often have to do with the number of trays, or the image area, or the resolutions available, etc.

When you send a document to a printer, the RIP does its job and out comes the page or pages. But today's digital workflow is much more complex and multiple RIPpings are often the norm. In a CTP workflow, the document might be RIPped to a color printer for color proofing, RIPped to an imposition proofer, RIPped to a remote proofer, and finally RIPped to the platesetter. In most cases this involves four different RIPs and four different imaging engines and four chances for variation.

Over time, two paths to RIP development developed from:
- Adobe licensees
- Adobe clones

In both cases, the RIP includes a core set of functions based on the PostScript interpreter. From there, developers have added increasing functionality. Here are some of them:
- more efficient graphics handling
- more efficient picture handling
- halftone screening with different dot structures, angles, and algorithms
- stochastic screening
- trapping
- imposition
- statistics and other reports

RIP evolution

The PostScript page description language was developed to communicate the appearance of text, graphical shapes, and images to raster-based output devices equipped with a PostScript interpreter. A single page description can be used on any PostScript-compatible printer from a 300 dpi laser printer to a 3,000+ dpi imagesetter or platesetter or digital printer. In our opinion, another reason for its success is that it supports high-end printing. Computer-to-plate and digital printing as we know them could not have developed without a standardized page description language. PostScript is a *de facto* standard in that it is the basis for prepress as we know it. RIPs take in PostScript files and output page bitmaps.

PostScript printer description files

Each application usually creates and stores files in its own internal format, not PostScript. When you print a job, the application uses a PostScript driver (called a PPD for PostScript Printer Description) to translate its data into PostScript. Depending on what computer or application you use, the printer driver could be installed as part of the application, or, more commonly, the printer driver is installed in the System folder for any application to use.

PostScript is device independent . . . to a point. When you print, you print to a specific printer that has very specific features such as certain resolutions, page sizes, minimum margins, choice of paper trays, etc. Although the PostScript driver can send the PostScript job to any printer, it can't specify a tabloid page for a printer that does not have a tabloid tray, for example. To access features specific to the printer, PostScript uses PPDs which are stored in the System folder.

Some printer-specific information that a PPD might include in order to output to a printer:
- input paper trays
- page size definitions
- print areas for each page size
- output paper trays
- duplexing (double-sided printing)
- default resolution
- resolutions available
- black and white or color output
- halftone screening functions
- default screen angles
- screen frequency combinations
- custom screening definition
- default transfer functions
- default font
- color plates to be output
- image reduction or enlargement
- selection of special functions
- stapling or finishing options

At print time, you select the PostScript output device and select a PPD (or a PDF in older versions of QuarkXPress). If you later want to print the same job to a different printer, all you need to do is select a different printer with a different PPD.

PostScript interpreters and RIPs

When the RIP receives the PostScript file for processing, it needs to convert that file to bitmap data. PostScript printers, whether 300 dpi laser printers or 3,000+dpi platesetters, need a PostScript interpreter to translate the PostScript code into the bitmap data needed to print or image the page. Raster data prints a page as a pattern of tiny printer spots. To place these spots, the RIP maps out the page as a grid of spot locations—this is called a bitmap. Any specific spot can be defined or located by its address based on x,y coordinates. To image a page, the output engine either images a spot or does not—zero or one, on or off. Data of this type is called binary, because only two values are used. The term bilevel bitmap means spots. Composite data means pixels—spots with levels of gray.

Output media

The most commonly used types of imaging media in laser output imaging recorders are:
- resin coated (RC) paper
- positive or negative film
- plate material (polyester or aluminum)

Resin-coated (RC) paper has a silver-based, light-sensitive coating on a paper substrate. It is then coated with a resin to insure durability. It is usually exposed in positive mode, producing black characters and images on a white background. It is usually pasted onto a carrier board to make camera-ready artwork. To make a printing plate from RC paper requires a camera shot of this reflective artwork to produce the negative film for stripping and then platemaking. RC paper is used for type and line work only, or for some black-and-white halftoned photographs. Newspapers have used RC paper to output screened halftones in position so that only one camera shot would produce the entire film of the paper with text and pictures.

Film is a sheet or roll of polyester (plastic) with a silver-halide light-sensitive coating. It can be imaged positively or negatively, depending on the printing plate to be used on the press. Negative-working plates are most common, which means that users output negative film. Plates are considered to be either positive-working or negative-working, depending on how they react to light. A positive-working plate requires a positive film image; a negative-working plate requires a negative film image. High-quality, long-run magazines and other users may use positive-working plates.

In the early 1990s, dry processed film was introduced but it has not become prevalent in use. The advent of computer-to-plate and digital printing is having an effect on imagesetter installations and eventually on film use. All new imaging technologies are filmless. Many capstan and drum recorders can also image polyester-based plate material. These plates work well with run lengths of up to 10,000 impressions for paper-based material, and up to 50,000 impressions for polyester. Aluminum plates require a special platesetter.

Photomedia development and processing

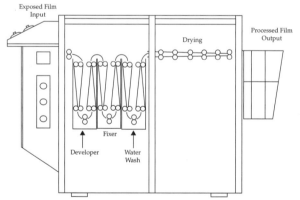

Once the film image recorder images a page, it advances the imaged media into a light-tight takeup cassette (to be transferred to a processor) or to an online chemical processor. The processor feeds the media through a developer tank (to develop the image), a fixer tank (to halt the developing process), and then a wash tank (to clean off any remaining developer or fixer chemicals). The media then feeds through a dryer, and exits into a receiving tray. You can then use the film media to strip into flats and signatures, make proofs, or when approved, to make printing plates.

Photographic processing

Factors that affect film processing quality include cleanliness, temperature, media speed, and chemical replenishment rate. Cleanliness is the single most important factor for good output quality and processor life. The processor must be cleaned on a regular basis since dirty chemicals do not perform as required and result in underdevelopment or stains on the media. If the processor's rollers get dirty, they can leave marks on the media, or they can get gummed and cause jams. Proper temperature is also essential for media development. If the developer is too cool, media will be underdeveloped; if too warm, overdeveloped. If the fixer is too cool, it won't stop the development process adequately and media will overdevelop.

Most processors have an automatic replenishment system to keep the chemicals potent. Chemicals require a proper replenishment rate. You can adjust the rate used to replenish the chemicals based on your use. If you replenish chemicals too slowly, they become exhausted and underdevelop the media. If you replenish them too quickly, you use up your chemicals faster than necessary. Media should move through the developer tank, fixer tank, and wash tank at the proper speed for optimum development. If it moves too fast, it will underdevelop; too slowly, it will overdevelop. Most media packaging or data sheets provide recommended times to develop that brand of media. You can use the specified development time to set the processor speed. Make sure you keep the processor clean.

Computer-to-plate (platesetters)

The demands of the industry never stop, especially when we have seen the ways in which other developments have taken place to cater to specific reproduction needs. Once the process for producing film flats in an automated and digitized way was proven to be successful with the imagesetters, the next logical need for the printing industry was a device that could image directly to a plate. Such a device is called a platesetter and the digital workflow that enables this to happen is called CTP (Computer To Plate). There are now several alternatives in preparing image carriers—to film, directly to plate (on or off press) or to purely digital printers.

Interestingly the history of the development of CTP goes back to 1974, when Lasergraph used two high-powered lasers to etch non-image areas off a letterpress plate, which was made of plastic. CTP technology had been attempted in the early eighties by some newspapers like the *Wall Street Journal,* and *New York Times.* In 1984, the EOCOM company showed a flatbed platesetter, which it later sold off to the Gerber company, now a part of Barco. Gerber showed the workings of a completely digital CTP system to the world in 1991 and Creo introduced thermal platesetting in 1995.

A loader holds the raw plates, which are separated by slip sheets to avoid scratches. A transport mechanism moves the plate to a location inside the platesetter which has a cylinder where the plate will be imaged. Imaging of the plate is done by laser beam. The exposed plates are moved by a transport mechanism to the delivery end.

There are three kinds of plate mounting systems in use, an internal drum and an external drum architecture, and a flatbed architecture. The difference in these systems is simply in the way the plate is mounted on the cylinder. In the internal drum architecture, the plate is mounted on the inside of the drum and in the external drum architecture, the plate is mounted on the outside of the drum. Of the 58 models of CTP systems in use today 24 are internal drum, 25 are external drum and the remaining (nine) are flatbed.

Direct to press

Heidelberg and Presstek came out with a technology called "Direct Imaging," or "DI" for short, in 1991. They called it the "system solution for computer to press" or is commercially called the direct-to-press technology. This technology supports taking the data stream from the computer that acts as its front end and imaging the plate directly on the press. The spirit of offset printing is very much alive in the QuickMaster-DI, the press from Heidelberg/Presstek which incorporates the direct imaging technology, as do presses from Scitex/KBA, Omni-Adast and Screen. A RIP converts the digital data into a bitmap and fires the laser beam onto the plate, which is mounted on the plate cylinder.

The plate has two layers, a base layer that is an ink-loving layer and a top layer, made of silicon, that is a water-loving or ink-repelling layer. The laser when fired on the plate burns the silicon layer, leaving the image receptive layer intact. Direct imaging technology uses waterless printing, although new processless plates will work with conventional lithography. When the press is in operation, the plate is in contact with the ink rollers that apply ink onto the image areas. The image is transferred to a blanket and then on to the substrate as in offset. The QuickMaster-DI uses a common impression cylinder as its internal architecture for the press. This means that this press has only one impression cylinder, instead of one for each color (cyan, magenta, yellow or black). This impression cylinder is in the middle and all the four blanket cylinders come in contact with this common impression cylinder. The paper travels between the blanket and the impression cylinder as in a conventional offset press.

Since the plates are imaged on the press, there is no reason that they will ever have to be moved horizontally or laterally for register. This is very important in the economics of running a press. A vast amount of press time is spent in the initial makeready of the job. Time being looked at as money these days, any saving in time has a direct impact on savings in money. Waterless printing as a process helps in getting brighter ink reflectance on the paper. The advantages of direct imaging are numerous.

Concepts of proofing

A proof is a sample print that is indicative of the final printed piece. Depending on the stage of the printing process, the type of proof may vary, suiting that specific need. However, the big issue in proofing is the one that the client signs off on. This is called a contract proof, because this proof is a contract between the client and the printer to reproduce the printing job as is. A lot of arguments stem from a mismatch between the proof and the final printed sheet. While some of this could be because of the printer's inefficiency, there are a lot of elements that are technologically mismatched in the first place. As long as the final reproduction device is different from the proofing device, proofing will be an issue.

As long as the industry relied on proofs that were made from the separated films, this problem of proof-to-print mismatch was not that emotional. This was because the films were the prime carriers of the image, so the image that was being transferred from the film to plate to paper was the same used to produce the proofs. However, with the advent of digital technology in the business of printing, along came the low-end desktop color printing devices. Most designers pulled a print off these printers (that now populate many office desktops), and now these became the proofs. These prints differ from the ones that you would get from a printing press. Designers have already gotten into this mode of checking their design and once they are satisfied with their output, they demand a similar look in the final printing. More sophisticated inkjet printers and the ones that use xerographic process are also being used for proofs.

The first shock that a commercial printer will get from these proofs is that they are all mostly from continuous tone devices. The icon of the printing industry—the halftone dot—is missing. Printers get their blood pressures up, wondering how they could match a print that does not even have a dot to the press sheet. There is proofing technology that plots a digital proof with halftone dots. The toner-based proofs do put in halftone dots, but in the real sense they are faked dots. They are not the same dots that are created by the halftoning process. Instead, they are a simulation of a halftone dot produced by the continuous tone device. These proofs do not have anything to do with the film separations, unlike their earlier counterparts that came off the color-separated film.

PREPARE

PROOF

PRINT

Proofing is a requirement when the job is going to be produced on a device other than your own printer. For digital printing, a proof is a "run length of one" and can be output at any time. When a printing press is the reproduction device, proofing is mandatory.

Proofing is the contractual prediction and verification, through simulation, of the expectation of eventual reproduction that is legally defensible. Before you commit your job to reproduction, you want to make sure it will output the way you expect. You need to know that the colors will be right and that all the text and images are in the proper place. You can make proofs at any stage of the job, from design initialization through final contract proof. For black-and-white output, you can use laser printer output, but for color, black-and-white proofs may be useful only for imposition proofs.

Critical issues in proofing

In a traditional print run, the job does not land on the press to be mass produced, until it has been approved by the client (the proof has been signed off). A proof should be an acceptable replica of what the press will eventually print. Traditional proofing systems use the same film negative or positive that is eventually used for making the plate that prints the final product, so there will be little challenge in matching the final product to the proof. With digital workflows taking over, you may have observed that none of the proofing devices ever use film. They all use the digital data from the computer, which is RIPped and printed by the proofing devices. These proofs have a marked difference from the press in the way they reproduce the image. The images are almost continuous tone and the presence of a halftone dot is missing in many cases.

This was not the case in the analog world, when film is used. This is probably why many print buyers are so concerned about approving a proof produced from a digital device. The added fear is that they do not see a halftone dot in the proof and thus make it less compatible with the press output. Some digital proofs can also be damaged by heat that may be generated inside the printer, or the colors may bleed. So digital proofing is still an area that needs a lot of catching up to be competitive with analog proofing. However proofing devices such as the KPG Approval, Scitex Iris, and Polaroid Polaproof have become well-accepted in the industry. Analog proofing is still quite prevalent because of the need for halftone dots, but digital color proofing is advancing very quickly.

Digital proofing

Color printers on the market today that are used for proofing use several different methods of producing color images. To proof color jobs, you can use one of these types of printers:

- In a dye-sublimation printer, ribbons are covered with dye. During printing, the ribbon passes over a thermal head. The elements in the thermal head vaporize the dye and transfer the dye-vapor onto the specially coated paper. The thermal head can vary the heat and vaporize different amounts of the dye to control how much dye is deposited on the paper. The ribbons are a series of magenta, cyan, yellow, and black dye sections. To print color, a dye-sub printer prints a color section, then feeds the paper back into the printer, prints the next section, refeeds the paper, etc.

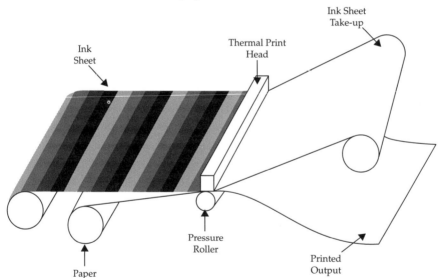

Ink Sheet Take-up

Ink Sheet

Thermal Print Head

Pressure Roller

Printed Output

Paper

Dye sublimination and thermal printers use a ribbon made up of color sections

- Thermal wax printers operate in much the same way as dye-sub printers. Instead of dyes, the printer ribbon is coated with colored wax. The thermal head heats the wax and that point of the wax, depending on the temperature of the thermal head, is transferred to and fuses with the paper. Thermal-wax ribbons are similar to the dye-sub ribbons in that each ribbon is composed of magenta,

cyan, yellow, and black wax sections. To print a page, the paper
has to pass by the thermal head four times (once for each color).

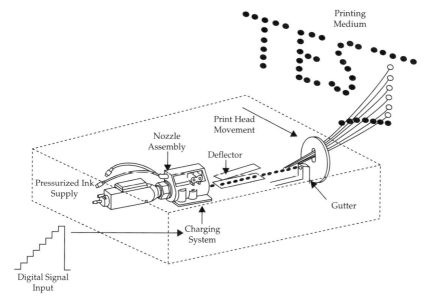

A continuous inkjet system

- Inkjet printers vary in size from desktop units capable of outputting page-size proofs to large-format units that can print wall-
  sized drawings or 4-foot-wide strips several feet long. Inkjet printers spit (continuous) or drool (drop-on-demand) ink onto the
  paper or other substrate.
- Color laser printers provide a proof you can check for the general
  look of color, but you probably should not make color decisions
  based on it. Color laser printers and copiers use a drum or belt that
  conducts a charge when exposed to laser light. The scanning laser
  charges this belt or drum, which creates an image. Toner is electrically attracted to the charged areas of the image and repelled from
  others. The image transfers to the paper and is fused.
- Other digital proofers use ablation (burn off one layer) or other
  technologies to image color proofs with halftone dots. All of the
  technologies described do not show the halftone dot since they are
  continuous tone printers. A trend has been to develop materials
  that can be imaged in the computer-to-plate recorder.

Bits are the building blocks of digital imaging

Another word for "digits" in a computer is the word "bits," or binary digits. To picture what a bit can do, the following illustration may help. Imagine a piece of white paper with many crossed grid lines on it, thus forming a mosaic of empty boxes in rows and columns. Using a black marker, you could fill in some squares and leave others blank, thereby creating a pattern. By creatively choosing some and leaving others, you could easily create a crude face, or the letter "A." If you had enough patience, you could create an intricate pattern of filled squares which looked like the Mona Lisa.

```
        X                    0 0 0 1 0 0 0
       X  X                  0 0 1 0 1 0 0
     XX XX X                 0 1 1 1 1 1 0
   X          X              1 0 0 0 0 0 1
```

Computers are very good at filling such grid squares with numbers or also filling them with colors. Let's say that the number one tells the computer to fill a square with black and the number zero tells the computer to leave it blank (white). Now, instead of actually filling squares with a marker, you can type a one or a zero, and the computer does the filling for you in its memory and on its monitor screen. With appropriate hardware and software, the computer can interpret your every motion, as you draw, and fill the correct boxes. It changes your motion and content and ideas into numbers (that is, digits). The digital revolution is all about numbers: making images from numbers.

One of the most fascinating things about computers is the speed at which they can do such jobs. The time it takes to blink your eye is about the time that it takes a computer to "read" about a half-million numbers from its memory, and then to display them as light in front of you. However, somehow, you must provide this set of "image numbers" for the computer to work with. You must somehow tell it what you want. A computer is simple minded (and even using the word "mind" is a compliment.) It is the application software which does all the number work and lets us do the fun stuff.

Pixels are picture elements

Each square of the grid in the example above can be called a picture element. This way of building a digital image "mosaic" is very common. Each element or tile of the grid is called a *pixel* (short for picture element.) The finer the grid, the more pixels that you'll need to fill, and the finer and more detailed the patterns that you render. With mosaic tiles, the further that you stand away, or the smaller and more numerous they are, the better the picture will look. The same is true in digital imaging. The more pixels that you have to fill, the better your image can look. In an intricate color image there will be thousands of such elements which make the picture.

Gray levels

Thus far we have discussed only binary *bits*—on-off, one-zero; black-white—two "levels." In order to create pleasing images of all types, we will probably need more, just like different values are used in art drawings and illustrations. In drawing, there are two basic ways to do this. First, the illusion of gray value can be created even with black pen on paper by varying amounts of cross hatching or stippling. This varies the amount of white paper which remains visible, and thus creates an illusion of gray. The second common technique is used in pencil drawing when pencils of different hardness are used. Techniques similar to both of these "tricks" are also used in the graphic arts.

Different shades of gray are created in conventional printing (for instance, a newspaper) by varying the sizes of small "halftone dots" (we'll explain this term later), even though the press can only print black spots on white paper. A computer monitor screen is capable of fine control over the brightness of each pixel. This is similar to the "pencil hardness" technique.

By assigning different numbers (other than 1 or 0) to a pixel, it can represent varying levels of gray. Exactly which trick is used to fool your eye depends on whether the image is rendered on the computer screen, or goes to print. It is as if each pixel can be shaded with a pencil that has a different number indicating the shade that it can put down on paper (or the monitor screen, etc.) Pixels that are not just binary bits are stored in the computer as *bytes*. A byte is usually a number from 0 to 255. Bytes are simply a way for a computer to be able to work beyond a zero and a one. (Actually, bytes are still made up of a string of eight bits, but that's one of those things you don't really need to know about.) Going from bits to bytes is much like going from the alphabet to words, and then going on to the works of Shakespeare (except that the computer could not even begin to go there.) These bytes and gray levels are important—because with a fixed number of pixels in an image, shading capability at each pixel can add valuable information or "quality."

An image made up of pixels stored as *bits* is sometimes called a *bitmapped* image. However, an image with pixels made of bytes, is *not* a bytemap. It is sometimes called a grayscale image, if it is a single color. It has greater *bit depth* than a bitmapped image, which just means it has gray values. Color images are stored in computers in various ways, but terms like "24-bit" or "36-bit" refer to color images with intermediate tones (that is, "gray" levels.)

Making sense of the digital ga-ga

Pixels, tiles, spots, grains, dots, bits, pits, bytes, samples, re-samples, rasters, lines, curves, angles, and cells—oh my. Bitmaps, bit depths, grayscales, gray levels, screens, gray tones, contones, halftones, quartertones, and duotones—RGB, CMYK, Lab, AM, FM, A-Z—oh no. Let's go through it step by step.

Contone means continuous tone

Contone and continuous tone refer to the same thing. When the tonal gradation of an image is continuous from white to black, we call that image a contone image. This also means that we have several intermediate levels of gray between white and black. These varying gray levels give a feel of the image being continuous in its tones between white and black. Examples of continuous tone images are photographs, wash drawings created from water color or oil paintings and images created with a spray gun.

In a computer, the bytes are used to map out computer grayscale images, wherever shading happens. The words grayscale, gray-levels, bitdepth, and tone are very close. A bitdepth refers to the hardness of your pencil shading. A bit depth of 1 bit refers to the pixel shading that has been either turned on or off. Note that even though the bit depth is 1 bit, there can be two possible levels—on or off.

When shading is used in an image as in a contone image, depending on the levels of gray that are required, there will be a bitdepth higher than 1. White is a level too, don't forget.

Halftones are dots of varying sizes

To print, we need paper (white) and ink (assumed black). So printing line work is no challenge, as it has only two tonal levels. All the white areas will be taken care of by the color of paper, and the image areas will be printed in ink that is black in color. However when continuous tones need to be reproduced, the photomechanical process creates a series of dots in varying sizes to simulate grayness. These varying sizes of dots create the illusion of producing tones of various shades. A cluster of smaller dots creates an illusion of a lighter gray and a cluster of larger dots creates an illusion of a darker gray.

Lets us first examine the original copy itself—the continuous tone photograph. Under a powerful microscope, not just a magnifying glass, you will see that the image in the photograph is actually composed of small grains of silver halide. More grains in an area creates a dark area and fewer grains in an area creates a lighter area.

In process color printing, there are four sets of halftone dots that are overlapped to create the illusion of grays.

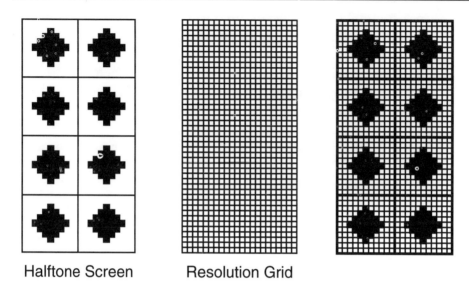

Halftone Screen   Resolution Grid

The halftone dots are based on the underlying resolution grid

There are many ways to create various tones with a pencil; the same is true with digital image pixels. A halftone dot is one way and the most common. If we now go back to the pencil and paper story, we can imagine filling one grid square, in each of the top and bottom left and right corners with black ink. The page still looks white with four small dots in the corner. If we now start to fill in a few more of the squares that touch each of the first four, we would now be creating four bigger dots. If we continued, the four dots would get bigger, and the page would look darker. Eventually the page would be filled with black dots and the entire page would be black.

The four dots that grew from nothing to make the entire page look dark can be called halftone dots, gray tones in an image can be simulated by assigning different values to a pixel, which can be turned on or off. The pixels are much smaller than the halftone itself, for many of these small pixels join together and form a halftone dot. The halftone dots themselves are much too small and can be seen only under magnification. An image created this way on the page can appear to be nearly equal to a photograph.

With many tiny pixels in the grid, we can print many levels of gray on paper. Please take note that in this case we used only two levels of pixels—either on or off, white or black. All we did was fill the squares (bit=1=on) or not fill them (bit=0=off). Yet we were able to create many levels of gray.

Dots refers to halftone dots

As we saw earlier, an image with grays in it that is printed on a printing press is created with halftone dots made up of spots called pixels. The task in halftone printing is to keep the size of dot as invisible to the eye as possible. Four characteristics of the halftone dot are useful to understand in order to produce good quality graylevel images. They are:

- dot size
- dot shape
- screen angle
- screen frequency

Halftone dot size

The size of the halftone dot determines the tone that will be reproduced. A smaller dot produces a lighter gray (highlight), a medium-sized dot produces midtones and the larger dots produce the darker or shadow areas in an image. In conventional halftoning (photomechanical methods), the camera room technician had the skill to control the size of the dots as they were shot. By using chemicals such as pottasium ferrocyanide they could reduce the outer diameter of the dot, thereby making it slightly smaller to give the desired detail in areas that were filled up during chemical processing. This was called "dot etching."

Halftone dot shape

A dot is usually considered to be a perfect circle. Yes, such dots are called round dots. But dots of other shapes are also used. More commonly dots that are elliptical or diamond in shape are used. This is because the shape of a dot has an effect on the way it can grow during the printing process.

When going from film to plate or from plate to blanket to paper, there is some spread of the dot by light or by ink

A 40% Dot On Film

The Same 40% Dot Becomes
A 57% Dot When Printed

The phenomenon above is called "dot gain." A round dot, especially in the shadow areas, has little space to grow, and it tends to fill in much faster. This is because the shape of the round dot permits it to grow all around its periphery. You end up printing tones that are darker than they should be. The shape of an elliptical dot is an ellipse or oval. This elongated shape allows it to grow more in the elongated sides. Therefore elliptical dots are used when fine tonal renditions are desired, like reproduction of facial tones.

In the earlier days of halftoning when a specific dot shape was desired, they were produced by using a separate screen that had the particular dot shape. Special effect screens were also used that offered dot shapes as lines, mezzo, dust, bricks, etc. In today's digital world, the screening computers in the scanners generate dots of varying shapes. Also many image programs on the desktop allow for changes in the shape of the dots. The shape of a halftone dot can make a difference in the appearance of an image. Usually a particular dot shape is chosen to make an image appear more natural, for instance, to avoid a tonal jump in flesh tones. Other times a dot shape is chosen for special effects, to make the image appear less natural.

Dot shape is very important in the printing of high-quality halftones. When printing images on newsprint, such factors as rough paper stock and less accurate presses can result in higher dot gain. A well-behaved dot and the proper pre-compensation for dot gain can result in a clean, well-rendered image instead of one that is muddy.

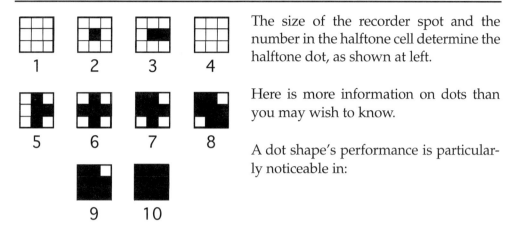

The size of the recorder spot and the number in the halftone cell determine the halftone dot, as shown at left.

Here is more information on dots than you may wish to know.

A dot shape's performance is particularly noticeable in:

Highlights. Your very lightest highlights should be as smooth tonally as possible and hold a 2% to 3% dot reliably. These highlights give extra "punch" to the image. A good highlight dot should provide enough geography for the ink to adhere to the paper with smooth tones. These are the smallest halftone dots that can be printed.

Midtones. These areas should be smooth, without perceptual tonal jumps. If this occurs, which isusually noticeable in flesh tones, shadows look filled in and gradients in skin tones look mottled, instead of smooth. At the 50% level some dots increase in size enough to touch. Other kinds of dots, round, elliptical, square, do not touch at the 50% level.

Shadows. These are the darkest areas of the image. Halftones should hold a dot without plugging, or filling with ink. A fine shadow dot provides extra detail for greater realism.

In the PostScript system, the dot shape is determined by a PostScript operator called a spot function. The Raster Image Processor calculates the dot shape based on the spot function. In one of the two types of square spot functions, halftone dots are shaped like squares through the tint scale. But in the other, halftone dots start out as circles, and grow to squares in the midtones, and then circles again. How it works is less important than the resulting image that you can produce.

A halftone is any image—such as a photograph—that exists as a series of small dots of varying size and color density that serve to simulate the appearance of continuous gradations of tone. Halftones are necessary in the reproduction of photographic images; most printing presses cannot print continuous tones, so photographic images must first be converted to a series of dots in order to be effectively printed. Lightness and darkness of portions of an image are effected by varying the size and density of the dots; small dots spaced far apart produce light areas (highlights), while large dots clustered more closely together produce dark areas (shadows).

Halftones are produced either as film positives or negatives by photographing a continuous tone original through a halftone screen or fine grid. The screen pattern and frequency of the dots that are produced determine the ultimate quality of the reproduction. A 150-line screen, for example, will produce 150 rows and 150 columns of dots, or 22,500 dots per square inch. Halftones can also be produced electronically, using digital data.

In digital halftone production, a halftone dot generated on an imagesetter or laser printer, comprising a collection of smaller printer spots. Since digital output devices generate images as a series of very small spots, each halftone dot must be composed of smaller printer spots. These printer spots are arranged in discrete "cells" or grids, which correspond to the halftone dots. The number of printer spots in a particular cell can be varied; the more printer spots that are grouped in a halftone cell, the darker the larger the cell appears.

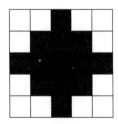 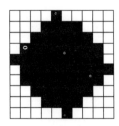

Two halftone cells, comprising 25 printer spots (left) and 100 printer spots (right). The larger the matrix, the greater the number of printer spots, and the greater the number of gray levels.

The basic indivisible unit of some printed images—commonly photographs—produced by photographically exposing or electronically imaging a continuous tone image to a screen, which breaks the image up into discrete dots.

Since most printing processes are incapable of printing continuous tone images, such images need to be broken down into individual dots of varying shades of color or gray, each tiny solid dot printing discretely and which together give the illusion of a continuous tone image.

Strictly speaking, the smallest fundamental unit of a halftone image, a small point of color, black, or some shade of gray which, when combined with many other dots of varying color and shade, form an image.

Although more technically referred to as spots, in order to distinguish them from halftone dots, computer screen pixels, the smallest portions of light that a scanner can detect, the smallest bits of toner that a laser printer can print, and the smallest areas that an imagesetter or a plotter can expose are also often referred to as dots.

Dot area density

The size of a halftone dot, expressed as a percentage of the total surface area, which can range from 0% (no dot) in highlights to 100% (solid ink density) in shadows. By carefully measuring the dot area in various regions of an image at various stages in the reproduction of an image, dot densities can remain consistent.

In digital halftoning, dots (in this case called cells) comprise much smaller printer spots which, depending on the resolution of the output device, can be used to create dots of various sizes and densities. Varying the number of spots that make up a halftone cell can work to fine-tune the dot densities by increasing the number of shades of gray available as the number of spots in a cell is increased. Dot area density is also known as dot area or dot density.

Enlarged view of a halftone image shows variations in dot area density and how they relate to the appearance of shadows, midtones, and highlights.

A printing defect characterized by halftone dots that print larger than desired, imparting to the printed image a darker tone or color, caused, in offset lithography, by increased pressure between the blanket cylinder and impression cylinder of an offset press, or in other processes by ink feathering or spreading as it penetrates the surface of the substrate. Dot gain can have many causes, one of which being the use of paper that has too great a porosity or an ink that has too low a viscosity. Some types of offset printing plates, in particular bimetal plates and positive-working plates, are better at compensating for dot gain than others.

Dot gain typically increases the diameters of dots by the same amount, regardless of the size of the dots. However, the larger the circumference of the dot, the larger the area around the dot that will increase, the result being that middle tones tend to be the dots most dramatically affected. In multi-color printing, dot gain can affect proper registration, so many prepress operations commonly reduce the dot sizes in the middle tone areas so as to compensate for gain (called dot gain compensation). Some often-encountered dot gain percentages include:

- coated sheetfed lithography at 150 lines per inch: 15%
- uncoated sheetfed offset lithography at 133 lines per inch: 20%
- coated web offset lithography at 133 lines per inch: 22%
- newsprint web offset lithography at 100 lines per inch: 30%

The variety of dot gain mentioned above is called physical dot gain, as the size of the dots physically increases. Another, optically perceived phenomenon is known as optical dot gain. Dot gain is also called dot spreading and press gain. The opposite effect is called sharpen.

A means of allowing for the effect of dot gain by reducing the size of the halftone dots on halftone color separation films. Dot gain is often the most pronounced in the middle tone regions of an image, and it is typically these areas that undergo dot size reduction. The percentage of the dot size gain varies according to the printing process (i.e, sheetfed or web offset lithography) and the paper characteristics.

Screen angle

Under a magnifying glass you may notice that the halftone screen runs in a particular direction. Scientific studies have found that when the screen is run at a 45° angle, the human eye can least detect the dots, which is why monochrome jobs are usually printed at a 45° angle. The same angle cannot be used for all the colors when printing in color. Every separation color is printed at a different angle.

The reason being, when two or more colors are printed, the screen angles would run on top of each other. The crisscrossing causes an objectionable pattern called *moiré*. A technique that minimizes the noticeability of moiré is to separate all the process separation colors by a difference of 30°. The conventional angles are:

- black   45°
- magenta   75°
- cyan   15° or 105°
- yellow   0° or 90°

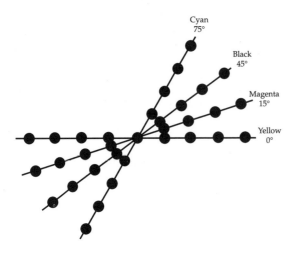

However, yellow, being the lightest of the four colors is separated by a difference of 15°. In conventional halftoning, screen angles were adjusted by rotating the glass screens to the desired angles. The later versions of contact screens came with screen angles already built in. In the digital world the software offers various screen angles. Unless you know why you need to change a screen angle, you would be best advised to leave the default angles as prescribed by the application program or the output device.

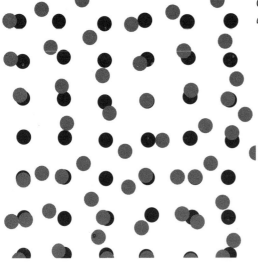

Get the screen angles wrong and you get the dreaded moiré

When overlaid, the dots on the four films (cyan, magenta, yellow, and black) produce a pattern.The only pattern that matters is the rosette. Rosettes are what makes color printing color printing. A rosette is formed by the four halftone screens placed at different angles and the resulting pattern simulates the appearance of color.

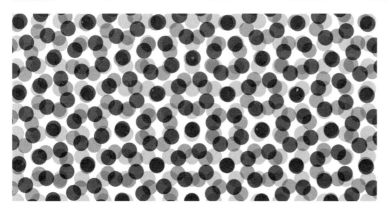

This illustration shows the four colors forming a rosette, which may be hard to see in b&w

Closed and open rosettes. There are two types of rosettes: open (clear-centered) or closed (dot-centered) rosettes. Open rosettes, because they have more tolerance for errors that might be introduced at the press, produce better results for most types of images. The extra room in the open rosette provides more tolerance for small press shifts (a shift of half a dot's size can cause moiré). In addition, the open centers help avoid ink trapping. Incorrect overlapping of dots and ink contamination problems are more prevalent in closed rosettes. Images with a lot of shadow detail work best with closed rosettes, which are less visible, and help provide more detail in the shadows, although image data in the highlight areas may be reduced. In the color separation process, dot patterns can cause problems. If the screen angles are not precise, patterns created by the combination of two or more screen grids cause moiré which may interfere with the image.

Screen frequency

The printed halftone image when viewed with a loupe (magifying glass) will clearly show you that it has been imaged as dots in a series of lines. These lines are the the lines from the output device, as the imaging device lays the dots in a series of lines as it images. The number of lines in which an image has been produced is called the screen frequency, usually measured in lines per inch (lpi). Determining what frequency you need to image is dependent on the type of stock on which you will eventually print. Rough surfaces, such as those used in daily newspapers, use a coarse screen in the range of 75 lpi to 100 lpi.

Most commercial offset printing that strives for good print quality is usually printed in the 133–150 lpi range. Very high quality printing, including fine art printing, are printed in 200 and above lpi. It is important to note the choice of screen frequency based on the type of stock, the printing process, and the quality of print desired. It is a fallacy that the greater screen frequency means better print quality. It is true to some extent, but should be backed by other factors as mentioned above. Using a higher frequency on a lower quality substrate like newsprint will only produce blotches of ink, as the stock is very absorbent. A printer can advise you on the screen frequency that should be used based on all these factors.

Spots are there or not there

To the human eye it is the dots that make the image. But what is it that makes the dot? A spot is the smallest addressable size of an output device, which when grouped together creates a dot. In other words, when several of the tiny spots of an imaging device are clustered together, they form a halftone dot. This cluster of spots is not resolvable by the human eye. So they appear to be a dot. We saw that the measure of halftone dots was in units of lpi; the unit of measurement of an output device is measured as the number of spots per inch or dpi in short. Unfortunately, the industry jargon of dots per inch is a misnomer, as the dots are usually confused with the halftone dots. A specification sheet of an output device like an imagesetter may say that its resolution is 1200, 2400, or 3600 dpi. This means that the device can address that number of spots per linear inch.

Pixels are picture elements

The tiniest area that can be addressed in a computer is called a picture element, or simply *pixel* for short. This is the lowest level of addressability on a grid, and determines the overall reproduction quality. Just imagine a large checkerboard. Each square within the checkerboard can be assigned a value. But each square can only have one value, either on or off. When a group of adjoining pixels, say a 5x5 square is fired by a laser beam, there is now the opportunity to assign a value to this entire cell. A fully exposed pixel (all cells) is black and an unexposed pixel (no cells) remains white. By individually addressing each pixel, the cell can have varying values, and size. This is the equivalent of dot size in conventional halftoning that produces a particular gray level. When the spot size is smaller, more pixels can be addressed in a linear inch. Which in turn can create more gray levels. Spots or pixels make dots, halftone dots.

Halftone dots revisited

Having discussed halftones earlier in their conventional use, let's now take a look at halftones that are produced digitally. All issues that were addressed in terms of dot size, dot shape, screen frequency and screen angle are very much applicable in digital halftoning too. They are just created differently. Remember that dots are often made up of many bits, that is, digits which tell the computer how many grid boxes to fill to make the right size dot on paper.

Halftone dots can be found on paper, film and plates but not monitors or scanners.

You could say that halftone dots have bit depth, like a monitor. Each spot on the screen can be turned on or off or somewhere in between. It is however difficult to put those "inbetween" values of ink on paper because you have paper that is white and ink that is black.

We therefore use the technique of halftoning to create an illusion of those "inbetween" tones during printing. Halftone dots are made in rows and columns.

Dot cells in rows and columns are superimposed on top of a bitmap grid. Each dot is made up of a cell of many smaller bitmap areas. Depending on the bitdepth of the cell, larger or smaller dots can be printed. If we looked at the rows of dots, we could call them dots in a line; which is from where we derive the terminology lines per inch (lpi), the unit of measurement to measure the screen frequency.

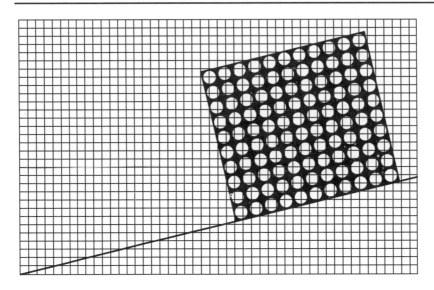

Halftone dots and the imagesetter grid

Finer halftone screens require higher screen frequencies and lower screen frequencies result in halftone screens that are coarser. To printers, frequency is usually a result of the type of paper used to print the image: newspapers use an 85-to-100 lpi screen to print halftones, while glossy magazines using slick paper and need a finer screen—they may print halftones by using 133-to-150 lpi or higher. For very high quality color printing, screen frequencies of 180-to-200 lpi or more are used. To digitally convert a photograph into a halftone, the halftone grid is superimposed on an image, almost as glass screens were used in conventional processing. Each halftone cell is then assigned a dot of different sizes to represent the image area in the cell. In total, the dots simulate the original image. Some cells are cyan, some yellow, some white, but all at different levels of gray based on the doyt size. The color for each cell is determined by the percentage of each of the process colors.

The size of halftone cell is based on the screen frequency and the image recorder resolution. Each of the halftone cells is comprised of many recorder spots (created by the image recorder laser beam when it is focused on paper or film or plate). Each of the recorder spots within a halftone cell can be on (producing black or a color) or off (producing white). The combination of recorder spots accumulates to form a halftone dot of a specific size and shape. To create different shapes, the recorder turns the platesetter or imagesetter spots on in pre-determined patterns.

These patterns are determined by a mathematical algorithm called a spot function, one for each dot shape, such as euclidian, round, diamond, elliptical, and square. A halftone dot is made up of the recorder's spots. The bigger a halftone dot, the more recorder spots are being used to make it.

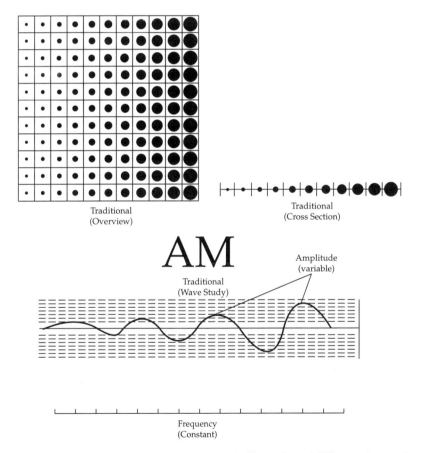

Traditional or Amplitude Modulation uses halftone dots of different sizes to simulate gray. The frequency is contant but the amplitude varies.

AM versus FM screening

Conventional halftone screening is called Amplitude Modulation screening. Amplitude means size and AM screening breaks up an image into halftone dots of varying sizes to simulate the original image in print. FM screening, on the other hand, keeps spots the same size and varies the frequency, or number, of spots and the location of those spots to simulate the original image. In FM screening, the concepts of screen angle and frequency no longer apply. The spots are randomly placed, and there is no direction (no screen angle) to the spots and FM screening is perfect for high-quality color work. Some printers who offer waterless printing use FM screening in conjunction with the waterless process because of the lower dot gain associated with that process. Waterless printing's lower dot gain counteracts any FM dot gain.

To emphasize:

FM Screening has same size dots with variable spacing

AM Screening has variable size dots with equal spacing

Stochastic screening

As we said, stochastic screening, called FM (Frequency Modulated) screening, lets you print high quality color images at lower resolutions by using a different approach to screening technology. Unlike amplitude modulated (AM) screening—that varies the size of the dot to simulate different shades of color—FM screening keeps the dot size the same and varies the number of dots used. The word stochastic means "random variable" or "to aim well" and stochastic screening uses randomly placed dots instead of the traditional halftone dots aligned along the traditional screen angles. Stochastic and FM screening have become synonomous.

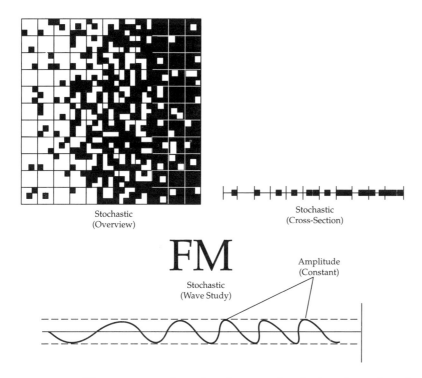

Stochastic
(Overview)

Stochastic
(Cross-Section)

FM

Amplitude
(Constant)

Stochastic
(Wave Study)

The concept of stochastic screening is that dots placed randomly will not cause moiré patterns. FM screening products apply advanced algorithms to determine the optimum placement of dots to appear random, yet not cause visual artifacts. With the advent of CTP, and one less level of dot gain, FM screening is hot.

File management, storage, and transfer

The basic level in which a document is stored today is the file. The biggest problem that concerns the creator and the service provider alike is the issue of file management. At no point in time is a desktop operator ever satisfied with the amount of disk space (storage) available for use. The problem is compounded for a service bureau that has to accept jobs from its clients. They have to have sufficient memory available to open, process, and save the jobs. Large-capacity storage devices that are plentiful these days offer some relief for this problem. It is however a wise decision to manage the files from the beginning itself. This would save a lot of trouble, time, and money.

Usually files are sent to the service provider on a disk to output to films. The problems start here if not checked well by the designer. Usually a document consists of text, images, some graphics, etc. A designer should take care to put all the images in the same folder as the page layout. When this is not done, you will encounter problems during printing. The page layout program file links to the image file during printing. Even though you may have been successful in printing out from your computer at the time you saved your job, the same may not work with the service provider's system. This is because your page layout program may have linked to the source file of the image on your hard drive. When the file is transported to another computer this link is snapped. The system replaces your image with a low-resolution image of your monitor (72dpi). When this image is output, the result is pixellated. Yuk.

Keep file sizes small

When you want to crop your image it is recommended that it be done in the image editing program. Even though you can do this in the page layout program, don't forget that your full-size image is still there, even though your page layout program does not show this to you on the screen. It just hides the rest of the image outside of the picture box that you have created. The real issue comes up during RIPping. The RIP has to actually rip the entire image and crop the portion selected. This is a burden for the RIP, and of course you end up paying for all that time. Don't get ripped by the RIP.

The same problem occurs when you want to rotate an image. You would be better off rotating it in your image creation program than doing it in your page layout program. RIPping is the biggest issue. When you add more computation work for a RIP you could crash the RIP too. When possible, it is preferable to avoid placing this burden on the RIP. (Also remember that you will be paying for all the unncessary computing time on the RIP.)

Choosing the correct resolution of your image is a vital step in file management. More is not always better in the graphic arts industry. Oversampling—that is, passing more data than can be used—does you no good. In fact you create a swelled-up file when you over-sample, and an increased file size that comes with its own inherent problems. Transfers take longer, RIPping takes longer, and the chances for errors can increase especially if you are transmitting your files. It is easier to manage files that are smaller.

Another common problem that is faced when sending out your work using a media is that of fonts. To print, it is important that the service provider has the same fonts that you used. In the event that they do not have the same fonts, the output device will substitute a font that it considers close to the one you used. In many cases, the font substitution is so close that you may not even realize that a substitution has taken place. But you will notice that the text has overflowed and has affected your layout. It is a good idea to provide the fonts that were used in the same folder.

Then when the output processor reads your file, it also links to the fonts folder. Remember to include both printer fonts and screen fonts. The printer is obliged to return fonts after use. The key is that the printer (or the service provider) will not hold that borrowed font in their system after the intended use. It is otherwise considered an infringement of property rights.

To avoid some of these common problems it is a good idea to flight check before sending your work out. Other methods include sending a PostScript file or better still a PDF (Portable Document Format) file.

Storage

The job is done, or waiting for an approval; where do you keep the file? By allowing the file to reside on the hard drive of your computer, you are consuming precious storage space. Also the more space that is consumed by the hard drive, the more likely that files may become fragmented, which may slow the speed of data access. Any storage medium is a backup medium. There are no storage devices that are 100% safe. While some are more reliable than others, it is your need that decides your choice of medium. Is you need for fast immediate access or do you need to store the work for future use? And of course how big is your file size and how many files are there?

Floppies have been the most elementary form of storage device. They are inexpensive, but notoriously unreliable—never save to only one floppy. Since floppies can accommodate only 1.44 MB of data, that's hardly anything for a typical graphic arts user.

Magneto optical disks are more robust than floppies. They can hold more data, usually in the order of 128 MB or 230 MB. They are called MOs for short and they combine the properties of a magnetic tape and that of an optical drive. An MO is more reliable than a floppy and is widely used by the prepress industry.

Zip disks have become popular of late. They are basically tape drives that can store 100 MB of data on a single disk. Because it is relatively inexpensive and is more robust than floppies and MOs, it is being widely accepted in the industry.

Jaz drives are pretty much an industry standard now when you need to cart larger amounts of data around. A Jaz disk can store 1 GB of data. Since large files are becoming common in the graphic arts industry, the need for storage media of this magnitude has made them popular.

CDs or compact disks have been a popular medium for storage and retrieval of data for a long time. A CD can accommodate 650 MB of data. With the price of the CD burners dropping each day, the use of

CD as a common storage device is increasing. CDs are considered a reliable medium for back up and archival purposes. They occupy very little space and are less susceptible to climatic variations than other media. CDs are used in the industry for large amounts of data and in sophisticated storage devices such as Juke boxes and servers.

File transfers

The most common form of providing a file to a service provider is with a disk. The files sent to a service provider can be native (that is, editable) files or TIFF files or PostScript files or PDF files. By sending a native file, there is an option for the service provider to make any changes that you may want. But there is also the risk of getting some of your formats altered by the outside source, however well experienced they may be.

Incorrect fonts could cause a text overflow if the same fonts are not used by your service provider. PostScript files are more secure as they contain all the elements in the file. Missing fonts which are the biggest headaches for the service provider, are a non-issue if embedded in the PostScript file. However a PostScript file is very voluminous and that could be an obstacle when sending over transmission lines. With faster transmission lines and with fiber optic cables, moving larger files speedily and reliably may become a lesser problem.

It is better to be aware of the problems that exist to provide solutions for more effective workflow. PDF—or better known as Adobe Acrobat—is taking care of many of these problems, and is becoming an excellent solution for transfer of files. Important to note in file transfers is whether you are compressing your file or not. Compressing the files makes the file size smaller and facilitates faster transmission of data. But there can be a loss of data when compression is done. There are many programs now that offer compression and decompression of files. These programs also give you the choice on the amount of compression that is desired. File transmission and file transfer are part of the same problem—getting files from where they are created to where they are produced.

Concepts of pre-flight check

This is a fancy term that we have borrowed from the airline industry. Before an aircraft takes off, it goes through a whole bunch of check-out procedures to ensure that all is fine. This preventive check (hopefully) gets all the passengers and crew back on ground safely after the flight. Just as this routine is important for an aircraft, the prepress industry too felt that a similar check should be done to all files before they are sent through the systems of a process house. A pre-flight check saves a lot of time and money for the clients as well as the process house. The files in question are put through a series of tests that tell whether all the fonts, images, and other elements needed to print perfectly are present.

The earliest forms of a pre-flight check were conducted by experienced prepress staff. Today there are utility programs that are commercially available to do a pre-flight check. These recognize the potential problems that may exist in the file. They also tell you a possible solution to rectify the problem. It is recommended that the designers conduct a pre-flight check themselves before sending their files to the process house, even though the file will be subject to a check there also.

The real objective is to prevent a problem from happening in the first place. It is important that the file is built correctly in the first place. Pre-flight check software cannot remedy the problems in the files.

Imaging issues

Not all imagers produce the same kind of image. Imaging quality is the result of factors like resolution, spot size, and addressability.

Resolution. This is ability of an imager to render detail. But it is not an independent factor. Addressability and spot size play a determining role in resolution.

Addressability. In a given area, say a linear inch, the number of marks that an imager can address is termed addressability. This is important because the more the spots in a given area, the higher the output resolution. The same is true for image capture—the more spots in an area that can be addressed allows you to acquire more data.

Spot size. A spot is not to be confused with a dot. In fact it makes several spots by the laser beam to produce a halftone dot. A spot is the smallest mark that an image setter can lay on film. The finer the spot (measured in microns) an imager can lay, the greater the detail that is capturable. When you have too large a spot size, they may overlap with the next row of laser spots and you may lose a lot of gray detail. This results in images having details in fine highlight and shadow areas filled up.

Laser intensity. This refers to the power of the laser to produce a solid black, the ability of the laser to have a high density on film. This allows you to control the amount of light that needs to be given to a particular type of film.

Accuracy. This is the measurement of the ability of an imager to lay a mark on a particular spot on the substrate. It is very critical in jobs that demand high levels of registration or when using a higher frequency.

Repeatability. This is the ability of an imager to lay the mark on the same spot on all four sheets films or plates. If this is not achieved then proper registration between various colors of a separation set will not work. Repeatability is measured in mils.

Dot gain, linearization, and densitometry

Densitometry can be used to monitor the imaging system, both to maintain a high level of quality and to counteract dot gain. Linearization is a method used to adjust the imaging system to ensure proper gray scale output. Dot gain is the tendency of halftone dots to grow slightly as they are reproduced in any of the production stages. Dot gain is usually associated with dot gain on press, but it occurs in prepress production and there can be several causes:

- Underexposure at the imager or underdevelopment in the processor both produce smaller halftone dots. When these film negatives are used to burn a plate, the resulting dots are bigger than they should be.

- Making contact copies of negatives can cause halftone dots to change size as light passes from the emulsion of one piece of film to the base of the other.
- Poor vacuum drawdown when making a proof or plate leaves an air pocket between the negative and the proof sheet, causing light to spread and thus create a larger dot.
- Choosing the wrong spot shape can exacerbate optical dot gain in tints or large areas of single color, especially as any of the three CMY colors approach 50% density.

Densitometry

Density describes the darkness or light-absorbing ability of images on a medium and is measured on a logarithmic scale from 0.0 to 4.0. You use a densitometer, which is like a volt meter for measuring the tranmission of light, to take the density readings. In prepress, densitometers measure the density of imagesetter film that is used to expose a printing plate. The target maximum density (Dmax) is 3.75 +/− .2 to ensure that the image is properly exposed and to prevent a partial exposure of the plate, in which case the non-image areas of the plate would begin to print after some number of copies. On the other hand, overexposure of the film would cause the image to spread and print with dark edges.

On the press, densitometers are used to measure the color bars in the marginal areas of a press sheet. The press operator measures the solid colors to find the Dmax, the 25%, 50%, and 75% tints to find the dot gain, and the overprints to measure ink trapping. The press is then adjusted accordingly. Densitometer readings may be taken during the press run to make sure the correct values are held, as the densitometer will show any shift before it becomes visible to the press operator's eye.

You can then use these density measurements to adjust your system. For example, if you find the density of the film is too great, you can adjust the exposure value for the image recorder. You can also use density readings from the film to determine if the photomedia processor needs adjustment. Once you've calibrated your imagesetting system, you can measure the results of a test page run on your press. This density tells you the total dot gain. You measure image density with either a transmission or a reflection densitometer. Transmission densitometers measure the amount of light passing through film. Reflection densitometers measure the amount of light bouncing back from the surface of the printed page. Both types of densitometers measure the image density by calculating how well the black area absorbs light.

Today, the measurement and control of color is also measured with colorimeters and spectrophotometers. The prepress and preparation process aims to get a job ready for the reproduction device. It requires an understanding of the technology of the reproduction system as well as the technologies for capturing, processing, and assembling images.

The big picture

All of the prepress issues come down to how you create pages and documents for eventual reproduction. On the next page is a simple chart that shows that the platform relates to the layout program which relates to the image manipulation program, and all of these relate to fonts, and imaging engines and plug-ins and XTensions and utilities.

It all comes together on a workstation where the document becomes a reality in terms of its assembly and then, through a myriad of smaller programs, gets to reproduction.

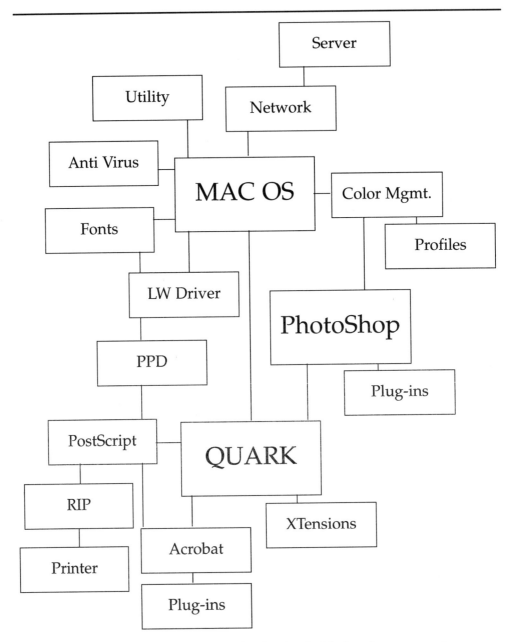

All the pieces of desktop prepress are interrelated, using the Macintosh as an example.

Chapter 3

PRINTING PROCESSES

A printing process describes the method adopted by a system to transfer the image on to a substrate (material). This also means that a printing system will have a medium that carries the image in the first place before it enables the process of reproduction. Getting this printing surface prepared is dependent on the printing process. Over the years, many different ways of putting ink on paper developed and these evolved to be the printing processes. The mechanics adopted under different systems are so different that they cater to specific applications in the market. For a long time the printing industry recognized five major processes. These were :

- relief printing (letterpress, flexography)
- planographic printing (offset lithography)
- recess printing (gravure/intaglio)
- stencil printing (screen)
- digital printing (toner and inkjet)

Relief printing—letterpress

As the name of the process says, the image areas are in relief and the non-image areas are in recess. On application of ink, the relief areas are coated with a film of ink and the non-image areas are not. With pressure over the substrate to bring it in contact with the image area, the image is then transferred to the substrate. If you can picture how a rubber stamp transfers ink to paper, then you understand the principle of letterpress and flexography.

Relief printing was the earliest form of printing and remained dominant for a very long time. The movable type of the hot metal era were all used with letterpress. This printing process takes its name from the manner in which the process was employed, primarily for type, and later engravings.

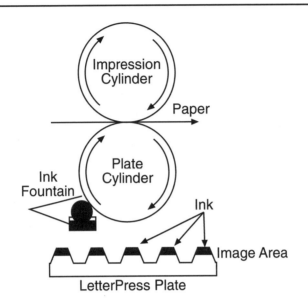

The plate profile is shown at the lower part of this illustration. In some cases the plate was formed as a cylinder for high-speed printing

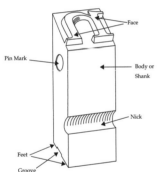

Text is made up of movable type. Types are made from an alloy of lead, antimony, and tin. A block is made of zinc or copper, in which images that are not obtainable in movable type are etched. Logos, diagrams, and illustrations are made from engraved blocks.

A letterpress printed product can be identified by the indentation that it creates in the paper. This is due to the mechanical pressure applied to the paper. In spite of this, letterpress produces images that are sharp and clean. It is a direct printing process, which means that ink is transferred directly from the printing surface to the substrate.

Letterpress is still used to some extent for embossing, imprinting, and special-purpose reproduction.

Flexography

This process adopts the same principle of relief printing and is therefore similar to letterpress. The printing surface is made of rubber instead of metal. The plate (the printing surface) is imaged from film or laser. Rubber plates were replaced by photopolymer plates during the 1970s as was the case with letterpress printing. Flexography is largely used in the packaging industry, where the substrates used are plastic, aluminum, foil, etc., for which the rubber plates are more suitable, due to their being soft. Usually flexography prints rolls of paper or foil instead of cut sheets.

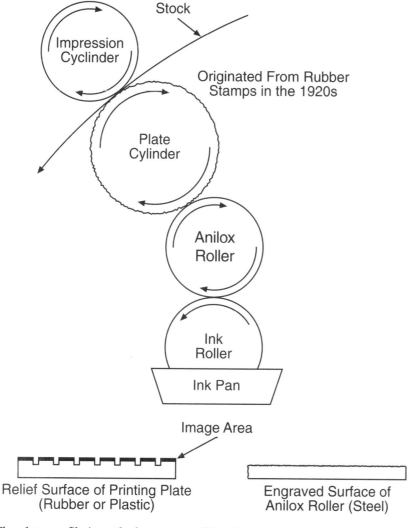

The plate profile is at the lower part of this illustration and the process is shown above

Flexography features:
- Printing from wrong-reading raised image, flexible plate direct to substrate
- Principal applications: almost any substrate which can go through a web press – tissue, plastic film, corrugated board, metal foil, milk crates, gift wrap, folding cartons, labels, etc.
- Recognition characteristics: as a relief printing method, has recognizable, but slight, ink halo effect around letters and solid color areas
- Two categories: wide web (18 or more inches wide) and narrow web
  - Wide web flexo market: flexible packaging, newspapers, corrugated boxes
  - Narrow web market: primarily labels, high-quality process color
  - Some flexo corrugated box printing is sheetfed

The continuous, repeated imaging capability, along the length of the web substrate makes flexography very suitable for products such as wallpaper and wrapping paper.

Planographic printing—offset lithography

Lithography is the most dominant of the printing processes. It accounts for over 60% of the printing market. When people refer to printing, especially color printing, they usually think of lithography. As mentioned in our first chapter, lithography was invented by Alois Senefelder. Lithography is a chemical process and almost opposite to that of letterpress which is more of a mechanical process.

Lithography works on the principle that oil and water do not mix. A lithographic plate is treated in such a way that the image areas on the plate are sensitized and as such are oleophilic (oil-loving); and the non-image areas are treated to be ink repelling or oleophobic. During the press run, the plate is charged twice; first by a set of dampening rollers that apply a coat of dampening solution and second by a coat of the inking rollers. During this process the image areas have been charged to accept ink and repel water during the dampening. The same happens to the non-image areas that start repelling ink as they are coated with water. (Remember the basic principle on which lithography works.)

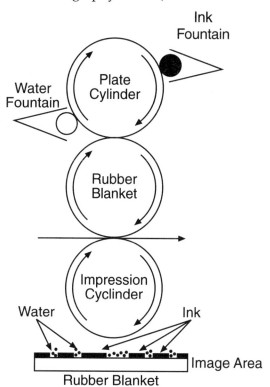

The plate profile is shown at the bottom of this illustration and the process is shown above it

Plate, blanket and impression cylinders

The lithographic process operates with three basic cylinders. They are the plate cylinder, the blanket cylinder, and the impression cylinder. All these are plain heavy metal cylinders. The plate cylinder has the printing plate wound around it. This plate is the carrier of the image that needs to be printed. In other words, it is the equivalent of the types and blocks of letterpress.

The blanket cylinder has a rubber blanket wound around it. This facilitates the transfer of the image from the plate to the blanket, and thereupon to the paper (or other substrates), when the substrate is passed between the blanket and the impression cylinder. The blanket provides the required resiliency to compensate for the unevenness of the substrate used. This is an advantage for the process, as even poorer quality stock can be used in offset printing. The impression cylinder is just a bare cylinder that acts to provide the necessary pressure to impress the image from blanket to the substrate. Pressure settings are varied between the impression cylinder and blanket cylinder when stocks of varying thickness are used.

Image transfer

The image areas accept ink and transfer them to the blanket. The orientation of the image in the plate is readable. When transferred to the blanket it becomes unreadable and in the next revolution, the image is transferred to the paper that travels between the blanket and the impression cylinder. The image is first set off from the plate to the blanket and then set off from the blanket to the paper. For this reason, lithography is also called offset printing. Since the image and the non-image areas on the plate are both in the same plane, lithography is also called a planographic process.

Types of offset presses

There are two ways in which paper can be fed to an offset printing press; either in the sheet form or in the roll form. Presses that feed paper in the cut mode are called sheet fed presses and the presses that feed paper in the roll mode are called web fed presses. Some of the presses can print on both sides of paper and they are called perfecting presses. Many of today's presses have the capability to print many colors as they have been configured with the plate, blanket and impression cylinder configurations many times over. A press that has one of this set is called a single color press, and presses that have multiple sets of the above mentioned combinations are called multicolor presses. They are usually in the two-, four-, five-, six-, eight-, and now ten-color configurations.

The plate used in lithography usually has a flat surface and is called planographic. There is no physical or mechanical separation between image and non-image areas. The plate material can be paper, plastic, or metal.

Printing unit

The printing unit is the section of the press where the print is generated and applied to the substrate. On a single color lithographic offset press, this is usually done with three cylinders called the plate, blanket, and impression or back cylinders. The plate cylinder has four primary functions:
- hold the plate in register
- come into contact with dampening system
- come into contact with inking system
- transfer inked image to the blanket

Dampening system

The purpose of the dampening system is to apply a very thin layer of water or moisture to the plate. The water is actually a special mixture of chemicals called fountain solution. The fountain solution keeps the non-image areas of the plate desensitized and printing clean. The separation between printing image area and nonprinting area is accomplished chemically by having:
- Image areas repel water and accept ink (hydrophobic)
- Non-image areas accept water and repel ink (hydrophilic)

Dampening types

- Contact or non-contact
  - Non-contact (popular on web presses)
    Brush (Harris) or spray (Smith)

- Contact dampening
  Conventional or continuous
    -Conventional has a reciprocating ductor roller. The rollers can be fabric covered or bareback. Fabric can be a thick cotton cloth called moelleton or a thin parchment paper sleeve
  Continuous dampening
    - Continuous is also called flooding nip
    - Direct plate-feed
    - Indirect inker-feed (integrated, Dahlgren)
    - Some combination of both (bridge)

Perfecting

Printing on both sides of a sheet of paper in a single pass through the press is called perfecting. In office imaging, laser printing, or photo-copying, this is called duplexing. Sheetfed presses usually perfect sequentially. Webfed presses perfect simultaneously. In order to perfect on a sheetfed press, the sheet of paper must be flopped or tumbled end-for-end inside the press. The tail or back edge becomes a new gripper or front edge. Any size sheet error essentially becomes doubled when done with a perfecting cylinder.

Inking system

The purpose of the inking system is to apply an accurately measured or metered amount of ink to the plate. Each process requires a special type of ink and method to apply it to the image carrier. Some inks are thick like a heavy paste and others are fluid. Some systems continuously bathe or immerse a roller or cylinder while others intermittently supply a limited and metered amount of ink.

If the ink is a thick paste, then it can be distributed by a series of soft rubber rollers. If the ink is a fluid, it would drip off the rollers due to gravity. Fluid inks require miniature wells or cups to transfer the ink. These wells can be part of the image carrier itself or a special type of inking roller.

The ink film thickness determines the strength or density of a color. There are two separate controls for overall or global (sweep) and localized increases or decreases in ink volume (keys). Here are some of the factors involved in ink distribution:

Fountain roller (ball)
Fountain blade
Ink keys
Ductor roller
Ink train
Oscillating or vibrator rollers
Form rollers

Ink distribution by printing process:

Offset lithography	paste ink & rollers
Gravure	fluid ink & doctor blade to remove excess ink on top surface
Flexography	fluid ink & anilox roller to apply ink to rubber relief plate
Screen	paste ink & rubber squeeze blade to force ink through porous mesh
Letterpress	past ink and rollers
Digital	liquid or dry toner powder

Image transfer

Each printing process has a method to transfer the ink from the image carrier to the substrate. Some do this directly while others have no contact at all with the substrate. Direct image transfer systems require a wrong-reading image carrier so the image on the substance is correct or right-reading.

Offset lithography	indirect, "offset," right reading
Gravure	direct, wrong reading
Flexography	direct, wrong reading
Screen	direct, wrong reading, because screen is two-sided and translucent
Letterpress	direct, wrong reading
Digital	direct, offset, or non-impact

What does offset mean?

Offset is the method of transferring an image from the plate to the substrate through an intermediate rubber blanket. When lithography was first invented, it was not an offset process, but a direct process. If desired, all of the printing processes could be "offset." The blanket cylinder has two primary functions:
- hold the rubber blanket
- transfer ink from the plate to the substrate

Looking at the various printing results

Letterpress	Same as flexo but hard metal type may deboss backside of paper.
Offset lithography	Text and line art is sharp and crisp with excellent edge definition. Halftones have high resolution screen rulings of 133–300 lpi for halftones.
Gravure	All images, both halftones and line art are screened. Solids may look wormy, screen tints may look "snowflaky" from dot skipping.
Flexography	Outside edges of solid type have a darker halo ring or outline.
Screen	Ink film thickness is very thick and can be felt. Top surface of ink may have a rough texture because of the pattern of the screen.

Waterless offset

With this concept, the use of water is eliminated from the process. Image areas are in recess from the non-image areas. The problems that are associated with ink water balance, paper expansion due to moisture content caused by water in the dampening solution, etc. are overcome with waterless offset. This concept was developed in the late 1960s by 3M as a dryographic process, but they stopped marketing because of the poor scratch resistance and durability of the plates. Plates were developed by Toray Industries of Japan in 1973. Toray made positive working plates that were more durable, had better scratch resistance, allowed longer print runs, and produced better quality. By 1978 they marketed positive working waterless plates, and by 1985 they were able to offer negative working plates.

Aluminum is the base material for the plate, and the plate is not anodized like conventional offset plates. A light-sensitive photopolymer coating is given to the aluminum base. Over this there is a very thin layer of silicon, approximately 2 microns. The plate is protected by a cover sheet, which is approximately 7 microns. This cover sheet need not be removed during exposure, and does not cause an appreciable dot gain, or undercutting during exposure.

Exposure and development

The waterless plates are made from either positives or negatives, depending on the plate type used. The plate is exposed to actinic UV light. During the exposure, the bond between silicon and the photopolymer is broken. The silicon loosens its hold on the photopolymer. The plate is developed by a chemical process that consists of tap water solution for lubrication and a glycol-based solution for treatment with a dye solution, which recirculates and is not discharged from the processor. These plates have the ability to hold a dot ranging from 0.5% to 99.5%.

The finished plate has the image areas in its photopolymer layer and the non-image areas in its silicon layer. The nature of silicon to repel ink, suits its role wonderfully in a waterless plate system. The image areas are in a recess and are protected by silicon walls. Since the image areas are protected by this wall, individual halftone dots have less capability to grow, thereby minimizing dot gain on plate. These plates are capable of producing very high screen frequencies, in the region of 200–300 lpi with negative working and 400–600 lpi with positive working plates.

Waterless press

Any offset press that has a dampening system on it can be used for waterless offset printing. Temperature and humidity control in the press room is critical in waterless offset between 80 to 88 degrees F. This is considered the optimum temperature range for inks and ink rollers in a waterless system. Each unit of the press has a different temperature, with black needing the hottest, yellow the coolest and cyan and magenta in between. When printing with good stock, we can expect good results. Since the non-image areas of the plate are made of silicon, they tend to get scratched when using poorer quality stock. This is due to the fibers from the paper scratching the silicon layer. The same problem can be caused by abrasive particles that may be used to dry ink (pumice powder).

Offset lithography features
- Printing from right-reading planographic (flat) plate to blanket and substrate
- Basic principle: "ink and water don't mix"
- Principal applications: publications, packaging, forms, general commercial printing, labels, books, etc.
- Recognition characteristics: sharp, clear images

Waterless offset
- Silicone surface of non-image area on a plate—recent advances in inks, plates, and presses make this a rapidly growing process
- Advantages: no fountain solution; yields cleaner, purer, more consistent color; improved color contrast; reduced dot gain; high gloss levels; reduced makeready, and running waste; faster job changeover times
- Requires special ink and plates, adapted presses
- Waterless-capable presses able to run both waterless and conventional
- Strong growth projected for high-end commercial sheetfed and heatset web offset

Sheetfed offset trends
- Press automation increases competitive advantage. Most automated features deal with makeready, nonproductive costs, and turnaround time.
  - Programmable, automatic blanket and roller washing
  - Semiautomatic and fully automatic plate changing
  - Presetting systems for fast format changes
- Improvements in feeder, sheet transfer, and delivery systems increase running speed to 10,000 to 15,000 impressions per hour.
- Digital press controls allow virtually total press supervision and control from central workstation
- De facto standard for multiple printing units on new sheetfed presses in six color units with inline coating unit. Placement of presses with seven, eight, or more units is increasing.

- Higher number of printing units accommodates more complex design and color applications.
- Increased demand for short run lengths.
- Sheetfed printing squeezed between efficient web offset operations and by digital non-impact printing processes and color copies.

Web offset trends
- Continued development of automated control systems expected for all aspects of web offset production, from makeready through drying, folding, stacking, and delivery.
- Press speeds of 2500-3000 feet per minute now possible.
- Successfully entering into competition with sheetfed at lower run lengths, and with gravure at higher run lengths.
- Waterless offset becoming more widely accepted.
- Opposing trends: regionalization of printing (in some part due to increasing postal rates) may keep run lengths, press sizes down; consolidation of printing plants may drive up need for longer runs on higher speed, wide web presses.
- Wider webs—54 and more inches wide—becoming more commonplace.
- Average run length has dropped by as much as 25% 1990–1994.
- Short run lengths (under 20,000) and extremely high run lengths (20 million) are economically feasible, depending on circumstances, with web offset and will be typical by 2000.

Direct imaging technology

Heidelberg came out with "Direct Imaging" which they called the "system solution for Computer To Press" (a different kind of CTP, essentially Computer to Plate on press). This technology takes the data stream from the computer that acts as its front end and images the plate directly on the press.The spirit of offset printing is very much alive in presses that incorporate the direct imaging technology. The plate is mounted on the press, but is quite different from conventional versions. The plate is in a continuous reel form that is wrapped externally around the plate cylinder. The image is on the surface of the cylinder. The plate has two layers, a base layer that is an ink-loving layer and a top layer, made of silicon, that is an ink-repelling layer. The laser when fired on the plate burns the silicon layer leaving the image-receptive layer intact.

Digital Front End (DFE)

The front end of the press is a computer that controls the digital data into the press. A RIP converts the PostScript data into a bitmap and fires the laser onto the plate, which is already mounted on the plate cylinder. The imaging head has 64 infrared laser diodes (16 diodes per color x 4 colors) that take the raster data and fire up the plate. The plates can be imaged in either of 1270 or 2540 dpi resolutions.

Direct imaging technology uses waterless printing. When the press is in operation, the plate is in contact with the ink rollers that apply ink onto the image areas. The image is transferred to a blanket and then onto the substrate as in offset. The QuickMaster-DI uses a common impression cylinder as its internal architecture for the press. This means that this press has only one impression cylinder, instead of one for each color (cyan, magenta, yellow or black).

The impression cylinder is in the middle and all the four blanket cylinders come in contact with this common impression cylinder. The paper travels between the blanket and the impression cylinder as in a conventional offset press.

Direct imaging

The laser technology which is built into the direct imaging press from Heidelberg forms the heart of this entire technology. Heidelberg has been a long-time known leader in the printing press arena. They have been and are a leader in the conventional offset field, but had not made a big dent in the digital work environment. However, they have had the insight to bring to our industry the strengths of conventional offset and combine it with the strengths of digital technology. In doing so, they and their partner Presstek, harnessed the combined power of these two technologies and thus was born the technology of "direct imaging."

Register control

The satellite construction of the press ensures that the paper is gripped once preventing transfer from one unit to the other. This feature of the press minimizes the chances for misregister. Another key issue to minimizing or practically eliminating misregister from the press is in the basic technology of direct imaging itself. Since the plates are imaged on the press, there is no reason that they will ever have to be moved horizontally or laterally for register.

This is very important in the economics of running a press. A vast amount of time is spent in a press during the initial makeready of the job. Time being looked at as money these days, any saving in time has a direct impact on savings in money. Waterless as a process helps in getting brighter ink reflectance on the paper. The advantages of direct imaging are numerous.

Although the press is now available in a slightly smaller sheet size (18-3/8"x13-3/8"), which is a limiting factor, the technology is a sure success. Now a new company called 74 Karat has been started by Scitex and KBA Planeta and they have adopted the direct imaging technology in their press. A key development that has been incorporated in 74 Karat is that they have built a press that is much larger that the QuickMaster-DI 46-4. Heidelberg has launched a 74 cm press, matching Karat's present size.

This press will have five- or six-color printing capability and images at 2540 dpi resolution. With many jobs being printed requiring more than four colors, Heidelberg's decision to provide the special color unit will be welcomed by the industry. This press will have an automatic plate mounting mechanism, with automatic plate washup, which will save considerable time. It is called the Speedmaster 74-DI. Direct imaging is a technology that has to be watched.

Recess printing—Gravure

Gravure is another direct printing process, like letterpress with, however some major differences. The image is directly transferred from the image carrier, which is usually a cylinder, onto the substrate. Gravure is called intaglio because the image areas are in a sunken area and the non-image areas are in relief. This must sound like an exact opposite of the letterpress process. In a way, that is true.

Press construction

A gravure press is constructed with two cylinders per unit, a printing cylinder, which carries the image and an impression cylinder like in the offset process, that applies the required pressure to transfer the ink. Gravure cylinders are usually made of steel. This cylinder has a number of tiny cells in it, around 50,000 to a square inch. The cells are protected by walls that are in relief. The surface of the cylinder is plated with copper to hold the image. The image is transferred photographically to the electroplated copper surface. The non-image areas on the copper are chemically etched or mechanically engraved to form the cells. Each cell varies in its depth, and this enables each cell to transfer varying densities of ink to produce tones. The ink used in gravure is in a liquid form.

Doctor blade

The printing cylinder rotates in a trough of liquid ink. During this motion, the inks fill the cells of the cylinder and inks the image areas. However, the non-image areas also get inked as they are in relief. This excess ink is wiped clean by a blade called a doctor blade. The doctor blade is positioned at an angle over the cylinder so that when the cylinder rotates, the excess ink that was picked up by the non-image areas are wiped clean.

In the continuing motion of the cylinder, the paper (or the substrate) is fed in between the printing cylinder and the impression cylinder. By pressure, the ink in the cells is forced out onto the substrate. Since the printing image is made of copper, which is quite expensive, gravure is usually used for very long-run jobs which it handles well because the image is placed on the cylinder directly, and on copper, which is a strong metal. Traditionally gravure has been used by markets that have a need to produce long run and consistently good quality printing. Packaging and some long run publications therefore employ this printing process.

Most gravure presses are web-fed. Some are as large as 16 feet wide. The gravure process is used for specialty products like wall paper and vinyls. Gravure presses can print at incredible speeds like 2500 feet per minute. So one can imagine that unless the job calls for huge numbers to be reproduced, in high quality, gravure as a process cannot be chosen.

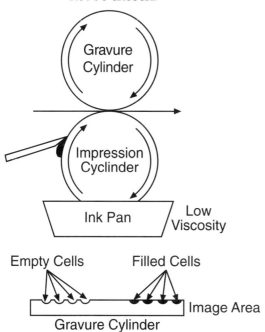

The bottom of this illustration shows the gravure plate profile. The top of the illustration shows the gravure process. Note the doctor blade removing ink from the impression cylinder.

Gravure features
- Printing from wrong-reading recessed image cylinder direct to substrate
- Three major segments: publications, packaging, and specialty product printing
- Principal applications: packaging, long-run magazines and newspaper inserts, catalogs, wallpaper, postage stamps, plastic laminates, vinyl flooring
- Recognition characteristics: serrated edge to text letters, solid color areas
- Relatively short makeready times on press; high color consistency; continuous, repeated image
- Cylinders last forever, making repeat runs very economical
- Cost of making cylinders remains high, making gravure expensive for jobs that are not repeated or not extremely long
- Trend is toward removing chemistry from cylinder-making procedure, increased use of water-based inks
- Breakthroughs anticipated in electron-beam engraving and photopolymer-coated cylinders

Stencil printing—screen printing

This is a process that is used by many artisans for short-run jobs. It is such a less expensive process that many screen printing units are operated out of garages. But that does not mean that screen printing cannot offer good quality printing. It is a pretty simple process to understand and operate.

Basically if you have seen how printing is done from a stencil, then you have probably seen the process of screen printing. The process is pretty much photographic in the image creation stage and it is mostly manual at the printing stage.

The image that needs to be printed is first captured on a photographic material, a positive usually. A silk screen is stretched tightly by hinging around a wooden frame. The process derives its name from this silk screen, which was used as the image carrier. The positive image is then transferred to the screen and developed. The image that has been transferred to the silk screen is on the porous area of the screen. The non-image areas are blocked out during the stage of image creation itself.

The screen is laid over the substrate that is to be printed and ink is poured on the frame over the screen. The ink is then wiped across the surface of the screen using a device called a squeeze. A squeeze is a wooden device that has a rubber blade. It facilitates the smooth flow of ink over the screen. Since the screen is porous in nature, the ink flows through it. Because the image areas are porous, they allow ink to flow through them. This ink is thus printed onto the substrate beneath.

Printing capability

Since the printing surface in the screen printing process is very flexible, it allows printing on three-dimensional objects too. This is something that the printing processes discussed earlier cannot offer. A substrate that is two-dimensional and flat is all that can be fed into those machines; in the case of screen printing, the printing surface itself can be wound around the substrate. So objects like cups, mugs, watches or other irregular-shaped products can be done using the screen printing process.

Although this description of screen printing may sound quite simple, in actuality there are screen printing presses that are as automated as any other printing presses. Multi-color printing presses employing screen printing process with capability to print on different substrates like polyester, metal, and pressure-sensitive materials are today a common scenario. These presses are equipped with online corona (electrostatic) treatment, and can even combine ultraviolet drying in some color units.

Screen printing features
- Printing by forcing ink through a stenciled screen mesh image directly onto substrate
- Principal applications: can print on any substrate; point-of-purchase displays, billboards, decals, fabric, electronic circuit boards, glasses, etc.
- Ink formulation, screen mesh count, and image type are major quality factors
- Recognition characteristics: heavy, durable, brilliant layer of ink

Other printing processes

The above-mentioned four printing process were considered the major printing processes for a long time. This was due to the fact that other forms of outputting ink on paper did not really have the ability to compare with the quality that these processes could produce. Moreover, the ability of other processes to produce color was very limited.

Over time other processes evolved to cater to specific market needs, and with their ability to reproduce color, they were extended to serve specific printing markets. They are all used mostly as proofing devices and without an exception they are all digital devices. One of the prime differences between the already discussed processes and the following is in the image carrier. In the traditional printing processes, the image is on a surface that produces multiple reproductions as replica to the one on the printing surface. The digital printing devices have the ability to vary the image every time they need to print. Let us take a look at some of the other technologies that could put ink on paper. For the present, we will call these *digital printing processes*:
- dot matrix (including limited color)
- electrostatic (including color)
- laser printing (including color)
- dye diffusion
- thermal printing
    - –thermal wax transfer

- inkjet
    - bubble jet printers
- other recorders

Dot matrix

These were the early forms of outputting a document from a personal computer. Used largely in the office environment, they did (and do) a pretty good job. The printers have a series of hammers in the print head. A color ribbon, usually black, is placed in front of the head. On instruction from the computer to print, the hammer whacks the ribbon against the paper placed behind it. The ink from the ribbon is thus transferred to the paper. The character or images are constructed by a formation of small dots. The quality of the output is quite poor, and the noise that is generated by the printer is quite disturbing. Types do not look sharp and the problems are worse when printing one color over another. The quality of image transfer deteriorates with aging of the ribbon and/or the hammer.

Electrostatic

A laser beam creates a selective charge on a selenium drum when exposed to laser light. The charge takes place in the image areas. The equivalent of ink is a toner particle. This toner particle gets attracted to the charge in the drum. When the substrate is fed into the machine, the toner particles transfer from the drum onto the substrate. A lot of document copying and printing work is done this way, and is also called photocopying, because multiple copies of a document are created by the use of light. Color electrostatic printers adopt the same principle to reproduce color and, depending on the equipment, the paper may pass through the machine four times, in a single writing station, or once in a multiple-pass station. These printers can print good line work, as they have a high addressability. Some of these printers print 600 dpi.

Laser printing

This is electrophotographic imaging as in copying machines, with the printing machines driven by computers. When the document is sent for output, a laser beam charges the printing drum by applying a static charge to the photoreceptive drum. The areas that received the charge tend to attract toner particles, and the image is transferred to substrate. For permanency, the toner-based image is heated and fused with the substrate.

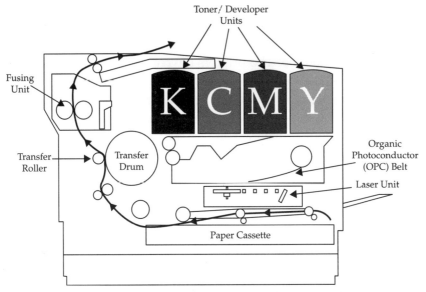

Laser printers can be desktop-based or higher-speed and very much like presses

The early models of laser printers which produced good quality copies had one drawback. The speeds were not very attractive for high volume requirements. Now high-speed printers are available like the Xerox Docutech 135 and 180, as well as Docucolor 40 and 70/100 which can be used for production work. They all use the laser process principle. Though claimed to be high-speed printers, they do not compare with traditional printing process speeds. Nonetheless, they are quite popular in the short-run, and on-demand printing markets.

Thermal printing

If you have seen the way something gets printed from a fax machine, then you have pretty much understood this process. A specially made paper that is coated with a dye is used in this process. When the paper is heated it turns black. So, during the imaging process, the image areas are heated and the spots on the paper turn black, giving us the reading matter printed. This is also a popular method employed for generating labels and barcodes. Because the process involves an induced change in the state of the substrate (paper), the process is limited to printing only in single color.

Dye diffusion printers

Originally this process was created for printing on fabrics. It uses a color donor ribbon that transfers the dye to the substrate by the use of heat. The temperature is usually very high, in the region of 400 degrees C. By varying the temperature on the print heads, varying intensities of color can be printed. This can produce a feel of continuous tone printing. This process has a good potential, as the inks used in dye diffusion printing have a color gamut greater than that of photography. However the flip side to this technology is that it is expensive, slower, and requires special substrates to print on.

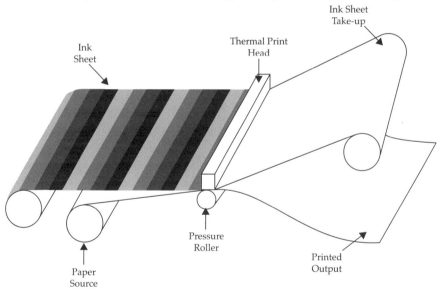

Thermal and dye diffusion printers have special ribbons with alternating color areas

Thermal wax printing

This process is somewhat similar to that of a dye diffusion printer, using wax as the medium of "ink transfer." A metal drum is divided into a grid that addresses a pixel to a spot on the grid. Every spot on the grid is assigned a color value. The pixels in the grid heat up and melt the wax in the ribbon, which is transferred to paper. These waxes are transparent, which makes it advantageous for these prints to be used as overhead slides for projection. Some of these types of printers have a three- or four-color ribbon to print from. They both produce color prints, but the one with four-color ribbons has more visual appeal than the tri-color ribbon printer.

Inkjet printing

This process works by spitting small droplets of ink on the surface of the paper. The amount of ink that is to be spewed on the substrate is controlled by a computer. There are three kinds of ink jet printing:

- continuous inkjet printing
- drop-on-demand inkjet printing
- phase-change inkjet printing

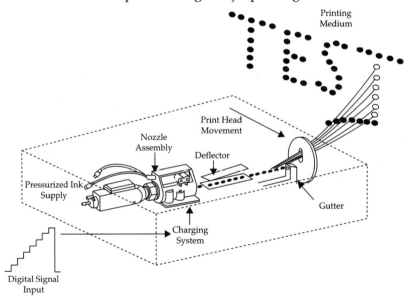

Continuous inkjet "spits" the ink at the substrate

Continuous inkjet printing "spits" liquid ink in a continuous fashion, and the pressure of the spurting of the ink is controlled by a vibrating device and the ink is spurted from an orifice which also determines the size of the droplet that will ultimately land on paper. All of the ink is fired from a single nozzle. This produces print which makes good line work and solid colors, which is acceptable for some low-end applications of the market. When it comes to printing fine images and multi-color printing, the drawback in the process stems from the single nozzle rather than an array or group of them. And that is what happens in continuous array ink jet. Every droplet's size is controlled by a single nozzle. Because of multiple arrays, speeds can be increased, and this gives better productivity. An array of continuous ink jet printing nozzles can also be attached to high-speed printing presses for specialized printing like barcoding or personalization.

Drop-on-demand inkjet printing

The ink is forced out of the orifices onto the substrate only where it is required. This is done by one of several methods. The inks used in this process are water-based. When heated, the water in the ink vaporizes and forms a gas bubble. This causes a droplet of ink to be pushed out of the orifice in the chamber, which will have to be replenished. The replenished ink then goes through the same process till it is pushed out. Because of this alternating method of throwing out the ink and then replenishing the chamber, the process slows. Another drop-on-demand ink jet printing method uses a piezoelectric plate. This plate carries the ink, and on an electrical current being passed, the size of the plate is deformed. The deformation of the plate reduces the volume of the ink in the plate and causes it to spill a drop. The drop of ink lands and dries on the substrate. This kind of inkjet printing is commonly used for large billboards and posters. The quality is acceptable.

Phase-change inkjet printing

The process derives its name because the ink changes its state from solid to liquid to solid before it actually lands on paper. These printers use a waxy kind of an ink in the ink chamber. This wax is heated and the ink changes to a molten state in a reservoir. When the print head receives an electrical signal, the volume of the reservoir reduces, causing the molten ink to be ejected. The reservoir is filled when there is no charge. Based on the signal received from the computer, the print head either turns on or turns off the electrical signal. Thus, the ink ejection from the reservoir is controlled. Since the ink is wax-based, it gels well with the substrate and does not penetrate the substrate. Up to 600 dpi can be addressed by this process, and it produces sharp and saturated images. As the ink settles on the surface of the substrate, its thickness can be felt; this also adds to the feel of the image printed on it. However, if handled, the print is subject to abrasion and can get damaged.

Bubble-jet printers

Bubble-jet printers are relatively low cost devices that produce color prints on plain paper. Low cost per page and low cost of the printer are the primary attraction of these printers. They are also limited in reproduction size, in that many bubble jet printers can print only up to a letter size (8.5"x11"). They can be used for applications like inhouse work, or for reports, but certainly cannot be used for contract proofs.

Slide or film recorders

Film recorders produce slides, in color and monochrome, as negatives or positives. When only one slide is needed, it can be easily produced with your camera. However, when a number of slides need to be duplicated, the need to maintain consistency and standards become critical. The basic image is created digitally in a computer and is imaged on a photographic medium for as many times as the number of copies needed. The recorders function like a camera though they do not capture light the way a camera does. Instead of aiming at the scene to be captured, the recorder aims at a Cathode Ray Tube (CRT). A light-sensitive emulsion is exposed from the beams of the CRT and this emulsion is sent for processing, the same way a conventional photographic film is processed. A recorder that has come in to cater to the high end of the market is Light Valve Technology (LVT). The film that is to be imaged is wrapped around a cylinder as in a scanner. The drum spins at a high speed, and the film is imaged by narrow beams of light through electronic light valves that modulate the amount of light that should image the film.

Ink

Every printing ink is formulated from three basic components:
- colorant (pigment or dye)
- vehicle
- additives

Pigments or dyes give inks their color and make them visible on the substrate. Without pigments, printing could occur, but it would be pointless since the image would be almost invisible. Vehicles carry the pigment through the press and onto the substrate. Without the vehicle, there is no printing, period. Additives include silicone, wetting agents, waxes, driers and other materials used to enhance performance characteristics such as drying speed, color development, slip and mar resistance. Of the three, vehicle formulation is most critical to an ink's performance on the press.

Colorants are the visible portion of the ink. They may be dyes, but more often are pigments. They may be in powder form (dry toner), in a concentrated paste dispersion known as a flush, or in a liquid dispersion. Red, blue, yellow, and black are the most frequently used colors in printing and together create purple, green, orange and other colors during the printing process. Other colors are used, but in much smaller quantities. The red, yellow, and blue colorants are almost exclusively synthetic organic pigments. The black used in printing ink is carbon black—a soot generated through burning natural gas or oil.

While not as visible as colorants, vehicles are just as important to the ink. Made up of oils (petroleum or vegetable), solvents, water, or a combination of these, they carry the colorant through the printing press and attach it to the paper or substrate. Most vehicles contain resins which serve to bind the colorant to the printing surface. The vehicle is the portion of the ink most responsible for tack, drying properties and gloss. Additives can include waxes, driers and other materials which add specific characteristics to an ink or to the dried ink film, such as slip and resistance to scuffing and chemicals.

Vehicles are complex blends of natural and synthetic solvents, oils, and resins, and are manufactured with strict attention to cycle times, heating and cooling. They can account for up to 75 % of an ink's content. Ink formulators can choose from hundreds of materials, alone or in combination, to create an infinite variety of vehicles, each with distinct properties suited to different printing applications. The vehicle is responsible for an ink's body and viscosity, or flow properties. It is also the primary factor in transfer, tack, adhesion, lay, drying and gloss. More than any other element in a formulation, the vehicle determines how well an ink does its job.

An ink's vehicle determines its rheology, or flow characteristics—whether it is liquid or paste, long bodied or short. This has a direct impact on the ink's movement from the ink fountain through the roller train, and its transfer from roller to plate, plate to blanket and blanket to substrate. The faster the press, the more critical these transfer properties become. As speeds increase, ink misting tends to increase as well. Increased shear and heat build-up on faster presses have the potential to cause an ink to break down, leading to dot gain, toning and other print quality problems.

Printers desiring to use lighter weight, uncoated or recycled stocks for economic or environmental reasons complain that the softer surface of these stocks makes them prone to water absorption, dot gain and picking. Using an ink with inappropriate tack and transfer properties because of an inappropriate vehicle compounds the problem.

Ink formulations differ depending upon printing process and application. Printing presses used in the various processes require different flow characteristics or rheology for the ink to travel in an optimal fashion through the press to the substrate. Letterpress and offset lithographic inks are fairly thick or "viscous." On press, they move through a series of rollers called the ink train where the action of the rollers spreads the ink into a thin film for transfer to the blanket and/ or plate and onto the substrate. Flexographic and gravure printing inks are more fluid, so that they flow easily into and out of the engraved cells on anilox rollers (flexo) and print cylinders (gravure).

All inks are made up of pigments, resin vehicles, solvents, and other additives, but the most important properties are color, color strength, body, length, tack, and drying. Color is determined by pigments, which are finely divided solids. Important characteristics of pigment include specific gravity, particle size, opacity, chemical resistance, wettability, and permanence. Body refers to the consistency and stiffness or softness of inks. Inks can range from stiff ink like that used for lithography to very liquid ink like that used in flexography. The term that is associated with this is viscosity.

Viscosity is the resistance to flow, so that a high viscosity ink would not flow. Length is associated with the ability of an ink to flow and form filaments. Ink length ranges from long to short. Long inks flow well and form long filaments and are not ideal since they tend to mist or fly. Short inks do not flow well, and tend to pile on rollers, plates, and blankets. Ideal inks are somewhere in the middle of the two types. Tack refers to the stickiness of the ink, or the force required to split ink film between two surfaces.

Tack determines whether or not the ink will pick the paper surface, trap properly, or will print sharp. If the tack is higher than the surface strength of the paper, the paper may pick, split, or tear. When putting down more than one ink on a page, the ink that has the higher tack should be put down first. Tack can be measured using either an inkometer or tackoscope. The final property is drying, but the ink must first set before it actually dries. Some newer drying systems include ultraviolet and electron beam radiation.

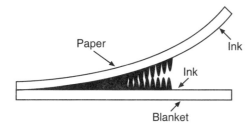

Tack is the relationship between ink, blanket, and paper

Ink drying

Ink drying is a very important function when considering what to use. Inks can dry by absorption, oxidation/polymerization, evaporation, solidification, and precipitation. During the process of absorption the vehicle drains into the sheet, leaving the pigment trapped by the fibers in the surface of the paper. There is really no true drying, which is why newsprint comes off on the reader's hands. When ink is dried using oxygen, it attacks the carbon atoms. This is called oxidation. The oxygen break down the double bonds of the atoms found in the drying oils, which causes the ink to dry. Sometimes the solvent is evaporated using heated rollers or dryers that cause the inks to dry, and is called evaporation. If the ink then needs to be chilled after going through a set of heat rollers the process of drying is called solidification. Finally, precipitation depends on the actual precipitation of resin from the ink vehicle by addition of moisture. This method is incompatible with the dampening solution on an offset press.

There are a wide variety of inks used for different purposes. Radiation inks have been developed to eliminate spray powder in sheet-fed presses. There are two types of radiation inks
- UV curing
- electron beam

UV curing inks dry when exposed to large doses of UV light. These inks are expensive because of the costly active ingredients. Electron beam curing inks are a good alternative to UV inks. The main cost is the high capital cost of getting the equipment to run these inks. Heat-set inks are quick drying inks used mostly for web presses. The solvents in the ink disappear after a drier heats them. Once the solvents are gone, the pigments and binding resins are fixed to the paper so the ink does not spread. Another type of ink is high gloss ink. These inks contain extra varnish, which give them a glossy appearance.

There are still many problems with printing inks although they have been around for centuries. The most common problems in the pressroom include:

- hickeys
- picking
- piling
- tinting
- scumming
- ghosting

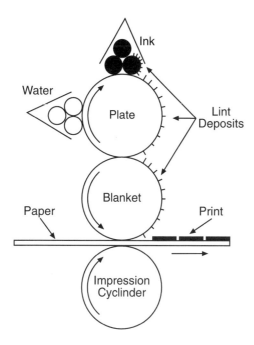

Hickeys are caused by dirt. Ink cans should be closed to prevent debris from getting in the ink. Picking transfers debris from the paper back through the ink and onto the paper again. Piling happens when the ink fails to transfer from the blanket to the paper. Tinting is caused by the emulsification of ink in the dampening solution and results from poorly formulated ink. A common remedy is changing inks, though adding a binding varnish may help. Scumming occurs when the non-image area takes up ink instead of remaining clean. Ghosting (mechanical) occurs when there is uneven ink take-off from the form rollers.

Lint deposits can transfer to the paper

The substrate used for each printing application and its end use further dictate the raw materials chosen to formulate an ink. Non-porous substrates such as plastic films and glass cannot absorb ink vehicles and require inks which dry either through evaporation or by polymerization (UV or EB). Often solvent-based, these inks are frequently formulated for additional performance characteristics. Inks used on soap wrappers, for example, must be alkali resistant; inks on liquor labels must be alcohol resistant; inks on food containers that will be heated in ovens or microwaves must resist high cooking temperatures.

Newspaper inks are formulated to dry by absorption; that is, the ink oils are absorbed into the newsprint. This process leaves the colorant sitting on the surface, and without the binding properties of resins or drying oils, it tends to rub off. For magazines, catalogs and brochures, the demand is for high quality paper, glossy printing with vivid colors that do not rub off readily. Here the printed ink is often subjected to heat to assist in drying. These properties dictate a different and more costly set of raw materials.

Many printers have made the switch from alcohol to alcohol substitutes in their fountain solutions for environmental and health reasons. If they did not communicate the change to their ink suppliers so that an adjustment in ink could be made, they may have been surprised to find a deterioration in print quality—increased scumming, tinting and toning.

Using sophisticated laboratory instruments—rheometers, viscometers, inkometers, and surface tensiometers—ink formulators can test vehicles to closely predict performance characteristics. The final test of any ink, however, will always be on the press, when the full combination of variables (ink, press speed, substrate, plate chemistry, fountain solution and even the ambient temperature and humidity of the press room) come into play. Close cooperation and continuous communication with ink suppliers will minimize potential problems and ensure that the vehicle in the ink you are using is the right one to get you where you want to go.

Inkjet ink

Inkjet printers fall into the larger class of non-impact printers. There are many techniques for printing without use of plates and pressure. These non-impact printers are used largely for computer printout and copying requirements and also include electrostatic printers, laser printers, thermal, and others. Inkjet printers are among the most important of non-impact printers. The are used to produce or reproduce variable information on a wide variety of substrates, paper, gloss, and metal, and textiles. For the last thirty years, inkjet has been predicted to be the next major printing technology.

Inkjet printers are used for many applications including mass mailings as well as home usage. Ink jet printing uses jets of ink droplets driven by digital signals to print the same or variable information directly onto paper without an imaging system. The ink is sent out of the printhead either by a pumping action, by a piezo electric crystal, or by vapor pressure. In the continuous process, electronic deflectors position the drops, while drop-on-demand places the ink only when needed. The bubble-jet printer you may own at home just drools the ink onto the paper. Once the ink is dropped onto the paper, the ink sets through absorption, spreading, and evaporative drying. Inkjet currently is the key contender for low-speed, low-cost desktop full color. The main categories of inkjet systems are listed in the following chart:

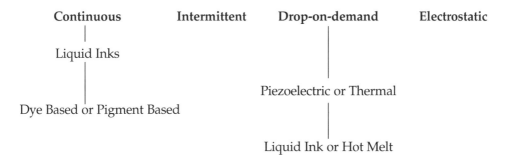

Inkjet inks are made of water-soluble dyes, polyethylene glycol, diethylene glycol, N-methyl pyrrolidone, biocide, buffering agent, polyvinyl alcohol, tri-ethanolamine, and distilled water. Since the dye must be water-soluble, this leads to poor water fastness on paper. Hewlett-Packard changed their ink formula in their HP DeskJet for a large improvement in water fastness. A problem is that of wicking, which is ink spreading away from the dots along the fibers of the paper. One way to reduce this problem is to change to hot melt/phase change inks.

Hot melt/phase-change inks are used in drop-on-demand desktop printers, but are aimed at high-quality full-color printing on a range of substrates. The phase change refers to the fact that the ink dye or pigment is contained in a binder that is solid at room temperature.

This principle requires a low viscosity ink. The inks are jetted as a hot liquid but cool almost instantly upon hitting the surface.

Inkjet technology is really not one technology, but two. The first is continuous as mentioned before. This method produces small characters at high speeds (up to 2000 characters/second). This method allows the printer to apply variable data to a job. The basic idea of this method is called oxillography. Using oxillography, ink is pressurized through a small nozzle, about the diameter of a human hair, and pulsed to form a uniform stream of regularly sized and spaced drops. These drops pass an electrode, which can induce an electrostatic charge on any droplet. Only drops that are used for character formation are charged. As the drops continue, they pass through an electrostatic field induced by two deflector plates. These plates deflect the path of the droplets by an angle proportional to the charge. By changing this degree of applied charge (changing the degree of deflection), characters can be formed on a moving substrate. Uncharged drops are deflected back and collected to be used again. There are some problems that are associated with this method of inkjetting. These problems are as follows:
- The need for sophisticated equipment for dry conditions to avoid loss of ink solvent in nozzle.
- Stationary items cannot be printed.
- The print is not solid and looks a lot like a bad dot matrix.

The second technology is drop-on-demand. This technology produces images using water-based inks for on-line printing of bags, boxes, and other items used for distribution. The drops are not deflected from one head, but from multiple heads, otherwise known as a raster. The firing of the ink is computer controlled to form the character. Drop-on-demand is slower than continuous jet, and the water-based inks require an absorbent substrate. There are limitations on this method of inkjetting
- coarse printing
- slow speeds
- only print on absorbent substrates

Rapid development is taking place in the area of continuous jet printers. These printers will be able to do quality multi-colored graphics,
although at low speeds. More developments also seem to be taking
place in continuous multiple inkjet systems. This system prints with
100 nozzles. In this system it is the uncharged droplets that are
placed onto the paper, not the charged droplets. This should increase
print accuracy, as there is no deflection between particles. Drop-on-
demand developments are focusing in on smaller dot sizes in order
to achieve smaller characters that in the traditional method. In order
to do this, the number of heads is increased, though it prints at slower speeds. The latest technology includes the touch dry ink jet which
uses 32 jets to apply thermoplastic ink, which eliminates problems
associated with solvent-based inks. The medium is held in the reservoir in the form of dry pellets, which are heated just before printing.

System	Colors reproduced	Resolution/DPI	Application
Continuous	26,000–16.7 million	150–300	Pre-film color proofing
		Photo realistic	
		Transparencies	
Drop-on-Demand	26,000–16.7 million	160-400	Short run color printing
Electrostatic	4,000–16.7 million	300-100	Short run printing
		Color overheads	
		Office copy work	
		Durable signature	

Inkjet has many benefits as well as problems. Benefits include low
price for equipment, high print quality, use of plain paper, and low-
cost consumables. Problems include that of having water-based inks
which are too volatile and dry in the nozzle and dry slowly. In the
future we can look forward to high resolution at a low cost, reliability, fast drying black ink, speed, and possible continuous tone color.

Inkjet printers transfer color to a page by squirting ink onto the paper. The different methods of applying the ink are known as liquid and solid inkjet. Both of these methods apply ink only where it is needed; this results in a variable cost per page. Liquid inkjet uses liquid ink that drys on the paper through evaporation. Liquid inkjet consists of two techniques known as pulsed inkjet and thermal inkjet. Pulsed inkjet uses hydraulic pressure to control the ink sent to the print heads and then to the paper. Thermal inkjet uses a heating element normally located in the ink nozzle that causes the ink to form bubbles. Once the bubbles become large enough, they are forced from the nozzle onto the paper. The problems with this technology are non-uniform spot shape and color density that is lost when ink is absorbed into the paper. Another shortcoming is that the ink remains water soluble and will smear if exposed to moisture.

Solid inkjet uses ink that is solid and must be melted before it is sprayed onto the paper. This ink solidifies quickly when exposed to room temperature and results in a better dot than liquid inkjet. The ink is dropped on the page using a print head which contains nozzles of each color. The ink hardens as soon as it makes contact with the paper. Once the page has been completely covered, a cold roller applies pressure to flatten the ink and strengthen its bond to the paper.

Inkjet has has two major subcategories: drop-on-demand [DOD] and continuous, further defined by the size of the finished product. Drop-on-demand ink jet heads have an array of tiny jets (240, 300, 600 per inch, depending on resolution) that each emit a single droplet of ink at an extremely high rate. Pressure difference caused by reducing the volume of ink in a reservoir causes this phenomenon. There can be multiple heads for printing process colors; however print speed is relatively slow (under ten ppm) because of the difficulty controlling each droplet and amount of time needed for the ink to dry.

A variation in the drop-on-demand technology is bubble-jet, where the ink is actually boiled and the resulting drop fired at the substrate. Still another variation is solid inkjet. Ink is contained in solid sticks which melt when heated. The resulting liquid is fired in the same way as the water based ink products, but instead of absorbing into the substrate, the ink resolidifies on contact. The printed piece is often three dimensional. This process works on almost any substrate. With continuous ink jet, ink is fed as a continuous stream. The stream is separated into droplets which are then electrostatically charged and deflected by magnetic fields to control the placement on the substrate. Unused ink is recycled.

Toner

Electrostatic, electrophotographic, and xerographic printers all use electrical charges transferred to a nonconducting surface that either attract or repel the toner. There are several types of electrostatic processes: direct electrostatic, color xerography, and ElectroInk.

The imaging material is a thermoplastic material (containing lampblack) that is used to create an image. The first toners were used in 1938 when Chester Carlson and Otto Kornei performed their experiments with electrophotography using a powder to transform printed images to a paper sheet. These experiments were conducted from 1944 until 1948. In 1950, Xerox released the product of these experiments, the first xerographic reproduction equipment. Since the introduction of the equipment, toner has become one of the most widely used reproduction vehicles.

There are three major groups of toners:
- dual component
- mono component
- liquid

Dual-component is the most common type of toner used today. It is made up of two distinctive parts—toner and carrier beads. There are three major ways of developing dual component toners, the most common of these being cascade development. It is based on triboelectrification, which is the process of exciting toner particles by causing an electrical charge (static) through the use of friction. The triboelectrification process causes excited particles to cling to read carriers. Toner is 3–30 μm in size, depending on the desired resolution of the printed image. The higher the resolution is, the smaller the toner particles needed. Dual-component toner is used in over 90% of the current xerographic copiers and digital printers. Printers such as Xeikon and the Xerox Docutech use dual-component toners for the development of their images.

Color xerography uses a pre-charged drum or belt that conducts a charge only when exposed to light. The scanning laser is used to discharge this belt or drum which creates an invisible image. Toner containing small iron particles is magnetically attracted to the appropriate areas of the image and repelled from others. This image is then transferred to a roller which collects all four colors. The image is then electrostatically transferred to plain paper where it is fused by heat and pressure.

The monocomponent toners differ from dual-component toners in that they do not require the use of carrier beads for development. There are several ways to charge monocomponent toners, induction, contacting, corona charging, ion beam, and traveling electric fields. The easiest and most commonly used of these is induction charging. Through induction charging, a conducting particle sitting on a negative surface becomes negatively charged. Because the opposite charges repel each other, the negatively charged particle is repelled by the negative plate and drawn to the positive plate. Through this process, particles lose their negative charges and become positively charged. Once toner particles become charged, they can be transferred to the substrate. Most low-end printers use one of these monocomponent toner-charging methods.

Direct electrostatic printers apply a charge directly to specially coated paper. Liquid toner particles are then swept across the paper and stick to the charged regions. Repelled toner is removed from the page before the next color pass. After all colors have been placed, the toner is then fused. This technology can be easily modified for large format printing. Liquid toner provides the advantage of finer toner particles that can be used to achieve high resolution output.

Liquid toners are comprised of toner and solvent. It is the use of solvent instead of developer that causes them to be liquid. Liquid toner solvents are nonconductive and primarily made up of thermoplastic resin particles, which are suspended in a saturated hydrocarbon. In many respects liquid development is related to or considered with powder-cloud development. In both cases, freely moving charged toner moves under the action of an electrostatic field.

Indigo ElectroInk is a variation of xerography that uses liquid toner. The liquid toner is charged electrostatically and brought into contact with the photoconductor where it is either attracted or repelled. The colors are imaged to an offset blanket from which the composite color image is then transferred to the paper media. This liquid toner offers the advantage of delivering very small dots that can produce very high resolutions. The Indigo E-Print 1000 is based upon this technology.

Thermal transfer devices include thermal wax transfer and dye sublimation. Thermal transfer technologies use a three- (CMY) or four- (CMYK) color ink-coated ribbon and special paper which are moved together across a thermal head. Wherever the thermal head applies heat, the ink fuses to the paper. This technology requires 3 to 4 passes across the thermal head depending on the use of a 3 or 4 color ribbon of ink. The result of this process is single-bit dots of the primary colors. The QMS ColorScript 230 is an example of a thermal wax printer.

Dye sublimation uses a similar technology, except that the inks used change to a gaseous state. This requires the thermal head to deliver a much higher temperature but results in finer control and smaller dots which can deliver multi-bit color. This results in continuous tone color. The gas that carries the color and tone entirely covers the dot being imaged. If less ink is carried, the dot changes in tone. In contrast, thermal wax would cover only half the dot area and the rest of the cell would remain white. Fresh consumables (a ribbon in most cases) used for each image result in a constant cost per page, regardless of the number of colors used.

For several decades, ink manufacturers have sought new raw materials which address economic and environmental considerations. For example, vegetable-derived oils such as soy and linseed oils have been used in place of petroleum-based oils in some formulations, water is replacing volatile solvents in others, and pigments are selected to eliminate heavy metals from inks, particularly those used for food or toy packaging. The adaptation of technology to individual process or product needs can be complex. The successful implementation of electronic printing technology requires an appreciation of a wide range of scientific disciplines. The interaction of ink or toner with the print mechanism and substrate needs careful consideration. The prediction of final print quality and its control will need evaluation. With all of the variables in printing press, substrate, and end-use requirements, inkmakers face an exciting challenge.

Will inkjet printing ink and toner compete commercially with offset lithography ink? There is an appeal here because it eliminates rollers, dampeners, and plates; it requires no film. On the negative side, however, are the costs of the equipment, the limited resolution of the currently popular ink jet printers, and limitations in inks. The graphic industry anticipates continued improvement in inkjet equipment in the areas of ink technology and costs.

Digital printing is becoming very popular since the introduction of the Indigo and Xeikon presses in 1993. These digital devices use toner, which is similar in principle to that used in a copy machine. But how does the fine powder stay on the page? Chester F. Carlson created the photocopier methodology. He found that in order to get copies of something it either needed to be rewritten or photographed, and knew there had to be a better way. He first looked at photoconductivity for the answer, and realized that if the image of an original were projected onto a photoconductive surface, current would only flow in the area the light hit. In October of 1937, his first patent was created for what he called electophotography. Chester hired Otto Kornei to help him out. Otto took a zinc plate and covered it with a coating of freshly prepared sulfur and wrote the words "10-22-38 Astoria" on to a slide in India ink. The sulfur was given a charge and the slide was placed on top of the sulfur and under a bright light. The slide was removed and the surface was covered with lycopodium powder. The powder was blown off and there was an almost exact image of "10-22-38 Astoria."

In order to preserve the image, Carlson took wax paper and heated it over the remaining powder. The wax was cooled and was peeled away, creating the first photocopy. This method created a blurry image though and Carlson wanted better dry ink. A fine iron powder was substituted and mixed in with ammonium chloride salt and a plastic material. The ammonium was to clean the image and the plastic was designed to melt when heated and fuse the iron to the paper. This was the first toner and in order to produce different colors, different tones were used.

Toners are pigmented bits of plastic about ten micrometers in size. The manufacturing of toner is a multistep process consisting of mixing pigments and internal additives with the base toner polymer, which breaks the pigmented polymer into particles of the desired size. The most important step is blending the pigments and other internal additives with the polymer binder at the right temperature so that it flows, but has a high viscosity. If the temperature is too high the pigment will not disperse as well.

The name electophotography is classified under patent class 355, subclass 200. It is defined as a device wherein the electrical conductivity, the electric charge, the magnetic condition, or the electrical emissivity of a light-responsive medium is selectively altered directly by light reflected from or transmitted through an original, whereby a visible or latent image is formed on the medium and persists after exposure. In simpler terms, a photoconductor acts as an insulator, retaining a charge of electricity. Areas of the surface contacted by light lose their charge. The remaining areas with charge attract oppositely charged particles of toner that is transferred to the paper. For most printers using this method, the drum is re-imaged for each sheet, unlike in lithography where the same image is produced multiple times.

There are various types of toners and development systems available on the market. Dry toner printers use a form of magnetic brush system to carry toner/developer from the supply to the development zone. These utilize non-magnetic toners carried on a magnetic iron which provides charge by rubbing contact or magnetic toners which contain a proportion of magnetic oxide. Dry powder toners are made up of the following components:

Constituent	Function
Magnetic Oxide	Colorant, provides magnetic counterforce transport; readability
Pigment	Color black, hi-light, filler
Polymer Binder	Fusing, toner stability
Charge Control Agents	Charge stability
Surface Additives	Lubrication/cleaning, toner flow

With these toners there are significant temperatures necessary in xerography. The first is the temperature at which the image is fixed to the paper. Anywhere above this temperature the toner is very fluid and splits apart. Once it splits, it then is left on the fuser roll and attaches itself to the next page. Toner also has some problems that differ from those of inks. Particle size also has a lot to do with the quality that you can get from a machine using a dry toner. Particle size usually ranges from 10–20 mm in diameter. Particle size any larger than this will usually produce jagged lines and dots. Toners which produce smaller dots take longer to make, and cost more.

Another type of toner is liquid toner. These toners are charged, colored particles in a nonconductive liquid. Liquid toner particles are much smaller than those of dry toners, and are capable of smaller particle sizes ranging from 3 mm to submicrometer sizes. Liquid toners are used in copiers, color proofing printers, electronic printers, and electrostatic printer-plotters. Liquid toners are made up of dispersants, resins, charge control agents, and pigments. The dispersants must be non-conductive in order to not discharge the latent image as well as interact with any other materials used in the process. The resin is used as a vehicle for the pigment or dyes to provide stability, and aids fixing of the final image.

The charge control agents are added to the toners to impart charge on the toner particles. Metal soaps are a common material used as a control agent. Finally, the pigment controls the color of the toner. Important factors of the pigment include particle size, dispersibility, and insolubility in the toner dispersant.

Liquid toners could be combustible, rather than flammable because of their high flash point. If evaporation does not occur and comes in contact with flesh, slight irritation may occur. Devices that use liquid toners are well-ventilated, or re-cycle any hydrocarbons through an internal system.

A major imaging problem is that charge voltage decay between the time of charging the photoconductor, exposing, and toning can affect image density and tone reproduction, as the amount of toner transferred is dependent on the exact voltage of the charge on the image at the instant the toner is transferred. The second deals with the toner chemistry. Because the chemistry is not understood, variations in batches of the same toner occur. In liquid toners the isopar that is used to disperse the toner is a volatile organic compound, which may require venting and is subject to Environmental Protection Agency regulations.

The process and the product dictate what type of inks you can use. A conventional lithographic press, an inkjet system, or a digital printing press are not only used for different applications, the inks used are all different. This will affect the quality and the other printing attributes. In almost every electronic printer, the consumable (the ink) is specific to the device.

Digital presses

Variable data

Digital presses have one unique capability that conventional printing processes cannot deliver. In a digital printing device, every copy that is printed is imaged that many number of times. Which also means that the printing surface is imaged once for every copy that is printed. This is in contrast to the conventional printing process where the printing surface is imaged once, and multiple copies are generated from that printing surface. It is this feature in a digital press that slows down its production. But the uniqueness of this feature opens up a new opportunity, which is exploiting the necessity to image every time for a copy. Since every copy needs to be imaged on the printing surface, every copy can also be varied on the printing surface. Which opens up a whole new world of printing capability—variable data printing.

Imagine all that one could do with variable data. Specially targeted messages can be printed for a select audience, instead of printing static data that may not be completely targeted to a particular audience. You can now have your brochure specially printed for you. The press will print your name, address, and even have contents in the copy that have been personalized to suit your tastes. Variable data includes images. The key to producing efficient variable data is handling powerful databases. There are off-the-shelf programs like Print Shop Mail, and Darwin (Scitex) and extensions to QuarkXPress like Datamerge that promise to exploit the potential of variable data. We have to keep in mind that though the potential of variable data is humongous, we are at an evolving stage of this great possibility. Digital presses provide this capability, which conventional printing processes can never do.

Digital printing features
- Digital printing is a rapidly growing segment of printing.
- Principal applications: short-run, on-demand printing.
- A digital printer can be defined as one that inputs a digital data stream and outputs printed pages.

- The broad categories of digital printers include electrostatic, inkjet, and thermal. But we can also say that any printing process that takes digital files and outputs spots is also digital.
- Interdependency with digital presses will likely create major changes in the operation of the printing industry and increase the volume of digital printing.
- Xerox DocuTech, Xerox Docucolor, Indigo E-Print, Xeikon DCP, Scitex, Agfa, Chromapress, and Canon CLC-1000 are among current major electronic systems.
- Digital masters made directly on press, printed with waterless offset lithographic process, characterize short-run direct imaging printing presses.
- Cost of digital presses and consumables impact competition between digital printing and offset lithography. Run length, turnaround time, and bindery needs/solutions are major cost factors in this competition.

On-demand printing involves short notice and quick turnaround. In the printing industry, print-on-demand can be defined as "short notice, quick turnaround of short, cost-competitive print runs," which all results in lower inventory costs, lower risk of obsolescence, lower production costs, and reduced distribution costs.

Most traditional printing does not satisfy this criteria and does not result in these advantages. The disadvantage of traditional long-run printing is that the reproduced information becomes obsolete, which requires the disposal and re-manufacture of new material. In the United States, approximately 31% of all traditional printing is thrown away because it is outdated. This number includes 11% of all publications, 41% of all promotional literature, and 35% of all other material. Although print-on-demand is a more sophisticated phrase for the printing industry, there is no specific technology that is used to perform such a job. On-demand printing (also known as demand printing) can be produced with a traditional press because the customer does not care so long as the quality is acceptable, and it is done quickly and economically.

Digital printing is any printing completed via digital files. A digital press may be capable of printing short runs economically, but digital printing on printing presses is well-suited for slightly longer runs.

When comparing on-demand printing and digital printing, demand printing is economical, fast, and oriented to short runs. On the opposite end, digital printing is printing from digital files, but is not restricted to short runs. Demand printing can be done with digital files or conventional film or plates; however, digital printing is done only with digital files.

Variable printing

Variable information can be printed by digital presses, which are presses that print digital data. On different pages you could have different names and addresses. This cannot be accomplished by traditional printing. With traditional printing, the prepress work is performed, the plates are made, and they are run on the press. The end result is thousands of pages that are identical. The information is static. The capacity to print variable information, which results in variable printing, is the key factor of customized printing. To accomplish customized printing today, conventional pages or static pages are run through high-speed inkjet devices for variable information. Many digital presses offer this ability. Unlike inkjet devices, digital presses are not limited to six or twelve lines of copy, but some can customize the entire page.

The basics of customized printing is the combination of variable information with output devices that do not require intermediate films or plates. They are true digital printing systems in that all or part of the image area can be changed from impression to impression. Short run can best be defined as one that is less than 5,000 impressions. Almost 56% of commercial, book, and office printing, including duplicating and copying, falls in the category of run lengths from 500 to 5,000 impressions. Presently, only 2.8% of this printing is done in four or more colors. By the year 2000, the amount of four-color printing in this run-length market will increase to approximately 11.5%.

Traditional printing presses usually operate in the long-run category; however, this trend seems to be changing. In order to stay competitive in this growing industry, printers are attempting to compete with moderate or even short-run categories. While most traditional presses will have difficulty meeting the needs of the short-run category, this is where a new market is developing. It is projected that the short-run wars will take place in the 100- to 3,000-copy range. The on-demand process consists of the client supplying electronic files or camera-ready materials and specifying how many copies of the publication will be needed. The printer produces the publication directly from the disk or camera-ready artwork and delivers it within a specified timeframe.

Currently there are three specific on-demand strategies in our industry: on-demand printing, distributed demand printing, and on-demand publishing. "On-demand" means that the data is stored and printed in electronic form. It does not necessarily have to be an electronic file, but usually it is a digital file which provides the effectiveness of the short run. The second strategy, distributed demand printing, requires that the electronic files be transmitted to other locations, printed, and distributed locally.

These publications can then be stored, printed, and shipped locally as needed. The third and final strategy is on-demand publishing (also known as demand publishing), in which the data is stored in paginated form and transmitted for immediate printout. This is done by large-volume magazines. Portable Document Formats, such as Adobe Acrobat, are being used to distribute the print-ready document files.

Electronic printing allows variable data printing. Traditional printing does not. Let us now compare the major features of the three traditional printing processes as we move into a discussion of packaging:

	FLEXOGRAPHY	GRAVURE	OFFSET LITHOGRAPHY
Substrates	Wide variety, can print on most packaging materials	Wide variety, can print on most packaging materials	Limited, not easily adapted to films or laminated packaging materials including polyethylene, paper, foils, and laminates
Impression Pressure	Light "kiss" impression pressure	Heavy pressure in printing nip	Relatively high pressure in printing nip
Plate life/ Run length	Avg. plate life between 1-2 million impressions	Avg. cylinder life between 3-4 million	Avg. plate life between short and long run available up to 300,000
Press Size	Many web widths available; widths range from 6″ to 90″ (wider for corrugated)	Many web widths available; widths range from 2″ to 110″ (wider for vinyl flooring)	Standard format size; sheetfed up to 60″ web-fed 11″-60″
Cut-off Repeat length	Variable repeat	Variable repeat	Standard format/fixed cut-off
Speed	Product dependent: toilet tissue–3,000 fpm;	Product dependent: publication–3,000 fpm vinyl flooring–50 fpm	Product dependent: sheet-fed 12,000 imp/hr 2500 fpm pressure-sensitive labels-150–300 fpm
Ink	Fast-drying fluid ink solvent, water, and UV curable dry trapping	Fast-drying fluid ink solvent, water dry trapping	Heat-set and non heat-set paste ink wet trapping
Digital imaging	Laser engraving and laser exposable available	Heavily utilized	Yes, on press and off press

Packaging

Packaging graphics are the last and possibly the most important advertising many products receive. Flexographic printing technology is used on a wide variety of materials for a great variety of packaging applications. Arguably, it is the flexographic process's "flexibility" that is its greatest advantage. Soft compressible printing plates, fast-drying fluid inks, and a simple, efficient ink delivery system give the flexographic printer the ability to reproduce high quality graphics on many different surfaces.

During the last decade, the dollar volume of products produced by the use of the flexographic printing process has been growing at a rate of approximately eight percent a year, a rate unparalleled by any other printing technology. Some of this growth is due to the increased need for packaging and packaging graphics. However, another source of new business for flexography is products that have traditionally been printed by the other major printing processes—gravure and offset lithography. Print buyers are beginning to recognize flexography as an economical, high-quality alternative to gravure and lithographic printing.

Packaging buyers have begun to hold the flexographic printer to the same high quality standards as lithography and roto-gravure. This means that the flexographic printers will have to consistently deliver high quality graphics. Specifically, tone reproduction is expected to be the same resolution in flexography as that printed by lithography and gravure. Historically, the flexographic printing process has been used for low-cost/low-quality packaging graphics. In fact, the stigma of being a "cheap" printing process has caused some packaging buyers to ignore flexography when selecting a process for higher quality graphics. Even within the industry a culture shift from low-cost/low-quality to low-cost/high-quality has been slow to come about.

Adding to the problems flexographers find when competing with other printing processes is the fact that there are no established standards for flexographic printing. Some standards that may be helpful include trapping, dot gain, and specific values for process color inks. The fact that the flexographic industry is without these standards complicates communication between buyers, suppliers, and printers, and makes quality consistency very difficult.

The recent move to "desktop" design has also introduced new problems for flexographic printers. With the use of the computer it has become relatively simple for the novice to create attractive new package designs. Unfortunately, many of the novice designers are ignorant of the limitations of the printing technology that will be used to mass-produce their designs. Also, many designs that appear attractive on a computer monitor are impossible to reproduce on a flexographic printing press due to press registration problems and ink limitations.

When a designer who has experience creating a package design to be printed by offset lithography or gravure applies the same design principles for a flexographically printed graphic, they may be creating problems for the flexo printer. Without the benefit of research into production methods and equipment, an otherwise simple design for gravure or offset would pose many printing problems for flexo.

Traditional printing processes

The three most commonly used printing processes are lithography, flexography, and gravure. Each of these processes has its own inherent advantages and disadvantages. To better understand the primary differences in each process, one needs to compare three key areas: the ink, the ink delivery system and the image carrier.

The most commonly used printing process (based on the number of printing presses currently in production) is lithography, sometimes called offset lithography. Lithography is used heavily in the publication industry for printing magazines, catalogs, and many daily newspapers as well as a number of other applications like annual reports, advertising, and art reproduction. Lithography is also often used for packaging such as folding cartons, labels, and bags.

Offset lithography is classified as a "planographic" process. That means the printing plate or image carrier used for lithographic printing holds both the image and non-image on one flat surface or plane. The image areas of a lithographic plate are chemically treated to be attractive to the lithographic paste ink, while a fountain solution or ink-repellent chemical protects non-image areas from inking.

In a lithographic printing press, a paste ink is applied to the image areas on the plate, the image is then transferred to a blanket (hence the term offset), and then to the substrate. Lithography has been a favored process because it can reproduce soft tonal values on coated substrates. Another highly prized feature of lithography is its ability to print 300-line screen images with excellent fidelity.

Gravure packaging

Gravure, sometimes known as roto-gravure, is the second most commonly used process in Europe and the Far East, and the third most commonly used process in the US. The gravure process prints perhaps the widest variety of products of all processes. Gravure is heavily used in the magazine printing industries and also prints many of the inserts in the Sunday newspaper. Vinyl flooring and woodgrain desktops and paneling are also printed by gravure. An offset gravure process is used to print the M on M&M candy and the printing on many medicine capsules. Gravure is used for many of the same packaging applications as those of flexography. Gravure is used for:

- Publications
- Products
- Packaging

The gravure printing process is classified as an "intaglio" process. An intaglio printing process recesses the image below the level of the non-image areas. A gravure image is etched or engraved into a copper plate or copper-plated cylinder. All gravure images are etched in a cell format on the gravure cylinder. By varying the size and depth of each cell, the gravure press can vary tones. Often, after the copper is etched or engraved, the plate or cylinder is plated with chrome to add durability and run-length to the gravure cylinder.

In a gravure press, a fast-drying fluid ink fills the recessed cells, a thin metal strip called a doctor blade clears the non-image area of ink, and then the image is transferred directly to the substrate under heavy impression pressure from a rubber-covered impression roll.

Gravure has been an outstanding choice for printing process color for mass-circulation magazines and newspapers. Gravure-printed postage stamps are another example of the fine print results of roto-gravure. Many plants have blended flexography with gravure to produce exceptional print results on packaging materials.

The flexographic printing process is classified as a relief process. A relief printing process is characterized by the image areas being raised above the surrounding non-image areas. Letterpress is also a relief printing process, the primary differences between letterpress and flexographic printing technologies are:
1. Plate hardness—the letterpress plate is hard and non-compressible; the flexographic plate is soft and compressible.
2. Ink—the letterpress ink is a paste consistency; the flexographic ink is a fluid, about the same consistency as paint.

In a flexographic press, an ink metering roll called an anilox is brought into light contact with the raised image areas of the flexographic plate by an adjustment controlled by the flexographic press operator. The flexographic press operator then moves the plate into light contact with the substrate to cause image transfer.

Flexographic packaging

Flexographic printing units in use today are simple in design and easy to understand. The following components makeup a flexographic printing unit:
- fountain roll
- anilox roll
- doctor blade
- dual doctor ink chamber
- plate cylinder
- impression roll

There are three types of flexographic printing units being used today: two roll, two roll with doctor blade, and dual-doctor chambered systems. The two roll units are usually found on older flexo presses, and on narrow web presses. Narrow web presses doing process color work will probably be equipped with two roll units and doctor blade, and more modern wide-web presses are equipped with the dual-doctored chambered system. Each of these printing units may preform acceptably; however, a doctor blade system should be used when doing screens and process color flexographic printing.

To understand each of these printing units, it is important to first understand the "heart" of the unit, the anilox roll. The surface of every anilox roll has been engraved with a tiny cell pattern, cells so small they can only be seen under magnification. The size and number of these cells determines how much ink will be delivered to the image areas of the flexographic plate, and then to the substrate. An anilox roll is either copper engraved and then chrome plated, or ceramic coated steel with a laser engraved cell surface.

On a two-roll flexographic printing unit, the rubber-covered fountain roll rotates in a bath of fluid flexo ink. As the fountain roll rotates, it drags a supply of ink from the ink pan and delivers it to the cells of the anilox roll. The relatively soft, rubber-covered fountain roll is held in tight contact (nipped) with the anilox roll. As the anilox rotates past the nip point, excess ink is "wiped" from the non-cell area by the fountain roll. Once past the nip point, each cell is filled with ink, and a measured, repeatable amount of ink is available to the printing plate. On the press, the flexographic press operator moves the "metered" anilox roll into light "kiss contact" with the image areas of the flexo plate, and then moves the plate cylinder into light "kiss contact" with the substrate to achieve ink transfer. The steel impression roll supports the substrate during ink transfer.

When a doctor blade is used with a two-roll unit, the nip between fountain and anilox roll is opened to allow the ink to flood the anilox and fill the cells. The doctor blade, a thin metal or polyethylene blade, then comes into contact with the anilox to sheer excess ink from the non-cell areas. When the flexographic press is equipped with chambered doctor blade inking units, the fountain roll and inking pan can be eliminated, and ink is delivered directly to the anilox through an enclosed chamber.

Anilox cells

The best flexographic printers select anilox rolls for their press after carefully evaluating the type of printing they intend to do, and the type of substrate they will be printing on. Often the flexographic printer will perform test runs to determine the ideal type of anilox roll in an effort to maximize graphic elements related to screen ruling, solids and spot color, type, and substrate.

These are the important characteristics of an anilox roll:
- Cells Per Inch (CPI)—The number of cells in a linear inch. CPI counts will range from 140 CPI to 1200 CPI. A general rule of thumb is as the cell count increases, the ink delivered to the plate decreases. To achieve adequate ink densities, a flexographer printing linework on absorbent corrugated linerboard would be using anilox rolls at the low end of cell count (160, 180, 200). If the corrugated printer was required to print halftones at 55 or 65 linescreen, the anilox roll would have to be replaced with a roll of higher cell-per-inch count (280, 300, 360). Another important concept is that as line screen resolution increases, cell per inch count should also increase. For instance, a process color graphic on a polyethylene frozen food bag may be printed at 133 lpi. For best results, and in order to avoid "flooding" the halftone dots with ink, the cell count of the anilox roll that inks the 133 lpi printing plate should be at least 550 or 600 cells per inch.
- Cell Volume—Cell count and cell volume are related. As a general rule, as CPI increases, cell volume decreases. Anilox cell volume is described by a theoretical or measured volume, and reported as Billion Cubic Microns (BCM) per square inch of cells. Typical BCM ratings for printing applications range from a low of 1.8 to a high of 14.

Using our example of the flexographer printing linework on absorbent corrugated linerboard, the low cell count anilox being used may have a cell volume of 10.0 BCM, and the process color on polyethylene at 133 lpi, and a 600 linescreen plate may be inking with an anilox cell volume of 2.8 BCM.

- Cell Angle—Anilox cells are engraved in a linear pattern, and at various angles. Typical anilox cell angles are 30°, 45°, and 60°. It is important to understand that the screen angle of the printing plate and the cell angle of the anilox roll can combine to cause an objectionable moiré pattern, even if only one-color halftones are being printed. Many anilox roll suppliers produce a random cell (no-angle) anilox that may be used for limited applications.

While an anilox cell angle may be selected to help avoid moiré, the problem of moiré is usually avoided by angling the separation screens. Research and experience has shown that the 60° angle allows for more complete ink transfer, and is becoming the preferred cell angle for flexographic printers. There is currently no other single component of the flexographic process that will have as significant an effect on flexographic print quality as the type of anilox roll being used.

Plate cylinders and repeat length

All flexographic presses, with the exception of corrugated and newspaper presses, have a variable repeat length capability. This variable repeat length is possible because the plate cylinder on a flexographic printing unit is removable and interchangeable with plate cylinders of different diameters. The flexographic package printer can minimize substrate waste by having an adequate inventory of plate cylinders of various diameters, and choosing the cylinder size that best fits the print dimensions. Most lithographic presses are limited to a fixed repeat length (often called a "fixed cutoff"). The plate cylinder used for most lithographic presses cannot be changed to conform to various package sizes. In this case each package layout and design must fit into the "fixed" dimensions dictated by the press and plate size of the specific lithographic press.

Flexographic plates can be mounted around the entire circumference of the plate cylinder, and images can be arranged to print a "continuous repeat," void of any seam area where the plate ends butt. Continuous repeats can also be accomplished by using laser-engraved design rolls. Flexographic presses can be built in several basic configurations: Stack Press, In-line, Common Impression Cylinder (CIC), and Corrugated.

Stack Press	One to eight color units Web can be printed on both sides with some stack presses Traps should be no less than 1/32" for thin films Often in line with other converting operations, including polyethylene extrusion, lamination, rotary and flatbed die cutting, and sideseal bag converting.
In-Line	Up to twelve color units Often used for printing thick substrates, like corrugated, paperboard Can print two sides (with the aid of a turn-bar) Often in line with other converting operations Not recommended for printing thin packaging film materials
CIC	Four to eight color units limited to one-sided printing Ideal press for hairline register at high speeds on thin, stretchable films Longer make-ready times required because of the inaccessibility of the printing units
Corrugated	Usually no more than four colors All corrugated presses are sheet fed Widths up to 120" Less accurate register capabilities Limited to one-sided printing

Multicolor capabilities

Flexographic presses commonly come with multicolor capabilities. Recently the flexographic industry has experienced an increase in installations of six and eight color presses. In some limited applications, as many as twelve colors can be applied in one pass through a flexographic press. From a creative design perspective the possibilities for eye-catching color are greatly enhanced by a printing process offering so many color capabilities. Combinations of four color process and spot colors, multiple spot colors alone, or high fidelity process color printing allow the designer a great deal of creative latitude when designing a graphic to be printed by flexo.

It is important to note that for transparent film substrates, the chances are good that one of the color stations will be required to apply a white backup or "choke" plate. Without the white backup, colors would appear flat and transparent. The white plate is a characteristic unique to processes utilizing clear or colored substrates.

Another important color characteristic of flexographic inks is that they are usually made from opaque or semi-opaque pigments. The color sequence usually adhered to for flexographic printing is lightest to darkest colors in the press units. Overprinting two or more spot colors will most likely result in the creation of an objectionable "mystery" third color in the overprint areas.

Reverse-side printing

An exception to the rule of lightest-to-darkest color sequence occurs when a spot color or line art job calls for "reverse-side printing." Reverse-side printing means the job is reversed laterally and printed on a clear substrate like polyethylene, polypropylene, or polystyrene. After printing, the graphics will be displayed from the "reverse" or substrate side, rather than the side of the substrate where ink has been applied. This technique is often used for non-food packaging, or for applications where another film will be laminated to the printed film.

Flexographic plates

There are a many types of flexographic printing plates, with the primary differences being the material from which the plate is made and the plate thickness. The type of plate material to be used to print a flexo job is decided by the flexographer after consideration of the graphic elements they are asked to reproduce. Although few flexo printers print from both rubber and photopolymer plates, many have two or three types of rubber or photopolymer materials for platemaking.

Another important characteristic of all types of plates is durometer (a measure of the hardness or softness of a plate). Printing plates (rubber or photopolymer compound) are soft and are of concern to graphic designers. Dot gain is affected by the durometer of the plate being used. Plates of higher durometer (harder), will print with less dot gain than softer plates. However, lower durometer plates transfer solid images more smoothly and completely than high durometer plates. The plate thickness is dictated by the flexo printer's type of press and plate cylinder inventory. Generally speaking, wide-web printers print from thicker plates than do narrow-web printers.

Molded rubber plates

The molded rubber plate has been used for flexographic printing since the 1930s. However, the introduction of the photopolymer plate in the 1970s marked the beginning of a period of steady decline in the use of the rubber plate.

From a design perspective, the important characteristics of molded rubber plates include:

- Molded rubber plates shrink shortly after they are removed from the molding press; consequently, plate films should be adjusted to compensate for shrinkage. The amount of shrinkage depends on the type of rubber being molded, but is typically 1.5%–2.0% along the grain of the rubber and .5%-1% across the grain of the rubber. To ensure accuracy, the exact shrink factors should be communicated between production artists and plate makers.
- Resolving capability of a rubber plate is limited to the 120-line screen.
- Molded rubber plates may be more difficult to register in the plate mounting step than photopolymer plates.

- Prints from molded rubber plates can only appear to be continuous repeat if images are nested in the job layout design, to hide the plate seam.
- It is difficult to mold accurate rubber plates larger than 24"x 36", consequently designs larger than 24"x36" must be done by piecing together multiple plates for each color.

Laser-ablated plates and design rolls

A design roll is a rubber-covered roll that has been imaged by laser ablation. The design roll is seamless, and can carry images around the entire circumference. The laser ablation imaging process is direct-to-plate. This process can also improve register capabilities. The specified trap between colors can be accurately achieved, bleed can be handled, registration marks can be provided as part of the design and eyespots or other devices can be placed precisely.

Laser-ablated design rolls are often used for long-run jobs that require continuous printing, and can be run in combination with other flexographic plates. Direct-to-plate laser ablation can also be used for imaging plates rather than an entire roll. However a laser-ablated plate must be mounted on a plate cylinder and will not be seamless. Laser-ablated plates are often used for short-run jobs and for spot coating on flexo or offset presses.

From a design perspective, the important characteristics of laser-ablated plates and design rolls include:
- Resolution is limited to a 100-line screen for tone reproduction, but can be a 200 to 300 line screen for tints.
- Laser-ablated image carriers do not require film output.
- Laser-ablated design rolls can be a truly continuous repeat design; laser-ablated plates require nested images to give the appearance of continuous repeat.
- Plates or design rolls imaged on a circumference do not require distortion.
- Laser ablation can be performed on both rubber and sheet polymer materials.

Photopolymer plates

Today, the photopolymer plate is the most frequently used plate for flexographic printing. There are two general categories of photopolymer plates available, sheet and liquid. The main difference between the two is the physical state of the raw material from the supplier. Sheet photopolymer is supplied in a solid state, while the liquid plate is supplied as a liquid which has about the same consistency as honey. The liquid solidifies when exposed to ultraviolet light. From a design perspective, the important characteristics of photopolymer plates include:

- Photopolymer plates have guaranteed resolving capabilities of a 150-line screen. Some high-end flexo printers have actually printed from plates with a 200-line screen.
- Prints from photopolymer plates can only appear to be continuous repeat if images are nested in the job layout and design to hide the plate seam.
- Most of the newest plate positioning and register devices rely on a "one piece" flexographic photopolymer plate.
- Some service bureaus and flexographic plate makers presently have the capability of filmless, direct digital imaging for conventional (non-laser-ablated) sheet photopolymers.

Platemounting systems

Offset lithography has long been able to take advantage of pin register for quick accurate color-to-color registration. The first commercial device for mounting and proofing rubber printing plates was probably developed in the 1940s by Franklin Moss, founder of the Moss-type Corporation. Until the recent adaptation of pin register and micro-dot register systems to flexographic plate mounting, color-to-color register was entirely dependent upon the skill level of the plate mounter. Many platemounters became highly skilled, while others were less accurate in plate positioning and registration, resulting in poor registration on the press.

The concepts of pin register and micro-dot register were developed to make accurate plate mounting fast and easy for everyone, even the beginner. Pin register requires a systems approach. That is to say that each prepress station, right up to the critical plate making and mounting stage has to adopt pin register or micro-dot line-up techniques. Pin positions or micro-dot targets must be accurately transferred through each step of prepress.

Mounting tapes

Mounting tape is the two-sided adhesive used for affixing flexo plates onto the plate cylinders. Mounting tapes also come in a variety of types and thicknesses. Two general types of mounting tapes are "hard" tapes and compressible tapes. A compressible tape is actually a thin layer of foam coated on both sides with an adhesive. The thin foam layer acts as a shock absorber to minimize over-impression on the flexographic plate. By contrast, hard tapes offer no shock absorbing characteristic and are only used to adhere the plate to the cylinder.

Research of various mounting tapes has shown surprising findings. For instance, one test of five different mounting tapes found solid ink density variations from 1.34 to 1.66 by simply changing mounting tape. Dot gain is greater with harder tapes than with softer tapes; usually, the less dot gain the better. Soft cushion tapes, however, do not provide for a uniform ink transfer in solid printing areas, often causing pinholes.

Cylinder preparation

Each cylinder should be checked for condition and accuracy before a plate is mounted on it. Cleaning, checking for defects, and checking for accuracy before mounting the plate will often save material waste, press time, and extra work.

- Cleaning—Plate cylinder surfaces should be thoroughly cleaned to provide the best possible surface for plate mounting. Improperly cleaned cylinders can cause inaccurate plate pressures by trapping ink or other foreign matter between cylinder surface and mounting tape. A cylinder surface with oil, grease or any other residue on it will not allow proper adhesion of the mounting tape and will eventually lead to plate lift. When cleaning a cylinder, it should be noted that many water-based inks require some type of detergent to rewet dried ink for cleaning purposes. Often these detergents leave an invisible residue or film on the surface of the cylinder that inhibits adhesion of tape to metal. Final cleaning of the cylinder surface should be done with a solvent that will leave no residue.

- Gears—Gears should be kept clean and well lubricated. Make a practice of noticing the condition of each with each job change. If they are removable, make sure they are tight when replaced.
- Total Indicated Runout (TIR)—Good pressroom practices includes the use of a dial indicator to check cylinder circumferences and bearing accuracies. Runout of each plate cylinder is important. Recommended tolerances for runout have been +/–0.001" for line work and +/-0.0005" for halftones; however, with today's more demanding quality requirements a good practice is to always work at halftone tolerances.

Substrate and substrate influence on flexographic printing

Substrate is a generic term for the packaging materials printed by flexography and other printing processes. These materials aren't necessarily chosen for their printing characteristics, but because they're functional. Thanks to flexography's versatility, there is almost no material that has not or cannot be printed by it. It has been said that if any material can be put in a roll, it can be printed by flexography. The quality of a printed product is affected more by the substrate than the type of process that applies the graphics. Packaging industries utilize a wide variety of substrates to satisfy the demands of a wide assortment of packaged products. Substrates can be classified into three general categories:

Paper/paperboard
    kraft linerboard (corrugated)
    clay coated kraft (corrugated)
    solid bleached sulfate (SBS) (folding carton)
    recycled paperboard (folding carton)
    coated paper (labels, gift wrap)
    uncoated freesheet paper (paperback books)

Polymer films
  polyethylene (PE) (dry cleaner, bakery, and textile bags)
  polypropylene (PP) (snack packages, candy wrappers, cookie
    packaging labels)
  polyvinyl chloride (vinyl films) (labels, wall coverings)

Multilayer/laminations
  metallized papers (gift wraps)
  metallized film (snack food bags)
  polyethylene coated SBS (milk cartons)

The important characteristics of substrates as they relate to the packaging printing process are:

Color

A printing ink is significantly influenced by the color of the substrate on which it is applied. The flexographic process is often used to print corrugated containers with unbleached brown kraft linerboard exteriors. Color matching on these types of material surfaces is difficult to achieve.

Paper/paperboard—White, brown kraft, and a variety of colored papers.

Polymer films—Can be clear, white, combinations of white and clear, or colored.

Multilayered/Laminations—The color characteristics are decided by the topmost layer with reflective qualities. Foils and metallized papers or films are silver, or tinted to a colored finish.

Whiteness/brightness

The whiteness or brightness of a paper is the paper's light reflective qualities. Even on bleached or coated papers there are differences in the whiteness or brightness of a sheet. Paper containing a high percentage of recycled fiber may appear to be more off-white than paper made from 100% virgin fiber.

- Paper/paperboard—Whiteness and brightness increases with bleached and coated papers. Optical brighteners may also be added to paper to increase brightness.
- Polymer films—White films can vary in opacity, which will affect brightness. Clear films require a printed opaque white ink under color images. Colored films are not be included in this measurement.
- Multilayer/laminations—Decided by the topmost layer of film or paper with reflective qualities. Foil and metallized printing surfaces require a printed white ink under color images.

Opacity

All substrates have a measurable opacity rating. Opacity is the ability of a substrate to prevent light transmission. The more opaque a substrate, the less light will pass through. A color printed on paper or film with a low opacity rating will be influenced by what lies beneath the substrate.

- Paper/paperboard—Thin lightweight papers have lower opacity and will be more prone to ink show-through.
- Polymer films — On clear substrates, opacity depends on the opacity of the printed white ink layer. The opacity of white or colored films depends on the film manufacturing process; films may be made white or colored by adding the appropriate colored resin to clear resin during the extrusion process. Darker films may tend to be more opaque than lighter films, but all films can be manufactured with high opacity.
- Multilayered/laminations—Usually high opacity is achieved by the multiple layers of opaque or semi-opaque substrates.

Smoothness

Smoother substrates allow for the printing of higher line screens. Rough, irregular surfaces such as newsprint and corrugated liner board require coarse screen rulings. Defects in smoothness can be described as either macro or micro. Macro refers to irregularities that can be seen with the naked eye; micro refers to a very small area with defects not readily seen with the naked eye.

Because the flexographic ink is fluid and generally not regarded as tacky, fiber pick (a problem common to lithographic printing) is not an issue.

- Paper/paperboard—Newsprint, corrugated linerboard, and paperboard are relatively rough. Calendered and coated papers are the smoothest.
- Polymer films—Polymer films are the smoothest printing surfaces, consequently roughness is not a problem; however, ink adhesion sometimes is a problem.
- Multilayered/laminations—The smoothness is dependent on the substrate used as a printing surface.

Absorption

On substrates with little or no absorption characteristics, the ink will dry at the surface providing more saturated color and less dot gain for halftone printing. Papers with low absorption rates are referred to as having high "hold-out." This means the paper holds or prevents the ink from being absorbed into the sheet.

- Paper/paperboard—Corrugated, newsprint, and paperboard are very absorbent. Calendered and coated papers are less absorbent and exhibit high ink hold-out.
- Polymer films—Polymer films are non-absorbent and exhibit the highest ink hold-out.
- Multilayered/laminations—Absorption characteristics are dependent on the substrate used as a printing surface.

Gloss

Coated papers and films have gloss characteristics that influence the gloss of the inks that are applied to them. High gloss finishes are very shiny, and tend to be reflective. Matte or low-gloss finishes can be applied to all substrates by matte coatings, and uncoated and uncalendered papers have low gloss.

- Paper/paperboard—Calendered and coated papers are high-gloss while corrugated linerboard, uncalendered newsprint, and paperboard have low-gloss qualities. Gloss can be increased after printing by applying an overprint varnish or lamination.

- Polymer films—Films are higher gloss than the highest gloss papers. Films can also be produced with a matte finish.
- Multilayered/laminations—The gloss of the printing surface is dependent on the substrate used as a printing surface; gloss can be increased after printing by applying an overprint varnish or lamination.

Caliper

Caliper is the thickness of a substrate. Caliper is usually measured with a micrometer. Thin sheets of paper may have a caliper as small as 0.002", and thicker sheets may have a caliper of 0.010". Paper with caliper readings greater than 0.010" are often referred to as paperboard. The caliper of paperboard may be as much as 0.030". Polymer films are by definition thin. Dry cleaner bags are 0.00065". The thickest calipers used for flexible packaging are 0.005" to 0.006".

Thin films require printing conditions with very accurate tension controls. Paperboard caliper should be uniform and free from low spots that will lead to print skips (voids) on the flexo press. For all substrates, caliper uniformity is critical.

- Paper/paperboard—Thinner papers are more consistent in caliper, paperboard may have inconsistencies in caliper.
- Polymer films—Thin films are susceptible to stretch during printing. Caliper inconsistency will cause misregistration, and print wrinkle problems.
- Multilayered/laminations—Caliper increases as layers are added. Extremely thin layers may be laminated together to attain required barrier and printing surface properties.

Flexographic design considerations

Trapping

Trapping is the overlap of color to avoid misregistration during printing. Misregistration is caused by substrate handling and tension problems on the press, irregular or inconsistent plate elongation from one color to the next, inaccuracies in the plate mounting, and limited register capabilities. A preliminary test run and analysis of the press will determine the registration tolerances. Typically, a designer will build traps into the file if the job is a simple one, otherwise trapping will be handled by using an option in a drawing or trapping software program like Trapwise or DKA Island Trapper, or handled entirely by the prepress service bureau. The best trapping applications allow for partial traps—where only the areas of an image that require trapping are affected, while leaving all other areas at their original dimensions.

Traps serve the same purpose in packaging as in commercial printing. There are two primary differences: 1) in packaging there are generally more colors, and 2) with flexographic printing, larger traps are required to compensate for misregister. Guidelines when designing for flexography would include avoiding tight registration requirements, creating sufficient trap for anticipated misregistration, designing with the dominant color printing over the lighter color, and avoiding trapping of gradations. Trapping may cause a dark line where the colors overlap.

A label printed on a narrow-web press should be trapped at a minimum of 0.005"—some require as much as 1/32", or 0.031" compared to average traps of 0.002"–0.005" for lithography. A typical trap area for a job on wide-web polyethylene might be 1 point (1/72", or 0.014"). However, if an objectionable dark trap line is created by the 1 point overlap, the designer may plan for a trap of .5 points. Trapping for linerboard or corrugated may require 1/64" to 1/8".

Typography

The soft flexographic printing plate, irregular substrate surfaces, and the fluid flexo ink can have a profound negative impact on text-sized type printed by flexography. The line strokes of smaller point sizes of type often increases during the printing process because of the compressibility of the printing plate and the fluid nature of the flexo printing ink. Negative or reverse type often tends to become pinched or fills in. In extremely adverse situations (poor press equipment or rough irregular substrates), lettershapes may begin to appear rounded and lose their shape.

It is the problem of impression pressure on the printing plate in the printing nip that causes most of the deformation of type. Smaller point sizes of type are most adversely affected and require attention.

For wide-web polyethylene printing, typical minimum type sizes are:
- Positive type—six point for sans-serif fonts and eight point for fonts with serifs.
- Reverse type—nine point minimum (it may be a good idea to spread 9 point reverse minimum type). For narrow-web printing, some fonts may be printed as positives as small as three point type, while others may lose shape at six or eight points. Use bolder fonts instead of light-weight versions.

When designing a job to be printed on corrugated, it is best to choose a medium weight typeface, and to avoid serifs for any type that is smaller than 18 point. A good rule of thumb is to avoid type that is made up of stroke widths less than 1/32" for positive type and 3/64" for reverse type. All type should be set at normal letterspacing.

To help compensate for the "weight gain" of flexographic type, it may be possible to use the trapping technique of spreads and chokes. Chokes are used on positive type, spreads are used on negative type. Some programs, such as Freehand and Illustrator, allow the designer to adjust the thickness of the type. This type effect can be achieved by selecting the text, converting to a "path" and then specifying a value for the"width" for the outer and/or inner "stroke" of the type. In some cases, these programs allow the designer to simply select the type and choose a desired effect such as "heavy" to thicken the selected type to print bolder.

In prepress design, some compensation can be done by choosing either a lighter face or a bolder face. For example, if bold positive type is desired, use a medium weight face. If a medium negative type is desired, specify bold face on the desktop. However, should this technique of selecting style attributes be used, make sure the printer font selected is installed on the output device to be used in the production process.

Letterspacing must be considered when designing for flexo. In offset, letters can be squeezed together to form a denser appearance on the page. The same spacing printed in flexo may cause the letterforms to merge together to become unacceptable. However, when printing fine-serif type with major letterspacing, the serifs may begin to lose their shape. Ideal letterspacing occurs when letters are close enough together to lend support to each other while under the pressure of the printing nip, yet not so close that they begin to join together under that same pressure.

Whenever possible, sans-serif fonts are preferred for flexo printing, however, the larger the point size being printed the better the chances that the font will reproduce as desired.

Unofficial industry standards and recommendations for type:
- Six point minimum for positive type, nine point minimum for reverse or knock out on wide web.
- Four point for positive, six for reverse on narrow web.
- When using small size type, avoid fonts with fine serifs or delicate strokes.
- Kerning may cause squeezing across cylinder. Avoid tight line spacing.
- Letterspacing and/or line spacing may increase slightly in the curve dimension due to plate elongation during the plate-mounting phase.
- All positive text should be printed in a single color if possible.
- Avoid placing fine type on the same color plate with line work and solid printing areas.
- Specify type thoroughly and accurately to the service bureau or flexographic prepress department.
- Avoid reversing type out of two or more colors unless a dominant color outline is used.

Plate distortion and elongation

From a prepress and design perspective, one of the most important characteristics to understand about flexography is the phenomenon of plate elongation. As a flexographic plate is mounted on a plate cylinder, a natural elongation occurs in the curve around the cylinder direction. Consequently, if the printed design is meant to be a circle, the image must be compensated by distorting (shrinking) the image in the around-the-cylinder or curve dimension, and the image on the resulting plate films may appear to be oval. After proper distortion factors have been applied and the plate has been mounted and printed, the oval will elongate to form a circle. The same distortion requirements hold true for all images. This is a general formula used for calculating plate elongation:

$$\frac{\text{factor based on plate thickness}}{\text{cylinder repeat length}} = \text{stretch per inch}$$

Sample calculation used for rubber plate distortion;
- T =Plate thickness with mounting tape; π carried to 4 decimal places = 3.1416;
- R.L. = Repeat Length of the plate cylinder

Plate Thickness	=	0.107"	Repeat length = 18.8"
Mounting Tape Thickness =		0.020"	
TOTAL		0.127"	

$$\frac{\pi \times 2\,T}{\text{R.L.}} = \frac{3.1416 \times 2(0.127)}{18.8"} = 0.0424"$$

This means that for every linear inch of plate used in the around-the-cylinder or curve direction, the images will increase at the rate of 0.042"/inch. To apply the calculation to a design measuring 12 inches in the curve dimension:

12" x 0.042" =0.509"

This means that plate films should output to measure 11.490" in the curve dimension, or 95.7% in the curve dimension, and 100% in the other dimension (ignoring any plate shrink as discussed in the Flexographic Plates section). Software written specifically for flexography can compute plate distortion factors and apply them to each color separation.

This formula shows that as the plate thickness increases the stretch factor increases, and as the cylinder repeat length decreases, the stretch per inch increases. The flexographic industry is currently using a variety of plate thickness in combination with a variety of mounting tape thicknesses. The type and thickness of the plate being used is dictated by the type of press being used and the type of work being printed on the press. Some typical plate thicknesses for some of the larger flexographic printing markets are:

Combined board corrugated	0.250", or 0.107"
Wide-web flexible packaging, preprint, and folding carton	
	0.107", or 0.067"
Narrow-web label	0.067", or 0.045"
Newspapers	0.024"

These are only examples of plate thicknesses currently being used. Recently there has been a trend toward thinner plate technology for flexographic printing.

There exist today many software packages with the capability of shrinking or distorting an image in one dimension. To be sure that the design will be the correct size and shape, the design has to be output to film after plate thickness has been determined and the proper distortion factor applied. The plate distortion step should be performed as close to the film output or plate setting stage as possible, and can be performed by the raster image processor (RIP) operator using distortion software. The actual distortion process need not be of concern to the designer.

Halftones and screening

The flexographic printing process historically has been recognized for its ability to apply spot color and line art graphics to a wide variety of substrates, especially those used for packaging. However, it is the recently improved capability of high-quality, economical four-color process printing that has given the flexographic process an edge over other processes for packaging graphic applications in full color.

Dot gain

All printing processes are subject to the natural and unavoidable occurrence called "dot gain." Dot gain can be described as an increase in the diameter of halftone dots from the film to plate and a further increase in size from plate to print. For example, when the image setter outputs a 50% screen film dot, the flexographic plate-making exposure step may cause that 50% film dot to "grow" to become a 51% dot area on the plate. This is a small and relatively insignificant gain in comparison to plate-to-print gain, where a 50% film dot may eventually print on a flexographic press as a 65% or greater print dot.

Halftone dots can be generated in a number of shapes including the square dot, the elliptical dot, octagonal dots, and symmetrical and asymmetrical round dots. Square dots begin to join at 50% (arranged in a checkerboard pattern), and the connected areas continue to increase as the dot area increases. Dot gain occurs at the perimeter of the halftone dot; as individual dots join, the perimeter area increases, causing a large density jump at the dot area where the contact first occurs.

Dot shapes. Without question, a round dot screen is the ideal for the flexographic process. There are however different versions of round dot screening software. Individual film dots on the best round dot screens for flexography do not begin to touch until they reach the 70-75% region. Most design software can provide for a round dot; however, dot shape should be determined as close to the platemaking step as possible, either at the film imagesetter or the platesetter. Consequently, the same type of dot should be available on the RIP and imagesetter, or platesetter.

The fluid ink and compressible plate used for flexographic printing tend to increase dot gain, making dot gain compensation an especially important step for high quality tone reproduction. Each different substrate printed by flexography will also influence dot gain characteristics.

It is important to understand that dot gain compensation is different for each printing process, for many different substrate surfaces, and often for different printing presses within the same process. Fortunately, dot gain is predictable and compensated for by a color separator, or adjusted for compensation in Photoshop, or in RIP-based calibration packages like Agfa Calibrator.

One of the most important considerations for a successful four-color tone reproduction is an understanding of the ink hue and dot gain differences that exist for the flexographic printer. When high-quality tone reproduction is important, the best results are obtained by first performing a preliminary press test run called a "fingerprint."

A fingerprint of the press will provide important information to the color separator or the desktop designer. By printing a target of this type under controlled conditions, color separation films can be adjusted to compensate for flexographic dot gain and ink hue.

Highlights

Another important consideration when color separating for the flexographic process is the placement of the minimum highlight dot. Most photopolymer flexographic plates are capable of holding a two percent highlight dot. Since the highlight areas of a flexographic print show the most dot-gain, it is extremely important that the minimum highlight dot capabilities be discussed with the printer before separations are made.

Vignettes

Flexographic highlight dot gain makes it difficult (if not impossible) to print a fade-away to white paper without a harsh break at the highlight edge. When designing for flexo, it is best to fade off the end of the design, or border the highlight end of the vignette.

A vignette or blend

Screen ruling and substrate

The selection of the proper screen ruling is critical to four-color process flexography. Screen ruling capabilities are most often dictated by the type of substrate being printed. The corrugated industry, for example, prints halftones screened at 45, 55, 65, or 85 lines-per-inch. Flexographic newspaper printers print halftones screened between 65 and 100 lines per inch. Flexible packaging on film-based substrates is commonly done at 120 to 150 lines per inch, and high-quality label printers have the capability of printing 200 line screen images.

Anilox cell count and separation screen ruling should be correlated to achieve the best flexographic print. A general rule of thumb is that the separation screen ruling should be no more than 25% of the anilox that will be used to apply ink to the plate. The ideal from an ink-application-to-the-plate perspective is to have a minimum of four anilox cells on top of each halftone dot.

Screen angles

Cells are engraved on an anilox roll at one of three possible angles 30°, 45°, or 60°. To avoid anilox moiré, film or plate screen angles should be at least 7.5° away from the anilox cell angle. Cyan, magenta, yellow, and black screen angles should also be set at angles at least 15° apart from each other.

Stochastic screening

Stochastic or Frequency Modulated (FM) screening for flexography may offer some advantages over conventional half-tone screening. FM screening eliminates the possibility of moiré, and also allows the flexographer to print high-fidelity color. High-fidelity color is a technique used to extend the printed color gamut by printing a total of six or sometimes seven process colors. The multicolor capabilities of flexo and the random dot pattern of a stochastic screen to avoid moiré make high-fidelity color an excellent design option.

The dot size used for FM screening is extremely small and comparable in size to the highlight dot of conventional screening. The flexo highlight dot is subject to excessive dot gain. Consequently, FM screening for flexography should not be attempted unless the printer and color separator have performed press fingerprints to determine the ideal dot size to be used, and accurate dot gain compensation curves.

A final point about films made for flexographic plate making: The polymer plate material is very soft and will easily trap air between the film and the plate during the plate exposure. Consequently, when making films for sheet photopolymer plates, a special "matte emulsion" film must be used to avoid out-of-contact areas during plate exposure.

Step & repeat

The concept of printing the same image multiple times across the width of a web and around the entire repeat length of a cylinder is known as "step and repeat." Package printing industries apply this concept in combination with variable repeat length and variable web width capabilities. The ideal is to maximize substrate usage and productivity by fitting as many repeated images on the flexographic plate as possible.

Often, a technique called nesting will be required. By placing duplicate package layouts or label graphics strategically between other layouts or graphics, the job can be designed for maximum productivity and minimum material waste. The best method of nesting images is to cut and paste original graphics. This step in the flexographic prepress process is done in the production art stage. Most standard layout programs do not have the capability of step and repeat. Step and repeat can be performed on some illustration programs and by specialized software that will create templates to allow the production artist the ability to impose multiple images for film output, while working within the confines of web width limitations and plate cylinder repeat length.

In the past, multiple sets of flexographic plates were made from one set of films, and imposition was performed in the plate mounting stage. Today, photopolymer plates and pin register or micro-dot plate register systems require one-piece plates, and one-piece plates should be made from one-piece films. The need for large one-piece films for wide web flexographic printing applications has brought about the need for large format imagesetters and film processors.

The flexographic printing process is sometimes prone to a quality problem known as "plate bounce." This problem is especially prevalent when lead edges of the printing plate run parallel to the printing nip, and can be avoided by a layout technique called staggering the plate. Not all designs will allow this technique, but when possible, staggering the plates may provide for higher press speeds. Another technique used for minimizing plate bounce is the use of "bearer bars" in the non-image areas. Bearer bars provide continuous contact between the plate surface, the anilox, and the impression roll.

Die-cutting & converting

When designing graphics for a die-cut label or die-cut folding carton, an artist must take care to place all graphical elements in the correct positions. A die-cut folding carton is an excellent example to illustrate the fact that the first requirement for design is that it conform to the shape of the package.

Packaging engineers often use computer aided design (CAD) systems to design folding cartons, corrugated containers, or rigid paper boxes. CAD files can be exported to illustration programs to provide the designer a two-dimensional layout of the job.

The designer should remember that eventually the design will be converted to a package, and each package forming process has special considerations that may be adversely affected by the design of the package. Some important considerations when designing for a job to be a die-cut box or converted to a bag include:

- Bar coding—Bar coding can be created on the desktop or provided through another outside source. In either case, bar codes should run parallel with the web direction, and should be cut back to compensate for flexo gain characteristics.

- Bleeds—For die-cut jobs it is important to have a copy of the die being used. This will allow the designer the opportunity to see where packages fold and join, and where bleeds will be required. The amount of bleed required depends on the press being used. Bleeds can be created with standard illustration programs.
- Cut areas—Because flexographic printers do in-line flatbed or rotary die-cutting, the die must be held in register with the colors being printed on the package. Important graphic elements should not be placed too close to cut areas.
- Glue areas/seal areas—To assure sealing when forming a folding carton, glue areas should be free of ink and varnish. Polyethelyne bags are often heat sealed. All areas in or near a heat seal should be free of ink. Heat sealing is also done on some folding cartons; for example, milk cartons are laminated with polyethylene and will be heat sealed at the seams. The design should be void of ink in the heat-sealing areas.
- Score lines—Die-cut folding cartons usually fold at score lines. The designer should consider a score line a critical registration area.
- Varnish areas—Many folding cartons or labels require the application of an over-print varnish. In some cases, variable information like freshness dating or product coding will be added during packaging. Often these areas must be free of varnish. This application requires a special "spot varnish" plate.
- Windows—Die-cut windows should be clearly indicated. A window used for folding carton or label work presents problems in the die-cutting operation. Before designing a window, check with the printer or package convertor to make sure that windowing is within their capabilities.

Prepress output

After a design has undergone the required production art trapping, distortion, and imposition steps, it is ready for film output or, in some cases, it is ready to go directly to digital flexo platemaking. Imagesetters used for the flexographic process have some unique requirements.

- Accuracy—The nature of the flexographic process includes a number of areas that might lead to print misregister. When precise register is required, the imagesetter being used should be the more accurate drum imagesetter, rather than its predecessor, the flatbed capstan imagesetter. However, capstan devices are suitable for single-color jobs with less demanding register requirements and are especially useful for unusually long jobs. Capstan devices can output film up to 80", while drum scanner lengths are limited to the circumference of the imaging drum.
- Size—The imagesetter should be large enough to handle the largest films required for platemaking.
- Film—The imagesetter must be capable of handling 0.007" matte emulsion film.
- Calibration—It is imperative that the imagesetter be properly calibrated. Film dot percentages below 10% should not vary by more than 1% from the required dot area. Film dot area over 10% should not vary by more than 3% from the required dot area.
- Uniformity—Light screen tints should be a uniform dot percentage, with no variation in size between individual dots.
- Shape—The imagesetter and RIP screening information should be capable of outputting a "hard" round dot.
- Resolution—Resolution should be adequate for the screen ruling to be output (1200–3600 dpi).
- Processor—Because flexographic plates require a relatively lengthy exposure, the film density becomes an important factor. Imagesetter exposure levels and film processing chemistry should be adjusted to provide D-Max areas of 4.0 and D-Min of 0.04 or less.

Proofing

"Proofing" for a flexographic job is not always a clearly defined activity. Historically, a flexographic proof had been a plate proof made on a mounter-proofer during the plate mounting procedure. This practice continues today in many wide-web flexo applications. The mounter-proofer proof is not appropriate for color matching. Instead, this proof is used internally to verify plate register, plate quality, and plate content. This type of proof is not used for customer approval.

A "contract proof" is a facsimile of the job a printer agrees to reproduce; the customer and printer sign a contract for printed material based on a contract proof. The typical "contract" proofing system used for offset lithography is not suited for flexographic package proofing. Basically there are three general problems associated with offset proofing when applied to flexography.

- Substrate—Most proofing systems proof to a limited number of substrates. Flexographic package printing is done on a wide variety of substrates, and colors proofed on any substrate other than the one to be printed will show color variation when compared to the live press run.
- Spot Color Matching—Film-based or digital proofing systems are based on CMYK toner applications. Many of the packaging graphics are line art and spot color, not screen tints of CMYK.
- Halftone Dot Gain Compensation—When a proof of a process color graphic is required, most film-based proofing systems are not calibrated for flexography. Proofing systems like Imation Matchprint and DuPont Chromalin were designed for offset lithography. These systems were designed to replicate dot gain as it would typically occur in offset lithography. To use these proofing systems, the flexographer has to output two sets of films: one set compensated for flexographic dot gain (cutback dot percentages) and sent to platemaking, and one set with increased dot percentages to replicate on-press dot gain, used for proofing.

Most flexographic printers use cutouts and "dummy" mock-up packages for proofing purposes. Digital proofs can be made from an inkjet or dye sublimation printer and used as a facsimile for the mock-up. When critical spot color matching is required, the flexographic printer will often provide the client with a catalog of colors applied to the substrate to be used. These colors may be variations of conventional color matching systems like Pantone, or Focoltone, they may be colors formulated by the printer, or they may be colors requested by the buyer. In any case, spot color matching should be visually evaluated and numerically verified by color measurement instruments.

Halftone film-based systems can be used for process color flexographic proofs; however, the current systems will continue to require that two sets of films be produced—one for plates, and one for proofing. Digital proofing systems (both halftone and continuous tone), when used within a color management environment, can be manipulated to output contract proofs for flexographic printing. When used in a color management environment, digital proofing can eliminate the need for an extra set of films for proofing purposes.

Packaging conclusions

The flexographic printing process has evolved from letterpress to become the most adaptable process currently used for packaging graphics applications. Because the process is unique, there are many unusual design features that should be considered during the prepress stages of a flexographic printing job.

Add to the unique flexographic design features the design features that are unique to packaging requirements and those that are unique to various substrates and design can quickly become a nightmare. In order to create successful designs for a flexographically printed job it is useful for the design and prepress personnel to have a basic understanding of the process, and its unique design considerations.

The design and prepress personnel may also find it useful to understand those features of a flexographic printing system that offer a wider latitude of design considerations, like that of multicolor capability. The most important areas of flexographic design are as follows:

Trapping. Generally speaking, traps need to be larger for flexographic printing than traps for the other printing processes. The type of press being used for printing and the substrate being printed also should be considered when deciding what trap measurements are appropriate. The best register (and so the least amount of trap requirements) can be achieved on a common impression cylinder flexographic press. Traps for prints to be done on an in-line or stack press should be larger than those intended for a CIC press. Thin films of polyethylene are the most difficult substrates to print without stretch, consequently these films may require larger areas of trap than designs to be printed on more stable films such as polypropylene.

Typography. The flexographic plate may cause type to distort somewhat during the printing process. A natural and unavoidable stretch occurs in the web or machine direction when the flexographic plate is mounted. This plate stretch may cause an increase in line spacing to blocks of text composed in that direction, or an increase in letterspacing when text is composed to run parallel with the web direction. Abnormally high pressure in the printing nip can cause a significant increase in the weight of type selected by the designer. Reverse type may be "pinched" by the excess pressure. Wider webs and rougher substrates like paperboard are especially prone to excess pressure being applied in the printing nip.

Plate elongation. Unlike any other printing plate, the flexographic plate will elongate or "stretch" during the plate mounting process. The elongation for each design must be compensated for in the prepress stage. General axioms to apply are:
- The thicker the plate, the more the stretch.
- The smaller the cylinder to be used for platemounting, the more the stretch.

Halftones. The flexographic plate has its own dot gain characteristics; each substrate will also contribute to differences in dot gain and tone reproduction. Highlights are also a challenging area of print for the flexographic process. Special care should be taken when generating film separations for flexographic printing. The best results for halftone printing can be achieved by first performing a "fingerprint" test run of the flexographic press in question. This test will provide the color separator with the information necessary to apply the correct gamma for the printing conditions. The rougher the substrate, the greater the dot gain. The durometer of the plate being used and the type of mounting tape also have a significant influence on dot gain.

Screen angles. The cells of the flexographic anilox roll are engraved in either a 30°, 45°, or 60° angle; these cell angles make a one-color moiré possible. Common practice when screening for a flexo job is to re-angle screens by either adding or subtracting 7.5° from standard offset screen angles.

Many unique packaging considerations are important to design and prepress for flexographic printing. The following techniques are often used for packaging design and prepress.

Step and repeat. Many smaller packages or labels are often printed multiple times on wider webs. When step and repeats are necessary, images may be turned 90° or 180° to allow for the best fit and least amount of waste.

Stochastic screening. Stochastic screening may be used when printing high-fidelity color or when printing multiple screen tints. Halftones for corrugated are best suited to stochastic screening techniques.

Die-cutting and converting. Package printing usually is only one step in a package conversion process. When designing graphics for packaging, special requirements must be considered. For polyethylene and other substrates that will be heat-sealed, it is important to keep heat-seal areas free of ink. A folding carton to be die-cut should have all image elements located such that when the box is formed they will appear on the correct panel. It is also important to keep glue areas free from coating or ink that may interfere with bonding.

Paper issues in reproduction

Runnability

Runnability is the ability of a paper to run through a press efficiently with no loss of productivity or increase in downtime. Runnability affects the profitability of a job and is a major concern to the printer. There is a difference between purchase price and user cost. A paper can have the greatest print quality characteristics but if it can't be run through the press, it is of little value. This is because of the large area of surface contact with the rubber blanket and stiff, tacky, paste inks.

Lithographic paper requirements. Conventional lithography uses a dampening or fountain solution to wet the plate's non-image areas so they stay ink-free or clean. Therefore, the paper must resist weakening of its surface strength due to repeated exposure to moisture from each successive unit.

Water resistance. Excess water or poor water resistance can cause the coating of the paper to soften, weaken and leach out onto the blanket. This causes piling and milking. Calcium carbonate (limestone) is a common coating and filler ingredient. Being an alkaline, it will increase the pH of the fountain solution and cause other print problems.

Offset litho paper requirements. Lithography, especially sheet-fed, uses thick, paste inks that are very tacky. Therefore, the paper must have good bond strength to resist rupturing of its coating or fibers from the surface. Of all the printing processes, lithography deposits the thinnest film of ink—about one (1) micron thick when dry. A micron is 10^{-9}m or .00004 inch. Therefore, any loose surface dirt or contamination such as fizz, lint, or slitting and cutting dust will show as an aesthetic print defect.

Gravure paper requirement. Image areas are engraved below the surface of the cylinder so paper must be very flat and smooth to make good contact with the well opening to transfer (pull out) ink. Gravure inks are very fluid and have little tack to pick up coating and fibers.

Paper should have sizing so fluids inks don't feather. Comparing coated and uncoated stocks:

Coated paper	**Uncoated**
Has a mineral coating	Has no coating
More expensive	Less expensive
Smoother surface	Rougher surface
Higher gloss	Less gloss
More holdout	More absorbent
Better image quality	Poorer image quality
Stronger surface	Weaker surface

Basis weight

Basis weight is a measurement of weight of some unit of area. It is the weight (in pounds) of a ream (500 sheets) in the basic size for that paper grade. It is important because paper is solid by weight, not linear distance or surface area by volume. Basis weight tolerances are +/- 5%. The US system of basis weight is very confusing because of the difference basic sizes for each grade category:

Basic paper sizes

Bond, ledger, writing	17"x22"
Cover	20"x26"
Bristol	22.5"x 28.5"
Index	25.5"x 30.5"
Newsprint, tag	24"x 36"
Coated, text, book, offset	25"x 38"

The metric system uses grammage, which is grams per square meter (g/m^2). For a 25"x38" basic size, the conversion factor to go from basis weight to grammage is to multiply by 1.48. Multiply by 0.675 for g/m^2 into lbs. A 100 lb book paper is equivalent to a 148 g/m^2 and a 50 lb is 74 g/m^2.

Substance weight usually applies only to writing grades of paper (bond, duplicator). It is the same as basis weight. "M" weight is the weight for 1,000 sheets, not 500. M weight is twice the basis weight.

The thickness of cover grades is measured in thousanth of an inch. Ten (10) point is .010". Thickness is often called caliper and it is measured in points or mills which is a thousandths of an inch (.001"). Bulk for book papers is expressed in the number of pages per inch (ppi) for a given basis weight. 50 lb book paper can vary from 310 to 800 ppi, .003" to .0013" respectively.

Paper grain direction

The grain direction, or alignment of paper fibers, affects the feeding and transporting of paper through the press. You want to handle paper on sheetfed presses at very fast production speeds of 15,000 impressions per hour (iph). The wrong grain direction can cause a loss in productivity.

If 25"x38", then the grain is long
Fold a sheet in both directions
   Cleanest fold is with the grain
Tear a sheet in both directions
   Cleanest tear is with the grain
Cut two strips in different directions
   Most rigid or stiffer strip is with the grain
Moisten only one side of a sheet of paper
   The paper will immediately curl and roll with the grain

The grain should run parallel to the printing cylinders or along the longest dimension which is called grain "long."

Why grain long?

The sheet must follow a relatively tight "S" curve as it wraps around the impression cylinder on its way to the transfer cylinder. If the sheet is grain long, it is more pliable and will gently follow and conform to the "S" curve. If grain short, the sheet is stiff and rigid and will slap against the cylinder. The wet ink surface will then mark and scratch. If the paper absorbs moisture it will expand mostly in the cross-grain direction. This makes the sheet of paper longer front-to-back. The packing beneath both the plate and blanket can be adjusted to compensate for the size change so images will now register and fit properly.

Finishing & bindery

Substrate and printing issues affect bindery and finishing. When folding you want to fold parallel with the grain to prevent cracking, especially on black solid colors. Perfect bound (hot melt) books should have grain direction parallel with the spine or back bone. Sheetfed presses require flat paper to prevent feeding, register, and printing problems. Paper should lie flat and have no curls, buckles, waves, or puckers. Flatness is very related to moisture content and relative humidity (RH). Mechanical curling on roll or reel set is greatest near the innermost core or reel where paper is wound very tightly around a small diameter. Tail-end hook is caused by forces of tacky ink splitting when the sheet is peeled off the rubber blanket at a sharp angle. It is especially noticeable on heavy coverage near the tail end of the sheet.

At the wet end (headbox) of the papermaking machine, paper is almost 99.5% water. At the dry roll end, paper is only about 5% water. The amount of water contained in a sheet of paper is called its moisture content relative humidity (aka RH); the amount of water or moisture in the air at a given temperature is called the relative humidity or RH. Cold winter months are usually dry. Warm summer months are usually wet or damp. Many printers have little or no control of the environmental conditions that affect paper.

Dimensional stability

Paper is hydroscopic which means it breaths and acclimates with the surrounding environment. The exposed outer edges of a pile or load can either absorb or release moisture while the inside of the pile, which is protected, remains unchanged. This causes the paper to swell and expand or shrink and contract in size.

Wavy edges on paper is caused by an increase in RH of the atmosphere in the pressroom. Wavy edged paper causes mis-registration on press or poor fit between colors. It usually occurs at the back corners and gets progressively worse, thus fans out. Severe cases cause wrinkles starting at the lower center and progressing diagonally to the outer back corners.

Conditioning and trimming paper

Paper must first be brought into temperature equilibrium before it is opened up and exposed to the humidity of the environment. Conditioning depends on the volume or amount of paper and the relative difference in temperature between the paper and air. Six cubic feet of paper takes 72 hours (3 days) to condition at 50 degrees difference.

Sheets should be both square and accurate to size. Front-to-back dimension is critical on sheetfed perfecting presses. Many printers trim stock for accurate size.

Cleanliness

Paper should not have any loose surface contamination such as dust, lint or dirt. If it does, the result will be voids in print areas called hickeys, fisheyes, or donuts. Many times this is caused by a dull rotary slitter or flat blade knife. It shows up as contamination on the blanket at the outer edges of the sheet only. Hickeys come from three different sources:

- paper
- ink
- dirt

Strength

Strength is primarily determined by how well the inner fibers are bonded or closely intermingled together, more so than thickness. Web- or roll-fed presses that are under high tension need a lot of tensile strength so web breaks do not occur. Weak surface strength tends to pick and cause hickeys, or delaminate and split apart. Stretch (elasticity) is the amount of distortion paper undergoes under tensile strain or tension. It is important in web or roll printing because paper is under a constant pulling stress. Stretch is generally greater in the cross direction (CD) than in the machine direction (MD).

Print quality

Print quality is defined by those factors and characteristics that influence the appearance of the printed image on the paper. Some print quality problems are unjustly blamed on the paper when some other factors, such as ink, blanket, or press, are really the cause.

Whiteness

Whiteness is the ratio of red, green and blue reflectance. Likewise, it's also the amount of cyan, magenta and yellow density. It is important in full four-color process printing that the paper be as white as possible so it can reflect all the colors in the spectrum. Printing is a subtractive process. White can be many different colors. White can be very neutral and balanced or it can have a predominant cast or hue.

If the paper is "cold" it is toward the blue side (CIE + b*).

If the paper is "warm," it is toward the red side (CIE + a*).

Brightness

Whiteness is the ratio of RGB reflectance. Brightness is how much blue light only is being reflected. Adding blue to a yellow paper makes it whiter (neutral) but less bright. The TAPPI (Technical Association for Paper and Pulp) specification calls for measuring brightness (% Ref.) at 427 nm. If the brightness is over 87%, the paper can be classified as a number one (#1) sheet. Titanium Dioxide (TiO2) is a popular additive that makes paper whiter, brighter and more opaque. Calcium carbonate (limestone) is a more practical and less expensive alternative for paper filler and coatings. Paper mills sometimes add fluorescent brightening agents (FBA) to paper to make them look whiter than they really arc. For a fluorescent material to fluoresce, the light source much contain some ultra-violet (UV) energy. Natural daylight is UV rich. Fluorescent agents are also used in specialty inks.

Opacity

If the paper is not opaqued but translucent, the image from one side can be seen on the other. This is called show-through and can be very distracting to the reader. As the paper caliper or weight increase, whether from fiber or filler, opacity increases because more light can be absorbed. Calendering reduces opacity because air spaces, which act as light traps, are collapsed. Strike-through is when the ink physically penetrates through a sheet of paper, not the light.

Smoothness

The smoothness or roughness of paper greatly affects printability. This is less so for offset lithography because the pliable rubber blankets can easily transfer ink into the low valleys. Surface texture can be measured, quantified, and profiled with instruments. Gloss is the amount of specular or mirror reflection a surface has. The flatter or smoother a surface is, the more gloss or shine it will have. Calendering increases smoothness and gloss because the rough surfaces are polished flat. More calendering of coated papers changes the paper's finish from matte, to dull, then gloss, to finally ultra-gloss. Paper gloss is measured at a 75 degree angle of geometry. Heatset web inks have poor ink gloss.

Formation

Formation is the term used to describe a paper's fibrous structure, uniformity, and distribution. Formation is judged by transmitted back lighting, such as a light table. Uneven clumping of paper fibers is called "wild" and will cause mottled printing because of the difference in ink absorption due to paper fiber concentration or density. Back tap mottle is a sporadic problem where the paper is blamed. It usually occurs in purples or blues. Pulling a single impression of just cyan or magenta shows no mottle, but together, it's mottled. The still-wet ink is non-uniformly back trapping onto subsequent blankets.

Two sidedness. Printers want paper to be as similar as possible for both sides of the sheet. This is because of sheetwise, work & turn, and work & flop impositions and layouts. Colors on facing pages (reader spreads) must match at the cross-over. Fourdriner-made paper is two sided because of the effects of the felt and wire side on water drainage.

Absorbency & holdout. Paper, by its very nature, has an affinity for inks, especially the liquid inks used in flexography and gravure. There must be a delicate balance or compromise between the paper's ability to absorb ink and its holdout. Too much of one and not enough of the other will cause several different print quality problems to result.

Too absorbent. If the paper absorbs too much ink then the solid images will appear weak and flat with little gloss. Halftones and screen tints will have excessive dot growth or dot gain and look dark, dirty, plugged up and filled in. Uncoated papers and newsprint may act like a blotter.

Holdout. Holdout is the ability of a paper to allow a fresh, wet ink film to sit on the top surface of the paper and not be quickly absorbed into the paper. If so, the ink will dry with a higher density (darker), and more gloss (shine). The more fluid the inks or more absorbent the paper, the less holdout there is.

Ink mileage

Paper holdout determines the mileage or ink consumption rate. It is very similar to an automobile's gasoline mileage. The more holdout, the better the ink mileage. One pound of black ink should cover 360,000 square inches of area on coated paper, but covers only 150,000 on newsprint.

Set-off

Set-off occurs when the fresh, wet ink film on the top surface of a bottom sheet makes physical contact with the bottom side of the next top sheet and the ink transfers. The image will always be wrong reading. Set-off occurs when there is too much holdout, an ink film that is too thick, an ink that dries too slowly, or cold paper.

Blocking

Blocking is a severe case of set-off. Blocking occurs when the wet inks dry in contact with each other and effectively have been glued together. Because the sheets stick together they cannot be easily separated without damaging the image areas. Usually, these sheets must be thrown away.

Spray powder

A printer can prevent set-off and blocking by using a fine white powder that is sprayed onto the top surface of the sheet. This anti-set-off spray powder prevents the sheets from making any physical contact.

It allows air and oxygen to flow between the sheets so they can dry faster. The powder is usually a corn starch. If too much spray powder is used, it dries in the ink and makes it very rough, almost like sandpaper. This can cause abrasion when two pieces run up against each other. It also detacts from the gloss of the inks. Excess powder can also cause problems on the second pass through the press.

Racking or traying

Sheet-fed printers try to avoid set-off, blocking and excessive spray powder by running small lifts in their press delivery. This is called racking or traying. Paper is very heavy and small piles or lifts keep the weight and pressure to a minimum. These piles are separated and supported by metal angle braces and plywood boards.

Chalking

If any ink takes too long to dry, the thinner viscosity vehicles, oils, solvents and other ingredients that bind or adhere the ink to the surface drain into the paper. The result is a dry ink that is mostly just pigment powder and can easily be rubbed or scratched off. This is called chalking.

Blistering

Heatset web offset presses dry the inks by passing the web through a hot, open flame gas oven. Blistering occurs on coated paper when there is heavy ink coverage that seals the sheet closed. Any moisture trapped inside the sheet suddenly vaporizes, turning into steam and rupturing the paper surface. Blistering is likely to occur when:
- the paper is coated
- there is a lot of heavy ink coverage on both sides of the paper or substrate
- there is too much moisture in the paper
- the dryer oven temperature is too hot
- the web speed is too slow

When you get right down to it, paper seems simple but it is rather complicated.

The digital movement

The age of electronics and computers has changed the way printed products are created and produced. Since the early 1980s, printing and publishing technology has been evolving new methods for production digital imaging. Before going further, let's define what exactly a digital image is. The term digital literally means "composed of numbers," so a digital image is an image that is composed of numbers. Every file, whether it be an image, a sound, or a text file, is nothing more than a string of binary digits. By modern convention the binary digit 0 is used to represent an image element, the binary digit 1 is used to represent a non-image element. Binary digits are called bits. A byte is a binary numbers represented by eight bits, it can have 256 possible values ranging from 1 to 255.

Digital images

Scanner

Images can be digitized by a scanner. A scanner captures an image and converts it into a computer file of binary values (0s and 1s) that correspond to the brightness of the image at various points, pixels. The ability of the scanner to "see" variations in brightness depends on how much information is stored in a pixel, an amount called pixel depth. The deeper the pixel, the more information it can store.

Digital image type	Pixel size	Tones/colors
Binary image	1 bit	2
Grayscale image	1 byte	256
RGB color image	3 bytes	16,777,216
CMYK color image	4 bytes	4,294,967,296

Digital photography

Digital photography is another way to digitize images. Digital cameras and cameras backs are used to photograph subjects using charged couple devices (CCD) that record the coupled images as electronic voltages. These analog voltages are converted to digital signals that can be fed directly into color correction software that produces images without the need for films or scanners.

Digital type

All output devices today are raster-based. This means that they create type and images as patterns of spots or dots on paper, film, plate, and other substrate. In 1985 Adobe introduced PostScript as a language for driving raster-based output devices, and for producing typefaces as vector-based outlines. Almost all digital fonts now fall into 2 main categories:

- PostScript or Type 1 fonts are scalable outline fonts which are defined using PostScript's bézier curves and work best with Raster Image Processors (RIP) because they do not need to be converted to be RIPped and output.
- TrueType fonts are also scalable outline fonts but they are based on quadratic curves. Created by Apple, these fonts must either be converted to Type 1 before being RIPped or a True-Type Rasterizer must be used to create the bitmap for the output device.

When data is stored in a file, it is usually structured in a manner that is tailored to specific types of information. It is also structured in a manner that allows recovery of the data with a reasonable degree of efficiency. There are various document structures that feed into the digital printing process.

Text data

In order to maintain effective and consistent results in the exchange of textual data across multiple platforms, an encoding scheme must be used to represent alphanumeric characters as a set of binary digits. ASCII eventually become the standard and is now used in most personal computers.

The ASCII (American Standard Code for Information Interchange) describes a coded character set which is primarily intended for the interchange of information. The character set is applicable to all Latin alphabets; eight bits are commonly used to represent each character in ASCII code.

Graphical data

Bitmaps
A bitmap is described as a rectangular array of pixels, which are used to form an image. In a bitmap, the pixel depth specifies the number of colors the pixel can show; 24 bits or 3 bytes (RGB) is often used as a practical maximum for the number of colors that should be required in any bitmap image. Once an input device such as a scanner or a digital camera has captured a bitmap image, it can then be manipulated using different types of software tools. These tools range from simple paint packages that offer a limited range of editing capabilities, to sophisticated photo-editing packages that offer a suite of complex editing and special effect tools. Common bitmap file types are TGA, BMP, PCX and TIFF (Tagged Image File Format).

Vectors
In computer graphics, vector data usually refers to a means of representing graphic entities such as lines, polygons or curves, by numerically specifying key points to control their generation. There are many common vector file types. Example: Auto CAD DXF, Auto CAD DWG and Wavefront OBJ.

Metafiles
Metafiles usually contain both bitmap and vector data. Metafiles are widely used to transport bitmap or vector data between hardware platforms. Some examples of the common metafile types are RTF, WGM, Macintosh PICT, and EPS (Encapsulated PostScript).

PostScript
The revolutionary product developed by Adobe Systems was a computer language called PostScript and a process that could interpret PostScript page descriptions and generate a data stream to drive a digital printing device such as a laser printer or film writer. The PostScript page description language has become the heart of desktop publishing and electronic prepress. It standardized the language that each application program outputs by developing RIPs for many different printers and output devices.

The RIP, or raster image processor, is really the PostScript programming language compiler. It interprets the file and executes its commands, which are to draw objects on a page. The end result of RIPping is a bitmap for the entire page that tells the output engine where to place dots. Digital imaging makes all direct-to outputs possible by replacing photography when used to image films, replacing films when imaging plates, and imaging plateless systems directly.

Digital printing is divided into three main categories of technologies:
- direct-to-plate off-press
- direct-to-plate on-press
- direct-to-print

DIRECT-TO-PLATE

There are two categories of direct-to-plate technology, direct-to-plate off-press and direct-to-plate on-press.

Direct-to-plate off-press

Direct-to-plate systems are the logical answer for longer run sheetfed and web offset printing, at least for now. That's why we are most likely to find commercial and publication printers, who use special cylinder-to-press approaches, print runs in the millions. Offset printing has been a bit behind because the CTP equipment hadn't been available. Direct-to-plate or computer-to-plate (CTP) means that electronic information from a file is sent in PostScript form to an off-press platemaking device. There plates are written, exposed, and processed so they are ready to hang on an offset printing press. The platesetter exposes the plate using a precisely guided and focused laser beam to deliver the data. CTP can save time and money, and can yield improvements in quality and consistency.

Direct-to-plate on-press

Direct-to-plate on-press, called direct imaging presses, is a system that uses plates that have already been "hung" or put in place on the plate cylinders on a press. Once hung, these plates are then imaged with the digital information for the print job. Before the plates can be imaged, the digital information has to be prepared. The electronic files, generated on the desktop computer and delivered in their native applications, first go to the printer's desktop workstation. There the operator performs a flight check, final imposition, and conversion to PostScript. Next, the PostScript files are digitally separated and bitmaps are generated via the RIP to a server and subsequently transferred to plates on press. Each plate is mounted on each press unit and imaged simultaneously. In direct imaging press, the prepress steps of film output and off-press plate are eliminated.

The technology used to image digital information from the press computer directly to each plate is called laser dot imaging. It was developed by Presstek. Laser dot imaging was first brought to the market on the GTO-DI from Heidelberg.

DIGITAL PRINTING

Once the plate is made, however, the image reproduction process is a purely analog affair. Ink is transported from reservoir to plate, and then from plate to substrate by mechanical means. Modern printing process may incorporate a number of digital subsystems to monitor and control color register, paper tension, paper density, and other important variables. However, the image information that the press transfers to the substrate does not have to exist in a digital form. Analog printing presses often employ computers to help them do their job more efficiently, but they do not need computers to tell them what to print. We do not consider modern lithography or gravure processes digital, even though the images they reproduce almost certainly were in digital form at some point earlier in the process.

Direct to print

Direct-to-print or digital printing is the production of printed materials directly from digital information residing in an electronic file in a computer. Put another way, it's the output of digital information from an electronic file onto a substrate of some kind. Until now, most direct digital printing devices, with the exception of imagesetters, produced continuous tone output. Imagesetters use lasers to expose graphic arts film, special paper, or plate materials with digital information. When the film is reproduced, the halftone dot structure is in place and the project is ready to be assembled into a film flat, which is then subsequently imaged to make a printing plate. If plate materials are imaged, the job is ready to go to press. Images printed by one of the traditional printing processes must have a halftone dot structure to be reproduced. Digital printing has this capability, so it's finally become printing to commercial printers as well; they can have their dots and digital too.

Traditional printing does not allow us to print variable information. With traditional printing, the prepress work is performed, the plates are made, and they are run on the press. The end result is thousands of pages that look exactly the same. This information is not variable; it is static. In contrast, many of the digital presses (presses that print from digital data) can print variable information. On different pages we can have different names and addresses. The ability to print variable information which results in variable printing is the critical component of customized printing.

For years, printers have been reporting that press runs are becoming shorter each year. A commercial printer's average order fell from 20,000 press sheets in the early 1980s to 5,000–10,000 press sheets today. No one talks about the customers who forgo ordering a printed product because they really need about 1,000 copies or less. Shorter printing runs evidently do not mean that people are buying less print—the printing industry is putting more ink on paper every year; people seem instead to want to buy more of less—they want more short runs than long runs.

On-demand printing
On-demand is a term that means different things to different people. In a general sense, the concept of on-demand is basically one of short notice and quick turnaround. In the printing industry, it is also associated with shorter and more economical printing runs. When all of this is combined, the definition becomes "short notice, quick turnaround of short, economical print runs." When all criteria are met, it results in lower inventory costs, lower risk of obsolescence, lower production costs, and reduced distribution costs.

Distribute and print

By combining digital printing with telecommunications, one can greatly reduce the delivery timetable of printed product. Most printing plants today use a print-and-deliver approach; the job gets printed, loaded on trucks or put in the mail, and delivered to the customer or their audiences. With digital printing and telecommunications, the customer or an electronic service bureau can design the pages, assign them to forms, and send the images electronically to many local printers for production. This new approach reverses the process of deliver-and-print, and gets the message into the hands of audiences quicker.

Fast turnaround

A few years ago, turnaround time at a commercial printer was 14 to 21 days, today it is about 10 days. For many projects, even that time does not work. When we add that reality to the decreasing size of the print orders, we can see why digital full-color printing is the right process at the right time. Digital printing is very fast—as a rule of thumb, two-sided full color print runs of 500 11"x17" sheets will take less than a half hour to go through these machines. And when the printing is completed, the product is ready for finishing. What must be factored is the time to flight and prepare the file for printing.

Personalization

One way a company can distinguish itself from the competition is to add perceived value to its product or performance. It can do that with improvements, innovations, and pricing options. Direct the message to the target audience as individuals (personalize it) and you also add value. Marketers, especially cataloguers, would like to use their databases in more sophisticated ways. Specially versioned catalogs, based on a consumer's previous purchases, credit history, and demographic information, are supposed to be the waves of the future. Short run, personalized digital printing becomes a tool to test these pieces before a full-fledged roll out. Shorter-run specialty catalogs, those with final print runs of 5,000 to 10,000 copies, can even be printed digitally in five or ten different editions of 1,000 each, with fewer pages of well-chosen merchandise.

Chapter 4

DESKTOP PUBLISHING

We are bombarded by the products of many creative professionals. If creative professionals did not exist, the weekly trek to the grocery store would be even greater drudgery than now, with all of the boxes of cereal looking the same, all of the magazines with the same lack of style, and all of the ads looking pretty drab. Creative professionals are the people who make us conjure up the images in our minds of breaking free from the corporate work week and heading off to the mountains in our rugged sport utility vehicles. All work of creative professionals, whether tangible or intangible, has an enormous impact on the sale of most products and processes.

The efforts of creative professionals manifest themselves as tangible items such as posters, billboards, point of purchase displays, catalogs, magazines, newspapers, books, product packaging, but also and more importantly, as intangible products like logos, and even company identities. Creative professionals involved with newspaper, magazine, and book design are producing a salable product, and therefore have slightly different concerns than those working on promotional campaigns.

Creative individuals can work as freelance artists, who are selected on a job-to-job basis, often dependent upon their style and previous work. Creative professionals can also be employed by an advertising agency where they work full-time utilizing their individual talents on any project that may be in-house at any given time. Creative professionals may also generate stock work that is filed and available for use upon payment of the artist. The artist and the customer have several options in their involvement in the project from initiation to completion.

A promotional project may take several routes to its completion. The customer may choose to contract an advertising agency that has a greater understanding of the design and production processes available. At this point the customer relays the information to the advertising agency about the product or process they are promoting, the audience they are trying to reach, and the medium they are using to contact this audience. The advertising agency utilizes their expertise in the design and production aspects of any job and makes recommendations on the promotional campaign. The advertising agency maintains contact with the customer throughout all phases of creation and production to ensure that the final product is acceptable. The advertising agency either utilizes their in-house artists, uses stock artwork, or contracts freelance artists to generate all elements and final design of the promotional package. The advertising agency also maintains contact with any outside production facilities involved in the production of the final product, whether they are prepress or printing facilities.

In some cases, a customer may decide to contract creative professionals and production facilities on their own. In these instances, the customer must dedicate more of their time, and maintain much greater involvement in the production of the final product. Rather than paying an advertising agency to monitor and manage the schedules of all creative professionals and production facilities, the customer is in fact paying themselves to perform that function. The customer must shop around for the individual artists that are economically and creatively most suited for the production of their job. They must determine how the final product is going to be manufactured, find the production facilities equipped to handle their job, and then determine who will manufacture the product.

Whether an advertising agency or a customer directly are shopping for creative services, there are several groups of creative professionals that may be contacted. They can be roughly grouped into four categories: photographers, designers, illustrators, and copywriters. It usually requires the collaboration of professionals from each of these groups to generate effective finished products.

Photographers

Photographers are a group of creative professionals who possess talents in capturing images. These artists have a variety of production relationships, and an even greater variety of tools available to them. The photographic industry has existed for many years and continues to evolve at a rapid rate, with the industry becoming more and more an electronic workplace, creating many new options for photographers. New technologies open up new creative possibilities of image creation and manipulation. Especially the continuing introduction of digital technologies into photography has opened up unexpected dimensions. It becomes obvious that the digital workflow has become popular, although there is still work for conventional photographers.

Tools of photographers

Photography started out as a very rudimentary process. Reflected light passing through a lens for a measured amount of time creates a latent image on a silver-based image carrier, usually glass or metal, which then has to be chemically developed to produce the permanent image. Although the products and processes have been greatly improved, the basic theory remains the same in today's conventional photography. Today's photographer uses various films, cameras, and lenses, and then uses specific darkroom techniques to properly develop the image. Basic exposure compensations and color correction can be performed in the darkroom before prints are made.

After negatives and prints are produced, the image must be scanned to generate a digital file to be useful in electronic page layouts. Photographers who provide a full range of services may scan the images in-house, color correct, manipulate if necessary, and supply the customer with a color proof, but more commonly the photographer's transparencies or reflective prints are sent to service bureaus or commercial printers to be digitized and proofed for customer approval. This process traditionally yields good results, but introduces several new processes in which errors may occur.

The digital photographer uses technology that eliminates the entire film and processing step. A digital camera allows reflected light to pass through a lens, but it utilizes charged coupled devices to image an electronic storage device that is loaded into the camera. The images can be downloaded onto a computer hard drive or storage device, and manipulated immediately using imaging software. These digital images can be transferred via dedicated lines or the Internet directly to the designer who can immediately use them in their page layouts. The entire scanning and proofing process is effectively eliminated at this point. Digital photography equipment itself remains quite expensive, but it also demands another investment of the photographer. The digital photographer must invest more money to purchase computer hardware and software, and they also must invest much of their time to become educated and remain current in the use of the hardware and software. Although the initial investment is greater for the digital photographer, they are able to offer more complete service to their customers.

Responsibilities of photographers

Photographers, both digital and conventional, have several responsibilities to their customers, whether they are advertising agencies or direct customers. In some cases photographers must set up the subject of their work, and in other instances photographers are directed to capture events or processes while they are in progress. The photographer is responsible for capturing multiple images and providing some sort of color output for the customer to view to determine which images are best for their final project. If the photographer is not able to digitize the image, they must prepare a transparency or print for the service bureau or printer to scan.

Illustrators

Illustrators are a group of artists who utilize conventional and digital tools to generate artwork. The basic parameters of this artwork are determined and conveyed by the customer or advertising agency, and the individual illustrator solves the design problem in their particular style. Because each illustrator has a slightly different style, this is commonly the determining factor when selecting an individual artist for a particular job. In today's visual world, the works created by graphic artists are among the most powerful vehicles for communicating ideas in our society.

Tools of illustrators

Illustrators may use very conventional tools such as pen and ink, graphite, watercolor, or charcoal. The illustrator determines which tools to use based upon the actual content of the illustration, and the overall feel of the finished product, as conveyed by the customer. The illustrator may be given strict guidelines about the style of their work, and the guidelines they need to follow for future digitizing of their artwork, or they may be left to their own means.

As the digital workflow is becoming more prevalent in the design process as a whole, more illustrators are utilizing digital tools to generate their artwork. These new computer tools do not generate the artwork on their own. The computer is a tool. Like pencils, airbrushes and other tools of expression, computers do not generate work by themselves. It takes a skilled creative professional, trained to produce high-quality results. Talent, persistence, experience, and technological understanding are all required. Iillustrators who decide to take the plunge into the digital world need to invest in the hardware and software, and educate and keep themselves up to date in the operation and maintenance of all of the equipment.

Responsibilities of illustrators

Illustrators have multiple communication responsibilities. They must be able to communicate with their customer to determine not only the look of their final artwork, but how it should be prepared for the designer or printer. They must also communicate through their artwork the assets of the product or process they are illustrating. Illustrations are often utilized in instances where photographs cannot be taken; to display internal assemblies, processes in action, or cut-away renderings. They are also used when a stylized effect is necessary.

Copywriters

Copywriters are a group of creative professionals who possess talents in effectively communicating the assets of a product or process to an audience. They may also create an audience when one may not exist. They help form product identities. The graphic image by itself cannot carry a message without the interaction of words. Copywriters utilize the written language as their primary tool. They have learned the rules of the language, and know when they can break them. They use their own creativity to combine words that will best convey the message the customer wants portrayed.

Responsibilities of copywriters

Copywriters are responsible for generating clear and concise text for use in a variety of promotional campaigns. They are dedicated to producing a positive product image, and creating a need for products that may have otherwise remained unknown. Copywriters are responsible for creating positioning statements, brand names, slogans, jingles, captions, and many other text segments. Professionally written copy can sum up the benefits of a client's product or service in a lively, persuasive tone, in easy-to-read terms. Professional copywriters can also eliminate jargon that might confuse or discourage potential customers.

Designers

Designers are the group of creative professionals who generate the frames that holds all of the elements of the other creative professionals together. The designer creates the final layout with all of the work of the other creative professionals, and much of their own work in place. The designer has the ability to manipulate all of the images supplied to them to best fit the final layout. The designer is the final link in producing a final page layout that conveys the image and information that the customer desires. A layout is the glue that pulls design elements together and broadcasts a client's message. Good layouts can be clean and simple, using fundamental principles of design, or they can be injected with sophistication and pizzazz, using advanced technological skills. The designer, then is the craftsman that applies the adhesive.

Tools of designers

Designers have many tools available to them. Their first concern is to use the basic design elements available to any graphic designer, regardless of the computer hardware and software they use. These are typography, color, size, photography, and illustrations. Typography is not the actual message of the written word, but it is key in relaying the message. The text must be clear and legible and even interesting and entertaining. There is more to typography than just the message in the words. Typography is a key design element.

Color is another critical design element. Designers can successfully use color to create relationships, add interest, and draw attention to their design. Color can compel, connote or calm—and especially communicate. It can make your client, and your audience, get your idea, see the benefits of your product, absorb your imagery, read your typography—get your ideas.

The final design elements are those generated by other creative professionals, photography and illustration. These two elements, although created by other artists, can be slightly altered in size and cropping to fit the final layout. The other artists may be contracted separately, but are expected to keep the final project in mind when preparing their work. In some instances the designer works with the other creative professionals, and in other cases receives only digital files or hard copy from them, and is responsible for making a cohesive design from all of their elements.

Responsibilities of designers

Graphic designers have responsibilities to their customer as well as to the manufacturer of the final product. Designers have dedicated themselves to create a final product that displays the assets and creates a positive image of the customer's product, service, or process. The designer must maintain contact with the customer throughout the process, and particularly when a final proof is available for the customer to approve before production begins.

The designer has a responsibility to the manufacturing facility to be educated on all file types, and to know which type to use in different situations. The designer must prepare all information for imaging files and must be accessible if questions arise. The job of the designer may seem simple, but there are many things to keep in mind. Digital files can look deceptively simple. Things are not always as they seem and what you see may not be what you get. Laser proofs or color proofs do not always output the same way on an imagesetter, even though the same file is used. The computer monitor images never match the hard copy images, even when calibrated correctly.

All of the creative professionals mentioned, whether knowingly or not, have a great impact on the printing industry. They can make the lives of the people manufacturing the final project joyful or miserable. It may be helpful to begin with the end in mind. The final design must be acceptable to the customer, make good use of illustrations and photography, and be well-designed, but it must also be able to be manufactured. If the product cannot be completed, all of the work of the creative professionals is for naught.

Most creative professionals are required to either supply their images in digital format or make sure they meet all of the requirements of a service bureau or commercial printer who will digitize the images for them. Creative professionals may send digital files to the printer via Internet or phone lines, which speeds up the production. The decrease in production time benefits all involved. Customers get their product more rapidly, creative professionals are able to generate more artwork in less time, and the printer is not as pinched in the amount of time they are allowed to manufacture the product. If there are last minute changes, they can be sent to the printer electronically, and there is no lost time waiting for the changes to arrive at the printer. The digital revolution is positive for customers, creative professionals, and printers alike.

The creative professionals mentioned all have interactions with one another and the customer. They must coordinate production schedules, artwork, and file formats, and must communicate all necessary information to have a successful final product. Effective interaction between customer, creative professionals, and printer is key to a positive working experience, and a successful final product. The world of desktop publishing is changing at an ever increasing rate because of rapid technology leaps in computers. Hardware and software has enabled many to take on more or all of the prepress work that was once reserverd for trade shops and specialized service providers.

The work being ouput can reveal professionalism or, in some instances, not. The computer has allowed prepress work to move from the servive provider using high-end extremely expensive computer systems, to desktop computers that rival the performance of the high-end workstations. But all the technology in the world does not help if you do not know what you are doing.

As computer systems have become more advanced, the borrowing of technology from other disciplines such as information technology and computer science has created more sophisticated systems that support the requirements of the graphic arts industry. We all know that in today's workflows computers play a pivotal role. Be it in the area of text creation, text editing, image creation, image manipulation, or printing to various output devices, there are computers all over the place.

All computers regardless of structure have the same basic hardware components in the computer processor—bus, mother board, memory, etc. These components, regardless of the platform, perfom the same basic function. The major components of a computer follow. If you are familiar with them, skip over this section. But if not, read on and learn about the basic components of the computer system.

Platforms

There are three types of workstations used in the graphic arts:

- Macintosh
- PC/Windows
- UNIX

The platforms or workstations used in creative and prepress production can be PCs or Macintosh or even UNIX workstations. Macintosh platforms still dominate the creative and prepress industry because of the Macintosh operating system and its ease of use. Page layout and photoediting applications and the PostScript page description language are now available running under Windows on the PC or MacOS on the Macintosh. PCs and UNIX workstations support printing formats and graphic applications, many of which do not work with each other easily. The Macintosh made it easier for graphic arts services to support their customers and many still have difficulty handling PC-based files.

Some high-end page layout and image editing applications also run on UNIX workstations because they offer more power, multiprocessing, and greater stability (fewer system crashes), but you have to learn the UNIX operating system, which is like learning a strange new language. Although UNIX workstations have been used as RIP platforms and file servers, they traditionally have not been used much as prepress workstations, although there are a few cases where very sophisticated software is run under UNIX. The goal of WindowsNT has been to offer an alternative to UNIX and those prepress applications that were originally developed for UNIX are also being offered as WindowsNT applications.

Macintosh

Power Macintosh computers use the PowerPC processor, a microprocessor designed by Motorola, IBM, and Apple. The PowerPC family contains several different processors that conform to the PowerPC standard at different levels of performance. They use one of these models: 603, 603e, 604, or the 604e PowerPC processors. The "e" indicates a processor with a larger and faster memory cache.

PC/Windows

A PC meant that the computer employed the same internal architecture as an IBM Personal Computer. Today, PC is a generic term for any desktop computer. Although Macintosh computers are PCs, the term typically indicates a computer that uses an Intel processor and runs a Microsoft operating system: either one of many DOS-related operating systems, or one of the versions of Windows. Some major manufacturers of PCs include:

- Compaq
- Dell
- Digital Equipment (now Compaq)
- Gateway
- Hewlett-Packard
- IBM
- NEC Packard Bell

There are many PC manufacturers, and many will assemble a custom PC made from parts you specify. Two things generally make a PC a PC as of this book's publication date, but this will probably change:

- Windows 95, Windows 98, and WindowsNT
- Intel Pentium and Pentium Pro processors

Windows

The original Windows (up to version 3.1) was an operating environment that required MS-DOS to run. Today most off-the-shelf PCs are pre-loaded with Windows 95-98. Even though you no longer need MS-DOS, Windows 95-98 lets you run DOS applications for backward compatibility. Windows 95-98 and Windows NT are 32-bit operating systems, whereas Windows was only 16-bit. The difference means that Windows 95-98 and Windows NT can transmit more data at one time, which provides significantly more speed. If you need power and security, use Windows NT. If you need compatibility with most software applications, use Windows 95-98. You will want the performance and crash-resistance of WindowsNT for demanding prepress applications. It is also used for servers and RIPs in prepress applications.

UNIX

UNIX is the granddaddy of all workstation operating systems. It usually runs on high-powered workstations available from H-P, IBM, Sun, Silicon Graphics, Digital Equipment, and Data General, among others. The Pentium Pro and PowerPC processors now bring PCs and Macs closer to the power that was once only available on the more expensive UNIX platforms. The UNIX operating system was developed at AT&T to allow multiple users to access the same computer. Over several years, most of the major computer companies (IBM, Digital, Data General) developed their own versions of UNIX to run specifically on their equipment. UNIX became quite popular in universities and research departments, mainly because AT&T literally gave it away to stimulate applications. The UNIX operating system is complex. In the 1990s, NeXT released products that ran on UNIX systems, but hid UNIX (like Windows hides PC DOS).

Prepress tasks that need processing power (such as trapping and RIPping) are available on UNIX workstations, which also perform as file and print servers. For example, the Dalim software using the Silicon Graphics workstation lets you run trapping, page assembly, color correction, and high-resolution photoediting. Prepress applications, such as Adobe Photoshop and Adobe Illustrator, are also available in versions that run under UNIX. UNIX-based workstations do not necessarily run all UNIX applications. You can't run a Silicon Graphics application on a Sun workstation unless the application has been specifically ported to that workstation. PCs and Macs have become fairly standardized and WindowsNT OS running on a Compaq PC works the same as WindowsNT running on a Gateway system, for example. UNIX is individually implemented on each company's platform.

You need to consider these factors when purchasing a workstation:
- CPU (central processing unit) speed
- disk capacity
- operating system
- expansion slots
- expansion options

Inside your computer system

Inside of every desktop computer system there is a microprocessor. This is a silicon chip, which looks like a canapé, that contains the CPU and some special-purpose memory. These are mounted on a board called the motherboard. There is a system clock in the microprocessor that regulates the speed of operations. For all specialized functions that a computer system performs, special add-in cards can be fitted on the motherboard. There are provisions on the motherboard to take on these special add-in cards. These slots are called expansion slots. To connect the computer with other external devices like keyboard, mouse and printers, there are the ports. From the ports, connection to other devices can be made. To get the computer powered up, there is a power supply and to keep the computer from overheating, there is a fan.

Micro processors are made from wafer-like silicon chips that are 0.004". The silicon layer is etched into patterns that are miniature versions of transistors and other elements that combine to make an integrated circuit. The microprocessor is the heart of any CPU. The increasing power of microprocessors is what makes computers more and more powerful by the day. The manufacturers of micoprocessors are Intel, Motorola, IBM, Digital Equipment Corporation, Hewlett-Packard and Sun Microsystems.

Computer hardware

The heart of any computer system is the central processing unit or CPU. The CPU provides two important functions.
- it processes data
- it controls the rest of the parts of the computer system

It consists of an arithmetic/logic unit (ALU) and a control unit. The primary storage for the computer is also lodged in the CPU. The primary storage of the computer temporarily stores the data and program instructions. The ALU takes care of all processing that is done in the computer. Essentially a computer performs math functions and logic functions. These are performed by the arithmetic/logic unit. The control unit in the CPU coordinates and controls all other parts of the computer. For example, the control unit assigns various tasks for other parts of the computer that will be required to perform various roles.

CPU

The speed of a processor is measured as clock speed listed as a number of Megahertz (MHz). PCs are available in models from 75 MHz to 500 MHz or more; Macintoshes range from 150 MHz to 330 MHz. A computer contains many different areas that process and transmit data and instructions. To move data from one point to another, the computer creates a pulse, a pattern of high and low voltages; one high voltage pulse followed by one low voltage pulse is called a "clock cycle." This cycle continuously repeats. The clock pulse instructs the computer when it can send data. For each high voltage pulse, the computer can send data or an instruction along its path within the system.

The faster the clock pulses, the faster data and instructions move, and the faster your computer runs. If a computer can issue one million cycles within a second, that computer runs at 1 MHz. A 200 MHz computer can issue 200 million cycles within a second. Faster is better but more expensive as well; although, I just bought a faster computer at a price cheaper than my older computer. A RIP workstation can take advantage of the faster speeds, but a faster processor won't increase your typing speed when running a word processor.

Clock speeds

Clock speed refer to the speed of the system clock. Clock speeds are measured in Megahertz (MHz), which is the equivalent of one millionth of a second. The importance of clock speed in a computer is the ability of the computer to interface with other parts of the computer that are much faster or slower. Computers for use in the graphic arts should be purchased with the fastest clock speed possible because most graphic arts applications require heavy-duty processing and if it is slow, the operator will be wating for the computer to complete every change that is made to the file that is being created or worked on.

Expansion

The computer workstation includes a board that contains the CPU (the processor), memory (RAM and cache), and all the chips required to run the computer. It should also have several empty slots where you can plug in other boards to increase the capabilities of the workstation. For example, you can install a video board to support a specific monitor, a Photoshop accelerator to speed up image manipulations, a network interface card to connect the workstation to your network, a sound card, or a modem.

Bus

Bus refers to the pathway in which the electronic impulses travel in a microprocessor. Buses are the pathways that connect the input devices, output devices and storage devices. The width of the bus is crucial, because the wider it is (referred to as "bus width") the more electronic impulses that can travel along it, and the faster the processing that is possible.

The current industry-standard bus used in workstations is the PCI (Peripheral Component Interconnect) bus. Both Power Mac and Intel-PCs can use a PCI bus, which means other vendors need to design only one card for their product (be it a modem or a sound card). The previous standard for the Macintosh was the NuBus; the previous standard for Intel-compatible PCs was the ISA (Industry Standard Architecture) bus. Many PCs still support the ISA bus by providing a combination of PCI and ISA slots. Because ISA was a standard for so many years, thousands of developers sold millions of cards for use in ISA slots. Many cards in development and for sale today still use the ISA bus. USB is the new Universal Serial Bus and is replacing SCSI.

Memory chips

The primary storage that we saw earlier is like a microprocessor that has embedded in it thousands of transistors. These are usually semiconductor chips that are mounted on circuit boards and then plugged into the motherboard of a computer. These chips are relatively easy to produce, hold much less memory, and are therefore relatively less expensive than the microprocessor. The memory chip can be varied in storage capacity and speeds, and over the years we have seen the ever increasing power of these memory chips. Speeds of the memory chips are measured in nanosecond (ns). The lower the number, the higher the speed achievable by that memory chip.

RAM

RAM stands for "Random Access Memory" and is the memory chip used in the primary storage. There are two kinds of RAM chips: DRAM and SRAM. DRAM stands for Dynamic Random Access Memory and represents the vast majority of the memory chips used in primary storage for computers. SRAM stands for Static Random Access Memory and is a specialized chip used for specialized functions within the primary storage. RAM is called so because any area of the chip which contains data or instructions can be directly accessed and its contents retrieved. RAM memory is volatile, in that the memory functions as long as power is supplied to it. When power is turned off, RAM cannot function and all the information that it holds will be wiped out. The primary storage holds information only until a function in the computer needs to be performed. Data is constantly going into and out of primary memory.

RAM is a vital component to a computer used in the graphic arts. There can never be too much RAM in a computer system because it allows the accessing and retrieving of files to occur at a much higher rate. In the end it speeds up your computer system and tasks which makes the computer more efficient at producing work.

Some systems require RAM chips to be installed in multipiles of two where other systems can install one chip at a time. Also, computers have an upper limit that the system can handle, which requires thinking ahead about how much memory will be required. If, for example, your system only has three slots you don't want to put the smallest chip in all three slots because, if a memory upgrade is needed, some or all of those chips will have be replaced and money will be wasted.

Memory

A workstation requires several types of memory. It needs memory to store applications and data currently being used, and it needs memory to process work. A workstation needs:

- RAM Random Access Memory, or system memory
- VRAM (Video RAM)
- cache

A computer uses RAM (Random Access Memory) to store the instructions of any applications in use plus the data content of any files currently in use. Power Macs and PCs can have several applications open at a time, allowing you to switch between editing a photo and placing that photo in a page layout. RAM comes in two types:

- SIMMs
- DIMMs

SIMMs (Single Inline Memory Modules) come in 30-pin and 72-pin models depending on the workstation, and come in units of 1 MB, 4 MB, 8 MB, 16 MB, and 32 MB. DIMMs (Dual Inline Memory Modules) have 168 pins and usually come in unit multiples of 16 MB, 32 MB, or 64 MB, allowing you to install large amounts of memory in the workstation. PCs with Pentium processors use 72-pin SIMMs. Older model PCs (like the 386 and 486 models) use the 30-pin SIMMs. Most Pentium and PowerPC based workstations use DIMMs. The type of RAM you can install depends on the workstation.

How much RAM do you need to start off with? All of it. It depends on what applications you plan to run. You need enough memory to run the operating system and as many applications as you think you'll need open at one time, with gigantic files open as well. For example, you may often have your page layout application open and the photo manipulation application so you can alternate between the two with a 70MB file. Utilities and extensions need RAM as well. Breathing requires RAM, so get as much as you can.

Memory Requirements for commonly used programs *(all trademarked)*

Software	Minimum Memory (MB)	Recommended Memory (MB)	Platform
Adobe			
Photoshop 5	32	64	M/W
Photoshop 4	32	64	M/W
Photoshop 3	32	64	M
Acrobat (Windows)			
Exchange	8	16	W
Capture 2.0	16	16	W
Reader	8	16	W
Catalog	8	16	W
Distiller 3.02	16	16	W
Acrobat (Macintosh)			
Exchange	4	16	M
Capture 2.0	16	24	PPC
Reader	5	16	M
Catalog	4	16	M/W
Distiller 3.02	6	16	M
After Effects 3.1	16	32	M/W
Dimensions 3.0	16	32	W
Dimensions 3.0	24	32	PPC
FrameMaker 5.5.6	16	32	M/W
FrameMaker+SGML 5.5	24	32	M/W
FrameViewer	16	24	M/W
Illustrator 8	32	64	M/W
Illustrator 7	32	64	M/W
ImageReady	16	32	M/W
PageMaker 6.5	8	24	M/W
PageMaker 6.0	8	24	M/W
PageMill 3.0	16	16	W
PageMill 3.0	8	8	M

Software	Minimum Memory (MB)	Recommended Memory (MB)	Platform
PhotoDeluxe Business Edition	16	16	W
Adobe Photo Deluxe 3.0	32	32	W
Adobe Photo Deluxe 2.0	16	16	M
Streamline 4.0	16	32	W
Streamline 4.0	8	12	M
Type			
Font Folio 8.0	8	8	M
Font Folio 8.0	8	8	W
Type Manager Deluxe			
Type On Call 4.2	8	8	M/W
Type Basics	4	4	M/W
Type Manager Deluxe 4.0	8	8	M/W
Web Type 1.0	8	8	M/W
Type Reunion Deluxe	8	8	M
Macromedia			
Freehand 8	16	24	M/W
Fontographer	6	6	M/W
Meta Creations			
Kai's SuperGOO	16	16	M/W
Kai's Power SHOW	16	16	M/W
Kai's Photo Soap	16	16	M/W
Art Dabbler	16	16	M/W
Painter 5.5 Web Edition	16	32	M/W
Painter Classic	16	32	W
Painter Classic	12	20	M
Kai's Power Tools 3	16	16	M/W
Expression	12	16	W

Software	Minimum Memory (MB)	Recommended Memory (MB)	Platform
Corel			
Draw 8	32	64	PPC
Draw 8	16	32	W
Draw 7	16	32	W
Draw 6	20	20	PPC
Ventura 8	16	32	W
Ventura 7	16	16	W
Photo Paint 8	16	32	W
Photo Paint 7 Plus	16	32	W
Photo Paint 6	8	16	W
Photo Paint 5 Plus	8	16	W
Print Office	8	16	W
Print House Magic Deluxe	8	8	W
Print House Magic	8	8	W/PPC
Graphics Pack II	16	16	W
XARA 2.0	16	16	W
XARA 1.5	8	8	W
DK&A			
Inposition	32	32	PPC
Ultimate Technographics			
Impostrip	16	16	M
Impostrip	8	8	W
Trapeze	64	64	PPC
Trapeze	128	128	WNT
UltimateFlow	16	16	M
UltimateFlow	32	32	WN
Printdesk OPI	16	16	M
IMPress	16	16	M

Software	Minimum Memory (MB)	Recommended Memory (MB)	Platform
Quark			
XPress 4.0	12	12	W
XPress Passport 4.0	12	12	W
XPress 4.0	5	8	M
XPress Passport 4.0	8	10	PPC
XPress 3.3	8	10	M
XPress 3.1	4	4	W
Microsoft			
Publisher 97	8	8	W
Publisher 98	8	8	W
Imation			
Trapwise	32	64	M
Trapwise	128	128	WNT
Color Central-server	32	32	M
Color Central-server	64	64	WNT
Color Central-client	2	2	M/W
PressWise 3.0	12	12	M
PressWise 3.0.2	12	12	PPC

You will always need more RAM than the software manufacturers recommend. It is said that the amount of RAM needed is about three times the size of the largest image or document file you work with. Plan for your memory requirements in advance. Do not wait for a production crisis.

VRAM

VRAM (Video RAM) is used to process the data for your computer monitor. The video card includes a processor dedicated to controlling the monitor, and it needs memory as well. The computer needs to store a value for each pixel on the monitor. The amount of VRAM needed depends on the size of the monitor and its resolution. 4MB of VRAM can support a monitor resolution of 1280x1024 dots at 24-bit color.

Cache

Cache memory is another level of memory. It is high-speed active memory that the processor can use to accelerate processing. The processor can access cache memory faster than it can access RAM, so the more instructions and data it can store here, the faster it runs. A workstation has an internal cache (called level 1 cache) memory built directly into the processor, and external cache (called level 2 cache) mounted on the motherboard. Some workstations allow you to add additional external cache memory. Level 1 cache is faster than level 2 cache, and level 2 is faster than RAM. Adding more cache memory to your workstation speeds up its performance.

RAM extenders

Think of them as Viagra for memory. No matter how much memory you have installed on your workstation, you may get the "Insufficient Memory" problem when trying to launch an application. If you have QuarkXPress running on your Power Macintosh, with your e-mail and screen saver running, and you want to check a color image, you try to launch Photoshop, but you don't have enough memory. So, you quit XPress, launch Photoshop, check the photo, quit Photoshop, and then re-launch XPress. Ungood. Adding RAM can alleviate this problem. You can also use RAM Doubler from Connectix. It allows the workstation to use memory assigned to another open application but which isn't actually being used. It manages memory to allow you to run more applications at a time, but cannot assign more memory to a single application than is physically installed in the computer.

Operating systems

When a computer is fresh off the assembly line and devoid of any software, it can do absolutely nothing. Accepting characters from a keyboard, displaying data on the screen, loading or executing a program are simply beyond its capabilities. It is the operating system, the set of software routines lying between the application program and the hardware, that makes all these functions possible. The operating system imposes rules that control the computer's hardware, the data, and the communications with the operator or user.

An operating system is divided into four subsystems, each of which manages four distinct kinds of resources within the computer system. The size or the configuration of the computer system aside, every one of these subsystems must carry out the following tasks:

- monitor its resources continuously
- enforce the policies that determine who gets what, when, and how much
- allocate the resource when it is appropriate
- deallocate the resource, or reclaim it, when appropriate

System software

The coordination of all the components of a computer system is handled by the system software. The most important of these components is the operating system. All the basic functions that a computer performs, like loading, storing, and retrieving files and carrying out other instructions, are all part of the operating system. All application software must be installed on an operating system. Every application software module that we use is very operating-system-dependent. This means an application can be run on specific platforms only and cannot be swapped to other operating systems. This is a current problem in the graphic arts industry because three major diffrent computer systems are in use: Windows/NT, Macintosh, and UNIX, which require different computer systems if more than one kind of operating system is needed.

Multitasking allows several different programs to be run all at the same time. While one program is printing to a printer, another program can be updating a text file. Resource sharing allows the user to share files or programs, so they can use a file in more than one program simultaneously. The resource—file or program—can be shared. Multiprocessing utilizes the services of two of more CPUs that are linked to carry out certain instructions, thus processing more data faster with multiple computers. Computers that employ multiprocessing can execute different functions from a program at the same time.

To perform multiprocessing the computer systems need very sophisticated operating systems. Time sharing is another method that allows multiple users to share the resources of a CPU. By this method the CPU provides each user a small amount of time and then moves over to the other user. Within this short period the CPU processes all that it could process for that user and moves over to the next user to process their need before returning to the first user. Since the time provided for each user, called a slice, is usually a very short period, the user will never notice the time lag. By this method the CPU is used efficiently, and is not allowed to be idle.

The operating environment

A Graphical User Interface (GUI—pronounced goo-ee) uses pictorial icons that when clicked using a mouse, activate the various functions. GUI icons are used to represent files, programs, and even commands. This makes it easier for the user to interact with the computer. No longer do users have to remember long strings of commands. All they have do is look for a particular function icon, and click on it. When the user clicks on the icon, the system software decodes the command and instructs the computer to execute the function asked for by the user. This does not necessarily mean that an absolutely raw operator can easily understand everything on a computer that has a GUI, but GUIs have definitely cut down the learning time for users and also the operating time to execute tasks.

GUIs were made popular by Apple with the Lisa and then with their first model of Macintosh computers. The rest of the personal computer market took to using GUIs much later. The operating system (DOS and MS-DOS) of the PC environment did not support GUIs for a long time; they were introduced to the PC world with a system called GEM (remember Xerox Ventura software?) and then later Windows. In fact, Windows is not an operating system in the fullest sense. It is a shell that sits on top of MS-DOS, which is the operating system. A shell is a software program that has GUI and acts as a link between the GUI and the operating system. These shells are used with older operating systems that do not have a GUI.

Most of today's GUIs create a computer screen that very much resembles your desktop. There are files which can be dropped into folders, and each of them can be named as you would name your files traditionally. These files and folders can be moved around anywhere on your desktop by the pull of a mouse. And then there are the menu bars at the top that help the user to request the various functions available. Some of these menus also have a submenu, which is nothing but more options for the specific function. There are two kinds of operating systems:

- Proprietary operating systems
- Portable operating systems

The type that we have been talking about all along is the proprietary operating system. In this type, the operating system can work only with certain types of computers. All software that can be used will have to be made to suit this operating system. So for a specific application, say an image editing application, if a program is developed, that program can run only on one kind of operating system. To get the same application working in another operating system, the application program will have to be programmed to suit that operating system.

In contrast to the proprietary operating system is the portable operating system. The portable operating system has the ability to run on any kind of computer. The greatest benefit that the portable operating system offers is that an application program can be run on different hardware platforms, but it will still have the ability to present the same kind of interface and functionality. This feature is referred to as interoperability and is becoming the trend of information technology.

Windows

Windows gave PC users the features of a GUI but Windows 95 was no longer a shell that sat on top of DOS and acted as the interface between the operating system and the GUI. Windows 95 also offers a degree of multitasking and allows the user to move information from one program to another more efficiently.

Window NT

WindowsNT has found a growing following in the graphics world as a server, RIP, and workststation because of its superior advanatges and pricing. It is more than a version of the popular Windows 3.1 OS and it is 32-bit. It is a faster operating system and is able to take advantage of multiprocessing capabilities and is an extremely stable platform to work on. A feature that the Macintosh still lacks is true multitasking. Unlike the Mac, when an application crashes the computer often needs to be restarted. WindowsNT is able to quit the crashed application and still remain stable enough to keep the system running.

Mac System 8

This is the operating system of Apple Macintosh computers, and has supported the use of the GUI ever since its inception. It may be that the GUIs of the industry are compared with that of the Macintoish. The Macintosh system is the most commonly used computer system in the graphic arts and has a large following. This is not directly related to its capabilities anymore, but initially it was because of the GUI and as the other systems caught up to the Mac, it was already entrenched in the graphic arts.

Monitors and accelerators

For most prepress applications, you absolutely need a color monitor. If you produce only black-and-white jobs, you can get away with a grayscale monitor, but this is not a common approach. Design and prepress professionals have color monitors. The monitor generates all the colors you see by combining red, green and blue. Each dot of color on the monitor is made from one red, one blue, and one green phosphor. For each of these phosphors, the monitor can vary the intensity of the light applied to that phosphor. For most monitors used in prepress, each phosphor can have 256 different levels of intensity. When combined with the other two phosphors for that dot, the monitor can generate over 16 million different colors by varying the intensity of energy activating the three phosphors. The one color (if it is a color) you cannot view on the monitor is white. If you look at a white area, it is really a very light blue or gray.

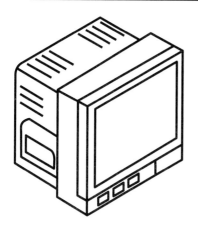

Color monitors are evaluated by:
- resolution
- color depth
- screen size
- refresh rates
- display acceleration

Monitors are big and klunky. Flat panel displays are just starting to enter the industry.

Resolution

A monitor's resolution is measured as a number such as 700x800. 700 is the number of dots in the horizontal direction and 800 is the number of dots in the vertical direction. A "dot" is a combination of one red, one green, and one blue phosphor (called a pixel) which combine to make different colors. The monitor can vary the brightness of each phosphor to vary the color of that dot. To make a cyan color, the blue and green phosphors would be about 60% to 70% of the maximum brightness, with the red phosphor off. Dot pitch is the distance between pixels, measured as a number such as .25mm (millimeters). The closer the pixels are to each other, without overlapping, the sharper the images that are displayed. The more dots the monitor has, the better it can display color.

Color depth

Color depth defines how much memory is used to store the value of a color for a dot (made up of 3 pixels). For example, if you use 1 bit of memory, that bit can be either 0 or 1 (computers store data in binary), meaning the pixel can be completely on or completely off—zero or one. A monitor with a 1-bit color depth is strictly monochrome. If the monitor has a color depth of 4 bits, it can store only16 values, too few to split between color pixels, so such a monitor would be a very coarse grayscale monitor with only 16 shades of gray. At 8 bits, each dot can hold any of 256 different values. For a grayscale monitor, this level of gray may be sufficient for many applications that don't require color. 256 shades of an individual color provide a good range for the monitor. For color, you need 256 shades for each of the three pixels that make up a color dot on the monitor.

24-bit monitors are what you want. The memory can hold 8 bits of data for each of the red, green, and blue colors that make up a dot on the screen. The intensity of the red phosphor can vary through 256 levels of intensity, creating 256 different shades of red. Combine this with 256 different shades of green and 256 different shades of blue and you have a monitor that can display over 16 million different colors. You can adjust the intensity of the red, green, and blue pixels to create 16 million colors. The data for an entire screen of displayed information is stored in VRAM.

If your monitor has a resolution of 1000x1000, that's 1,000,000 different spots. Each spot has 3 pixels, each with 8 bits of data, so you need 24,000,000 bits, or 3,000,000 bytes, or 3.0 megabytes, of VRAM to store the data of one screen. If you only have 1MB of VRAM, you can't use the full display capacity of the monitor. If you have 3 MB of VRAM, you are all set. For a 1280x1024 monitor using 24-bit depth, you need at least 4MB of VRAM.

Refresh rates

The phosphor that makes a pixel gradually decays after being excited by the beam. If the red phosphor was lit 100%, it would soon fade and eventually disappear. Therefore the computer continually redraws the image on the screen. If the workstation takes too long to redraw the image, you may be able to see the image fade, get bright, fade, get bright and so on, resulting in a flickering image. To avoid flickering, the monitor must have a refresh rate of at least 75 Hz (the number of times per second the image is redrawn). Hz mean Hertz—it used to be cycles. Higher numbers draw more frequently.

Screen size

Monitors come in various sizes, such as 14", 17", 19", 20" or 21". Like TV sets, these values measure the length of the diagonal of the screen. Although a monitor may by 21", the screen space, or the area the screen uses to display, is slightly smaller. The curved edges of the monitor can't be used to display anything. Many monitor manufacturers now list the actual screen size (the screen area that can be used to display images) in addition to the physical size of the monitor. Flat panel displays use LCDs (Liquid Crystal Displays, which are common on laptops).

Display accelerators

Displaying detailed, complex images on the monitor can take time to process and display. To improve the performance of video-intensive operations, you can install video accelerators (in addition to the video card) or, if you use Adobe Photoshop, accelerators specifically designed for that application.

Input

You can use many devices to enter information into your computer, including:
- keyboard
- mouse
- trackball
- touchpads
- tablets
- voice recognition

The most basic input device is your keyboard. You can purchase a minimal keyboard, a standard keyboard, or an ergonomic one. Ergonomic keyboards provide wrist support and usually have a split keyboard to allow you to hold your hands more comfortably while typing. If you don't do a lot of typing, you don't need an ergonomic keyboard. The minimal keyboard eliminates the vowels. Only kidding. These are really cheap keyboards without the F-keys and the numeric key pad. They are a waste of time and money. The minimal and the standard keyboard layout is called

QWERTY (from the upper row of letters). This layout was developed when typewriters were first designed. The layout actually slowed down the typist so that the keys would not jam. With today's electronic keyboards, the mechanical restrictions are no longer valid, but the layout has become so entrenched that it is still the preferred layout for keyboards. An alternative layout, the Dvorak layout, arranges the letters so that the vowels and the five most frequently used keys are on the same row. The home row of Dvorak is AOEUIDHTNS. Proponents of this keyboard layout claim that it can dramatically increase typing speed. You can purchase keyboard remapping utilities (available for most platforms, including PCs and Macs) and labels to convert a standard keyboard into a Dvorak keyboard. We have never met anyone who has ever done this.

Your workstation needs a mouse, or a trackball, or a touchpad. Mice or mouses are configured as one-button for Macs, two-button for PCs, and three-button for UNIX workstations. Trackballs and touchpads have become popular alternatives to mice. A trackball works like a mouse except you use your fingers to move the ball instead of sliding a device containing a ball across a mousepad. A touchpad lets you use your finger to control the cursor, wherever your finger goes on the touchpad, the cursor goes on the screen. Finger taps work the same as mouse clicks.

You may want a graphics tablet. You "write" on it with a stylus (similar to a pen) or a puck. Your "writing" appears on the screen as you stroke the tablet. Using a tablet allows you to create artwork much as you would if you used a piece of paper and a pencil or paintbrush. The pen or stylus transmits the information to the graphics application. You can also access certain functions, which are mapped to the tablet, with a touch of the stylus.

Storage technologies

File sizes for graphic files and print-ready jobs are increasing in size. Users in the industry needed a way to move these large files off their computers to others at another location while not affecting their own machine. One common approach is to use removable storage media.

These devices come in all types from a CD-ROM to large removable drives in some kind of array. They have a great use in the graphic arts because they allow large files to be taken to other locations for output while freeing up your computer. Secondary storage devices can also hold more data and programs at lower prices. With the multitude of media types available for storage, you can select the type or types that best suit your needs. Different industries patronize a set of media and those media have automatically become standards in those industries.

Data storage

The size of your files varies depending on whether you're laying out pages, editing high-resolution graphics, or entering text. High-resolution graphics take up a lot of disk space. Even if you use some form of automatic picture replacement, you still need storage for document files, fonts, software, and utilities. Backup systems go hand-in-hand with storage. If you have a 2GB drive with all the high-resolution graphics for this month's production and no back-up, a disk crash could be—I don't even want to think about it. You have several options for your storage:
- fixed hard disks
- floppy disks
- removable high-capacity disks
- RAID arrays
- magneto-optical disks
- CD-ROMs or DVDs
- digital tapes

The technology of storing information has advanced in the past few years and continues to do so. The goal is to save the most data in the least space at the least cost in the most reliable manner. If you need to transport data, say, as delivering a job to a service bureau or to a printer, you also need to make sure your media, most likely removable cartridges, are compatible with the drives used by your service provider. Please ask first rather than just showing up with a box full of old SyQuest 44s.

Fixed disks

An internal fixed disk is installed within the cabinet containing the rest of the computer and runs off the system's power supply. An external fixed disk connects to the system usually using a SCSI or USB cable. You can easily share an external disk by plugging its SCSI cable into a different workstation (Power Macs can share with Power Macs; PCs can share with PCs). A typical PC or Power Mac comes equipped with a 4–8 GB internal fixed drive. Most disks are now in the multi-gigabyte range.

Removable disks

A removable fixed disk can increase the amount of storage available to the workstation simply by inserting another cartridge. You can remove the disk to transport it easily to another site, such as a service bureau. Removable disks include:

- SyQuest cartridges (44, 88, and 200 MB)
- Iomega Zip, Jaz disks (100 MB for Zipand 1 GB or 2 GB for Jaz)
- Magneto-opticals (128 MB to 256 MB)
- Imation SuperDisk floppies (130 MB)

SyQuest drives were the original general-purpose removable media. When floppies could only store 1.4 MB of data, you could use a Syquest cartridge to store 44 MB of data, enough room to back up the hard drive of an old Macintosh II. The SyQuest drive can use 44 MB, 88 MB, and 200 MB cartridges. SyQuest also offers a drive for 1.3 GB removable cartridges, plus drives for 3.5-inch 230 MB cartridges. You do not find these around very much. File sizes keep expanding faster than disk capacities.

Zip drives from Iomega support removable cartridges the size of a 3.5-inch floppy disk, except these disks can hold 100 MB of data. Because of the compact size, Zip cartridges have become common as backup media and to transfer files between locations. Iomega also makes Jaz drives that use 1 GB or 2 GB cartridges. These cartridges are about the size of two 3.5-inch floppies on top of each other. Zip drives are now commonly installed in PCs and Macintoshes. The Apple iMac does not even have a floppy disk drive.

RAID (Redundant Arrays of Inexpensive Disks)

RAID, Redundant Array of Inexpensive Disks (really), is two or more disks that look like a single disk. RAID disk arrays provide greater speed and security for your data. RAID types:

- RAID-0, has no redundancy and spreads the data across several drives. These disks speed up data writing and retrieval, but provide no data security. If one disk goes bad, none of the disks can be used.
- RAID-1 writes data to two disks at the same time. If one drive fails, you can use the backup disk. This requires twice as much disk space for a specified amount of data.
- RAID-3 writes parity data on one of the drives. If one drive fails, you can reconstruct the data from the other disks. The parity disk cannot be used for data storage. If two disks fail before the data has been rebuilt, you lose all the info on all disks. The probability of two drives failing is low.
- RAID-5 allows many different write operations to occur at the same time. These disks are optimized to handle many small read/write operations. Parity is spread throughout the disks instead of on a single disk within the array.

Magneto-optical disks

The material of the active layer retains magnetism and it is the magnetic state of the storage element that is changed. During recording, the laser beam heats the focus spot to a critical temperature at which the medium no longer retains magnetism. When the spot cools it becomes magnetized again in a direction which depends on the external magnetic field. That field is produced by current or by a permanent magnet. The same process is repeated to erase a recorded element, but with the external magnetic field reversed so that the element is returned to its state. The coil current is reversed as the laser beam passes from one element to the next, and the existing data is overwritten just as in magnetic disks. It is difficult to reverse the current rapidly, so a disk sector is totally erased during one revolution of the disk; with the external field in one direction all signal elements are heated by the laser to return them to the zero state.

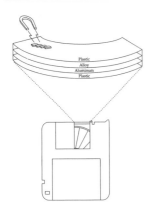

Magneto-optical disks work differently from fixed and removable disks (based on Winchester disk drive technology). A disk drive writes to an optical disk by shining a laser that heats up the material to magnetically change the reflectivity of the disk where the data is written. When the material cools (very quickly), the disk can't be affected by magnetic fields (unlike floppy disks or removable cartridges), providing reliable, long-term data storage. To read the data, the drive shines a laser (not as powerful as the laser that writes the info) and reads the different levels of reflected light. A bit can be high-reflective or low-reflective, resulting in binary data. An optical cartridge can store from 230MB to 2.6GB, depending on the specific drive.

CD-ROM

(Compact Disk Read Only Memory) CDs are likely to become another standard. SyQuest, magneto-optical disks and Iomega Zips are popular media used in the desktop publishing industry where a need to transport files from the designer to the service bureaus exist. Let us now take a look at some of the media used as storage devices and how they operate. Almost every workstation sold today comes with a CD-ROM drive. Many software applications and image libraries come on CD-ROMs. You'll need a CD-ROM to install software on the workstation, and if you use technology such as Photo CD, you'll need the CD-ROM to retrieve artwork. A CD holds 650MB worth of data. To store files, specifically the high-resolution graphics that take up so much disk space, you can also use CD-R, which allows you to write a CD once, but you can't overwrite it. These types of drives allow you to create your own image library by storing thousands of images on a single CD, and you can retrieve those images as many times as necessary. Also, some graphic arts trade shops write completed jobs on CDs to return to the customer for archiving.

CD-E (erasable) technology allows you to erase a CD and write new information. In effect, a CD-E drives works much like any hard drive, except that it works with a lot more information. CD-E drives are just now becoming available. You may see CD-ROM drives with a 2X,

4X, 6X, 8X, or 16X rating. These numbers indicate how many times 150KB/sec the CD-ROM drive can read. A 2X drive can read 300KB/second and a 6X drive can read 900 KB/second.

Digital audio tape

Digital audio tape is a media that had become very popular for recording music digitally, but still maintaining a tape format. It is the same ability of this media to record sound digitally that enables it to store data. A Digital Audio Tape (DAT), which is about the size of a credit card, can store about 1.3 GB of computer data. DAT is a metal particle tape that has been widely used in high quality audio tapes and in 8mm video. Because of its relatively small size, a DAT drive can be built into a desktop machine in the same space that is occupied by a 3.5" floppy disk. DAT tapes are well suited for applications such as backup, software distribution, and exchange of data. Its storage capacity is approximately nine times that of 1/2" reel-to-reel tape or 1/4" cartridge tape. Access time required to locate a given file is about 20 seconds on average.

Tapes are traditionally used as system backups. Tape drives allow you to store a lot of files at the cost of ease of retrieval. A DAT tape can store 2-4 GB. A DLT (Digital Linear Tape) tape accommodates up to 70 Gigabytes of data, depending on the model. You can purchase a tape changer to expand the storage capacity to six or more tapes. Such a system could hold .25 TB (terrabytes, or 25,000,000,000,000 bytes) of data. Depending on the speed of the tape drive/changer, it could take anywhere from several hours to a couple of days to back up that much information. Tapes are the oldest known form of storing data on a secondary storage device. They are made of thin mylar coated with ferric oxide that can be magnetized.

These tapes record data sequentially, which means that if the data that needs to be retrieved lies at the end of the tape, you have to wait until the head reads the whole length of the tape. The tapes are available in 1/2" and 1/4" widths. They are either spooled in large reels or are in cartridges. The magnetized and non-magnetized spots on the tape represent the presence or lack of data. Tapes record data in a column separated by nine tracks, one for each bit of information plus a track for the parity bit. The tapes are known to degrade when kept for prolonged periods due to a chemical process. The binder systems used in tapes are based on polyester polyurethane. These degrade by a process called hydrolysis. Humidity is another factor that affects the life expectancy of the tape. Floppies are like the magnetic tape divided into tracks. These tracks are in the form of concentric circles. They are further divided into pie-shaped wedges called sectors.

Data cartridges

These look pretty much like a normal audio cassettes. They have become a popular means of backup and archival storage. Because they are relatively inexpensive, they have become popular with home users and the small business community.

Ablative recording

The disk consist of a glass substrate and a special alloy used as the recording layer. A high-power laser beam is focused on the recording layer which melts under the immense heat generated by the laser, forming a pit. The rim of the pit is molten metal. When reading the media, the low-intensity read laser reads the pits and the land areas of the surface and notes the changes in the reflectivity. The lands are interpreted as 0s and the pits are interpreted as 1s.

Phase change recording

This uses a medium that has two states, an unstructured state (amorphous) and a structured state (crystalline). The crystalline state is more reflective than the amorphous state. When focused laser thermal energy is applied, it reverses the state of the recording layer and produces a change in reflectivity. To write, the laser will thermally reverse amorphous state to the crystalline state. A similar example would be that of water and ice. The material is the same but can be altered by temperature. It becomes critical to accurately control the laser power, as the transition temperature range is very narrow.

Bubble forming recording

Two layers, a die-electric sublayer and a sputtered overlay of heat-absorbing material, form the substrate. A laser beam is focused through the die-electric sublayer onto the heat absorbing layer. The heated spot in the absorbing layer vaporizes and the adjacent spot creates a subsurface bubble. This change in the reflectivity of the sublayer is what is read by the low intensity laser during the read process.

Dye polymer recording

A dye polymer recording media is typically constructed of elastomer and thermoplastic layers. The dyes in each layer absorb different wavelengths of light produced by a pair of lasers in the read/write head of the optical drive. A change in reflectivity occurs when the medium is heated by the write laser, thus changing the molecular structure and effectively creating a logical 1. The bit is erased by reheating the spot with the erase laser thus restoring the layer to its original reflectivity or logical 0 state.

WORMS

Refers to an optical disk technology that allows you to write data onto a disk just once, after which, the data is permanent and can be read any number of times. A single Write-Once Read-Many (WORM) disk can store from 600 MB to over 3 GB. WORM optical devices were originally introduced for use in the digital audio and video market. WORM will not permit rewrite or erasure of data once written. This technology, because of its nature, is well-suited for archival applications where data must be retained, not changed.

The reading and writing of data on the WORM disks is performed using a semiconductor diode laser. A laser beam is turned on and off in accordance with the bit pattern in the data. When the beam hits the writing layer, the exposed area is heated, causing a change in reflectivity. This change in reflectivity is used to distinguish between 0s and 1s during the reading phase. WORM technology uses the ablative method of recording. The life of WORM media varies. Generally the life of 12" WORM media is for 10 to 30 years. However, all manufacturers are accelerating the life of the media. Various types of substrates are used in optical disk including air sandwich, glass, acrylic, polycarbonate, and aluminum.

Digital Video Disks

There has been a lot of fanfare on the arrival of this new media. It is believed that major Hollywood picture studios were consulted on the system for what the next generation of the video storage format must do. Hollywood came back with requirements that the new formats must store more than 135 minutes of video, have better picture quality than laser disks, feature 5.1 channel digital surround sound, and have the capacity to carry between three and five language sound tracks.

Storing such large amount of data posed a problem, said the engineers at Toshiba. Data to be squeezed closer together was not a problem, but not possible on a disk constructed the same way as a CD. CDs are made of 1.2mm thick piece of plastic with a metallic surface glued to one side. When the temperature changes as when the disk is placed in a warm player, the disk warps slightly. While this was not a problem by itself, the data that would have been placed very closely would cause errors because of the warping problem.

To overcome this, engineers designed a disk that had two plastic layers each 0.6mm thick with a metallic layer sandwiched in between. This technique not only prevents warping, but also it provided for better bit detection, because the laser had to travel through less material. DVD is expected to create new opportunities for motion picture companies, advertising agencies, and computer hobbyists. With the launch of DVDs, most motion picture companies are releasing their old and new videos on DVDs. They are expected to cost less than the video tape with as much as four times the quality.

Input/output technologies

Pen-based systems

In pen-based systems, instead of typing the data into the system, the operator simply writes on a pad. In another category of input device that uses pen-based system the user writes directly on the screen. The screen is a specially built tablet that accepts data when written on. The writing device is like a pen, and the screen acts like a pad. These pen-based systems give the user the same writing experience that they would otherwise have using a note-book and pencil (or pen). Pen-based systems are very clearly targeted towards the mobile worker, where the information gathered by them needs to be updated in their company's system in real time. So they have become popular with courier companies, insurance agents, and sales representatives.

Digitizing tablets

These devices are a combination of pen-based systems and touch screen technology. All input functions like writing, drawing and designing can be done using digitizing tablets. These devices consist of a puck (hand-held device made of plastic and glass with intersecting crosshair) which the user holds in the same way as a mouse and writes on a pressure-sensitive tablet. In some cases, the puck is more like a pen or stylus, and from the amount of pressure that the user applies on the tablet, the input is taken accordingly. As is the case when using a pen or crayon, the more pressure is exerted, the darker the color or thicker the line. This device is quite useful in the design segment of the graphic arts.

Output devices

Output devices help the computer communicate with us. They do this by displaying the results of the input we have given the computer. Display technologies include VDTs (Visual Display Terminal), and CRTs (Cathode Ray Tube). Most display terminals use CRT, like the one used in your television. It is basically a huge vacuum tube in which electron beams fire either red, green, or blue phosphors, based on the data or image that is transmitted to it by the front end computer. How intense the beam is depends on the data sent from the CPU of the computer. We see the image on the screen when these beams hit the phosphorous coating on the screen, which is illuminated. The combinations of these glowing phosphors is what we see as images, text or design patterns on our screens. CRT is relatively inexpensive, but they are bulky and consume space on the desktop. Besides, the quality of the phosphor is very much dependent on the age of the tube. As the tube ages, the colors shown on the monitor become quite unrealistic. That does not mean that in deciding color critical issues in printing, one cannot trust a brand new monitor. Some can get pretty close.

FPDs

FPD stands for "Flat Panel Display" and these units are less space-consuming and lower in weight than the CRTs. FPDs are constructed from sandwiching two flat sheets of glass with an active display element located between the sheets. FPDs use a matrix addressing system whereby the CPU sends signals to transistors that are placed around the border of the screen. These transistors control all the pixels in a given column or row. Liquid crystal display (LCD) is an example of FPD. LCD uses an oily substance as the active display element between the glass, and this substance responds to electrical fields by reorienting its molecules to transmit or block ambient light or backlight to create an image.

HDTV

HDTV stands for "High definition television." There is now a move to convert computer monitors and television screens into one display technology. HDTV offers a much larger screen format, with full pictures that have colors that are more vibrant than the present television quality. Digital technology is the backbone of this technology. Images and sound will be produced completely digitally and will also be transmitted and received completely using digital technology. It is expected that within the next ten years or so, HDTV will have completely replaced current televisions.

File formats

In the modern prepress environment there are a wide variety of different applications that can be used to accomplish the same task. All of these different graphics programs write a wide variety of different file formats that can be used for a wide array of different applicatioons. Some of the files are for low-resolution use on the web where others are for use when outputting to high-resolution devices.

This wide variety of graphics formats is due to a number of factors such as file limitations, proprietary hardware and software, and economic factors. One problem that the graphics arts industry has moved away from is the proprietary file formats that only worked on particular systems—nothing but the particular system could read or access the file.

These kinds of systems are still around but for the most part do not exist in the desktop publishing enviroment. Most of these proprietary systems, known as CEPS (for Color Electronic Prepress System) systems, have been replaced by the abilities of the desktop computer. These systems had their place but with the shift away from closed systems, it's no longer feasible to use systems that write file formats that can only be accessed by a select set of systems or services.

The use of proprietary systems reduces your ability to shop around for the best service organization to deal with for prepress and printing work. You may be locked in. With the move from proprietary file formats, a number of file formats were created that fulfilled specific functions from TARGA files to EPS files. All of these different files have unique requirements that allow them to support special circumstances. An important thought to keep in mind is to use a file format that is capable of storing your work in the right enviroment but also is one that the user can access and use with no trouble or special applications that will open the file but, by doing so in a roundabout way, could alter the file.

Bitmapped file

The most basic type of graphic is the bitmap. It is essentially a grid of dots—a mosaic made from many tiny black and white or colored tiles, or bits. The tiles are called pixels, or picture elements. Lines are built up as rows of adjoining pixels, and all shapes are outlines filled with black and white, gray, or colored pixels. You change a bitmapped image by replacing tiles. The optical illusion of nonexistent colors or grays is achieved by dithering, or mixing tiles of nearby colors or shades of gray. Dithering looks at the colors or grays in one row of tiles and the colors or grays in an adjacent row and then averages the two rows to create a third row between them.

Black and white bitmaps need only one bit to describe each pixel—zero or one. A single bit per pixel doesn't provide enough information to specify a color or shade of gray. Images containing 256 grays or colors require 8 bits per pixel, and photographic-quality full-color images require 24 bits per pixel to specify any of 16.7 million colors. Depending on resolution, color and grayscale bitmaps require significant volumes of storage.

Bitmaps have a fixed grid-like or mosaic nature and can produce unsightly results when an area of the bitmap is moved, enlarged, or rotated. When you move part of a bitmap, you tear up tiles and put them somewhere else, leaving a hole. Moved tiles overlay or replace tiles. If you enlarge a bitmapped graphic, it looks like big dots. If you shrink the bitmap, some of the tiles overlap others. Any change to a bitmapped image becomes jagged and distorted.

Printing a bitmap gives you only the resolution you started with. Low resolution bitmaps print at low resolution; even on high resolution output devices. If you print a 300 dpi image on a 1,200 dpi printer, you will get 300 dpi. On a 2540 dpi imagesetter, that 300 dpi image looks like heck. Most professional systems only use bitmaps for pictures. Pixel use lets you achieve artistic effects that resemble those of traditional color painting. Image manipulation programs work on bitmaps, which are also the graphic format for scanned images.

Bitmaps are even more confusing because the term is also used for:

- Type fonts produced as a fixed size and style, which cannot be resized. This format is not used very much today for fonts.
- The result of raster image processing—where every laser dot is placed on a grid for the imaging engine, indicating whether that spot is on or off.

Raster files are bitmapped files that hold information for every pixel in the image. This type of file is resolution-dependent and the higher the resolution, the larger the file size, because it is holding information for every pixel in the image.

Vector graphics

Object-oriented graphics are typically produced by drawing programs. They overcome the limitations of bitmaps. The images are composed of mathematically described objects and paths, sometimes called vectors. Object-oriented applications store your strokes as a list of drawing instructions compiled from menu choices and mouse actions. Everything you draw, move, or change updates an internal file that lets the program keep precise track of each item in the drawing.

You can enlarge, reduce, rotate, reshape, and refill objects, and the program will redraw them with no loss of quality. Moreover, you can manage objects as if each item were drawn on a separate transparent sheet. They are freely movable over the surface of a document and can be stacked and partially hidden by other objects without being permanently erased.

The advantages of object-oriented art extend to the printing phase as well. Instead of dictating to the printer where each pixel should be, the program mathematically describes the object and lets the printer render the image at the highest resolution possible. Thus, unlike bitmaps, object-oriented graphics (usually line art) are resolution-independent. Object-oriented images printed on a 2540-dpi imagesetter look far superior to the same object printed on a 300-dpi laser printer. Object-oriented graphics are the natural choice for illustrations, line art, business graphics, etc. Object-oriented images have smooth curves, grayscale shadings, and tints.

TIFF

TIFF files are versatile bitmaps. The Tagged Image File Format is the most commonly used format for storing bitmapped or picture images in various resolutions, gray levels, and colors. It does not store object-oriented images. TIFF was created specifically for storing grayscale images, and it's the standard format for scanned images such as photographs—now called TIFF/IT. TIFF has different levels based on the number of colors or grays they can contain. It is a composite format.

Monochrome TIFF stores 1-bit images, but the black and white pixels can be dithered in a variety of patterns to simulate grays. Dithered patterns limit the degree to which you can edit and scale an image. Grayscale TIFF typically holds 256 grays. It's the best choice for graphics used in page layouts, because most page layout programs can adjust the contrast and brightness of grayscale TIFF images.

Color TIFF handles 16.7 million colors. With EPS, it is one of the top two formats for images that will be color separated. Some programs save TIFF images with subtle variations from the norm, but TIFF/IT has changed that. TIFF is not used for storing text or object-oriented graphics.

Tag Image File Format for Image Technology (TIFF/IT) is an ANSI standard that builds on the Aldus 6.0 version of TIFF (Aldus came up with the idea) and carries forward the work done on DDES (Digital Data Exchange Standards) and IFEN (Intercompany File Exchange Network). TIFF/IT provides an independent transport mechanism for raster images and integrates high-end and desktop publishing formats. In practice, TIFF/IT should make it easier to exchange data between high-end and desktop environments.

TIFF is a format for storing and interchanging raster (as opposed to vector) images. This usually refers to data that comes from scanners and frame grabbers, as well as photo-retouching and paint programs. TIFF describes images in a number of formats and also supports several compression methods. It is not tied to proprietary products and is intended to be portable. It is designed so that it can evolve as new functions become necessary. It is the tags from TIFF which made the format attractive to the supporters of DDES. Because TIFF has been designed to evolve, it is possible to create new tags for TIFF/IT to satisfy requirements of high-end systems. The tags describe each pixel in terms of color, graylevel, and other attributes.

By August, 1986, the first version of TIFF was approved. Microsoft played a role in the drafting of TIFF, and later formally endorsed TIFF for Windows. This helped establish TIFF in both Macintosh and Windows applications. While Aldus was finalizing the 6.0 specification in 1992, the IT8 committee of the American National Standards Institute (ANSI) was working on TIFF/IT which was approved in 1993.

The TIFF/IT format is made up of three primary components. Only the first component (CT) is actually part of the TIFF spec:

- Contone image (CT)—Each pixel is described by four bytes, one for each of the four process colors: cyan, magenta, yellow, and black (CMYK). This format is equivalent to TIFF CMYK previously known as TIFF s (separated TIFF).
- Linework image (LW)—High-resolution, multi-colored contone, graphic and text elements described as run length compressed data. LW is superimposed onto CT during color separation. While LW pixels may be assigned a color, they may also be assigned to be either opaque (to block out the CT below) or transparent (to let the background CT show).
- High resolution contone image (HC)—Run-length coded format which is commonly used for masking or trapping. The resolution of this format must be high to avoid stairstepping at the edges of masked images.

Another component is described:

- Final page (FP)—Describes a complete page formed by superimposing CT, LW, and other information.

LW and FP have no equivalent formats in the old Aldus TIFF. These file formats are unique to raster-based file structures of high-end systems. PostScript linework is usually reproduced with vectors. In addition, PostScript has no use for the HC format because masks are generally described using vector clipping paths. Given that LW formats are not used in PostScript, it would be superfluous to include them, or the FP format, in TIFF.

There are also three monochrome or binary components of TIFF/IT. These come from work done in DDES and are similar to their color counterparts except that their formats take advantage of the reduced amount of data associated with monochrome and binary images.

- Binary line art (BL)—Binary line art (or run-length encoded bitmap) image or file. Each pixel is represented by a single value.
- Binary picture (BP)—Binary picture (or byte-packed bitmap) image or file. Each pixel is a single bit.
- Monochrome picture (MP)—Monochrome picture (or continuous tone) image or file. Each pixel is represented by a single byte.

The ISO standard proposes two levels of conformance:

- TIFF/IT is intended to support a transport-independent means for the exchange of various images used in the prepress, printing and graphic arts fields, typically between CEPS (color electronic prepress systems).
- TIFF/IT P1 is also intended to support a transport independent means for the exchange of various images but for prepress, printing and graphic arts and additionally desktop publishing and information processing.

TIFF/IT allows the exchange of files with a wide variety of characteristics. P1 removes some of the flexibility of TIFF, but makes those files simple to read. P1 has more restrictions which make it simpler for receiving, but more complex for sending.

While high-end systems generally use raster formats alone, in the PostScript world both raster and vector formats are common. LW files are not line art in the PostScript sense. In PostScript documents, line art is created as PostScript code (which describes the lines, curves, and fills of a piece of line art). This vector PostScript line art is resolution-independent (that is, it can be output on a variety of PostScript devices and still produce the best quality that the device can achieve). Historically, traditional high-end systems work with raster data only. This means pixels, and lots of them. Scanned images contain many pixels, each of which can represent a range of colors.

These scanned continuous tone images are relatively large, but because they are ultimately halftoned, the scan resolution does not have to be extremely high. Line work (since it includes items with well-defined edges like text, rules, and logos) needs higher resolution to avoid stairstepping. To merge the line work convincingly with the contone data, not only does the spatial (that is, scan) resolution have to be high, but the tonal resolution (that is, bit depth) also has to match the continuous tone scan.

This results in a large file. As an example, a 300 dpi, 1 square inch, CMYK file requires about 350 KB of storage space. By increasing the resolution to 1,800 pixels per inch (about what a line work file requires), the file size increases by a factor of 36 to 12.4MB (An 8x10 inch file at that resolution would be a gigabyte in size.)

LW files, because they contain repetitive areas of the same color, are easily compressed using run-length encoding methods. The same is true of the files used for trapping and masking. They also are of great size, and they benefit greatly from compression. The size of LW and CT files is one obscure technical reason why PostScript has had such great success. For most desktop applications, it just made a lot more sense to create line work with vectors than to create humongous raster files.

TIFF/IT is a collection of formats, some with roots in the high-end, some with roots in the PostScript world, all joined together through a common file structure. Why did the industry think that it was necessary to bring these elements together in a standard?

The main reason is ease of interchange. But, TIFF/IT also allows powerful high-end formats that take advantage of DDES to break the bonds of magnetic tape. TIFF/IT could also simplify direct-to-plate and direct-to-press operations by providing a stable raster format which is desirable for a number of reasons:

- In computer-to-plate and computer-to-press environments it is costly to have a PostScript error occur late in the process. A stable raster file can be passed to a recorder with less chance for error.
- Imposition, trapping, color correction, and adjustments for press conditions can often be handled more easily with a raster file.
- It is generally easier to estimate the output time of a raster file based on its size. When PostScript vectors are RIPped, even though the file size may be small, the job still may take a long time to output.

TIFF images can be transferred from the PC to the Macintosh and vice versa. It was designed to travel across any machine architecture. TIFF is a file format capable of representing several kinds of scanned data. Currently, there are two kinds of TIFF data: bi-level—black and white—data and grayscale data. Grayscale images consist of an array of pixels and each can represent one or more shades of gray. The pixels of a gray image are usually 4, 6, or 8 bits deep, representing 16, 64, or 256 different shades of gray. This makes grayscale images useful for storing photographs.

PICT

PICT is not an acronym and is the oldest generic file format on the Macintosh. It is based on QuickDraw, the Mac's native graphics language. PICT objects and bitmaps can be white, black, cyan, magenta, yellow, red, green, and blue and can hold bitmaps with resolutions greater than 72 dpi but most are 72 dpi.

PICT2 is an extension of the PICT format, and it has two subtypes: a 16.7 million-color version, commonly called 24-bit PICT2, and the more prevalent 8-bit PICT2, which holds 256 colors. PICT2 sets no limit on the resolution of bitmaps except that imposed by the application. With 8-bit PICT2, a custom 256-color palette can be saved along with the image data, enabling any PICT2-wise application to recreate the original screen appearance.

Some programs do not save a custom color palette when exporting an image, and some importing applications ignore the custom palette. In these cases, when the image is opened by the new application, its colors will be determined by the current color palette, which can create color-shift and output problems. Color shifts could also occur when a chunk of 8-bit PICT2 from one page is pasted into another 8-bit PICT2 page.

PICT2 is usually a better choice for presentations, in which the final image is viewed on-screen for multimedia or on a slide, than it is for publishing. It is readily imported but poorly supported by publishing applications. Page-layout programs offer contrast and brightness adjustments for grayscale art, but not if it's in PICT2 format.

PICT is used by many screen capture programs to take a snapshot of what is on your monitor at that moment.

PostScript

In the early 1980s, Adobe Systems, Inc. developed a method to describe typographic images as vectors or outlines, thus allowing type to be infinitely modified and distorted. Previously most type had been bitmapped, which allowed no change in size or style. At the same time, they introduced the PostScript language, which described pages in coded form in order to print those pages on raster-based printing devices. The PostScript language consists of over 300 verbs or commands that instruct the program to move to certain points, draw lines, fill boxes, select type, etc.

A PostScript interpreter processes the PostScript language file for printout.

A PostScript file is a purely text-based description of a page. In many applications, you can create a PostScript file from the Print dialog box. You can open this file with any word processor and modify it (if you know PostScript).

Here is a typical PostScript file. It begins with the required %!PS:

```
%!PS                    230 360 moveto          250 407 lineto          290 360 lineto
newpath                 %create 2nd box         270 407 lineto          closepath
210 360 moveto          230 407 lineto          270 360 lineto          gsave
%create 1st box         250 407 lineto          closepath                 .60 setgray
210 407 lineto          250 360 lineto          gsave                   %fill with gray
230 407 lineto          closepath                 .70 setgray              fill
230 360 lineto          gsave                   %fill with gray          grestore
closepath                 .80 setgray             fill                    0 setgray
gsave                   %fill with gray          grestore                1 setlinewidth
  .90 setgray             fill                    0 setgray               stroke
%fill with gray          grestore                1 setlinewidth          }repeat
  fill                    0 setgray               stroke                  /Times-Roman findfont
grestore                1 setlinewidth          270 360 moveto          24 scalefont
0 setgray               stroke                  %create 4th box         setfont
1 setlinewidth          250 360 moveto          270 407 lineto          230 450 moveto
stroke                  %create 3rd box         290 407 lineto          (My Gray Scale)
```

Lines that begin with the % are comment lines. Note that the value or variable comes before the command. The result of this little program is:

My Gray Scale

When you click the print command of any job, the page is converted to PostScript code and sent to the printer's RIP. You can save the page or document as a PostScript file—the same one that would have been sent to the printer—for later printing. You don't need the originating program to print a saved PostScript file. The PostScript file can be fed directly to a PostScript printer with a PostScript download utility. Unfortunately, there's no preview image, and the graphic essentially loses its editability, so you should always keep the original version of an image or a page in the native format of its originating application. A saved PostScript file includes all type and graphic information. If dialog boxes for printing have been properly selected, a PostScript file is best for remote printout. There are then several "flavors" of PostScript format:

- Click the Print button and your document is converted into a PostScript file and sent to the printer.
- Select "Save" instead of "Print" and the PostScript file is saved to your disk. You can open it in any text-based program and see it in all its glory.
- Art, design, and other programs can save the PostScript file to disk and include a view file. This is an EPS or Encapsulated PostScript file.
- You can convert the saved PostScript file to a portable document format using the Adobe Acrobat Distiller program. This creates a PostScript file with a view version that can be opened on Mac or Windows systems and read with the free Adobe Acrobat Reader.

EPS

A benefit of EPS (Encapsulated PostScript) is that special functions such as transfer curves, screen rulings and separation information can be embedded in the file that can't be changed once it leaves the creator of the file. But once a EPS is created it can't be edited very much except for size, cropping and distortion. Encapsulated PostScript is a PostScript file with a preview. It is used for storing object-oriented and bitmapped artwork. EPS has two subtypes: ASCII (text-based) and binary (hexadecimal). Object-oriented programs (such as Illustrator and Freehand) that offer an EPS Save option often use the ASCII format.

An EPS file in ASCII format usually contains two versions of the graphic. One is a resolution-independent PostScript (text) description for printing on a PostScript device. The second version is a low-resolution bitmapped PICT preview that can be displayed on the monitor without PostScript interpretation. This method enables page-layout programs to import, crop, and scale EPS graphics while using the pict image for visual feedback. If an EPS file has no embedded PICT version of the graphic, the importing application displays a gray box as a sort of placeholder.

If an object-oriented image is saved in the EPS format, it will retain its resolution-independent printing quality, and in most cases cannot be ungrouped, refilled, or recolored. It can be resized, distorted, or cropped. Because EPS files are self-contained, most popular programs that perform color separation accept and color separate EPS files. Binary EPS is similar to the ASCII version, containing both a PICT preview image and the actual graphic. Instead of being a text-based description, the printable graphic is stored as a stream of numbers that represent the pixel attributes. Binary EPS is voluminous but well suited for outputting bitmapped color images for four-color separation. A binary EPS color bit map uses about half the disk space of its ASCII EPS counterpart. Many programs have a specific save option for binary EPS.

DCS

Where OPI works with TIFF images, Desktop Color Separation or DCS is a file format that creates four-color separations by saving images as a set of Encapsulated PostScript or EPS files. It is used to exchange color data between retouching, separation, and page layout programs.

DCS is a format developed by Quark to allow images to be stored with the color data in a pre-separated format. The composite preview image is stored in one file. The individual CMYK color plates are stored in separate files. The composite file can be at full-resolution or a low-resolution version of the composite, depending on the application that created it. DCS 2.0 keeps the color plate information in separate tables. All of the data is stored in a single file, with header comments that specify the individual offsets.

The page layout application can send only the color plate in question to the printer, saving time in data transfer and RIPing. Scitex CT systems manufactured by Scitex in general use proprietary file formats which are only understood by Scitex systems. Applications supporting the HexaChrome six-color model store their files as DCS to ensure that layout applications print all of the layers.

Unlike TIFF, which originated from the work of committees, DCS was basically the work of Quark, Inc. in response to a request by CyberChrome Inc. of Branford, Connecticut, which had created a DOS-based color separation system for the desktop. Cyber-Chrome wanted a format for bringing separated color images into a QuarkXPress file. The basic specification, which Quark, Inc. made freely available to other developers, includes five linked EPS files: CMYK versions of the separated image and a composite master file that allows users to print low-resolution composite files on a color printer. This standard also is called five-file EPS or EPS5.

The advantage of DCS is that it allows an image-editing program to perform color separation and pass it through to final output with its integrity maintained. Users can choose which of several image editing programs or systems they want to use to create DCS separations independent of the final creation of the page and the separation of color elements on the page, such as type or line art.

The DCS format was adopted by Adobe Systems as a standard method of output for the first version of Photoshop. DCS provided a convenient way to prepare separations in Photoshop before rasterizing the PostScript file in a page layout program. This division of labor saved processing time, and a combination of Photoshop and QuarkXPress became popular among designers and prepress services for outputting pages with color images. Users have said they wanted to see some reduction in DCS file size because DCS files contain bitmapped data for each file of the CMYK separation, and most also include a complex, 8-bit, 72-dpi, four-color view file.

PDF

At the end of the 1980s, there was a great deal of work done in the development of some method that could take a page and send it cross-platform, cross-program, and cross-application to be read on any device. The page would be "frozen" in form. Theoretically it would be the same as the file that was originally created. The files would be extremely small compared to the original source files before being converted to a portable document format. It would employ a JPEG lossy compression offering levels of compression. This file would have huge possibilities, especially in the prepress area. See the chapter on Workflow for more detail.

JPEG

The Joint Photographic Experts Group developed the JPEG file. This format was created for a standard for color and grayscale images; it only works on continuous tone images. The big advantage of this file is the compression that the file allows. It uses a lossy compression scheme that will throw out data to compress the file as much as 10:1.

The user is given the choice of how much compression to apply to the file. At the higher levels, there is noticeable image degradation.

Compression

A variety of compression methods are used:

- Run-length (sometimes abbreviated as rle, run length encoded)—Run length data compression methods decrease file size by encoding sequences of identical symbols. For example, in a bilevel image, the image is composed of only two types, black and white. In some cases, there may be sequences that include long strings of either black or white characters. Instead of encoding a sequence of 20 white pixels as: ####################, this string could be encoded as 20#s. Two examples of run length compression methods are: PackBits and CCITT Group 3 one-dimensional Huffman coding. PackBits is a byte-oriented run-length compression scheme used with Apple Macintoshes. CCITT Group 3 is a two-pass coding method where frequently occurring items are given shorter codes than less frequently occurring items. Bilevel images can be compressed with either PackBits or CCITT Group 3. Grayscale can't be compressed using CCITT Group 3.

- LZW—LZW stands for Lempel, Ziv, and Welch (the names of the compression scheme's creators). LZW is designed to be able to compress all kinds of data, including images of a variety of bit depths. LZW is lossless, which means that there is no loss of quality due to compression. LZW works quite well on bilevel images; however, for grayscale and full color images (particularly those images with a lot of detail) LZW may not be able to offer significant amounts of compression.

  LZW is an adaptive compression method which means that the compression technique is dynamically adjusted based on the content of the data being compressed. LZW is also termed a dictionary method of compression because it creates dictionaries which are used to compress commonly repeated data.

- JPEG—The Joint Photographic Experts Group approach was developed to create a standard for color and grayscale image compression. It is effective only on continuous-tone color spaces. JPEG is a variety of algorithms, each of which is targeted for a particular class of image applications. These algorithms fall into two classes: lossy and lossless.

    Lossy—These algorithms are based on discrete cosine transform (DCT). Though they involve the loss of some data, they provide substantial compression without significant image degradation.

    Lossless—These algorithms use a two-dimensional differential pulse code modulation (DPCM) technique. JPEG as used in TIFF also provides for the use of the Huffman coding model.

One important characteristic that affects these files is the compression scheme used to compress the file. Compression schemes fall into two categories: lossless and lossy. Lossless compression allows the file to be compressed but when it is done no information is lost. Lossy compression works by removing some of the data so the compression algorithm is much more effective but image quality can suffer.

Run-length encoding is another lossless compression scheme that decreases the file size by encoding sequences of identical numbers. After the compression takes place no image data is lost, but the compression may be limited.

JPEGing a JPEG may not be a great idea, since you are compressing what has already been compressed to start with. The result will not be satisfactory.

File extensions

You can often identify a graphics file by its descriptor extension. DOS-based systems usually include it as part of the file name automatically; Macintosh systems tell you in the "Get Info" box. You should get in the habit of putting a period and a three-letter extension that tells you what the file format is. It helps to have an immediate knowledge of what you are dealing with. Here is a list of some of the more common file extensions and the file formats that use them.

Bitmapped file formats

GIF (.GIF): Used for pictures that are transmitted by modem from commercial online services.

IMG (.IMG): Bitmap GEM format. Used by Corel Ventura Publisher.

MacPaint (.MPNT): Bitmap format limited to a resolution of 72 dpi.

PCX (.PCX, .PCC): Bitmap format developed by ZSoft for PC Paintbrush.

TGA (.TGA, .PIX): Format for images created on TARGA video boards from Truevision. Because of their resolution, files can be very large.

TIFF (.TIF): Tagged Image File Format. Probably the most common bitmapped file type. Now a standard called TIFF/IT.

Object-oriented file formats

CDR (.CDR): CorelDraw format.

MacDraw (.DRWG): Format used by MacDraw.

CGM (.CGM): Computer Graphics Metafile. A standard graphics file format for high-level systems.

DFX (.DFX): A format for CAD files.

EPS (.EPS): Encapsulated PostScript.

GEM (.GEM): Developed by Digital Research as its operating environment.

HPGL (.HPG): Hewlett-Packard Graphics Language. Originally for plotters.

PIC (.PIC): The Lotus format used by Lotus 1-2-3 for graphics and charts.

PICT (.PCT, .PIC): Bitmap format used by the Macintosh.

PICT2 (.PI2): Advanced PICT format that can handle color.

SLD (.SLD): AutoDesk's slide format for AutoCAD.

WMF (.WMF): Windows Metafile Format. Microsoft's common graphics file format for applications that run under Windows.

There are a lot of other graphic formats out in the industry. Some, such as Scitex CT, are a proprietary format; others are supposedly non-proprietary but aren't used much on the Mac side or in graphic arts like the TARGA file. All these different file formats make it hard for the pre-press house to get their customer's jobs out on time and it also can make it expensive. To have all these different applications around just so one weird file can be read and dealt with is inefficient and costly. But a large part of the industry is using some version of the TIFF file and the EPS file format.

As more and more professionals are doing their own prepress work because the cost of technology has come down and they want more of the control in their hands, they have to be aware of the different kinds of formats and when it is appropriate to use each. They should avoid using proprietary formats because there is a good chance that the service provider will not be able to read the format and then the job time will be wasted as the file is converted over to one that works in their environment.

As a rule of thumb, right now, images should be in TIFF, and vector art saved as EPS—these are very general guidelines, but every service provider will be able to read either of these two formats.

Discussion of file formats

Working in a modern prepress environment is a thrilling experience. Creative folk will end up sending in almost any file type that you can imagine. The assumption is: if I have this program, everyone must have it. This results in a wide variety of different graphic formats. One of the most usual problems that occurred in the past was receiving a file that couldn't be read. This stems from the use of proprietary and non-proprietary hardware that write different formats.

That is why a variety of more or less standard file formats were created. File formats are categorized by the type of graphic that is being stored to disk. Raster files are bitmapped files which hold information for every pixel in the image. These type of files are resolution-dependent and the higher the resolution, the larger the file size because it is holding color and grayscale information for every pixel.

On the other hand vector-based graphics store the points of the shapes that were created in x, y locations in relation to the page that was defined. Information is not being stored for every pixel. It stores the shape and the tagged information, such as line weight. This type of file is resolution-independent, which allows the file to be output to a variety of different devices.

One important characteristic that affects these files is the compression scheme used to compress the file. Compression schemes fall into two categories: lossless and lossy. Lossless compression allows the file to be compressed, but when it is done no data will be lost. Lossy compression works by removing some of the data out of the file so the compression algorithm is much more effective, but image quality can suffer but the file sizes will be smaller. For images going to the web, compress to your heart's content. For high-end printing, compression must be used very carefully.

The most widely used file format for saving images is the Tagged Image File Format (TIFF). It stores raster-based images. With Aldus and Microsoft involved, it made the format successful because both the Mac and the PC side were addressed.

Out on the market is TIFF/IT which is a newer variation of the TIFF file concept. This addition was made to allow tags or unique characteristics to be added to the file. It allows for the transfer of files between desktop publishing and high-end publishing systems. Another variation is the TIFF/IT P1 which is the same as the original TIFF/IT but places certain restrictions on the file to make it a little more limiting in what it can handle—specifically ads that are part of pages and publications.

The PICT file is Macintosh's first graphic file format and generally is used for low resolution applications. But we can forget about PICT. Apple's plan is to use PDF as the screen format in OSX—the next big operating system for the Macintosh.

The Encapsulated Postscript (EPS) is a PostScript file with a preview. It allows vector or raster data to be stored in this file with a color preview. DCS is EPS in a pre-separated workflow. This file format allows raster-based programs like Adobe Photoshop to create color separations and allow them to pass the images right through the layout file at printout time.

Up to now EPS files did not store the font data. With the current version of Illustrator and via Acrobat 3.02 you can.

But forget about EPS. It will be replaced by PPDF—Placed PDF. This is a format that may even give TIFF/IT-P1 a run for the money for digital ads. Microsoft is about to introduce a utility program that converts almost any graphics format into another graphics format. Users have applied Photoshop for that purpose for years. We are working very hard to find workarounds to get to the file format we can actually use.

The object must be files that are resolution independent, which allows the same file to be output to more than one output device without changing anything.

A benefit of the EPS is that special functions such as transfer curves, screen rulings and separation information can be embedded in the file that can't be changed once it leaves the creator of the file. But once a EPS is created it can't be edited very much except for size, cropping and distortion.

Another variation of the EPS is the Desktop Color Separation (DCS) that was developed by QuarkXPress. This file format is made up of five parts which are the four CMYK separations plus a low resolution composite color preview. This file format allows raster based programs like Adobe Photoshop to create color separations and allow them to pass the images right through the page layout program to be RIPped. It saves time RIPping the final job because the images are already separated.

But all this is being addressed in the new Acrobat 4 version. It will even embed ICC profiles. We are getting smarter about the way we save and transport graphic files. It only took a decade.

As more and more non-trained graphics people are doing their own prepress work because the cost of technology has come down, and they want more of the control in their hands, they have to be aware of the different kinds of formats and when it is appropriate to use different formats so there will not be problems as it is sent through the production process.

In other words, it is all changing.

As the industry is changing, so are the tools that are used on a daily basis to create, manage and output the jobs that need to be printed. Software is one of the most difficult tools to keep up with because it is constantly being updated. Software is the key to this whole desktop publishing revolution and without it, it wouldn't be possible to do.

Some software is very generalized in what it can do, whereas other applications are very specific and do nothing else. Usually software that does virtually everything is not the best choice because it has to do everything, and therefore it doesn't do one thing great. A very specific application that is designed for one task will usually have the most capability in that one job area.

Software is very job-specific in many cases because it has replaced many of the manual methods used in the past. Software can be categorized by the main job that it performs:

- designing/illustration
- photo manipulation
- page layout
- trapping
- imposition

Content creation (Art and design)

Tending the creative flame

Art has always been and will always will be an integral part of graphic communication. This chapter will not be dwelling at length on this aspect, but we felt it is important to be mentioned here. From time immemorial graphics has been a powerful tool that has enhanced the quality of the printed word. Graphic designers have used various tools that helped them create some wonderful images. They were certainly of artistic value and the artists themselves were very skilled personnel. Computers today offer a number of tools for the artist community and desktop computers are very popular in graphic design and development.

Digital graphic design and prepress

Many graphic designers quickly embraced the digital technology, which aided the process of creation of art, while giving them many options to work with. Graphic artists became more proficient in the use of computers, storage devices, memory related issues, operating systems, lightings, seatings, *et al*. With more of traditional art moving the digital way, the boundary between digital graphic design and prepress diminished. Both communities started using similar equipment and programs.

The pace of the digital world is awesome and breathtaking. It can definitely cause stress for the novice, or even the professional. The holy grail of fine art and creativity is sometimes lost in the technology. But, a determined and hard-working designer may very well discover that the tools are only means to an end and then exploit them for all they are worth.

The reality of learning, growing, and creatively succeeding in the new digital world can be difficult. There are still those who make mechanicals, only now there are fewer services who know what to do with them. The only realistic solution is to practice and learn in order to master the new medium. This is all it is, a new art medium. In this book we hope to teach, to convince, and excite you about it. The power for one individual to draw and to illustrate and to make your imagination public through art has never been greater in the history of the world. This is only the beginning of the next great post-modern art movement. And to answer the question "Where is art going next?" can be summarized in one word—DIGITAL.

Creating images

A printed product has images that are created either as line work or as continuous tone images. Line work consists of just two levels: white which is the color of paper and black, which is the color of ink. Here the image does not have any shades in between. These images are created by artists who skillfully draw by using lines, curves and other geometric shapes. They also vary the thickness of the lines to give a better rendition of the images.

In some situations images are created as a continuous tone image. A tone refers to all the intermediate levels that are found between a black and white. These levels, usually in varying degrees of gray, give a feel of the image being continuous. Since the tonal gradation of the image is continuous from white to black, these images are called continuous tone images.

Examples of continuous tone images are photographs and wash drawings created from paintings that may either be watercolor, acrylic, or oil. Some artists use an air gun to create continuous tone.

In today's digital world artists use programs such as Painter, Photoshop, Freehand, and Illustrator to create images from scratch. These programs help the artist to draw the image, size it, color it and even manipulate the image. The computer gives the artist a wide choice of a palette for colors. Moreover, the tools offered by these programs are similar to the traditional tools that were used by the artist; it's just that these modern tools are so convenient and fast.

These programs let artists create lines, apply tints, size drawings, and eventually output them to an output device. The control that many of these drawing programs gives are so versatile that sometimes the artists are able to perfect their creation, something they would have found difficult when creating them manually.

The advent of PostScript in 1985 gave a new life to the artist (and novices as well) which revolutionized the world of desktop publishing. It provided the underlying infrastructure that made drawing less streneous. Creating a perfect straight line, circle or other geometric shapes were made simple by defining the coordinates. And this motivated many new "artists" into the industry. Images and text could be created at the highest resolutions of the output devices to which they would eventually be output.

Other ways

Apart from creating images from scratch, images can be photographed. Traditional photography called for shooting the image and processing the latent image chemically.

Digital photography, with which images are captured today, does away with chemical processing. A digital camera captures an image somewhat like a scanner. Scanning an image and manipulating an existing image are other ways by which images get created these days. We will be discussing digital photography, scanning, and image manipulation in detail later.

And then there are the libraries that come with many software application programs which offer you a variety of ready-to-use graphics and objects, called clip art. Professional artists may not need to use them, but the variety and quality that is offered today should suffice for the average computer user.

Creating and importing text

The first task in building a page is placing the text into your layout. There are a number of word processing programs that allow one to input the text. Among those are programs like Microsoft Word, Write, WordStar (remember that?), etc. Also, the page layout and editing programs like QuarkXPress and PageMaker allow inputting of text. It is important to take note of some filters that you may need to work with when you switch between word processor and pagination program. Usually people compose their text in a word processor and later import it into a pagination program. This is because it is so simple to compose text using the word processor. Other attractions are that there are better dictionaries and grammar aiding tools in the word processor.

Once the basic page is composed, and the text is developed, it is exported to the pagination program, where the tools are better suited to creating a professional document. There are more tools here that enable the importing of images, graphs, and other objects within the document. Objects that have been imported into the page can then be resized, rotated, tinted, or given a shadow.

A crucial issue is that of fonts. There are two types of fonts that are widely used. They are the Type 1 PostScript and the True Type fonts that are used extensively on desktop computers and with PostScript printers. When these fonts are used interchangably the user gets into font conflicts. Both create fonts using an outline, which facilitates resizing as well as enabling them to be printed on low-resolution as well as high-resolution output devices. Since all printers used in the printing industry are PostScript devices, most printers and designers use Type 1 fonts. This is especially so since their work does not call for printing on high-resolution output devices.

Computer-ready art

Designing and layout: combining images and text

You will often have text created from a word processing program, images that were created or edited with an image creation program, and drawings and illustrations that were created in an illustration program, all to be combined into a single page. Putting them all together is the task and the challenge. In the early days of desktop publishing, this was considered a revolution by itself. Color adds to the complexity that a page layout program needs to handle. QuarkXPress and PageMaker have been the dominant players in the industry for a long time.

Although many word processors also have the ability to import images, the page layout programs offer more sophisticated capabilities. They have the ability to import images from a variety of file formats. They are also better when it comes to dealing with typography. Some of the present-day page layout programs can accept multiple master fonts, a new breed of font technology, that has the ability to extend two or more of the features (like bold, condensed, expanded . . .) of the typeface within itself.

The page layout programs should also be able to support some of the more commonly used color models. When a document is being used for printing from a printer, the program needs to support a CMYK model. If the document is being created for an application like being used online, then the program should support an RGB color model. Even in printing situations, artists use special colors that cannot be created with the CMYK color model.

In those situations, the programs should support the Pantone Matching System (PMS). Since page layout programs are being used extensively by the printers, one of the key tasks that is expected of the program is its ability to do color separation. The images and text that were created in various programs also come in with color.

These colors will have to be eventually separated into the process four colors (CMYK) and, if called for, they should be able to prepare special plates for the special colors. The real challenge in color for a page layout program is its ability to color separate color photographs and transparencies. QuarkXPress is most successful in the printing industry for being the pioneer in performing color separation from color files. Although this capability is offered in the page layout program, one is better advised to do color separation in Photoshop, with the separated image pasted into Quark. This would save a lot of time, which in a production environment is of immense value.

Ilustration programs

Designing programs are broken up into the type of graphics that they make, vector or raster. Most of the major applications are vector based, though there are a few on the market that are raster (pixel based applications) such as Painter 5.0. The major vector applications are Adobe Illustrator and Macromedia Freehand, which are the two competing programs in the market currently.

Vector art is composed of a series of points that are made up of Bézier curves that are used to create objects. Both applications are fully capable of producing work that meets professional standards. Using these programs, users can work with text, objects, and layers. Very complex work is created by these programs on a day-to-day basis. They both support all the different color systems such as RGB, CMYK, Pantone, CIE LAB, etc. And recently both have supported the PDF file format as well as work with HTML for web-based work.

Image editing

Image editing programs are dominated by Adobe Photoshop and a small percentage of the market is owned by Live Picture. Photoshop's latest version has gone through many revisions, each time enhancing the program and making it more capable. Photoshop is a pixel-based editing program that edits each pixel on the screen every time a change is made to the image.

This makes the files large and slow to work with when not using a "high performance" computer that can process large amounts of data quickly. Photoshop is a jack-of-all-trades when dealing with images because of the wide variety of things that can be done with it and well. Important functions are retouching, color correction (global and selective), color separations, and image manipulation, which allows the user to make images of other images.

A basic example of this is putting a person's head on someone else's body. This is a very simplistic example of image manipulation but the layers function makes a lot of the manipulation possible because it allows the user to put images on top of other images and work on each one independently. When the work is finished, this multilayer image is merged into one composite layer. Photoshop acts as many people's color separators because it does a good job of color separations when set up correctly, and allows many people to do the needed color corrections and other work that was traditionally performed by other people in the production process.

Page layout

The page layout program takes all the images, art work, and type and brings them together into pages for a layout. These programs offer no image editing ability, so prior to bringing work into these programs it must be ready to be output. QuarkXPress and Adobe PageMaker are the two applications that are currently being used in the industry, with Quark being dominant. Both of these programs allow almost any conceivable page design to be done. These programs offer great control over the type so "proper" typography can be produced.

These programs are linked to the file formats that they import TIFF, EPS and JPEG. These programs also will separate the entire page into color separations. As with the other programs they work with all the different color systems such as RGB, CMYK, HSB, Pantone Matching System, etc. A unique feature that is mostly found in QuarkXPress are XTensions. These add special functions on top of the application. What this allows are specialized tool sets to be added to the application to enhance it and customize it for the work that you generally perform.

In a general operation description, the user begins the process by importing pages and specifying the size and configurations of the desired imposition. The specifications are established by the characteristics of the printing press and folding capabilities of the printing plant. Other important configurations are related to the binding process used. Characteristics like gutters, margins and allowances are examples of these binding configurations. Finally the last stage is the production of film, plates, or, in the case of some digital presses, output directly to the press cylinder.

The digital revolution is upon us. From art and design to print-ing and publishing, the graphic arts world has been reduced to bits and bytes. We now live and work in or near cyberspace. Today, the creative originator makes digital files as a byproduct of the creative process; the printer receives digital files as input for the reproduction process. What should unite these two groups often divides them.

Commercial printers receive over 80% of their work in digital form but there is no consistency. We have to re-educate the cre-ative community about proper preparatiom.

Why do some jobs run effortlessly and others do not? The ability of the art professional is a big part of it. Those who know the secrets to QuarkXPress and Adobe PageMaker, Photoshop and Illustrator, among other programs, can create what are called "responsible" pages. An irresponsible page mixes Pantone and CMYK colors in a gradient blend, specifies 212-line screen halftones, has 39 typefaces with missing EPS files, and traps all colors indeterminately. One must prepare pages and documents based on meaningful standards of quality but also on pragmatic standards of reproducability. Can the pages be output by the replicating system successfully?

Another element in successful output is the pre-flight and analy-sis ability of the commercial printer or prepress service. Their attention to detail in re-setting all dialog boxes to the proper printout device, making certain all files are present and account-ed for, and assuring that the document will actually print. Printers are also offering newsletters, seminars, training sessions and consulting for their customers in order to increase the com-munication between creator and manufacturer.

Creative pages are useless until they are output to film (to make a plate), directly to plate (to go on press), directly to plate on press, or directly to digital press — or even to digital file on disk or online service. Newer reprographic technologies will only accept digital files and both creative professionals and print professionals will have to work more closely. We need to bridge the digital divide by communicating with each other and making technology work for us. The goal of this small book is to help you understand the various elements that make up pages and documents and how they are used to disseminate information in the brave new digital world.

Chapter 5

THE MYSTERY
AND MAGIC OF COLOR

Why would we call color "a beast"? Why is it that we can often get easily lost in color space? Even stating answers to these two questions is not simple. There are tremendous volumes of human literature, and consequently awesome decades of "person-years" of effort, that have been devoted to the goal of achieving intimate knowledge of color. Many extremely intelligent and famous people have tried to put all of the questions about color to rest. Yet, today's bottom line is that many questions still remain—and it is still "a beast." It is still easy to get that unlucky "lost" feeling. A true knowledge and understanding of color is a daunting task. We should never underestimate the task we continue to face in attempting "good" color reproductions. On the other hand, do not fear. After all, color is often an artist's passion, but it is just another human perception.

Color is a beast partly because it is neither fully in the realm of science, nor is it entirely in the realm of art and aesthetics. The problem is possibly that color has much to do with the mind. (Much to the frustration of many physicists and engineers.) Color is often studied methodically in a field of science called "psycho-physics." Physics and psychology together, oh my.

We can often get lost with color because there are so very many expert opinions and an equal number of opinionated experts. Each has their own perspectives, each their own language, each lives in their own favorite "color space," and each has their own "axe to grind." To live peacefuly with this beast we need to remember only one simple thing: Color is just a part of basic human functioning, like breathing. One does not need to know astronomy and cosmology to enjoy looking up at the stars. Remember that the same fundamental idea is true of color. It is the psychology-physics thing, and human relationships, that tend to make color complicated. A standard language (and culture) for communication is the key which all color experts must seek, including the artist.

Since we are interested in reproducing color, not just enjoying it, we need to examine this beast in some more detail, as best we can. We'll start with the basic question, "What is color?" The answer is really quite simple. It often surprises some people who thought they knew it. Color is a psychological sensation which is caused by light energy entering the human eye. Color is a human experience. To experience color you must have three basic things:
   - A sighted human being, who is not "color-deficient."
   - An object or "scene."
   - Light. (You might think about this and say that you don't need #2 if you are looking directly at a light source, like a computer. However, most "light sources" that we can think of are also objects.)

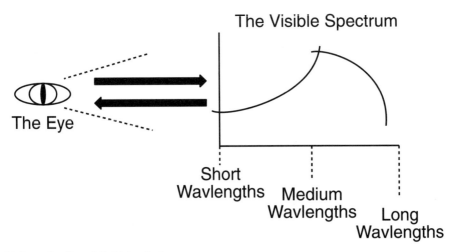

Light and reflected light is what we see

Light is defined as the part of the whole spectrum of radiation which is visible to humans. Please, feel quite blessed that our eyes do not "see" radio waves, or infrared radiation, or X-rays, or cosmic rays. If they did, the "color-beast" would be much worse, and even harder to tame. An incredible range of radiant energies exists in nature. It is called the "electromagnetic spectrum." The relatively tiny portion of this vast energy spectrum that we can "see" is called "light." It is essentially the rainbow colors.

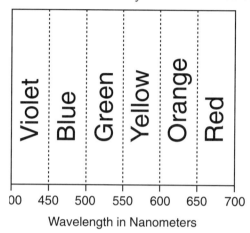

Wavelength in Nanometers

Back in 1666 Sir Isaac Newton used a triangular glass prism to recreate these rainbow colors in his laboratory, from a ray of sunlight entering his window. This experiment was an important beginning to color science. Color art and color perception, of course, were already quite well established at that time. If you look closely, the rainbow consists of three major bands of color that we've called red, green, and blue.

Other color bands like yellow and orange also are visible, but these are narrow, and are only very small fractions of these three major bands. The key related fact here is that our eyes contain three kinds of vision cells ("cone" cells) which happen to be sensitive to red, green, and blue light. There is an important relationship between the rainbow, our vision, and the magic number three. So, we have just met the beast, and he is us. The fact is that various mixtures of red, green, and blue light stimulate the corresponding cells in our eyes, and then we experience color. Simple, huh? In technical terms, it is often called "trichromatic vision."

To recap, without human observers, there are no eyes or vision. Without light, there is no red, green, or blue stimulation for vision. Finally, without objects, we have black empty space. Note that people who are totally color-blind are rare, for they would not have any functioning cone cells. (They wouldn't necessarily be blind, since there are other cells in the eye, called rods, which can detect light, but not color.) Other people have only some of the cone cells functioning properly. For example, they might have only the red and green sensitive cones. These people are partially colorblind, and would see only certain colors which happened to stimulate the cone cells that they had working. All of this physics, cell "physiology", and brain processing, is the science of vision. It can easily get even much more complicated. We won't go into all of that here. As we've said, color can be an awesome beast.

The electromagnetic spectrum

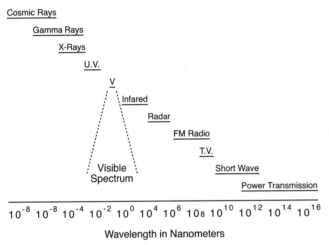

Cosmic Rays

Gamma Rays

X-Rays

U.V.

V

Infared

Radar

FM Radio

T.V.

Visible
Spectrum

Short Wave

Power Transmission

$$10^{-8} \ 10^{-8} \ 10^{-4} \ 10^{-2} \ 10^{0} \ 10^{4} \ 10^{6} \ 10_{8} \ 10^{10} \ 10^{12} \ 10^{14} \ 10^{16}$$

Wavelength in Nanometers

We see roughly 350 nm: gamma, xrays, ultraviolet, visible spectrum, infared, microwave/radar, T.V., short wave, sound

The spectrum is 11 Km long.

So color is just a human sensation. Science can only do so much with sensations. It's still trying to figure out all of the answers to physics. The appearance of a color cannot yet be totally "measured" or "specified," as such, perfectly with any instrument. (Human "instruments" are still the best.) Neither can a color nor the appearance of a color be perfectly "reproduced" by any means. These statements might surprise many readers. Nonetheless, they are true, and image scientists and printers alike must reluctantly agree. However, all is not lost. This beast can still be tamed. "Good" color reproduction is still attainable. Only perfection eludes us. Printers have been dealing effectively with these limitations for years. Excellent color reproductions are made by using sound technical methods, a delicate balance of art and science, careful craftmanship, process control techniques, and experience. It is neither easy nor simple to accomplish it, but nonetheless, it can be done. It will usually mean good cooperation and communication with many key members of a team. It can rarely, if ever, be done solo.

Basic color reproduction theory

Basic addition and subtraction

Oh great. Now we're doing math. Well, actually— yes, it is true, we are. However, we'll try to stop with simple addition and subtraction. It is almost that simple. Sir Isaac Newton produced rainbow colors from white light with a prism. We're just going to explain the basics of how to reproduce any one (or more) of those possible colors. Building upon what we've just discussed above, we'll explain two fundamental "theories" currently used to reproduce colors as they are needed. These fundamentals are hardly "theory" anymore. They're actually quite well understood by color and image scientists.

Understanding "additive" and "subtractive" color is important to color reproduction. It will also explain the basic difference between working with colored light (for instance, a rainbow or a computer monitor) as compared to working with inks or paint on paper or canvas.

Additive color theory corresponds well with how the human eye perceives colors, as we've just explained above. Start with colored light. Suppose you have three color "flashlights" which can produce red, green and blue beams. We're simply going to reverse Newton's 1666 experiment. He took sunlight and created a rainbow with the prism. If we now project the three different flashlight beams, red, green, and blue, onto a white surface, then where the three colors overlap we'll perceive white. Newton's experiment does work in reverse. Where green and red lights overlap we detect yellow (green and red = yellow is somewhat surprising, isn't it.). For green and blue overlapping lights we observe cyan. Finally, where blue and red overlap we perceive magenta. If we then vary the relative amounts of each of these three colors we can obtain as many colors as it is possible for the eye to resolve. Thus, three "primary" colors can be added together in various amounts to make many visible colors. This is the "additive" theory.

The same principle is true on our computer monitors. If all of the tiny red, green, and blue pixels are turned on at once, it creates a white screen. In the same manner, various adjustments of the amounts of the three primary pixel lights added together will produce the millions of colors available on your monitor. This again describes the additive color principle. Note carefuly that we said that the pairs (2) of the three primary colors (red, green, blue), will add together to produce cyan, magenta, yellow. These are going to be the main colors we'll use in printing inks. Here, they are the "secondary" colors created via the additive system. We will recognize that they become the "primaries" for the subtractive system below.

So, what about this subtraction? Ink on paper, artist's paints, and photo prints can re-create a rainbow of colors for our eyes by "subtractive" priciples. However, an important fact to remember is that the net result to our eyes is identical. Ink or paint produces an image which still sends colored light into the eye. This light stimulates the red-, green-, and blue-sensitive cone cells, which in turn produces the human experience of color. In other words, from the perspective of the human eye, the "experience" of the colors is the same. Red, green, and blue cone cells are stimulated by red, green, and blue light.

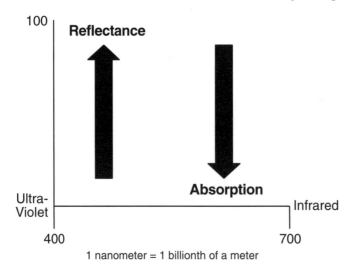

The RGB world is reflectance; the CMYK world is absorption

We now need to explain the difference between subtractive and additive color. To explain subtractive color, we begin with white light. The white light usually comes from a white surface such as paper. Paper is white because its surface is reflecting the right "additive" combination of the red, green, and blue light to our eyes. The light comes from some white light source (for instance, a lamp or the sun). To create subtractive colors then, we use three primary "colorants" (that is, ink, paint, or dye): cyan, magenta, and yellow. These colorants act like the colored glass in the flashlights used above—they only allow certain specific colors to pass through to our eyes. They are like a special type of Newton's prism which takes in white light and then allows only some of the colors to come out. Each colorant absorbs about one third of the "white" visible light spectrum and transmits the other two thirds. So, if we take cyan ink, for example, it absorbs red light. Magenta ink absorbs green light.

If a solid area of color on a printed page has both cyan and magenta on it, then most of the red and the green light from the paper will be absorbed. What color is not absorbed? What's left? Blue, of course. It's just subtraction. Subtract red and green and you get blue. Many of the other colors which can be made using the colored "flashlights," can also be made by using inks, dyes, or paints to subtract colors from white light in this manner. Again though, the visible result can be accurately described as simply combinations of red, green and blue light heading into the eye. The difference is that this light is produced by "subtracting" the colors that are not needed from the white light coming from the paper or canvas.

Therefore, for any specific matching color, whether reproduced via additive or subtractive principals, a similar mixture of red, green and blue light goes into the eye, stimulates the cone cells, and will give the same sensation. The difference between additive and subtractive color may seem trivial. In fact, in some ways it is. However, as you read on, you will hopefully discover and understand the following fact: Many of the problems encountered in color reproduction can often be traced to a poor understanding of this simple difference between additive and subtractive color reproduction. The whole trick is in the word "matching."

Color imaging systems

Our world is sumptuously filled with natural color. Our bodies and mind comprise the fundamental human color imaging system which captures light and processes it to give us all of the visions of our colorful world. This sophisticated processing is done by the optics of the eye and the intricate physiology of the light-sensitive cells combined intimately with the powerful computing power of our minds. This is the ultimate color image processing system which all other color reproduction systems try to emulate. However, all other systems fall short. It is this human system which defines our whole discussion and endeavor of color reproduction and science. From our human point of view, it is this system which is the perfect ideal which all others strive to imitate. Seeing is still truly believing.

Now that we understand some of the basics of the nature of color, and the fact that colors can be recreated from combinations of three primaries, where do we go from here? How is the color of images accurately reproduced? The process of color image reproduction can be broken down into three basic steps: capture, processing, and output. The first of these is "capture." Since the human system is the ideal, we try to capture all of the same color and light information that the eyes would capture. The usual goal is to try to capture as much image information as possible in order to accurately represent the scene to someone at a later time. In other words, to "re-produce" or re-create the original image as if you were there.

This "original scene" might be one in nature, or it might be some previously captured record of such a scene, like a photo or art image. This task can be attempted in many ways, ranging from direct digital camera capture, conventional photography, to scanning of previously captured images. At this step, the use of red, green, and blue filters is common in order to capture the light in a way similar to the cone cells in the eye. It should be quite obvious that if less (or wrong) information is captured, compared to what would have been captured by the eyes, then there is no good chance of accurate reproduction.

The next step in color reproduction is the processing step. The processing step must somehow take the captured light information, preserve it, and prepare it for output (that is, re-creation of the scene). In human vision, the "processing" is done by the complex combinations of the eye optics, the way the cone cells work, the intricate interconnections ("wiring"), and finally the brain itself. In order to effectively mimic this ideal, any other color system must be very careful to accurately account for and preserve the captured information as it prepares, computes, and processes it for the next steps. In modern digital color reproduction, the information we speak of is often some data code. Every one of the details of turning captured light information into this code is important. Similarly, any computing or transformations of this data are also crucial. Color information is often lost or altered in this processing (that is, storing, computing, transporting) step, even though it might have been captured quite properly. This is the cause of many color reproduction errors.

The final step is the output. This is the actual reproduction of the original. In the human system, "output" seems to be instantaneous. The scene is "out there" (that is, beyond the body), and we look at it, and we instantly "see" it. In humans, the "output" of the system is the virtual image we see in our mind. In every other system imaginable, the goal then must be to capture, process, and re-create an identical stimulus for the mind's eye of the viewer. This is done with paints (artist), ink (print), and dye (photos), using skill, knowledge, and technology. The hope and the goal is that the reproductions will induce the same vision of the original in the mind of the observer. If we think about this, it is incredible that we even attempt to try it. It is even more incredible that we often succeed. Professional artists, photographers, and printers can, and often do, reproduce colors amazingly well.

In this book, we'll try to describe the practical details of these color image reproduction steps. Done properly, the steps will ultimately lead to exact recipes for placing the correct amounts of CMY and black(K) ink onto paper. As described above, these inks will then hopefully subtract exactly the right amount of color from the white paper and send the rest of the light to the eye of the customer. Then, again hopefully, the customer will be pleased. However, remember, the fact still remains that "perfect" reproduction is impossible. We must therefore attempt to skillfully fool the observer's eye and mind into accepting our image. It is usually a challenging—and beastly—quest.

Great gamuts

What is a "gamut" anyhow?

It has been estimated that humans can see about 10,000,000 different and distinct colors. These millions of colors define the largest gamut possible. As stated, other types of radiation like radio, gamma, X-rays, UV, IR, etc. are "out of gamut" for humans. A gamut then is simply the total collection of possible colors which any color reproduction system can do. Since color depends on human vision, the human vision system has the largest gamut of all.

Spaces, solids, models, and systems

Munsell and the desert island

The topic of color inevitably leads to a discussion of "color spaces." What is color space? It can be confusing, but it is not a magic word that only geeks can understand. Again, remember our guiding principle: color is a human experience. Color "space," color models, color solids, gamuts, systems, etc. are just various ways to organize, study, and communicate color or color concepts.

Imagine yourself stranded on a desert island with plenty of time to spare. The island beach is covered with millions of pebbles of every possible color. At first you'd just look at the stones and enjoy the colorful beauty. Then, possibly, you might start to think about how to "organize" the stones into some kind of meaningful order. What arrangements would you be able to make with the colored stones? This thought experiment is often used to explain the basis for color order systems, which are also called models, solids, and spaces.

So let's arrange the stones. First, you might notice that there are stones with color, and ones that have no color (e.g. whites, blacks, greys), so you make two piles. You look at the pile of colored stones, and you sort out piles of color groups, like reds, yellows, greens, greys, blues, etc. You then look at the pile of colorless stones, and realize it would be easy to sort them from black to grey to white. With the same thought in mind, you see that in each color pile (the reds, the greens, yellows, etc.) there are lighter ones and darker ones, so you make smaller groups of lighter color, darker color, and some in between. You think you are done now, but you look at the little light and dark groups and see one more thing you can do. Looking closely at each one of these lighter- and darker-colored piles, you see that some of the stones look almost gray, with very little color. Others in the same group seem to have "pure" color. You are done.

So what did you learn? Colors can be lighter or darker. This is called "value" or "lightness." Colors can be red or yellow or green, etc., and this is called "hue." Finally, they can be purely colorful, or can be dull and close to grey or white. This is called "chroma," or "saturation." Thus, we have learned that color can be ordered or organized in three ways or dimensions. To repeat:

Take stones on a beach
Divide the stones by color (hue)
Divide the stones by lightness/darkness (value)
Then divide the colors by how much color is in the stones (saturation)
This color model still is a reference for a visual uniformity
Numerical scales are associated with each of the values
This makes it possible to refer to a color by a definitive co-ordinate
Tri-stimulus values
One value measures the color
One value measures the strength of the color
One value measures grayness

An artist/teacher named Albert H. Munsell methodically arranged colors in the form of a three dimensional "tree" shape in 1913. His colored "pebbles" were rows of small painted squares. The "trunk" (center pole) was colorless, with black at the bottom, white on top, and grays in between. The colors or "hues" (reds, yellows, greens, etc.) were hung around the trunk, each at its own angle around the centerline. Finally, in each color group, the pure colorful colors were near the outside, and the drab, nearly colorless ones were close to the trunk. This tree-like, flattened sphere shape, is sometimes called the Munsell color solid. It is simply one way of ordering colors in a methodical way which corresponds well to the way we perceive them. It is very similar to the desert island experiment.

In addition to this arangement of colors in three dimensions (value, hue, and chroma), Munsell also numbered the painted chips and pre-scribed simple rules for identifying each color. Now, he could write 5 Y 5/10 and it would mean the paint chip in the yellow branch with a value of 5 and a chroma of 10. So now we have "order," and we can make an order for a specific color. We now have a code for each color, such that if you called me on the telephone, and wanted me to send you a certain color, you could just give me the Munsell code, and I would be able to send it to you. However, without doing the desert island sorting and the Munsell numbering, how would you possibly be able to tell me which color you wanted? What words would you use? It would probably take far too many words and hand waving (over the telephone?) to get just the right one.

The following is a list of properties necessary for color models to be successful:
- Models should be independent and perceptually uniform.
- Models should be scaled for hue and saturation and grayness.
- Models should support a separate (apart from chromaticity grayscale value.
- Models should be able to support a white point correction for different printing substrates as opposed to just the image's white point.
- Models should be as objective as possible, with the considera-tion of a standard observer.
- Models should support the ability for an image to move into and out of the color space with relatively small amounts of computing.

- Ease of computing should not be compromised for accuracy.
- Color space should use image bits efficiently and with minimum data paths.
- Color space should be able to be competitively compressed.
- Color models should make use of regular quantization schemes.
- Color models must be able to support additive color spaces.

RGB

Another color space. Another system. Try not to panic, but there are dozens more. But don't worry too much about it. These are just different methods to work with and organize color; they are just different tools. Their goal is always still the same: To produce the perception of the correct color in the mind of the observer. Referring to the telephone call for a Munsell color above, how would we be able to "deliver" that specific Munsell color without using the actual paint chip? As we've explained, the additive color system using red, green and blue light can produce millions of colors. In order to match the color we need, we must know the exact correct amounts of red, green and blue light, and to be able to accurately produce them somehow. The computer monitor CRT is the most widely used example of this additive RGB system.

In the computer, RGB digital color data is often coded using 8 bits to represent the relative amounts of each primary. Thus with 8 bits for the 3 primaries (RGB), it becomes "24-bit color." Each primary has a decimal value in the range of 0–255. This type of image data is sometimes refered to as "RGB data" or an "RGB file" or "mode." This type of data has the advantage that it is immediately compatible with the way computer monitiors and TVs work.

At first thought, this all makes sense and it seems straightforward that we'd be able to create the Munsell color we want, if only we knew the formulas. Therefore, one problem with RGB is to determine these correct formulas for the mixtures of RGB light. This leads to two more problems. First, the "lights" are not always the same. Each CRT, for example might have slightly different red, green, and blue "phosphors" used to create light. Second, even if all of the RGB lights on all monitors were exactly the same, the intensity of those lights for a given value of 0-255 is different. And this is only the beginning.

Sounds hopeless, doesn't it? If the goal is to exactly match a color, such as a Munsell paint chip, it is often inadequate. If the goal is to only give an "idea" or an approximation of color for creative purposes, then the system works fairly well. CRTs and the RGB system are only as good as the attention to all of the details in the image reproduction system, that is, capture, processing, and output. However, it is a fact that even with the maximum amount of care and calibration of the entire system, RGB monitor color can rarely be relied upon to accurately reproduce colors exactly. Be careful.

CMYK

If reproducing colors using the additive RGB system is difficult, then what about the subtractive CMY system? Photographers, printers, artists, and others use it daily to reproduce color on paper or other white surfaces. If done properly, it works fairly well to represent and reproduce original colors. As we've explained above, after the ink, paint or dye absorbs their share of the white light spectrum coming from the paper, what remains is R, G, and B, which enters the eye. The secret, and the problem to be solved is to somehow be able to calculate the correct amounts of CMY needed for each color. In most color systems, RGB filters are used during the capture or input phase of the color preproduction process.

These filters essentially replace or simulate the human vision response, as if someone were actually viewing the original. This trick is called "separating." Throughout color reproduction systems, the many various forms of records of this RGB filtering are often refered to as "separations." In printing, the records used just before output, which contain the calculated "recipes" for the correct amounts of CMY (and K-black) ink to be placed onto the paper are called the separations. The separation films usually have halftone dots at this stage of the process. (Sometimes, the film step is eliminated and separations are written directly to the printing plate.)

When C, M and Y inks are placed in the same area, theory predicts that all of the spectrum should be subtracted, and the observer should see black. In fact, the observer will see a dark brown which may or may not be called black. The reason for this is that all inks, dyes, and paints are not "perfect" subtractive filters. (That should not be a surprise.) The flaw is that all inks absorb extra light which they theoretically should let pass, and they also do the opposite. In other words, they let colors of light pass which theoretically should be absorbed. This results in "unwanted" color, and is one reason a perfect black can't be made from CMY. Therefore, we use black inks with the colors to compensate for this phenomenon. Black ink is also used to boost the density of dark areas without resorting to larger total amounts of ink, which can cause printing problems.

CIELAB

With the above explanations and discussions, you can probably begin to see the problem with trying to achieve perfect color. First, we don't fully understand or agree upon color science and theory, even though we've come a very long way. Second, it is essentially impossible to "capture" color exactly like the human vision system can do it. Third, it is difficult to translate, compute, and keep track of (process) all of the color information that is captured, even with computers. And finally, both the RGB and the CMYK systems that humans have devised to ouput and actually reproduce originals are also lacking in terms of color. What all of this means for us is not hopelessness and despair. It simply means that we are attempting something which is not simple or trival, and that we must do everything we can do to put every link of the chain in place as best we can.

The CIE was established in 1931 and the abbreviation stands for Commission Internationale de l'Eclairage, which in turn stands for The International Commission on Lighting. It is a "standards" organization. At the simplest level, they saw the many problems in color specifications, communications, and reproduction. They took a new approach, in an attempt to fix the problems. Their new approach is still used in a modified form today, and is the foundation for the best we can do in dealing with the "color monster."

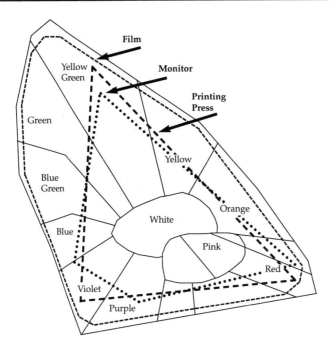

The concept is simple: a "standard observer," viewing colors under standard lighting conditions, who speaks a common language that we can all understand—the language of numbers. Sounds reasonable, right? So, who is this person?

CIE and the ICC and other spaces (for instance, RGB). Remember: they all describe the same thing.

Color matching systems (Pantone, etc.)

A very popular way to discuss color that uses a visual system is the swatch books used in the creative side of the graphics business. A unique problem with color printing was how to describe a particular color to a printer while not being able to see what the color would look like printed. This stems from the fact that everyone views color differently and has a different set of memory color that they refer to when describing color. So swatch books came out, such as Focolotone, Truematch and Pantone color matching systems. Pantone was the the one who invented the use of these color swatch systems.

These are two main types, one used for spot color printing where a special ink is used instead of the the traditional four-color process inks. Spot colors are often added in addition to the four-color process inks. Also these color matching systems have process color sets so designers can pick a particular color out of these swatches which have a reference number like Pantone CV18 regardless if it is a spot or process color. This allows the color to be specified to the service provider showing the exact color that is needed and there are no problems communicating color because each side of the process is using the same set of colors. So it is much easier to match a job to the designer's specification.

These sample books come with thousands of color combinations, different stock and ink sets such as metalics, fluorescence, and pastel. This system helps in taking the guesswork out of what a particular color will look like because they allow very close comparisons to see what they will look like approximately. These swatch books are needed when these matching systems are being used in an application program such as QuarkXPress. When the job is being created, the swatch books allow the designers to choose the color they want in the computer system, but they are looking at the monitor, which we know not to trust. So the swatch book is used to see what this color will look like printed on a particular substrate (paper).

These color matching systems are in all the major page layout and illustration programs which allows the user to easily choose whatever matching system that they want to use., depending on what system the service provider uses. A word of caution: if these swatch books aren't updated regularly at both ends, the designer and printer, there will be problems communicating what you want. This is because colors are added, numbers change, and as they age the colors fade, changing the appearance of the color.

Because of the human perception system, color is viewed differently from individual to individual and is affected by surroundings and lighting. All three of these conditions add variability in evaluating color, and especially when looking at proofs or at the actual printed job. This variability makes it almost impossible to view the identical work when a designer has one set of viewing conditions and the pressroom another. They will see the color differently and this will cause problems in discussing the color. This is especially a problem when people are dealing with critical color that will make or break the look of a job. If these decisions are being made under different viewing conditions, there is no way for the color to match the printed piece. Viewing color must be standardized so when people are viewing color they are under the same conditions, which makes it easier to communicate color to the client and to the prepressroom.

Back to some techie stuff for a minute:

RGB color model
A cube with RGB values on opposite corners

The CMYK model
Same as a RGB color cube
CMY values are on the opposite corners of the complementary RGB colors

The HSV color model
Hue (color of the color)
Saturation (how much of the color)
Value (general lightness and brightness)

CIE and L*a*b* or L*c*h*, XYZ, XXY, etc.
An attempt to create a uniform color space
The XYZ space is more linear and L*a*b* is more abstract and three dimensional

Completing the color transform
Here is an example of how many transformations happen in a color workflow:
RGB of scanner to L*a*b* (profile connection space)
To RGB of monitor to L*a*b* (profile connection space)
To CMYK of application to L*a*b* (profile connection space)
To CMYK of output device

Viewing

Standards are set up specifying the lighting and the viewing conditions for viewing color. The only part of the system that can't be controlled is the human observer, because every observer of color views color differently due to physiological and psychological conditions such as memory colors which associate certain objects with a particular color. Everybody has a little different idea of what green grass is supposed to look like and viewing colored objects in a standardized environment takes a lot of the variability out of the system.

Standard lighting

Lighting is the most important component of standardized viewing because the same proof viewed under tungsten, fluorescent, and incandescent lights will all appear different even thought the proof is the same. This difference due to lighting has caused a standard to be used known as D5000 or D50 lighting, measured in Kelvins, and it is specified at 5000 degrees Kelvin. Surroundings also affect how color is perceived as having a standardized background also takes another variable that could influence how color is seen by an observer. A standardized viewing background is one that is a neutral gray. These standards are often met by using a viewing booth that has D50 lighting and a neutral gray background.

Using these standards throughout the production process will help eliminate problems when color is being described because it will prevent the problems of viewing the same work under different conditions and having them appear different as a result. Applying these standards is a form of quality control that can easily be put into place in all parts of the production process that deals with color. One little inexpensive tool of the trade that is recommended is a metamerism patch which will tell the user if the lighting is D50 or not. This is because the patch will change color if the light is not D50. It is just another tool to control the the whole process.

High Fidelity color

The ability of the four-color process to reproduce RGB colors is limited. Many times the resulting colors are not what customers expect. Most of these times, the hue is correct but the saturation or the brightness is not satisfactory. Here is when High Fidelity color comes into play. HiFi color is the reproduction of images with more than four colors to achieve better results than the four-color process.

In 1987 Harold Kruppers introduced Color-Atlas, a seven-color process designed to use red, green, and blue along with cyan, magenta, yellow, and black in an effort to expand the color gamut. This method allowed the use of traditional halftone screening because it never takes more than three inks to produce a single color.

In 1990 at Drupa, Linotype-Hell demonstrated a seven-color printing process, and in 1992 Mills Davis and Don Carli established the Davis HiFi Project with the sponsorship of several industries. The advances in HiFi separation sofware, increases on RIP and computer speed, the introduction of stochastic screening, and the evolution of waterless printing promoted the interest in the HiFi Project.

HiFi color was first used to reproduce art, and it will affect those applications that need critical and accurate color. Potential markets for high fidelity color are some glossy catalogs, annual reports, high-quality books, trading cards, labels, packaging, maps, displays, posters, scientific imaging, textiles, and greeting cards. Some areas, such as image capture, are very well addressed. Images can be captured in RGB or CMY form, but capturing the optimum digital data is very important because it is very difficult to color-correct multiple separations. An alternative is to color-correct prior to separation. The image is separated using special separation software. There are three general forms to generate HiFi separations:
- Big Gamut CMYK process
- CMYK+Special Color process
- Pantone's Hexachrome process.

Big Gamut CMYK uses different approaches to increase the gamut. One of them is just the use of CMY additional plates to give it an additional hit to overprint areas of the CMY original plates. CMYK+Special process uses seven color separations, CMYK + RGB. As with Big Gamut, it also it takes advantage of bump plates to create overprints.

Pantone took advantage of the fact that in the United States there are more six-color presses than seven- or eight-color presses, and came out with a HiFi six-color process. Pantone Hexachrome process has a significant advantage over the other processes because it uses a six-color ink set of CMY plus orange, green, and black to achieve a larger gamut and increase the color saturation. It also has the most separation options.

Famous color conversions: *Living on the wild side*

There are six important criteria to achieve good color:
- gray balance
- tone reproduction
- tone compression
- color correction
- image sharpness and detail
- memory colors

Gray balance

Gray balance is the ability to reproduce a neutral gray of an area in the original as a perfect neutral gray. This means that there has to be a proper balance of Y, M, and C (get used to initials) in the separation when printing with the correct feed of a solid in the separations. A gray balance test is done to determine the correct level of usage of Y, M, and C to achieve the correct gray. To come to the correct level, a test using the exact plate, press and inks must be used in the same way it is done in production conditions. The gray balance test is referred to by other names such as neutrality test, equivalent neutral density (END) or tone reproduction and neutral density (TRAND) chart, which is the test target of the Rochester Institute of Technology.

Usually in a gray balance test there is a greater percentage of cyan and an equal but lower percentage of magenta and yellow. This is an important issue in the reproduction of color, because gray balance has a direct relationship to color reproduction. For when printing a neutral gray with the proportion of the tri-color mentioned above, one is expected to reproduce the gray faithfully. A typical gray balance percentage would be . . .

	Highlight	Midtone	Shadow
Cyan	7%	63%	97%
Magenta	5%	50%	90%
Yellow	5%	50%	90%

. . . when printing on coated stock on a web offset press. These figures cannot be taken as gospel, and will have be fingerprinted to individual presses and printing conditions. When proper gray balance is not achieved in the separation, while the grays don't reproduce faithfully, a cast of the color that is disproportionate to the gray balance will be seen. One may then experience a bluish gray, a magentaish gray, a yellowish gray or gray that has a combination of the faulty colors. While these problems can be seen in the neutral areas, the same will be translated in the other areas of the image where there are hues also. So, a highlight that should have been a white may end up being reproduced with a cast. A greater assumption in color reproduction would be that if you have achieved gray balance in your separation, then your color systems are calibrated well enough. It is thus more critical to correct one's gray balance first before venturing into any color correction activity. For if any color correction is done without doing gray balance properly, one is certain to be tampering with colors blindly, for you may never know the levels of your corrections.

Tone reproduction

Tones are the various levels of gray that can be seen between a pitch black and a pure white in a monochrome image. In a color image they are the various shades of CMYK that make up the different levels of the image. In addition to achieving exact match of colors, reproducing these tones is a challenge to the printer. It becomes so much more of a challenge due to the innumerable areas where variations can take place in printing. Therefore reproducing the tone faithfully as in the original is termed tone reproduction. It is important to note here that to achieve a good tone reproduction, there has to be a correct rendering of contrasts.

Contrast is the number of tones that can be found in a reproduced piece, be it on a photographic paper, film, plate, or a printed sheet. This is determined by the number of tones that can be found between the highlight and the midtone areas. A human eye detects the various tones found in this region better than the tones that are between mid-tone and shadow areas. The reproduction of correct tonal values is crucial.

Making the job of tone reproduction precise is an inherent difficulty in the printing process called "dot gain." This refers to the increase in size of a dot in the printed sheet from what it was on the film or plate. Dot gain occurs for many reasons on the press and the middle tone (around 50%) is the area where dot gain has the most effect. Which means a midtone area that is expected to be printing a 50% dot prints as a 70% dot. A gain in the size of the dot to 20% is happening here.

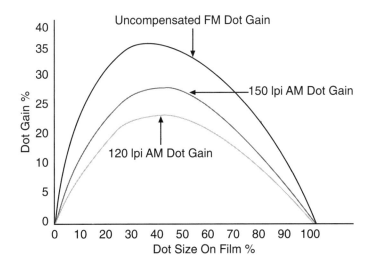

Dot gain is a reality in ink-on-paper reproduction, and must be calculated

When a dot gain of this magnitude happens on the printed sheet, it is quite natural that it has a direct effect on the tone reproduction. Translated, we will now be printing a deeper gray (70%) in the 50% area than we expected to. In other words, our tone reproduction will be in variance with the original. To compensate for dot gain, and to reproduce the tones correctly, the 50% dot needs to be placed in another location. That would take care of the midtone dot so that after printing and due to dot gain, the intended 50% dot would still print in the desired midtone area. If this compensation is done correctly, the tones would be reproduced correctly, with the right contrast in the image.

Tone compression

Like the dot gain we discussed above, we have another inherent problem in the printing process. That is the inability of the printing process to produce a solid density that may match an original. For instance, if the solid (shadow) density of an original is 3.0, then the solid density of the printing process should also be 3.0, to give a good reproduction. Unfortunately, even with printing on good coated stock using four-color process inks, we can achieve a maximum of 1.80 in the printing process.

To make matters worse, we also get different kinds of originals from the market, originals that have different density ranges. Typically a color bromide print (photographs) would have a density range of 1.90 and a color transparency would have a density range of 3.0, something that far exceeds the capability of the printing process. In order to reproduce the original as closely as possible in the printing process, we need to make certain adjustments in the separation process itself. So that when reproduced, we have a print that looks "quite similar" to the original. This adjustment is called "tone compression," even though the solid ink density does not, in densitometric values, equal the shadow density of the original.

Color correction

This term is so loosely used today that any change in color that is called for in the original gets generically termed "color correction."

While this is not totally wrong, it is better to understand the meaning and causes for color correcting. The prime reason why color correction is done is to overcome the anomalies in the pigments of the process inks, usually termed "hue error." In other words what hue error means is that every ink in the four-color process set does not reflect or transmit the correct amount of light.

Theoretically, according to the subtractive color theory, every ink absorbs one third of the primary color from the spectrum and reflects the remaining two thirds. Translating this complex reasoning in the theory, a process cyan ink would delete red from the spectrum and reflect the other two colors, namely blue and green. This combination of blue and green combines to give off what we see as cyan. Similarly, magenta absorbs green from the spectrum and reflects red and blue (magenta), while yellow absorbs green from the spectrum and reflects red and blue (yellow).

While this is an absolute theory, in reality the exactness with which each color is expected to absorb or reflect does not happen. Since the inks are contaminated, a cyan is not a pure cyan by itself. It has in it a certain percentage of magenta and yellow. This is applicable for the other two colors as well, though it is much less in yellow. The excess of unwanted color that each of the process colors carry is the contamination, and this needs to be removed. Correcting for these hue errors in the ink during the color separation process is called "color correction," and this is the primary reason that color correction is done.

Color correction is done by removing that percentage of magenta and yellow contamination in the cyan ink, and so forth in the magenta and yellow separations. The following is a depiction of the hue error in process inks.

Cyan	= Cyan	+ Magenta	+ Yellow
Magenta	= Magenta	+ Yellow	+ Cyan
Yellow	= Yellow	+ Magenta	

Magenta ink usually has the greatest amount of contamination with more yellow pigments in it. And yellow has the least amount of contamination in it.

As mentioned earlier, while some people refer to changing of colors to suit a particular need as "color correction," it should now be clear that the colors would have reproduced poorly in the first place even without having to adjust them for the specific need. This is why it is a good idea that the color separator is informed well in advance of the color set that is going to be used eventually during printing. This is also because different color sets have differing hue errors in their sets.

Image sharpness

A very important and noticeable aspect in the reproduction of good quality color printing is the sharpness in the reproduction. If the details that are in the original are not reproduced in the same manner in the original, there is every likelihood that the print will not be accepted by the client, even though other factors of good reproduction like tone reproduction and color correction functions may have been done well.

Image sharpness is directly affected by the way the image was sampled (during scanning) in the first place. If the image was sampled with fewer picture elements (pixels), there is a possibility that you would not have captured enough information in the picture that would eventually reproduce with lesser detail. While there are very many causes to losing detail during the printing process (for example, using absorbent stock), the separator should be made aware of these issues much in advance.

The separator can then apply certain detail enhancement techniques that are available in today's software so that the final image does not suffer from insufficient sharpness.

Memory colors

Color is a subjective issue that very often it is the subject of many a disagreement. This is because each of us sees a color differently, more-so under different lighting conditions. An important aspect when talking about color is memory colors. These are the colors that come to one's mind when you think of the subject. As an example we think of blue when we are talking about sky. We all know that sky could be orange or dark. But blue is the color that hits our mind as soon as we think sky. This is called "memory colors," as these are the colors that one's memory recalls from its directory, based on past experiences.

Memory colors are an important issue when we discuss color, because our minds have been programmed in one way or another from our past and our minds may interpret a color based on the memory color more than the color that our eye may see. Though this phenomena may happen without our realization, it is an important concept that we need to understand. A lot of disagreement in color usually happens more with the hue than with the color. During the press approval stage one gets to compare the printed sheet with the approved proof for the match in color. Although one is expected to literally perform this comparison, and is something we believe, research has shown that is not exactly what happens. The observer starts to compare the printed sheet in front of them to their memory colors. Since this activity happens so subconsciously, it appears to the observer that they are in reality comparing the printed sheet with the signed-off proof.

Memory color is an important criterion to be considered in the separation process for obtaining good reproduction. Since an average observer goes through the above-mentioned experiences in color judgment, it becomes important for the color separator to keep the factors of memory colors in mind when preparing the separations. For even though the separation may not be an exact match of the original, that could be what the client may be looking for, based on the memory colors that may be affecting the client. In such situations the task and expectations of the color separator become that much more challenging.

Steps in color correction:

Step 1
Highlight selection
Image-adjust-curve
Find an area in the image you want to correct
Adjust the curve to get desired results
Click OK

Step 2
Shadow selection
Image-adjust-curve
Find an area in the image you want to correct
Adjust the curve to get desired results
Click OK

Step 3
Cast correction
Image-adjust-curve
Identify a cast by evaluating a neutral area in the image
Use the gradation tool to remove the offending level
Click OK

Step 4
Tone correction
Image-adjust-curve
Identify a tone issue (highlights/shadows too dark or light)
Use the gradation tool to adjust the general brightness and lightness
  of an image
Click OK

Step 5
Color correction
Image-adjust-hue/saturation
Use the saturation slide bar to correct under/oversaturated colors
Click OK

Step 6
Unsharp mask
Filter-sharpen-unsharp mask
Adjust the values according to the image final output size and output requirements
Click OK

UCR, GCR, & UCA

Dealing with grays is a major component of color printing. Here is a short introduction to Under Color Removal, Gray Component Replacement and Under Color Addition. A more expanded section is the chapter on image capture.

UCR affects the neutral shadow areas of an image, not the entire image. C, M, and Y are reduced, replaced with an increase of black in the black separation. The values are chosen to comply with SWOP (Specifications for Web Offset Printing) specifications for UCR, and thus result in a maximum printing dot (all four inks) of 300%.

One reason UCR is used is to avoid press problems (especially wet-on-wet) due to excess ink coverage. Without UCR, total four-color coverage (that is, maximum dot, also called "total ink limit" in Photoshop) could exceed 300%. This can cause serious press problems such as ink tack problems (poor wet-on-wet trapping) or problems caused by slow drying (for example, set off), or plugging of shadows due to dot gain. With UCR, and the SWOP limit of 300% total, these problems can be reduced or avoided. UCR also means that the press makeready time is shortened and neutral areas print more consistently. Ink costs can also be reduced, since total ink use is less, and black ink can be cheaper than the color inks.

When you compare a UCR proof to a control, that is, a proof with no UCR applied, the neutrals appear cold, being slightly "warmer" in the control. Shadow densities are slightly higher in the control (due to higher total print dot). In the three color area, the neutrals are much lighter, due to the reductions in CMY. The highlights are not affected visibly, and the colors are closely matched.

GCR also replaces CMY with black, but it affects the entire image. In color areas, the "gray component" or "unwanted color"of three-color mixtures is removed, along with an equal amount of the other two wanted colors. This "extracted" CMY is replaced by black, since CMY in equal amounts is a "gray component." The practical benefits of GCR are similar to those already cited above for UCR. Also, in addition to more stable neutral areas, GCR can also provide better color control in long runs, resulting in less hue shift. GCR is more powerful an effect than UCR since it affect the whole image, and often 100% is excessive.

The replacement of all of the gray component CMY with black can cause the image to become too cold. To compensate, less GCR can be used, or UCA can be used to add CMY back into the neutral areas to compensate for hue shifts and to put some warmth back into blacks and neutral shadows. A GCR three-color proof could be dramatically different from both the control and that of the UCR scan. In the four-color area, the black and neutral areas were much colder, without the brown hue. The black also was higher in density. There was a hue shift in the red fabric, but the other colors quite closely matched the original. There was increased detail. The three-color CMY half had very saturated colors, all areas were colored, it lacked detail, and there were no grays or neutrals. This gray and detail information would have been carried by the black separation.

Digital proofs

Color proofs are essential links between the designer and the print provider. It is a method of judging the appearance of an upcoming printing job before it reaches the press. A few years ago these proofs used to be exclusively analog but now, with the development of digital workflows in the printing industry, digital proofs became a necessity. Desktop publishing software is opening the doors for more creative ideas. Graphic artists and designers now have the tools to manipulate images in their own computers. Such capabilities increase the necessity to observe their jobs much earlier in the process to correct errors without the high costs associated with film, chemicals, and proofing materials. The desktop revolution and the introduction of new digital proofing technologies have prompted the development of a variety of possibilities for color and text proofing. New proofing systems include liquid inkjet, color laser, thermal wax transfer, dye sublimation, and continuous inkjet printers, among others. Understanding the practical applications and the limitations of each one of these technologies is very important to evaluate the results of a specific proofing device.

Another advantage of the use of digital proofing systems is the possibility of approving a design in different locations, using digital networks instead of postal or shipping services, saving time and money. But the most important thing to take into account when evaluating a digital proof is to know how the process that generated it simulates or distorts final printing conditions. Today digital proofs are meeting the high quality required by commercial publications. Some approval systems, like KPG Approval, generate halftone dots, enabling the viewer to observe moiré patterns, diffuse highlights, plugging of shadows and excess amounts of any process color in specific image areas. Other systems that do not meet these characteristics but are considerably less expensive are being extensively used by designers and printers that cannot afford high-end equipment. These systems are more likely to be used as pre-proofs.

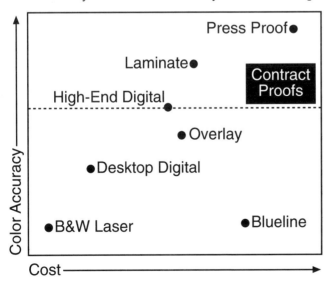

Color proofing has many alternatives, but the primary one is the contract proof which assures fidelity to the final reproduction process

Pre-proofs and proofs

Digital output devices can be divided in two major groups. The first group is those devices that produce prints which show the designer only a perceptible design composition. These devices produce what is known as preliminary proofs or "pre-proofs," also called "for position only." The second group can be referred to as contract digital proofers, and they give prints that exhibit accurate color and, in some cases, true halftone dots and screen angles. These technologies are not totally accepted by the entire graphic arts industry, especially by high-quality printers. However the increasing use of digital workflows and computer-to-plate, coupled with the better capacity of these devices to more accurately compensate for press characteristics and substrates, is promoting the adoption of digital proofing.

Graphic artists and designers must know what technologies should be used for each different need. Some technologies are accepted as pre-proofs and other technologies are accepted as feasible contract proofs. The technologies associated with pre-proofs are thermal wax printers (Tektronix Phaser); electrostatic devices (EFI Fiery and CLC); desktop inkjets (Hewlett-Packard) and color laser printers (QMS Magicolor). The technologies that may be accepted as contract proofs are dye sublimation printers (Imation Rainbow); continuous tone inkjets (Iris) and digital halftone devices (KPG Approval).

The main uses of pre-proofs are to judge the effect of an overall color design, to check the placement of design elements, to observe text flow, to check color breaks for spot colors, and to provide reference in design composition. In contrast, feasible contract proofs are used to judge the color reproduction quality, check the registration, and determine precise composition size.

Advantages of digital proofing

Because of the increasing number of printers or proofers available in the market, designers and prepress professionals have access to these technologies now more than ever. The price range of these devices is from less than $1,000 to $250,000. Furthermore, the capacity of digital proofing to produce proofs at any stage of the process contrasts with conventional methods that are capable of producing a proof only after the film is processed. Making films for conventional proofing methods can take a few hours. With digital approval systems, the time to make a proof varies from one minute to 30 minutes for higher quality systems, like Kodak Approval or Iris 5015. The cost associated with conventional proofs includes film, developers (chemicals), and special proofing base sheets. These materials are far more expensive than the total amount of toner, wax crayons, special substrates, and color transfer rolls used by digital devices.

Proofing before film output

Working with conventional workflows implies that proofs are only possible after film is output from an imagesetter. If these films are considered incorrect after proofing, the costs of producing new proofs imply new films and more time to produce them and this is neither practical nor inexpensive. With digital proofing systems you can obtain the proof you want without the costly film and time.

Remote proofing sites

On occasions, the same job has to be proofed at different sites. For example, if the project is to be printed at various locations or the design has to be evaluated by a client with more than one office or by a group of people at different locations, the same digital file is used for all of them. The results will be the same as long as the different machines are calibrated to the same standards required by the prepress provider or the printer. This remote proofing approach is used not only for midrange or high-end proofers but also for low-end devices; this is helpful for designers in different locations in making decisions about imposition or page layout. This strategy also avoids costs and turnaround times associated with express mail.

Registration

Misregistration is not a concern in digital printers or digital proofers. In conventional proofs, however, it is common to find some registration problems. Registration problems occur because conventional proofs are made superimposing four laminate overlays, each one with one process color. The laminate overlays are aligned according to the "eye" of the printer or technician, which also brings variability to the process. Digital proofs eliminate this human factor.

Printing conditions

Printing conditions refer to the characteristics of the press and consumables that will be used for the final production. Characteristics like dot gain, substrates, and ink are to be taken into account during the proofing process. Conventional proofs, however, do not have enough capacity to adjust to all these printing characteristics. In contrast, digital proofs are controlled by calibration software that compensates more accurately for dot gain and substrate and ink characteristics. Most digital printers can use different kinds of stocks, which allow them to simulate real substrate conditions.

Conventional proofs are limited to a few substrates, with different degrees of whiteness, on which it can perform a proof. Additionally, only digital printers can proof a stochastic screening process. Stochastic screening processes use spot/dot sizes so small that they cannot be resolved by the materials used in conventional proofing.

Disadvantages of digital proofing

Although the printing industry is now moving towards the implementation of computer-to-plate technology with offset lithography, many printers still use imagesetters and films to make their printing plates. If a digital contract proof is being used by one of these printers, special care must be given to the film, to avoid mishandling, scratches, or fingerprints that could alter its quality or performance.

The raster image processor and its software determine the shape of the dots and the screening characteristics that produce the final film halftone screens on the imagesetters. It is very probable that the digital printers' raster image processor will produce different screen patterns compared with the ones produced by the imagesetter's.

This can cause color inconsistencies and image fidelity differences between proof and printed piece. Inconsistency problems can occur even if the proofing system produces halftones, due to differences in screening patterns. Sophisticated software is available to adjust differences in color or image accuracy and match the final press sheet. Digital workflows depend on digital files. If a file is altered, unintentionally or intentionally, the color, design element space, and graphic characteristics data are very likely to cause problems. Similarly, if file data is modified after a digital proof is done, the following proof or film results will differ from the first proof. Therefore, special attention must be given to the manipulation of these files to keep track of all the changes that are made.

Acceptance of digital contract proofs

Digital proofs are facing the same acceptance problems that conventional methods like DuPont's Cromalin faced a decade ago. These proofing systems had a slow acceptance at the beginning but then they were fully accepted to the point that today they have become almost a standard in the industry. With new digital workflows and the introduction of CTP technology, the need for digital proofs is growing in almost every segment of the printing industry. However, the process of adaptation to this technology is slowed by the human nature of printers.

Many printing companies and their customers are still reluctant to adapt to this technology, some because they are natural conservatives and some because they just do not cope well with all the changes. The first area of the industry to accept digital contract proofs was gravure printers. Gravure process does not use films to create images so it never had films to make proofs. For that reason, gravure printers embraced digital proofs very quickly.

The acceptance of contract digital proofs in the field of offset lithography is determined, on one hand, by the type of digital prepress process and, on the other hand, by the quality requirements of the job being printed. Digital prepress, based on the process, can be divided into two types—one uses imagesetters and film output while the other is a computer-to-plate system. In terms of quality, each process can be divided into three categories.

The highest quality level, which requires more color accuracy and image fidelity, is just beginning to accept mostly halftone digital contract proofs, which is considered to be accurate enough for these reproductions. In a midrange to high quality printing, which involves periodicals, books, and several commercial printing applications, computer-to-plate systems are also being used extensively. On this quality level, digital proofing is enjoying broad acceptance. Halftone-based as well as continuous inkjet proofing constitute the commonly used proofing methods.

Finally, in the printing that requires the lowest color accuracy level, like newspaper advertisements, magazine inserts, etc., digital proofs have found more acceptance than in other levels. The devices used are the cheapest ones (dye sublimation and inkjet printers).

Considerations for four-color process printing

Four-color process jobs reproduce spot color by combining cyan, magenta, yellow, and black. Digital proofing systems must be calibrated with the press on which the final job will be printed. Custom or spot color created by computer software will be displayed using the four process colors unless these applications are printed directly from the illustration program. When the application is imported to a pixel-based program, like Adobe Photoshop, spot colors are automatically converted into CMYK colors. Lower quality stocks such as periodicals affect enormously the quality of color images due to the great ink absorbency of these substrates. These factors have to be taken into consideration even where the proofing system is calibrated to a specific press or printing process.

Influences on image quality

Printer maintenance

Maintenance of digital printer devices has an important influence on the quality of the reproduction. The maintenance task is more or less difficult according to the complexity of the device. A more complex device needs professional service. This activity is directly related to the replacement of consumables like toner cartridges, developer cartridges, photoreceptive drums and belts. For example, as toner colorants are consumed, the densities of text and images are reduced. As parts become dirtied, chances are that colors will become dulled. In the case of laser printers, the dirtiness of the photoreceptive drum will produce casts over the reproduction.

Some devices are equipped with self-cleaning features; however when needed, maintenance for these machines can be done only by skilled technicians. Midrange and high-end devices require the establishment of regular maintenance schedules to assure their higher color and image qualities and repeatability capacity. Repeatability is the capacity to repetitively print consistent quality output. Only by regular maintenance can output repeatability be achieved.

Viewing conditions

The light source under which proofs and general color images are observed has an enormous impact on their appearance. Proper light and a proper surrounding environment are needed to judge contract proofs and, in some cases, pre-proofs. Some considerations in this regard involve the following concepts:

Metameric colors. If the colors of two monochromatic objects match under one light condition but do not match under another light condition, the two colors are considered to be a metameric match. They can match, for instance, under incandescent and halogen light but not under fluorescent light.

Whatever the situation could be, it calls for the use of standardized light conditions or for the use of a constant light source while evaluating proofs, prints, or transparencies. The use of constant light throughout the entire graphic arts process contributes to color accuracy and quality and avoids confusion during the creative and production processes.

Black bodies. The whole concept of standardized lighting conditions is based upon the color temperature of a light source. A black body is defined as a hollow chamber whose color depends on its temperature rather than its composition. The color of black bodies changes with changes in temperature. When unheated, their color is black. When the temperature of these objects is raised to 5000K, a black body displays a white light which is equivalent to the light that the human eye perceives as daylight. This white presents a balance between the amount of the primary bands of the visible spectrum—that is red, green, and blue. Due to its color balance, a 5000K light source is extremely important for viewing artwork and color reproductions. An object illuminated with this kind of light is considered to be neutrally illuminated.

The use of different sources of light can affect the appearance of a colored object. For example, a blue object will appear to be deeper bluer and greener under fluorescent light due to the lamp's excess of blue and cyan colored light emission. The 5000K light source is a standard. It was developed by the American National Standards Institute (ANSI) and is the standard lighting source under which artwork, proofs, and press sheets are viewed. A 5000D lamp displays the same color temperature as a black body at 5000K, this kind of light emulates what the human eye perceives as a sunny, bright day. The letter D stands for "daylight." All bodies exposed under these conditions are neutrally exposed, which is very helpful for detecting image inaccuracies.

The viewing booth

A viewing booth consists of a 5000D-equivalent light source placed inside of a booth painted a neutral gray. The environment, or the surrounding space where the booth is located, also has an important influence on viewing conditions. Its light should be lower than the booth light, and it should also be gray. The reason for this is that any colored object inside the room will reflect some light over the objects being observed, altering their color characteristics.

The human factor

Opinions about image quality always differ from person to person. Standard viewing conditions were created to narrow those differences. However there are still other human factors that interfere with the judgment of a printed piece or proof. Memory colors are those colors associated with objects that our mind tells us should have a certain appearance. The green of the grass, the red of the apple, the blue of the sky are examples of memory colors. Different people may have different opinions about the appearance of these colors. It is important that there be an agreement among those people judging color accuracy in regard to memory colors.

Influence of artwork borders

Copy framed with a heavy dark border gives the impression of having more contrast or brightness. On the other hand, light borders tend to display less contrast or brightness. If an artwork is mounted in a posterboard, the posterboard should be neutral gray, otherwise, it can affect the contrast perception of the color. It is important to keep in mind this influence when for any reason the print being observed has a border of any kind.

Adjustment to the light source

The human eye has to be allowed to adjust to the lighting conditions. It could take a few minutes for the human eye to adapt from dark lighting conditions to lighter conditions. If we do not allow this to happen, our color perception can change during the observation process.

Color summary

Digital terminology and tips

- Pixel means picture element
- Spatial resolution is the number of image pixels per unit in a horizontal and/or vertical direction. This is expressed in ppi or epi.
- 1 millimeter (mm) = 1/1,000 meter
- 1 micron (μ) = 1/1,000,000 meter
- 1 nanometer (nm) = 1/1,000,000,000 meter
- Wavelength of light = 350–700 nm or 0.35–0.7 micron
- Bit (b) - one bit
- Byte (B) - eight bits

What is density?
- Lightest and darkest range that comes from a substrate or image; 0.0 means completely clear; 4.0 means utterly opaque
- Density of 1.0 = (10-to-1 ratio)
- Density of 2.0 = (100-to-1 ratio)
- Density of 3.0 = (1000-to-1 ratio)
- Density of 4.0 = (10000-to-1 ratio)
- All this means is PMT that has a density range of 4.0 is using 10 times the data as the one using 3.0
- Lost data is usually lost in the shadow detail

Some issues that contribute to colors not matching
- Different input devices creating different output values
- Monitor adjustments
- GCR and UCR
- Total ink coverage
- Re-mappings of unprintable colors differ
- RGB to CMYK conversions
- Differences in proofing device profiles
- Viewing conditions introduce flawed color judgement
- Density changes ink-induced hue errors
- Variable ink sets
- Paper color
- Dot gain

The nine golden rules of color separations
- Set expectations
- Specify tints as percentages—not Pantone
- Ask for help
- Garbage in = garbage out
- Process color cannot yield all colors
- Look at the fine type and the type in reversals
- Quote all work that is being done
- Tell folks what you want, not what you don't want
- Sign all proofs

Separations—black plate selections

- The black's highlight point: set the black's 5% dot to the cyan's 35 to 50% dot (the density is .70 to 1.0).
- Use this to enhance shadows in highlight areas (in the quarter tone areas).
- The darkest black printer should read 70 to 80% (do not exceed these values unless there is some sort of UCR happening).
- The mix of 95C, 87Y, 87M, and 60K will equal 350% ink coverage (easily printable on good coated stock).
- High-key should be set to 80%; low-key should be set to 70%.

UCR & GCR

- UCR subtracts neutral CMY values only (shadow areas).
- GCR affects the whole tonal range and does not just affect the neutrals (GCR does affect chromaticity).
- Improves print and visual contrast as well as print conditions.
- Removes CMY from areas where black is printing.
- Is advantageous because you do not need to use as much ink (cheaper) to produce black.
- Dries faster so you can ship the product faster.
- When applied correctly, UCR and GCR can roll back the final CMY densities as much as 60% to 70%.
- UCR subtracts neutral CMY values only in the shadow areas; active in shadow areas—good with images that have a lot of chromaticity.
- Use UCR because you don't want black dot in 3/4 tones or lighter.
- GCR affects not just neutral CMY but causes a chromatic change across the entire tonal range.

Six steps to successful color

- Select a highlight point
- Select a shadow point
- Cast correction
- Tone correction
- Color correction
- Unsharp mask

The steps for highlight selection
- Find area that should be white with detail
- Controls the appearance of the brightest spots of an image
- Makes the difference between a clean scan and heavy scan
- Watch out for specular highlights
- No dot is needed to describe the area (white paper is okay), like a reflection in metal glass or water
- Do not confuse this area with the starting point of a scan
- If you choose, you will have heavy highlights and mid-tones; putting a dot in the specular highlights reduces the contrast of an image
- Quickest way is to look at a white area and place a dot in it
- Don't forget about the specular spot
- Be careful of too much magenta in highlights, as it will make the highlight look pink
- Yellow alone makes the highlight turn greenish
- One way to balance the white is to show gray
- Most transparencies have a color cast; do you want to keep the cast, neutralize it, or cut it back?
- If there is a scene that has a lot of white in it as the important subjects you want to print—in order to neutralize it
- What looks white in the viewing booth should not reproduce white no matter what the scanner sees
- White is a memory color (you don't want to have pink or green highlights)

Methods for finding a shadow point
- Find the darkest part of the image
- Scan a gray scale strip and calibrate to the 95 percent swatch
- To get a shadow point that does not have a color cast make: cyan 95, the magenta, yellow in the high 80s to low 90s
- If there is no shadow, use the border of the transparency
- If the original is a color print, use the gray scale that usually works
- For high-key images, set the cyan to 100 percent, magenta and yellow at 92-95

The 3-6-9 rule
- 3% - slight changes
- 6% - medium changes
- 9% - massive changes

Note: this rule is good for tone and cast corrections

The six steps for tone/cast correction
- Gradation tools
- Working with a transfer curve
- Quarter tones (from highlight to mid-tones)
- Decrease to add brightness and contrast
- All tonal correction is meant to correct photographer's exposure problems
- Use neutral viewing

Tone correction
- Tone correction affects the general brightness/darkness of the image (no color shift)
- When the correction equally affects the CMY separations that is tone correction
- Tone correction is when you need to lighten/darken up the image a half-step
- Tone and cast corrections are good to perform when the highlight and shadow point selects are correct
- Increase tone correction to strengthen colors in a high key image

Histograms
- Each section on the scale represents one specific gray level (or color)
- If the histogram is smooth, then there will be good tonal reproduction
- If the histogram looks like a comb, there will be posterizations

The six steps for color correction
- Perform this step after the other four steps have been performed

- Color correction should not affect neutral, whites, or shadows
- Color correction is meant to affect highly saturated/unsaturated areas
- If you want to affect a very saturated color, move the lighter color value only 3 percent

Three types of controls for unsharp mask: amount, threshold, smoothness
- Sharpness increases contrast between neighboring pixels
- If there is a lot of detail in the image, use lower amounts
- Threshold (a point where an action begins or changes)
- All values outside the range will be sharpened/not smoothed
- High threshold will mean fewer smoothed areas, the result is a sharper image
- Sometimes you need to turn off the smoothness controls so you do not defeat the purpose (a product shot of a rug)
- Smoothness/radius
- Decreases the contrast of adjacent pixels

When to unsharp mask
- When the image's final print size is larger, use more unsharp mask; when smaller, use less
- When the image has lots of detail, use less unsharp mask; when the image has less detail, use more
- With people's faces, do not unsharp mask the cyan plate

Color is black magic

To print color we must convert RGB to CMYK, but to view it on a monitor we need to go back to RGB. To proof it, we go back to CMYK. Today we have an abundance of color management tools and color utilities but no one stands out as the one system that can do all that we want it to do. We try to capture color and print color by the numbers, converting and transforming from one device to another via Look Up Tables (LUTs) or Profiles or some other set of tables of equivalence. It's like translating text from English to Japanese and then to Australian. A better analogy may be that of making film dupes—eventually the numbers get fuzzy too.

We use the term RGB to mean any tristimulus color model, including CIE Lab, which is three dimensional in its representation of color. CIE is based on the so-called standard observer at some theoretical illuminant level, which could range from candlelight to atomic burst. We work in a narrower world and could never separate each and every viewer illuminant. The CIE Color Appearance Model ranges from 10 to the minus six all the way to 10 to the plus six, yet most of what we see is about 100 steps somewhere toward the middle.

Color is the most subjective area of publishing. We all see things differently, under different lighting and environmental conditions. Color is opinion-based. Spectrophotometry, the science behind the language of color, assures color professionals of getting exact color matches in design, prepress, and printing. While densitometers are useful for quality control, spectrophotometer measurements are more complete.

Many monitors use D65 illuminants that approach 6500 Kelvin. Viewing booths are at D50 or 5000 Kelvin. So what are we all really seeing? We certainly are not calibrating color for thousands or millions of print readers. We are calibrating color for one print buyer who becomes the ombudsman for the thousands or millions of eventual readers. You know who we mean: the person who signs off on the proofs. They are the only color model that matters.

To be or RGB

To go from RGB to CMYK we use chromatic maps for each and every printer. This requires non-linear transformations. The RGB color is a curved line and it must be mapped to a straight line (CMYK). The formula is intimidating. You go from RGB to a Look Up Table— LUT— to get an xyz white level and then do three calculations on L and a and b and then through another LUT to get C (which is 1 minus R), M (which is 1 minus G) and Y (which is 1 minus B). But that leaves Black. The old photomechanical scanners used filters to go from RGB to CMYK. Later color scanner makers sold their own flavor of black generation.

We spend a lot of money in the printing industry performing pre-separation and then trying to monitor and maintain it throughout the printing process. There is logic that says leaving the images in RGB and then making the conversion to CMYK in the RIP makes sense. An RGB file is about one quarter the size of a CMYK file and it contains more color information than the CMYK file. Let us begin now to research and implement RGB workflows for the new century.

Way back when

Color separation was originally produced with graphic arts cameras. Then the scanner came into use. That led to digital color and the ability to edit and manipulate color on computers. All three of those historical approaches were based on pre-separated CMYK workflows. We think there is a fourth generation: digital color using RGB.

We live in a multimedia world. The Internet browsers use GIF and JPEG. Interactive media uses PICT or screen images. Print uses TIFF. Television uses NTSC. PhotoCD uses YCC. The need to switch among multiple image formats becomes more of a necessity every day. Print is only one form of communication and images are being re-purposed routinely. Having a format that easily converts from one file type to another makes sense. Having a smaller file makes sense. Having a format with more color data makes sense.

Why have we not changed our ways? Printers and print buyers do not change easily. If it works, leave it alone. Pre-separated workflows almost work. Most of us are trained to handle them and there is a confidence in the ability to control what will happen. But the time has come to surrender the old ways and to start down the path to new ways. As an industry, we are considering high fidelity color with six or more inks on bigger and bigger presses. We are re-considering stochastic screening as computer-to-plate evolves. We think there will soon be new approaches to four-color process printing that starts with RGB and stays with RGB until the press. It may eliminate UCR and GCR as it linearizes color and creates a whole new approach to black generation. It may eliminate screen angles as we know them. Consider this the manifesto for a new age of color printing.

Chapter 6

IMAGE CAPTURE

In 1827 the Frenchman Joseph Nicephore Niepce developed heligraghs, the forerunner to the photograph. Photography is the technique of producing a permanent image on a sensitized surface by the means of the photochemical action of light energy. Light energy is used to form an image by exposing a photochemical, typically silver-halide (referred to as emulsion), creating a latent image on the film (emulsion on a supporting base). The light energy is brought to the film though a lens that focuses the light entering the camera body. The camera body is a light tight box containing the film and the controls that vary exposure and movement of the film. When the film is exposed, this produces a latent image that is still sensitive to light. The latent image is then developed by a chemical process that oxidizes the silver-halide crystals into a permanent, non-light sensitive image carrier. The image on the developed film can then be used to create multiple copies of only the image, scanned into a computer for digital applications, or processed to be used to create an image capable of being printed in a newspaper, magazine or other printed material. Modern photography is a highly developed form of image capture that will be used for years to come, but it has benefits and disadvantages as with any technology.

The primary benefit of photography is the ability to store vast quantities of information on a small piece of film. This information is in an analog form, meaning the image is produced by natural light waves that vary regularly and continuously over the entire visual spectrum. After the film is developed it can be archived or copied for other use. Another benefit is the relatively low cost of the basic capture device. A large format camera and lenses typically used by professional photographers is from $5000 to $10,000. The compact size of the camera and lenses make for a portable unit, so field applications are easy to perform. On the negative side, photography is still regarded a combination of an art and a science because of all of the variables involved in the production of an image. The variables in photography can not be seen in real-time because the film needs to be developed after all of photographs are imaged. These variables often make it necessary to take many photos of the same object using differing camera adjustments to insure a quality image for final use, creating waste in consumables, personnel and equipment time. The overall time involved in taking the photograph, developing it and making the image ready for production is extensive. Other problems with standard photography are the impact on the environment created by the chemicals in the film itself and the required developers. Many of these chemicals are toxic: For example, the silver-halide that forms the emulsion is a heavy metal carcinogen and a very expensive waste product. The most important drawback is that the permanency of the image would not allow for any form of image editing. With the advent of the personal computer, a new category of image capture has begun to address these problems.

In 1981 IBM Corporation popularized the first home or personal computer. These machines were developed as an inexpensive tool to aid in the basic needs of an office or home. They did not have the ability, either in power or software, to perform tasks involving graphics capture or manipulation. Not until 1984, with the introduction of the Macintosh built by Apple, was it possible to work with electronic images. Instead of using silver salts imaged by light, then developed to create a hard copy, the principles in electronic imaging involved a computer that uses a series of numbers to represent a digital or non-continuous point within an image; a myriad of these points is used to form the electronic image.

The scanner was the first effective form of digital capture. The form, quality, and cost of the scanner has changed over the years, but the principle on which they work has changed little. An image, usually a photograph, is placed within the scanner, either on a drum or on a flat piece of glass. Light is reflected off (or through, in the case of transparencies) the image onto a set of light-sensitive diodes that form the photo array commonly called a charged-couple device (CCD). The CCD is a semiconductor that produces an electrical output proportional to the amount of light striking each one of its elements. Each diode responds much like a grain of silver on conventional film, except that it converts this reading into a digital value that is then sent to the computer for storage and editing. Color scanning usually entails three individual scan passes, one each for red, green, and blue.

The number of diodes in the CCD is the limiting factor for optical resolution. Resolution is expressed as the number of pixels per inch. The more pixels per inch (ppi), the higher quality the image will be. A primary limiting factor in the number of pixels used is the size of the electronic file. With a color image requiring a minimum of 24 bits per pixel, the file size can become extremely large. For example, an image that is 8.5x11 inches scanned at 100 ppi will have a file size of 2.8 megabytes, the same size image scanned at 600 ppi would be over 100 megabytes. As the sophistication of the scanner and the accompanying software has improved, the use of interpolation of the scanned images has artificially increased the maximum ppi capabilities. This increase does still impact the overall file size, but can be used to generate output at a high enough resolution for the modern output systems including raster image processors (RIP) or computer-to-plate systems (CTP).

Early generation scanners were costly, slow, and had poor resolution, but that has all changed. A generalization of the classes of scanners can be broken down to: Inexpensive ($100-$1000) for home or small business use, mid-range ($1000-$10,000) for lower quality printing output, and the high-end ($10,000-$250,000).

Inexpensive scanners are produced by many of the home or PC computer builders. All of the low-end scanners are of the flatbed type. Items to be scanned are placed on a sheet of glass, much like a photocopier, then a lamp illuminates materials from below. The reflected light is focused onto the CCD, converted to digital output, and sent to the computer. Few of these scanners are capable of scanning over

600x1200 ppi optically and may have the software to interpolate. Because the typical enduser is a small business or home user, the maximum page size is only 8.5x14 inches. Transparencies may be scanned with only limited results. The dynamic range, or the ability to discern subtle shadow detail, is low.

The mid-range scanners are more often produced by printer equipment suppliers. Some of the more common companies are Agfa, Epsom America, Heidelberg, Konica, Minolta, and Umax. These scanners are still of the flatbed variety, but have much improved optics, CCDs, and software packages. Typical optical resolution is over 2500 ppi and interpolated upwards of 9600 ppi. Transparency capabilities are almost equal to the reflected in regard to dynamic range and color representation. Agfa has developed software they call Total Film Scanning technology to improve the color of negative scans. When scanning a negative the user selects from a list of film brand names and type to create an optimum scanner setup. Within the software is also an aid in proofing: Color Tune and ICC profiles are accessed to specify component color calibration (monitors, printers). The bed size is made larger for either larger originals or to allow for batching. Batching is when multiple images are placed on the unit at the same time. This multiple capture can aid in the speed with which images are digitized, because each image is defined as an individual, not an inclusive image. Mid-range scanners are used for projects not demanding extreme quality, but are popular due to the ease of operation. Versatile and feature rich, the advanced software still allows for almost push-button ease.

High-end scanners are very specialized and driven by proprietary systems. Most of the scanners at this level are of the drum type. Manufactures of this type of scanner include Creo, Heidleberg, Howtek, ICG North America, and Scantronics. Optical resolution can be as high as 10,000 ppi with an interpolated resolution exceeding 24,000 ppi. Such high resolution is most often needed when an original image is small, as in a 35mm negative, and requires enlargement. With the less expensive scanners, significant enlargement is not possible because of the low resolution and lower total dynamic range.

The optics found in the drum scanner permit transparencies to be equal to reflective images with resolution and dynamic ranges surpassing those found on many presses. Drum scanners use a cylinder that has the image placed either inside or outside of it, turning as the sensor is drawn down the length. The sensor type is no longer a CCD but now is a photomultiplier type (PMT) unit. This form of sensor device is very accurate in discerning color and has a dynamic range. Highly trained people are required to operate these systems at the level of complexity involved with the setup and digitizing of the images. Proprietary software and hardware driving the scanner means few people are trained for their use. Only high-end quality companies can afford to purchase and operate scanners of this level. The latest addition to the scanner at this level is the ability to scan in halftone films. Halftone images are specially developed images suitable for creating the printing plates for a press. This ability is called copydot, meaning an image can be captured on a dot-for-dot basis.

The trend in the printing industry is to create a digital-only prepress world. Through this need for only digital information, a weakness of the scanner is brought to the forefront: It can scan only flat objects that must fit on its glass or inside its drum. For any object that does not meet these restrictions, the user has to use an analog camera with film, develop the film, and either scan the transparency with a high-end scanner or convert the film to a print to be scanned. As with any other time, a perceived need brings about change. Designers developed a technology that combined digital scanning capabilities with the three-dimensional capability of the analog camera.

The electronic camera has two different families: still video and digital. Still video is for low-end home use and is more common than the digital camera, which is a relatively new development. The basic difference between the two is that the still video camera uses a magnetic storage device, such as a floppy disc, to produce an analog electronic file versus directly creating a digital file. The analog file is then converted by a software package into a digital file. The primary reason for the use of this camera is that the type of sensor array allows for an instant image capture analogous to the film camera. Still video cameras can be used out in the field to image still or moving objects. The system is of poor resolution quality because of the limitations of the sensor. The sensor technology is based on television capture systems, so it is limited to a horizontal line resolution of 525 total. In comparison, a 35mm negative would contain over 3000 lines. Companies producing the cameras are mostly producers of film cameras such as Canon, Minolta, Kodak and others. These systems are acceptable for home use or Internet imaging but are inadequate for publishing use, so the digital camera was introduced.

The first true digital camera was the Dycam, introduced in 1990 for about $1000. This camera was very limited, having only grayscale images with lower resolution than the still video. Today's cameras are averaging in price upwards of $60,000, imaging in color with very high resolution. The color image is produced using a CCD, as seen in the scanner, by making three passes over the object to be imaged. This object is usually placed in a light-controlled studio similar to a film camera studio. Through the use of software the image can be previewed on a computer monitor and any adjustments can be performed before the image is digitized.

The digitized image can be directly brought into many publishing programs including Photoshop, QuarkXPress, Photosuite and others. With these programs, an image can be manipulated and edited for publication. The advantage, and also disadvantage, is the image is fluid: It can be altered in as many ways as an artist chooses without any permanent change to the original file. The primary drawback to this system is the inability to capture real-time images. Only still objects under controlled circumstances can be digitized at this time.

In this new digital realm of desktop publishing, images need to get into these desktop publishing systems by being converted into some type of digital format. With the advent of the desktop publishing system, there has been a big shift from the traditional color separators doing image capture and color separations, with very expensive PMT-based drum scanners, to the designer doing all of these with relatively inexpensive equipment at their location.

This is a recent change because only the color separation houses had the capital and technical expertise to manage the kind of image capture and processing that we mentioned earlier. But as the desktop computer became more popular, the cost plummeted and the first desktop scanners hit the market. These desktop scanners however used a technology called CCD (Charge Couple Device) that was at variance with the PMT (Photo multiplier tube) technology adopted by the high end drum scanners. These CCD scanners became so less expensive that today one can purchase a CCD flatbed scanner for under a thousand dollars, whereas the drum scanners are well over a couple of hundred thousand dollars.

This change from the color separator doing the scans to the designer doing the scans came about with the advent of low-priced desktop scanners. With the advent of Adobe Photoshop, anyone could do the color separations themselves to convert their work from RGB to CMYK or whatever they need. While they are able to cut out a step in their production process, they are also cutting out the expertise of the color separation house for scanning. While the desktop scanners took scanning out of process houses, the bigger damage that this technology has done is in not creating the knowledge level that is needed to get a good scan.

These were the skills that were possessed by the process houses. One of the primary reasons for this dismal state is the low price at which one can buy a desktop scanner. When a knowledgeable and skilled scanner operator costs several times more than the cost of the scanner, these desktop scanners that flood the market are operated by people who have less formal training in the capture of images. But this situation has actually cost more to have the job done right because it was not done right the first time. This chapter will highlight some of the finer nuances of image capture using different kinds of scanning devices. We will also touch upon an emerging medium in image capture—digital photograhy.

Digitizing process

In almost every communication medium there has been a transformation from the analog world to the digital world. We saw the first of these transformations in the audio industry where audio tapes were replaced by Compact Disks (CDs) and in the telecommunications industry where the copper twisted wires that carried the audio signals were replaced by fiber optic cables that carry digital signals. The home entertainment industry, too, is going through that transition from carrying the analog information on tapes to digital information on Digital Video Disks (DVDs).

Being a key player in the communications business, little wonder that the printing industry is also shifting from the analog world into the digital world. The bridging of the two worlds came about with the scanners.

Digitizing

Before there were scanners, the image information was captured using process cameras. Therefore one can say that the primary task of scanning is to convert an analog image, which is in the form of light signals, into digital information (bits). A very important factor to good color image reproduction is the quality of the image that is scanned. Being one of the first stages in the graphic reproduction process, it is crucial that the image is captured well enough at this stage to be imaged later. In spite of the innumerable software programs that are available in the market, very little can be achieved from an image that is scanned poorly.

A digital camera is essentially a portable scanner. It captures reflected light and converts it into digital signals. Scanners and digital cameras are digitizers.

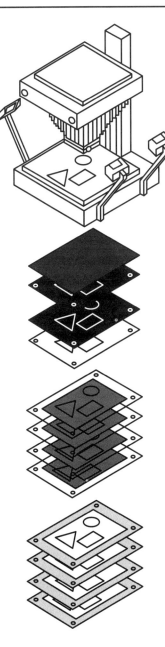

The graphic arts process camera shoots each separation through a different filter to get the four film negatives. These were then stripped into film flats and used for exposure to plates.

Today almost all image capture is done via electronic systems.

It is a myth that with some of the sophisticated software now commercially available even novice operators can achieve good quality scans. There is still the need for expertise to create a completely electronic prepress workflow—you need an electronic method for including images, whether those images are stock photography, product shots, line art graphics, or photographic images as prints or transparencies. In the past, these elements were scanned on high-end drum scanners that also produced film. The color separated films produced by these scanners would then be manually stripped into the rest of the flat.

Scanners

A scanner takes a physical image—either a photograph, a 35mm slide, a print, a transparency, or line art—and, using a light source, electronically converts that image into binary data that can be used to store the image on a computer. The type of scanner you need for your jobs depends on the types of originals you want to scan. Desktop scanners come in these major categories:

- drum
- transparency
- flatbed
- handheld

Desktop scanners do not usually have the built-in automatic scanning controls that traditional high-end scanners have. The scanner typically comes with control software, and many scanners come with color editing and manipulation tools that you can install on your computer. Some use Adobe Photoshop with a plug-in for controlling the scanner.

What makes a scanner?

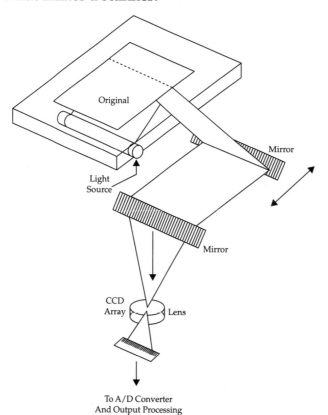

The fundamental principle by which a scanner functions is broadly the same, irrespective of the type or manufacture of the scanner. The copy (original) is illuminated by white (incident) light. The incident light, on hitting the copy, reflects (in a reflection copy) or transmits (in a transmission copy) the amount of light that is reflected off or transmitted through the copy. This light is sensed by small electronic devices placed in the scanner called detectors. Typically high end scanners use photomultiplier tubes (PMT) and the desktop scanners use charge coupled devises (CCD).

These detectors capture the image information in the form of picture elements (pixel) and convert the light energy (photons) into electrical energy (electrons). Most color scanners use 8 bits for each color channel (red, green, and blue), and are called 24-bit scanners. High-end scanners use 36 bits, or 12 bits per color channel. The quality of the final reproduction determines the scanning resolution.

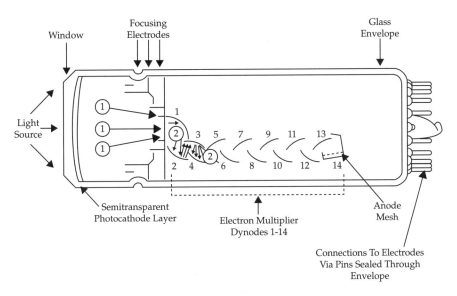

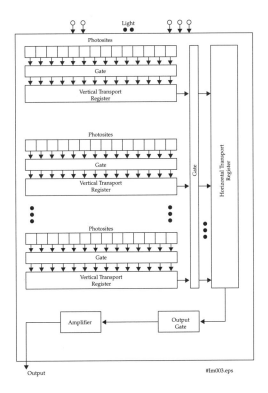

A photomultiplier tube above; a CCD below

Scanners measure resolution in dots (actually spots) per inch (dpi), sometimes called samples per inch (spi). The more spots in an inch that can be scanned, the higher the resolution and the more detail that can be captured. Another aspect of scanner resolution is the number of bits per spot the scanner sees.

Once a spot has bit depth it becomes a pixel. A pixel (picture element) is the smallest spot on the original that the scanner can detect. An 8-bit scanner uses 8 bits of binary information to register and store the value of a single pixel. An 8-bit scanner can detect 256 shades for each pixel. 8-bit scanners are only used for black-and-white images.

The types of scanners that are in use can be broadly classified into three categories:

- high-end scanners
- desktop scanners
- midrange scanners
- hybrid scanners

High-end scanners (aka drum scanners)

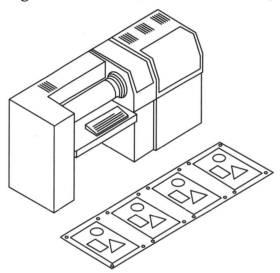

A high-end scanner outputs film—or data

These were the first of the scanners that came to the graphic arts industry. A high-end scanner consists of an analyzing (scanning) unit, a color computer, a screening computer and a recording unit. From the configuration of these scanners, one can make out that scanning and recording on film are done on a single piece of hardware. Earlier models of the high-end scanners were made as a one-piece unit, though the latter models separated the recording unit from the scanning unit for better productivity.

Analyzing unit

The analyzing unit consists of an analyzing (scanning) cylinder on which is mounted the copy. A multi-directional light source that converges to create a point source light is used to illuminate the copy. Depending on whether the copy is reflective or transmissive, the light source is placed, either in front (reflection) or behind the copy (transmissive). The light signals from the copy are analyzed by an array of photomultiplier tubes that pick up the image information. These PMTs are highly sensitive devices which capture fine information found in the copy. In fact, the employment of this analyzing technology clearly separates the high-end scanners from the other categories.

Color computer

Some of the functions that are done by the color computer include under color removal (UCR), gray component replacement (GCR) and detail enhancement. The image information which would at this stage be in RGB (red, green, blue) mode, gets converted into CMY (cyan, yellow, and magenta) mode. Black separation (K) is done by a mathematical computation. This is critical, as the printing process uses the CMYK color space, whereas the images that are captured in the raw form (photography) and those that are scanned are both in an RGB color space. Some of the functions that are done by the screening computer include identification of highlight and shadows, screening and tint laying information, screen ruling, screen angling, dot shape determination, linearization, magnification (enlargement and reduction), and modulation of the laser.

Recording unit

This unit consists of a recording cylinder with an exposure head facing it. In the exposing unit, the laser head exposes light onto the film. Once the scanner determinants are decided and the scanner is set to go, recording (exposing) takes place simultaneously while the analyzing head scans the image. Two of the more popular lasers that are used for recording are Argon blue laser and Helium Neon red laser. Only the older high-end scanners actually output film separations.

Desktop scanners (aka flatbed scanners)

Now you know why scanning came to be done at the desktop, attempting to do away with the huge high-end scanners. With desktop scanners the copy is placed on a flatbed from which copy is scanned, just like placing copy on a copier platen, which is one reason why they came to be called flatbed scanners. These scanners employ an analyzing technology called charge coupled device (CCD) to read the image information reflected from the copy. CCDs are linear in nature and are placed in arrays. Each array is sensitive to a particular level of gray. And there are the CCDs that have a tri-linear array, one each for reading red, green, and blue information respectively. Depending on whether it has a single linear array or a tri-linear array the scanner can be categorized as a monochrome scanner or a color scanner. A single linear CCD can read varying levels of gray while a trilinear CCD has the ability to read all the color information from the copy. The (CCD) technology employed by digital cameras and video cameras is the same as that used by scanners.

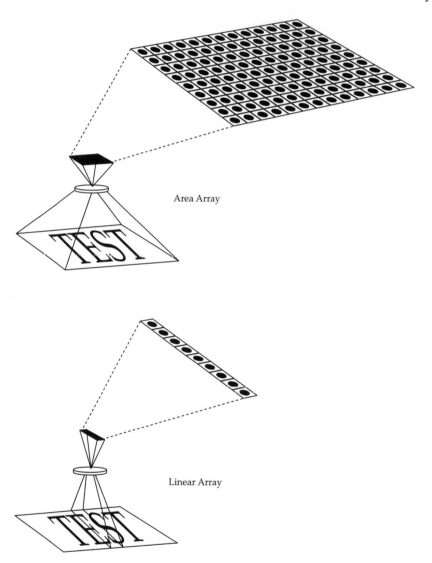

Area Array

Linear Array

Scanners can operate by way of an area array that looks at the entire page or a linear array which steps across the page, looking at each spot

Light sources used in desktop scanners are fluorescent-based. The copy is placed on the bed of the scanner face down (for reflective copy). The copy is illuminated from the bottom and the reflected light from the copy bounces on the CCD array placed below. The scanner captures the image information and sends it to a desktop computer for further processing. For transmissive copy there are special devices that accommodate the copy and illumination is from a separate head over the copy.

The second part of scanning from a desktop scanner is the desktop computer. Popular in the graphic arts industry for this purpose is the Macintosh computer and their clones. Personal Computers (PCs) are also used for this purpose. These desktop computers have the software that converts the image information captured by the CCDs from an RGB mode to a CMYK mode. UCR, GCR, detail enhancement, and color corrections are all done from this computer.

This information is saved as a file and sent to a Raster Image Processor (RIP), which converts the data stream into bitmapped data. The rasterized image is sent from the RIP to an imagesetter which actually images the data on film. As you can see, while it may appear that the desktop scanner is much smaller than the high-end scanners, in reality the desktop scanner by itself is nothing more than the scanning unit of a high-end scanner. It needs the support of a desktop computer, a RIP and an imagesetter to produce the "almost the same" kind of an output as a high-end scanner. The "almost the same" is because one should not assume that the output from a recording unit of a high-end scanner and that from an imagesetter are the same.

Advantages of high end and desktop scanning systems

One primary advantage of high-end scanners comes from using a drum as the method of scanning, which makes scanning much faster. And the other, probably the most important reason why they are called "high end," is because of the quality that can be achieved from these scanners. PMT technology is the source of this quality. Here are some of the scanning systems:

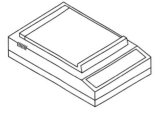

Scanners fall into a handful of categories, mostly based on their capability. At left is a simple flatbed scanner, color or black and white—today, mostly color. Handles flat prints with ease.

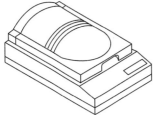

For slides or transparencies, you need an option that backlights the original so the scanner can "see" it.

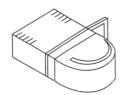

Or you can get a scanner that only handles slide or transparency images, but not prints.

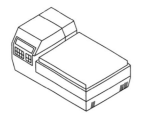

Flatbed scanners have been increasing in capability, and now compete with drum scanners.

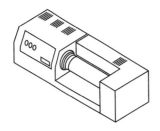

Drum scanners handle reflection (print) and transparency material, often at the same time.

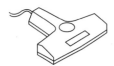

Lastly, hand scanners were popular at one time for text scanning. It only looks like a vacuum cleaner.

Where scanning takes place is as much an issue today as how scanning takes place. For many years, the price of the high-end scanner mandated a central facility that handled many scan jobs. As the price of scanners declined, the scanning process moved closer and closer to the creative originator. Today, low-cost desktop scanners with superior capabilities have allowed scanning at the point of document origination. But the file sizes have remained large and this has forced some users to use centralized scanning services applying the automatic picture replacement approaches like OPI and DCS (to be discussed later).

Midrange scanners

Midrange scanners were developed to combine the high-quality deliverables of high-end scanners and the flexibility offered by desktop scanning systems. Born was a new breed of scanners that began as flatbeds, evolved into drum scanners and has now returned to high-end flatbeds.

Drum scanners have their scanning done on cylinders using PMT technology but they are housed just like a desktop scanner; the scanning unit does not have anything more than the scanning function. Beyond this function, the color separation task follows the same path as with the desktop scanners.

Hybrid scanners

A fourth category of scanners is called "hybrid scanners." Well, they are not a type by themselves, but have been configured to be a system that links the high-end system to the desktop environment. The data that is generated after the image has been scanned (that till now was done on the high-end scanner) is linked to a desktop computer for image manipulations and other features that the desktop workflow allows. So these scanners essentially have only the scanning unit built into them and they look like a detachment from the recording unit of a high-end scanner. One reason that this system is advantageous is the size of the scanning drums that are available only in the high-end scanning systems. Some fine art scanning needs a large scanning drum/bed.

While the high-end scanners can accommodate large copy, they cannot perform all the image manipulation functions that are possible in the desktop work environment where low cost and high flexibility are now commonplace.

The underlying technology of color separation in a scanner is the same as in the conventional process camera—filters. Be it a PMT or CCD, the white light passes through the filters placed on the PMT array or on the CCD array and is separated into the CMY color space. While many of the scanner features discussed here appear to be sophisticated, they all have their roots in the conventional photomechanical color separation methods of the process camera era. Some of the terminologies used in today's digital work environments also derive from their traditional analog counterparts.

Drum scanners

Desktop (or beside the desktop) scanners evolved from the expensive high-end scanners used in service bureaus for the past few decades. The technology has evolved to a point where both the cost and size of drum scanners have come down dramatically, although they are still more expensive than flatbed scanners. Drum scanners can scan both reflective art (such as prints) and transparencies, from 35mm slides to 16x20 inch material or larger. Most are 11x17 inch.

Typical drum scanners can scan color and black-and-white originals at high resolutions (4000+ dpi). The more bits of data (gray levels) the scanner can save for an image pixel, the higher quality the scan. Typical drum scanners use 12, 24, or 36 bits per pixel. To scan using a drum scanner, you mount the reflection or transmission artwork on the drum, securing it with mounting tape and oil. The drum revolves around the scanning mechanism, and the scanning mechanism moves along the drum by means of a lead screw, an accurate method of transport used in all high-end scanners. It is also common to have the scanning mechanism revolve around the drum. The contact is immediate and there is minimal room for error due to refraction or focus. Most drum scanners use PMT (photomultiplier tube) technology, but CCDs are also in use.

A transparency scanner typically produces high-resolution (up to 4800 dpi), 8-, 12-, 16-, or 24-bit color scans of 4"x5", 2.25"x2.25", and 35mm film positive and negative transparencies. Some transparency scanners support the full range of resolutions and film sizes; others are restricted to 8- or 12-bit color, or only scan 35mm films or larger chromes.

Multiformat transparency scanners allow you to scan everything from 35mm slides all the way up to 4"x5" or larger transparencies. These scanners use CCD (charge-coupled device) technology most often.

Flatbed scanners

These scanners, typically called large-format flatbeds, range from 8-bit black-and-white scans to 36-bit full-color scans. Flatbed scanners usually are used to scan reflective art, although many also include adapters that allow them to scan transparencies. As with transparency scanners, flatbed scanners use CCD technology.

On flatbed scanners, the artwork is placed on a flat glass bed and the bed itself moves past the scanning mechanism. Artwork is held in place by mounting boards, scanning plates, or simple gravity, none of which is as accurate as the surface-to-surface contact of the drum.

How scanners work

Scanners use two types of technology: PMT (photomultiplier tube) are inherited technology from the high-end scanners of the past, and CCD (charge-coupled device).

For both technologies, the scanner divides the original image into a very fine grid, usually a square grid. Each cell in the grid is assigned a set of values, based on the main color and gray levels in that cell, using its red, green, and blue components (or a gray value for black-and-white images). For example, a single cell may be a shade of aqua. In this case, the information recorded for that block would be the values of red, green, and blue that make aqua (mostly shades of green and blue).

In general, PMT and CCD scanners differ in these ways:

- PMT scanners have had a greater dynamic range than CCD scanners; they can pick up more detail across a broader tonal range, especially in the shadow areas of an image.
- PMT drum scanners usually cost more than CCD scanners.
- CCD arrays contain many individual sensors, which can vary slightly in sensitivity. Newer CCD systems are engineered with better tolerances and compete with PMT systems.
- Most drums can accommodate several originals, so you can save time by batch scanning. Some high-resolution desktop scanners only can scan one original at a time.

PMT scanners

The term photomultiplier tube refers to how the scanner converts light intensity from the scan into electrical voltage. A vacuum tube takes in light, converts it to an electrical signal, and amplifies the signal; if it takes in a single photon of light, it may output the equivalent of hundreds of photons based on color depth.

To scan an original, you mount it to a clear drum and insert it in the scanner. The scanner has light sources both inside and outside the drum, and an analyzer head inside or outside the drum. To scan a transparency mounted on the drum, the light passes through the transparency to the analyzer head. To scan reflective art mounted on the drum, the light source reflects off the artwork to the analyzer head. As the drum spins at speeds of several hundred rpm, the light and analyzer move together along the length of the drum. A sensor scans a tight spiral path along the entire surface of the drum. The number of samples per revolution together with the speed at which the sensor moves along drum determine the resolution of the scan.

When the sensor detects light, it splits the light into three beams. The beams then pass through red, green, and blue filters, and then into photomultiplier tubes. The PMT converts light energy into an electronic signal. PMTs can detect differences in light intensity across a range from light to dark. This "dynamic range" enables PMT scanners to capture detail from the light highlights to deep within the shadow areas of original images. The scanner stores the electronic signal as binary data in a format that can be used by a computer.

CCD scanners

Transparency and flatbed scanners use CCD technology to capture images. A charge-coupled device is a solid state electronic device that converts light into an electric signal. Each array has thousands of CCD elements arranged in an array, usually a single row. Most scanners use a trilinear array that has a row of elements for each of the three primary additive colors (red, green, and blue.)

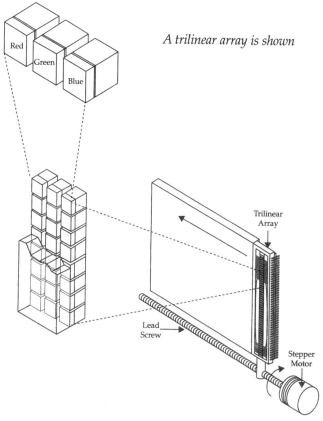

A trilinear array is shown

To use a CCD scanner, you mount the original on a glass plate or mounter, whether it's the glass surface of a flatbed, or a slide or transparency holder. The scanner shines light through red, green, and blue filters, and then through a transparency (or bounced off of reflective art) and into the CCD array. As the sensor moves across the original, the scanner "samples" a line of image data—actually each spot of a line. The resolution of the scan depends on the number of elements in the array, the size of the image being scanned relative to the size of the image as captured, the spacing of the stepping, and the speed that the sensor moves down the length of the original. All combine to capture the greatest amount of information.

Let's start a scan

Scanners can scan images at a variety of resolutions. Scanner software or photo image programs can perform functions such as enlarging the image or removing color casts. You do not have to, nor should you, use the highest resolution for every scan. After you make a few scans at the highest resolution, you'll realize:

- High-resolution scans take up a tremendous amount of disk space.
- High-res scans take longer to transmit to the output device and longer to process through the RIP.

What resolution do you need for your originals? The answer depends on how you plan to reproduce the image and the ratio of the original image's size to the final output size. If you plan on displaying the photograph on a web page, you only need about 72 dpi resolution—using anything higher produces unusable data. In fact, scanning for monitors is almost too simple. If you plan to print the image on newsprint at 1016 dpi, you will need more data. If you plan to use the image in a magazine that outputs full color at 2540 dpi, you'll need a lot higher resolution. You can use this formula to determine the scanning resolution for any original:

Scanning Resolution = LPI x Sampling Ratio x Enlargement Ratio

This formula works for all types of originals. The components:

Scanning resolution: It's better to have too much data than too little data, but this also means you may be carrying a lot of overhead. Image editing applications allow you to resample an image, which means that the software reduces the resolution of the image for you, which also reduces the file size. You can always reduce an image's resolution later, so you could start out with a high resolution and then downsample. You can increase an image's resolution, but you won't increase the detail unless you rescan the original. Going down is easy; going up is impossible.

If you typically reuse images in a variety of sizes, you could always scan at the same high resolution and then resample for each size or crop instance.

Line Screens: LPI (lines per inch) is the line screen you plan to use when outputting the image to film or plate. This value depends on the resolution of the recorder and its resolution is a completely different issue from scanning resolution. Jobs printed on coated stock might need a 133 lpi screen, while jobs printed on newsprint might need an 85 lpi screen.

Sampling Ratio: This is the rate at which the scanner samples data from the image, with 1.0 being a one-to-one sampling. To make sure the scanner reads enough data, use a sampling ratio from 1.25 to 2.0, depending on your quality requirements. 1.5 provides enough data for most commercial quality work. If the image is complex, you might want to sample at 2.0. If your line screen is going to be extremely high (200+ lpi), sample at 1.25 to reduce the size of the file.

Enlargement ratio: The enlargement or zoom ratio is how much bigger or smaller the image will be as compared to the original. If the final image is to be exactly the same size as your scanned image, use a 1 in this part of the formula. If your final image is twice as big, use a 2, and so on. If you plan on reducing the size of the image, use a fraction. For example, to reduce the size of an original by 90%, you would use 0.9 in this part of the formula.

Essentials for scanning

One of the most subjective areas in the printing industry is the understanding and application of color in reproduction. The key to applying color is the issue of light. What happens when there is an absence of light? Or there are degrees of light which affect color and tone. Because its effect is subjective, color can be interpreted in many ways by the observer, based on a number of factors, most of which involve light. A good understanding of color and related issues therefore is important to produce a good scan. The following pages cover important issues in color as they relate to scanning.

Finer aspects of image capture

While all the issues that we saw earlier are important for color separation, the placement of the highlight dot (the lightest area) in the original is of utmost importance. A good part of the quality of separation lies in the correct placement of the highlight area. Quality is affected by the wrong choice of the highlight in the original. For that matter, an original may not even have a highlight area. Where a wrong highlight has been chosen, in spite of later achieving good tone reproduction or color, practically nothing can be done to save the image. You may have to go back to the scanning stage and start the capture process all over again. All scanning programs let you define the highlight.

What is a highlight area?

The lowest density that can be found in the original that is white or is supposed to be a white is called the highlight area. The reason why we say "supposed to be a white" is that many originals may be carrying a color cast. This cast may not present a white as white but as the color of the cast. Also note from the definition that the area with the lowest density is not necessarily the highlight area. That area could be a light pink! To know exactly where the highlight of the copy lies is a very important step in capturing an image faithfully in the scanning process. It is preferable to maintain a white in the highlight area. Some originals may have a color cast and some may not even have a highlight area, so the task of assigning the highlight to a particular point in the original lies with the scanning program and a good operator. If the client prefers to have their original reproduced as is (that is, with the cast), then the highlight can be ignored. However, that is not the usual case, and clients insist that the color cast be removed and a clean, fresh image be reproduced.

Using a step wedge

The use of a step tablet or step wedge helps in the process of placing the highlight in the correct spot on the original. A step tablet is a neutral carbon dye transmission scale which has several steps of gray ranging from a pure white to pure black in density increments of 0.15. Pure white on the step wedge shows a density of 0.00 and pure black shows a density of 3.00. This wedge is used with copy that is transmissive in nature. Similar in characterestics to the step wedge is the gray scale that is used for reflection originals. These targets placed alongside the original can quicken the setup time in the scanner when determining the high placement. Another way to determine the highlight in the copy is to densitometrically measure the highlight area in the copy. Depending on the type of copy, a reflection or transmission type densitometer can be used.

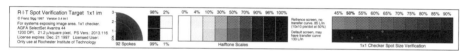

Highlight placement

Possibly the simplest way to place the highlight is to place it in the white area of the copy. But that does not really give us the correct highlight. Classical examples of problem images would be in jewellery and cutlery shots, where there are fine reflection spots. These spots gleam and throw out a reflection that does not have any details. Such spots are called specular highlights and should not be used as a determining area to place the highlight.

A good way to place the highlight dot is in the 0.30 density area of a step tablet that is placed by the side of the copy. By assigning the highlight gray balance values of cyan=7%, magenta=5% and yellow=5% (these numbers can be different, set to different systems) at the 0.30 density, we are forcing the scanner to look at the 0.30 density area as white. This again cannot be taken as the magic number for all originals.

If the highlight of the original is different from that value, we will not be accurate. So it is important that the highlight be placed at the correct density that the original carries. When the highlight is placed at 0.15 density for an original whose truer highlight is at 0.30, we end up with a reproduction that is too dark. Similarly, we can get one that is too light when the highlight dot is placed at 0.50 density area for an original that has a highlight density of 0.30.

Color casts

Color casts are very apparent in the highlight area, and are spread across the entire original image. The color cast is most noticeable in the highlight area of the original because our memory colors tell us which areas need to be white. And when they are not white because of the cast, we are able to distinguish them clearly. There is no corresponding ability to identify casts in the shadow areas because we cannot easily distinguish tonal color differences in the shadow areas.

There are several reasons why you get a color cast in the original. Some of them are:
- improper storage of the film before/after exposure
- improper lighting conditions when the original film was shot
- the photographic emulsion used "push processed" chemistry
- the emulsion was processed using exhausted chemistry
- the emulsion was processed using contaminated chemistry

The earlier mentioned technique, letting the color separator select the highlight point, works when originals need to be reproduced "as is." Then one is reproducing with whatever color cast may be present. By assigning the highlight gray balance values to a highlight area of the original, we eliminate the color cast. This is because the operator is telling the scanner to see the assigned area as white. This technique removes most of the color cast, but some remains in the shadow area. This may not matter, as the human eye cannot detect this flaw. It is an excellent way to remove color casts, but is something that the operator should not decide unilaterally, but in consultation with the originating client.

Shadow placement

Shadow placement (the darkest area of the image), another important step in the separation process, determines tone compression. Tone compression is essential in the separation process and shadow placement is the technique that facilitates this compression. Successful tone compression is the result of the placement of the shadow dot in the correct location in the image copy. The results of the gray balance test determines in which density area of the copy the shadow dot should be assigned. A gray balance shadow dot of

cyan	=	97%
magenta	=	90%
yellow	=	90%
black	=	80%

has to be assigned to a designated density area in the copy. Correct placement of the shadow dots is critical; a wrong placement of the shadow dots produces poor results that do not match the copy. If the shadow dots are assigned to a density area lower than that in the original, then there would be too much tone compression and the image is likely to look very dark. The contrast would be too great. Note that contrast is a factor that is determined by the highlight to midtone range. By placing the shadow dot in an area that is higher that that of the copy, not enough tone compression takes place and the resultant reproduction will look light and washed out.

Midtones

It is not possible to produce an exact match of the tones in the printed sheet to those of the original because one cannot put the same density of ink on the sheet as is on the original. Therefore, the art is to alter the tones during the separation process so that in print they would appear to be similar to the original. In other words, we try to match the contrasts in the original in the separation process. Research has proven that human beings can distinguish subtle differences in the highlight-to-midtone regions more than in the shadow regions, which is why the separation professional pays greater attention to capturing the highlight-to-midtone regions.

Fingerprinting the press

The printing process itself introduces several variables in the reproduction process. These cause a change in the tones that were created during the separation process. The end result could look very different from the way the separation was prepared. Therefore it is a good idea to understand the printing characteristics of the press before beginning the separation process. This allows for some compensation to be done at the separation stage so that the image eventually prints as desired.

This activity is called "fingerprinting the press," and it is a very important task that every printer should do. This information needs to be provided to the scanning operators before they prepare the films. Important in fingerprinting is that all operations done should be repeatable.

Keyness of the original

Keyness refers to the tonal values in the original and their locations. High and low key are the two kinds of keyness that can be seen in different originals. A copy that has most of its tones in the highlight-to-midtone region is termed a "high key" copy. A copy that has most of its tones concentrated between midtone and shadow is termed a "low key" copy. There is no issue when the client wants to reproduce the copy as is. When the client wants to achieve good tone reproduction, the separator must know where to place the midtone dot.

By nature, a high key needs more contrast, which means that the density range between highlight and midtone needs to be shortened. The separator would therefore have to place the 50% dot at a lower density value in the original. A low key original would need a longer highlight to midtone and therefore the midtone dot needs to be placed at a value higher than is on the original. By placing the midtone dot at the correct location (in other words, compensating for dot gain), you automatically have taken care of the keyness of the original. It is with some experience that one could determine where exactly the midtone dot needs to be located.

Color correction

Color correction is the process of compensating for the hue error in the printing inks. To determine the extent of this flaw in a printing system, a test target like IT-8 could be scanned in along with a normal transparency and proofed, using the proofing system that is used in production. These test targets are specially prepared originals and have certain color patches and fine targets aimed to be reproduced well in the printing process.

Special care should be taken to choose the proofing system so that the hue error in the printing system matches that of the proofing system. Otherwise, we would be comparing two different systems, and the compensation done in the separation will not do the image justice when printed. If this test is done with an Ektachrome transparency, then the settings done (after getting good results in the test) would be valid only for Ektachrome emulsions for that particular type of ink set. A change in any of the these parameters requires a new test to determine the new values that need to be compensated for in the separation.

Printing inks and hue error

We saw earlier that the printing inks are not pure in their pigment content and carry a lot of impurities. And we called those impurities hue error. This can be measured by reading the solid ink densities of the printed sheet using a densitometer. A formula to determine hue error would be:

$$\text{Hue error} \quad = \quad \frac{\text{Unwanted density}}{\text{Wanted density}}$$

Yet another way to determine hue error is :

$$\text{Hue Error} \quad = \quad \frac{M - L}{H - L}$$

where
H = High reading,
M = Middle reading
L = Low reading

Magenta is usually the most contaminated of the ink set having a hue error of 50%, followed by cyan which has a hue error of 33%, with yellow being the least contaminated of all with a 10% hue error. Note that these numbers are not universal and will be different with different sets (maybe in different batches, too). But the universal fact is that every process ink set has hue error. The extent to which it varies is what is different.

Scanner controls for color corrrection

Scanner controls depend on the type of scanner that the process house or the printer possesses. While the high-end scanners offer color correction controls on the hardware itself (though they are internally driven by software), the desktop and midrange scanners offer color correction features in the software. The following are the types of color correction that can be made:

- general (or global) color correction
- selective color correction

It would be appropriate at this juncture to understand the concept of "wanted colors" and "unwanted colors." Wanted colors are the colors that are required to produce a particular hue. For example, to produce the hue green, we would print yellow over cyan. In this case, yellow and cyan are the wanted colors and the color that is left out is the subtractive primary color; that is, magenta is the unwanted color. When a small percentage of the unwanted color is mixed along with the wanted color, it produces a darker shade of the hue. In reproducing fine detail, these unwanted colors add the detail. On the other hand, when we want to make a hue purer or saturated, we deduct a percentage of the unwanted color from the combination that produced the required hue. Another term that is used to describe the unwanted colors is "gray component."

General color correction

When a color is altered in the scanning process, it affects all other colors that are present in the image. As an example, if you want to increase the cyan to improve the color of the sky, all other areas that have a cyan in them, like green, blue, and cyan areas not needing the increase, are also affected by this change.

Selective color correction

When only a particular color in the image needs to be altered, then selective color correction is done. In the above case, only the sky areas of the image can be increased or decreased in a particular hue without affecting other hues. However, if there is an object in the image that has similar hue, it is bound to be affected. Almost all of the modern desktop publishing image manipulation software have the ability to do something called "fine field color correction," applying a color change to a particular hue in a particular object.

Detail enhancement

Resolution is a term that is grossly misused in the graphic arts industry. It is important to draw a distinction between the various terms that refer to resolution. They are:

lpi	=	lines per inch, which refers to halftone screen ruling
dpi	=	dots per inch, which refers to output device resolution
ppi	=	pixels per inch, which refers to resolution of the video monitor
spi	=	spots per inch, the number of spots the imaging device places to form a halftone dot

Detail is also referred to as edge enhancement. The theory behind this is that when contrast is created between the edges of two pixels, it results in the image being perceived as sharper. The reasons detail may need to be enhanced include high magnification, which enlarges the pixels and thereby creates an unsharp image; preferences by the author or editor, who may seek additional detail that may be lacking in the image; or simply that the image was not captured with a sufficient number of samples in the first place, which is something that cannot usually be repaired by adding detail.

In image manipulation software like Adobe Photoshop there is a filter called unsharp masking that takes care of image sharpness. Contrary to how it sounds, this filter actually sharpens the edge details. Unsharp masking as a terminology in the desktop publishing world actually derives from the days of conventional camera separation. In those days, color separation was done using process cameras with filters.

There were two kinds of color separations, called the direct method and the indirect method. Without delving deep into either of these techniques, we will explain the derivation of the term "unsharp masking."

O'Brien effect

A mask, which is another photographic material, is prepared in the positive form of the color separation negative. This mask is bound with the separation negative and a positive is shot. This mask is called the unsharp mask as it is actually unsharp in nature. What it does is create a sharp boundary between two areas that actually needed to be sharpened. Those areas would have been worked on earlier. This difference in a light boundary that is placed between two similar densities that existed in the color separation negative gives off a feeling of contrast in the final positive. This effect is called the "O'Brien effect." The O'Brien effect states that a dark border, placed between similar densities, will give the perceived effect of greater contrast.

Although there are no photographic masks used in the digital world, similar effects are created using the aperture in the scanners. The scanners have two apertures, a smaller aperture and a bigger aperture, the smaller one being the scanning aperture and the larger one is the USM aperture or Unsharp Masking aperture. The high-end scanners provide the option to choose from a variety of apertures. The smaller the aperture, the greater the detail in the image. In the desktop world, the programmers of the application programs that do this function electronically have given the same name of unsharp masking to the filter. Because there are no apertures in typical desktop scanners, the function of unsharp masking is done from the computer. The programs offer three controls to carry out detail enhancement. They are *amount, radius,* and *threshold.*

The sharpening function is offered by all the systems, but they all perform the function in their own way. In short, the conventional camera separation does it using physical masks, the high-end scanners perform these functions mechanically using special hardware, and desktop systems use special software to accomplish sharpening. It is important to understand that each image manipulation software offers its own way of performing the sharpening functions and it is a good idea to get familiar with the package first.

Under color removal (UCR)

Theoretically, when overprinting yellow, magenta, and cyan we are supposed to get a black. But from experience we know that this is not what happens. We end up with a muddy brown which is why we add a black to get that solid black. However we also do not print a solid of all the colors with a black to produce a black. Depending on the printing system, the separator chooses an ideal Total Area Coverage (TAC) value. This means the sum of the shadow dots in all the colors does not exceed the limit set by the operator. This is usually set around 300% (again do not go exactly by this number).

In a normal separation the shadow area would be something like cyan=97%, magenta=90%, yellow=90%, and black=80%. If these percentages are summed, they amount to more than 300%. Beyond a TAC of 300%, the black that the human eye sees is still the same as what it would have been at 300%. We only add a greater amount of ink over the given spot. This not only does not add any further value to the printed piece, it also causes additional problems in printing. Because of the unnecessary additional ink, there will be drying problems that could result in setoff, etc. Moreover, the expensive inks (cyan, magenta, and yellow) are used in an area where they are not even recognized by the human eye.

Under Color Removal (UCR) takes care of these problems. The color computer in the scanner looks at the neutral area and takes away the percentage of cyan, magenta, and yellow in areas that can be replaced with black. By doing so, the pure black areas in the original are printed with only the black ink, and the expensive three color inks are saved. UCR affects the neutral areas only and does not affect the color.

Gray component replacement (GCR)

Gray Component Replacement is another special function that is performed by the color computer. GCR is a term that was originally coined by researchers from Rochester Institute of Technology. It is also referred to by other names like achromatic separation and integrated color removal (ICR).

Originally introduced in 1984 by Dr. Rudolf Hell, this feature was incorporated in the Hell scanners. As a theory, GCR existed many years ago. The problem of implementing GCR was the computing bottle neck, as computation of the algorithms needed called for some powerful computers. Around 1984, Hell was acquired by Siemens, the German giant with strengths in computing. This acquisition helped Dr. Hell implement GCR and incorporate his feature in the scanners.

Getting to what GCR does, the color computer looks at the shadow area of the trichromatic separation (C,M,Y) and takes away the common amount that is shared by these three colors and replaces it with an equal amount of black. This may sound a bit complicated, but it is the ability of the color computer to do the compensation in black that would determine the quality of the GCR separation. Little wonder that the industry had to wait for a powerful computer system to work out the algorithms. Using GCR three-color separation lacks shadow in them whereas the black separation is very heavy.

This is very unconventional compared with the traditional separation, where the black separation is usually a skeleton black. Use of GCR calls for some constraints as different scanning systems recommend that different percentages of GCR be applied. However, the result of a GCR separation and the traditional separation should match. There should be no confusion that one produces a better result than the other. The advantages of using GCR will be felt in the printing floor alone.

Digital photography

As mentioned earler, an emerging form of image capture in the graphic arts industry is digital photography. We felt that even though we will not be able to cover the entire gamut of this topic, a good-coverage of digital photography would be very relevant in this chapter. This term could mean different things to different people. In the traditional sense, photographing was essentially done using a camera, films, and processing chemicals within a darkroom. With digital photography, even though the camera remains (though modified), other components like films, processing chemicals, and darkrooms do not feature at all. The images are captured electronically and processed in a computer. As Agfa puts it, digital photography is a migration from silver-based imaging to silicon-based imaging.

If that is about all there is to photography, what does this change in state of an image capture mean to the printing world? As we saw earlier, the similarities between a conventional camera and a digital camera ends with the camera itself. No films, no processing and no darkrooms. But is the camera itself any different? Yes, even though many of the components of a traditional camera are still there. Lens, aperture, shutter and the body are still found on digital cameras. But the camera which traditionally held film to capture the image has been replaced.

In order to record image information, a digital camera uses a CCD, the same CCD technology that we saw being used in the desktop flatbed scanners. The CCD has a number of elements built into it. This determines the resolution of the camera. A CCD that has many elements is expensive, which in turn shoots up the cost of the digital camera. But these elements are required to capture the image information. The more elements there are in the CCD the more resolution and better the image quality that can be expected. There are a couple of ways that digital cameras capture image on the CCD.

Static array CCD

Some cameras use a static array CCD, where several elements are arranged in rows and colomns. The image is captured in a single exposure. This method is fast and less expensive. The flip side to using a static array CCD is that the photographer is limited to the number of elements available on the CCD of the camera.

Scanning array CCD

The other digital camera technology is the scanning array CCD. As the name implies, capture of the image is done by a scanning mechanism. The camera will necessarily have to be mounted on a tripod. The camera scans the object while the scanning array CCD records the image information as picture elements (pixels). This is facilitated by an electric motor that moves in very small steps to record light. By this scanning movement of the CCD, smaller pixels can be recorded, and the elements used for image capture can be maximized. A greater resolution can be obtained using a scanning array CCD.

Resolution

Several low-cost digital cameras that are in the market naturally offer lower resolutions. They would be in the region of 307,200 pixels (640x480). While this could be acceptable for simple jobs, the more expensive digital cameras needed for professional photography can offer a resolution of 20 million pixels. A simple comparative of what these resolutions may mean, when compared with traditional photography: An equivalent of a fine grain 35mm transparency would have a resolution of 20 million pixels. Naturally these cameras are very expensive and are used by only the professionals. They also require enormous computing, storage, and processing capability.

Photo memory

The question then is how many pictures can I take? This was quite a simple issue when we dealt with traditional cameras. Depending on the film that you purchased, the manufacturer told you that this roll of film has 24, 36, or whatever number of frames that could be used to capture images. With digital cameras, the situation becomes different, with its capacity determined by the amount of memory that your camera has.

So, a dinky little $300 digital camera will have hardly 1MB of memory with a low resolution. That should give you around eight under-sized pictures. So, what do you do after that? Do you need to buy another camera, like in the case of a disposable camera? No, you will have to clear up that memory in the camera to shoot/capture your next round of image information. This means that every time you exhaust your memory, the file will have to be downloaded into your computer's hard disk or onto other storage media. Some digital cameras provide you with specialized memory cards that help increase the camera's memory capacity. These cards are not for permanent storage and the image will have to be eventually moved to more permanent storage devices. So, while we saved on films and processing, we will have to now invest in memory. Although it may be a wash as to whether we invest in memory or file cabinets.

Back to the desktop

Once the image is captured using a digital camera, it has to be downloaded to a desktop computer. Depending on the software that the camera offers, the images may have to be downloaded one at a time. However, some cameras are offering batch downloading, which saves time and effort. The images have to be decompressed as they are retrieved after downloading. Suitable software extensions will have to be installed in your computer to decompress the images during the retrieval process.

A filmless world

Several segments of the photographic market that were using silver-based emulsions have already moved to digital photography. Where image quality is not of paramount importance, and speed and convenience dominate a market's priority, digital photograhy has been a success story.

In spite of all the media hype about a filmless world, we are definitely not there. Digital photography is still at its infancy. Even though some very expensive cameras in the $28,000 to $45,000 market do produce some stunning images, we are not yet on the road to a filmless world. The image quality-to-cost ratio is still a big divide in the continued patronage of film-based image capture. The image quality that one could get from a 35mm SLR camera with certain enhanced features in the $800 range would need a digital camera of today's competence in the region of $30,000. This price difference is diminishing, with improved hardware and software features. When this difference becomes small, a filmless world could emerge.

Digital cameras and scanners

With digital cameras capturing the image information in a similar manner as a scanner, will the need for a scanner vanish in the years to come? One important aspect that needs to be highlighted is the sensor that is used by both the technologies. We saw earlier that scanners that did high-end scanning used a PMT, whereas the low-priced desktp scanners used CCD technology. And without exception all digital cameras use CCD technology for their photosensitive semiconductor. The quality levels that could be expected of a PMT far exceed those of a CCD.

In spite of the inroads that digital cameras are making in the photographic and graphic art industries, with the assumption that the future of digital photography will include more advanced devices with sophisticated features and better prices, there are still hundreds and thousands of images that have been captured with film. These images will need to be scanned. And then there are the fine art works that will still call for high-end scanning. The technology of digital photography will continue to embrace the finer features of high-end scanning. This will no doubt pave the way for better quality images that could be captured faster in the future. Scanning will complement digital photography and they will coexist.

Chapter 7

FINISHING

Before you start, you have to finish. You must plan the total job before you start. Before you can design a document you must develop a page imposition based on:

- the final trim size of the document
- the binding method to be used
- the method used for duplexing or perfecting
- the size of the press sheet
- the folding that will be applied

Finishing and binding

The imposition design depends in part on the binding method. Some of the most popular binding methods include:

- stapled flat sheets
- collate and cut
- perfect binding or tape binding
- saddle-stitching
- folding
- case binding of books

Imposition

There are other binding methods as well, but you will most likely deal with the binding types above. Some jobs do not require binding as they are just flat sheets, and they are easy to handle. A poster or a single two-sided sheet does not need to be bound after it comes off the press, although you may still need to fold it. Imposition is the arrangement of individual pages or units in a press sheet, in such a way that when folded and trimmed, pages are in correct order and orientation. There are many forms of this; however, there are a few that are common. These are sheetwise, work-and-turn, work-and-tumble, signature, multiple-image, and ganged-image imposition.

Imposition nomenclature

Size	Defines how large the job is and its dimensions (height and width).
Page count	How many pages.
Paper size	Defines the type of paper, its size, and thickness (caliper).
Stock	Defines the classification of the paper (book, cover, bond, newsprint, etc.)
Basic size	Each stock has its own standard basic size. The basic size is used to calculate a standard measure of paper weight, known as basis weight. For example, the basic size for book stock is 25x38 inches.
Basis weight	The weight of 500 (1 ream) sheets of basic size.
1, 2, . . . "n" up	refers to the number of repeated pages that are included in the same press sheet. For example, if you are going to print a brochure "2 up," it means that on your press sheet you have two brochures.

Register and alignment

Many people assume that the sheets of paper that are bought from the mill are perfectly square, but this assumption is usually wrong. Printers depend on register to reproduce images with quality. Most offset lithographic presses align sheets against the leading edge and one side. To accomplish this a side guide is used on the press, with a mechanism that pulls the sheets of paper against the side guide, ensuring that all sheets of paper enter the machine in the same position. This practice is extremely important to image registration and alignment, particularly if the paper is not precisely squared.

Gripper edge

When a sheet of paper is in the feeder, going to enter the press, before it is taken by the grippers it is stopped for a few seconds and its leading edge is aligned with the press grippers. Therefore, the leading edge is called the gripper edge. This is the most precise alignment line from head to tail. Printers usually mark this edge with a couple of Xs. The edge on the tail is called the wild edge, and is the least precise alignment from head to tail. You must account for the gripper edge when planning the sheets and image area that will be possible from a large sheet of paper.

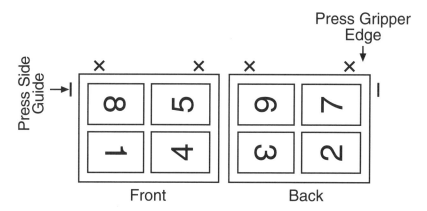

A typical front and back imposition

Side guide

As we mentioned before, the paper is aligned against the leading edge and one side. When the paper enters the press it is jogged (pushed) against a side guide. This side of the paper is marked with a short solid line in the illustration above.

Types of imposition

Sheetwise (also known as work-and-back)

This is probably the simplest type of imposition. It is used when the sheet and the image are near the maximum press size. Printers first print one side of the sheet, then the operator must back up the sheets (that is, print the flip side) by turning them upside down and changing the plates. Finally he prints the other side. In this case, imposition is almost forced because there is no alternative but to fit the images in the space available. So two sets of plates are required for each printing unit. With this procedure, the gripper edge remains the same when the sheets are backed up. This is very important because it facilitates the registration from front to back with a common edge.

Work-and-turn

This method is much more efficient than the first one because there are important time savings associated with it. In this imposition, the pages need to be at least two up, or an even number. The press sheet is divided in two halves, right and left. On one half of the sheet, say the right one, the front of the job is printed. On the left side the back of the job is printed. So, we obtain a back and a front in each impression on the same side of the sheet of paper. When the sheets are printed on one side the operator flips the sheets side to side, and prints the back side of the sheet, without changing the plates. This way the back side will be backed up on the previous printed front side. The same for the other side. Here is an example:

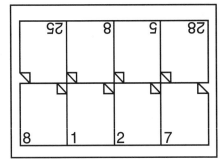 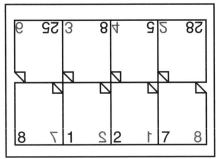

Work-and-Turn Signature
Both Sides Printed
From Same Plate

Printed Press Sheet
(back page shown
in grey numbers)

This imposition saves time and materials since there is no need for an extra set of plates. Adjustments for the press due to the side change are minimal. The gripper edge remains the same, as in the case of sheetwise. The only problem with this imposition is that the ink must dry enough before the sheets can run the second time.

Work-and-tumble

Work and tumble is a variation of work and turn. In this case, however, the press sheet is divided in two halves, but instead of right and left, it is divided in front and rear. The press sheet, as in the prior example, winds up with a back print and a front print on the same side.

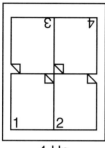

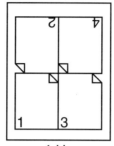

4-Up	4-Up
Work-and-Turn	Work-and-Tumble

The sheets are then flipped from head to tail to be printed again, on the other side, using the same set of plates. The side guide remains the same but switches the gripper edges. Therefore is very important that the sheets are perfectly squared. To achieve this it is necessary to pretrim the paper before printing.

Allowances for this type of imposition tend to be bigger since the gripper edge changes head to tail; in other words, you have to use the same allowances for both head and tail. This is also the kind of imposition used in sheetfed perfecting presses that print both sides of the sheet in one pass through the press.

Signature imposition

In signature imposition, four or more page units are put on a plate so that when the printed sheet is folded and bound, the pages will read in proper sequence. The way to make sure this happens is to fold and number dummy signatures of all the sheets required to make the book. It is important to be sure that the folder will fold the same way you fold the dummies.

Multiple image imposition

In this imposition, two or more identical images can be run at the same time. This is particularly useful when the finished sheet is at least half the maximum sheet size of the press. This imposition is mostly used when the run length is large since it reduces the running time substantially. One of the most common applications is in packaging or label printing.

Ganged image imposition

Ganged imposition is the positioning of different images, even from different customers, in the same press sheet. Obviously all jobs have to have the same paper specifications and same set of inks. This imposition will reduce waste, makeready time, and running time. The drawback is that with this kind of operation, it is not always possible to turn the job very quickly, since it is necessary to wait for various jobs to fill up the press sheet.

Folding

Folding layout

Every printed material reaches the finishing department in the form of flat sheets. Folders are used to transform these flat sheets into signatures, folded brochures, etc. There are many ways to fold paper as well as many different kinds and sizes of paper sheets. Binders should have a documented outline for locating pages on the sheet so that the pages will have a logical sequence after folding. This outline is known as the folding layout plan, and is nothing more than a guide for imposition. Most binderies have these plans printed, giving instructions and basic layouts of pages.

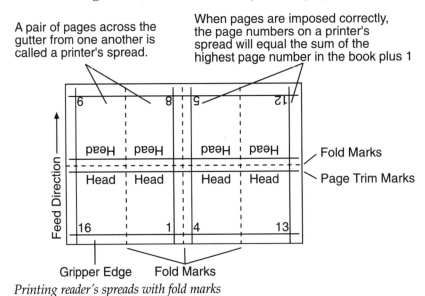

Printing reader's spreads with fold marks

Paper weight is another factor, besides sheet size and equipment, that determines how many pages a signature can hold. It is obvious that the heavier the stock, the smaller the sheet, and thus the fewer pages the signature will contain. The most common numbers of pages per signature are 8, 16, 32, and 64.

Implications of paper grain

During paper fabrication, the fibers tend to arrange themselves in the direction of the movement of the Fourdrinier machine's screen. Folds that are made parallel to the paper grain are better than folds done against it. It is always better to run the first fold parallel to the paper grain. In some instances, particularly with heavy stocks, an extra micro perforation is made to help folding against the grain.

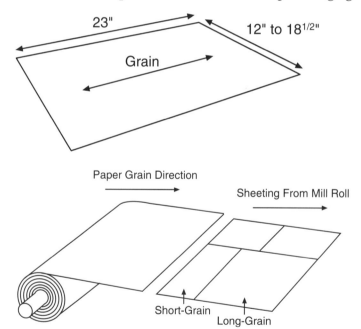

Folder types

Although folding machinery can be very complex and varied, we can divide folders into two general categories:
- tape/knife folders
- buckle folders

Tape/knife folders

Sheets are fed one by one into this machine, where they are pulled by a tape that carries them. When the sheet is in position, a dull blade comes down, forcing the sheet of paper in between two rollers. These rollers catch the paper, making the first fold. There are subsequent tape, and blade mechanisms, positioned perpendicular to the first one, that make the next fold. If a sheet of paper is folded once, we have four pages; twice, we have eight; three times, we have sixteen; four times, thirty two; and so on.

Buckle folders

As in the previous case, sheets are fed individually, this time into a slot at higher speed. When it reaches the folding position, the forward advance is blocked, causing the sheet to fold a little, just enough to get caught by a pair of revolving cylinders, which folds the paper in the correct position. The operation is repeated again in subsequent slots. This folder is widely used for small signatures, endpapers, and brochures that have odd sizes and shapes. This folder is also capable of doing parallel and combinations of parallel and right angle folds.

Binding

Sewing

Sewing is a binding process used mostly for hardcover bookbinding and is the binding that has the greatest durability and good open flat characteristics. There are two kinds of book sewing, Smyth sewing and side sewing.

Side sewing

In side sewing the thread is passed through the book thickness from one side of the book to the other side. This is a very strong and rigid binding, which is cheaper than Smyth sewing. The signatures are put together to form the books, which are inserted as the entire books, not the separated signatures into the sewing machine in a straight line past the sewing head, where they are drilled and sewn.

Smyth sewing

Smyth sewing ties signatures together by passing a thread through the folded edge of each signature, from the outside to the inside and outside again. This binding is very flexible, which allows the book to lie flat and stay open. In Smyth sewing, signatures are fed one by one into the sewing machine, and sewn in consecutive order to form an entire book at a time.

Perfect binding

Perfect binding is a type of book binding that uses an adhesive on the spine to link signatures and pages together. With this binding process, the backs of the signatures are ground off and glue is applied along the spine to secure all the pages.

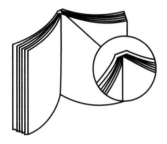

The first step in perfect binding is gathering. The signatures are fed into the binder's feeder either manually or automatically. The signatures are then separated and delivered to a conveyor, which picks up all the signatures for a single book and transports them from station to station until they reach the adhesive binder station.

The backbone, which is the part of the book that receives the glue, has to be critically prepared. Normally the backbone preparation is done in two steps, milling or shredding, and roughing. The idea is to expose as many fibers as possible along the edge of each page. An important design consideration is to plan extra space between pages for the grinding process.

The adhesive application can be done in different ways. Some jobs need more than one glue coating, some do not. Hotmelts, which consist of resins, film former, plasticizer, and fillers, are often used. This glue is heated to approximately 380 degrees to be applied to the spine of the publication. Perfect binding is very popular for books. You could have a self cover, which means that the cover is the same as the paper used for the text, or you could have a separate cover of heavier weight.

Covers

Most covers used with perfect bound products are soft covers. Soft covers are generally made of a heavier stock than the inside stock. If the cover is heavy enough, some kind of scoring is necessary to help the cover lay open. Covers are fed in-line and glued automatically. Therefore it is necessary to register the cover with the rest of the publication. After gluing, the cover needs to be pressed against the inside to assure that it is pasted correctly. The last step is trimming to the final size of the publication.

Paper grain and perfect binding

As we already mentioned, paper does change dimensions when it captures moisture from the environment. The changes, however, are noticeable in the opposite direction of the grain. Therefore, once the signatures are glued together the spine does not change dimensions, the paper grain should never be perpendicular to the spine.

If you fail to follow this advice your product will fail. Paper will absorb moisture and will start to grow in the opposite direction of the grain, however, the paper is restrained to the spine size, and therefore the sheets of paper will wrinkle and will display waviness. The same problem applies to the cover as well.

Will the publication stay open?

In theory, perfect-bound materials will never stay completely open. Hotmelt adhesives, the most commonly used in perfect binding, contain no solvents, hence they remain solid at normal temperatures. This makes the publication tend to close. If someone tries to open flat, leafing through would place too much strain on the glued edges. This could break the spine and damage the entire book. Developments in adhesive technology are helping binders in this sense. The use of cold emulsion adhesives, like PVA, polyvinyl acetate, and warm PUR, polyurethane, and other adhesives, can improve the open flat characteristics of perfect-bound books. Another factor in open flat books is paper grain. If paper grain is not parallel to the spine it certainly will not help the book or publication stay open. The lay flat capability is an important user requirement.

Otabind and RepKover

Otabind is a binding process that improves the regular perfect binding. This method uses flexible PVA adhesives and allows the spine to float inside the soft cover structure, permitting the book to open flat. The cover is not pasted to the spine, but to the sides of the first page of the publication. This reduces the strain on the spine, allowing the book to open much more easily. The back of the cover does not suffer either because it is completely separated from the spine.

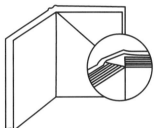

The first and last pages however, will tend to remain closed and joined to the cover, since the cover is glued to them. Therefore it is wise not to include any critical image in these two sheets.

RepKover is a variant of Otabind. In this case the inside cover is reinforced in advance with a strip of cloth pre-mounted on the spine area. Since the bound book block floats inside the cover, this structure does not damage the spine, or the cover. The use of PVAs is recommended. An even better approach would be to combine this method with PUR adhesives. With RepKover the problem with the first page is eliminated, giving more freedom to designers. RepKover is more expensive than the other method since an extra operation is necessary. However, books will have a much better appearance and will open flat.

Do solvents migrate?

Solvent migration is a phenomenon that is related to the interaction of the hotmelt glue and lithographic ink solvents. The result of this interaction is a debilitation of the binding glue, which results in falling pages and detachment of the cover.

Paper porosity allows hotmelt glue to travel away from the spine in the same way ink solvents permit ink to penetrate into the fibers. When these two, ink solvents and hotmelt, interact, the glue is susceptible to degradation. Although sometimes a perfect-bound book looks perfect just after binding, it is possible that this problem will occur within the next few weeks.

This is because sheetfed lithographic inks can take several days, even weeks, to dry completely. On the other hand no problems of this nature occur with inks used on heatset web offset presses, because the majority of ink solvents are extracted from them while printing.

To prevent this problem, printers and binders can take some precautions. The most reasonable is the following: if ink must bleed into the binding edge, strip it out at least 3/16 inch on each side of the fold. This precaution should prevent solvent migration problems.

Perfect binding allowances

Allowances are guidelines for printers and binders which specify extra space in certain critical areas to compensate for misregistration, inaccurate positioning of signatures at the bindery, and distortions typical of each particular binding method. Allowances also refer to procedures geared to optimize the finishing processes. These allowances have to be planned before printing to avoid problems later in the process. Therefore, although finishing is one of the last operations, it should be accounted for in the first production steps.

Signatures must always be folded first in the direction parallel to the grain. Depending on the bindery, the allowance for grinding in spine preparation should be at least 1/8 inch. A more typical number is 3/16 inch. Allowance for bleedings should be at least 1/8 inch, on all external sides of the page. Crossovers should be carried out only on those pages that are facing each other on the press sheet, to avoid color switches and ensure perfect registration between left and right pages. If an image must bleed into the binding edge, and hotmelt is used to glue the spine, it must be stripped out 3/16 inch.

Saddle stitching

Saddle stitching or saddle-wired binding is the simplest binding method for publications with low page count or for publications that use extremely thin paper. Saddle stitching is a process that stitches through the spine with metal staples. If the publication contains more than one signature, these are nested one inside the other and stitched together.

A design consideration is to compensate for the creep of inside signatures. Another is the allowance for a lap. A lap is an extra portion of paper in just one side of the signature. In other words, one side of the signature should be larger, so that the center page can be found easily by the automatic stitching machines.

Signatures are opened and hung on a chain (saddle), which travels from one station to another, picking up the remaining signatures, until the stitching station where all signatures are stapled. The last station is the trimming station where the publication gets trimmed on the three remaining sides, after being stitched.

Among the advantages of this binding method is that it is very economical and fast. In addition, stitched publications always open flat.

Creep

Saddle stitched publications may present a problem related to the thickness of the paper, known as creep. The problem results from the fact that the inside signature will differ in size because the paper will extend further into the outside trim area. Therefore the back pages must compensate for this situation, otherwise the trim margins will not align.

There are no formal formulas to calculate creep allowances, although some advanced computer imposition programs compensate for creep. The best way to compensate for this phenomenon is to build a dummy with the same paper that will be used in the real job. Then, after folding, put the signatures inside one another, drill a small hole with a puncher and measure the difference. The results are decreased bind margins on the inside signature and larger ones on the outside.

Perfect binding versus saddle stitching

Choosing between these two binding methods involved technical aspects as well as aesthetics. Whatever method is chosen however, the job must be carefully planned for the chosen binding method to avoid mistakes.

Number of pages, format, type of paper, paper grain direction, type of press, imposition, signature layout, inserts, and cards are just some issues that a good planner has to take into consideration before deciding which binding method will be used.

Advantages of perfect binding

Signature imposition is not critical.
Binds single sheets and cards.
More than one binding option, PUR, PVA, etc.
Permits spine identification.

Disadvantages of perfect binding

Paper grain is critical. Probably is the biggest constraint.
Does not lie flat if hotmelt glue is used.
Has a minimum thickness of 1/8 of an inch.
More expensive.
Hotmelt is not environmentally friendly.

Advantages of saddle stitching

Paper grain direction is not critical.
Paper will not buckle.
Always lies flat.
Fast and economical.

Disadvantages of saddle stitching

Has thickness limitations.
Requires adjustments for creepage.
Inserts have to be tipped in.
Requires laps to open signatures, which increases waste.
Requires a minimum of four page units and a bindfold.

As we can see, paper grain is a major inconvenience for perfect binding. Therefore, the advice of this author is to consult always with bindery experts about this issue during the planning stages of your work. All these considerations aside, it is recommended that if the publication thickness is 1/2 inch or greater, the product should be perfect bound.

Inserting

Inserts are extra pages that need to be included in publications but do not belong to any signature. Usually, they are extra illustrative materials and can consist of just one flat sheet or a separated folded piece. These materials need to be attached to the publication before the final assembly of the book.

Tipping

To tip is nothing more than to paste the insert onto facing pages in the signature. A small strip of glue is applied to the binding edge of the insert, which is then pasted to the binding edge of the signature. This can be done either inside or outside the signature pages. Tipping outside is less expensive than tipping on the inside because it can be done by machine. Inside tipping has to be made by hand since the signatures must be opened to place the insert in the inside. While a machine can tip thousands of inserts in one hour, by hand it is only possible to tip a few hundred in the same time.

Hard cover bookbinding

Casemaking

To build a case for hardcover books it is necessary to have board, cloth, and glue. Boards are cut to the size of the book and cloth is cut with a 5/8 inch extension on all four sides. Additionally, the cloth cut should account for the spine space, which is the thickness of the book plus 3/8 inch in each side of the spine board. The spine board is cut with the width of the publication. The boards are glued to the cloth in place along with the spine board, which is placed between the two larger boards. Then the extra cloth around the boards is folded and glued to the inside of the case.

If some decoration is to be made to the case, this is the moment to do it, before it is cased-in with the text. Decoration can be made with foil stamping or any other image stamping procedure. In luxury editions, leather is often substituted for cloth. Today the process of casemaking is done by machines that can reach a production rate of approximately 30 covers per minute.

Casing-in

Casing-in is the process by which the inside text of the book is mounted in the hardcover bookcase. Each book is fed into a machine where glue is applied to the endpapers and the joint. Endpapers are extra sheets of paper, generally of a heavier stock, that are added to the body of the book, acting as support and link between the cover and the inside book. Then the case is placed like wrapping around the inside book, which is forced into the case. The endpapers are adhered to the inside part of the cover. At this stage books are inspected for defects.

Finally the book has to dry. To help the permanent setting of the book, pressure is applied to the books for periods as long as twelve hours.

Building-in is the same process described at the end of the casing-in process, the difference is that building-in is done automatically by building-in machines in just a few minutes instead of several hours. Building-in machines take the books after the casing-in machines and inspection. The machine has pressure plates and heated formers that pull the cloth into the joint and pressure the book at the same time. The plates clamp the books for a brief moment and then release it. The process can be repeated twice or three times depending on the drying required.

Binding on-demand for digital printing

On demand printing has emerged as the result of two major requirements. The first is to reduce delivery time, the second is to reduce the number of volumes produced and still be cost effective. It is demand print that achieves inventory reduction by printing shorter runs, which print in less time than longer runs. Digital printing and digital prepress have eliminated many bottlenecks in the print production workflow. Therefore the jobs arriving at the bindery departments are smaller and come at a faster pace. Customers also request faster turnaround times. To keep up with restrained time frames, binders have had to either automate their conventional operations or adopt new bindery methods.

Bindery methods for on demand are primarily mechanical methods, such as spiral, comb, and channel binding. Saddle stitching and tape binding are also used because of their convenience and simplicity.

In-line and off-line finishing

In-line finishing methods are finishing methods incorporated into the printing machine. These methods need to be completely automated to keep pace with the machine's speed. In some cases, the finishing part is not included in the machine itself, but is somehow attached to the printing device's delivery.

Off-line finishing methods are considered extra operations, and the finishing equipment is separated from the printing device. The decision to use one or another method will depend on many factors, such as the type of work (for instance, quality requirements versus speed of delivery), finishing capabilities of the print shop, etc.

In-line finishing capabilities can be as simple as stapling in one corner or as troublesome as tape binding and perforating. A factor that influences the finishing for digital printed products is the sheet size. Sheet sizes for digital printing are much smaller than those for lithography (8.5x11 or 11x17 versus 23x38, respectively); therefore, planning for on demand finishing should be easier than for bigger presses. However, because each printed piece is unique, there is not much room for errors.

In-line stapling

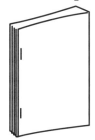

This is the simplest binding operation that can be incorporated into a digital printing machine. Staples are fed from a roll of wire, ensuring a large supply. The most common position for the staple is the upper left corner of the job. The staple can be horizontal or vertical.

Side stitching is another option, and consists of locating two or three staples along the left hand edge of the book. Although this method gives a better book appearance to the job, it will not open flat.

Hole drilling

A very simple finishing method is just drilling three holes for three-hole binder placement. This procedure is done off line using heavy duty drilling equipment. A printer could also use predrilled paper, but it represents an increase in paper costs.

Mechanical binding

Comb binding

Comb binding is the use of a plastic piece to hold pages together. It is very efficient for very short runs. The paper needs to be punched in several points, to wind up with a series of holes on the binding side of the book. The off-line equipment to punch the holes is very simple and can be used in an office environment. A plastic comb is inserted in the holes, through the thickness of the book. Automated machinery can perform this process in larger quantities. The drilling process sometimes can be integrated in-line.

This binding method allows a thickness range from 3/16 to 2 inches (approximately 500 pages), and combs are available in different colors, which gives a little bit more variety for design. The simplicity of this method, plus the possibility to incorporate thicker covers and its open flat characteristics, makes this process very convenient for short runs of presentations and publications.

Wire coil binding

With wire coil binding the book must be punched in a similar way to comb binding, then a wire is threaded through the perforations. This process is more durable than comb binding because there is no pressure on the spine.

Tape binding

Tape binding tries to emulate perfect binding, and can be performed in-line or off-line. A strip of flexible cloth tape that contains a heat activated glue is applied to the edge of a stack of paper. The glue will dry or cure almost instantly as it cools, making this process ideal for on-demand printing. This type of binding is found in-line in some machines, particularly in the Xerox Docutech series. This method offers a very high tensile resistance as well as open flat books. The tape strip comes in different colors.

Channel binding

Channel binding emulates traditional hard cover binding. As in hardcover books, the inside pages are inserted off-line into a hard cover. The cover has a metallic channel that, when compressed, grips the interior pages and holds them to the cover. The same metallic channel can be decompressed, if extra pages or inserts need to be included or removed. Covers are available in different spine thickness and colors, ranging from 0.20 inches to 1.3 inches.

In-line perfect binding

Some companies are already offering in-line perfect binding services. With this method you can bind books of up to 350 pages, which streamlines the production of on-demand books. When a complete interior is finished, it is automatically fed into the binder, the spine is ground and hot melt adhesive is applied, and the cover is then wrapped around. While the bindery is still in progress, the digital printer is printing the next interior, ensuring continuous production. Finally the books are transferred to the trimmer where the head, foot, and face are trimmed.

In-line binding also uses saddle stitching as well. The signatures are stapled through the spine, like many magazines or catalogs. Saddle-stitching is done by stapling the pages along the center fold. Take a magazine apart (remove the center staples) and look at the sheet of paper containing the front cover (the first page), and notice that the sheet also includes the back cover. This is a signature. When you prepare an imposition for a saddle-stitched job, you must take into consideration that the pages on a single sheet of paper are not consecutive. The term saddle comes from the part of the binding machine that holds the paper for stitching. Publications bound by saddle-stitching can be opened easily and lay flat when open. After about 100 pages, the publication is too large for saddle-stitching. In-line binding is an enabling technology for on-demand digital printing.

Press sheet sizes

For sheetfed presses, the press sheet is the large sheet of paper fed through the printing press which contains the pages from one signature. For webfed presses, the paper itself is fed from a continuous roll and the press sheet is a single signature cut from that roll, usually after printing. Digital presses are designed for either sheets or webs.

The signature

Imposition is the arrangement of all the pages in a job and a signature is a unit of organization within the imposition. Sheetwise, work-and-turn, and work-and-tumble layouts each consist of a single signature. Each signature consists of the pages for both the front and the back of the press sheet. Jobs with more pages in them than can print on a single press sheet are composed of multiple signatures.

An imposition that consists of 4-up signatures means that four pages are placed on one side of one printable sheet, the next four pages are placed on the flip side of that same sheet. Each sheet, or the pages printed on that one sheet, is a signature within the imposition. Depending on the folding and binding defined for the job, the pages within a single signature may not be consecutive—in fact, they will almost never be consecutive.

The size of the press sheet depends on the printing press. Some small presses can only print on sheets up to page size (8.5"x11"); other presses can print tabloid sizes (11"x17")—two pages. Larger presses can print 4, 8, 16, 32, or more pages on one press sheet. A typical large press sheet measures 32"x40". That size press sheet could contain sixteen 8-1/2" x11" pages (eight pages on each side of the sheet), with registration marks, space between pages, color bars, or other reference and fold marks.

Impositions should use the largest standard-size press sheet that the press supports. Each press sheet consists of as many individual pages as can fit on the sheet, although you need to reserve space for registration marks, density bars, folding marks, trim areas, and collation marks.

Folding the job—part two

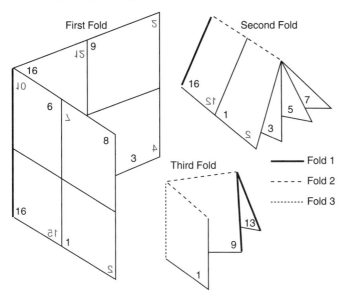

In printing, folds include more than just the folds you see (as in a newspaper or magazine where the paper is folded, but not cut, between two pages). If you print pages destined for a book (no folds in the final product) using an 8-up imposition (eight pages on one side of the press sheet), the press sheet would be folded 3 times after printing. Some jobs contain folds in the final product. In addition to jobs folded in the middle, your job may incorporate specialty folds such as an accordion fold or a map fold. These folds, plus the folds to get each page on the press sheet into position, must be designed into the imposition.

A large press sheet could contain a signature with 8, 12, 16, 24, 32, 48, or more pages. A press sheet with two pages on each side needs to be folded once; a press sheet with 4 pages needs to be folded twice; a press sheet with 8 pages needs to be folded three times, and so on. The folds must be slit to separate the pages (unless the publication is being saddle-stitched). Saddle-stitched jobs must be folded. If a job destined for saddle-stitching is printed on an 8 page press sheet, two of the three folds need to be slit; the center fold isn't slit.

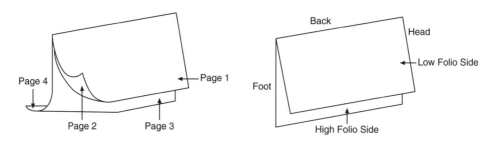

Folding a signature for binding often requires a lap for the binding machine

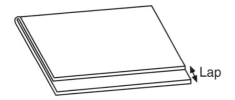

Types of impositions

There are as many possible impositions as there are ways to fold and cut paper into brochures, book, publications and other priunted products. As we move toward digital output technology, the secret to its success will be in the bindery. Here are some of the most common impositions:

- 2-up layouts
- 4-up layouts
- 8-up layouts

The number of pages you put in a signature depends on the size of the press sheet, the size of the page, and the distance between and around pages.

2-up layouts

A 2-up imposition means there are two pages on each side of each signature. The plate containing the front of the signature is mounted on the press and the paper is run through the press and printed. The plate containing the back of the signature is mounted on the press and the paper, which has now dried, with the unprinted side up, is fed through the press again. When printing four-color jobs, the four-color press would have a plate for each color in the job (four for each side of the signature) mounted and would print one side of the signature, then the other side of the signature (after side one dried sufficiently). You would also need additional plates for any spot or custom colors used in the job.

You could also have a 2-up work-and-turn layout. For this layout, the two pages on the front are the same, and the two pages on the back of the signature are the same. For example, side 1 has two page 1s and side 2 has two page 2s. After printing, the pages are cut apart and you end up with twice as many "pages" as press sheets.

4-up layouts

This layout is usually designed for a job that is to be saddle-stitched.

4-up imposition, saddle-stitching

To print a press sheet, you need front and back signatures for each color (one plate per side for black-and-white printing, four plates per side for process color printing, and additional plates for spot or custom colors). After printing each side of each of the signatures, and folding, the sigs are collated and bound.

4-up signature-printed and cut

For other job needs, you could create a 4-up layout that has all the same page on each side of the press sheet—front of the signature has four page 1s, back of the signature has four page 2s. This lets you print four complete units at one time, so one thousand sheets yield four thousand finished units. You can design a 4-up layout to support the work-and-turn or work-and-tumble printing methods.

The 4-up press is called a 26-inch press because the sheet is usually 19"x26" and the image area is just over 17"x22" for four 8.5x11 inch pages plus bleeds, trim, marks, etc.

As with all impositions, the best one for each job must be determined by the printing, folding, and binding methods.

8-up layouts

When you have larger press sheets (or small pages), you can fit many pages on each side of a sheet:

- 8-up work-and-turn
- 8-up work-and-tumble
- 8-up saddle-stitch
- 8-up collate-and-cut

8-up work-and-turn

The work-and-turn layout produces two each of four individual pages on each press sheet. After the first side of the press sheet is printed, the same plate (or four plates for process color printing, plus additional plates for spot or custom colors) remains on the press and the press sheets are turned over (after drying) and fed through the press again.

8-up work-and-tumble

The work-and-tumble layout is similar to the work-and-turn, except that the paper is flipped top-to-bottom rather than side-to-side after the first side is printed.

8-up saddle stitch

If the saddle-stitched job contains sixteen pages, you could use the same layout as the sheetwise layout. However, if the job includes more than that, you need to use a layout that places the first page and last page next to each other, the second page and second to last page next to each other, and so on, so that when the press sheets are folded, slit at all except the center fold, and collated, the pages occur in the correct order.

8-up collate and cut

When the job will be collated and cut prior to binding (perhaps to be spiral bound), each 8-page press sheet (16 pages total, 8 pages each side) consists of a unit of 16 pages. When that press sheet is folded and the pages are trimmed, you have the first 16 pages of the job. The next signature consists of pages 17 through 32, the second sig the second 16 pages of the job.

Imposition marks

The press sheet needs more than just the pages to be printed. If the sheet needs to be folded, fold marks must appear outside the page area as a guideline for setting up the folding machine. Process color jobs need registration marks for the colors, and color bars help the press operator evaluate the job while it's on the press. A press sheet should contain these marks in addition to the pages to be printed:

- job information
- color and density bars
- crop, center, and fold marks
- registration marks

Not all marks need to appear on all press sheets. A black-and-white job doesn't need registration marks. The sheet may also contain other informational marks determined by the specific job.

Color bars

When a job includes halftones, the press sheet will have density bars outside of the page area. The printer inserts these. Gray scale density bars should be included on both black-and-white and process-color work. Color bars must be included on a process color press sheet. The press operator uses these marks to continuously check the job as it prints. By measuring the gray balance shown in the gray scale density bars and the color combinations, the operator can adjust the press as necessary to maintain the best quality for that press. Color bars come in many shapes and sizes, and may include several combinations of colors: tints, overprints, targets, slur marks, and more.

Crop and fold marks

For jobs that need to be folded, the press sheet should show marks at the location of each fold. Also, virtually every job that prints needs to be cut to size after printing. Marks outside of the page area, such as color bars and registration marks, need to be trimmed from the paper before the job is bound. Every signature must have at least crop and fold marks for the cutter operation. Single-page sheets must also have them if there is bleed or the image area is less than sheet size.

Registration marks

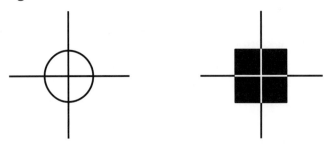

When printing four-color sheets, or even five- or six-color jobs, the press sheet must have registration marks. These marks appear in the same location on each plate for the page and allow the press operator to determine if the four (or five, or six) plates are printing in proper registration. When in register, the cyan, magenta, yellow, and black registration marks print on top of each other and should show as a single black mark. If one of the plates is out of register, the registration mark shows the problem.

Job information

To help identify the job, each press sheet should contain text that describes the job—including the customer name. For jobs composed of several signatures, the number of the signature within the imposition can be printed (signature 1 of 8, for example). For sheetwise layouts, the words "Front" and "Back" also help identify the sheets when printing and collating a job.

Some simple folds

On the adjacent page are some simple folding suggestions for a single sheet of paper and how it can be handled to create some interesting layouts.

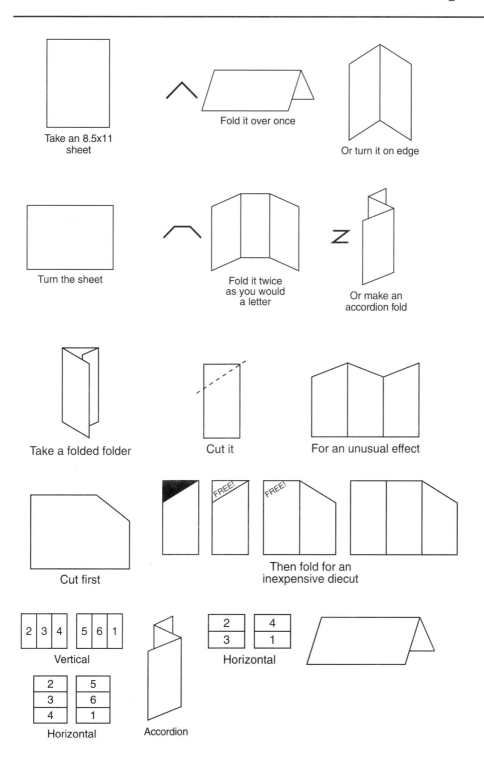

Take an 8.5x11
sheet

Fold it over once

Or turn it on edge

Turn the sheet

Fold it twice
as you would
a letter

Or make an
accordion fold

Take a folded folder

Cut it

For an unusual effect

Cut first

FREE!   FREE!

Then fold for an
inexpensive diecut

2	3	4	5	6	1

Vertical

2		4
3		1

Horizontal

2	5
3	6
4	1

Horizontal

Accordion

Paper

Although end use requirements are important in determining the paper to be used, the various printing processes also have their own inherent paper requirements.

Sheetfed Offset Lithography. This printing method uses tackier inks than other methods, so the paper must have high surface and internal bonding strength. It must also have high water resistance to maintain its surface strength in the presence of water from the dampening system. The paper surface must be free of dust, lint, or other debris, to keep foreign material from piling on the blanket or upsetting the press's chemical balance. If successive printings on each sheet are required, the paper must have high dimensional stability, and its equilibrium moisture content must approximate the relative humidity of the pressroom, to prevent register misalignment. Long-grain paper is also required for multicolor jobs.

Web Offset Lithography. Many of the same considerations as for sheetfed offset printing are required for paper destined for web printing. Web printing inks are generally not as tacky as those used in sheetfed offset, there is less moisture involved in web printing, and the paper moves faster through the system than in sheetfed printing, the result being that web presses can handle lower basis weight papers, and papers that are lighter have less pick resistance. The moisture content of web rolls tends to be lower than paper used for sheetfed offset printing, to reduce moisture loss and web shrinkage. High-speed web presses also reduce many of the problems inherent in sheetfed offset printing. But web printing requires paper rolls that unwind with even tension and flatness, and have a minimum of defects to prevent web breaks. It is generally damage to rolls that causes the most problems in web offset printing.

Gravure. Because of the nature of gravure printing (ink is transferred to the paper from ink-filled cells engraved in the press cylinder), smoothness of the paper surface is the most important criterion. Compressibility and softness are also crucial. Minute pits or depressions in the paper's surface can cause incomplete ink transfer, as can low compressibility. Gravure presses, however, print well on low-quality, lightweight papers.

Flexography. Flexographic printing can handle many different types of papers. Flexographic inks are not very tacky, so pick resistance is not a major concern. (Paper rolls used in rollfed flexographic presses must be free of the same defects as those used in web offset printing.) Flexography is used for many types of packaging, wrappers, cartons, corrugated boards, and books.

Screen Printing. Screen printing can handle many different types of surfaces. Smoothness is not a critical issue, but may affect ink drying. Crucial considerations for screen printers are sheet flatness and freedom from curling or wavy edges. The ability to withstand and maintain dimensional stability during heat-based ink drying is necessary. Thickness is also a consideration when using heavy inks, so as to prevent warping.

Letterpress. Like paper needed for gravure printing, paper destined for letterpress printing must have an extremely smooth surface so as to allow complete ink transfer. Inks used in letterpress tend to be heavy, so the paper surface must be able to prevent spreading of halftone dots. The paper must also be able to withstand the pressures imposed on it during printing. (The ability to accept letterpress images is called a paper's impression tolerance.) Since inks are heavy, the paper must have high pick resistance, and high surface cleanliness. Supercalendered coated papers or coated papers with high finish are often used for fine halftone printing.

Electrostatic Printing. Electrostatic printing, including photocopiers, laser printers, and other forms of non-impact printing based on electrostatic attraction of toner, requires little more than paper that will not curl or cause other feeding problems at high or low speeds—runnability issues similar to those for other printing processes. A specific requirement for electrostatic printing paper is high electrical resistivity. Paper is made specifically for use in electrostatic printing machines (sometimes called xerographic paper).

Inkjet Printing. A requirement of inkjet printer paper (used primarily in addressing, coding, and computer printouts) is that it absorb ink quickly and minimize spreading and feathering so as to produce sharp images. Specially coated papers are manufactured specifically for use in high-resolution inkjet printers.

End-use requirements

There is a vast number of end uses of paper, and even within types of paper products there are a variety of factors that determine what type of paper should be used. Here are a few of the larger paper markets and some general guidelines for the paper(s) used for each.

Advertising. The paper used must be aesthetic and functional. If multicolor printing is to be used, paper suitable for multiple passes is required, and must also possess the desired texture and color. Offset lithography and gravure processes are most frequently used, so the paper must also work functionally and economically with the appropriate process, and conform to the customer's issues of print quality and cost. Advertising that includes return mail cards must meet postal thickness requirements.

Books. In addition to printing and binding requirements, aesthetic factors must also be taken into account. The subject matter should dictate the paper texture, finish, and shade. Illustration matter must be on such paper that allows for acceptable reproduction. Bulk is a consideration, as the signatures must fit into the predesigned case. High-bulk paper is generally required for low-page-count fiction and children's books, while low-bulk papers are required for high-page-count encyclopedias and Bibles. Opacity, consistency of shade, and strength along binding edges are also important. Groundwood papers are used for low-quality short-life books, while books destined for long-term archival and storage are typically printed on alkaline papers. Endleaf papers that secure the pages to the binding must be strong and tear-resistant. Book covers and dust-jackets must have high durability and tear resistance. Coated-one-side (C1S) label paper is used for printed book jackets. A type of coated one side paper, also known as bristol paper, is used for paperback covers.

Business Forms. Special paper, called business forms bond is used primarily for business forms. Quick ink absorption is a special consideration. Multiple colors are used for separate copies, and issues of tear resistance and ease of perforation are important. Clear transfer of carbon images or, increasingly, carbonless images is also necessary. Forms used in optical character recognition (OCR) systems must provide compatibility with OCR scanning equipment.

Cartons and Containers. Printed paperboard and rigid containers provide packaging for cigarettes, cereals, candies, milk, cosmetics, and pharmaceuticals. Print quality and aesthetic considerations are of prime importance, as are FDA regulations. They must also be able to withstand procedures such as die-cutting, folding, scoring, gluing, laminating, and processing on high-speed packaging equipment. They must also be highly rigid and strong, resist fading and abrasion, repel moisture, be chemically inert, non-toxic, and sanitary, as well as be compatible with flexography, gravure, letterpress, and sheetfed and web offset lithography.

Catalogs. Low basis weight papers are used for mail-order catalogs, for postal cost considerations, and catalogs distributed through other means use a variety of other basis weights. Newsprint-type paper is used extensively, and catalogs are mostly printed by web offset and rotogravure printing processes.

Checks. The surface of check paper must be uniformly smooth, and allow for writing, printing, typing, and the printing of magnetic ink character recognition (MICR) ink. It must also be strong enough to withstand repeated handling and check sorting. The regular considerations of its predominant printing methods—letterpress and offset lithography—are also required.

Company Reports. Annual reports and other corporate print jobs must use paper that will cleanly reproduce financial material and illustration matter (such as graphs or halftones). Ease of reading numbers (either in tabular or pictorial form) is the prime consideration, and different types of paper can be used in the same report, depending on the availability of paper that will meet all the required needs. Glossy papers, because of their glare, are typically not used. Offset lithography is the primary reproduction process, which adds additional considerations to the choice of paper stock.

Envelopes. Standard envelope paper is often used, as are coated and uncoated book papers, and papers that match accompanying letterhead and stationery. Preprinted envelopes for direct mailing and other uses are printed with their accompanying material and as self-mailers on business forms paper, and are often done all at once on a web press. The paper requirements also include other aesthetic and functional requirements, as well as the ability to withstand repeated handling and postal sorting equipment. Envelopes are printed by offset lithography, flexography, letterpress, thermography, and steel-die engraving, adding further considerations.

Greeting Cards. In addition to aesthetic considerations, paper used for greeting cards must have high folding endurance and be adequately stiff and rigid. Textured surfaces, like vellum, are also required, as are operations such as embossing, bronzing, flocking, die-cutting, and thermography. A papeterie type of paper is used for greeting cards, and offset lithography is used almost exclusively for printing, with the occasional use of letterpress and screen printing.

Labels and Packaging. Label papers must be able to withstand printing, varnishing, lacquering, die-cutting, embossing, and automated labelling equipment, and must adhere well to their intended surfaces, as well as be compatible with their primary printing processes—gravure, letterpress, sheetfed offset, flexography, and, to a minor extent, screen printing. Packaging uses include wrapping paper (decorative and otherwise), book dust covers, food wrappers, etc. All must have adequate strength, and high ink holdout. Box wraps must endure lamination, and food wrappers must comply with FDA regulations. All must be compatible with flexography and rotogravure, the primary packaging printing processes.

Legal Forms and Financial Reports. Low basis weight, high-opacity papers are typically used for business prospectuses, financial and stockholder reports, and other corporate jobs. Permanent and durable high-grade bond and ledger papers are used for legal documents such as contracts, leases, wills, mortgages, etc. All must be compatible with letterpress and offset lithography, the primary printing methods for such documents.

Maps. The requirements for map paper are dimensional stability (to keep the scale of miles or other required measurement scales accurate), high tear resistance, tensile strength, and folding resistance (so the map will survive extensive handling, unfolding, and refolding), and high wet-strength (a must for maps intended for outdoor use, such as camping or hiking). Maps are almost always printed using offset lithography.

Menus. The two most important requirements for menu paper are aesthetics (a variety of specialty papers, such as imitation parchment, are used, depending on the pretensions of the restaurant) and stiffness (for ease of reading in an upright position). Menu paper should also possess a high degree of tear resistance, tensile strength, and folding endurance (to keep menus intact with repeated handling). It's also probably a good idea for menu papers to have a high degree of wet strength. Menus must also endure embossing, stamping, and printing using letterpress or offset lithography.

Newspapers. Most newspapers are printed on high-speed web presses, using primarily inexpensive groundwood pulp-based newsprint. High opacity, good printing cushion, and rapid absorption of ink are necessary considerations. The source of most web-printing problems comes from inadequate winding of the paper rolls themselves. Paper having inconsistent bulk throughout the roll will unwind with uneven tension and cause deformations in the printed image while on the press, and even cause web breaks.

Newspaper Supplements. Newspaper supplements are printed on "roto news" paper designed for high-speed rotogravure presses.

Roto news paper is produced with a higher filler content, and is calendered to a high finish, as required for rotogravure printing. Sunday supplements and magazine sections of newspapers, such as *Parade* magazine, use supercalendered uncoated rotogravure papers.

Periodicals. High-circulation magazines are printed on high-speed, rotogravure presses, and lightweight papers are often used to keep down mailing costs and provide print quality. Often, coated groundwood paper is used. Covers and advertising inserts are typically printed on higher-quality coated papers and reply-cards on postal bristol or other heavier-weight card stock.

Phone Books. High opacity and low thickness are requirements, and lightweight uncoated mechanical pulp-based papers are used for phone books. The ability to reproduce small type legibly, as well as clear advertisements in yellow-page sections, is important. Most phone books are printed on web offset presses.

Postcards. Heavy bristol papers (such as postal bristol) are used for postcards, which must not only accept pen-and-ink readily, but also be stiff and rigid enough to withstand postal sorting equipment. Coated-one-side bristols are used for picture postcards, and offset lithography is typically the printing process used.

Sheet Music. Prime importance is high whiteness and brightness, opacity, and the paper must be free of dirt, which could be construed as notes or other types of musical notation. Pages must remain flat when bound. Sheet music is printed using offset lithography.

Stationery and Letterhead. Aesthetic and functional requirements are necessary considerations for business and personal stationery. Letterhead is commonly printed on watermarked chemical pulp bond, or watermarked cotton-content bond. Envelopes and other paper products are designed to match the letterhead. Acceptance of pen, typing, and, increasingly, laser printing are requirements. Personal stationery is typically printed on white or pastel papeterie, a filled uncoated paper with a smooth, vellum, or embossed finish.

Tags and Tickets. Depending on the specific end-use requirements, most tags, tickets, punch cards, etc., use tag papers, which have the highest strength and durability. Depending on the desired print quality, coated tag stock may be used, and wet strength may be required. Tickets and laundry tags need to be stiff and durable, yet also tear properly at perforations. Letterpress and offset lithography are the primary tag and ticket printing processes.

Paper grades

Paper is categorized by its end use characteristics and its basis weight into a variety of different grades. There are hundreds of different grades and subgrades, but there are a few common, basic paper subdivisions. Each grade has a separate set of available basis weights, and one particular basic size at which the basis weights are calculated. Some of the common individual paper grades are bond paper, bristol paper, coated paper, cover paper, duplicator paper, imitation parchment, index paper, ledger paper, manifold paper, mimeograph paper, newsprint, offset paper, onionskin, safety paper, tag paper, text paper, vegetable parchment, and wedding paper.

Paper and printing problems and defects

All the paper properties listed earlier work in concert to increase or decrease a paper's printability and runnability. Both of these factors contribute to various printing defects affecting both print quality and trouble-free running of paper through a press. Here are some of the most common printing problems caused by paper imperfections: Defects due to blanket contamination, or particles of paper debris, lint, pickouts (the pulling of particles of paper or coatings from the paper surface), or debris from elsewhere in the pressroom contribute to hickeys. The accumulation of particles on the blanket, called blanket piling when it is present in such quantity as to cause a degradation of print quality, is called either whitening, when it occurs in the non-image area of the blanket, and image area piling when, as its name indicates, it occurs in the image area of a blanket.

The appearance on a printed sheet of undesirable images is called ghosting. Printing problems resulting from premature contact between the paper and the blanket—called prekissing—results in halftone blemishes such as doubling, or the printing of a phantom halftone dot slightly offset from the proper halftone dot, which distorts the printed halftone image. Slurring is a smearing of the edges of text or line art, while dot slurring is the smearing of halftone dots, both types of slurring typically occurring at the trailing edges of the images in question. Paper with inadequate pick resistance or low basis weight results in printing defects called waffling, or embossing, and back-edge curl (or tail-end hook), in which the pull of a tacky ink as the paper is peeled from the blanket pulls the image area of the paper with it, and creates distortions in the paper.

Other similar problems include picking, in which bits of paper are ripped out and stick to the blanket. In web presses, ink tack also contributes to delamination. Paper that has a wild formation can cause graininess of halftones, in which halftones dots are not printed uniformly. Ink chalking is a problem of coated papers that occurs when ink drying is hampered by an incompatibility between the ink and the paper coating. (Other ink-related distortions include ink setoff and blocking, mottle, show-through, tinting, and misregister. Problems with ink drying include dryback and blistering.)

Problems that affect the runnability of paper include curl, wavy edges, and other problems related to dimensional instability. In web offset printing, a primary cause of runnability problems is roll defects.

All of these various aspects mentioned above work together in the manufacture and printing of paper. There is a lot of technology in a piece of paper.

Runnability issues—milking

- Milking—occurs on coated papers when the binders in the coatings become softened by moisture on the first print blanket. This allows the following print blankets to lift binder and coating pigments out of the sheet. The non-image areas can become thick enough on the blanket to interfere with ink transfer from the plate to the blanket.
- Milking/whitening—is also seen with uncoated papers as well. Calcium carbonate and starch will lift off the sheet, if improperly bound, and begin piling, as with coated papers, on the blanket.
- Cleaning the blankets can be difficult with normal press washes. It is best to use warm water and solvent. The carbonate can also wear the plate over time or cause "blinding" which is the removal of the image.

Runnability issues

- Contamination
  Milking and edge buildup on a web offset blanket.
- Poor trimming
  Poor trimming on folio or web paper can result in the loose fiber/filler breaking away during printing and collecting on the blanket which then results in print contamination.
- Cutter debris
  Cutter debris will show one straight edge. This material will break loose and move inward on the offset blanket resulting in contamination.
- Synthetic fibers
  Synthetic fibers from a new or damaged felt appear "shiny" on the offset blanket. Like wood fibers, they will "plug" up halftone screens if excessive. Synthetic fibers are very long compared to wood fibers. The small white fibers are wood, the long ones are synthetic.

Print quality issues—mottle

- Gloss mottle is a galvanized ink appearance with uncoated paper caused by poor paper formation. Areas of fiber and nonfiber result in ink soaking into some areas and not others as a galvanized effect.

- Back trap mottle is irregular and unwanted variations in ink density caused by uneven absorption of the substrate and printing in succession onto blankets with no overprint ink. Four or more color presses generally show this problem. This generally is the result of poor coating or base paper absorbing the ink at different rates
- Wet trap mottle is caused by the overprinting of one color onto another color with tones and solids. Wet trap is more apparent in high-contrast areas in the affected solid or tone. This is more of an issue with coated papers.

Runnability factors—ink

- Ink mileage is affected by the type of paper you print on (coated or uncoated). Paper holdout determines the mileage of the ink. The better the surface holdout, the better the ink mileage. One pound of black ink, assuming identical solid ink densities, covers approximately 360,000 square inches on coated paper but only 150,000 square inches on uncoated newsprint.

Chapter 8

WORKFLOW

Unlike other manufacturing assembly lines, graphic arts workflows do not follow a general model of the production process. Every printing plant is different. Every workflow is different. And every job is a surprise. With conventional workflow, the production process used to start with the printer or the prepress house. They received different kinds of artwork or raw text, and their job was to set type, scan images, build pages, make film and plates and finally print the job. They knew how to scan the images, whether transparencies or reflections, positives or negatives. They knew what colors were "reproducible," what the variability of the process was, and what file formats to use. The printer and/or the prepress service had almost everything under control.

Today we see the integration of the image creator with the production process itself. Most jobs today arrive in digital format. Designers as well as graphic artists are integrating computers into their work. Content creators are now doing some tasks that used to be done by printers or prepress houses, so printers and prepress services are losing control over file preparation for printing. And that file preparation controls the entire process.

Digital workflow for printing often comes down to two basic approaches: raster and vector. There are almost 20 different raster-based file formats available in the Macintosh version of Photoshop alone, many with configurable subsets—plus vector formats. All of these formats come together in a container of sorts, which holds all page elements and combines them. The container application may vary throughout the workflow, which results in two distinct types of job control—component files, which are created by the designer or creative professional in the initial preparation, and consolidated files.

Component files

Component files for high-end printing are assembled using QuarkXPress or PageMaker or Illustrator or FreeHand (the latter two for packaging) and FrameMaker or Corel Ventura Publisher for object-oriented, text-intensive documents. The components are raster and vector files.

Consolidated files

Consolidated files are used to bring all of the component files, both raster and vector, into a single format—a container— that is accepted by an output processing system, a RIP or CEPS system. The consolidated format has been PostScript, but PDF is now an alternative. PDF and PostScript come from the same roots. Font handling, color handling, resolution, target output device, and compression must be set up in advance in order to achieve an acceptable consolidated file.

In PostScript, altering the consolidated file after creation requires re-creation from the original component files. PDF started the same way, but now there are many tools for editing PDFs. When PDF lacked these tools, CT and LW formats, either in CEPS native formats, or as TIFF/IT files, found a reason to remain in production. These formats stayed in use because of the requirements of specific output devices. However, raster files are uneditable and voluminous and this can affect network performance. CEPS raster-based CT and LW files have a limited set of editing tools, usually based on proprietary systems. TIFF/IT has no editing tools. PostScript never really lent itself to interactive editing, although there were some attempts on the part of third-party developers. PDF is moving rapidly via plug-ins to provide high levels of editability.

Embedded elements

Vector files are usually saved in EPS; raster files have loads of options, with production efficiencies such as image replacement, data compression, and color management. It is almost impossible to control the file formats from clients; it is useful to try to control those used in internal operations.

Editability

The need to make changes to a job (sometimes after it has been shipped) is not really funny. Author's alterations, printer's errors, or Murphy's law make editability an issue at every stage in the process. With automated production processes, it is vital that we get the job right as far up front as possible and then have the ability to make changes at each step if necessary.

Embedded elements

While vector files are usually saved in EPS, raster files have many options, changing not only the specific format, but enhancing production with items like image replacement, data compression, and color-managed files. Now that we are moving to digital photography and scanning very early in the process, we must re-think the way in which we capture and apply our files. We repeat that it is almost impossible to control the file formats from clients; it would be useful, at least, to try to control them in our internal operations.

If technology helps us work faster, better, and more efficiently, why is it that it doesn't always work, particularly in graphic arts? Because we have too many variables. In the printing industry there are many variables that affect the production process. Although is important to notice the amazing technological developments that are helping printers and service bureaus to serve their clients better and faster, it is also very important to point out that this is a developing industry, which lacks a great deal of standardization. Every user is king.

Islands of automation

The ultimate and ideal workflow is a totally digital workflow. Unfortunately in this industry, in only a few instances is this the case. Traditional print publishing is plagued by incompatible equipment and disconnected islands of automation that electronic publishing has created, unintentionally, as entirely new forms of digital bottlenecks.

This last sentence contains two key terms, "islands of automation" and "bottleneck." Starting with the first one, islands of automation refers to those highly automated processes inside the workflow that do not have continuity with the other steps or processes that follow in the workflow. It is like having computer-to-plate technologies and not having reliable digital proofing. The benefits of having a filmless and time-effective platemaking process are diminished by the fact that some customers require a film-based proof. The second definition is bottleneck. A bottleneck is any process or workstation with capacity less than or equal to the demands placed on it. Capacity is the measure of the system output. For example, on a printing press, it is the number of impressions that it can produce in a time frame, usually an hour.

Every process is composed of many steps. Every step or production operation has a certain capacity. The capacity of each of these operations is not the same. Some stations work faster than others, meaning that at some point some workstations will be idle while others will be overloaded. In the case of islands of automation, we may have very fast, highly automated processes linked with slower processes that will constitute system bottlenecks. The problem with bottlenecks is that they determine the capacity of the entire system. If in my system I have very fast workstations linked to others that are not so fast, the capacity of my system equals the capacity of the slowest workstation, not the fastest. To be effective, workflows should be entirely automated. In the printing industry, we talk about automation, digital file transfers, etc., but the full benefits of the technology will not be seen if a fully digital workflow is not in place.

Why workflow automation?

Automation permits the combination of complex and simple tasks that do not need manual intervention. The reason we should do this is lower costs and faster deliveries. However, in graphic arts, there are probably as many exceptions as rules. Exceptions are those jobs that do not run easily through the workflow. Managing exceptions is more difficult. They are more expensive than managing regular standardized processes because they require operator expertise and intervention. This concept applies not only for the production process alone, but also for customers, since they now have to archive, retrieve, manipulate, and reuse digital information. They must also deal with exceptions and lack of standardization.

Workflow design

We can have as many workflow models as we wish. The bottom line is that when designing a workflow, it is necessary to analyze the different steps that are encountered most frequently. Then, identify the individual processes to produce the desired results, and finally design a workflow, or a group of workflows, which can handle those steps in an efficient manner. The idea of workflow design is not to streamline each task in order to save time in each step of the process, but rather to automate the entire process. The whole is the sum of its parts. The following section details the many steps involved in workflow for printing and publishing production.

Typical tasks in a print production environment

Preflighting

Preflighting a job is nothing more than checking if the digital file has all the elements necessary to perform well in the production workflow. Many software programs are designed for this task. Among other items, these programs check if the fonts are embedded, if all images are present, with the right format (RGB or CMYK), etc. The idea of preflight checking is to avoid mistakes before the job reaches the first output production steps. Preflight checking attempts to avoid problems by fixing them up front.

Color management

Color management has been an area of controversy. It has became more popular recently as digital printing and digital proofing become more popular. As it is used in this book, color management is the effort to match color as it is captured by various devices, displayed by various monitors, and output from various different output devices for a given job. It is important to maintain the consistency of quality of the same image across different media and output devices. Today, color management is based on profiles for encoding color as it relates to a specific image to and from specific devices.

PostScript file creation

Most jobs are created in some sort of page layout application like QuarkXPress or PageMaker. Most RIPs (Raster Image Processors) do not understand applications—they "speak" another language, PostScript. Therefore, at some point, it will be necessary to transform those application files into PostScript code. When you click *Print* the application program builds a PostScript file from your screen image, the underlying data and some information from the operating system. In the graphic arts, when you print, you are sending PostScript code.

PDF file creation

PDF is an excellent file format for file exchange. As we will discuss later in this chapter, it is one of the most versatile file formats due to its portability and cross-platform characteristics.

Trapping

When you have adjoining elements of different colors, registration is critical. The problem is that press registration is not one hundred percent perfect; therefore it is necessary to overlap these colors to compensate for misregistration, and we call this image trapping. Today trapping is accomplished using different software packages. Some are more sophisticated than others, but the question is when in the workflow is trapping done. Some do trapping before RIPing, some do it while RIPing, and others after. Approaches depend on the configuration of the workflow, but for the most part, it will depend on the kind of applications and products service providers provide.

Imposition

Imposition is the arrangement of individual pages on a press sheet, so that when it is folded and trimmed, the pages are in correct orientation and order. To impose is a responsibility that should not be taken lightly. As in the case of trapping, there are advanced imposition software packages that do this automatically. However, this task can be done manually in the application software, depending on the type of operation.

RIP

The RIP (Raster Image Processor) takes in high-level page description files and outputs low-level data streams that can be fed directly to a digital printer, imagesetter, or platesetter for image rendering, or to a video display to be viewed. The RIP has three main internal functions interpretation, creation of the display list, and rasterization.

- Interpretation: in this stage the RIP interprets the PostScript code. It decodes PostScript and prepares the information to the following step, the display list.
- Creation of the display list: creation of an intermediate list of objects and instructions before rasterizing. It is a list of objects in a page description file that have a determined order. The order the page elements have in this display list is the same order in which they will be displayed or imaged.
- Rasterization: the conversion of graphic elements into bitmaps for rendering on a monitor, digital printer or imagesetter. In other words, the RIP takes the display list and converts it into pixels. This stage is necessary because every output device needs to generate spots, dots, or pixels.

Proofing

A proof is an output of the job before it gets printed. There are different kinds of proofs available that range from conventional proofs, which are film-based, to soft proofs, which use a calibrated monitor, to digital proofs, from a digital proofing printer.

Remote proofing

Sometimes the person who okays the proof is in a remote location. To avoid mail delays, some firms use remote proofers at their customers' sites. Files are transmitted over a digital telecommunications network. Once the client receives the file, they can output it on paper, using a digital printing device, or simply display it on a monitor (soft proof). The file that is sent can be an application file, a PostScript file, or a PDF file. This file can have either just the resolution necessary to output on the proofing device, or the full resolution of the final reproduction device. File size is an important issue for file transmission over digital networks; therefore, it makes more sense to have just the resolution needed to output on the proofing device. In any case, the most important consideration is to have the proofing devices accurately calibrated to the printing conditions of the press or digital printing device on which the job will ultimately be produced.

Corrections

The aim of a proof is to detect any error or mistake in the file prior to printing the job. When corrections need to be done, decisions have to be made quickly. It is necessary to have excellent communication between customer and producer. Remote proofing, and digital proofing in general, is helping to speed up the process of correction and re-proofing. Therefore, it is important to have corrections as a task in the workflow with a clearly defined methodology. If film is still used, it is output by an imagesetter, after the RIP stage. Film can be outputted either on single spreads or on full size imposed page. The film is then used for plate exposure, or for making analog proofs.

Plate output

Today there are two methods for producing a plate: the conventional way, using film, and the digital way, using a computer-to-plate device, also known as a platesetter. With a totally digital workflow, the second way is more suitable; however, many printers still use film due to the capital investment required. With computer-to-plate technology, film is eliminated from the production workflow, which represents many advantages for printers, and eliminates one level of variability in the system. Another issue with computer-to-plate is proofing. Proofing has to be done digitally; however, digital proofing, although it has improved in the past couple of years, is still not completely accepted as a contract proof by some critical customers. They demand a halftone-dot-based proof.

Blueline proof

The purpose of a blueline proof is to check final imposition and verify if there is any element missing or misplaced. The blueline can be printed in many paper formats: it can be a print of a single page or a big print of the entire press sheet imposition. These proofs are not intended to judge color or print quality in any aspect, they are just to verify the position of the elements in the page or the imposition.

Printing

Printing is the last task in a print production environment. Today we not only output using conventional printing methods, like offset lithography, flexography or gravure, but also we have a variety of optional digital printing devices available. Digital printers and presses use different technologies, and instead of ink, they use toner or inkjet ink.

Storage

Storage refers to the warehousing of electronic files from already completed jobs. Files can be stored on computer hard drives, CD-ROMs, tapes, or magnetic diskettes. Many storage technologies have been developed in recent years, however graphic arts files are known for huge sizes, and therefore storage can still be a problem more in the finding and retrieval than in the actual storage.

These are the most typical tasks in a print production workflow. Some others are omitted here but probably they are a subcategory of the ones we just mentioned. As you see, each one of the tasks has its own requirements. Workflows can be very different from one print shop to another. Each one may combine tasks that are highly automated with conventional or manual methods or they can have a fully digital workflow. The content creator must be aware of these issues before creating the file for printing.

One of the promises of PDF does lie with the originators. If they convert their layout program pages into PDF properly, and properly is the operative word, then workflow can be truly automatic. We must assume that some originators will not make good PDFs (and they probably did not make good application files either), so PDF may begin when a job is accepted by the prepress or printing service. Many new utility programs will allow PDFs to be fully edited (except for certain layout features like justification and hypenation) for changes and corrections at the last minute.

Variable data printing

Print no longer has to be simply a long-run, broadcast-oriented information distribution medium. Print is able to deliver a specific, targeted message to a specific, targeted audience.

At the front end, master pages must be formatted with provisions for entering information that will vary from printed unit to printed unit. Information must be imported from a database to fill the variable areas of the layout. Most of the programs for variable-data printing provide some way to define portions of QuarkXPress or PageMaker layouts as subject to variation.

Personalization is an outgrowth of the mail merge features dating back to word processors of the 1970s (and to "player-piano" type-writers of the 40s and 50s), which made it possible to merge a standard letter with a list of names, addresses, and personalized salutations. Personalization on today's digital color presses mostly takes the form of supplementing name and address data with other text in specific areas of a static page layout. The source of the variable information is a database or a delimited, sequential list of fields. A more advanced approach to personalization is adding not just text, but other content objects to the page, such as photos, graphics, scanned signatures, etc. They are retrieved from a database for placement in the layout.

A different aspect of variable printing is sometimes described as custom document assembly, or versioning. This has been done in the office for years. Word processors in the 70s assembled individual paragraphs into reports, customized insurance policies, and other materials.

Short runs of specific layouts can incorporate variable data with some of the data varying from page to page, while other content is common to a series of pages. Many programs define the variable objects on the master page as a variable content box. Data areas on the page must be predefined (usually as rectangles of a fixed size). The database data is then linked by a variable data program and the master layout and the variable data are combined, either in the page (which then needs to be rasterized for each impression) or in the RIP.

Soon pages and layouts will be generated on the fly according to the defined content. The static master page must be rasterized and each of the variable-page components must also be rasterized fast enough to keep up with the print engine.

The RIP requirement becomes more complex as graphics and color-separated photos are included as components that vary from unit to unit. Print server configurations such as Barco's and new multi-processor RIP configurations such as Adobe's Extreme are working in this area. For now, most pages to be printed are prerasterized, assembled on the fly, and input to the print engine.

The ability to pass these huge amounts of raster data through the pipeline to the print engine in such a way as to ensure that the device can run at its rated speed is the other major challenge. This task is complicated by the size of the pipeline to the print engine, that is, the maximum speed of data transfer to the engine, which at this stage of the technological evolution of engines is generally much slower than is required for true productivity.

The suppliers of digital color printers and presses have chosen a unique method for handling variable data and producing custom documents. They all face other technical considerations that contribute to the complexity of the overall variable-printing workflow, including the ability to handle input from a variety of database formats and mechanisms for ensuring and verifying job integrity.

Digital workflow is evolving rapidly to meet the demands of automated presses, printers, and systems. The printing industry must be competitive with mass media. It must be able to handle long and short runs, static and variable data, now and not later.

The RIP

Almost every imaging device available today is a raster imager, using spots to build text, lines, pictures, etc. Thus, every imager must, out of necessity, have a RIP, whether it is a lowly desktop printer or a giant computer-to-plate (CTP) system. And every RIP is just a little bit different. Many are based on Adobe's design, with some additional features, and some are legally derived from public information on the PostScript language. These have been called PostScript clones. Most of the small or home office market is dominated by Hewlett-Packard's PCL printer language, a PostScript wannabe and many of the high-end CTP systems use non-Adobe interpreters.

When you send a document to a printer, the RIP does its job and out come the page or pages. But today's digital workflow is much more complex and multiple RIPpings are often the norm. In a CTP workflow, the document might be RIPped to a color printer for color proofing, RIPped to an imposition proofer, RIPped to a remote proofer, and finally RIPped to the platesetter. In most cases this involves four different RIPs and four different imaging engines. And four chances for variation. Plus, there are "flavors" of PostScript based on versions from Adobe licensees and others who are not licensees.

RIP evolution

The PostScript page description language was developed to communicate the appearance of text, graphical shapes, and images to raster-based output devices equipped with a PostScript interpreter. PostScript has become dominant in the computer printing world because of its device-independence and resolution-independence.

Device-independence means that the image (the page to print or display) is defined without any reference to specific device features (printer resolution, page size, etc.). A single page description can be used on any PostScript-compatible printer from a 300 dpi laser printer to a 3,000+ dpi imagesetter or platesetter. In our opinion, another reason for its success is that it supports high-end printing. Computer-to-plate and digital printing as we know them could not have developed without a standardized page description language.

Most applications that can print to a PostScript printer also let you "print" to a file. Printing to a file means that the application (or the computer running the application, with the help of a PostScript driver) converts the job data into PostScript commands and saves the data as a file instead of transmitting the code over a cable to a printer. You can then download the file to any PostScript printer to print it out. Downloading is different from printing in that no data conversion (from job data to PostScript) takes place, the file is merely sent to the printer. This allows you to directly send PostScript streams to printers, without opening any application program. The PostScript file contains all font and image data and can be stored on a disk and sent to a graphic arts service. Most computer platforms have a variety of PostScript downloaders available.

PostScript is device independent . . . to a point. When you print, you print to a specific printer that has very specific features such as certain resolutions, page sizes, minimum margins, choice of paper trays, etc. Although the PostScript driver can send the PostScript job to any printer, it can't specify a tabloid page for a printer that does not have a tabloid tray, for example. To access features specific to the printer, PostScript uses PPDs (PostScript Printer Description files) which are stored in the System folder.

Some printer-specific information that a PPD might include:
- input paper trays
- page size definitions
- print areas for each page size
- output paper trays
- duplexing (double-sided printing)
- default resolution
- resolutions available
- black and white or color output
- halftone screening functions
- default screen angles
- screen frequency combinations
- custom screening definition
- default transfer functions
- default font

QuarkXPress also uses another file to relate printer-specific information: a Printer Description File (PDF), which is not to be confused with another subject of this book, the Portable Document Format, also a PDF. (Confusing, isn't it?) QuarkXPress uses data from both the PPD and PDF to generate PostScript for output. At print time, you select the PostScript output device and select a PPD (or a PDF in QuarkXPress 3.3 or below). If you later want to print the same job to a different printer, all you need to do is select a different printer with a different PPD.

Hardware and software RIPs

There are so-called hardware RIPs and software RIPs. The distinction is not always clear. Initially all RIPs were proprietary, with a CPU, disk, RIP software, and related hardware enclosed in a cabinet and attached to an imaging recorder. There was no monitor and no keyboard, although a keypad and LCD panel on the recorder did allow some level of interface. You connected your network to the RIP and away you went. Then someone decided that they could sell you the RIP software and you could install it in your own computer. Usually they supplied a special computer board and cable to connect to the imager. The latter approach was called a software RIP.

PostScript 3

In September 1996, Adobe Systems Incorporated announced its newest printing systems solution, which includes the next generation of Adobe PostScript called PostScript 3 (the word "level" has been dropped). Adobe's integrated printing system solution focuses on changing the printing experience by allowing OEM customers to build best-in-class printing solutions and providing users the ability to print complex graphics and Web content, when and where they need it. Adobe has gone beyond offering a page description language to providing a total systems solution for delivering and printing digital documents.

Adobe has developed an advanced level of functionality in Adobe PostScript 3 to accommodate the new digital document creation process which includes varying sources, complex composition, and virtually unlimited destinations. Users are now accessing content for use in digital documents from varying sources including electronic mail, web pages, intranets, online services, content providers, and digital cameras. Document composition now includes not only text, but also complex graphics, clip art, corporate logos, Internet content, multiple fonts, scanned images, and color. Finally, the digital document's destination can be to printing systems anywhere in the world, such as personal printers, network printers, service bureaus, pay-for-print providers, or data warehouses for electronic archival.

Enhanced Image Technology, a PostScript 3 feature, insures that documents print faster, easier, and with optimal quality. A key benefit to the user is that EHT recognizes image objects and automatically optimizes processing to deliver the highest possible quality, and at the same time speed return to application. Adobe PostScript 3 will include new imaging features that support the increasingly complex documents available via the Internet, support for three-dimensional images, photo-quality grayscaling, smooth gradients in graphic objects, image compositing, and full-color spectrums.

PostScript 3 will support direct processing of web content, including HTML and PDF. It will also extend the resident font set to provide compatibility with the resident fonts of all leading operating systems, enhancing performance by reducing font downloading. PostScript 3 provides users with a more robust ability to manage individual pages within a document, thereby improving control over the printing process.

Extreme neé Supra and the future of RIPs

The high-speed data requirements of digital presses, large-format film "imposetters" and computer-to-plate systems demand radical changes in RIP and workflow architectures. Developers are also trying to eliminate PostScript processing bottlenecks and accelerate deadline production times. RIP suppliers have been converting PostScript into contone (CT) and linework (LW) files via proprietary methods or converting PostScript into some editable internal format in an attempt to make the RIPing process more efficient.

There are lots of alternatives out there. Covalent Systems' Job Monitor Protocol is a standard framework for collecting data from jobs as they pass through a series of steps and for transferring the data to business systems. Prepress production environments could collect critical information, such as how much time was spent on image editing at one workstation and color correction at another, and transfer it to a business system for analysis and billing. All of this is available now if you stick with the selection of proprietary systems and custom interfaces between them. Another proposed standard, CIP3, covers the interaction among processes at the front-end prepress operation, the press itself and the back-end finishing operation. CIP3 is being promoted by Heidelberg, with the support of other press and finishing-equipment suppliers, in addition to front-end system vendors such as Agfa.

Adobe's Extreme RIP architecture is a major step in RIP evolution. It is built around the 3.0/3.x version of Adobe's Portable Document Format. PostScript is an interpretive programming language; PDF is a compact, noninterpretive format designed for fast imaging to a screen. PDF has lacked the ability to handle high-resolution images easily and to handle screening for print—both of these are included within Extreme. Extreme also connects web and print publishing, as both will use the new version of PDF used as the plug-in to web browsers.

Working with PostScript

Not all PostScript is equal; code generated by Photoshop conforms to Document Structuring Conventions (DSC), some from QuarkXPress does not. Page structure can't be easily determined. Extreme converts such files automatically into PDF format, allowing separate processing. Extreme incorporates both Adobe PostScript language and Adobe Portable Document Format (PDF) for production printers, and Adobe PrintMill, an intranet-based printing and printer management solution. When you create a page in QuarkXPress or PageMaker, you are interfacing with the program as displayed on the screen. The GUI describes the page on screen for the user. However, when you click Print, it is PostScript code which defines that page as it is sent to the printer or imagesetter. You can even save the PostScript file to disk and read it (if you can decipher it). But a page described in PostScript is nearly uneditable without an understanding of the programming language itself. Admittedly there are unique people out there who can edit PostScript. PostScript is a voluminous file format. Placing a single "a" on a QuarkXPress page and "printing" the page to an ASCII file produces at least 16 pages of type.

Outputting PostScript

There are four choices for outputting a file from an application (find all of them below):

1. Click Print and send the file to a printer on your in-house network. This is a great option if you're publishing a single copy for yourself. Or even a couple of dozen copies for the staff.

2. Send the application file to an outside service, but make sure you send the image files and all of the screen and printer fonts. This file can be changed by the service bureau, making its integrity questionable.This approach not only opens the door for further unpredictability, but it also raises some tricky legal issues. Due to font licensing, the service bureau must install the fonts you use and/or supply, print your job, and immediately remove those fonts from their system. This must be done for each job and each time the file is printed. What if the service bureau has purchased a license to the same font? For instance, you supply a document which uses Garamond. Whose version of Garamond is it—Adobe's, ITC's, Monotype's or some overnight type house's? If you don't specify and/or the service bureau doesn't have the correct version of your typeface, a font substitution will occur. Possible repercussions of an improper font substitution could be the reflowing of text, sometimes destroying the original design. Or maybe you like Courier, the ultimate font substitution.

But service bureaus deal with application files because they can open them, preflight check them and make changes.

3. Save the file to disk as PostScript code, which incorporates the images and fonts, and send it to an output service. This is a

viable option if you have a very large external storage device to save all of that PostScript information. (Remember, a single "a" generates 16 plus pages of PostScript text. Well, that's not really fair, because the 16 pages of code could support many text pages. But, PostScript code is voluminous, nevertheless.)

A drawback to this method is the lack of "correctability." If the correct page setup options were not chosen at the time of PostScript generation, the page may not reproduce as desired. Often, designers don't know the specifications of the imagesetter or output device of the service bureau. Without this information, specifications regarding page size, crop marks, line screen ruling, and many other variables can't be set. And once the PostScript file for that document is generated, it's too late. What if only a part of a page or a graphic created in a drawing program needs to be placed into a page layout application like QuarkXPress or PageMaker? Thus was born the Encapsulated PostScript file—a file representing one page with, or in the early days without, a preview image. This allows you to save a graphic in a standardized form and place it into a composite document where it can be scaled and manipulated to fit. However, the EPS file does not save font data and many artists have seen their beautiful graphics output with Courier because the original font was not available at the RIP. So, the EPS was portable only to a point. Adobe Illustrator now saves EPS with the font data as does Acrobat Exchange 3.x. And the new Placed PDF could replace EPS.

PostScript conclusions

As a platform-independent page description language, PostScript has emerged as a de facto standard. Today, PostScript accounts for 95% or more of the final output of all commercial publications. On the downside, PostScript is extremely variable and page-dependent.

There's no doubt that PostScript has brought on revolutionary advances. But with every revolution comes the need for further refinement. Even Adobe admits that PostScript has many deficiencies for the role it is currently playing. The use of PostScript has far surpassed Adobe's original intention, and thus, they are in the midst of solving problems and advancing their core technology in order to fulfill the expectations of today's digital workflow demands. The wide variety of applications, platforms, and typefaces has caused many headaches for the publishing industry. There are just too many places for things to go wrong.

While you can easily move documents around by e-mail, network, or disk, you can't assume that everybody has the right fonts on their system, or that they have the right program to open your document, or even (in a cross-platform environment) the right setup to receive the document. You could spend a lot of time and money installing the same software and fonts, plus the requisite extra hard-disk space and RAM, on every system to allow document portability—and then train people on each program used to create the documents in the first place. But of course, this setup is inefficient and you don't have the capital to implement it, and neither does anyone else.

PostScript serves its purpose as a way to describe document pages in a design-rich fashion. But in today's world of ever-increasing efficiency, the need for speed, and the customer's insistence on jobs being printed "yesterday," research and development into document handling is a neverending process. Files need to be transferred from place to place quickly, predictably, and efficiently. With the increasing use of digital presses, CTP technology, and completely digital workflows, the need for platform-independent digital file transfer standards is becoming more and more urgent.

That brings us to the fourth alternative for communicating with graphic service providers and the outside world, the Portable Document Format.

   4. Create a PDF of your file.

More about this approach later in this chapter. But let us now look at some of the areas of workflow infrastructure.

Telecommunications

Once your job has been created, how do you get it to the service provider? Many people in graphic arts still use a courier service, such as FedEx, or another service of that kind. This practice can result in high costs, especially when the same file has to be sent back and forth several times for corrections or any other changes. More important, however, is the fact that important deadlines usually have to be met and all this process creates delays in turnaround times. In addition, during the sending and receiving process, files have a high risk of being lost or damaged.

To dilute the risks of sending and receiving files, couriers are being replaced by a much friendlier way of getting your files to the service provider: telecommunications. Using some sort of "line" sending files via a computer can be done in a stressless fashion. Jobs can be sent anytime; if something is missing it can be easily re-sent to fix the problem; if corrections are made, the creator can view the document before output. This all happens without the parties meeting face-to-face.

But not everything works perfectly with telecommunication technology. The one drawback to this technology is the transmission time—that is, the time it takes to send the job over a line to its destination. Today it is common to have files in the hundreds of megabytes; sending such a large file over a wire is not very efficient, and special dedicated digital lines intended for high-speed transmission are required.

All transmission technologies are measured at certain speed rates in either kilobytes per second or megabits per second. These figures are assuming perfect conditions, which is rarely the case. Therefore, the user should be advised that the transfer rate quoted is usually for a perfect world, which very seldom happens in real life situations, due to noise in the line, high loads, etc.

Data signals

When we talk of data signals, these are signals that need to be transmitted from one computer station to a nearby printer or to travel great distances to reach other communication devices there. Broadly, the signals that can travel over communication lines can be divided into two categories:

- analog
- digital

Analog signals: Traditionally, communication devices like radio and television have used analog signals to transmit. In an analog signal, the data travels in the form of a wave. The height of a signal is called amplitude, which can be modified. The number of waves (or cycles) in a given period is called the frequency and can also be modified. By modifying the amplitude and frequency the signals are transmitted as information.

Digital signals: A digital signal is a burst of on/off signals that creates a square rather than a wave. Every burst of signal represents a bit and the absence of a burst represents a zero bit. They are more accurate than the analog signals and are much faster.

Modems

Since transmission can be done digitally, the advantages of using digital transmission are enormous. However most of the infrastructures for telecommunications that have been already laid are analog, which means that the conversion to digital transmission can be very expensive. But we can circumvent this problem by using a device called a modem. A modem is a piece of hardware that converts analog signals to digital signals and back to analog.

Modems are retaking their importance with people's growing interest in the Internet. Furthermore modems are being extensively used for the transmission of less voluminous or less critical data via the World Wide Web. Today new technologies are improving the information transmission over ordinary telephone lines. Modems with a transmission speed of 56.6 Kbps are replacing the 28.8 Kbps devices, and it is expected that the speed will increase to 100 Kbps. This speed is now available only on special lines. Modern modems are being built with a voice and data recognition protocol that allows the switch between voice and data in less than one second. This is particularly important in those cases when a transmission is done using both data and voice. An application of this is technical support using show-and-tell explanations as a help.

Another feature is digital simultaneous voice and data (DSVD), which permits the transmission of voice and data at the same time using just one line. However, data transmition is done at a lower speed. A future characteristic of modems will be a videoconferencing standard that will give the advantages of the voice and data protocol and will support small images.

In the US, cable TV companies are now joining computer companies to bring the broad bandwidth used for television to computers at home via cable modems. The speeds of cable modems can be 10 times higher than special T1 modems. However, the speed will depend on the type of system used and on the number of users logged on.

In the graphic arts industry, however, some points have to be taken into consideration. First, present cable modems are fast only for receiving data. The data transmission is too slow, approximately 19.2 Kbps, which is not enough for interactivity. Second, in order to improve the two-way transmission, it is necessary that the entire cable change from analog to fiber optic, and this could take a couple or more years in the US.

Lines and connections

T1-lines: ISDN (Integrated Services Digital Network). ISDN is a digital communications network that allows the traffic of analog (voice) or digital signals at the same time. This worldwide network is used for the transmission of large volumes of data, which involves heavy processing demands. ISDN works with cable working at T1 satellite speed that gives it a speed of 10 MB of information per minute.

The digital protocols that allow ISDN lines to carry voice and data faster than the speediest modems have been around for nearly a decade, but users are still labeled as early adopters for installing ISDN. The most common ISDN line, Basic Rate Interface (BRI), has two 64-Kbps channels for data transmission rates of up to 128 Kbps. That translates to file transfers of about 1 Mbyte a minute, or two to four times the speed of a V.34 modem.

That speed can be improved by file compression and by the new crop of PCI adapter cards for Power Macs, which can bundle as many as four ISDN lines for a total of eight 64-Kbps transmission channels.

While ISDN has spread in Europe—first in prepress and then in other industry segments—in the United States, the regional telephone operating companies have been slower in updating switches with ISDN to provide nationwide service coverage. Phone companies have lagged at pumping up technical support to aid users with ISDN installations.

Compounding the difficulty for earlier adopters of the technology was a lack of interoperability. While service providers are supposed to follow the ISDN specification promulgated by the International Telecommunications Union, not all have adhered to the letter. In California, for example, Pacific Bell's slight deviation from the specification means its BRI ISDN lines run at 56 Kbps per channel rather than the normal 64 Kbps. Despite the slow start, analysts see a bright future for ISDN. About 250,000 ISDN installations were completed by the end of 1996, and it is anticipated that there will be 1 million lines by the end of the century.

In the publishing world, ISDN's biggest draw is its ability to replace overnight courier services and magnetic disks with a faster file delivery mechanism. ISDN has been used in the last few years by advertising agencies and reproduction and design bureaus to send files to printers and to send files to clients for proofing and approval.

Strong demand doesn't remove installation stumbling blocks and operating problems, but there are strong signs that US regional telephone operating companies realize ISDN's potential and are redoubling coverage and support efforts.

It might also be easier for converts to survive the ISDN installation process, now that the phone companies and equipment vendors have agreed on a set of ordering codes that make it easier for installers to pinpoint the correct line interface for each customer's equipment and application.

Smaller companies without a telecommunications manager or consulting budget may have the rockiest installation road. After potential users find out if service is available in their area and learn about some of the installation pitfalls, the question is which type of connection to consider: point-to-point links based on adapter cards or a WAN (Wide Area Network) using ISDN-enabled routers.

Forming a WAN with ISDN has its own set of advantages, including the ability to offer file transfers to the entire network and the ability to multiplex lines together for greater aggregate bandwidth. On the downside, however, routers must use some of the ISDN pipe for standard network messaging, and in AppleTalk's case that can lead to considerable bandwidth loss. Many companies offer ISDN services: Ameritech, Bell Atlantic, Bell South, Pacific Bell, Southwestern Bell, and U.S. West, among others. But ISDN now has a major competitor: ADSL.

ADSL and SDSL (Asymmetric & Symmetric Digital Subscriber Line).
ADSL lines do not need cable other than the local copper telephone line. Faster than T1, an ASDL line has the download capacity of 6.144 Mbps, but uploads at 500 Kbps. It is useful for surfing the web but it is not recommended for digital imaging and high-quality video conferencing due to its asymmetrical bandwidth. AT&T developed the Symmetric Digital Subscriber Line to solve this problem. Symmetric bandwidth stands for the line capacity to receive and deliver at the same bandwidth.

ATM (Asynchronous Transfer Mode). ATM is a way to package and deliver data. This service also uses either the local area network (LAN) or the wide area network (WAN). Global information can flow in an uninterrupted way at speeds from 1.544 Mbps to 1.2 Gbps. ATM is being used extensively in the corporate world and its potential is also expanding to desktop publishing applications.

Wireless connections

Today satellite transmissions are still not as viable or cost-effective as cable-based transmissions. In the future, however, it is very possible to have complex wireless networks. The existing wireless networks are restricted to highly specialized applications, and are capable of transmitting data at 115.2 Kbps, using infrared technology.

Long distance carriers are particularly keen on catching the air wave, because they have national networks but lack direct connections to individual telephone and cable households. AT&T announced that it would invest $137.5 million in a satellite broadcasting service, Direct-TV. MCI paid $682 million for an orbital slot to offer its own high-powered satellite broadcasting service. Sprint and its cable partners reorganized their alliance to focus on wireless rather than wired services—even changing the venture's name to Sprint Spectrum, an allusion to the radio-frequency spectrum used by wireless services.

The popularity of wireless stems partly from the fact that the business has already grown so rapidly. The cellular industry that made McCaw so rich went from almost nothing in 1980 to a $20 billion business in 1996. And in the last few years, refinements in digital technology have also made wireless transmission suitable for a broader range of services, including computer-precise television transmissions and high-speed data transfer. Even after the telecommunications market is fully deregulated in the US, the high cost of stringing wires or laying cables, and the expected resistance of the local cable and phone-wire monopolies to interlopers, will make it tough for long-distance carriers, local telephone companies, or cable operators to break into each other's traditional land-line markets.

The Baby Bells own the wires that link into most American households. Would-be rivals like long distance carriers can either negotiate to lease capacity on the local network, try to duplicate the network or find ways to bypass it. To duplicate that kind of a network, they must dig up streets or put up telephone poles. So far cellular has been too expensive to become a viable competitor to local phone service, but personal communications services may have a better shot.

PC networks, using digital radio transmissions for voice and data communications via small hand-held devices, can serve many more customers simultaneously than current cellular networks. This, and the cut-throat competition as several wireless companies compete in many of the larger metropolitan markets, should result in prices much lower than cellular companies have typically offered.

Networking

To create a network is, in essence, to connect computers and other communication devices in a way that many users can share common resources.

Local Area Network (LAN) and Wide Area Network (WAN)
There are two basic types of networks.
- Local Area Network (LAN)
- Wide Area Network (WAN)

Local Area Networks: These networks connect hardware and software, via communication channels within a close proximity. An example of a simple LAN is two computers linked with a telephone wire and connected to a printer. The network could be in a single floor, or several floors within the same building, or even a few buildings, but within close proximity. The connectivity is usually created using copper twisted wire or coax between these devices. In a slightly bigger network, the network could consist of connecting a few computers, a file server, shared hard drives, laser printer, storage devices, color printer, and possibly an imagesetter. Software runs the network and manages all the activities in the network.

LANs when used properly reduce the cost of expensive hardware, software, storage devices and color printers that could be shared, thereby applying the resources of the organization effectively. LANs help users to share programs and files. This minimizes traffic inside the office and less paper needs to float around. However, LANs need properly trained operators to manage them. From a security angle LANs do not offer the best protection of confidentiality.

Wide Area Networks: When there is a need to connect to wider locations, say communicate with the entire world, a LAN cannot do justice. For those corporations that have worldwide operations, when they need to communicate with each operating division as though they were in one building, WANs come in handy. The biggest of all the WANs and the most popular of them is of course the Internet. It connects millions of small computers and users worldwide.

Computer systems hold all kinds of information within them. When all this information needs to be shared by a much larger audience, the Internet helps access and transmit the data. Every computer that has an Internet connection becomes a member of the huge network. Through this network, any information that resides in any one of the computer systems can be accessed and used by all other computer systems around the world. Users from any part of the globe can share resources such as databases and the results of scientific research. Electronic mail (e-mail) is a very popular Internet application that benefits a great many users.

Topology

Topology refers to the layout of the network in which a LAN can be arranged and made to work. Basically there are three types of topologies that are used in a LAN. They are:

- star
- bus
- ring

Star: This type of a network topology has its roots in an earlier computing era, when a mainframe or some large computer would be the central computer to which several small computers would be connected. These small computers would draw most of the information from the mainframe and do the processing. It helped organizations that had a huge chunk of database and needed to process it locally. In this topology, the main computer is the hub and has all the information and any of the other intelligent terminals can be used interchangeably. It becomes useful when one operator of a terminal is away, but another user from the central computer can access that operator's information and work can move along. The biggest exposure using a star network is that when the hub computer crashes, it brings computing capability to a halt.

Bus: This is the most common of all topologies used in a LAN. A bus network aligns all the computers and other communication devices along a single channel. The connectivity is by copper twisted wire, coaxial cable, or fiber optic cable. Ethernet is a proprietary technology that is used by most bus networks. They can transmit about 10 megabits per second with new versions up to 100 Mbsps. When data is transmitted it is "broadcast" in both directions. There is special network software which ensures that the intended data reaches the target computer. An inherent drawback of bus networks is that data can be transmitted by only one computer at a time. If more than one computer transmits data, the data may collide, and it will have to be transmitted afresh.

Ring: All devices in this network are connected in the shape of a circle or ring. It creates a closed loop, into which each computer is connected. With this topology, any computer in the network can communicate with any other computer. The problem of data collision is avoided in the ring network by the use of an electronic signal system that it adopts called a token. In this system, every message that is sent on the network is attached to the token. When a computer is ready to transmit, it checks the signal to see if the token is free. The computer attaches its message to the token and transmits it. When the computer which the message is intended for is reached, it frees the token and puts it back to the network. A drawback of the ring network is that if a single link on the network fails, the entire network fails.

Networking Macintosh computers

In the Macintosh environment, the simplest and least expensive network approach is LocalTalk, which is built into every Macintosh.

You can construct a simple network of two Macintosh computers using LocalTalk with PhoneNet-compatible connectors—common telephone wire that connect computers, and the same wire that is used to connect a telephone to the wall jack. You can also use the same connectors to connect computers to your printer and share it. Unfortunately, it is very slow.

A LocalTalk-based network can be as simple as two computers and a printer connected together. With LocalTalk, computers and printers may be over a thousand feet apart, depending on the quality of the cable used. Computers are strung together, or daisy chained, using the connectors. If additional computers or printers need to be added to the network, they can be daisy chained into the existing connections.

This type of connection is inexpensive, but not very fast. The speed of the communication between computers is 230,400 bits per second. This may seem fast when compared to the fastest modems available, but it may not be fast enough. An alternative is to use Ethernet, a much faster networking technology—at least 43 times faster than LocalTalk. 10-Base-T Ethernet is at 10,000,000 bits per second; 100-Base-T is at 100,000,000 bits per second; and 1,000,000,000 bps Ethernet is not far away. Fiber optic connections are being applied by early adopters. With its high speed data transfer rates which can outperform copper wire, optical fiber will clearly become the new method for transmitting data.

A Macintosh-based network using Ethernet does not connect computers and printers together by daisy chaining them—they are connected into a hub. A device known as an Ethernet Transceiver is used to connect the cabling to the computer. For the Macintosh to use an Ethernet network, it must have an Ethernet card installed. Most recent Macintosh computers are delivered with a built-in Ethernet card. Most computer stores or catalogs can supply the card and instructions for installing it. The Ethernet Transceiver connects the card in your computer to the cabling of the network. The maximum distance supported by Ethernet is 500 meters.

Once the Ethernet network is physically set up, the Network Control Panel in the Macintosh is used to select Ethernet rather than built-in LocalTalk. With Ethernet in place, the only difference the user will notice is improved performance. One of the computers on the network is designated as the Server, and the other computers are its Clients. Usually, the fastest computer should be the Server.

Networking Windows computers

The networking picture in the Windows environment is more complex. The physical aspects of networking are almost the same as the Macintosh environment but LocalTalk is not used in the Windows environment. The networking method built into Windows for Workgroups or Windows 95 is known as the Microsoft Windows Network. This method is similar to AppleTalk in appearance and operation. The printer is connected directly to a computer, rather than to the hub itself. In the PC environment, the computer allows the connected printer to be shared. Any computer on the network can then connect to the shared printer and print. Most Ethernet cards for PCs come with a connection on the card, so a transceiver is not needed. Certain newer Macintoshes are also configured this way.

AppleTalk and the Microsoft Windows Network are known as peer-to-peer networks: any computer can be a server, and any computer can be a client. A computer can also be a server to one computer and a client to another at the same time.

Security

In all these types of networks a critical issue that gets a lot of attention is the issue of network security. Since data gets transmitted long distances over physical and non-physical media, there is always a potential that the data could be intercepted, damaged, or manipulated. Computer viruses can harm the quality of data and the damage could be devastating as the virus could easily spread over a vast number of computer systems very quickly, since the connectivity through the Internet is enormous. As much as the boon that networks provide us, it is advisable to watch out for the bane as well.

Servers

Digital has to be stored, managed, processed, and transferred to produce a job. Servers are necessary to network or to connect to different workstations. These workstations can be scanners, proofers, imagesetters or other computers. Servers can perform four different functions: file, print, application, and database.

A file server's function is to store a large number of digital files and share the data or some applications with other workstations on the network.

An application server's function is to perform a certain task when files, from the network, are sent to a specific folder in the server. One of the most used applications is image trapping.

A database server's function is to handle all file tracking functions. This kind of server uses a multitasking operating system such as UNIX or Windows NT for graphic applications.

The print server's function is to spool all the printing files from the network to a central area until the printer is free. The spooler allows monitoring the printer and scheduling jobs for printing with the purpose of allowing various workstations to use the same printer.

Choosing a server

On a network, a server is a computer with a large amount of disk storage that has shared software and information. Other computers on the network are clients and access the software or information as needed on the server. Choosing the right server and equipping it properly are the keys to the success of a LAN. A server is usually a computer that holds the bulk of the LAN operating system and shares its resources with workstations. Usually a single server:

- stores shared files
- stores software
- links to printers or other output devices
- links to tape drives and storage media
- links to modems
- links to RIPs

All connected users share these resources. As a LAN grows, these functions are spread over many servers and separate data management and communication servers may be needed. One of the first decisions is whether to buy:

- a standard PC or Macintosh as a dedicated server and tailor it with third party add-ons
- a PC or Mac designed as a proprietary server unit
- a Sun Computer or Silicon Graphics workstation as a server
- an NT running on a PC compatible or DEC Alpha hardware

Dedicated servers

Networking methodologies use a dedicated server. In this case, one computer (typically a very fast one) is designated as a dedicated server. All other computers that attach to it are clients only. This technique is used for larger networks that demand higher performance than the one that can be obtained with peer-to-peer networks. With a dedicated server, all shared files are on the server, and the client computers access it for their information. A server will usually have a network operating system installed on it (Novell, Lantastic, NT, etc.) and the monitor and keyboard will be removed. The Server will automatically start its software on power up, and only service requests from the network. Printing is shared as before, except that in very large networks, another computer is usually designated as a Print Server, and services only printing needs.

Proprietary servers

Because proprietary server options are designed for a particular LAN operating system, you avoid incompatibilities that crop up with a standard PC. For example, some third party back-up systems and power supplies do not work very reliably with certain LAN operating systems. Proprietary units are optimized for their specific LAN operating system.

A print server receives jobs from a user on a network, stores the job in a queue, and then forwards the job to an output device on the net-work—most networks have multiple output devices, from very low-resolution laser printers to high-resolution imagesetters and platemakers. Features such as queue management, statistics report-ing, printer setup, and file storage for later printing are common. When the printer is ready, the computer sends the first packets of data which the printer receives and processes until the job has been sent to the printer. If you are the ninth person waiting to print, the wait could be enormous. However, most computers allow you to print in the background.

Background printing means that when you select *Print*, the comput-er saves the job to a temporary file and a separate piece of software handles communicating that file to the printer when the printer becomes available. You can continue working on the computer while the job prints. When the computer needs to send data to the printer, the application running in the foreground may have to pause, tying up your computer. Within a few years, true multitasking will be available on most systems. In addition to releasing your workstation faster from print processing, a print server should also be able to per-form queue management.

Queue management

A print queue is a series of jobs waiting to print. A print server usu-ally manages multiple queues, either for the same printer or for dif-ferent printers. A print server can have different queues for a single output, each with an individual setup. A print server usually has dif-ferent types of queues:
* Active—jobs print when the output device is available
* Hold—jobs print when the administrator releases them
* Completed—printed jobs remain stored on disk for archiving or reprinting
* Error—jobs that could not print are stored for review

The active queue is used when you have a job to print and you want to print it now or as soon as the device is available. You can use a hold queue, for example, if you want to print jobs overnight. That way, jobs that need to get out during the day get sent to the active queue, and jobs waiting in the hold queue get sent when the network load is lower, or when higher-priority jobs have finished printing. A completed queue lets you hold onto jobs for future printing; and an error queue holds the jobs that could not print because of a printer error, a PostScript error, or a network error. When the error is fixed, you can resend the job. The hold queue, in particular, lets you manage the printing services on your network. Jobs can be sent to the print server computer, but won't print until the system administrator directs them to the appropriate active queue. This type of queue works for jobs requiring special attention, such as special media (film or plate) or switch settings. They can be held until the system administrator has the output device set up properly.

Multiple print queues

The ability to support multiple print queues allows you to designate queues for specific print devices, so you automate job routing and eliminate manual switching. For instance, you can have a queue for a plain-paper device and one for a film device. During the proofing stages of the job you send it to the plain-paper queue; for the final pass you send it to the film device.

To manage all these queues, the print server should be able to:
- delete jobs in a queue
- redirect jobs from one queue to another
- change priority of jobs in an output queue
- view the status of jobs in the queue
- enable or disable any of the queues

In addition to managing the jobs within the queues, the print server should let you tie specific printer options to a queue. If you have a high-resolution imagesetter, you might want to have different queues for low, medium, and high resolutions, depending on the job's requirements. Then, you only need to select the queue that is called "2400 dpi film," for example, and the job automatically goes to the correct output device and prints at the correct resolution. For plain-paper laser printers, you could have different queues for the different paper trays. For digital color presses like the Xeikon DCP, Agfa Chromapress, or Xerox Docucolor, you could have multiple devices with certain types of paper in use.

By including a printer configuration in the print queue, jobs always print the way you want them to print. For an imagesetter, you can use printer setups to make sure all the RIP settings are set correctly. The print server lets you set page orientation, negative or mirror image modes, resolution selection, and page grouping before a job is sent to the imagesetter. A print server should be able to set any of the options available from the RIP's software. The print server also maintains statistics about each job, providing the user with a report on printing times, number of pages printed, source workstation name, date and time of job, and more. This report could be in a format that can be imported into IBM Lotus, Microsoft Excel, or other programs for billing or accounting purposes. Prepress service bureaus charge by the minute for jobs that exceed expected runtimes and a print server's job log provides the exact runtime for each job.

Network infrastructure

Current networks on either cable or wire. Cables and wires are extremely important because they are the connection between the workstations and other electronic devices, including other remote networks. Cables can be coaxial or fiberoptic; wires can be shielded twist pair or unshielded twisted pair.

Twisted pair wire refers to two insulated copper wires twisted together. However a twisted wire may contain up to 100 or more pairs of twisted wires. It is widely used for local telephone wiring. This wire is capable of transmitting only one signal at a time.

Coaxial cable is a three-layer insulated cable, each layer is surrounded by another cable, and so on. It is similar to TV wiring.

Fiber optic cable is a totally different approach. This cable is made of thin glass fibers that transmit light. Because data is transmitted via light beams, fiber optic cables have the advantages of speed, high connectivity, and interference resistance. The disadvantage is that this technology needs the most expensive network interface cards. The cost is expected to decrease due to the fast growing fiber optics industry as capacity will play an important role in the future.

The network components include an operating system, an interface card, cabling and a protocol standard. The most common protocols are Ethernet, widely used in the graphic arts industry (0.5 Mbps); Token Ring, used on complex computing environments, and FDDI, a new standard developed for fiber optic networks. They define the movement over the network and over other components.

Network implementation

The role of digital networks in publishing is to provide a way to process digital pages in an automated manufacturing environment. Customers should be able to enter the specifications of a particular job and use communications lines to send the files. Such a system requires a high level of technical expertise and its characteristics will depend on the demands of each individual operation of the organization. The implementation of systems like this can only be done by professionals. There are several specialized firms that assist other organizations in the implementation of network systems.

The World Wide Web is now providing opportunities to market and distribute products over this electronic media. The success of these networks will depend on the web's capacity to share increasing volumes of information as fast as possible.

There are two different types of Internet access, direct access and indirect access. Indirect access is when the computer is connected to a bigger computer or server, via modem. It acts like a terminal of the main computer.

Direct access is when the computer itself a node on the network. Other forms of direct connections include SLIP and PPP. The first one is more common for PCs and the second for Macs. These two connections give you direct access to the Internet via a modem, but still depend upon a host computer, which has a direct, high-speed connection to the Web.

Server and client computers

Computers in a network can be considered server computers and client computers. Since their objective is to send and receive information from and to different locations, servers usually have more disk space and faster connections than clients. The client computers require less power because they usually provide information to just one person or a small group of persons.

Since today many computers can perform as either servers or clients and software is needed for both sides, the terms client and server apply also to programs. Clients are then programs that request information and servers perform the processing needed to serve the request.

Open Prepress Interface (OPI) servers

Work with high-resolution images may be very inefficient, especially when moving digital files over a network. High-resolution images have large amounts of data causing bottlenecks in the prepress workflow. An open prepress interface (OPI) server is a prepress production tool that permits the use of low-resolution images to facilitate the workflow on certain applications. These low-resolution images are derived from high-resolution ones but their size is radically smaller, allowing the transmission over digital networks to be much faster.

Although faster networks and file compression techniques have given some improvement to transmission speeds, file size problems in data transmission have been compounded by the addition of supporting applications like trapping and imposition. Therefore, OPI is still a valuable solution for many prepress operations that do not require the use of high-resolution images.

OPI was initially developed to allow customers using proprietary high-end color workstations to interface more easily with desktop publishers. At the time images were scanned, the scanner would create an additional low-resolution image along with the high-end image. These low-resolution images were called For Position Only (FPO) and would be transferred to the desktop publisher to be included in applications like page layout. After the layout was determined the files were sent back to the high-end system for output. At this stage FPO images were replaced by the high-resolution images retaining the position, scaling, and rotation specified by the layout design software.

Today OPI has completely moved to desktop-level systems and includes print server technology, which permits the conversion from low-resolution (FPO) to high resolution to be postponed until final production stages. This feature increases considerably the productivity in the prepress production environment.

High-resolution images are kept on the standard server while FPO images are used in page layout programs. The result is a much smaller layout file that is very easy to transfer across networks. At the same time, on the main server, the high-end image is available for any direct operation like color correction, retouching or any other image manipulation function. When the layout and the high-end image are ready, the layout is sent to an OPI server queue where the FPO is replaced by the high-resolution image. Another benefit of the small size of the layout file produced with FPO is that these files open faster for other prepress production steps like imposition and image trapping.

Open Prepress Interface (OPI)

OPI allows users to store high-resolution image files on a central image server, a computer dedicated to the storage and management of these files, and then use a callout file (that includes a low-res preview of the high-res image) in the page makeup application. When the job is printed, the workstation sends only the small amount of data associated with the callout file.

The OPI industry-standard convention defines how to embed instructions in a PostScript output file to tell the output device where and how to merge the various text and graphics components of a page. OPI enables users to work with low-res preview images in their page-makeup programs, and keep the high-res graphic images close to the imagesetter. This maximizes workstation productivity and minimizes network traffic.

OPI originated at Aldus, now part of Adobe. PageMaker users wanted a simple way to use high-quality color photos that had been scanned on high-end scanners, without having to bear the data burden that accompanies those images. So Aldus decided it made more sense to use PageMaker to design the layout and compose the text, then add a few commands to tell the output system how to position the color files. In general, OPI works with TIFF files. OPI supports all the cropping and sizing commands issued in the page makeup program. When the page makeup program creates a PostScript output file of the job for the printer, it appends these commands, along with the pathname and filename, as PostScript comments in the job stream. When the OPI-compliant output system reads these computer comments, it acts upon them by retrieving and merging the high-resolution image.

DCS and OPI

Many OPI solutions also support DCS (Desktop Color Separation), an industry-standard convention for handling color separations created with desktop publishing programs. DCS originated with Quark as a way to manage color separation files. DCS works with EPS (Encapsulated PostScript format) files. In producing color separations, DCS-compliant programs—such as Photoshop—generate a set of five EPSF files. These five files include a main, or "composite" file, as well as a file for each color separation: cyan, magenta, yellow, and black. The composite file contains the names of the cyan, magenta, yellow, and black EPS files and the pathname to their storage location, PostScript commands to print a non-separated version of the image, and a 72-dpi PICT version of the image for viewing on the screen.

In a typical DCS operation, the user places the composite image in the Quark file. When the user prints the job, Quark sends the color separations instead of the composite image. OPI systems that also support DCS enhance this operation by allowing the color separation files to be stored on the server, so Quark does not have to transmit these large files at print time. Quark sends only the callouts, containing the pathname to the separation files, and the OPI-compliant imagesetter fetches those files accordingly.

Document management

Information is a critical tool for business and entertainment purposes. Today information can travel as fast as light. It can be modified and expanded to satisfy users needs and, more importantly, it is more available today due to the existence of multiple distribution channels. The large networks of information that include online services, cable modems, electronic media, and small circulation media, are dependent upon personal computers.

Information providers and creators have now new ways to expand their business. To create, convert, disseminate, and re-purpose their content, these users have to also manage the tools available for digital information. Here is a brief list of elements that are considered publishable content: photos, text files, video clips, charts, statistics, diagrams, and illustrations.

To convert this information into digital content, a prepress service provider takes the original content and converts it into a form suitable for communication (printed pages, web pages, CD-ROM, etc.).

Regardless of the form in which the content will be distributed, publishers and designers will have large numbers of digital files taking an enormous amount of disk space. Often these content providers do not have the capacity to archive these large amounts of data nor do they have the skills to handle digital content, especially when the files are so voluminous. Tools for effective management of their digital documents are now a necessity.

Additionally, knowing how to manage its digital content can bring wealth to a company. There are many benefits from it: ability to enter global markets through efficient distribution, the decrease in production and distribution costs, the use of shared content over networks, increased flexibility, a reduction in archiving space, and the opportunity to transfer content to online services, such as the Internet, for marketing and distribution.

Digital ads

The Committee for Graphic Arts Technologies Standards (CGATS) has announced that Subcommittee 6 of CGATS has selected Adobe System's Portable Document Format (PDF) as a basis for a standard to address the industry requirement for digital distribution of printing data. CGATS formed SC6 to meet a need to develop standards to permit transmission of digital ad data electronically. The Digital Distribution of Advertising for Publications (DDAP) Association has been lobbying for the use of industry standards to allow digital ad distribution for some time. SC6, in response to this need, is developing standards that will allow for digital ad distribution as well as facilitate digital data exchange of composite page data for other print applications.

SC6 has finalized the user technical requirements to summarize the needs of the industry. Based on these requirements, two standards have been written. One focuses on the exchange of raster data based on the work of IT8 and ISO TC 130. TIFF/IT-P1 (ANSI IT8.8-1993 and ISO 12639) are the basis for this work, which will allow the exchange of rendered pages targeted to a variety of printing processes in a transport-independent format.

The challenge of transferring a combination of object-oriented data and raster data concurrently has been more difficult to resolve. The solution will be a second standard, titled "Graphic technology exchange of digital page data in final form using PDF." The standard will detail a transport-independent exchange mechanism based on Adobe's PDF data exchange format. The PDF format is open-ended and allows TIFF/IT-P1 raster data objects to be packaged within a

PDF file and linked to PDF objects. The application software that accepts the PDF, such as Adobe Acrobat, could view the TIFF/IT-P1 information with an appropriate TIFF/IT viewing plug-in.

The PDF was developed to meet the needs of many industries transferring, in a device-independent form, data targeted for rendering by a variety of different rendering engines from personal computer screens to printing presses. PDF is a file format used to represent a document independently of the application software, hardware, and operating system used to create it. PDF, the Portable Document Format, is a publicly available specification by Adobe Systems.

Key elements included in the CGATS standard:
- Fonts will be included with the PDF to assure rendering with the correct font and font metrics.
- Faster data will be accommodated by incorporating or calling external files, including TIFF/IT-P1.

Data to be exchanged will include single colors or CMYK process colors with color rendering.

Differences between PostScript and PDF
- A PDF file may contain objects such as hypertext links that are useful only for interactive viewing.
- To simplify the processing of page descriptions, PDF provides no programming language constructs.
- PDF enforces a strictly defined file structure that allows an application to access parts of a document randomly.
- PDF files contain information such as font metrics, to ensure viewing fidelity.
- PDF requires files to be represented in ASCII, to enhance document portability.

PostScript and PDF are closely related as they have the same roots. PostScript is needed in order to produce PDF files for use in a prepress environment. The Acrobat Distiller strips out important imaging information concerning images contained in the resulting PDF file and plug-ins are needed to add functionality back into Acrobat so that the PDF file can be used in a prepress environment. One such plug-in commonly used in Acrobat is "addPS." This allows users to have more control over how files are imaged on a film imagesetter. Making a PDF file is a relatively simple process. The long way involves saving your document in PostScript form and then opening it in Distiller. The easy way is to use the PPD printer driver which does both things automatically.

To improve performance for interactive viewing, a PDF defines a more structured format than that used by most PostScript language programs. PDF also includes objects, such as annotations and hypertext links, that are not part of the page unit itself but are useful for interactive viewing.

Creating a PDF file

The two most common methods of creating a PDF are either through the application software in which the document was created or from PostScript files made from the document. Many applications can produce a PDF file directly. The PDF Writer, available on both Apple Macintosh computers and computers running Microsoft Windows, acts as a printer driver. The PDF Writer shows up as a printer in the Macintosh Chooser window. The user needs to choose that "printer" to create a PDF file. The user then "prints" their file to the PDF Writer and an electronic file is produced. This is similar to "print to disk." The PDF file is platform-independent; it can be viewed or printed from Macintosh, Windows, PC, and UNIX platforms.

For more complex documents that involve high-resolution images and detailed illustrations, the PDF file must be created differently because of limitations of the system software. The application Acrobat Distiller was developed for this situation. Distiller was designed to produce PDF files from PostScript files that have been "printed to disk," that is, saved as a file in PostScript format. The Distiller application accepts any PostScript file, whether created by a program or hand-coded. The Distiller produces more efficient PDF files than PDF Writer for some application programs.

Prepress issues

PDF files can contain color separation information by saving specific color information as individual PDF pages. This is the manner in which the color separation process must be done since there is no color separation engine in Acrobat Exchange, Reader, or Distiller to perform the color separation at output or when files are being distilled. Page layout applications used in conjunction with a PostScript driver can create a distillable PostScript file that can contain multiple pages of color information. For four-color printing, the PDF file contains four pages that correspond to the four color process inks. If the document has more than four colors, the PDF file would then contain more individual pages for the additional color information. Each color is given its own page in the PDF.

The PDF file format has difficulties in translating trap information from some original applications. To apply traps in Adobe Illustrator one must convert the text into outlines. The application then no longer considers this information as text and treats it as a graphic element. Some of the high-end imaging capabilities of PostScript have been left out of the PDF file format.

Output

The Distiller strips out certain information in the process of making PDF files. A plug-in called "addPS" adds PostScript information to a PDF document that describes what the screen frequency and angle should be for the PDF file being imaged. This plug-in is used to send PostScript files to a RIP allowing the user to specify the default line screen and angle information of the imagesetter and RIP. The next file that is imaged at the imagesetter would be imaged according to those specifications. A separate PostScript routine needs to be sent each time a new color is imaged because the angles need to be offset for each separation. If an imagesetter cannot set the screen frequency and screen angles without the help of a page layout application, "addPS" or some other utility must be used.

Workflow models

Workflows can take many configurations depending on factors like the software used and, more importantly, on the needs of the user. In this section we comment on various approaches that intend to solve workflow issues. We describe the most traditional approach all the way through to more sophisticated solutions that include PDF files as the basic architecture.

Traditional model

1. Workstations running OPI-capable application programs place images on the OPI or image server over the network.
2. Any workstation on the network sends the job to the appropriate print server queue.
3. The print server spools the job, releases the workstation, and transmits the job to the appropriate output device.

Transmission time is very fast because the job contains only a low-resolution image and a callout of the image. The RIP with the OPI integrating function reads the callout in the job and connects to the image server as directed. Because the same workstation may be used as both the image server and the RIP, the integrator needs only to retrieve the image from its disk and merge the high-resolution image into the job stream as the page is printed.

Once the publication is output, what happens to the images? In the old days, they were archived to tape. Today, publishers and service firms are interested in the future of their images. That means they want to store them in such a way that they can be found quickly, accessed rapidly, and converted (re-purposed) to various file formats for print or presentation. If your prepress group has only a couple of workstations, you keep the files you need on those workstations. If you have several workstations, you probably need to share files, create image databases, and improve network performance when sharing those files. You need servers.

- file servers
- print servers
- OPI servers

File servers. When you need to find a file, it's nice to know where to look. A centralized file server that stores high-resolution images, fonts, layouts, and completed jobs can increase everyone's productivity. You can use any workstation that can share files as a file server. Both the Windows NT (server version) and the Power Macintosh platforms incorporate file sharing as a standard. If you use a Windows NT platform as the server, Macs can also access those files. You can also equip the server and workstations with several utilities, such as RunShare and Extensis Portfolio (formerly Fetch), to make file sharing easier and quicker.

The most important feature for a file server isn't a high megahertz rating (although it helps), but a fast I/O speed. You can increase a workstation's I/O performance by using fast hard drives or disk arrays and SCSI accelerators. For critical applications where you can't ever let the server go down, you can configure it with an uninterruptible pwer supply (UPS) and hot swappable drives—drives you can replace without shutting down the computer.

Print servers. Everybody knows what it's like to send a long document to the printer: you used to sit there and wait while the computer flashed printer status messages in your face. You were basically out of commission until the printer released the computer. Print servers solved this problem by spooling print jobs from around the network and sending them to the appropriate output device. When you print your document, you actually send it to the print server; the print server accepts the job and releases your workstation right away. You get back to work; the print server continues to accept and print jobs from all users on the network.

The term spooling has nothing to do with winding something threadlike around a cylinder. "Spool" is actually an acronym for Simultaneous Print Operations On-Line. Every print server has a spooler. Print servers are necessary for maintaining a productive prepress department. A print server receives jobs from a user on a network, stores that job in a queue, and then forwards the job to a printer on the network. The device could be a low-resolution printer or a

high-resolution imagesetter. Those are the basics. A useful print server also includes such features as queue management, job logs, printer setup, and often can also store files for later printing.

Open Prepress Interface (OPI) servers. OPI addresses the problem
inherent with any electronic graphics production environment—the
large amount of data in image files. This data burden impedes productivity in some systems:
- It ties up the workstation while the image file is being printed.
- It creates a network bottleneck any time the image file is transmitted, whether to another workstation for page layout or to
  the output device for proofing or final imaging.

The OPI industry-standard convention defines how to embed
instructions in a PostScript output file to tell the output device where
and how to merge the various text and graphics components of a
page. OPI enables users to work with low-res preview images in
their page-makeup programs, and keep the high-res graphic images
close to the imagesetter.

To work within the OPI model, you create jobs like this:
1. Make up pages using any of a variety of desktop publishing
   programs. On these pages, compose and fit all the editorial
   content, line work, charts, ads, and other page elements.
2. Place photos or other high-resolution graphics on the page
   using a screen-resolution preview FPO image, which is a low-
   resolution TIFF image created by a color-separation program
   such as Photoshop.
3. Send the job to the imagesetter.
4. The imagesetter, using OPI interpreter software, reads the
   pathname, fetches the high-res image from the server, and
   merges the image in position with the text and line work.

The preview is sometimes called a callout file, proxy image, FPO (for
position only), or a view file. This preview image resides on the
workstation, and its storage path and filename must match the storage path and filename on the server.

In general, OPI works with TIFF files. OPI supports all the cropping and sizing commands issued in the page makeup program. When the page makeup program creates a PostScript output file of the job for the printer, it appends these commands, along with the pathname and filename, as PostScript comments in the job stream. When the OPI-compliant output device reads these comments, it acts upon them by retrieving and merging the high-res image. Many OPI solutions also support DCS (Desktop Color Separation), an industry-standard convention for handling color separations created with desktop publishing programs. DCS originated with Quark as a way to manage color separation files.

DCS works with EPS (Encapsulated PostScript) files. In producing color separations, DCS-compliant programs—such as Photoshop—generate a set of five EPSF files. These five files include a main, or "composite" file, as well as a file for each color separation cyan, magenta, yellow, and black. The composite file contains the names of the cyan, magenta, yellow, and black EPS files and the pathname to their storage location, PostScript commands to print a non-separated version of the image, and a 72-dpi PICT version of the image for viewing on the screen.

Color Management Systems

To prepare jobs for color printing, you often use a variety of devices: scanners, monitors, color printers, and imagesetters. The data for a color image goes through several transformations as it moves from one stage in prepress production to the next, from the scanner, to editing on the screen, to printing a proof, to running film or plates.

Each device in your prepress system can produce a certain range of colors. The color range, or gamut, is device-specific and varies somewhat between similar devices (such as different scanner models), and varies dramatically among different devices (such as scanners, monitors, and printers). If you scan a photograph of an orange hat, the scanner uses a set of CCDs or PMTs to capture the data that represents the color orange. When you display that image on your screen, the orange data is represented by the monitor's RGB phosphors, which give the image a different hue from the original photo. When you print the image on a color printer, the orange data is represented by the printer's toners, and yet another hue appears. A color management system translates these device-specific colors into a common visual language that can be used at all stages of prepress production, with the assurance of predictable color reproduction.

The International Color Consortium (ICC) was established in 1993 by several leaders in the prepress color industry, including Adobe, Apple, Kodak, Microsoft, and more. The ICC's goal is to create, promote, and encourage the standardization of an open, vendor-neutral, cross-platform color management system (CMS) architecture. A CMS works by creating device profiles for the equipment used in the color prepress production process. The color profile for each device describes the color range supported by that device in relation to a device-independent standard, usually the CIE color standard. The profile allows the CMS to translate the colors used by the device into a color-independent space. When one device uses a color that another cannot reproduce (such as a bright color on the monitor that the printer simply can't duplicate), the CMS automatically selects the closest reproducible color. When each device is profiled in the CMS, the result should be consistent, reproducible color output.

Networks and communications

Prepress systems generally require a network. Even if it's only to connect one workstation with one printer, that connection is essentially a network. Most prepress groups have a lot more devices. To connect the scanners, workstations, servers, and output devices, you need a fast, efficient, and reliable network. When Apple introduced Apple-Talk, users were amazed that networking could be made so easy. AppleTalk worked fine for passing small files back and forth, but in the prepress production environment, where color images can be 30, 40, 50, and more megabytes in size, LocalTalk's 230 Kbps just could not carry the load fast enough. Ethernet, on the other hand, using high-speed TCP/IP, can handle data at significantly higher speeds. Combine AppleTalk with Ethernet and you get EtherTalk, AppleTalk protocols running on Ethernet cabling.

Ethernet is a type of Local Area Network (LAN) and is defined by the Institute for Electrical and Electronic Engineers in IEEE Standard 802.3. This standard defines the rules for configuring Ethernet and how devices on the network communicate with each other. To create an Ethernet network, you select a cable type, a protocol, and the hardware to control the network.

Most Ethernet networks use a bus topology where each device on the network connects to a backbone cable. Each end of the cable must be terminated. Ethernet cables can be any one of these cable types:

- Thick Ethernet (also called ThickNet or 10 base5) uses a relatively inflexible coaxial cable about 1/2" thick. The maximum length of each ThickNet segment is 1640 feet. For longer networks, you need a repeater, described below.
- Thin Ethernet (also called ThinNet or 10Base2) uses a thin coaxial cable with twist-lock and tee connectors. ThinNet cable is much like the regular coaxial cable used by most cable TV systems. The maximum length of a ThinNet segment is 606 feet. As with ThickNet, you can add a repeater to the network to create a longer network.
- Twisted pair copper wire (also called 10BaseT) is currently the most efficient and popular cabling method used on Ethernet networks. 10BaseT uses a star topology (each device connects to a hub) and unshielded twisted-pair cabling. Twisted-pair cabling is the same wire used to connect telephones, so it's widely installed in the walls of many buildings. The maximum length of a device from the hub is 330 feet.

Each LAN can only use one type of cable, although you can add a bridge or router to the network to connect two networks that use different cable types. For devices on the network to communicate, they must use the same protocol. A protocol defines how computers identify themselves on the network, how data moves over the network, and how the data is processed when received. Commonly used protocols include TCP/IP, AppleTalk (EtherTalk), and IPX (used by Novell in Netware-based networks). The details of how these protocols work is different, but they all can use the same physical cabling.

As such, you can use more than one protocol on the same network. For example, you can have UNIX workstations using TCP/IP and Macintosh workstations using EtherTalk on the same network. Each device on the network, workstations and other devices, needs an interface card and software to interface to that cable type and use the needed protocol.

The cabling types listed above describe how long each network segment can be before performance degrades. To extend the length of the network, you can use repeaters or bridges. To connect networks of different types, you can use a router. You need a gateway to connect to the Internet or another Wide Area Network (WAN). You can purchase devices that perform one or more of these functions.

A repeater is about the size of a modem and extends the length of cable on a network. For instance, if you need to run ThinNet cable farther than 606 feet, you can use a repeater to gain the extra distance. The repeater amplifies and retransmits the signal, letting it travel beyond the normal limitations of the cable.

A bridge can be used to join two networks of the same type (such as two Ethernet networks) and also functions as a repeater. The two networks can use different cabling types, such as ThinNet and 10BaseT, but they must use the same protocol. Also, the networks can use different transmission speeds.

A router connects networks of the same type or of different types (such as a LocalTalk network and an Ethernet network).

A gateway is a combination of hardware and software that connects two different types of network protocols (such as connecting an AppleTalk network to a network using non-AppleTalk protocols, such as TCP/IP or DECnet). The software in the gateway translates the protocols from one network to the protocols of the other.

Prepress systems are also linking OPI servers to image archives. An image database becomes important because users cannot find images based only on their file names. Some production pros can retrieve images on this basis, but designers may not. Without reliable image pattern-recognition technology, we have to rely on keywords, indexed fields and full-text queries of captions or description files. These are typically stored in a database (relational or fixed-field) and searched by a full-text indexing engine.

Server evolution and integration

It all started with one PC connected to one printer. Add more PCs and more printers and you have a system. A prepress networked system usually consists of multiple workstations, a file server, and a printer or printers connected by network cables.

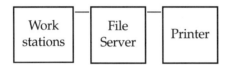

Sometimes a print spooler is added so that files destined for the printer are accepted by the spooler to release the workstation's application. The spooler then queues the job or jobs based on prioritization and sends them to the printer. The difference between a print spooler and a print server is based on the amount of time files remain on the disk. A spooler may delete files sooner than a server.

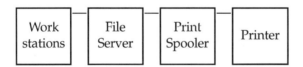

The printer on a prepress network is usually a PostScript-based printer and therefore has a RIP. Most desktop printers have the RIP inside the printer . . .

... while imagesetters and platesetters and proofers have the RIP as a separate unit, connected by a cable. Today, every raster-based output device must have a raster image processor.

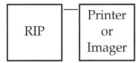

A server may be added to the output function to store RIPped files for later printout of the entire file of one or more of the color separations. This may be called a print server or a print spooler. We are going to call it a RIP server because it serves the RIP. At one time there was a RIP for each and every output device. Today, the trend is to try to RIP-once-and-output-many-times. So the RIP server functions as a print spooler/server, holding files for later printout or archiving.

The RIP server and the RIP may be integrated into one unit.

An OPI server could be added to the system for automatic picture replacement.

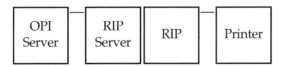

Or the OPI server and the RIP server could be integrated while the RIP is a separate unit ...

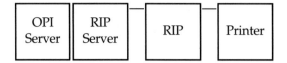

. . . or the OPI server, RIP server and RIP could be integrated into one unit.

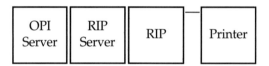

At various levels there could be more than one printer, proofer, imagesetter, digital color press, platemaker, or other output alternatives.

When the functions of OPI, RIP and print server are integrated into one server, we are going to call it a super server. It then is networked with the file server and the printer or imagers.

To the super server we add the final ingredient of PDF handling, trapping and imposition. The final system now takes form as a PDF server.

Adobe PDF will change the very nature of networks and servers and systems and prepress. With scripts or plug-ins, many routine tasks can be automated. For instance, a script might take a QuarkXPress file, open it, distill it, open Acrobat Exchange, perform a function, save it, then invoke server functions to trap the PDF, impose it based on the electronic work order, direct it to a proofer, and prioritize it to a print queue.

OPI servers, workflow servers, database servers, file management servers, and image servers. Servers are migrating to RIPping and archiving, and archive image databases are expanding to handle work in process. Print servers, once limited to spooling, now perform trapping and imposition and promise to eventually automate work-flow, as database-driven workflow software makes similar claims. RIPs once only RIPped; now they serve. Servers only served; now they rip. The result is that almost every server and almost every RIP system does almost the same thing.

Workflow is changing. Workflow software has migrated from text-based systems to prepress document production systems that help route jobs to the required queue or invoke processes when work is dropped in a queue or hot folder. The server is simply a central (net-work) function that can run background tasks like automatic trap-ping, or rasterizing (RIPping) a file for output to a printer, imageset-ter, platemaker, or whatever. File servers are based on UNIX or Novell networks, with Macintosh, PC/NT and UNIX workstations handling processing. Workflow may also mean setting up "hot fold-ers" to perform prepress functions and letting the server do the rest.

The server approach shifts the processing burden from individual workstations to a central server for more efficient printing and job handling. Sending files to the server takes seconds, even for pages with gigabytes of images. Software directs where and when each job is to print, inserts high-resolution scans precisely where they belong in the layout, monitors print progress, and maintains statistics. Queued jobs can be rearranged, placed on hold, deleted, or moved among queues with ease.

Hot folders

A hot folder is a folder or directory on a computer that is continually monitored for some activity. When a file is placed in that folder, the monitoring application performs a specified action on that file. For PDF, PostScript files get distilled. In an imagesetting environment, files placed in hot folders get RIPped and output to an image recorder. Usually, the hot folder can be set up to enable specific features on the RIP before the file gets rasterized and output by the image recorder. For example, the hot folder can set the resolution or screening for the job or distill at different parameters.

In a system without hot folders, users send jobs to the folders over the network. Before the job is sent, the user needs to make sure the system is properly set up to process that job—for a RIP, it would include the resolution, the imaging mode (negative or positive), the transfer function for that media, and any special screening (AM or FM screening) must be specified. If the user and the RIP are located in separate locations, changing these production setups could be time-consuming. A function used by more than one person for more than one type of job may need frequent changes in how it outputs jobs. Some jobs may require 3000 dpi; others may only need 1200 dpi. Black-and-white jobs likely don't need to use advanced screening; four-color separations may need FM screening enabled.

Hot folders are an important workflow tool. Once the hot folder is set up and defined, you just need to place files for processing into the hot folder—the computer takes it from there and the job runs using the correct setups. The hot folder doesn't even have to be on the same computer as the activity—but the computer does need network access to the hot folder.

In configurations with multiple RIPs and multiple output devices, or in busy production environments, hot folders can provide all the benefits of a stand-alone print server, without the added expense. All action settings can be tied to a hot folder. For RIPs, these settings include resolution, image modes, plate settings, page grouping, archiving, and recorder selection.

Scanning folders

When you set up the hot folder, you need to turn on scanning for that folder. There may be times when you don't want to scan folders. Users can still place files in the hot folders, but they won't be processed until the system is available and you re-enable scanning.

Changing workflows

Adobe has met the demands of changing communication technology by creating a RIP architecture for production printing systems, called Extreme. The main goal of Extreme is a high-performance, large production capacity, with a quick turnaround. In order to satisfy personalized printing expectations, Extreme must be able to handle large amounts of variable information for each different page, and it must be able to produce reliably and predictably. Adobe is working to reach these goals.

Extreme is a RIP technology which can process both PostScript and PDF streams. Files first enter the "coordinator" which determines whether the file is PS or PDF by its inherent page independence. The PS files go to the "normalizer" and the PDF files go to the "page store." The "normalizer" acts as Acrobat's Distiller and converts the PS file to a PDF.

These distilled files then continue on to the "page store" where all documents are stored as PDF pages. Pages are processed through the RIP into bitmaps and finally passed on to the "assembler" which dictates the flow of information to the marking engine. In addition to digital presses, Extreme's technology is applicable to large-format imagesetters, proofers, and platemakers, as well as digital printers.

The first implementation of a PDF workflow was the Agfa Apogee system. There are other workflows, but most users admit that PDF will play an increasing role in workflow automation.

Print production work flow

This is an outline of the most important areas of workflow. It summarizes many of the concepts and explanation in the previous pages:

Primary segments of printing production
- Pre-Press
  From design to production of the image carrier
- Press
  The process for transferring image to substrate
- Post-Press
  Final manufacturing processes: folding, conversion, binding, forming, die cutting, etc.

- Design of the product; of the document; of the page
  Product design considers form and function;
    page design considers aesthetics
  Most pages now created on computer, therefore page designs
    and use of color are becoming easier and more complex
  Blurred roles of client, designer, service bureau, trade shop,
    full-service printer
  Growing emphasis on re-purposing for digital media

- Document originator responsibilities
  Correct file creation programs for specific jobs
  File formats
  Fonts
    Who owns them
    Who provides them
    Schedule
    Requested schedule—promised schedule
  Who pays for what
  Color expectations
  File organization
  Colors
  Shipping files (compression)
  Incorrect page sizes, fold marks & bleeds
  No hard copy proof

Preflight check
Refers to a structured series of tests performed on a page layout
file before sending it off to be imaged

- Color
  Tone and color reproduction—converting continuous tone
    photos into halftone images
  Scanners—desktop through high-end—have replaced the
    process camera
  All halftones—b&w and color—must be prepared to specific,
    calibrated specifications for print quality

- Images
  File formats, image databases, document and image file links
  Image assembly construction: building in colors, tints, halftones,
    trapping

- Assembly
  Most pages now assembled by computer rather than in light
    table stripping
  Computer image assembly increases productivity and quality,
    reduces cost
  Overlapping roles of designers and printers in defining and
    including page elements

- Imposition production, not design responsibility
  Imposition: positioning page images on the press sheet to meet
    press and bindery requirements
  Manually position and register page films for entire press sheet
    or step-exposure units
  Imposition software is used with film imagesetters (4-up and 8-
    up are most popular sizes) and computer-to-plate systems to
    reduce dependency on manual processes

- Proofing
  Proofing—because people make mistakes, needs change, and
    image quality must be verified

Client (buyer) closely involved in these stages of production; different than other industries

Different proofing products for varied proofing needs; comps, intermediate, imposition, final/contract

Increased demand for digital proofing systems, especially in digital workflows

- Platemaking

  Analog platemaking from film images still dominant procedure for both conventional and waterless plates

  Computer-to-plate (CTP) capability is having rapid growth is many industry segments

  CTP's hot issues today are determining the real cost or return on investment (ROI) and re-engineering the workflow

- PDF (Portable Document Format)

  PDF files can be created with Acrobat Distiller, which converts PostScript files into PDF. Distiller effectively handles high-res images, gradients, and other artwork while creating a page-independent, highly structured, small file format for delivery.

  PDF files can be viewed, edited, enhanced, and printed with Acrobat Exchange.

  PDF files can be viewed and printed with Acrobat Reader, a free downloadable application.

- PDF in the workflow

  PDFs meet the demands for CD-ROM, DVD-ROM, Web, and print publishing.

  The same PDF file can be used for digital proofing, imposed film imagesetting, computer-to-plate, black and white document printer, color printer/press, Web viewable and printable documents, CD-ROM files, and achievable formats.

  PDF files can be distributed for the remote printing and proofing with the assurance that each site will print uniform and predictable document.

- Pressroom issues
  - Growing emphasis on color printing and impacts the pressroom capability and productivity
  - Overlapping competition among digital printing, sheetfed offset, web offset, and gravure presses
  - Automation of press operation: reduced make-ready and running waste
  - Growth of waterless offset technology, on-demand printing needs

- Post-press
  - Binding: the work required to convert printed sheets or webs into books, magazines, catalogs, and folders
  - Types of binding methods: side-and saddle-stitch, perfect binding, case binding, mechanical binding
  - Finishing: the operations required to make displays, greeting cards, folding cartons and boxes, labels, and other specialty items
  - Types of finishing operations: die-cutting, folding, gluing, scoring, perforating, embossing, laminating, foil-stamping, varnishing
  - Design determines the "what"—the appearance, form, and function. Production determines the "how" of print finishing and binding methods.
  - Finishing and binding operations and specifications are planned long before final image assembly and platemaking, presswork
  - There can be either/both on-line and off-line finishing and binding operations for any printing process and product. There are numerous variables based on specific job needs.

- Planning a project
  - Special requirements
    - Binding (Wire-O, or perfect binding require different manufacturing paths)
    - Die cuts
    - Metallic ink

- Press and other specifications
  Offset lithography, flexography, gravure, screen printing
  Digital printing for on-demand and variable data
  Digital may require different screening
  Because of the output devices capabilities screens should be
    optimized during the creation of the documents
  Longer runs are not as problematic as short run we have much
    more experience
  If there are file issues, when do you start and stop charging?

- Creating the job
  Document originator responsibilities
  Applications for desktop color prepresses

- Preflight workflow issues
  Preflight can take a long time if department is busy
  The plant may not understand that preflight is not production
  We have to preflight according to the manufacturing path
  Once we have preflighted we are ready for production

Job enters the plant
  Electronically over a network
  Via a disk
    Once a bid is accepted the sales person receives the disk
    The job is given an order number for tracking

The disk is given to the prepress department
The files get preflighted
The disk is then preflighted via its forecasted manufacturing path
If the files are workable then the job is scheduled
If the files need work then the sales person is notified
Either the client does the work or the files are sent back and worked
  on by the client

The electronic file gets processed
Once the files are optimized for output they are PostScripted

The files get proofed
Color proofs are generated for customer approval
Provides a reasonable indication as to how a given set of data will
  appear when printed under a given set of printing conditions

The files get trapped
Trapping refers to how much overprinting or adjacent colors overlap
  to eliminate white lines between them
Spread versus choke approach

The files get imposed
The PostScripted files are then imposed via preps
Once imposed, a proof is generated
Check for imposition and document integrity
The proof is double checked
The files get proofed
    Files are proofed for position
    If the proof is OK then we output

The files get output
Once the OK is given we create the final product
    Digital Press
    Plate
    Film
       These files need to be post-flighted
       Then they get archived
       The job is then digitally archived

Preflight workflow issues
   Preflight can take a long time if department is busy
   The plant may not understand that preflight is not production
   We have to preflight according to the manufacturing path
   What happens is we shift manufacturing path
   Once we have preflighted we are just a hair away from production

Workflow section
  Who does what to the document
  Internal and external
  Who pays for mistake?
  Do corrections effect schedule?
  How is the archive achieved?
  How is the archive agreement met?

Workflow and standards must be made clear
  If the file passes preflight it should be the manufacturing plant's
    responsibility to work with the documents issue
  The prepress is responsible for the integration of a variety of
    applications, platforms, and networks

The job process

  Digital file entered into the plant
    • The file gets processed
    • The files get PostScripted
    • The files get imposed
    • The files are PostScripted
    • The files are proofed
    • The files are fixed
    • The files are plated

The files are preflighted
  The disk is then preflighted via its forecasted manufacturing path
  If the files are workable then the job is scheduled
  If the files need work then the sales person is notified
  Either the client does the work, or the files are sent back to be
    worked on by the client
  The electronic files are processed
  Once the files are optimized for output they are PostScripted
  The PostScript files are then imposed via imposition software
  Check for imposition and document integrity
  The proof is double checked
  If the proof is OK, then we create plates or film

CIP3

"International Cooperation for Integration of Prepress, Press, and Postpress," abbreviated as "CIP3"

Main component is the print production format (PPF)

It is meant to tie standards and protocols together

The information is meant to be used throughout the entire print manufacturing process

Who is creating this standard?

The discussions and research was started in 1993 with Heidelberg and the Fraunhofer Institute

This standard was meant to share the information that prepress uses throughout the manufacturing process

Guided by 28 members, at present

The requirements for the file format
- Ability to store raster image data, geometric data, and text
- Ability to code color information in a color system (for instance, CIE-L*a*b*)
- Ability to structure the information contained in the PPF
- Flexible and easy to extend through entire process
- Easy to generate—PostScript operators
- Easy to convert into a graphic representation for display
- Easy to print on a standard printer
- Easy to interpret
- Vendor-independent and platform-independent
- Uniform coordinate system for all types of information
- All file formats were considered, PostScript was chosen

What information is stored in a PPF?
- Low resolution preview image
- Curves of transfer of copy-to-film and copy-to-plate processes
- Position and types of register marks
- Color control and density measurement information
- Geometric data for cutting and cut marks
- Geometric data for folding and folding procedure
- Annotations and comments

The primary goal of the CIP3
- To reduce the effort required for the setup of different machines during the production of a printer product
- This means the electronic communication must be enabled between the different steps of production
- This is very important because a lot of data is already viable in prepress must be made accessible to any further manufacturing

How PPF works with PostScript
- The extraction of information from a CIP3 file based on PostScript will require a PostScript interpreter
- It is necessary to have a common CIP3 parsing library that interfaces with different applications
- The alternative is a more restrictive coding regulations for CIP3
- The structure of the PPF
    Header
    Prolog
    User-defined prolog
    Fold procedures
    Structure, attributes, and content
    End of file

Attributes of the PPF
- Within the CIP3 format the document's attributes are used to store information that characterizes the job
- To define an attribute it is necessary to specify the attribute's name and its values
- The attribute is bound to the PPF structure
- Attributes are optional or necessary

Folding data
- Data which describes the position of the sheet and the sequence of the folding procedure
- This data can be bound to a cut block section
- In the fold procedures section, which follows the user-defined profile section, folding procedures are defined
- It is possible to specify more than one folding procedure

- Each procedure is stored under a unique name that is referenced in the CutData and CutBlock file sections
- The cutting information contained information is only intended for the cutting procedure within the folding capabilities

The following data is stored as content:
- Continuous tone image with reduced resolution
- Display of the sheet to be printed with 8 Bit depth per color separation
- The image is meant for display only
- This comp is good to use as a dummy of the image. Check to make sure production has been completed correctly i.e. cut lines etc.
- Currently the OPI specification 1.3 is used for coding of the continuous tone images only, not other details

Register marks
- The position and rotation of each register mark are identified
- It is important that the register marks are defined so that their centers are on the point of origin of the coordinate system

Color and ink control fields
- Two basic types of measuring fields are supported
- Color measuring fields and density measuring fields
- Control strips can build up from these two basic fields
- Color and density measuring fields can be positioned on the front or back page of the sheet

Cutting data
- Cutting data is described by nested blocks
- This is applied at the lowest level of the PostScript hierarchy
- Cutting direction should be device independent, and the cutting images specified in the CIP3 format do not directly imply a certain cutting sequence
- The sequence of cutting has to be determined by a specialized application that also generates the cutting program
- This can be loaded and executed on by any cutting device

The CIP3 file
- The files can be parsed by a PostScript interpreter to extract specific information
- The image data and the transfer curves can be used to calculate the ink details and profile and preset it to the printing press
- The cutting data can be used to automatically generate programs for a cutting device
- The folding data can be used to automatically generate programs to control or preset a folding device

The CIP3 file can be printed on a normal PostScript printer
- This can only be done after appending a special prolog to the beginning of the file
- The printing depends on whether both front and back of the press sheet or only one side
- The details can be parsed by a PostScript interpreter to produce a description of the job
- This can be a job ticket
- The code must be PostScript compliant
- The information stored in the CIP3 file is hierarchically structured

File formats

TIFF
- TIFF is a family of image formats grouped under a single specification that was founded by Aldus Corporation.
- A TIFF file contains a directory, then a series of tags that specify certain types of data
- TIFF files support many color spaces, compression methods, and storage orders
- The most current version of TIFF is 6.0
- TIFF files will support clipping paths generated from Photoshop 4.0
- TIFF files support spot color channels

TIFF/IT
Tagged image file format/information format
Types for TIFF/IT
    1. Continuous tone (rastered)
        The pixels have an X Y co-ordinate
        The pixels may have as much as 4-bits of data (one bit per pixel)
    2. Line work (rastered)
        The pixels have an X Y co-ordinate
    3. HC high resolution continuous tone image
        Transparent color capability allowing the color underneath to be visible
    4. MP monochromatic picture
        Same as the CT except with color
    5. BP binary picture data
        XY 1-bit co-ordinate
        Bitmapped format
    6. FP final page format
        Uses a tag system to co-ordinate the various elements within the format

EPS
- Encapsulated PostScript (EPS) file is a subset of PostScript files
- EPS files include only a single image, with no device-dependent data
- The image is not scaled to a particular page size
- An Encapsulated PostScript file (EPSF) can also be RIPped with a showpage command
- (It should contain all fonts and dictionaries it needs)
- In general, EPS files are rasterized and vectored files
    Supports clipping paths
    Supports halftone embedding
    Supports transfer curves

DCS

- DCS is a format developed by Quark to allow images to be stored with the color data in a preseparated format
- The composite image is stored in one file
- The individual CMYK color plates are stored in separate files
- The composite file can be at full resolution or a low-resolution version of the composite, depending on the application that created it
- DCS 2.0 keeps the color plate information in separate tables
- All of the data is stored in a single file, with header comments that specify the individual offsets
- The page layout application can send only the color plate in question to the printer, saving time in data transfer and RIPping
- Scitex CT systems manufactured by Scitex in general use proprietary file formats which are only understood by Scitex systems
- Applications supporting the Hexachrome six-color model store their files as DCS to ensure that layout applications print all of the layers

Scitex

There are two formats used for exchanging data between different Scitex machines

1. Handshake formats
2. CT and LW versions of these files

Maintains the clipping paths Scitex CT images with SILOs (the Scitex term for clipping path) generated from the Scitex MaskCutter program

PostScript as a language

Just as the name suggests—first a noun then the verb

Portable document format (PDF)
  The PostScript is interpreted
  An object list is written
  The dot is written by the RIP
  Reader/with search
  Microsoft Office macros
  Exchange
Catalog capability
Scan OCR
Plug-in support

Trapping
- Trapping is a method of adjusting areas where two distinct colors meet so that press mis-registration won't cause white specs
- A trap either spreads (enlarges) the lighter color into the darker color or chokes (reduces) the lighter color into the darker color
- You use the choke trap if the background color is lighter than the object it surrounds; and you use the spread trap if the background color is darker than the object it surrounds

How to trap
To set your own traps
    You can set traps in the illustration, image-editing, or page layout application, or a dedicated trapping program

If you import an Ilustrator drawing into your Quark file, you cannot use the Quark tools to trap objects in the drawing
Quark will not take the graphics color content or boundaries into account when trapping native Quark elements to it
Dedicated trapping programs are attractive because designers and desktop publishers can use them
These applications come in two types: zone based and object based

Trapping types
The object based type of application converts a PostScript job (page layout saved from Quark or other application as a PostScript file) into bitmapped format

The trapping engine finds all the edges that need trapping

The applications can automatically decide the proper size, shape, and color for the traps, or it can allow you to enter specific trapping info on a per-job basis

Trapping zone based

Zone trapping

Choose the mode (black to overprint etc.)

The file gets a low resolution RIP

The application then analyzes the color breaks

Then from the color break info the application then creates a vector file

This file gets saved as an add on to the file if not RIPped

From the vector file the application either does a center line trap or right and left trap

The right and left trap act as choke and spread

To edit the traps you draw a box around with zones

Multiple edits are hard to perform with zones

This is similar to color pair architecture of Scitex

Tapping object based

- Low level RIP of the file
- The application then creates a database of the color densities
- Once the database is created, it stays with the file until it gets RIPped
- When the file is getting imaged, the trapping database interacts with the RIP to effect the trap
- This means the file is RIPped once

Trapping software features

- Batch processing using queue folders
- Manual overrides for all traps on an object level
- Automatic removal of existing traps
- Supports OPI, DCS, Scitex, APR, Color Central, Helios
- Supports unlimited spots and four process colors
- Traps both intersections or entire objects
- Direct color separations and printing

- Ability to "print" directly from page layout applications
- Automatic handling of metallics and varnishes
- Automatic trap color reduction
- Overprint inks based on user-definable basis
- Enhanced control over automatic trap settings
- Centerline traps under user control
- Automatic trapping of all EPS and nested EPS graphics
- Enhanced trap controls for text
- Full color over trap color, directions and width

Open prepress interface—OPI
- The OPI industry standard defines how to embed instructions in a PostScript output file to tell the output device where and how to merge the various text and graphics components
- What happens when using OPI?
  A low-res will be swapped out by the high-res file
  Any color corrections or manipulations you do to the low-res are ignored
- The main advantage is that the file sizes are dramatically reduced, this means you are not moving lots of file information around
- The secondary advantage is that it will allow you to assume the exact size and placement of your images in your final documents
- You can scale the image from 25% to 175% of the original scanned size
- If you need to do anything besides scaling or cropping within the layout program such as QuarkXPress or PageMaker, OPI types of workflows are probably not good for you

The workflow
- The scanner creates a low-res file in the imaging processing process
- Send the FPOs to be placed by the designers
- When the document comes back, the image server will swap out the low-res files with the corrected high-res files

- If you don't have a server to create OPI, you can use a Photoshop plug-in called Export PSImage
- This filter allows you to generate your own low-resolution, which you place in QuarkXPress

Automatic picture replacement
- APR is a system that creates a low-res electronic stat (proxy image) for use in a page layout application
- This low-res file is placed into your document in the exact position at the exact size it should be processed
- Once you have the low-resolution file, which is just an EPS, place that file in your document
- Send the document with the APR and the Scitex image server will swap out the low-resolution data with the current high-res data

Chapter 9

PUBLISHING

The business of publishing is the business of moving ideas from one source to the public. This movement of ideas often involves a transformation of these ideas from something that is abstract and theoretical to something that is understandable to many people. The task of formatting the idea in an understandable package which is accepted by the public is often the greatest challenge in the business of publishing. We see many forms of publishing, from traditional forms such as newspapers, books, and magazines to newer forms including television, radio, CD-ROM, and web pages. These different forms of publishing compete for the public's attention, making the market very competitive. All forms of publishing require a great deal of investment and organization. In the future, publishers are going to have to accurately identify the package they want for their publication based on the user's application of the information and produce it in the most cost effective way to reach their market while minimizing risk.

One of the oldest formats for publishing is the book. Books are a standard form of packaging information. The words are written on paper pages which are then numbered and bound on one edge. The numbers on pages in books allow for systems of organization and retrieval such as contents and indexes.

As a culture we are very comfortable with this format of information, possibly because it has been around so long. In reality books are a very practical and efficient way to store information. The information in books will be usable as long as the language it is written in is understood, giving them an almost unlimited life-span. The printed page does not require any additional energy or technology to function, unlike computers and television. Books are very portable, they can be taken almost anywhere. In many people's minds, books represent a high level of social stature, education, and intelligence. There is also a level of prestige associated with publishing a book which, in our current culture, is not found with other publishing formats.

Some people view the book publishing industry with the same romance as they view the book—that it is an industry that is concerned with spreading knowledge rather than making money. This is for the most part untrue. The publishing industry is like any other and in business to make money. The industry is large in that it supports many businesses. The structure of publishing is very complex and requires authors, editors, publishers, printers, binders, and booksellers to move the ideas to the market.

Authors are not necessarily at the beginning of the publishing process but are considered the controllers of the basic ideas. It is not necessarily the duty of the author to have the idea for a book, but the author needs to have the skill to take the idea from the theoretical and organize it in a logical way so other people can understand it. Within the industry authors can become specialized. Some authors may be particularly skilled in explaining the function of technical topics. Others may specialize in writing novels for entertainment. Once the manuscript is created it is considered the property of the author, unless it is a work for hire.

Publishers must negotiate reproduction rights in the form of a contract to print the manuscript. These contracts establish how the author is paid, usually by a percentage of the book's sale, known as a royalty. When an author is paid up-front before the sale of a book, it is known as an advance. This money is taken from royalties of future book sales. There is also a trend in the industry for publishers to sign book deals with authors. This can be compared to a sports team signing a free agent player. Publishers know that certain authors will attract a certain number of sales no matter what they write about because they are famous. This trend is good for those authors because they can force the different publishers to bid against each other and drive the price up.

Publishers control the process of moving the information from the private sector to the public. These people are responsible for deciding which ideas need to be published, what form they should be reproduced in, and controlling the quality of the production both in how it is written and how the final piece looks. The publisher controls most of the money in the process, because they take the most risk in the production of the book. The author, printer, and binder get paid by the publisher, and the bookseller receives their product from the distributor or the publisher directly. Taditionally this has meant that the publisher has to take a large risk in their business. Printers and binders usually get paid before the book hits the shelf and there is no way to be positive of a book's success.

The printers are the manufactures in the process. Ideally, printers are given composed pages by the publisher and asked to reproduce it exactly. This is not really the case; often printers play some role in controlling the quality of the piece. The biggest responsibility of the printer is to reproduce the work in the way the publisher intended. An additional part of the manufacturing process is the binding of books. This can be done by the printer or through an independent bindery. The amount of risk the printer takes in the success or failure of a book is limited, because they get paid a fixed amount regardless of whether the entire print run is sold or not. This is not always the case because sometimes printers will invest in the publication to get the business of printing. The bottom line is that the publisher is a customer of the printer, and printers will work with publishers to keep them as customers.

The first customers of the printed book are booksellers and libraries. Booksellers are often divided into categories depending on how they sell their product. There are wholesalers, retailers, book clubs, and other distributors. The types of booksellers have changed in the last few years and will continue to change. The business of selling books is now dominated by superstores which carry a large selection of books. These stores offer a very comfortable environment to review books. The result of this is that people view shopping for books as a form of entertainment. These booksellers have an enormous amount of power with publishers because they represent a big portion of the publisher's market. As a result they can demand lower prices for books. The booksellers are the portion of the industry which the publisher has the least amount of control over. The bookseller chooses how to promote a book or to promote it at all. Publishers also have to deal with the tradition of returning books. In this industry it has been established that booksellers can return unsold books after a certain period of time for a full refund. This allows the bookseller to order as many books as they feel like and return them at the publisher's expense. The luxury of being able to return books has encouraged the bookseller to over-order books to protect against shortages. There is also a trend towards purchasing books from sellers who work through the World Wide Web. The stores on the Web have a huge market without the overhead of operating storefronts.

The goal of the book publisher and book publishing industry should always be to minimize the risk they are taking with the books they publish. The profits from a book drive the industry, but it is very difficult to gauge the profitability of a book before it hits the shelves. The responsibility of gauging the market for the book rests solely on the shoulders of the publisher. The most important decision the publisher has to make is, is the market ready for the book, or is the book good enough to find a market. This is dependent on the content of the book and the condition of the market.

In publishing, as with all industry, reputation is very important. The reputation of a publisher is largely dependent on the titles they produce. This is often why some publishers are willing to produce a book that may take a loss but is considered "important" by society. These books serve a promotional purpose for publishers.

Books have different types or classifications. There are books for different purposes and that appeal to different people. Some of the basic types of books are trade, professional, juvenile, religious, and general paperback. Trade books are specific to certain areas of industry, for example, in printing there is the *Pocket Pal*, which explains much of the industry. Professional books may include reference books of legal precedents. Other categories appeal to certain groups such as children, or people of a certain religion. Lastly there are books that try to appeal to a general audience which are designed to entertain. These groups and types of books are important to the industry, because they can tell a publisher how, or if, a book should be produced and how it should be marketed.

Before a book is produced it must be considered by the publisher for production. The path a manuscript takes through a publishing house is often the way its content is judged and modified so that it is in a form that is ready for the public. The job of evaluating the manuscripts falls on the publisher's editorial staff. This group of people is responsible for deciding which books should be published and what changes need to be made to manuscripts to make them ready for the public. The first level of control the editorial staff has is in the manuscripts that they choose to let in the door. Most manuscripts that are considered are the pieces they have either requested or gone out and found. Many manuscripts are submitted to publishers, but are simply too great a risk or do not fit the publisher's profile. Once a manuscript is accepted, it goes through a series of readings. These reviews are designed to filter out unpublishable works and correct publishable ones. Readers can be on staff or hired and often have specialties. Readers can specialize in evaluating grammar, consistency, and validity of sources and facts. Editors can also consider the document's style. Often publishers have what is known as a "house-style" or a set for rules they follow to make their work consistent.

The publisher needs to consider the information they have in the manuscript. What is the information used for, and how is it used? This question is important because a book might not be the best way to package the information they have. An example could be if a publisher is going to produce stock market reports on various companies. A printed piece would enter a market it could not compete in, because it is static. Information published in an electronic format is dynamic and can be constantly updated. Before the publisher produces a book they must consider the type of information they have and its application.

Traditionally in the book publishing industry, deciding how many books to print has always been one of the most difficult questions. The selling price per copy of a book is one of the most significant factors in the sales of a book. The public will pay more for certain books and less for others. But the production cost per copy of a book is something that is not fixed, it varies with how many copies are produced and what manufacturing process is used to produce them. In traditional printing there are certain fixed costs that are the same no matter how many copies are produced and variable costs that increase with the number of copies made. Fixed costs include plates, overhead, setup, and the outside manufacturing, promotional, and advertising costs.

Variable costs include mostly the consumables like paper, press time, and binding material. The fixed costs are divided among the number of books produced. So the more books produced, the less cost per book. The problem is that often publishers look at the value of printing a large number of books and end up warehousing most of them before they throw them away. The alternative to producing too many copies is having to reprint a book. When a book is reprinted the fixed costs have to be paid again, representing a great increase in the cost per copy.

New printing technologies are changing how publishers look at the cost of printing small quantities of books. The greatest risk to the publisher is making a large investment in mass-producing a book the public may reject. This risk can be reduced if the publisher can produce a limited number of books to test the market. The fixed costs of preparing the printing press for operation have been greatly decreasing with new technologies. In the past the press's image carrier, the plate, had to be created through an expensive and time consuming process. New technologies that either mechanically create plates or produce the image carrier directly on the press (direct imaging) have greatly reduced the fixed costs of prepress operations. With digital presses, the cost per copy does not vary much at all. These presses have a toner-based system that can produce a different image each time at no real additional cost. These two new technologies do not replace traditional printing but do allow the publisher a marketing tool. A book can be tested on a digital press, which has a low cost per copy, on short runs, and, if the market likes it, the publisher can then take advantage of the value of printing mass quantities on a traditional press.

The introduction of digital printing has made on-demand printing a reality. If digital presses can have run lengths of one, it is conceivable that all our books can be produced as we request them. When a publisher considers on-demand publishing, they must consider the type of book and how it is purchased. The trick to on-demand printing is the demand part. Many books are sold not because a customer is looking for a specific title, but because they browse through a bookstore and pick out a title. These types of books will continue to be produced for this market but in limited runs. Books that are going to be requested and have limited shelf life will be produced on-demand, such as computer manuals.

Marketing of books will also be changing by the flow of information publishers receive about their customers. Companies are becoming smarter and smarter about marketing their products to very specific people. This is accomplished through the use of databases. Information about customers comes from many different sources such as surveys, business reply cards, and the newest and most powerful, the World Wide Web. The web is a powerful tool for gaining information about specific people. Most people have to give information when they sign up for a web service, and this biographical information can be used along with the topics they seek while online. If the web service provider knows that a customer is a doctor and they often look for sites about vineyards, they have a specific audience with a specific interest. If there are many other people that share interests with the doctor, then a publisher may want to address this audience with a book about wine. The publisher can get information about income levels by demographic areas, or even how much people spend on books, from either the Internet service provider or credit card companies. The publisher can then consider if they should produce a book priced at fifteen dollars or fifty dollars.

The information we gather about customers is also changing the way we promote books. In addition to finding audiences for books, we can promote those books to specific audiences. This is especially powerful when people purchase books online. As illustrated in the example above, the same customer who was identified as interested in a book about wine can be directly addressed when using the web for promotion of the book. The information about their interests triggers an ad for the book about wine to flash when they log on to the web. This allows the bookseller to address very specific customers with books they are likely to have an interest in.

New technologies are not all helpful to the book publishing industry—many represent a threat. We simply do not know the future of the printed book. Presently the greatest advantage the book has over other media is the comfort we have with it. Soon the advantage other mediums of publication have over the book will edge it out of the nonfiction marketplace. The biggest problem books have is that the information in them is old when you compare it to almost any other source. Digital media also offer more efficient search methods for research applications than any books. This is not a problem when you look at the market of books for entertainment, because the age of the information is not critical. Books used for research are a market that is going to be seriously hurt by new media. Why would anyone spend a large amount of money for a set of encyclopedias when they will be out of date in five years? This is where the industry is going to have to re-think how to serve this consumer.

Some people are greatly concerned over the future of book publishing. In recent years the number of forms publishing can take has increased. The book has competition from radio, television, magazines, newspapers, and the World Wide Web. In the past competition has affected the book's share of the market of packaging ideas and promotion, but it has continued to exist. At the present time in our culture books have a some advantages over other types of media. In addition to the affection we have for books, they offer some concrete advantages over other media such as portability, ease of use, a long life-span, and the fact that they do not require a large investment (such as a television) to present their information. Books also tend to have a higher degree of credibility when compared to other publications. The challenge for tomorrow's publisher is to look at the information they are given, decide which formats most logically support that information based on its application, and consider who is purchasing the final product and how. This analysis must be done by publishers when they decide which markets to promote books in. If publishers want to stay relevant and profitable they must use all the new technologies available to reduce the risks of publishing.

Intellectual property

The business of publishing is changing dramatically with the advent of new technologies, new markets, and new methods of doing business. The copyright system, which has quite an extensive history of its own, has been forced to change as well, in order to accommodate and support the new trends in publishing and disseminating information. If one thinks about the history of copyright and the paths it has followed, it really is quite interesting. Not so long ago, people were just concerned with books which were traditionally typeset and printed. Now, with the World Wide Web and digital printing capabilities, it is a much more confusing issue about how to maintain control over intellectual property.

Just think about how the invention of the photocopy machine changed copyright policies. People no longer had to buy a book or borrow it from the library to obtain its information and to indirectly pay for the rights associated with the work. They could now simply place the material on these neat machines themselves, and make as many copies as they desired, paying no attention whatsoever to any intellectual rights infringement. In the English-speaking countries, according to an ancient legend, copyright was first enforced in the year 567 A.D. In that year the ecclesiast Columba made a copy of a psalter in the possession of his teacher Finnian. A controversy arose and the cause was adjudicated by King Diarmud in the Halls of Tara, who held in favor of the plaintiff Finnian with the phrase, "To every cow her calf. . . ." The phrase "to every cow her calf" was also canonized, though in a different way. It is quoted in nearly every work on copyright, having as it does the kind of agricultural charm that appeals to city lawyers. The phrase, however, has a distinct significance. It recognizes, perhaps for the first time on record, the existence of such a thing as intellectual property.

It is important to understand where the concept of copyright came from in order to appreciate the changes that have occurred and what paths it might take in the future. Copyright began in the sixteenth century as a way to keep order among members of the book trade, which were organized as the Stationers' Company. The private concern of these guild members, copyright existed in this manner for over a hundred and fifty years through the support of the laws of press control and censorship. This method of private organization created a sort of monopoly on the book trade. Eventually, governmental sanctions were created which eliminated censorship as a means of "copyright control" for the protection of published works.

With mayhem on the rise because of the lack of protection, the British Parliament was forced to come up with an alternate plan to maintain control of the protection for intellectual property. There were two fundamental aspects to which copyright was directed—to provide order in the book trade for the members of a guild organization which had a monopoly of the trade and then to destroy the monopoly of that book trade.

As a response to the problem, Parliament came up with a "copyright statute" which was largely modeled on the stationer's copyright, however, it avoided another monopoly situation by incorporating two important changes: it would no longer be limited to members of the guild, and the protection that it would offer could never be revoked—it would be "perpetual" protection, within the scope of two terms of fourteen years each. The stationers' copyright had been an instrument of monopoly; the statutory copyright was intended for trade-regulation.

Today, the problems that copyright faces are indeed linked to its problems from the past. The greatest challenge facing the copyright system is to find an acceptable balance between the interests of three groups: authors, who give expression to ideas; publishers, who disseminate ideas; and the members of the public, who use the ideas. Copyrights are no longer a way for the government to control and monitor ideas, or for individuals or private groups to attempt to monopolize the dissemination of information, they are used to protect the expression of ideas for profit. In a society where there was no freedom of ideas, copyright protected only against piracy; in a society where there is freedom of ideas, copyright protects against plagiarism. Copyright, begun as protection for the publisher only, has come to be protection for the work itself.

CCC beginning

The purpose of copyright, as stated in the U.S. Constitution, is "to promote the progress of science and useful arts, by securing for limited times to authors and inventors the exclusive right to their respective writings and discoveries. . . . " The guarantee of monetary reward to creators for the utilization of their intellectual property is the legislative means for the promotion of the progress of the copyright system. When the copyright law was last revised, the US Congress encouraged the inception of a rights and royalty clearance system for reprographic uses. As a liaison between creators of original works and reproducers of those works, the Copyright Clearance Center (CCC) was enacted in 1978.

The CCC is a not-for-profit organization whose primary function is to facilitate compliance with United States copyright law. Currently, quoting CCC materials ". . . through its collective licensing programs, CCC provides authorized users with a lawful means for making photocopies from its repertoire of more than 1.7 million registered titles." The success of the CCC has been profound because of its structure as a central means for users and rightsholders to give and receive permissions and royalties in an organized and easily understood manner. A major goal of the CCC is ". . . to respond to the changing needs of [their] constituents, particularly in meeting the challenges of more sophisticated technologies. [Their] programs, each created in response to identified needs, are constantly evolving and expanding to satisfy the unique requirements of new markets, more advanced technologies, or current interpretations of the law."

In addition to the suggestion to create the CCC, Congress also chose to form a temporary committee to examine and thoroughly revise the copyright laws of the United States. The National Commission on New Technological Uses of Copyrighted Works (CONTU) was formed with the unique goal to provide the President and Congress with both the recommendations for and procedures required to increase the efficiency of the United States copyright law. CONTU was looking specifically to assure public access to copyrighted works used in conjunction with computer and machine duplication systems and to respect the rights of owners of copyrights in such works, while considering the concerns of the general public and the consumer.

The duties with which CONTU is charged could certainly not be easy as the pace of technological change in computer software and hardware continues to surpass the speed of legislative development and enactment. An additional issue is the cultural and definitional differences which exist between the legal and technical communities; these communities share neither training nor objectives and such differences make communication difficult. Aside from the issues that CONTU is concerned with, CCC must also deal with international rights concerns. The international scope of software markets and technologies has further complicated already complex legal issues. The United States has bilateral copyright relations with about 80 countries. Sixty of these countries adhere to the Berne Convention which provides for a minimum level of copyright protection without requiring notice or registration. Many countries have also ratified the Universal Copyright Convention (UCC), which requires that foreign works be afforded the same copyright protection as domestic works. However, under the UCC, a published work must bear a notice of copyright in order to receive protection.

The growth of the popularity of CCC's services since their beginning in 1978 has been enormous. The change in royalties paid from CCC programs from FY1996 to FY1997 alone was 23 percent—a record $35 million. Some of CCC's newest services have been most profitable. There has been a lot of change in the way that higher education provides textbook materials to their students. Custom built textbooks have become increasingly popular, and CCC has had a large impact on this trend. Strengthening [their] position in the academic community, CCC introduced a new set of bundled services—the Academic Licensing Service (ALS). ALS expands the scope of the Academic Permissions Service to include more flexible options for coursepack providers and users. For example, ALS will support a variety of fee collection and payment options to accommodate the range of budgeting needs among academic constituents. And it takes advantage of CCC's rights management technology to create licensing options for a broader range of rightsholders.

To simplify the permissions process for coursepack providers, CCC also added online capabilities via CCC Online. This interactive system allows a customer using the World Wide Web to select an item from their preauthorized repertoire or request a special item, determine the price for usage, and secure permission. Already, over 37 percent of the ALS business is transacted on CCC Online and that figure is expected to grow.

In order to provide support for the increasing use of digital technology in college and university environments, CCC introduced a new Electronic Reserves Program, which is part of ALS. The Electronic Reserves Program provides rightsholders with the power to control fees charged for the use of their works. This has been a huge improvement in the realm of digital permissions. As CCC has stated ". . . CCC's Electronic Reserves Program provides copyright owners with an essential means to satisfy user requests and ensure collection of their individually set fees. Users acquire permission through CCC to lawfully post copyrighted material on a campus intranet. Students may then access this course-related material via their computers using an assigned password."

Perhaps even more complicated than the permissions and copyright issues of literary works are those pertaining to photographs. In general, publishers have a history of having been inconsistent in acquiring rights to photos. The policies of acquiring rights to photographs vary from year to year, and from photo to photo. Even if photographs have been published, it is possible that the publisher might not own all the rights to the image, and innocently, they might not even be aware of this problem. In the recent past, the only way to determine the rights status of a particular photo was to manually search through old and incomplete records.

Photo rights can be very restricted and limited in ways unique to the medium. Photographers can grant rights limited to black and white reproduction, a specific size range, a specific resolution (number of dots per inch), or to publication in a specific sort of magazine. Limitations may also be imposed on the number of copies that can be reproduced, the time period during which the copies can be made, or the geographic area in which the copies can be circulated. Sometimes, the photographer is entitled to special fees for the reuse of a photograph.

CCC has also been active in its quest to provide a solution for the permissions of digital images, in addition to their goals involving literary works. The formation of Mira (Media Image Resource Alliance) by CCC aids world-class professional photographers as a resource to control on the use of their images, and the power to set their own fees for the use of their images. Mira is basically an all-digital stock photography agency. ". . . through its online permissions and ordering system, Mira enables users to obtain—securely and lawfully—fully digital, press-ready photographic images with just a few mouse clicks."

The success of CCC relies on their ability to keep costs low for their clients. If the costs are not kept reasonably low, then it detracts from the earning potential of their clients for reasons of business economics. "Thanks to the effective use of technology and streamlined business processes, [CCC] can simplify the process of providing usage information for users and minimize costs, thus maximizing returns to copyright owners." The success of a voluntary licensing and permissions system depends on the continuation of developing cost-effective programs for both rightsholders and users. CCC has demonstrated their ability to do this, while maintaining a high degree of operating efficiency, which is easily demonstrated through their record of receipts: CCC's receipts in millions of dollars range from $20 million in 1993 to $50 million in 1997.

Each year, CCC offers innovative new programs serving many types of copyright owners, a broad range of users, and works in multiple media. Leading edge technology is central to this effort. Today, this technology enables [CCC] to manage complex rights while providing straightforward permissions clearance services. Tomorrow, it holds the key to delivering new programs and products, serving the needs of new markets, and creating expanded royalty opportunities for rightsholders.

Digital organizational trends in publishing

In 1996, the Information Identifier Committee (IIC) was formed as a joint venture between the International Publishers Association (IPA) and the International Association of Scientific, Technical & Medical publishers (STM). The purpose of this joint committee was, ". . . to seek and facilitate international consensus on a system to identify units of information in the digital environment." It was determined that the system should both provide an electronic means of copyright management and support commercial activity over electronic networks. The mission statement of the IIC was: Publishers will engage in substantial commercial activity over electronic networks.

To facilitate this new aspect of publishing, works and parts of works which are bought, sold or accessed over digital networks must be identified according to an internationally accepted standard system. Such an identifier system will enable multiple applications such as the development of electronic copyright management systems, ordering and fulfillment, tracking, billing and payment schemes, bibliographic control and enforcement systems.

Throughout their work, the IIC studied many different means of identifying digital information. They studied not only systems devised within the publishing industry, but also in such related industries as the music industry. The Association of American Publishers (AAP) had been working on a system called the Digital Object Identifier (DOI) System, and this was the system which the IIC adopted in April 1997. The DOI System connects users, publishers, and information, via the Internet or any future networks. It consists of the names of the objects, or the DOI code number, and a directory of those codes called, appropriately enough, the DOI Directory. The directory can be accessed by the public throughout the world via the Internet. The object code itself is a two-part number, separated by a slash. On the left of the slash is the registrant's prefix, which is issued by the DOI Agency. The DOI Agency works in a way similar to the ISBN system. They are responsible for issuing these prefixes and ensuring that they are efficiently managed. On the right side of the slash, the publisher chooses the actual item ID number which should be unique to the object. Here is an example of what a DOI might look like: 10.65478/45920.

The DOI System's underlying technology is the CNRI Handle System. The Handle System is a distributed and scalable system which stores the names of digital objects and the information needed to locate those objects via the Internet. The most important characteristics of the Handle System are its scalability; its enforcement of persistent unique names; its ability to associate values with names so that users need only know one name to access information about versions, for example, or associated rights and permissions; and the system's optimization for speed and reliability. These important characteristics ensure that the DOI System will become a dynamic part of today's technology, and will adapt to future technologies.

The DOI directory can be accessed by the public on the Internet through a World Wide Web browser. With the browser, a customer or potential customer can find out information about an object by submitting a query to the directory. This query activates a chain of commands in the computer which will first forward the question to the appropriate publisher's DOI database, and then will return to the customer's browser with either the object itself, or information about the object, as requested. The ease of operating this kind of system for both publishers and the public has caused the DOI system to receive rave reviews about the new ease of facilitating copyright management and ownership issues. It also has been complimented on its ability to encourage and simplify scholarly research, and to promote digital commerce.

In October 1997 at the Frankfurt Book Fair, a group of publishers presented a demonstration of how they had begun to use the DOI system on a prototype basis. The system is continuously scrutinized in order to attain the best fit with systems that are already in place at many publishing houses, and to determine how the industry will receive the most benefits from the institution of this type of technology. It has been speculated by one publisher, that, "In the future, . . . access to the DOI Directory will be expanded to encompass interactive computer systems, for example, as a part of real-time multimedia presentations. Such expanded access could involve on-line negotiations over rights and interactions with payment systems as well as direct access to the desired material."

Once described as ". . . the license plate for digital content on the information superhighway. . . ," the DOI system can be used to identify a book, a chapter within a book, or even smaller parts such as paragraphs or even words or phrases. As Robert Badger of Springer Verlag, head of AAP's DOI Task Force said, "It's more than copyright management. . . . It's really for commerce. It can identify anything and it is easy for business and for individual consumers to use." While the system was developed by the AAP with, of course, publishers in mind, it was also designed with the idea that eventually it could be used similarly with other kinds of media as well: audio, images, video, and software. The AAP and IIC knew that this quality would be very important, the cross-media nature of the electronic marketplace. The DOI system is being looked at as one of the single most important advances in developing and expanding the electronic marketplace.

The expansion of the electronic marketplace has opened up an entirely new area for business growth. One new company, PubWeb, Inc., which is based in Woburn, MA, has seized the opportunity to become involved with the changes in electronic management of the publishing industry. PubWeb's specific industry niche is in developing the book-on-demand aspect of publishing. This area of business has become increasingly popular with publishers who, given the new digital technology, are now distributing and then printing, as opposed to how it's been done for the entire history of publishing, printing then distributing.

PubWeb works with any publisher or printer to arrange for printing books on demand. Essentially, PubWeb can be described almost as a broker. They handle the orders and then send them on to the printer. One of the most attractive features of PubWeb's services is that they account for all royalties and printing charges. PubWeb offers publishers the option of maintaining a database themselves of their own titles, or of having PubWeb manage a database of pages for them. The software which is the basis for PubWeb's operations is called NetPaper.

NetPaper is licensed from the Consortium for University Printing and Information Distribution, or CUPID. CUPID, while funded by Kodak, Sun, and Xerox, is managed and operated by Cornell University. The mission of CUPID over the past four years, has been to, ". . . design a client-server software application that utilizes the Internet to distribute and print high-quality documents." CUPID works by letting a user select documents from a publisher's website catalog. The user can then choose a printer which is convenient to them geographically, or simply because they prefer a specific printer. The NetPaper software finds the user's chosen documents from the publisher's secure web content server. When the file or files are found, NetPaper automatically accounts for all the copyright royalties and printing charges. NetPaper then sends the digital, print-ready file to the appropriate printer, with an accurate job ticket describing the customer's instructions.

Currently, the publishing area which has seen the biggest growth in the print-on-demand business is the higher education publishing market. There are several reasons why this business decision has been a popular one. Higher education publishers have suffered for years over the costs associated with book returns, high inventory, and increased unit costs due to smaller and smaller print runs. The most compelling motivation is that of the book return rate. "According to the Association of American Publishers, book return rates have grown to where they now are US publishers' biggest single expense —over thirty-five percent of sales."

It is no surprise, then, that higher education publishing is PubWeb's target market. PubWeb has taken advantage of their knowledge of the current statistics that ". . . the lost revenues and additional operating costs associated with high returns is compounded by the fact that used books represent over one third of all the books sold [in the higher education market]. Neither publishers nor authors receive revenue from the sale of used books."

Over the past twenty years, higher education publishers have found that decreasing percentages of students per class are buying "required" books. Today, the average sell-through rate (those books sold compared to those books produced) for a new textbook over the life of the edition has dropped to below 40%. The Association of American Publishers (AAP) and the National Association of College Stores (NACS) have identified a major factor in this decline: budget-conscious students tend not to purchase books unless they know a professor is going to use them extensively throughout the course. By contrast, when professors create a completely customized document, the sell-through rate skyrockets from 40% to over 85%.

Used college text books account for over a third of the higher education books sold, which translates into lost revenues of up to nearly $1 billion. With PubWeb's use of NetPaper, it is feasible that eventually all college professors will opt to create their own customized textbooks, possibly on a semester-by-semester basis, thereby decreasing or completely eliminating the value of used books. This is a very attractive possibility for publishers of higher education materials. Another great advantage to the "distribute then print" mentality is that millions of dollars can be saved by the publishing industry in shipping costs. It is amazing to think that never mind sending books across the ocean, it isn't even necessary to send a disk across the ocean. All business transactions can be done through the Internet. This saves not only the money directly associated with shipping costs, but the resources needed as well, not to mention the transport time that ocean freighting requires. These costs used to prevent some smaller companies from doing business abroad, but now the market is virtually open to anyone. It is also believed that the increased level of competitiveness will increase the efficiency of the business and decrease the costs. "By leveraging the Internet for electronic, not physical, distribution to authorized printers, NetPaper opens international markets in a new and exciting way."

The benefits of utilizing software such as NetPaper seem to be endless:

- With NetPaper, publishers can set a fee for their intellectual property and pass responsibility for printing and distribution to the bookstore or individual consumer.
- Out-of-print and out-of-stock titles can be given an eternal life with NetPaper. Whenever a book or document of any size is virtually inventoried and linked to the NetPaper network of printers, it can be easily printed on demand, returning a profitable revenue stream indefinitely. This increases the opportunity to publish more authors and titles.
- NetPaper offers all content publishers a profitable avenue for pre-publication, preliminary edition release, and test marketing of titles. Publishers can test and often prove that demand exists before making bigger investments in specific titles.

A competitor of PubWeb's NetPaper is the AAP's electronic commerce division, called PUBNET. PUBNET provides EDI (electronic data interchange) service to over 90 publishers. This list of publishers represents hundreds of subsidiaries and imprints. The AAP states that, "Over 3,700 bookstores, libraries, wholesalers, and schools are now buying books electronically through PUBNET, making it the largest EDI trading community of booksellers and publishers in the world." Very similar to NetPaper, PUBNET's database is geared specifically for the higher education market. Currently, there are over 340,000 titles in the PUBNET database. The PUBNET system is also electronically linked and prepared to take orders and monitor progress all the way through to fulfillment. The information is also available separately as a product information source.

On-demand approaches

Backing up a little bit on the historical time line, some of the earlier attempts at developing massive publishing databases were the Primis electronic custom publishing system introduced by McGraw-Hill in 1989, and the Instant Access proprietary software of Pitney Bowes Management Services (PBMS) which was used to create custom text books by four major publishers. In 1993, the Primis system was used by over 800 universities and colleges in creating customized text books.

When these two systems were developed, it was determined that processing a typical order from the Primis system took approximately 10 minutes, and a 300-page book from the Instant Access system took approximately 20 minutes to be processed. These systems were capable of taking PostScript formatted documents, inserting folios, paginating the material, creating tables of contents, and adding title pages—all automatically. The Primis system was usually networked to a Kodak 1392 digital printer, while the Instant Access software was most often linked to a Xerox DocuTech, and also a couple of Kodak 1392s. These electronic advances were just the beginning of the newer, more advanced megasystems of NetPaper and PUBNET.

While it is the belief of the authors that traditionally printed books will not "go out of style," it is also their belief that the educational textbook marketplace has been, and will continue to be, forever changed by these new database systems and the means of managing the rights of different types of intellectual works. It is also their hope that actions resulting from the improved efficiency and facility with which copyrights are being managed will encourage users to be more law-abiding than they have been in the past, perhaps due to the red tape that was once part of the process. This effective management should help to decrease the costs of rights involved with publishing works. This situation is similar to the software copying dilemma, which some people believe would be helped by lowering the cost of software so that people do not feel compelled to "save money" by illegally copying the software.

The rapid pace of technological change that the publishing industry is experiencing can only help to increase the efficiency and availability of products to be offered. Customers will continue to be delighted with the new options that they are given and publishers will continue to reap the rewards of lower inventory costs, and a decreased need for resources, among many other benefits. It is hopeful that publishers will recognize and be able to pass on some of these savings to their customers, thereby increasing the access to an even broader base of possible markets.

Magazines

The magazine, or periodical, is "a publication that is issued periodically, usually bound in a paper cover, and typically containing stories, essays, poems, etc., by many writers, and often photographs and drawings, frequently specializing in a particular subject or area, as hobbies, news, or sports." A magazine, typically consumer-based, contains material commissioned or written in-house, often determined months in advance. There are many types of periodicals, serving distinctly different purposes.

The magazine has and will continue to be a print medium that caters to our informational and entertainment needs on a weekly, monthly, or other periodic basis. They speak to us on topics ranging from business to health, world news to sports news. Practically every industry, career, hobby, or television series has a publication dedicated to the subject; this includes both the recognized world of your standard, glossy coated-stock newsstand magazine to the underground world of the homemade fanzine. The magazine publishing industry is a very lucrative industry, enticing many to pour money into a magazine that may or may not last through the year. New magazines are launched every year, with a marginal percentage of those becoming truly successful. With new and alternative types of media surfacing, from television to the web, magazines have quite a bit of competition. Television in particular, with its immediacy, mix of entertainment and information, and free (for broadcast TV) price, is a tough competitor.

Types of magazines

The magazine spectrum is broad to say the least, but can be broken roughly into two major subdivisions: consumer and business (trade). Smaller subdivisions include journals, newsletters, and the independently produced fanzine. Consumer magazines are periodicals of mass or specialized interest either sold or given free to the public. There are over 51 classifications for magazines under which all magazines are listed. While the mass-market magazines often face major competition from television, the specialized consumer magazine has a direct, intimate appeal that television cannot match. By offering a greater depth and closer perspective on a particular subject, the specialized magazine attracts a more loyal following than that which most specials or TV series could offer.

Business (trade) magazines cover the financial and commercial aspects of a particular industry or business. These magazines, when successful, possess a high ratio of advertising pages to editorial copy. Many utilize a controlled (free) circulation, rather than traditional subscriptions or newsstand sales; they rely on advertising sales as primary income. The resulting field is extremely competitive. These magazines often have much higher editorial and graphic standards than consumer magazines, using color graphics, illustration, and photography with the highest degree of quality.

Journals, a more scholarly venture, are usually started because a group of enthusiasts, most often members of a society (such as found in scientific or academic circles), wishes to disseminate information about their work and activities. Material submitted is generally not predetermined. These periodicals contain articles or papers that are primarily based on original research or scholarship. Journals have a small circulation and are usually nonprofit, funded by universities, grants, or foundations. Many journals do not accept advertising.

Newsletters are not typically regarded as a part of the magazine publishing industry, but fall under the description of a periodical. They average between four and eight pages in length, only one or two colors, and are sold by subscription or distributed for free. There is also a big trend towards electronic distribution of newsletters via email.

The fanzine (or "zine") traces its roots to the 1930s, when science fiction fans would create fanzines to share SF stories and communicate with one another. This form resurfaced with the emergence of punk rock in the 1970s, and continues to gain steam up until the present. Both these past and present instances all revolve around a group of amateurs that felt they were being neglected and took it upon themselves to cover their "scene." Zines are noncommercial, nonprofessional, small-circulation magazines that their creators produce, publish, and distribute by themselves as an alternative to commercial publications. Rarely turning a profit, more often losing money, zines are a labor of love of the creator, and will cover any and every combination of topics under the sun.

The physical size and shape of all of these types of magazines varies for every single title. There is no single accepted format, although a great many magazines will fall just shy of letter (8.5"x11") size. Size itself may be part of the selling of the magazine, either for its expanded format or its small, convenient size.

Size of the magazine industry

At any one point, it is difficult to precisely state the size of the magazine industry. The most recent figures place the number of consumer magazines at around 4,200. Business magazines have a similar figure. Newsletters number in the thousands, and zines, with a high launch and death rate and a lack of any real standard of measure, number between 10,000 and 20,000. According to the Oxbridge

Communications' National Directory of Magazines, the total number of magazine titles (excluding zines) in Canada and America alone is around 29,000. Recent figures for the dollar volumes of the industry were increasingly hard to find for any recent year, but a successful magazine generally makes a 10% profit.

Behind the magazine

Modern media conglomerates, such as Time Warner, hold much of the strength of the magazine industry. These giants are diversified enterprises which are much larger than a single title. They may have holdings in a number of magazines, television, and other forms of mass communication; magazines may only be a small part of their operation. In addition to the giants, hundreds of smaller publishing companies produce a wide variety of titles. These other publishing groups may also be home to several titles, or they may only provide one title.

The publisher of the magazine is usually the top executive who holds final authority over every department, from editorial to business. Magazine policy is made by the publisher; this person will usually be business-minded, and they oversee the entire operation. Generally, three people will report to the publisher: the editor, the advertising director, and the circulation director.

Each of these people heads a respective department responsible for some aspect of the production process. These departments can be a few people or a few hundred people, depending on the size of the magazine and the parent organization. Traditionally these departments are housed within a home office (these staff are considered in-house), but with downsizing and costcutting, many magazines are taking a "virtual office" approach. Currently, the traditional roles previously mentioned are undergoing drastic redefinition. With cuts in the size of staff, a larger breadth of roles is being assumed by the individual involved, and ideas of what it is to be editor, art director, designer, and sales staff are continually evolving.

Subscriptions and newsstands

Magazines are distributed either through subscriptions or newsstand sales. Circulations can range from small, unreported numbers to millions of copies per issue. Subscriptions often offer lower rates and extra promotions as a means of securing definite sales. Some forms of magazines, such as journals or trade magazines, are often distributed through free, controlled circulation. These magazines have a (relatively) guaranteed audience, and advertising pays for the costs of production. As stated before, scholarly journals may be funded by a related group or society.

At any time, newsstand sales can comprise more or less of the total sales compared to subscriptions, depending on the title. Newer titles depend on newsstand sales almost entirely (disregarding advertising as income) until they can build a subscriber base. Most magazines do make most of their sales income through single-issue purchase.

Advertising revenue

By and large, magazines generate a large portion of their revenue through advertising dollars. Billions are spent yearly on print advertising alone. Most magazines will run a 60/40 advertising to editorial ratio, although this number can vary in either direction. Television and the so-called new media compete with magazines for these dollars, forcing publishing companies to search for alternative means of generating revenue. This can include arranging sponsored trade shows, branching out into new media themselves, new product lines, and custom publishing.

Association/custom publishing

Technology allows the publisher to gather mass amounts of information about their readers and they are beginning to use this information to target specific segments and provide them with customized articles that ultimately increase loyalty and give the magazine an edge over the competition. Custom publishing takes a few basic forms. It might be an organization creating a magazine for a decidedly small audience. More often, it takes the form of a corporation or company underwriting the production costs of a magazine aimed at customers with a vested interest in their products. A good example of this is the inflight magazines produced by the airlines. This is referred to as "brand publishing." It is one of the fastest growing segments of the magazine publishing business and is proving to be a new source of high return both for the sponsoring company and the publisher.

Custom publishing is seen as a better method of direct marketing by many companies, as it has the "legitimacy" of traditional consumer publishing, but the content may be nothing more than a thinly veiled sales pitch for that company. However, many companies use custom magazines as a means of providing valuable information, not just on their products or services, but on items of interest to the targeted customer. Financial institutions are using the magazine format to replace traditional brochures; their efforts are being met with promising results. Companies wanting to change their image are producing magazines that are effectively helping to improve public opinion and show a new side of that company. With proven results and control of editorial content, many companies are willing to spend the extra money to fund the production of a custom magazine.

Cost savings

The last few years have seen dramatic changes in the business of publishing magazines. With desktop publishing technology becoming increasingly advanced, easy to use, and cheaper, the move to this technology has been driven by cost-savings. A number of trends have begun to prove themselves viable options to the traditional publishing model and are, in part, responsible for this shift.

Bringing more production tasks in-house not only saves the publisher and magazine money, but allows more independence of operation while giving more control over the quality and appearance of the magazine. Tasks like scanning, proofing, and RIPping can now affordably be done in-house, and it is estimated that "soft-proofing," digitally rendered proofs using strictly calibrated monitors to represent the color, moire, etc. of a page, will be perfected soon. Digital color proofing is closely tied to the trend in computer-to-plate (CTP) printing. More and more magazines are skipping the costly use of films and analog proofs and are moving their operations towards a completely digital workflow. More and more, advertisements are also arriving in digital form for publications. When the advertisers still insist on using film for ads, equipment such as copy-dot scanners can be used to scan the film into digital form for use with the CTP technology.

Well-organized image databases and image management are other areas which are seeing increased attention. They are now being used to incorporate and catalog not only still images but sound clips and movie files as the move towards multi-purposing and multimedia increases. This improves production and opens up new revenue options. Many times an off-the-shelf database application serves the purpose, but some publishers choose to have a custom application created for them.

Common software tools, such as QuarkXPress, Adobe Photoshop, PageMaker, etc., and better modes of transferring files have given rise to increased collaboration between in-house staff and workers throughout the country. ISDN, T1 lines, and dedicated commercial services are all higher speed communications systems which are making this a reality, decreasing turnaround time and drastically altering the publishing workflow. With this also comes the distributed workgroup and the rise of the virtual office. With more and more professionals desiring to stay in a geographic area or to spend more time with their family, publishers wanting to keep the in-house staff to a minimum, and the aforementioned communications systems, the virtual office is gaining popularity.

While not viable for all magazines, many publishers are finding that the virtual office is a wonderful new option. Benefits include increased productivity (with no one else to chat with, many workers find that more of their time is spent actually working), lowered costs, and the ability to hire talented professionals no matter where they live. Many times, editorial staff may never know what the other editors look like, despite constant interaction. Most magazines might be best suited with a mixture of the traditional and virtual office, with a home office and in-house design department, and a combination of freelancers and editorial staff working from home.

A huge issue with a completely digital workflow is preflight checking. The communications systems offer the ability to transfer data in the matter of seconds, but missing graphics, bad color specs, and font problems continue. The preflight process helps to combat these dilemmas, with a combination of off-the-shelf tools and manual double checking. With the increased affordability of technology, more smaller publishers are now able to jump into the industry and compete with the bigger, more established publishers. And with the ease and span of the World Wide Web and increase of online magazines, traditional publishers are seeing increased competition.

The future

One of the ever-present questions is whether the magazine will ever go entirely electronic. While some preach the end of print, this hypothesis continues to be proven wrong. Computers have made electronic versions of magazines more viable, but there are some basic places where a computer has yet to truly catch on; try taking a laptop to the beach or the bathroom. Magazines, and all print media, will hold on to these areas for quite some time. This is not to say that magazines will not try or succeed at producing versions that are digitally based; from the web to CD-ROM, new and old titles alike are being published daily. Some magazines are in fact trying to exist solely as a digital format, and electronic magazines, or e-zines, may exist solely on the web.

The World Wide Web

With the proliferation of e-zines and online companions to print magazines, the web helps provide readers with news and information with the click of a few buttons. It is giving magazines a helping hand in staying competitive with such mediums as television by offering the latest stories in a comparable timeframe. By also offering alternative and extra articles on the web, and snippets of what can be found in the printed version, many magazines are now creating a symbiotic relationship between the two, strengthening the magazine's presence. Some magazines have succeeded in using subscriptions for web-only material based on the ability to offer up-to-the minute information, but this represents a relatively small number. With its near limitless reach, the web offers a new tool for editorial and market research. Not only can a writer use services like Lexis-Nexis, but the sales force can use such things as online customer surveys for gathering information on a company they intend to pitch a product or service to.

CD-ROM and DVD

A number of titles are utilizing multimedia technology to produce either digital counterparts to an already established print magazine or new titles solely on CD-ROM. Relatively cheap and easy to produce, these types of magazines use programs such as Macromedia Director to author the magazine. CD-ROM magazines can now include sound, digital video, and interactivity to make an exciting new form of magazine. DVD offers even greater capacities for information and is making an impact in film-industry-based magazines. Due to the need for specialized equipment (for instance, a disc drive of some sort and computer), these forms are a little slower in catching on.

Magazine publishing has had a large impact on American society, throughout our history. It has served as a vehicle for change and exchange of information, and as a source of entertainment. Today it is an evolved form of mass communication, focusing on delivering information of increasing specialization. Enticing, this industry draws many into its ranks; some are rewarded, some are not. Currently in the midst of a big digital upheaval, this industry holds a lot of promise, opportunity, and excitement for those willing to take some of the necessary risks. The industry itself has grown more stable with time, and in general, more titles are being established than discontinued.

Chapter 10

NEW MEDIA

There are two viable media for electronic publications: CD-ROM and the networks (both the Internet and the various commercial networks, such as America Online and CompuServe). So many people are now using CD-ROM and/or the networks that they have become worthwhile ways to reach an audience. CD-ROM and Internet are available to all kinds of businesses, to professionals at all levels, and, most importantly, to consumers at large. A survey of technical program attendees at a recent major conference on computer graphics showed that 93 percent of those surveyed had CD-ROMs and 94 percent had full network access. CD-ROM and the networks are alike in the kinds of information they can present to their users, but they differ in their stability, their information access rate, their costs, and the ways in which products based on them can be marketed to a mass audience.

Electronic publishing offers a number of excellent opportunities for information publishers including:
- greatly decreased publication costs
- a way to publish that can't be put into traditional formats
- the ability to greatly increase the amount of information in a single publication
- a way to move into new approaches to organizing and presenting information

Perhaps most fundamentally, electronic publishing allows an author or publisher to integrate text, sound, pictures, video, animation, and interactive computing into a common paradigm and a common medium. Currently, documents that integrate all these capabilities are called multimedia or multimedia documents. All media and all processes, both computing and communication, are fused into a common digital domain.

Diverse kinds of information

Textual and numeric information. At the most elementary end of the spectrum are very large databases and archives of primarily technical data, in textual and numeric form. This type of publishing accounts for the majority of the electronic titles currently being manufactured, for example, census information, national telephone directories, legal decisions, laws and regulations, archives of government documents, and parts catalogs for computer, hardware, and auto parts stores. The information is often time sensitive and it is often already in usable machine-readable form. Putting this information online is a natural development and CD-ROM is a good medium as well, particularly if it is important to keep archival copies of the information. CD-ROM titles based on textual and numeric information are typically manufactured in disk pressing runs that are small and subscription-based (that is, an updated set of data on disc comes out monthly or quarterly).

Pictorial information. Many CD-ROMs containing pictorial information are also being manufactured today, and there are many archives of image information on the Internet. In some ways, these archives are similar to the text-oriented titles. They contain collections of information; examples include clip art, font collections and photography portfolios. However, the economic model for images is somewhat different from that of text. In fact, there seem to be many more models for pictorial CD-ROMs than there are for text-based products. Image titles may be distributed as shareware, as royalty-free images, as stock libraries that can be reused on a fee basis, or as stock libraries that can be used only by the end user.

Sound information. Sound is available for both online in the Internet and CD-ROM publications. Virtually all CD-ROM players can also play audio CDs, and information in audio CD format can be intermixed with information in CD-ROM format. Some recording artists are already beginning to create CD-ROMs that supplement their music with pictures or videos included on the discs themselves, and some artists are publishing their music through the World Wide Web.

Digital video

Digital video is another kind of information that may be provided either online or on a CD-ROM. Until now, video has been limited to small windows on the computer monitor, and to frame rates below 15 fps (frames per second). However, newer compression technologies and faster playback hardware have recently raised this threshold to full screen, 30 fps video—achieving a quality equal to, or better than, the home VHS video cassette recorder. Video can already be played back from a CD-ROM onto an ordinary TV set or computer screen. At present, there is some competition among available formats and play-back technologies, but it may be resolved in the near future.

The changing nature of information

Electronic publishing takes advantage of new opportunities to expand our notions of both technical and popular communication. Eventually, this type of publishing may change the very relationship between information and the document that conveys information.

Expanding communication opportunities

Putting technical materials online or on CD-ROM is the way to pub-lish longer papers and incorporate additional information that may have too limited an appeal to be included in printed journals. This additional information includes not only text, but also data sets, color images, video clips and research notes. The authors become more familiar with electronic media. As publishers are realizing that there is important information they can't convey in paper form, they include floppy disks and CD-ROMs as companions to their books, which is a convenient way to allow the readers to interact with the author's work, thereby helping them understand it more deeply and allowing them to draw their own conclusions.

Digital libraries

Traditional libraries serve their patrons in a number of ways: by building collections of materials for readers, by providing them with catalogs and indexes to these collections, by preserving a historical record, and by guiding the reader who has specialized needs. Digital libraries—shared collections of digital materials that may be widely distributed geographically—have the same goal but offer access to new document formats and new technologies to support access, catalogs, indexes, and expert assistance. There is quite a lot of activity in investigating and building digital libraries in universities, businesses, and government agencies. The idea is to build focused collections of digitized legacy documents, formal and informal reports, multimedia documents, and even data sets so that researchers and others can access and use these collections in unified ways with powerful tools.

CD-ROM and online publishing (Internet)

CD-ROM

The CD-ROM market is growing at a fast pace, and there are many different types of CD-ROM titles available today. These titles can be roughly divided into the following major categories: informational, educational, and entertainment CD-ROMs. The major qualities of CD-ROM that makes it an attractive medium for publishing are:

- a large and growing market
- the large capacity of the disc
- familiar editorial and publishing models
- low cost of manufacturing
- durability and stability

Acceptance in the market

There is now wide acceptance of CD-ROM as a medium, just as DVD, a competitor, is entering the market. More and more computer systems have CD-ROM players and the public is becoming accustomed to purchasing discs for education and entertainment. The rate of increase in the installed base of CD-ROM players has grown from about one million units per year in 1992, to six million or more a year in 1996. The *Wall Street Journal* estimates that there will be an installed base of more than 80 million CD-ROM units by the year 2000. The Digital Video Disc (DVD) system, which is compatible with CD-ROMs, was launched in 1996 and will be seeing significant sales by the end of the decade.

Large capacity. A CD- ROM provides a very large capacity—654.7 megabytes (MB). This capacity can be freely divided into any combination of text, sound, pictures, video, and software needed for a particular title. A 300-page book with 300 words per page, for example, contains 540,000 bytes and about 1,000 such books in ASCII text format can be stored on a single CD-ROM. Even with color images, a CD-ROM remains very competitive. With print books, there is a high cost of separating and printing high-quality color figures and their quality still falls short of the quality of the digital originals on a CD-ROM. A CD-ROM can also store images of higher resolution; the Kodak PhotoCD format, for example, can store about 115 images at 2,000 x 3,000 pixels each on a single disc.

Familiar editorial and publishing models. CD-ROM has become the preferred distribution medium for anything over a few megabytes in size. CD-ROM is preferred over floppy disks because it doesn't get erased or damaged and because it's cheaper than floppies to manufacture in quantity. It's preferred over online distribution because it doesn't take time and connection cost to download, and because the original copy can be kept offline without having to worry about accidental erasure.

Low cost of manufacturing. CD-ROM is inexpensive to manufacture. For a small run (about 1,000 copies), the total production cost might be less than $2.00 per disc. More elaborate kinds of packaging can add another $1.50 to this cost. Printing and binding books, on the other hand, is likely to run more like $10 or $12 in these quantities. The shipping and storage of finished discs is also much cheaper than for books. Publishers can manufacture discs in only the quantities needed and maintain small inventories. By contrast, in book publishing, the setup and make-ready cost is so high that most publishers are forced to manufacture larger quantities at one time and maintain larger inventories.

Durability and stability. CD-ROM is a remarkably robust storage medium. A disc suffers no physical wear while it is being played. And it is difficult to damage the reflective surface on which the information is stored. The polycarbonate plastic through which the laser passes is extraordinarily transparent and is not damaged by the the laser or other light, including sunlight or UV light. The only way to damage a disc is by scratching the disc surface.

Online publishing (Internet)

The vision of online publishing is that readers will have immediate access, from their homes or workplaces, to a body of knowledge that is being constantly updated by its authors. There are some very exciting opportunities to shape the nature of electronic publishing on the Internet. The Internet is the largest interconnected computer network in the world that provides information exchange. All the computer connected to the Internet can easily communicate with one another using the TCP/IP protocol, which enables connection among computers produced by different vendors.

The backbone network of the Internet was initiated by the ARPANet, which was sponsored by the U.S. Department of Defense in 1983. After ARPANet disappeared, NSFNET, a network connecting super-computer centers, assumed the role of the Internet backbone in 1986. Later, the Internet evolved to become a national research computer network in the United States that connected university research centers, academic institutions, and nonprofit organizations. In the late 1980s, the Internet began to expand all over the world.

Nowadays, people log on to keep up with their client; to order books, hardware, and software; travel; to research technologies and business opportunities; and to exchange an ever-increasing amount of e-mail with colleagues and friends. People like ordering certain products over the Web. If they know what they want, and if the supplier has an excellent reputation, web ordering seems very low risk and completely convenient. Large corporations are saving huge amounts in their procurement budgets by automating ordering via the web.

The ability of the Internet

The key to WWW is the use of a concept called hypertext. The fundamental concept behind hypertext is that information can be stored and retrieved in a nonhierarchical structure. So instead of moving through directories of information as FTP or Telnet does, hypertext allow to jump from one place to the next through a series of "links" around the world. Much of WWW goes on an Internet protocol called http, (HyperText Transport Protocol). The language used in http is called HTML, HyperText Markup Language. HTML is an application of SGML (Standard Generalized Markup Language), which is a powerful tool for defining and displaying documents for electronic information, development, and presentation. Many journals today are tagging their text and figures in SGML to make for easier electronic access and manipulation of the publications.

There is also the eXtensible Markup Language (XML), a subset of SGML, that provides many of the capabilities of full SGML but has simplified processing requirements to support the dynamic requirements of the web. A catalog publisher that is repurposing data for the web can use XML to mix and match information overcoming the limitations of HTML without the processing overhead that a full SGML would carry with it. XML will aid in the creation of custom catalogs, thus offering more bits of information from paper to the web.

Changes In Share of Media Revenues 1987–2002

Medium	Share (%)			Share change (%)	
	1987	1997	2002	87-97	97-02
Daily Newspaper	26.8	22.1	20.3	-4.7	-1.8
Weekly Newspapers	2.6	2.5	2.3	-0.1	-0.2
Consumer Periodicals	5.1	5.2	4.8	0.1	-0.4
Business/Other Periodicals	3.1	3	2.8	-0.1	-0.2
Directories/Yellow Pages	6.7	6.1	5.3	-0.6	-0.8
Catalogs	5	5.3	4.8	0.3	-0.5
Circulars	6.6	7.5	6.9	0.9	-0.6
Other Direct Marketing	6.5	8.7	9.3	2.2	0.6
Broadcast TV	20.9	20.7	19	-0.2	-1.6
Cable/Specialty TV	0.9	2.7	3.5	1.8	0.8
Radio	6.6	6.9	6.2	0.3	-0.7
Outdoor/Transit	0.9	0.6	0.5	-0.3	-0.1
Internet/Electronic	0	0.5	6.7	0.5	6.2
Miscellaneous/Other	8.4	8.3	7.7	-0.1	-0.6

Source: McCann-Erickson and Kubas Consultants Projections

Impact of the Internet on publishing

The Internet is attracting a growing interest among both consumers and businesses. The Internet has created a new excitement and buzz for communication media with every expectation of continued strong growth ahead. The Internet, and the associated World Wide Web (WWW), is rapidly changing how media professionals buy and use different channels. The Internet is attracting considerable attention in real life as well as in the media. The media model also projects significant increases in investment and usage of the Internet by both advertisers and consumers during the next five years. While there is considerable hype associated with the Internet, its most vital signs, as demonstrated by this headline, "Net use doubling every 100 days" (USA Today, April 16, 1998), indicate that the Internet will become a significant medium in the coming years. Increased use of the Internet or computerized databases will pressure conventional printed directories and catalogs. There are three important reasons favoring electronic catalogs and directories:

- the cost of production for electronic databases is relatively low
- these databases can be updated with minimal cost
- the cost of distribution is minimal

These are also negatives associated with the electronic catalog:

- color reproduction on PC screens can vary
- limited access and usage by many consumers
- computers can be more difficult to use than print

For example, because of the difficulties in reading text on computer/video screens, the use of inkjet or laser printers in business or in homes to reproduce Internet and other images and graphics will actually accelerate the consumption of bond or coated paper.

Internet for business

The Internet offers many advantages for companies that want to sell products, whether they are expanding a physical storefront or creating a company that exists only in cyberspace. The reasons for a company to have an online store are:

1. Reach a worldwide audience.
2. Do business with an affluent market.
3. Be open twenty-four hours a day, no time zone barrier.
4. Reach consumers when they are ready to buy.
5. Appeal to consumers who hate sales people.
6. Open new channel to distribution for the company.
7. Offer lower costs to consumers and beat competition.
8. Beat competitors to new markets because they are not online.
9. Reduce or eliminate inventory, warehouse, and money costs.
10. Interact with customers.
11. Engage the senses by using audio, video, and multimedia to create relationships and sell products.

Many types of business models are possible and successful on the Internet. A virtual store conducts business only on the internet, not on the street. For example, Amazon books (www.amazon.com) has $30 million in annual sales and grows at 34 percent a month. Online auctions sell every kind of product from computer products to travel vacations. Moreover, the internet is becoming a resource center for employers seeking new workers and for employees finding new jobs.

Advantages of the Internet

As an advertising and sales promotion medium, the Internet has a number of real and virtual advantages, including:
1. Size does not appear to matter in the virtual world—a tiny company can have a powerful Web presence.
2. The Internet is totally digital—data, graphics, images and even full motion video can be transferred around the Internet.
3. There are no geographic borders or boundaries on the Internet—an advertiser can have a global presence, irrespective of where the website may be located.
4. The Internet is highly interactive and involving—magical words for many advertisers and marketers.
5. Internet users tend to be young, well-educated, and represent the leading edge of innovation in society. Those now surfing the web after school will make the media and marketing decisions in the 21st century.

6. The Internet is relatively economical. For a small monthly access fee, people can "surf the net" for hours. Communications costs for users are negligible.

7. The Internet represents the "death of distance" as far as moving information is concerned. The Internet could become the next telephone or fax machine.

8. The Internet will benefit from increased activity based on evolving e-commerce and e-business applications.

9. The Internet appears to have amazing potential. The dynamics all seem to be positive.

Disadvantages of the Internet

While the Internet appears to have many advantages and benefits, there are some points to be concerned:

1. The Internet ideally requires both a powerful personal computer and high-speed modem for proper access. These are expensive and are found in less than 35% of U.S. households today.

2. Computers are difficult to use. They are extremely logical and do not tolerate ambiguity. Few people think the way that computer programmers would like them to.

3. There are technological glitches in how well personal computers communicate via the Internet. Claims of 100% compatibility and trouble-free communications are usually manufactures' hype and are not substantiated in the real world.

4. The Internet may become another passing fad, to be replaced by the next "hot new medium" to come down the technology highway. But the principle of a world fully linked for communications will persist. The net might vanish but something else would probably take its place.

5. Increasing telecommunications costs, more government intervention and companies starting to institute charges for what is currently available on the Internet for free can all be impediments to the Internet's future expansion.

6. The proven results of Internet advertising and successful Internet sales initiatives are relatively sparse to date. There is danger of the Internet's growth being hampered because it appears to deliver much less then what it promises.

Trends of Internet

The trend to more computer usage is inevitable as computer prices decline while their power and capabilities increase. Telecommunications are improving as well, which means faster data transfers and greater bandwidth. These trends will drive increased use of the Internet and e-mail by both businesses and consumers.

A number of retailers and other vendors are embracing e-commerce as a cost-effective way of selling or marketing their goods and services via the Internet. Another emerging concept called electronic business or e-business is also attracting attention. E-business links the Internet to the wealth of business information that all corporations house. Under e-business operations, customers and suppliers can access and share information electronically. E-business is an evolution of e-commerce. E-business is based on wiring business from the back office to the sales floor. The IBM Corporation is a strong proponent of e-business initiatives.

The Internet is a growing medium, adding more services and features each day. Net usage appears to be doubling every 100 days or so. Most advertisers believe they must have a presence on the Web. The Internet also provides a rapid response mechanism. The positive attributes of the Internet include its transactional and interactive capabilities. Another driving force is its use as an advertising medium will be the concurrent rapid growth of e-commerce and e-business.

The Internet will experience rapid growth because of several interrelated factors:

- Lower cost and more powerful personal computers will be found in a growing number of homes.
- Bandwidth has been increasing while the cost of Internet connections has stabilized.
- There are new transactional applications like e-commerce and e-business, which expand the offerings available on the Internet.
- The Internet has become such a popular topic of discussion, no one wants to be left out.

Digital becomes the universal standard

The shift from analog to digital in all forms of communication has become more pronounced as lower cost and more powerful technology is rapidly making many conventional production processes and practices obsolete. Telecommunications, photographic images, graphics, and text are now transmitted and stored electronically, with impressive time savings, cost efficiencies and improved accuracy (fidelity). More media and their suppliers are embracing a wide range of digital processes. Although digital television (DTV), for example, is coming slowly in some areas, it will revolutionize broadcasting, especially once convergence with the Web is complete.

Computers are an essential tool for business and are becoming one for living. However, although electronic document technology is available, traditional publishing is still used. Acquiring books is an indication of culture. Developing habits of reading books is one of the major goals of public education. Reading books and magazines is easier than screen. Books and readers can be brought together without any electrical outlet or batteries requirement. In the publishing industry, print media must take advantage of the long-term trends to increased computerization to build on their expertise and to strengthen their established franchise.

Market demands such as paper costs, postal rates, CD-ROMs, DVDs, the Internet, and on-line services have prompted customers to investigate alternative production and distribution options. A traditional printed product is one that utilizes plates, film, prepress, warehouse storage, and ground-based transportation. Nontraditional or alternative products could be defined as those not requiring plates, film, long press runs, warehouse storage, and transportation. Alternative products include recorded disks and on-line products, plus materials created by on-demand publishing and customized print.

When we talk about the new forces competing with traditional print, we have to look at on-line services, CD- and DVD-ROM publishing, and the World Wide Web. We have to think about the advantages of these alternative products or alternative media. By examining the advantages and disadvantages of traditional print and alternative products, we see how print can compete in the new communications world order. With advantages over traditional print, such as customization, cost, and timeliness, digital and variable printing could be considered an alternative media.

Interactivity is a new and fascinating subject. There are six advantages of interactive publishing: customization, timeliness, comprehensiveness, searchability, transaction, and economy. An argument could be made that the medium best suited to advertising is the medium that will grow at the expense of those media worst suited to advertising. If you believe that most print production (newspapers, magazines, marketing) is subsidized by advertisers, then you could say that advertisers influence the success of certain media. If it is true that advertisers influence the success of certain media and that interaction enhances advertising, then you have to wonder if advertisers will consider interactive new media (DVD-ROM, on-line) a better buy than non-interactive media (newspapers, magazines, etc.). Disk-based products offer more interactivity then most printed products. The ability to "mouse around" allows you to follow your own path through a CD-ROM. Printed products can offer some interactivity but much less then CD-ROMs.

By now you must have seen, heard of, or "surfed" a commercial on-line service (America OnLine, CompuServe, etc.) or the Internet. The emerging vision of our on-line future in "cyberspace" has been the cover story of almost every magazine. The big breakthrough began in 1993 with the creation of a new application on the Internet called the World Wide Web (WWW)—it is user-friendly and linked to other sites. Schools, government agencies, and now business can build what is called a "home page." The home page can be thought of as a store front in a shopping mall. It uses a graphic interface so you can see what is inside.

The other advantage is the linking or the "hyperlinking" ability. Unlike conventional on-line services which are basically one big computer, the Internet is made up of thousands of computers. You start reading an Internet page and you come to a word or sentence that is underlined and in a different color. If you "click" on this area with your mouse, you access another page, perhaps on another computer that discusses that word or sentence in more depth.

Web browsers such as Explorer and Netscape allow you to interact with the websites and other Internet resources with point-and-click ease. In one stroke, the web makes the Internet much easier to use and gives you the graphical tools to set yourself up as an information publisher. Internet activity has created a new communication medium. People looking for jobs are posting multimedia resumes to the web; companies testing new marketing strategies are creating electronic storefronts. The web is nothing more then a set of hyperlinked elements that conform to a standard known as the Hyper Text Markup Language or HTML. HTML is an application of the Standard Generalized Markup Language or SGML, a defined standard for platform-independent publishing that allows you to pass documents to other platforms and other media, such as disks. HTML documents include audio, video, text, graphics, and tables, as well as links to resources like e-mail, and other websites.

Multimedia

There seems to be much confusion about what multimedia really is. It has become a buzzword that people like to use, but don't necessarily know what it means. Simplistically, it means more than one medium or communication type is used. This definition is more the old style of multimedia, when a slide show with narration or a paper that included a graphic was considered advanced. Since there is now the ability to do much more than that, a better definition of multimedia is "the combination of two or more media types, to effectively create a sequence of events that will communicate an idea, usually with both sound and visual support. Typically, multimedia productions are developed and controlled by computer."

It is the advances in computer technology that have spawned the booming multimedia industry, because computers make it all possible. In the last twenty years, computer multimedia has developed from early specialized PCs that ran slide carousels, to the 1980s when manipulation of text and graphics began. In the 90s personal computers have developed enough to give anyone at home the ability to create sophisticated presentations incorporating graphics, video, and sound.

As computers advanced, storage mediums had to keep up. What good is it to create a wonderful product, if there is no way to transport it and share it with others. The underlying problem is that the file sizes grow immensely when items, such as quality graphics and sound, are added. The development of high-density floppy disks was the start of being able to store more complex files. These disks hold about 1.4 Mb, which seems quite small for today's standards but were very important when they were new. After these disks, the holding capabilities of the storage media grew by leaps. Older drives could hold 40 Mb or 88 Mb. 3.5" magneto-optical disks could hold 128 Mb. These storage versions have faded and been replaced by the current favorites. Newer disks that hold 100 Mb for smaller products and CD-ROMs which revolutionized the multimedia field with the storage of 620 Mb. CD-ROMs really have made the high-end multimedia products possible not only because of their large storage capabilities, but because they are produced very inexpensively compared to the other storage devices. New disks and drives are also much less expensive to produce and purchase than their predecessors.

There are certain components necessary in a computer system to consider it a multimedia-capable system. Macintosh- and Windows-based computer differences held back the advancement of multimedia for years. Multimedia titles were being developed for the Mac because the hardware specifications for each machine were known. The problem was that there were a great many more PCs than Macs and these machines had no standards for what hardware components they included, so software developers were hesitant to produce multimedia titles without these standards. To solve this problem, the Multimedia Personal Computer (MPC) specifications were developed beginning in 1990. By 1995 the minimum specifications for MPC level 3 were issued, including 8 Mb RAM, Pentium 75 Mhz processor,

540 Mb hard drive, quad-speed 600 Kbps transfer time CD-ROM drive, 16-bit quality sound, and 640 x 480 16-bit color display. Macs have comparable standards. Today, it is almost impossible to buy a PC with specifications as low as these, so compatibility isn't as big a problem now as it has been in the past. Multimedia products are marked with the MPC level needed so buyers will know if the product will run on their machine.

In order to produce high-end multimedia there is certain equipment that is necessary or at least highly desirable to have. These include a computer with a high-speed processor and 1024 x 768 pixel monitor, microphone and speakers, video or digital still camera, flatbed scanner, CD-ROM recorder, and high external storage capabilities. This equipment will allow the developer to create multimedia in a time-efficient way, in turn reducing production costs.

There are seven levels of multimedia production. Levels one and two are the simplest and become more involved as the levels increase with interactivity at levels six and seven. The levels are as follows:

Type	Level	Elements
Static	1	Black and white text and graphics
	2	Color text and graphics
Animated	3	Simple animated text and graphics
	4	Predigitized video and animation
	5	Authored video and animation
Interactivity	6	Input required from the audience on a group basis
	7	Input required from the audience through individual interaction

The level chosen to support a particular product depends on what equipment is available and what the purpose of the product is. The best rule of thumb in multimedia creation is: just because you can do it, doesn't necessarily mean you should. The developer must decide what is the most appropriate way to convey the information. If a handout is all that is needed it would be a waste of time and money to create a video presentation. Multimedia cannot make up for poor content, poor design, poor targeting, or delivery by a poor presenter.

When designing for multimedia, it can be important to know how large the files being created will be, especially when deciding how to store them. The average screen size is 13 inches, or 640x480 pixels. Monitors do come in much larger sizes than this, but a good guideline for designing multimedia that will be distributed to many people is to design for the average user. If the product is designed for a larger screen it won't fit properly on the smaller screens and is not useful for those consumers. This must be considered if the product will be distributed to many and the computer being used with the media is unknown. If you are designing for use on a specific machine with high-quality capabilities then it is fine to fully exploit what technology is available.

Along with the pixel size of the image used, the color depth of the monitor is also necessary to figure out the file size. The color depth of the monitor determines how many colors are available to use. The choices are 8-bit, 16-bit, and 24-bit, which have the ability to produce 256 colors, 65,536 colors, or 16.7 million colors, respectively. The minimum requirement for color depth is 16-bit, but it is best to only design for 256 colors because the pictures can load more quickly. The higher the pixel count and the greater the color depth, the better quality the graphic will have. In general, it is best to develop products that more people can use, even if they aren't the best quality that is possible to make. Once the pixel and color depth values are known the approximate file size equals:

$$\frac{\text{image size in pixels x color depth in bits}}{8}$$

Record all image file sizes to be able to estimate the size of the finished product and be able to plan for appropriate storage. Multimedia projects are developed using authoring tools. Level one and two multimedia can usually be created just with a word processor, but the higher levels need more involved programs to create them, ranging from low-level programming languages to highly developed tools to create multimedia. One analyst put these authoring tools and languages on a "user friendliness" scale. At the bottom are Assembler and machine languages. Up one step from these are C and C++ programming languages. These low-level programs are what are used to build the higher-level programs and make them possible. They really aren't necessary for the average user to know unless their interest is in programming or in developing their own product from scratch. Another step up are scripting languages such as ScriptX, Lingo, and HyperTalk. At the top of the scale are authoring tools that are so developed that they look like standard English and are the easiest to use with the least amount of training.

It is important to know what the function of the product is, because the developer needs to figure out how to present the information. Multimedia is not the ideal way to present very text-intensive materials. There are books on CD-ROM but most people find it tedious to read a lot of text off a computer screen. If multimedia still is the best choice for presentation, but parts of the information contain a lot of text, the method of dealing with the text is important. Instead of having screens full of text there are several options. Text can be placed in scrollable windows allowing the user to find out as much information from the text as they choose to scroll through. Pop-up information also can be used—as the user passes over a section of the media, related information pops onto the screen to extend the information presented. Whether the document is on-line or not, links can be included in the product. This also allows the user to choose what areas they would like to find out more about and link to these areas. If they are already interested, they will read more text.

Along with designing multimedia for the 640 x 480 resolution and 8-bit color depth standards, there are also more good general rules for the design of multimedia, many of which focus on reducing the file sizes. If the product will be used on-line, the color depth can be reduced even more, to 5 or 6- bit color, to allow it to download more quickly. Since multimedia is designed to be viewed on a computer monitor, there is no reason to include a graphic that is at any higher resolution than the monitor's 72 dpi. It is a good idea to save all images that are used at 24-bit color in a separate file. This allows the designer to have a full-quality original to refer back to if they want to make color changes in their 8-bit palette or to make a quality print of the image. Finally, it is very important to know what types of files the authoring tool being used accepts. Many will not read EPS files and only accept PICT or BMP files. If a file can't be read or converted, it is useless to the developer.

Once created, multimedia can be used for a large variety of purposes. There are four main categories of types of multimedia. These are entertainment/recreation, education, reference, and business functions. Entertainment is probably the area that most people are familiar with. Video games are all multimedia and they become more and more popular as they become more complex and graphic intensive. They are perfectly suited to utilize the abilities of multimedia. Multimedia can incorporate the fast action, vivid colors, 3-D animation, and elaborate sound effects that are essential to entertainment. It can also provide the rewards, recognition, and sense of accomplishment that are often part of entertainment titles. Recreation multimedia encompasses everything considered a hobby. Travel and sports information would fall into this category.

Education products can often be combined with entertainment for the hybrid known as "edutainment" or be focused solely on the learning environment. Many of these products are children's learning games that are designed to promote reading or math in a game-like setting. For the older learner, these multimedia education tools can help by supporting a variety of learning styles all in one. Education products can help the visual learner see the concepts that are being discussed in class, give the struggling student practice quizzes, or let one dissect a computer-generated animal rather than actually having to do the dirty work. As with all multimedia education products, the nonlinear abilities of the programs are ideally suited for learning.

Multimedia reference materials are a compact and inexpensive way of storing information that, if produced in more conventional ways, would take up a lot of room and cost a great deal, such as encyclopedias and phone directories or archives of images and movie clips.

The business applications are almost endless. Multimedia can be used for presentations to employees or clients. Company publications can be converted easily to multimedia forms making the presentation of possibly boring information, like financial reports, expressible in a more interesting form. The technology also makes it possible to dive into the marketing side of multimedia applications. Sales pitches can be much more impressive with the use of multimedia. Catalogs of products are a popular growing area. They can be very broad in their scope, perhaps more so than traditional catalogues, with the ability of adding sound to sell CDs or customizing an outfit in an on-line catalogue.

Training and constantly seeking more effective training methods can be accomplished through multimedia programs. Businesses are dependent on trained personnel to perform highly specialized tasks. They can be as simple as a presentation of company rules, policies, and procedures or as complex as simulated work conditions and role-playing situations. The growth of multimedia has no end. From the looks of it, the sales of multimedia-capable computers has been growing exponentially over the last several years. At the end of 1992 less than 1 million households had a multimedia computer. In four years the number of households grew to more than 24 million. This growth hasn't slowed and the hardware and software involved in multimedia are becoming more affordable.

Where marketing is concerned, the demand for multimedia capabilities and products is steadily growing as the prices of the products drop. The investment in a multimedia-capable computer or the upgrades required for an existing computer are well worth the cost because of the increase in productivity potential from a personal computer.

Multimedia allows the user to be in control. Users can skip around at will through the product, choosing which areas interest them and what they want to do or learn with the product. With this ability the product can be "individualized" for many users of the same product, since everyone can move at their own pace through their chosen paths. It also allows the user to take an active role in the use of the product. As example of the active role in an educational product could be, you could be using a multimedia title to study a Shakespeare play. You begin by reading a passage from the play, then you choose to see the passage acted out by viewing a digitized video clip of an actual performance. Finally, you decide to test your knowledge of the passage by taking a quiz—and getting immediate feedback. Based on the feedback, you decide to review the material again or go on to a new passage—an active process.

Physical media

CD-ROMs can store 650 Mb and DVDs can handle 4 or 5 gigabytes. But raw storage is practically useless without extensive searchability. This advantage is most clearly illustrated with reference materials such as dictionaries, encyclopedias—you can search the entire encyclopedia in less then one minute. The combination of search and retrieval ability and other new media advantages of CD-ROMs has already challenged one traditional market—the book publishing segment, the $800 million market for reference books like dictionaries and encyclopedias, where sales of CD-ROMs now exceed those of printed versions. Digital media has forced publishers to reevaluate their print production and distribution methods. Choices:

1. Recorded disks
    CD- or DVD-ROM
    Other (Disks with 100 Mb becoming popular)
2. World Wide Web services
    Conversion of text to HTML and images to GIF or JPEG
    Design and assembly of site
    Maintenance of site on server
3. Image bank services
    Conversion of images to required formats, PDF archives
4. Database services
    Maintenance or conversion of data
    Assembly of databases for personalized printing

 5. Design services
 Layout and graphic design for certain customers

DVD: it's called a medium because it's not well done

CD-ROM was called "the new papyrus" and it ushered in the multi-media age. The next generation is now (almost) ready and it is called DVD—"Digital Versatile Disc"—a new digital optical disc storage technology. It is the newest generation of consumer and computer electronics products and may replace the VHS player and video tape, CD-ROM discs and players, plus CD-A, and CD-R devices. DVD consists of five different formats: DVD-Video, DVD-Audio, DVD-ROM, DVD-R, and DVD-RAM.

DVD technology

DVD throughput is 10.08 Mbps to 40.32 Mbps. DVD multi-layer technology provides a significant increase in total storage capacity. DVD uses a laser with a shorter wavelength than CD-ROM and its "pits" and "tracks," which are used to store data, are smaller. Thus more data can be stored in the same physical area. The DVD specifications allow data recording on two layers, as well as both sides of the disc.

DVD-5 = 4.7 Gb (1 Side, 1 Layer)
DVD-9 = 8.5 Gb (1 Side, 2 Layers)
DVD-10 = 9.4 Gb (2 Sides, 1 Layer)
DVD-18 = 17.0 Gb (2 Sides, 2 Layers)
DVD-R = 3.95 Gb per side
DVD-RAM = 2.6 Gb per side

DVD-Video is designed to provide high quality, interactive playback of digital video, audio and graphic content with video quality that meets broadcast standards (720x480 pixels/frame at 30 fps) and audio using 5.1 channel Dolby Surround Sound that exceeds Audio CD (CD-A) standards. Interactive DVD-Video provides a higher level of interactivity than the Laser Disc or Video-CD formats. DVD-Video supports normal, pan-scan, and letterbox formats on both standard and wide-screen televisions. Up to nine unique video angles can be included. Navigation commands consist of a single instruction, or a combination of two or three instructions. Thus, multiple versions of a video, with different shots, angles, scenes, etc. can be included.

DIVX. DIVX is a proprietary extension to the DVD-Video format that provides additional features, including enhanced copyright protection through the use of DES encryption technology with a pay-per-view business model. A DIVX player has extra hardware for DES decryption, and a modem to call a central station. DIVX Discs "sell" for $5 each. Consumers can watch a title for up to 48 hours, then "rent" additional viewing periods for $3 and then exercise an option to "purchase" the disc for unlimited viewing on a single DIVX system. DIVX players call a central station to post new rental transactions on a regular basis. DIVX has two major owners: Circuit City & Ziffren, Brittenham, Branca & Fischer.

DVD-ROM

Most of the DVD-ROM titles currently under development use MPEG-2 Video, Dolby AC-3 Audio, and 24-bit high resolution graphics. Today almost all DVD-ROM-enabled personal computer systems include an MPEG-2 playback board. Ten different OEMs are shipping DVD-ROM drives, systems, and upgrade kits. Movies are considered to be a major market—just think, no more rewinding.

Re-writable DVD-R

There are a number of available options for writable and rewritable DVD options: DVD-R, DVD-R/W, DVD-RAM, and DVD+RW. CD-R media are compatible with all existing DVD-Video and DVD-ROM drives with 3.95 Gbyte capacity per side. No cartridge is required. Write-once means safe data to many users (cannot be changed).

DVD-R/W

Comparable to CD-RW and DVD-R with a phase-change recording layer. CD-Read and Write media is compatible with existing DVD-Video and DVD-ROM drives. Capacity is 4.7 Gb per side and 1,000+ rewrites are possible.

DVD-RAM

DVD-Random Access Memory media is not compatible with existing DVD-Video, DVD-ROM or DVD-R drives. Capacity is 2.6 Gb per side. Cartridge is optional, but recommended with 100,000+ rewrites. Less than $500 for drives and less than $100 for media.

DVD+RW

Comparable to CD-RW. DVD+RW media is not compatible with existing DVD-Video, DVD-ROM or DVD-R drives. 100,000+ rewrites are said to be possible.

Inside the DVD

"DVD" refers to Digital Video Disk, now called Digital Versatile Disk, or in popular terms, DVD, even though some people at one time called it Digital Vapor Disc (because of its prolonged absence from reality). But the DVD disk is our next high-density storage medium generation. The goal of electronics consumers and makers of computer peripherals, is to have a standard disk that will support a group of products that function in home computers, and as peripheral devices of TV, and eventually replace the CD-ROM, Audio CD, video game systems, and other tape products.

DVD has been in the works for approximately five years. Everything began in January of 1993 when, in Cannes, France, an audio disk was demonstrated recorded with MPEG-1 audio at double-density. In December of 1994, Philips and Sony announced a proposal for a high-density disk called MMCD. It was to be single-sided and dual-layered, and they envisioned it as appealing more to the professional electronic publishing, computer side of the market. In January 1995, they announced their SD, a double-sided disc, based on the videodisk, and targeted at the home entertainment market. There were more than two years of battle between major disc makers and content providers, when finally the DVD Video players hit the market in the US in March 1997.

The disk is the same diameter as a CD-ROM, but now it is possible to record on both sides. Each side holds 4.7 Gb, equivalent to seven

CD-ROMs, or 14 CD-ROMs if both sides are used. A double-layered version is also planned to hold 8.5 Gb per side, or the equivalent of 28 CD-ROMs if both sides are used. A CD-ROM cannot be recorded on two sides. The most important characteristics of the DVD are its bonded substrates, visible-light laser, and multilayered sides. A quality that distinguishes DVD is its double-side capacity, a feature that is made possible by bonding multiple substrates.

DVD has two thin (0.6 mm) substrates in a disk with the same thickness (1.2 mm) of a regular CD. Bonding provides two advantages. First, it is possible to create a disk with two different sides. With each side as thick as half of a CD, it is possible to use smaller pits to represent the data. This results in a higher data density, represented in exactly the same manner as a CD, but the thinnest DVD substrates will permit the use of a shorter wavelength light source (laser) because the pits to be read are smaller. In fact, they are approximately half the size (0.4 microns for the DVD versus 0.83 microns for the CD). Also, shorter pits leave more track-to-track space (0.74 microns for the DVD against 1.6 microns for the CD). The net effect is that DVDs have a capacity four times greater, because it has more pits per square inch, compared with CDs.

Multilayered sides. A DVD's capacity is further increased when more than one layer is placed on each side (each layer is 0.6 mm of plastic substrates). The inner layer reflects light from the laser back to a detector through a focusing lens and beam-splitter. An optional outer layer can be partially reflective and partially transmissive—passing some light on to the inner layer and reflecting some light back. DVD player designs incorporate novel dual-focus lenses to support two-layer operation, yielding 8.5 Gb in a single-sided DVD, or 17 Gb in a double-sided disc.

DVD devices are available in two substantially different variations. DVD video players look like a video or laser disk player (truly, because of this, a DVD is often referred to as a Digital Video Disc), and are designed for home applications. DVD-ROM drives look like a CD-ROM drive and are designed for use in PCs.

DVD disks use MPEG-2 condensation and provide approximately 135 minutes of video per side. It is expected to become the VHS tape of the 21st century in its expected rewritable versions. The music industry hasn't yet embraced the DVD structure because the audio CD is a digital medium that has enough room for the traditional number of songs offered in an album. Many audio purists say that before we will see the end of the analog LP days the digital sampling of audio material has to be really excellent to recreate the total sound spectrum.

As an example of the recording order in the DVD disk (also called track structure), we can use the following, where "I" is the Lead-in area (leader space near edge of disc), "D" is the data area (contains actual data), "O" is the lead-out area (leader space near edge of disc), "X" is the un-usable area (edge or donut hole), "M" is the middle area (interlayer lead-in/out), and "B" is the dummy bonded layer (to make the disc 1.2 mm thick instead of 0.6mm):

For a single-layer disc, with a continuous spiral direction from inside to outside of disc:

```
| ------------------------->
| BBBBBBBBBBBBBBBBBBBBBBBBBBBBBBBBBB          outer edge
| XXIIIDDDDDDDDDDDDDDDDDDDDDDDDDOOOXX         of disc
|
```

For a dual layer disc, we have two options: (a) Parallel track path (for computer CD-ROM use), with the same direction for both layers:

```
------------------------->
XXIIIDDDDDDDDDDDDDDDDDDDDDDDDDDOOOXX          Layer 1
XXIIIDDDDDDDDDDDDDDDDDDDDDDDDDDOOOXX          Layer 0
------------------------->
```

or (b) Opposite track path (for movies), with the opposite directions. Since the reference beam and angular velocities are the same at the layer transition point, the delay comes from refocusing. This permits seamless transition for movie playback:

```
<-------------------------
XXOOOODDDDDDDDDDDDDDDDDDDDDDDDMMMXX  Layer 1
XXIIDDDDDDDDDDDDDDDDDDDDDDDDDDMMMXX  Layer 0
------------------------->
```

The DVD is a great family of products, and we have been talking about only two. The first DVD device was the DVD-Video player, which is a player for television whose principal purpose was to play in theaters. A DVD disk only seems like a CD-ROM disk, but holds 4.7 Gb of data, enough to fill seven normal CD-ROMs, that means above two hours of digital video. The DVD-Video could also keep up to eight language's worth of audio tracks, and thirty-two subtitle tracks. Just as the compact disk changed the face of the music business, DVD-Video is transforming the video industry. A DVD disk is very cheap to manufacture (approximately 80 cents per unit for a DVD disk, compared to $2.20 for a VHS tape).

Among the new devices, we have the DVD-R/W, a standard proposed for the DVD rewritable disk by Pioneer. It has 3.95 Gb for side and one could write it 1,000 times. The hybrid DVD, whose specification leaves disk for a segment of DVD-video, contains computer data. This space allows a DVD-hybrid disk to really act like both a DVD-video and a DVD-ROM. All of DVD-R, DVD-RAM and DVD-RW are versions of the recordable DVD-ROM: DVD-R (record once, 3.95 GB) uses technology similar to CD-R and is compatible with almost all DVDs. The technology will improve to support 4.7 Gb for 1999, which is crucial for desktop DVD-ROM and DVD-Video production. DVD-RAM (erase and rerecord many times, 2.58 Gb) uses technology that is incompatible with today's DVD drivers (because of its reflectivity and differences in format). Also, because of their fragility, DVD-RAM disks are presented in a protective cartridge (like the magneto-optical disks). To summarize:

DVD-1 (8 cm, single side, single layer):	1.4 Gb
DVD-2 (8 cm, single side, double layer):	2.6 Gb
DVD-3 (8 cm, double side, single layer):	2.9 Gb
DVD-4 (8 cm, double side, double layer):	5.3 Gb
DVD-5 (12cm, single side, single layer):	4.38 Gb (4.7 Gb) of data, 2 hrs+ of video
DVD-9 (12cm, single side, double layer):	7.95 Gb (8.5 Gb), approximately 4 hours
DVD-10 (12cm, double side, single layer):	8.75 Gb (9.4 Gb), approximately 4.5 hours
DVD-18 (12cm, double side, double layer):	15.90 Gb (17 Gb), above 8 hours
DVD-19 (8cm, single side, single layer):	1.36 Gb (1.4 Gb), about a half hour
DVD-20 (8cm, single side, double layer):	2.48 Gb (2.7 Gb), approximately 1.3 hours

DVD-3? (8cm, double side, single layer):	2.72 Gb (2.9 Gb), approximately 1.4 hours
DVD-4? (8cm, double side, double layer):	4.95 Gb (5.3 Gb), approximately 2.5 hours
DVD-R (12cm, single side, single layer):	3.68 Gb (3.95 Gb)
DVD-R (12cm, double side, single layer):	7.38 Gb (7.9 Gb)
DVD-R (8cm, single side, single layer):	1.15 Gb (1.23 Gb)
DVD-R (8cm, double side, single layer):	2.29 Gb (2.46 Gb)
DVD-RAM (12cm, single side, single layer):	2.40 Gb (2.58 Gb)
DVD-RAM (12cm, double side, single layer):	4.80 Gb (5.16 Gb)
DVD-R Write-once (single side):	3.9 Gb
DVD-R Write-once (double side):	7.8 Gb
DVD-RAM Rewritable (single side):	2.6 Gb
DVD-RAM Rewritable (double side):	5.2 Gb
DVD+RW Rewritable (single side):	3.0 Gb
DVD+RW Rewritable (double side):	6.0 Gb
DVD-R/W Rewritable (single side):	4.0 Gb

No one unique company possesses the DVD technology. The DVD standard was developed by a consortium of 10 companies: Hitachi, JVC, Matsushita, Mitsubishi, Philips, Pioneer, Sony, Thomson, Time Warner, and Toshiba. Working groups with representatives of many other companies also contributed to the standard. In May, 1997 the consortium was replaced by the DVD Forum, which is now open to every company.

Codes

The big problem with the propagation of DVD-Video (because the other kinds of DVDs do not have this problem) is the use of codes to control its use in different countries, and to guarantee an exclusive market. That is why it has a requirement that the DVD include codes that can be used in geographical regions. There are six defined international regions:

1. Canada, USA, and Territories;
2. Japan, Europe, South Africa (included Egypt);
3. The Southeast of Asia, Oriental Asia (included Hong Kong);
4. Australia, New Zealand, Pacific Islands, Central America, Mexico, South America, Caribbean;
5. Soviet Union, Africa (also North Korea, Mongolia); and,
6. China.

The future of DVDs

Some people say that 5.2% of homes (5 million) will have a DVD-Video player in 2002; 2% will have a DVD-Audio player, and approximately 80,000 DVD-ROM titles available by 2005. For comparison, there were approximately 700 million audio CDs and 160 million CD-ROMs in use worldwide in 1997. There are approximately 80 million VCRs in the US (89% of houses) and about 400 million worldwide. There are approximately 250 million television sets in the US and 1.2 billion worldwide. A brief side-by-side comparison of the CD-ROM with the DVD, is shown:

	DVD	CD
External diameter [mm]	120.0	120.0
Substrate thickness [mm]	0.6	1.2
Pitch of the track [mm]	0.74	1.6
Wavelength [nm]	650.0	780.0
Lens correction error [%]	13.0	25.0
Capacity [Gb]	4.7,8.5	0.65 (CD-ROM)
	9.4,17.0	0.80 (CD Music)

DVD issues

Not all DVD-ROM systems are created equal. In one set of tests, the typical DVD-ROM title failed to play correctly on more than 66% of the available DVD-ROM systems. Unlike CD-ROM which had one developer with all others following that specification, DVD has multiple developers and competing "standards." Supposedly, CD-ROMs can be read on DVD readers, but this is not for certain for all systems. The fact that there are so many iterations may delay industry acceptance and application. There is no doubt that DVD will have an impact in both the consumer and business worlds, but it does have to get its act together.

CD-ROM and DVD

One of the authors bought a new apparatus a few years ago to play a special CD. The new apparatus was one of the first DVDs made by Philips and the disk was a game of interactive golf. During the play, no one realized that we were going into new digital technology, and that several years later would be the "top" in optical storage media.

Digital environment

Managed information, including digital images, drawings, and video, are creating a strong demand for better storage systems. Real time access (like RAM), backup (like disk or tape), and secondary storage (like WORM in 12" and 5.25", MO, CD-ROM, or DVD), among others compete for the storage dollar. Each storage medium can be classified according to their capacity, speed, durability, and cost. Nowadays, the most popular is secondary storage because backup exists because critical enterprises must support information against disaster events. CD, on the other hand, is a random access option. CD can handle of large files. Secondary storage (CD, WORM, MO, DVD) are designed for applications that require infrequent access to static information. Optical technology dominates the secondary segment because of its durability, cost by megabyte, and random access characteristics.

The CD-ROM

The CD-ROM is a preferred medium because it provides access to large amounts of information in seconds. The compact disk was introduced in 1983 in the Netherlands and Japan as a distribution medium for digital audio. In the fifteen years since, it has been adjusted to a CD-ROM and adopted like a delivery medium for text and data, photographs, and digital video. The CD-ROM is the basis for one of the most successful successor electronic products of all time, the DVD.

What has made CD-ROM successful started with improvements made to solve the CD-Audio problems. With CD-Audio plants already in place for replication, the CD-ROM could be made at half of the cost. CD-Audio makers, ready with their production line established, could create a CD-ROM in volume at low cost. With a capacity of 650 Mb (or the equivalent of 450 floppy disks or 20,000 scanned pages) and cost of less that $6.00 for blank disk (or less that $0.01 by megabyte or less than $0.0003 for scanned page), they invaded the multimedia world with the lowest cost per megabyte.

Manufacturing a physical CD-ROM is similar to injection molding, with a few differences. Making it a CD-ROM depends on the kind of information that it contains: defining content, identifying formats, gathering data on disk, and creating and copying images. Physically, manufacturing of music CD and CD-ROM does not vary greatly. A conventional disc is made of a 1.2-mm thick transparent plastic substrate and one side has a recording layer. On top of the recording layer is a reflective layer and a protective layer (together the latter two layers are less than 5 microns thick).

Characteristics that make a CD-ROM unique are portability and life cycles of up to 250 years. The non-erasable nature of the CD guarantees a legal audit trail to prevent fraud for security-minded institutions, included banks and insurance companies.

Likewise, CD technology is extremely satisfactory because it is a medium which guarantees a constant, synchronized stream of data, audio, and video, when the information has to be delivered digitally. Among the applications of CD-ROM, we have:
- Digital publishing (CD-ROM catalogs, etc.)
- Software and database distribution
- Document and image archiving
- Computer data archiving and backup
- Personal use such as original audio CD, video CD and CD-ROM creation
- Multimedia presentations
- Photo CD

SGML and HTML

In 1979, Charles Goldfarb, working for IBM, submitted to the American National Standards Institute (ANSI) a definition of a text-based methodology for defining and deploying process-independent document marking that he called GML, or Generalized Markup Language. The definition has been formalized and adopted as an international standard known as Standard GML, better known as SGML. Goldfarb had joined IBM in 1967 after working in a law firm for several years, and was leading a project to create a document management system for the legal profession.

The problem that he faced was that to get legal briefs from an IBM mainframe onto paper, highly process-specific programming was needed. While not a monumental problem in itself, when you take into consideration that three or more programs were needed to perform the legal research, and each required different coding in the documents being searched, things became quite difficult. And that is why Goldfarb went about developing GML, from which SGML was born.

So what exactly is SGML? Very simply, it is a highly defined, non-proprietary language for writing your own markup schemes. Markup is the text that is added to the data of your files in order to convey particular information about that data. In a word processor, the markup is the proprietary codes that the software inserts into your text files to indicate which words should be printed in a certain font, which paragraphs should be centered, where page breaks occur, etc.

SGML relies on the principles of descriptive markup where the markup is used to indicate the nature, function, or content of the data in a file, rather than saying how that data should be processed. SGML can be used to define the significance of a document's content rather than its appearance. Using SGML, a heading would be identified as a heading rather than a piece of text that has to be printed or displayed in 20 point Times Bold.

The markup schemes that you create using SGML in turn declare a set of rules which unambiguously state how the data must be marked up in order to be correctly structured. SGML-aware software can ensure that any markup in a file conforms to the appropriate set of rules thereby guaranteeing that the data in the file will be structured in a known way. If the set of rules you are working with declares that text defined as a "sub-section" can only occur within text defined as a "section," SGML-aware software will ensure the rule is obeyed during text creation and editing.

It used to be that owest-common-denominator approach to text interchange for files of different programs and platforms was ASCII. However, ASCII in its earlier standard 7-bit form only allowed for 128 glyphs and controls. There was also no formatting of text in different layouts, fonts, and sizes. Standard character sets (like ASCII) were all the standards that one needed to exchange the content of electronic documents. Despite its interchange capabilities, ASCII has many limitations.

In the post-Macintosh era, in the world that began as computer-assisted publishing in 1980, we need new standards with support for layout, typefaces, graphics, sounds, movies, hyperlinks and everything in between. Numerous incompatible standards for electronic document exchange exist and all those standards emphasize common appearance of documents: recipient and sender must see almost the same thing. SGML, in contrast, concentrates on document structure and totally ignores visual appearance.

It is this concentration on structure that sets SGML apart from formats such as RTF, PostScript, and Adobe Acrobat. This makes it a very powerful and flexible contender in many fields from multimedia to traditional documents.

One of the biggest misconceptions about SGML is that it is a standard document structure. It isn't and the reason it isn't is that no one standard structure could be useful to all authors and publishers. The structure that may be perfect for books might not ever fit the needs of letters and timetables. So SGML is an enabling standard, and it is up to the Document Type Definition, or DTD, part of the specific SGML application, to define what the tags (or codes) are and their relationships with each other. SGML does not set the specific structure of the DTD; it is up to users, industry groups, and committees to define the DTDs to be used for document interchange.

An example of a DTD is MIL-M-28001B, a specification required by the Department of Defense for submission of some technical manuals. There has been an HTML DTD since HTML 2.0 but browsers do not enforce it. HTML is an application of SGML, not a subset of SGML.

The reason HTML is widely known is that it is the document format used by the World Wide Web on the Internet. The World Wide Web, also known as the web, was created by the European Council for Nuclear Research (CERN) so that they could use the Internet to share information with other scientists throughout the world. The DTD they created was HTML, a deliberately simple set of tags that carried basic information such as type style and hypertext links.

The reason they used so few and such simple tags was so that the programs needed to interact with the Web could be small and simple, and so that use of bandwidth was kept to a minimum. In its early days, the web was quite small, and text only—thus there was no real need for complex markup. The web exploded because the first graphic-based browser, Mosaic, was introduced by the National Center for Supercomputing Applications. With Mosaic, it was possible to create much more complex websites with different fonts of different sizes, graphics, and other forms of multimedia such as sound and animation, movies, and computer programs.

The largest document

The World Wide Web is the world's largest "document"—with thousands and thousands of text "pages," graphics, audio and video files interlinked throughout the world on connected servers. It was met with great enthusiasm by academics and scientists and quickly grew beyond the bounds of CERN. Computer enthusiasts of all kinds started developing World Wide Web applications and promoting the World Wide Web across the Internet. It did not take long before all types of hypermedia became available for Internet enthusiasts to explore.

The web is based on the Hypertext Transport Protocol (HTTP), a protocol designed for sharing documents via a client/server model. Hypertext Markup Language (HTML) is simply the language that all World Wide Web documents speak. It is a set of tags that tell the navigational software how to display text, hypertext links, images, and movie clips. HTML was purposely kept simple; there are only a few tags for text markup, allowing navigational software to be minimal and thus inexpensive to write.

The simple tagging schemes of HTML allow novice web users to create their own documents. These homemade documents or home pages can be hyperlinked to any other home pages residing on a web server via their Uniform Resource Locator (URL).

HTML offers great flexibility in its tagging schemes. Tags are guidelines for how a web browser should display the material. Some tags are required by all web browsers, while other tags are optional. All web browsers are different. Mosaic, the first, was graphical, while others were text based. HTML describes what a document element is, not how it is to be displayed, so not everyone has to have the same capabilities to access web information.

Once the HTML document arrives at its destination, the browser can use whatever tags are appropriate to it and ignore the rest.

Reasons for interest

The pen is no longer the only implement mightier than the sword, and freedom of the press no longer necessitates a press. The mighty pen and ink printing presses are being challenged by a quirky language called HTML and the manifestations of it that are, in essence, a paperless and inkless press known as the World Wide Web. The printed medium is a wonderful source for disseminating information and will assuredly exist forever.

However, more glamorous, cheaper, quicker, and environmentally sound methods of communicating the same information are hitting the mainstream. One does not have to be a printer. One might be an electronic publisher, an information gatherer, converter, transformer, and deliverer.

This outlook creates a wealth of new opportunities and challenges. Repackaging information in new ways creates opportunities and develops new markets, and new audiences. Print, interactive multimedia, and online publishing are unexplored areas of opportunity, and now relatively unsaturated. However, collectively, these media preview the future of information delivery. The opportunities are manifold, limited only by imagination, endeavor, and available bandwidth. Currently, the web allows all these information technologies to merge, thus creating a new paradigm for information delivery.

The effective integration of digital media elements such as graphics, audio, and video into a website can be just as important as informative and well-organized text. When done properly, the incorporation of multimedia into a site can substantially increase its utility as well as its aesthetic appeal. However, poorly implemented multimedia can just as easily diminish a site's usefulness.

When dealing with multimedia elements, a number of issues must be considered. In stark contrast to ink on paper, publishing on the web can be described as instantaneous communication, distributed worldwide to potentially millions (projected to be billions) of readers in a content-rich, colorful, highly interactive format, produced at a unit cost too cheap to meter. There is only one problem: you have to know how to find it.

Data structure

The learning curve associated with setting up and maintaining a website is additive. As a website administrator or webmaster becomes comfortable with the site's basic functionality, more advanced features can be added. Implementing these features requires greater levels of technical expertise. Implementing mixed-media elements in a web document increases the overall file size of that document. The more elements that are included, the greater the file size.

This is the single largest issue confronting online information providers to date. The technology allows for inclusion of video, sound, and large graphics, but most connections are ill-equipped to download the data within a reasonable time frame. Some web browsers tackle the large graphics issue head-on. Users can specify whether to display the graphics or not. If a user chooses not to show the graphics, a small icon appears indicating that a graphic exists. This significantly reduces retrieval time.

Audio and video files are relatively large, thus exacerbating the file size issue. Content providers who include audio and video files within a document must seriously consider the end viewer when deciding the size of such elements. It is a general rule that potential downloaders are warned of any files over 100 K. Another important consideration for graphics files is their display size (height and width in pixels). Although it is directly related to data size, it is important to keep the physical size within reasonable limits so it looks acceptable on most viewers, some of whom have smaller monitors. Similarly, it is important to use reasonable length video and audio clips (less than one minute). Various software packages offer techniques on how to address this problem.

Data formats

Web publishers create their multimedia elements across the gamut of computer platforms utilizing literally hundreds of software packages. The resulting effect is a myriad of possible file formats facing the web publisher. Also, not all navigational software and supplemental or utility programs are suited to handle the different file formats. Certain standards exist that attempt to tackle this issue, like PDF.

Text-only users

A few web users still use text-only navigational software. In fact, until 1993, text-only navigational software was all that existed. It is frustrating for a text-only World Wide Web user to try to access information, only to find out that the particular site is only formatted for a graphical-based browser. These users are often ignored, reducing the value of a website. Strategies exist on how to best orient a website for all types of navigational software.

Given the growth of hand-held devices that can be linked to e-mail and the web, it is possible that web sites may very well have to maintain a text only mode in order for these devices to receive and display the information properly.

Other web issues

Although the World Wide Web has great support for graphics and hypertext links, it is still developing security to enable financial transactions to take place safely. It has cried for a richer markup language to handle tables and style sheets, and XML is coming. And it has required greater efficiency in expediting transactions. Although the web is touted as the next great information delivery vehicle, there are still many small problems that must be solved.

E-commerce is growing rapidly on the web and prognosticators say this will be the great enabling approach that will spur the growth of the online world..

HTML programming

Once the information is compiled, it has to be expressed as HTML documents so the web browser can interpret it. The Hypertext Markup Language is designed to specify the logical organization of a document, with important hypertext extensions. It is not a wysiwyg-based word processor such as Microsoft Word or Corel WordPerfect. HTML allows you to mark titles or paragraph marks, and then leaves the interpretation of these marked elements up to the browser. One browser may indent the beginning of a paragraph, while another may leave a blank line instead.

HTML documents are made up of a hierarchy of elements. These can be divided into two broad categories—those that define structure of the body of the document and those that define information about the document, such as the title or relationships to other documents. Elements are denoted by the tag <element_name>.

This is simply the element name surrounded by left and right angle brackets. Most elements mark blocks of document content for a particular purpose or for formatting: the above <element_name> tag marks the beginning of such a section. HTML documents are structured into two parts, the head and the body. The head contains information about the document that is not generally displayed with the document, such as its title. The body contains the body of the text.

Style issues

HTML is an application of SGML (the Standard Generalized Markup Language), which is used to describe the general structure of various kinds of documents. It is not a page description language like Post-Script, nor is it a language that can be generated by a page layout program. The focus of HTML is the content of the document, not its appearance. With a few minor exceptions, HTML does not describe the appearance or layout of a document. Initially, the designer of a web page had no control over line length, typeface, point size, or color. These characteristics were specified by the end user according to their web browser, personal preference, or system limitations.

Designers usually come from disciplines where they control the final output, and the thought of someone else controlling the final look of a document is awkward. Today, the originator can "lock" in much of the formatting.

Working in a text-only markup language with little control over the appearance of a document was frustratingly archaic compared with today's technology. You can acquire a number of drag-and-drop browser programs or one of the many programs that convert print-ready documents to HTML web pages.

But for the kind of environment that the web provides, HTML does have advantages over other forms of document publishing languages. For example, each HTML document is small, so it can be transferred over the Internet as fast as possible. Typeface or format information is not within the document thus allowing for faster loading and displaying. Also, HTML documents are device-independent and can be displayed on any platform. This is absolutely necessary considering that all types of computer platforms access information on the Internet. All that is needed is a web browser that can interpret HTML for that platform.

Inline versus external images

The IMG element allows an image to be inserted within an HTML document. This is known as an inline image and its function is to allow graphics to be included within a document and presented with the text. The opposite is an external image which is accessed through hypertext links that retrieve and display images in a separate viewing window. Both methods allow a user to display an image, and when used appropriately, can enhance a web presentation considerably.

There are two methods for downloading images. Interlaced GIFs appear first with poor resolution and then improve in resolution until the entire image has arrived, in contrast to images arriving linearly from the top row to the bottom row. The interlaced approach is great to get a quick idea of what the entire image will look like while waiting for the rest. Some browsers do not support progressive display as the image is downloaded, but non-progressive-display web browsers will still display interlaced GIFs once they have arrived in their entirety.

External images

The only inline image file format that all browsers can view is GIF. Linking to external images gives more flexibility in what image file format can be used.

A common practice with web pages is to provide a very small GIF image (a "thumbnail") inline on the page itself, and then link that image to its larger counterpart. This has two major advantages over including the entire image inline: It keeps the size of the Web page small, so that page can be downloaded quickly, and lets readers get a feel for the image and decide whether they want to download the whole image. This flexibility is an advantage when providing information to a large audience with myriad system setups and requirements.

Sound

Sound data is a digital representation of an analog signal, which is typically represented as a continuous waveform. When sound is digitally recorded, samples of the wave form are captured at fixed intervals. The more samples taken, the more information stored for each sample, the higher quality of the sound. Sample rate measured in kilohertz (KHz) describes the quality of the sound. Common sample rates are 11 KHz, 22 KHz, and 44 KHz. Sample size, usually in 8 bits or 16 bits, is the amount of information stored for each sample. For example, audio CD has 44 KHz and 16-bit sample size, which is very high quality sound.

An 8 bit ".au" file is currently the most common choice for putting sound files on the web. This format is supported by most of the sound-capable machines on the Internet. Second, this format produces a fairly small file that requires little bandwidth to transfer. AU files are of barely acceptable quality, as the 8-bit sampling causes them to sound comparable to transmission over a telephone. There are other sound formats supported by web browsers. It is important to note that most sound formats are specific to a player program, and sometimes to a specific platform.

Video

The four variables which affect the size of a video file are the length of the clip, the size of the frame, the color depth (256 colors, thousands, millions, etc.), and the amount of compression applied. Manipulation of all these settings determines what combination produces acceptable quality files with the minimum size.

Like other files, movie files can be identified by their file extensions. There are only two movie file formats that can be viewed from the Internet, that are international standard file formats for multimedia. They are MPEG and QuickTime.

MPEG is a very popular movie file format for PCs and stands for Motion Picture Experts Group. The members of this group come from more than 70 companies and institutions worldwide including SONY, Philips, Matsushita and Apple. They meet under the ISO to develop digital video standards for compact discs, cable TV, direct satellite broadcast and high-definition television.

QuickTime is an ISO standard for digital media. It was originally created by Apple Computer and used in the Macintosh. It brings audio, animation, video, and interactive capabilities to personal computers and consumer devices. QuickTime movies are real movies. This standard is more mature than the MPEG standard. Way back in December, 1993, Apple announced that it had begun demonstrating technology that will make future television and multimedia devices more compelling, interactive, and useful for people. Specifically, Apple demonstrated the integration of MPEG technology into applications using QuickTime technology. QuickTime for Windows is available for customers who use Microsoft's PC-based Windows operating system. QuickTime movies have the file extension ".qt" or ".mov."

The chief hardware component of a website is the host computer, which houses the site's content. The software program that runs on the host is called a web server. It interprets incoming requests and returns the appropriate documents. Server programs are available for most major operating systems, including UNIX, VMS, VM, Macintosh System 7, Windows 95, and Windows NT.

The major considerations in choosing a host are platform stability, performance, and amount of RAM (random access memory). Platform stability is most important. If the operating system routinely crashes under normal loads, the web site often will be inaccessible. In general, UNIX computers have the most stable and robust operating systems, but their stability can be outweighed by their cost and technical requirements. Macintosh and Windows machines are acceptable for handling light loads (with peaks of several hundred hits per hour), but are not recommended for higher loads. NT-based systems are competing against UNIX-based systems.

Most of today's business hardware and nearly every available UNIX workstation can handle the processor and I/O (input/output) demands of all but the most heavily trafficked web servers. However, the host computer's physical RAM can cause a bottleneck as the usage load increases. A basic web server platform should have at least 128 Mb RAM, and high-load computers should include 256 Mb RAM. To serve heavy loads, the host computer should be a dedicated web machine—one that is used exclusively for the web site. Under light loads, a host can be used for tasks in addition to its web server duties.

HTTP

HTTP (Hypertext Transport Protocol) is the primary protocol used to distribute information within the World Wide Web. It is a relatively simple, highly flexible protocol used to deliver information across the Internet. HTTP defines a simple transaction, consisting of the following four parts, to deliver requested information from a server to a client:

- The client must first establish a connection to the server.

- The client then issues a request to the server specifying a particular document to be retrieved.
- The server sends a response containing a status code and the text of the document if it is available.
- Either the client or the server then disconnects.

One main goal of HTTP was to provide a simple algorithm that would enable fast response times. To achieve this goal, HTTP was defined as being a "stateless" protocol—one that does not retain any information about a connection from request to request.

HTTP is also a "connectionless" protocol—limited to one request per connection. Unlike other protocols, such as FTP, the connection between server and client is broken after each request is made. This means that every time a client wants to fetch a document, it establishes a new connection to the HTTP server.

This is one of the main reasons why it takes so long to load HTML pages with many inline graphics. For each graphic, a separate connection is established and information is requested. While establishing a connection is not generally time-consuming, it can seriously affect performance for distant or heavily loaded sites.

Older clients, like NCSA Mosaic, waited until a connection was closed before they opened their next connection. However, all newer clients, such as Netscape and Explorer, open multiple connections and receive documents in parallel. Unless bandwidth is the bottleneck in retrieving documents, this behavior results in significant time savings when accessing sites loaded with inline images.

Data size

The amount of data that has to be transported for image or video files is the most important concern for web publishing. This is especially important because of the large number of users on 56 Kbps or slower lines. For them, it can take minutes to receive even medium-sized images, sounds, or video files. Browsers are beginning to cater more to users on slow lines by providing extra functionality. Most browsers let the user delay or completely turn off image-loading functions. Several second-generation browsers request images simultaneously, or in parallel, which significantly speeds the retrieval process. However, while these features help, content providers must carefully watch the size of the images.

There are a number of techniques for reducing the data size of images. Although the most obvious way may seem to reduce the image's total physical size, this does not necessarily yield substantial data-size reductions. An important issue to keep in mind when generating images is that different data formats compress images differently. For a particular image, the JPEG format may be significantly smaller than the GIF format, or vice versa.

Although it may not seem apparent, reducing the number of colors in an image can produce substantial savings in data size. By halving the total number of colors, the file size can be reduced by 10% to 30%. Luckily, the change in the number of colors usually is barely detectable to users. Because most browsers already limit the number of colors seen by users (typically 25 to 50 colors), reducing the number of colors makes an image more in accord with the browser display and speeds up loading. To fit within the windows of most web browsers, images should not be wider than six inches. Most image-editing programs can perform these functions. One popular and useful way to reduce the size of the graphics on a page is to use thumbnail images as links to the main images. Thumbnails are small versions (approximately one inch square) of images. Besides being small (2 K to 5 K), they can save time by letting users decide whether or not to retrieve the full image.

Basic structure of an HTML document

HTML documents are divided into two sections: a head and a body. The head contains information about the document itself, such as the title, indexing information, and ownership. The body consists of the document itself, the images, text, and links to other documents and files displayed by the web browser.

Head Section
```
<HTML>
<HEAD>
<TITLE>Sample Web Page</TITLE>
</HEAD>
```

The head section is opened and closed by the <HEAD> and </HEAD> tags. Information belonging in the head section should be placed between these two tags. The tags in the example above form a minimal head section, and should be included at the beginning of every HTML document.

Body section
```
</HEAD>
<BODY>
<H1>Introduction</H1>
```

The body section is started or opened and ended or closed by the <BODY> and </BODY> tags. The text and images of the document itself, to be displayed by the Web browser, should be placed within these two tags. The start tag should be placed immediately after the head end tag (</HEAD>), and before any images or text included in the document itself. A matching </BODY> must be placed at the end of the document, after any images or text included in it.

Tags ending a document
```
</BODY>
</HTML>
```

</BODY> ends the content of the document itself, and should be placed after any text or images that will be displayed by the web browser. </HTML> ends the page itself. The head and body sections are enclosed within the starting <HTML> and ending </HTML> tags.

Creating a basic HTML document

Open your editor of choice and type in the following code. Do not worry about what <H1> means, you will learn what it is in the next section. Once you are done typing, save the document with the appropriate .html (.htm for DOS) extension; for example, sample.html.

```
<HTML>
<HEAD>
<TITLE>Exercise 1</TITLE>
</HEAD>
<BODY>
<H1>Introduction</H1>
</BODY>
</HTML>
```

Open up your web browser of choice and select the function which opens local files (File/Open File in Netscape). Then, open the HTML file you created. Remember, you must save the file first in your text editor, then open it. For each iteration, you can also use the reload function of the browser. The graphical representation displayed by the Web browser should look like the one shown below. If it doesn't, look over your code and fix any mistakes. Our result from the above:

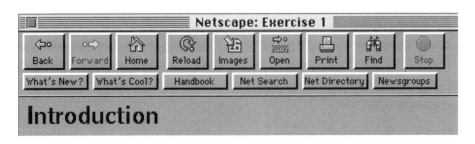

What are headings?

There are six levels of headings. The larger the number, the smaller the size of the resulting text (using a graphical browser). Examples of all six levels are provided below, followed by the tags that produce them. Headings are used to logically organize a page into separate sections for easier comprehension. Lower level headings in turn subdivide each section. Headings automatically create space between them and any text preceding or following them.

<H1></H1>   Level One Heading

This is the highest level heading. It is often used at the beginning of a document.

<H2> ... </H2>   Level Two Heading
<H3> ... </H3>   Level Three Heading
<H4> ... </H4>   Level Four Heading
<H5> ... </H5>   Level Five Heading
<H6> ... </H6>   Level Six Heading

```
<HTML>
<HEAD>
<TITLE>Headings</TITLE>
</HEAD>
<BODY>
<H1>Level 1 Heading</H1>
<H2>Level 2 Heading</H2>
<H3>Level 3 Heading</H3>
<H4>Level 4 Heading</H4>
<H5>Level 5 Heading</H5>
<H6>Level 6 Heading</H6>
</BODY>
</HTML>
```

The result of the above markup:

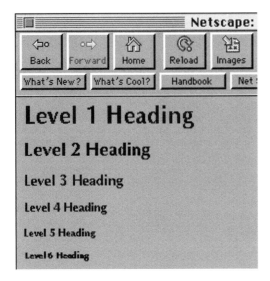

Controlling text spacing

HTML leaves the details of how to display a document (spacing, font selection and size, etc.) up to the program viewing the document. White space (such as tabs, spaces, and carriage returns or line feeds) is ignored. Therefore, specific tags marking paragraph and line breaks are used to define the structure of HTML documents.

Paragraph tags

The <P> tag starts a paragraph, and the </P> tag ends it. These tags typically create a space between any images or text preceding the enclosed text.

```
<P>
This is an example.
</P>
```

Line break tag

The line break tag causes any text following it to begin on the following line.

```
This is<BR>
an example.
```

Horizontal rule

The <HR> element is used to draw a horizontal dividing line completely across the browser window, no matter what width the window is set to by the user. This can be to logically separate blocks of text, or to separate an icon list from the body of the text. The HR element is said to be empty which means there is no copy to apply it to—you don't need a </HR> to close it.

Creating an HTML document

Create a simple HTML file using all the tags covered up to this point. You should have a comfortable feel for the basic structure and tagging schemes for creating HTML files. Save your document and view it with a web browser. If you have more than one browser on your platform or have access to other platforms, it is recommended that you view the document under each. Each browser displays HTML slightly differently and the differences may be surprising.

```
<HTML>
<HEAD>
<TITLE>Exercise 2</TITLE>
</HEAD>
<BODY>
<H1>A Primitives Portfolio</H1>
<H3>By Malcolm Jones Jr.</H3>
<HR>
<P>
The one sure thing about Bob Dylan is that there
is no sure thing. In a musical career stretching
over more than three decades, he has proven time
and again that he owns the most bottomless bag of
tricks in the business...
</P>
</BODY>
</HTML>
```

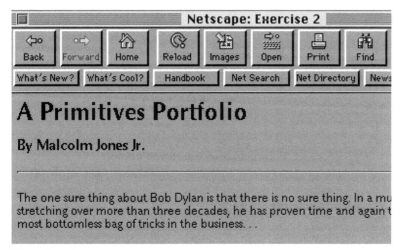

The output in Netscape

Character emphasis

HTML allows you to specify special character highlighting or emphasis (boldface, italics, etc.). These elements simply change the typographic rendering of the characters enclosed inside the tags. HTML allows you to specify these modes in two ways: logically (by the logical meaning of the special text you wish to mark) and physically (by explicitly specifying the style you want, such as italics, boldface, underline, etc.). Note that the logical styles may not be distinct (that is, different logical styles may be rendered in the same way).

Logical styles

The logical styles and examples of their renderings:

EM—Emphasis (usually italics).

```
<EM> this is example text </EM>
```

is rendered:

this is example text

STRONG—Stronger emphasis (usually bold).

```
<STRONG> this is example strong text </STRONG>
```

is rendered:

this is example strong text

CODE—Example of typed code (usually fixed-width font).

```
<CODE> this is example code </CODE>
```

is rendered:

```
this is example code
```

SAMP—A sequence of literal characters.

```
<SAMP> this is example text </SAMP>
```

is rendered:

```
this is example text
```

VAR—A variable name.

```
<VAR> this is example text </VAR>
```

is rendered:

this is example text

DFN—The defining instance of a term (often rendered bold)

```
<DFN> this is example text </DFN>
```

is rendered:

this is example text

CITE—A citation (typically rendered in italics).

```
<CITE> this is example text</CITE>
```

is rendered:

this is example text

Thus, <EM>, <STRONG>, <CODE>, <SAMP>, <VAR>, <DFN>, and <CITE> can be used to emphasize or change the typography of designated textual elements based on a description of their content.

Physical styles

The physical style elements, and their renderings, are:

TT—Fixed width typewriter font.

```
<TT> this is example text </TT>
```

is rendered:

```
this is example text
```

B—Boldface where available.

```
<B> this is example text </B>
```

is rendered:

this is example text

I—Italics

```
<I> this is example text </I>
```

is rendered:

this is example text

U—Underline (may be rendered as italic in some cases)

```
<U> this is example text </U>
```

is rendered:

this is example text

Other formatting markup tags

If a browser does not support these tags, the text will appear with no typographic changes. Browsers are programmed to ignore (and not display) tags they don't understand. Three of the most commonly supported examples are provided below.

Address
This element is used for address information, signatures, authorship, etc. The rendering of the contents is left up to the browser (indented, italic, right justified).

```
<ADDRESS> spms@rit.edu </ADDRESS>
```

is rendered:

spms@rit.edu

Preformatted text

The PRE element is used to enclose text to be displayed with a fixed width typewriter-like font. This is useful for presenting text that has been formatted for a fixed-width character display.

```
<PRE>
Chapter I      The Period
Chapter II     The Mail
Chapter III    The Night Shadows
Chapter IV     The Preparation
Chapter V      The Wine-shop
Chapter VI     The Shoemaker
</PRE>
```

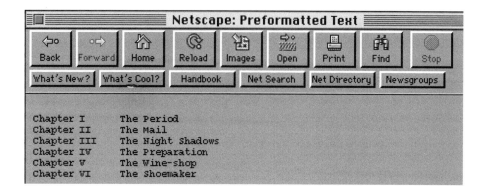

Block quote

The BlockQuote element allows quoted text to be rendered in an appropriate way. Typically this may be slightly indented, or italicized. BlockQuote also causes a paragraph break, and typically forces white space both before and after the quotation.

```
<HTML><HEAD>
<TITLE>BLOCKQUOTE</TITLE>
</HEAD> <BODY>
<H1>A Tale of Two Cities</H1><HR>
<I>by Charles Dickens</I><BR>
A story of the French Revolution<P>
<BLOCKQUOTE>

It was the best of times, it was the worst of times,
it was the age of wisdom, it was the age of fool-
ishness, it was the epoch of belief, it was the
epoch of incredulity, it was the season of Light,
it was the season of Darkness, it was the spring of
hope, it was the winter of despair, we had every-
thing before us, we had nothing before us, we were
all going direct to Heaven, we were all going
direct the other way--in short, the period was so
far like the present period, that some of its nois-
iest authorities insisted on its being received,
for good or for evil, in the superlative degree of
comparison only.
</BLOCKQUOTE>
```

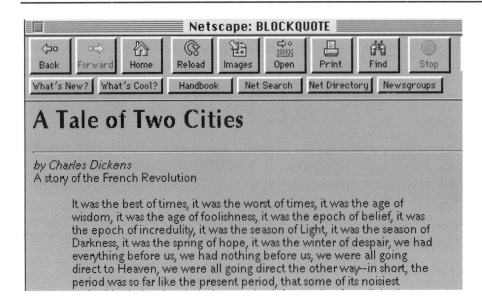

Lists

List tags cause standard items (such as bullets or numbers) to be inserted before the listed text. They can be nested within one another to create sub-lists (the effect of this on the appearance of a document differs with the browser that is used). The text of a list entry uses the same style and fonts as normal text.

Unordered list

Using an unordered list tag causes bullets (or the equivalent, if the viewer is using a text-mode browser) to be placed before the listed text. An unordered list is opened by <UL> and closed by </UL>. Listed items between them are preceded by <LI>.

```
<UL>
<LH>This is a list header!
<LI>Any
<LI>Text
<LI>Here
</UL>
```

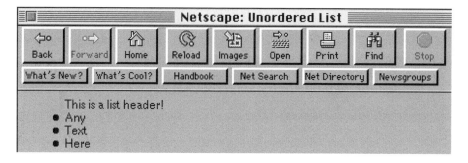

Numerically ordered list

Using a numerically ordered list tag causes numbers (starting from one) to be placed before the listed text. An ordered list is opened by <OL> and closed by </OL>.

```
<OL>
<LH>This is a list header!
<LI>One
<LI>Two
<LI>Three
</OL>
```

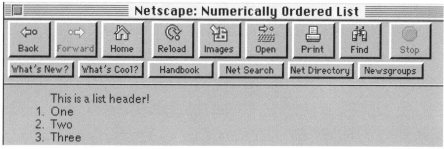

Directory list

This is used for short lists of items, such as file names.

```
<DIR>
<LI>alpha.html
<LI>beta.html
<LI>theta.html
<LI>zeta.html
</DIR>
```

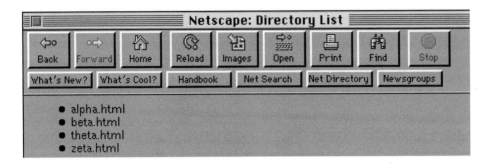

Definition list

Definition lists place nothing before entries preceded by <DT>, and indent entries following <DD>. A definition list is opened by <DL> and closed by </DL>. Listed items between them are preceded by <DT> (Definition Term) and then <DD> (Definition Definition). Use of <DT> without <DD> or vice versa is non-standard.

```
<DL>
<LH>This is a list header!
<DT>Term
<DD>Definition
<DT>Another Term
<DD>Another Definition
<DT>One More Term
<DD>One More Definition
</DL>
```

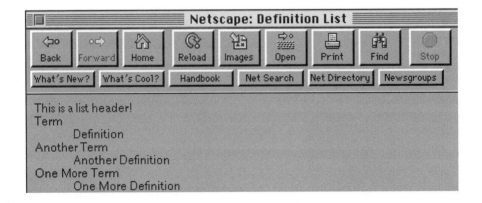

Hotlinks

A hotlink is a word, phrase or image which is highlighted by your browser indicating to the reader that more information on the highlighted item is available by clicking on that item. When you select or click on a hotlink, you are automatically transferred to the document (or image, etc.) which that hotlink points to (or if the selected resource is not something your browser knows inherently how to display, like a video for instance, an external viewer is launched which knows how to display the selected resource).

Hotlinks are created by placing a word, phrase, or image within a pair of anchors which associate the text with a URL (Uniform Resource Locator). A URL is an Internet address. Image hotlinks are called clickable images. A complex image can even contain multiple hotlinks (depending upon where on the image the user clicks), using image maps.

Hotlink concepts

A hotlink tells the browser what type of server is being used to present the file, the address of the machine the file is located on, and where it is on that machine. It also includes a label with which to select the hotlink. Links to other documents and files appear as highlighted text in a unique style when a page is viewed. When the person using the browser selects the link, the browser is automatically transferred to the file the link points to. The file can be located anywhere in the world.

This is the power of the World Wide Web: transparent linking of information resources to one another across the planet. The person viewing a document does not need to know how or where a resource is stored or what server is used to present it, they just select a hotlink and the file is automatically transferred to their machine.

Three things can happen at this point:
1. The browser itself displays the file (if it is a text file, another HTML document, or a type of content the browser is capable of displaying).

2. If the browser is configured properly, and recognizes the type of file that is being sent to it, a program capable of viewing the file is launched and the incoming file is automatically loaded into it (for example, a QuickTime video or audio clip).
3. If the browser does not recognize what type of file is being sent to it, or it has not been told what type of program to use to view the incoming file, the user is told this, and asked whether or not they want to download the file.

Hotlinks in practice

When creating links in HTML documents the link tag <A . . ./A> is used. The most common kind of linking among HTML documents is linking to other documents on the Web. Unlike most other tags the <A> tag includes some extra information about the link itself, called attributes. To link to other documents on the Web, the HREF attribute of the link tag is used. HREF is short for hypertext reference and is used to specify the URL of the file the link points to.

Absolute vs. relative URLs

A relative URL assumes the same access-method, server-name, and directory-path as the document the URL appears in. It indicates the position of the target URL relative to the current URL. For example, here's a URL to a file in the same directory as the document the URL appears in. Below is what a typical <A> tag looks like.

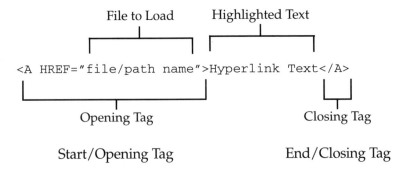

Relative URLs are also sometimes called partial URLs. They are used to point to information resources in the same directory or on the same server. Absolute URLs, on the other hand, are usually used to point to information resources on other servers. In practical terms, this means that you can use relative URLs to direct navigation between documents that you author and use absolute URLs to direct navigation to resources elsewhere on the Internet. A typical link with an absolute path looks like the one below:

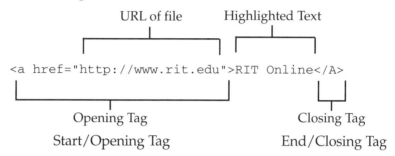

Creating links

This section demonstrates how to include both an absolute and relative link within an HTML document. Remember that both files need to be in the same directory (folder) for the relative path to work properly. For the absolute path, link to any web site you wish.

```
<HTML><HEAD>
<TITLE>Linking</TITLE>
</HEAD>
<BODY>
<H1>Linking</H1>
<HR>
<H3>Relative and Absolute paths</H3>
This Relative path connects me to <A
HREF="Exercise 2.html">Exercise 2</A>
<P>
<P>
This Absolute path connects me to <A
HREF="http://www.rit.edu">RIT Online</A>
</BODY>
</HTML>
```

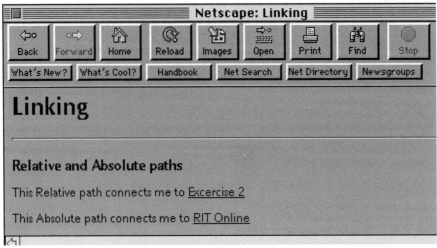

The distinction between absolute and relative URLs is totally hidden from the web server. When a user selects a relative hyperlink, the web browser uses the current URL to determine the access method, server name, and directory path, and sends only absolute URLs to the server. Relative URLs also give you the flexibility to move an HTML directory structure anywhere on the Web. And if you move your documents to another server, all the linking remains intact.

Graphics

Fundamentally, there are two different ways to present graphics—inline images and external images. Inline images are displayed by the web browser as part of your document and are automatically retrieved along with the document. External images are displayed by a separate viewer program (started by the Web browser when needed) and must be specifically requested by triggering a hyperlink.

Inline graphics involve the transfer of a lot of data and so retrieving them can be slow. Many web browsers let users optionally delay downloading of the inline images. With delayed downloading, inline images must be triggered by a hyperlink before they will be downloaded. When triggered, they still appear inline, not in an external viewer.

When contemplating the use of graphics within your HTML documents, you should consider the user community that will be accessing your web server. Will they be using graphics-capable web browsers, such as Netscape, or will they be using line-oriented web browsers? The decision is easier if one class of web browser dominates, but is more complicated if you expect people with both types of browsers to be using your web server.

Inline images

The inline image is just one more piece of information that is included in the autoflow and autowrap (text wraps around from line to line) of your HTML on the Web browser screen. In other words, an image is treated just like a word. So an image can appear in the middle of a paragraph. If you want the inline image to stand alone, you need to make sure you place <P> or
 HTML tags around it in your HTML document.

GIF

Although many different graphics file formats exist, most browsers will only recognize a few. In practice the only format common to all browsers is GIF (Graphic Interchange Format), devised by CompuServe. While this is the most commonly used format on the web, other graphics file formats have their strengths and some are likely to increase in popularity. Browsers that can display images in other formats, primarily JPEG (Joint Photographers Expert Group) are now common. GIF was developed to be a device-independent method of storing pictures.

GIF allows screen-quality, screen resolution graphics to be displayed on a variety of hardware and is intended as an exchange and display mechanism for graphic images. GIF is reasonably well matched to inexpensive computer displays, since it can only store 8 bits/pixel (256 or fewer colors) and most PCs cannot display more than 256 distinct colors at once. GIF does well on images with only a few distinct colors, such as line drawings and simple cartoons. A GIF picture file has an extension .gif.

JPEG

The JPEG standard is an excellent standard for most realistic images (photos for example, but not line drawings or logos). It uses a powerful, though nominally "lossy," compression method. JPEG is best suited for truecolor original images. JPEG stores full color information: 24 bits/pixel (16 million colors). Therefore, with full-color hardware, JPEG images look much better than GIFs on such hardware. JPEG files are much smaller than GIFs, therefore, they are superior to GIF in terms of disk space saving and transmission time. A JPEG picture file has an extension .jpg. Using JPEG for a photographic image for example can produce 10:1 savings compared to GIF, as well as permitting much better display quality on truecolor-capable displays. Netscape handles inline JPEG.

Placing inline images in documents

Inline images are specified in HTML using the <IMG> tag. Like the <P> and <BR> tags, the <IMG> tag has no closing tag. It does however, have flexibility in that it can include up to three attributes; SRC, ALIGN and ALT. The SRC attribute indicates the filename of the image to be included within the document. It is followed by an equal sign, with the filename in quotes. Name the file exactly. Also, the image file should be in the same directory as the HTML file. The <IMG> tag looks like this: <IMG SRC="filename.GIF">

```
<HTML><HEAD>
<TITLE>Images</TITLE>
</HEAD>
<BODY>
<IMG SRC="WBradley.GIF">
</BODY>
</HTML>
```

When inline images are autoflowing as part of a paragraph, you can explicitly control the alignment of the image with the text line by using the optional ALIGN attribute of the <IMG> tag. The three values for ALIGN are:

```
<IMG ALIGN=TOP SRC="filename.GIF">
<IMG ALIGN=MIDDLE SRC="filename.GIF">
<IMG ALIGN=BOTTOM SRC="filename.GIF">
```

TOP alignment places the top of the image even with the top of the current line of text, and so on. If ALIGN is omitted, bottom alignment is the default.

```
<HTML><HEAD>
<TITLE>Image/Text Alignment</TITLE>
</HEAD>
<BODY>
<IMG SRC="Horse.GIF" ALIGN=TOP>Text at top of an image
<HR>
<IMG SRC="hglass.GIF" ALIGN=MIDDLE>Text in the middle
of an image
<HR>
<IMG SRC="doggy.GIF" ALIGN=BOTTOM>Text at bottom of an
image
</BODY>
</HTML>
```

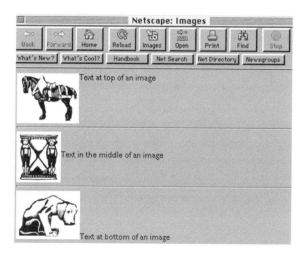

Image alternatives

Inline images can't be displayed on character-based terminals, as you would expect. Character-based Web browsers indicate that an image is in the autoflow stream by displaying:

```
[IMAGE]
```

However, you can override this default and make your inline images more meaningful in character-based Web browsers by using the ALT attribute:

```
<IMG SRC="filename.GIF" ALT="image description">
```

The HTML ALT option makes character-based Web browsers display the image description instead of [IMAGE]. You can also make the character-based browser ignore an image using a null ALT option:

```
<IMG SRC="filename.GIF" ALT="">
```

When a character-based Web browser sees the null ALT option, it ignores the image-insertion tag. The HTML authoring convention is that if you are going to insert inline images in your document, you should at least describe the image with a word or phrase for users with character-based Web browsers.

```
<HTML><HEAD>
<TITLE>Image Alternative</TITLE>
</HEAD>
<BODY>
<IMG SRC="prev.GIF" ALT="[Previous Page]">
<IMG SRC="next.GIF" ALT="[Next Page]>
<IMG SRC="help.GIF" ALT="[Help]>
<IMG SRC="quit.GIF" ALT="[Quit]>
</BODY></HTML>
```

The output in Netscape

Performance

It takes a lot longer for a web browser to retrieve an HTML document that has inline images than to retrieve one that does not. The larger the inline image, the longer it takes. In fact, the time is proportional to the square of the dimension (a four-inch-square image takes almost twice as long as a three-inch-square one). Many graphically-based web browsers cache inline images. So if the inline image has been used in previous HTML documents in the user's navigation chain, that image might still be cached. Caching also happens when the same inline image appears multiple times in the same HTML document. It is retrieved only once. External images are images that are not displayed inline as part of your document, but in a separate window, by an external viewer program. This is the technique to use if you have TIFF, JPEG, RGB, or HDF images and don't want to convert them to GIF. This technique is also useful for displaying very large GIF images. Instead of using the <IMG> HTML tag described earlier, include the URL of your external image file as part of the hyperlink. To display a JPEG image in an external window, you can include the following:

```
<A HREF="filename.GIF">hyperlink text</A>
```

The user needs an external viewer installed that knows how to deal with the incoming external image file. Also the web browser needs to know how to recognize the type of data that's arriving and how to start the appropriate viewer.

Images as links

If you include an <IMG> tag inside of a link tag (<A>), the image specified becomes a clickable link. One trick that's used to solve the performance problem of big images is to use thumbnails. A thumbnail is a small version of a figure displayed inline, which is a link to the full-sized image displayed externally.

```
<HTML><HEAD>
<TITLE>Images as Links</TITLE>
</HEAD>
<BODY>
<AHREF="hi_res.GIF"><IMG  SRC  ="thumb.GIF"></A>
Click on image to see high-res representation!
</BODY>
</HTML>
```

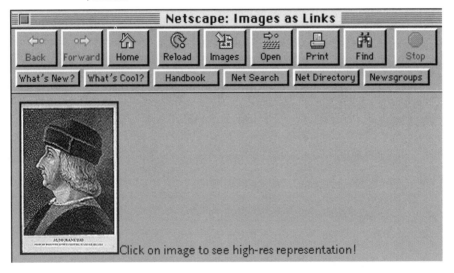

External objects (video & sound)

To specify an external object in HTML, you create a link to it just as you would another HTML document. In other words, you use an <A> tag with the HREF attribute.

<A HREF="external_file.ext">media file</A>

The file format, indicated by the file extension, of the external object is critical when linking to one within an HTML document. The file format tells the web browser what type of file to expect and the browser automatically launches a program that can present the object file.Wrong file extension, wrong player launched.

Formats

Like other files, video files can be identified by their file extensions. There are only two movie file formats that can be viewed from the Internet and they are international standard file formats for multimedia. They are MPEG and QuickTime. MPEG movie formats have the extension .MPG. QuickTime movies have file extension .QT and .MOV. These files can be played on both Macintosh and PCs.

	Format	*Extension*
Audio	AU	.AU
Video	MPEG	.MPG
	QuickTime	.QT or .MOV

Size and format indicators

It is considered good etiquette to label all large files (larger than about 500K). This applies to graphics, audio, video, and other large file formats. Because some clients can only accept certain data formats, it also is helpful to provide descriptors or icons that identify a file as image, audio, or video and to indicate its data format and size. This is especially true of very large files. It is extremely frustrating for users to download a 5 Mb video file only to discover that it is in a format not supported by their browsers.

```
<HTML><HEAD>
<TITLE>Exercise 4</TITLE>
</HEAD> <BODY>
<H1>Exercise 4</H1>
<HR>
<A HREF="sound.AU"><IMG SRC = "sound.GIF"
ALIGN=MIDDLE ALT=" ">Sample Sound </A>[64k]
<I><B>AU Format</B></i> <HR>
```

```
<A HREF="movie.mov"><IMG SRC="movie.GIF"
ALIGN=MIDDLE ALT=" ">Sample Movie</A> [4.3MB]
<I><B>QuickTime Format</B></i>
</BODY>
</HTML>
```

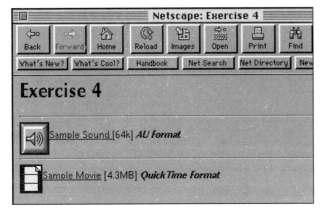

In conclusion

Multimedia is the synthesis of digital content and form for information presentation, exploration, and dissemination as applied to education, business, and entertainment. Many words are currently being used to label multimedia: cybermedia, intermedia, new media, hyper media, interactive media design, interactive multimedia, electronic media, computer graphic design, unimedia, multimedia, and digital media. They all essentially arrive at the same place: the distribution of products in electronic form, delivered on a medium (disk) or over a telephone line or network.

Technology is forcing many disciplines into new forms, shapes and relationships. A prime example is the present convergence of the entertainment, communications, and computer industries. There may never have been a time when change was more rapid and dramatic. Government, industry, and education are active commuters on the "information superhighway" (remember?). Multimedia is the computer integration of different forms of communication media for the presentation and dissemination of information and knowledge, for education, entertainment, simulation, and promotion.

Presentation. Multimedia can be used to present information in new and more interesting ways. It integrates full color, graphics, video clips, animation, type and sound. It provides new tools for conveying ideas and making points.

Simulation. Multimedia can be used to simulate control panels, gauges, and visual displays so that users can be trained in certain operational procedures before approaching an actual system.

Promotion. Multimedia can bring products "alive" and allow potential buyers to learn more about them through sound and video. More importantly, the potential buyer can interact with the program to get the information they want.

Education. Multimedia can be designed to be interactive and thus work with the student in the process of discovery. The program can help them navigate through the information in some orderly fashion while appealing to both eye and ear.

Entertainment. Multimedia is "MTV publishing" and for some in that it can be flashy, superficial, and confusing. But, it can also be games and some games can actually be educational.

The confluence of communication systems

Some societal and technological trends are evident:
- merging telephone, television, and computer-based technologies
- the advent of hundreds of channels of cable television
- the growth of distance learning
- the application of computers in teaching and learning
- the development of electronic publishing items, like catalogs, directories, and reference materials
- the dissemination of information in print and non-print forms
- the development of data highways, which will link academic, commercial and governmental users

Each of these areas increases the access of human beings to increasingly larger amounts of information and knowledge. To utilize this information and knowledge effectively, it will have to be organized and presented in new forms which take advantage of the increased capabilities of new information dissemination technology. These capabilities will have to be applied by a new breed of information developer, who will apply conceptual, aesthetic, technical and integration competencies to organize and design information for presentation.

The new information developer

This new information developer will shape content in exciting and innovative ways. They are the professionals who convert information into form. With a background rooted in typography, aesthetics, design, imaging, and presentation skills, and using the computer as an integration tool to assemble pages and screens, they will apply new approaches to information packaging and delivery.

Thus, there will be two levels of application:
1. Multimedia producers: they will convert content from others into new forms. They will work in-house or as commercial services.
2. Content developers: they will be publishers or teachers or others with content and they will either master the tools to put their content into form or they will utilize the services of developers.

There will be a need for a large pool of people trained in this technological approach. They will have to acquire these skills somewhere.

21 rules for interactive media

1. Capitalize on the users' frame of reference. Use icons and symbols that they understand. What can you do with an arrow that is new and creative? How do you indicate "Next Page" without saying it? Icon: A few thousand pixels doing the work of one or two words.

2. Be consistent with the outside world. Think of how normal people would normally act. Can you go beyond up, down, back, forward? Space travel? Time travel? Get me to the next page on time.

3. Have fewer, richer screens. Don't waste my time with a line of type, a glimpse of art, and thou beside me in the wilderness yakking.

4. Provide a common look and feel. Not the uniformity of the military, but a family resemblance to the milkman.

5. Provide navigational assistance. Provide a traceable path to and from wherever. You are here! Where's that?

6. Be consistent, consistently.

7. Efficacy: How will the user react? . . . interact? Overact? What is clickable? What is not.

8. Pretend that the program is a game. Make it fun, mysterious, intriguing. But not if you want to sell boots.

9. Aim for conceptual integrity. In other words, give the user some element of commonality on each screen so as to tie the screens together.

10. Give the user control of a complex program in a simple manner. Put the user in the driver's seat.

11. Reduce the users' need for rote memory, training, and documentation. We hold these icons to be self evident.

12. The purpose and use of a control should be obvious from its form. No user should have to try to figure out what it means or how it works. Thoughtless interactivity?

13. Good programs offer clues to location and navigation. Leave electronic crumbs for the user to follow. Don't be too cute. Don't be too sophisticated.

14. Bad programs confuse the user. Bad users confuse the program.

15. Good programs get the user involved. Keep your sense of humor . . . somewhere between Robert Benchley and the Three Stooges.

16. Make the program and its operation predictable. If A = B don't let it = C later on.

17. Provide rich and subtle feedback. When the user performs an action, let them know you care enough to send the very best. Users love a response to an action—it is an acknowledgement, a reward even.

18. Imagine a perfect solution and temper it with reality. Create the realistic solution and temper it with imagination. Have one foot in the real world and one foot in cyberspace.

19. Create escape routes so that users can back up or quit or just give up easily. This way out.

20. There is a thin line between real creativity and the need for psychiatric help. The real pioneers in multimedia design will not be recognized until they are dead.

21. Readability isn't everything; it's the only thing. Text is not art, maybe.

Chapter 11

CHALLENGES

On-demand printing

The idea behind on-demand printing is primarily one of short notice and quick turnaround. In the printing industry, print-on-demand can be defined as "short notice, quick turnaround of short, economical print runs," which all results in lower inventory costs, lower risk of obsolescence, lower production costs, lower scap rates, and reduced distribution costs. Most traditional printing does not satisfy this criteria and does not result in these advantages. The disadvantage of traditional long-run printing is that the reproduced information becomes obsolete, which requires the disposal and re-manufacture of new material. In the United States, approximately 31% of all traditional printing is thrown away because it is outdated. This number includes 11% of all publications, 41% of all promotional literature, and 35% of all other material. Although print-on-demand is a more sophisticated phrase for the printing industry, there is no specific technology that is used to perform such a job. On-demand printing (also known as demand printing) could be done with a traditional press because the customer does not care so long as the quality is acceptable, and it is done quickly and economically.

Defining digital printing

Digital printing is any printing on paper using spots, dots and pixels, from digital files. This usually involves toner-based printers (inkjet too). *On-demand printing* can be any approach, ink or toner, printer or press, where the printing is done in short runs as needed—delivered when you want it and where you want it. Almost all digital printing is on-demand, but very little ink-on-paper, press-based printing is so. Digital printing can produce fully variable printing and books printed one at a time. Presses may handle short runs, but every piece is the same. Printers can make each one different. The terms are used synonymously but you can see that they are not exactly the same.

Defining variable printing

Variable information can be printed by digital presses, which are presses that print directly from digital data rather than using plates. On different pages you could have, for instance, different names and addresses. This cannot be accomplished by traditional printing. With traditional printing, the prepress work is performed, the plates are made, and the job is run on the press. The end result is hundreds or thousands of pages that are identical. The information is static and, therefore, not variable. The capacity to print varying information on each copy of a page is the key factor in customized printing.

To accomplish customized printing up until recently, conventional pages or static pages had to be run through high-speed inkjet devices in a second process to add the variable information. But many digital presses offer this ability. Unlike inkjet devices, digital presses are not limited to six or twelve lines of copy; some can customize the entire page. The basics of customized printing is the combination of variable information with output devices that do not require intermediate films or plates. They are true dynamic printing systems in that all or part of the image area can be changed from impression to impression.

Typical lengths

Short run can be defined as one that is less than 5,000 impressions. Almost 56% of commercial, book, and office printing, including duplicating and copying, falls in the category of run lengths from 500 to 5,000 impressions. Presently, only 2.8% of this printing is done in four or more colors. By the year 2000, the amount of four-color printing in this run-length market will increase to approximately 11.5%. Traditional printing presses usually operate in the long-run category; however, this trend seems to be changing. In order to stay competitive, printers are attempting to compete with moderate or even short-run categories. While most traditional presses will have difficulty meeting the requirements of the short-run category, this is where a new market is developing. It is projected that the short-run wars will take place in the 100- to 3,000-copy range.

On-demand printing and publishing

Whether press or printer, on-demand jobs start out the same way. The on-demand process consists of the client supplying electronic files or camera-ready materials and specifying how many copies of the product will be needed. The printer produces the publication directly from the disk or camera-ready artwork and delivers it within a specified timeframe. Currently there are three specific on-demand strategies in our industry: on-demand printing, distributed demand printing, and on-demand publishing. "On-demand" means that the data is stored and printed in electronic form. It does not necessarily have to be an electronic file, but usually it is a digital file which makes the effectiveness of the short run possible. The second strategy, distributed demand printing, requires that the electronic files be transmitted to other locations, printed, and distributed locally. These publications can then be stored, printed, and shipped locally as needed. The third and final strategy is on-demand publishing (or simply demand publishing) in which the data is stored in paginated form and transmitted for immediate printout.

Future on-demand

An advanced definition of digital printing is any printing that uses a rasterization process to produce image carriers or to replicate directly to substrate from digital document files. The definition of on-demand printing now includes binding or finishing. In the end, on-demand printing requires both an imaging engine and a means of combining in consecutive, uninterrupted operations the printed pages into finished products—college textbooks, out-of-print books, insurance policies, research reports, business proposals, or any other reproduced products.

What is a portable document?

The underlying concept of document portability is that of printing to a file and distributing that file. As an analogy, take a sheet of paper with text and graphics on it and fax it. The sending fax converts the page images to dots and the receiving fax prints them out. If you have fax capability from your computer, a program takes the page image, converts it to dots and sends it to the printer. Now, save the last file we created—a representation of the page as dots—and instead of printing it to paper, put it on the screen. This document can be sent, viewed, and digested on screen by a large audience without any hint or mention of paper.

But there is something missing. Like any fax image, there is no underlying intelligence for the text. You could not search through it because it does not know an "a" from a hole in the paper. Searchability is something you want. You could use the application file, but then the receiver must have the same fonts you had, and the images must be provided and the applications must be at the same revision level.

Some portable document approaches saved a bitmap of the page as it appeared on the screen, the underlying ASCII text, and the font data. By having the text in ASCII format you can search for words and phrases. This is a major advantage over print. After all, the material in a book or catalog is not really information until you find what you want.

One aspect of portable documents is analogous to some of the "portable" TVs of the 1950s when you had a unit that weighed hundreds of pounds with a handle on the top. Even with compression, some portable documents are six to ten times larger than the original application file. True, the final file size is larger than the original application file counterpart, but the advantage is quite significant.

By creating an electronic document that carries all the needed components—fonts, graphics, and even a program to view and print the document—portable document software could eliminate the cost and time of printing, distributing, and storing paper copies, while adding the ability to find text and link multiple documents so information would be more accessible and more dynamic. Whether for use within a company for document exchange and distribution, or for use on bulletin-board systems, CD-ROMs, or fax-back services for user-requested documents, the possibilities for portable-document software are beguiling.

The portable document enters the market

In 1990, developers introduced portable document software. First came No Hands Software's Common Ground. Adobe later shipped Acrobat, and Farallon Computing followed with Replica. Other companies also had portable document formats. Adobe Systems dove into the competition in 1993 defining their Portable Document Format as a file format used to represent a document independent of the application software, fonts, hardware, and operating system used to create it. The software used to create this PDF was called Acrobat (actually, its original name was "Carousel").

Adobe's PDF was a third version of a PostScript file format. It took the PostScript file of the document and RIPped it (called distilling) to a new format that saved every page as an individual item, compressed the type and images, and cut out almost all the variability of the programming language. What remained was a portable document file that could be viewed on almost any platform, Mac or PC, running DOS, Windows, MacOS or UNIX. But the first version of Adobe Acrobat did not fully support high-end printing for color separations.

The PostScript code needed for production printing was not included. This did not hinder the use of PDFs to view the document on monitors or to print to monochrome and color printers, but it was not able to output a composite CMYK file as four monochrome PostScript streams to be sent to an imagesetter or a platesetter.

The ultimate portability

The printing and publishing industry saw more potential in the PDF than just looking at pages on a screen. Like the success of PostScript itself, the success of the PDF was based on capturing the high end of the printing world. Competitors to Acrobat saw only viewing as the problem to be solved. They forgot that paper was and always will be the only form of communicating to everyone in the world regardless of their lifestyle or location. Paper is the most democratic form of communication, since it does not restrict access because of technology or societal status.

Towards the ideal digital document

Adobe acknowledged the need to meet the demands of the high-end printing market. As a result of their working relationships with organizations such as the PDF Group and DDAP, Acrobat is emerging as the software capable of creating the near-ideal digital document.

The printing and publishing market expressed their needs, and Adobe listened. Acrobat 3.0 was released in November 1996 with added functions necessary for the high-end market. Acrobat 3.0 incorporates extended graphics state functions so that color separation can occur more effectively and OPI image comments can now be preserved. The PDF pages can be exported as an EPS for insertion in a page makeup program like QuarkXPress or PageMaker—only this time the font data is saved. In late 1997, Acrobat 3.01 was released and it fixed a few glitches and added a few new features. 4.0 is coming and it advances the franchise substantially.

Imagine an ideal digital document. How many headaches would be avoided, we thought, if there was a portable, page-independent, platform-independent file format which could not only preserve design richness, but also allow for "repurposability," searchability, predictability, and even some editability? This ideal digital document describes the Portable Document Format. PDF may not only be the aspirin for your headaches, but may also very well be the refinement of the PostScript revolution. PDF documents:
- preserve design richness
- create predictability
- maintain some editability
- create searchability
- allow repurposability (conversion from one medium to another medium—from front to web, for instance.
- allow high-end printing

Design richness

Preserving design richness entails maintaining the look and feel from creation to final output by properly reproducing all content information within the document such as bitmaps, vectored line art, and text.

Portability

Document portability is our concern. Computer users have suffered from a lack of formatted text, loss of graphics and lack of proper fonts installed on particular computers that are used to view and print documents. Documents have been somewhat portable through the use of ASCII and Rich Text Format (RTF) files, but content alone does not always convey the true message without formatting or design richness.

PDFing a file makes it "portable" across computer platforms. A PDF file is a 7-bit ASCII file, and may use only the printable subset of the ASCII character set to describe documents—even those with images and special characters. As a result, PDF files are extremely portable and compact even across diverse hardware and operating system environments.

Furthermore, PDF provides a new solution that makes a document independent of the fonts used to create it. Fonts can either be embedded or descriptors can be used. Embedding the fonts in the PostScript stage includes the actual font outlines in the file. Distilling this file will ensure that pages are displayed with type characters in exact position. The font descriptor includes the font name, character metrics, and style information. This is the information needed to simulate missing fonts and is typically only 1–2K per font. If a font used in a document is available on the computer where the document is viewed, it is used. If it is not available, two Adobe Multiple Master fonts are used to simulate on a character-by-character basis the weight and width of the original font, to maintain the overall color and formatting of the original document.

Font embedding does add some additional data to the document; however, it provides an important aspect of document portability—cross-platform font fidelity and the ability to print at any resolution. This means that the receiver of the digital page could have a high resolution color printer and print out pages as needed at a remote location. Pages could be created in one part of the world and then sent to a printer in the opposite hemisphere who uses the data to make high resolution films for printing. Plus, embedding all fonts assures text editability.

Editability

Last minute changes to a PDF can be made via a new plug-in for Acrobat Exchange called Text Touchup. Since the PDF is vector-based and includes the font name, character metrics, and style information, small type changes are possible. Full paragraphs cannot be edited due to the lack of reflow capabilities, but those small yet sometimes crucial changes such as misspelled words or incorrect phone numbers or prices can be made on a last-minute basis within Acrobat Exchange or with other plug-ins, such as Pitstop.

Predictability

Acrobat PDF eliminates the variability of PostScript and provides a foundation for effective digital print production workflow. A RIP interprets PostScript, converts it into a display list of page objects and then rasterizes the page into a map of on/off spots that drive the marking engine. When you distill a document into a PDF you are essentially doing the interpretation and display list functions as in the RIP process.

The resulting PDF is a database of objects that appear on a page and how they relate to each other—a print-specific file with extensions for OPI, image screening information, and more. The variability of PostScript is squeezed out and only the essence remains—which can be added back into the PostScript stream again for printout—just open the PDF and Print it. If your document can be distilled to a PDF, the odds are that it will output reliably on most PostScript RIPs.

Searchability

With Acrobat software, it is possible to find information instantly. There is a full-text search tool which allows the user to retrieve exactly what text they need. Hypertext links can be used to simplify web browsing and navigation features such as bookmarking and cross-documentation links are also included to help the user move through numerous documents faster.

Repurposability

Adobe's PDF for some time has been marketed as a web tool offering greater design richness over the HTML language constraints. PDFs can be downloaded to the World Wide Web and accessed through the free Acrobat Reader plug-in for the two most popular browsers. A document created for print output and distilled into a PDF can now, with virtually no changes, be used on a website. Sites can now be created with all the design richness available in page layout applications such as QuarkXPress and PageMaker. Open in Reader and print it out.

PDF and PostScript. Although PDF files require PostScript information for their creation, the resulting PDF files are different from their PostScript counterpart. A PDF file is not a PostScript language program and cannot be directly interpreted by a PostScript interpreter. However, the page descriptions in a PDF file can be converted into a PostScript file.

How PDF files work. The PDF file format is not a programming language like PostScript. You cannot send a PDF file to a laser printer directly because the file format contains information that a current PostScript RIP would not understand. The PDF does contain PostScript code, but the extra PDF data would inhibit the RIP from processing the document. A PDF file must be sent to a RIP through the Acrobat Reader or Exchange application. When output by Reader, the PDF is converted into a PostScript file and sent to the RIP just like any other PostScript file.

Perhaps in the future, the PDF would become the basic file format and the very concept of RIPs would change. PDF and PostScript are highly inter-related at present.

Creating a PDF file. The two methods for creating PDF are:
- PDFWriter
- Acrobat Distiller

The PDFWriter, available on both Apple Macintosh computers and computers running the Microsoft Windows environment, acts as a printer driver. The PDFWriter shows up as a printer in the Macintosh Chooser window. The user needs to choose that "printer" to create a PDF file. The user then "prints" their file to the PDFWriter and an electronic file is produced. This is similar to "print to disk."

For more documents that involve special fonts, high-resolution images and detailed illustrations, the PDF file must be created differently because of limitations of PDFWriter. Acrobat Distiller was developed for this situation. Distiller produces PDF files from PostScript files that have been "printed to disk." The Distiller application accepts any PostScript file, whether created by an application program or hand-coded. Distiller produces more efficient PDF files than PDFWriter for various reasons and it is recommended if you are going to print to film or plate or on high-end digital printers.

You can view a PDF file with Acrobat Exchange and Acrobat Reader. Acrobat Reader is a free downloadable file available from Adobe at (www.adobe.com). Copies of the reader can be shared with others. These two applications contain the interface that allows users to easily navigate through a PDF document, even those that contain thousands of pages. To improve performance for interactive viewing, a PDF defines a more structured format than that used by most PostScript language programs. PDF also includes objects, such as annotations and hypertext links, that are not part of the page itself but are useful for interactive viewing. There is about a 10-to-1 compression factor between the original application file and the PDF file.

Traditional methods for variable-data printing

Traditional Variable Data Printing (VDP) solutions borrow the metaphor of a form with fields that need to be filled with specific or personal data. Graphically, the form consists of fixed data, such as a logo, borders, background, and fields markers, possibly with field names. The personalized copy is generated by putting data into the fields. Such data typically represents information on one person, thus this data filling activity is called personalization. Automatic systems can personalize a form by retrieving the relevant record(s) from some database and inserting the information extracted from those records into the appropriate fields of the form.

The very traditional methods, the application we all know from various bills we receive, such as the telephone bills or junk mail that has our name in certain places, uses traditional print production methods for printing the empty forms, and simple digital printing (for instance, monochrome ink jet technology) in order to print the personal data onto the previously printed form. The single and most obvious disadvantage of traditional methods is the need to hold large stocks of printed forms. Changing the design of a form typically implies waste of pre-printed stock. Using different form styles, say for addressing different populations, is typically avoided or involves high costs of stock. Digital printing technology addresses these difficulties and offer new dimensions to personalization or variable data printing.

Page-to-page variability

Digital printing technology allows for printing, at the production speed of the printing system, pages that can be completely different from one another. This is in contrast to traditional printing systems which allow for printing, at very high speeds, pages that are identical to each other; the downside is that these traditional methods require significant preparations in the prepress phase, which eventually result in ready-to-print press plates from which one can make all those identical pages.

The page-to-page variability of digital printing opens up a significant new dimension to personalization or VDP printing. One does not need to preprint forms (and deal with the resulting stock maintenance issues). Instead, one could print, at the same time, the full page, form data as well as field content. Currently, the speed at which digital printing can generate full pages is slower than the speed at which traditional printing can emit those pages (the gap seems to be smaller as we approach the end of the millennium). This production disadvantage is expected to be offset by the savings one can gain due to avoiding stock issues, and the higher price one can charge due to the higher value of print that is gained from the flexibility in the design of forms or the ability to change them, say for addressing different populations.

A key challenge, faced by all vendors of digital printing systems, is how to make the inherent technology of page-to-page variability into a useful feature, and thus a solution and not just technology.

First-generation VDP solutions

First-generation solutions are based on implementing the forms metaphor. This is typical in two major products. One is the printing system developed by Xeikon in the DCP family of digital presses, the other is the forms technology in PostScript Level 2 from Adobe.

Xeikon technology: master page and variable fields

The Xeikon technology allows their press to receive the form part of a job as a master page, and the personal data (the values that go into the fields) as a collection of variable fields. The data flow requirement is that one first sends to the printing system the master page data, and then follows with a stream of data for the variable fields with proper breaks for different pages. The press generates pages by repeatedly (that is, per-page) merging the master page data with the variable fields data of that page. Assuming that the input stream of data for the variable fields adheres to a set of constraints defined by the vendor then this merge-and-print process can be done at the rate of the print engine.

A variant of the master-page and variable-fields implementation is when all data is pre-processed and stored on disks, prior to the print process. The print then goes directly from the pre-processed data, still having on-the-fly merge between variable fields data and the master page. Another variant is when the prepress process creates raster data for the full page, without the distinction between fixed (i.e., master) and variable (i.e., variable fields). The print process must be able to retrieve the full data for the pages at the machine's rated print speed. This last variant is really electronic collation.

Typical limitations of master-page (MP) and variable-fields (VF) technology are in the number of VFs per page, in the total page area covered by the VFs, in the overlap allowed between VFs, and sometimes in alignment constraint on the pixel address where a VF starts or ends. The severity of such constraints is reduced in the prepress-based processing and printing methods, where data is first prepared to disk. Here, however, a new constraint is introduced: the total number of pages that can be printed in a run. This constraint stems from the limitation of disk space.

These limitations, at the minimum, present tough challenges at the document design phase. One has to not only limit the design to the abstraction of a form and its instance data, but also adhere to limitations that come from the implementation on a particular engine (such limitations can be, for example, the inability to change MP during a print run). In our modern era, where document design and authoring is done independent of print peculiarities, and a formal language (typically PostScript) is used in order to convey, very precisely, the content and design to the printing system, the MP and VF limitations are even more severe.

Adobe's PostScript forms

The forms mechanism introduced in PS Level 2 language allows for specifying pages that consist of predefined parts (forms) and unique data per page. In principle, this is a major step forward compared to the machine-specific technology introduced earlier. It creates a machine-independent mechanism for formally stating that a page consists of some elements that had been previously defined and used. Forms suggests that the intended use was form filling applications, and the implementation is reasonable where the form defines the master page and it is relatively simple in its graphics content (for instance, b/w simple graphics and text form).

We think of VDP printing in terms of forms and their instance data. Using these metaphors for digital printing is a good starting point but not where the state of the art should be. It is clear that if personalization could affect not only instance data, but also layout, colors, graphics, and number of pages in a personal piece it will be more effective. And effectiveness of personalized print material is all what we are looking for in VDP jobs, since this is the key item which creates the higher value of the printed material. Such high value can be translated to higher revenues to the design or print providers.

The key challenge faced by developers of VDP solutions in digital printing is how to eliminate the various first-generation constraints on VDP print jobs while still maintaining the capability to print at machine-rated speed. This is the key challenge because meeting it will allow much simpler, yet more flexible document design phase, which leads to more creative (and attractive) documents, while not sacrificing the production aspect (that is, printing at the machine's rated speed).

The Scitex approach

Scitex has a full architecture for VDP solutions. It consists of a print specification language, called Scitex VPS, and a RIP that is capable of efficiently processing not only regular PostScript jobs or PDF jobs but also Scitex VPS jobs. The processing capability of the RIP is augmented by specially designed hardware but at the low-end or mid-range parts of the product line, it is all software processing. They have also developed a tool (application) that will enable the originators (that is, the creators or design providers) to be as expressive as possible. This tool is called Darwin. It is a QuarkXTension combined with a data and job manager called the Darwin Pilot. With Darwin, the designer can think of the full Quark document as the form (a very flexible one) and use the Pilot to define the rules by which document instanciation will happen.

To print, Darwin uses either PostScript (like Quark), or Scitex VPS. With Scitex VPS, Darwin can indicate to the printing system the distinction between fixed (or re-usable) parts and per-page, unique parts. This distinction allows the printing system (which includes the RIP) to process the print job very fast. The fundamental elements of the Scitex approach are the Scitex VPS language and the technology to process such print jobs efficiently. However, Darwin addresses a very important need of the originator's community, the need to effectively design VDP jobs. Scitex VPS is the means by which Darwin can indicate to the printing system what to print. Clearly, other authoring tools, desktop or custom, can use Scitex VPS for the purpose.

Scitex's approach is based on a generalization of the forms metaphor. Instead of thinking in terms of a form and its instance data, we think in terms of a set of predefined (per-job or per-context) page elements, and page-assembly instructions that specify how to build final pages out of page elements and unique data (inline, per-page). Instead of thinking in terms of single pages we think in terms of booklets. In other words, a booklet is an instance of the generic document. Booklets may have several pages in them, and not all booklets in a job must have the same number of pages.

A Variable Input (VI) job is not a set of pages, all using the same form template. Instead, a VI job is a collection of personalized copies, called Booklets, of a job-specific, generic document. Each booklet is personalized according to some specific unique data or record. All booklets of the job use, per-page, elements that are either unique for that page or come from a set of page elements (graphics, text, images, etc.) that were defined for the job. "Common and Unique Building Blocks (CUBB)" is the name for the forms and instance data metaphor. Using CUBB, a form can be defined as a page element, which will appear in all pages, booklets are of size 1, and the unique data is the variable fields.

In other words, CUBB is a more general approach that allows for much more elaborate and creative designs but still enables the simple forms metaphor. At first, one must distinguish between a document on the one hand, and its specification as a print job on the other. In the non-VI world, documents exist in their application domain. We are all familiar with Quark documents,

Word documents, or PageMaker documents. These are application-dependent representations of the document metaphor, which allow the user to author, view, modify, design, and, in general, have the illusion of working with real documents. A scientific way of stating this is that the various authoring applications provide their users with a document abstraction.

In this non-VDP world documents are printed by generating a formal representation of their content and design in a print specification language, typically PostScript. Then, the RIP in the printing system translates the print specifications to machine-specific instructions (or data) that place dots on paper. The key requirement satisfied by the printing system (and especially its RIP) is that what appears on paper is exactly what was specified.

A VI document is a set of regular documents. The set is defined in terms of a document template, a collection of data records, and a set of instantiation rules. A document template may be a single layout or a collection of possible layouts. Data records are the data out of which each regular document should be generated (for example, name, address, etc.). Instantiation rules define how to generate a regular document from a specific data record and the document template; they specify not only where and how to insert specific information from the data record but also drive automatic design rules that can pick a layout, for example, based on some information in the data record.

Scitex has developed Darwin as an authoring tool for VDP documents. It consists of a QuarkXTension and a data management tool called the Darwin Pilot. Other authoring tools are, for example, Atlas' Print Shop Mail. A common example of VDP documents and an authoring tool is the use of mail-merge in MS Word. In this case, the Word document with the place-holder for the personal data is the document template, the personal data entries in the external table are the data records, and the instantiation rules are simply the implied rule of replacing place-holders with the content of fields in the data record where the data record's field name matches the document's place-holder name.

Authoring tools for VI documents are important, not just as generators of unique print specification languages, but this is because the authoring of VDP documents without a special tool is a very tedious and error-prone process. This means that even if such VDP authoring tools use PostScript for doing the print, they still have value. Using PostScript for specifying the print jobs of VDP documents is possible but may result in an inefficient print process. This is because the print process has no information about the structure of the print jobs, and thus cannot take advantage of the fact that certain elements repeat on every page, etc.

Scitex VPS: Variable Print Specification

Scitex has developed VPS, an extension to the PostScript language, that allows for formal specification of VDP print jobs. The language allows for defining jobs that consist of booklets, each consisting of pages, each constructed by assembly of

- predefined global page elements
- local (i.e., per page) page elements
- unique, inline, data for the page

Every job defines a context which includes the collection of page elements that will be used in building pages for that job. Adding page elements to the job's context is supported by the VPS language itself. These page elements are the common building blocks we used earlier. So, one can think of a relatively small set of page elements out of which one could assemble quite a large number of pages. This difference between the cardinalities (size) of the set of page elements and the set of booklets (pages) is the key for the expected performance benefit.

Each time the process assembles a page out of pre-rasterized page elements it saves the RIP the time associated with rasterizing these elements. The performance gains depend on the complexity of these elements as well as on their size. Also, not having to re-RIP means also not having to re-send these over the network. This avoidance of network activity is a potentially significant saving by itself.

The VPS mechanism allows for defining pages using the forms metaphor. A form is one page element, and the variable fields are all isnline data. The VPS mechanism allows for much more general specification of VI print jobs. This generality is what allows authoring applications to present their user with quite elaborate design schemes, with almost no concerns about the actual mechanisms of printing. In other words, the abstraction presented by VPS is higher level than the forms-based abstractions, and it gives a lot of power to the designer/author/creator/originator. This higher-level abstraction is of course a challenge for the designer of the printing system, but it is exactly what gives the capability to produce print jobs more effectively.

Chapter 12

ADVANCED IMAGING

Raster file and bitmap file

A bitmap is a map of bits—by definition, a one-bit-deep raster file. We often think of bitmaps as the things that RIPs generate from raster and other data to send to platesetters and imagesetters. But bitmaps can be other things—for example, a common fax file (at least one without any grayscale data) is an encoded bitmap.

A bitmap is an array of pixels—each pixel is defined by its bit depth. It can be one bit deep (bilevel)—what Photoshop calls bitmap mode. This used to be called line art—it may or may not be in black and white (it could have been colored in Quark/PageMaker), and may or may not be at 100% (could have been screened back in those apps). It can be 8-bits deep (grayscale, aka monotone or index color). It can be 24-bits deep (RGB). It can be 32-bits deep (CMYK). A CMYK copydot image, for example, has four channels, each of which is bilevel (one bit deep).

A bitmap is a type of graphics file in which a separate value for each pixel of an image is stored in a bit or group of bits. Scanned images are stored as bitmaps. The word "bitmap" is used to define an array of pixels (not bits) whose individual values are defined in bits. In pre-press we use it to grasp the concept of black and white. Adding more depth to raster files, we arrive at what we describe as a contone or continuous tone image.

How can something broken up into little squares be continuous tone—usually considered for original art, which is usually continuous tone. Contone and continuous tone actually refer to the type of original image that we are attempting to digitize, and do not describe the data itself—after all, individual pixels are squares of uniform color; the tones do not actually flow continuously from one area of an image to the next, but the squares create the illusion of continuous tone when viewed from a reasonable distance. Although we in prepress use the term contone for a non-screened image, incorrect use of the term non-screened is possible. The images have a fixed resolution and are not really scalable, as one might think a true contone would be. With scalability in mind, neither is the original image— film grain and whatever. The term "contone" comes from a perfect, resolution-independent world and is used to describe an "imperfect" image.

Many of the problems that printers and their customers face is related to understanding the basic principles of how hardware, software and workflow combine to achieve results in the digital imaging process. We talked about archiving "raster images" that were one-bit TIFFs representing halftone dots, used as instruction sets for marking engines such as platesetters. Then we heard of the benefits of Scitex workflow, where ripped PostScript data is trapped, imposed and stored prior to the screening process that creates halftone dots. Using the definition that says that raster images are screened instruction sets to explain the RIP process becomes problematic when also describing the imaging process of continuous-tone (unscreened) proofing systems like dye sublimation printer demands. We began using the term "raster image" and the term "screened one-bit TIFF" to describe the instruction set that drives the marking engine.

Raster is a very general term meaning data in the form of a grid of pixels. It doesn't say anything about pixel depth (how many bits in each pixel), color space, composite or separated format, compression scheme, resolution, the geometry of the sampling grid (may be square but could be something else), or screening. It does mean that the data is not text or vector format. Raster data is what scanners generate. Raster data is also what you get when you "rasterize" a vector file or text—that is, toss out all that useful resolution-independent compactly-encoded information and reduce it to a grid of pixels that will serve you well if it doesn't have to be resampled, and will cost you in terms of quality if it does.

A bitmap is an array of pixels—each pixel is defined by its bit depth. Wouldn't that be byte-map? The "bit" part of the bitmap clearly defines it as bilevel as a bit can only have a value of 0 or 1. The term "bitmap" is really a more technical description of a particular form of raster file. In prepress, we use it to grasp the concept of black and white. Adding more depth to raster files we arrive at what we describe as a contone or continuous tone image. The term "raster-image" (or raster file) seeks to clearly define the differences between various representations of graphical data. Vector data or raster data generally define that the format is represented as pixels (spots of visual information), regardless of pixel-depth or order. While a bitmap is a raster-image, a raster image can be more than a bitmap.

Be careful of using TIFF or TIFF/IT to describe a general data type. They are accurate only if the file literally conforms to the particular specification. TIFF by itself doesn't say anything about the data type, other than that it is a raster format. TIFF files come in various forms—bilevel and contone. Likewise, CT/LW is sometimes used as a general term, other times to refer specifically to the Scitex format.

Let's use the terms "bi-level bitmap" and "contone raster data." Some use the term "CEPS rasters" to refer to CT/LW or TIFF-IT, but I'm sure that term makes some people uncomfortable. Let's use "bi-level bitmap" to refer to separated data that is screened for output to the markup engine. Unfortunately, some will still be confused by the fact that some RIPs use intermediate formats before screening the data on the fly for output to the markup engine. There is bound to be confusion between these formats (CT/LW or other) and "bi-level bitmaps" for users who never see anything but the expression of these data sets on film or plate. Let's make the distinction between image data and screened output data more clear. If we refer to image data as a "pixel map" or "picture element map" when referring to "contone raster data" and only use "bitmap" for separated, screened, device resolution data. That way we could refer to individual elements of a bitmap as "bits" which combine to make various shaped "screen dots."

People would be confused between binary "bits" and screened data "bits." Let's advance that the terms "contone" and "continuous tone" actually refer to the type of original image that we are attempting to digitize, and do not describe the data itself—after all, individual pixels are complete squares of uniform color; the tones do not actually flow continuously from one area of an image to the next, but merely create the illusion of continuous tone when viewed from a reasonable distance. Camera operators used the term "contone" to distinguish original art from halftone film or repro. An extension of this logic to the digital age allows us to use the term "contone" to refer to any unscreened image data types, including (but not limited to) CT/LW, TIFF, GIF, etc. The term "contone raster data" is specific to digital images where "contone" can refer to either digital or analog image data.

Before Adobe Photoshop, the term bitmap was widely used in the graphic arts industry to represent any file made of individual pixels, whether those pixels were only on and off or capable of multiple shades. Only after Adobe took the very literal translation of bitmap as being a map where only a single bit controls the value of a pixel did this new definition sweep the land. The term bitmap is commonly used in both manners, and we should clarify what we mean by "bitmap" when we use the term.

The contone raster image contains many pixels of various shades; these shades are used to determine the size of the post-screening halftone dots on most devices, but are used to directly drive the marking engine on continuous tone profing devices such as dye sublimation.

1. For data which is already screened, and at device resolution, the term "bi-level bitmap" is descriptive and unambiguous.
2. For data which is unscreened, "contone raster data" is my preference.
3. For two-component formats, like TIFF/IT-P1 or Scitex CT/LW, I have heard various terms: compound raster, dual raster, etc. Multi-resolution bitmap is another one.

Wide-format printing and its processes

More that 200,000 wide-format printing devices were sold in 1997. A six percent growth is predicted over the next four years. Wide-format printing has become a major player in the digital printing arena.

Wide-format printing, which is referred to as large-format printing, can be defined as the production and reproduction of documents that are 36" wide or wider. What is produced are large, color images that would most generally be considered impractical or even impossible to produce by conventional printing methods, be it offset, digital offset, or even screen printing.

The wide-format printer and its end result can range from very simple to very complex. There are plotters that produce simple engineering and architectural type drawings. At the high end, photoprinters are producing incredibly accurate continuous tone images.

Wide-format printing is being used for many applications. Users are graphic design studios, advertising agencies, prepress operations, corporate in-house art departments, architects, and engineering firms. Each user usually has a unique use for their printer. Creations include posters, banners, signage/art for construction areas, window displays, fine art reproduction, and engineering and architectural blueprints and drawings. And with these already established users and markets, new users and markets are being created and developed every day.

Wide-format printers can print on a wide range of substrates—from paper to canvas to vinyl—just about anything you can get through the printer. The printers offer a variety of resolutions, and handle colors ranging from the standard four-color gamut to eight-color gamuts.

Wide-format printing is now routine, applied by sign shops, screen printers and inhouse graphics departments.

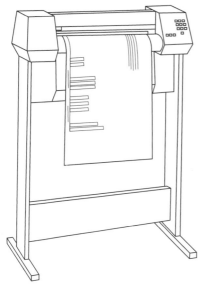

Wide-format printers, like the one at left, rely on two primary technologies to produce printed images—electrostatic and inkjet, with inkjet being the most common of the two. However, electrostatics is still an important topic, because it is still a choice.

Electrostatics

Electrostatics became a popular term with Chester F. Carlson's invention of Xerography. Electrostatics is the foundation of the concept of Xerography, which we know as the process of toner being electrically attracted and then fixed to a piece of paper.

Originally, electrostatics was used in creating decorative metal tiles, where electrostatic forces attracted powder to the tile, and then the powder was burnt into the surface when the tiles were furnace fired.

Electrostatics in printing is actually a function in the process of electrography, or electrographic transfer printing. This process involves the conversion of electronic signals to a latent image charge pattern on to a reusable dielectric material. The information is held to the dielectric material by electrostatics. Toner is attracted to the electrostatic charge, and then transferred to the the paper and fixed. The dielectric material is then made ready to repeat the cycle by cleaning the remaining residual toner and discharging the surface.

In the digital printing process, the use of electrostatics is a little bit different. The difference is that in digital printing, the transfer step is removed. This means that there is no transfer from the dielectric material to the paper. Instead, the toner is applied directly to the charged paper. Another form of electrostatic printing is known as Corona Powdered Electrostatic Transfer. This process takes place when paper is placed in contact with a photoreceptor and the back of the paper is flooded with ions carrying a charge opposite that of the toner. The opposite charge attracts the toner to the image areas on the paper. As the paper is pulled away from the photoreceptor, the toner will adhere to the surface with the strongest attraction. Where the toner sticks to the paper is the image area.

Inkjet

Inkjet is the more popular of the technologies used in wide-format printers. Although an acceptable definition of inkjet printing would be the process of an ink being sprayed onto a piece of paper, the technology of how that ink is moved through the cartridge to the jet nozzle and then to the paper is a much more involved process. There are four predominant inkjet technologies used for wide format: electrostatic, piezo drop-on-demand, thermal, and phase-change.

Electrostatic principles return to inkjet technology in the process of deflected inkjet. The same basic principle applies here as in electrography. However, instead of a converted latent image being placed on a dielectric cylinder, the latent image is now placed into a stream of ink droplets. The droplets then pass through a electrostatic field, causing a deflection of the droplets. This deflection directs the droplets to their proper location on the substrate. Unchanged droplets pass through the deflection field to a return path for reuse.

Piezo drop-on-demand inkjet

Piezo drop-on-demand inkjet technology works on the principle of an electrical reaction creating a mechanical reaction. Piezo is also known as PZT, for its chemical composition of lead zirconate titanate. In the drop-on-demand process, this electrical-to-mechanical conversion takes place at the PZT, usually a crystal.

When an electric charge is applied to a crystal, it undergoes minute dimensional changes, as either a contraction or expansion. The amount of contraction or expansion is determined by the polarity of the electrical charge applied to the crystal. This contraction/expansion creates a change in pressure in the ink inside the chamber. The ink's reaction to the volume/pressure change in the chamber determines how the ink is forced out of the chamber opening. Within a few milliseconds, the crystal shrinks and creates a vacuum that draws new ink into the chamber.

The advantage to using piezo technology is that it produces a smaller, more uniformly shaped dot. These factors provide a more accurate and higher quality print.

Many of the latest inkjet systems being introduced are piezo. Eastman Kodak and CalComp Technology jointly developed a piezo inkjet technology. The agreement is intended to leverage CalComp's Crystal Jet-based technology and Kodak's imaging science and color management technology.

Thermal inkjet

Thermal inkjet printing is mechanically very similar to piezo inkjet. An electrical pulse creates a reaction, and that reaction causes the ink in the chamber to be forced out of the chamber. In thermal inkjet, the reaction created by the electrical pulse is heat in a resistor. Heat causes the resistor to form a bubble, which separates the ink from the resistor. When the ink cools down, the bubble breaks, resulting in a pressure that forces a droplet out of the nozzle. Although this process may seem like it is taking a very long time, it is important to keep in mind that it is all happening in milliseconds.

Phase change

Phase change is another form of ink-jet printing. Phase change, like thermal inkjet technology, is made functional by heat. However, rather than using liquid inks, phase change uses solid waxy pigment. A heated resistor heats and melts the wax and the melted wax is jetted through the chamber's opening, onto the substrate.

Each technology, electrostatic and inkjet, has its advantages and disadvantages. Electrostatic technology has an advantage in fade resistance and printing speeds. However, one of the most important factors to consider is price. Initially, electrostatic systems were much more expensive to purchase than an inkjet system. Even though electrostatic supplies were less expensive than inkjet, the initial cost was often a major determinant in which users would purchase, regardless of quality and printing speeds.

Over time, however, advanced technology has made electrostatic printers more cost-effective than inkjets for a wide range of wide-format printing applications. A lower-cost writing head, and a single toner channel, and modifications in the writing technique enhance price and performance, reducing the initial cost to about one-third that of similar techniques of the past. Also, eliminating liquid toners and liquid disposal, reducing hydrocarbon emissions, and purifying and reconstituting ink concentrate improve ease of use, reduce environmental hazards, and cut supplies cost.

Inkjet ink for wide format printers

Ink selection plays an important role in wide-format printing. Each ink contains a vehicle and a colorant. The proper choice of each component will affect droplet formation and image quality.

The colorant of an ink can be either a pigment or a dye. Pigments tend to provide better contrast, have better light and water fastness, and adhere better to the substrate. This would make pigmented inks more suitable for outdoor use. Dyes tend to be more stable in suspension, and are less apt to clog in the tiny orifices of ink cartridges.

Carriers are aqueous and non-aqueous. Aqueous inks are preferred in systems like electrostatic deflection because they assist in the formation and deflection of drops, which tend to have high viscosity, high surface tension, and moderate to high conductivity.

Two more important characteristics of inkjet ink are viscosity and surface tension. These properties work hand in hand, but each also has its specific function in drop formation. Viscosity determines the way the tail of the droplet breaks away from the orifice of the cartridge. Surface tension determines characteristics such as drop formation, drop size, and drop shape.

Inkjet ink and substrates

As with ink jettability, viscosity and surface tension play a major role in ink-to-paper reactions. Factors controlled by these determinants are initial contact angle, wetting and wicking, smearing, and bleeding. These are all factors to take into consideration when combining inks with substrates. The substrate/ink interactions for ink-jets are very different from those of conventional printing. Drops hit the paper at a very fast pace and at high velocities, covering a moving substrate. Also, there is no pressure, to assist in impregnation of the substrate and drying by absorption.

Sometimes, inks and substrate don't work perfectly or as anticipated. The following is a list of various problems that can occur when inks and substates are improperly matched.

Fluorescing: Colors look brighter than they should. Could result from pH imbalance between the substrate coating and ink. Colors shift from original color expectations.

Mottle: Non-uniform media coating causes ink to be absorbed at different rates. Unevenness in color-fill areas.

Bleed: One ink color runs into another due to excessive dot gain and slow ink absorption. Poorly defined edges and lines and unwanted color mixes at junctions.

Pooling: Ink is unevenly absorbed by coating and swims on top of coating, almost like a puddle of water. Puddle defects in heavy ink coverage areas.

Feathering: Ink travels through coating and follows substrate fibers. Can be color-specific, unlike color-to-color bleed, causing loss of edge definition. The image has artifacts, thin spikes protruding past the printed edge.

Strike through: Ink travels deep into the substrate coating and is visible on backside of media. In addition to staining, the image may lose color gamut value and the media may cockle (wrinkle).

Repelling: Usually seen when inks are not compatible with one another. When dot attempts to lie on top of another dot, it is repelled and falls to the edge. Color shifts from the original and image appears grainy.

Banding: An image appears to have lines or pinstripes in the direction of the print. Usually found in gradients and color blends.

Choosing your substrate

Choosing the proper substrate for your job can make you the hero or the goat. A popular solution is to follow a procession of steps that ask the same questions each time through. The following is a typical example of these basic steps.

Step 1

Determine the image type and complexity of the image to be printed. Most images can be divided into three categories:

- Simple: Images that are made up primarily of lines and text: there may be a limited amount of small area fill. The key characteristic is the lack of large areas where the ink coverage is more than 100 percent. Typical examples include signs, CAD drawings, charts, and simple graphs.
- Complex: These contain detailed graphics, clipart and/or other image elements that contain large area fills and require reasonably accurate color matching. The key elements are significant areas with 100 percent or more ink coverage and/or the need to match colors. Examples are images with company logos, in-house posters/announcements, maps and advertising signs.
- Pictorial: Any image containing a photographic element or a very complex graphic. The key characteristic is that the image covers a large area and requires well over 100 percent ink coverage to print well. Examples are photo posters, back walls or signage, art reproductions, murals and point-of-purchase displays for trade show stands.

Step 2

Determine the primary use of the printed images. Use can be divided into five primary categories, which are, in turn, divided into three "image quality" levels.

- Indoor use: use for one week or less, or for over one week.
- Outdoor use: use for one week or less, or for over one week.
- Presentation, point-of-purchase, trade show: typically mounted on a substrate.
- Banners: Free-standing banners, normally grommeted and hung; can be used indoors or out.
- Backlit: Translucent images illuminated from the rear.

The image quality levels include:

- Cheap and cheerful: The least expensive medium that will provide an acceptable image quality.
- Wow: Image quality and color that will "wow" most audiences and give an outstanding result.
- Stupendous: When only the best image quality will do.

Step 3

Choose the best media type for the project. Although the types of media being offered seem to be increasing each year, there are certain categories that remain constant. Here is an overview of some of those, by type, characteristics, uses, and limitations. Various manufacturers/suppliers may label their specific products differently.

- CAD color bond: A bright, white paper good for lines and text; inexpensive. It will not, however, take heavy ink coverage; cockle and blend can occur. Uses: CAD, simple signs.
- Presentation bond: A bright, white opaque bond, weighted from 24 to 60 lb; will take moderate area fill. This medium is slow to dry when it has heavy ink coverage, and it can cockle under pictorial images. Uses: presentations, signs, low-cost graphics.
- Photobase: A totally opaque media available in matte, satin and glossy finishes; 5 to 7 mil calipers are common. Provides a quality image no matter how much ink. Can be difficult to laminate if not completely dry, and can be torn. Uses: pictorial images.

- Glossy bond: Bond paper with a glossy top coating and a barrier coat underneath; it will take much more ink that other bonds. Lighter than photobase media. Uses: Graphics, large area fill, some pictorals.
- Glossy film: A very bright, white, totally opaque polyester film, 3-5 mil caliper. Physically tough, this medium provides a superior image. It will, however, show finger marks, so it's best laminated for handling purposes. Uses: Whenever highest image quality is required.
- Clear film: Optically clear film, 3-5 mil caliper, that provides excellent image quality. This should be used only where transparency is needed. Uses: Overlays, window displays, backlit (with laminate).
- Adhesive film: Both glossy and clear films with adhesive backing, available in pressure-sensitive and cling types. Careful: Need care in mounting, and cling effect will not work on all surfaces. Uses: As for other films, but adhesive enables easy mounting.
- Backlit film: 4-10 mil translucent film, with the translucency set so that the image is visible with both backlight and reflected light; image quality is excellent. Note, however, that any flaw in the image will stand out; needs care in mounting in a light box. Uses: Backlit displays for trade shows, malls, airports, etc.
- CAD vellum: Semitransparent cotton paper that can be used for low-cost backlit applications. Images, though, must not have areas of high ink coverage. Image is not as good as film. Uses: simple, in-house backlits, window displays.
- Canvas: A heavyweight medium available in matte and satin finishes, this provides excellent image quality and is designed for pictorial images. Cutting is difficult, however, and care must be take when printing due to weight and thickness. Uses: Artistic look for any application; banners and hanging displays.
- Art paper: A companion product to canvas, this medium gives the look and feel of paper used for watercolor painting. Best mounted or framed; take care in cutting. Uses: Artistic look for photorealistic images.

- Vinyls: Available in various weights and finishes, available with peel-off adhesive backing. Designed for pictorial images, but image quality can vary; extra care is needed in lamination. Uses: Banners, hanging displays; use for physical strength.
- Foils: A thin base material with "glittery" surfaces that provide dramatic effects. Note that the colors in the image must be chosen carefully; also, laminating can be difficult. Uses: Special effects for signage, point-of-purchase applications.

Step 4

The final step involves entering all of the properties of a project into a chart that can outline the specific information described above. Other important factors to consider are lamination, media quality, availability, and price. Wide-format printers are usually fairly similar in appearance. However, each has certain characteristics and limitations. Widths range from 36" on up. Most models use both a cut sheet and roll media format. However, wide-format printers cannot print full bleeds, because a portion of the paper needs to be grabbed by a paper-handling mechanism. This margin ranges from a fraction of an inch to two inches.

Wide-format printers run at speeds measured in square feet per hour rather than in pages per minute. This is one factor to take into consideration when determining how much attention the printer needs when producing a job in order to make the printer cost effective. Ink capacity is another determinant. Capacity ranges from 20ml to a full liter. Some printers also come with the capability to self-feed rolls of paper.

As with any other printing process, image resolution is an issue in wide-format printing. Resolution is usually dictated by the intended use of the printed piece. Wide format output is usually viewed from a distance, so the resolution of wide-format prints can be much lower that that of letter or tabloid size pages without a noticeable loss of clarity. If you use your wide-format printer for color proofing, high-resolution models are available and will most likely serve your needs much better.

Quality and speed developments

It does not seem likely that over the next few years there will be very dramatic increases in the speed of inkjet technology, due to the basic printhead design. The trend will most likely be to double up nozzle counts to increase quality.

Many wide-format printers are designed for high-volume production, working in server and network configurations. More expensive models have the RIP built into the printer. Other models can be used with a variety of software or hardware RIPs. The RIP usually determines how much RAM is available. RAM amounts range from 8 to 256 Mb.

As with other printing operations, wide-format printing is becoming more of a cross-platform environment, with the ability to be compatible with Windows or Macintosh. The most common network interfaces are serial and parallel. Most printers also feature Ethernet or EtherTalk connections, but few offer SCSI or LocalTalk ports. Networking options, PostScript support, and additional RAM are often bundled with the RIP, available through either the printer manufacturer or a third-party vendor.

Slowly but surely, the applications for the tools and end products of wide-format printing have been expanded. Large posters and other related applications, including commercial and fine art and the continued applications of billboards and mass transit, have developed as part of the continually growing wide-format picture. The market is discovering that wide-format has few limitations.

An interesting consideration is that this growth of the wide-format market has not been planned, especially by the industry's manufacturers and suppliers. Instead, to a large degree, it has been the people who use wide-format technology who have started the fires and developed the new applications.

One of the primary drivers of the wide-format market is advertising. US retailers are looking for quick responses to their products and they're only stocking products targeted to the needs of their customer base. Retailers are trying to react faster to customer buying habits by changing their signage and point-of-purchase displays more often. Digital printing, especially wide-format, is an answer to their needs.

Superwide

For the superwide inkjet (40" and up), the market is highly specialized and so far, small in the U.S. Growth tends to be outside the U.S., especially Europe. Nevertheless, there is a developing market for superwide systems in the U.S. based on a new and poorly understood market related to the events industry.

Wide-format printing is an emerging technology. In the era of digital printing, wide-format is another option. Many markets can be served with wide-format printing. The printing industry itself sees wide-format as an attractive means to creating new business opportunities. As with any other technology, decisions on what to buy or implement, or what needs improvement, need to be informed decisions. Having an understanding of the technology, and then applying that knowledge to the wide array of specific product information available rather than knowing the buzzwords, is the best way to make those informed decisions. It has been predicted that wide-format printing will be the most revenue-generating segment of digital printing. In any case, the fact is that wide format is an exciting development, especially to those with creative intentions.

Inkjet is not the only approach to wide-format printing. Toner-based printing started 60 years ago, when Chester F. Carlson invented xerography. In greek "xeros" means dry and "graphein" means writing. The theory behind the technology is producing or reproducing images and text by the creation of electrostatic charge patterns, which then are made visible by charged marking particles. This means that there are no chemicals involved, except if you call the toner a chemical. And toner is one more approach for superwide printing.

When Chester Carlson allied with the Haloid Corporation his technology was patented. But very shortly, a product incorporating a variation of xerography, the RCA Electrofax, came on the market anyway using a paper with the photoconductor incorporated into it. The coating was a inorganic Zinc Oxide (ZnO). The coated paper served as the medium for both the formation of the latent image and the final image. Thus, they eliminated the transfer step that was found in the xerographic process.

Another approach was a process called Persistent Internal Polarization. Certain photoconducting materials can be polarized by the simultaneous presence of radiation and a field. Images can be created by either the selective polarization in exposed regions or by first producing a uniform polarization of the photoconductor surface followed by a depolarization image exposure. This process requires high exposures and the quality of the images made is not that good.

Still another process is photoconductive pigment electrophotography. In this process, photosensitive material is incorporated into toner particles that are dispersed in an insulating liquid or softenable resin. On exposure, charge is transferred from the exposed particles to the electrode so that the charge-reversed particles are attracted to the metal electrode. Xerography survived all these "attacks" from other processes.

Inkjet again

In inkjet, ink droplets are extracted from an orifice and propelled to a receiving surface. The ink goes directly to a receiver without rollers, ribbons, fuser systems, or any other apparatus. The basic requirements for inkjet printing are a method of creating ink drops and a method for selecting those drops that will deposit on the receiver. Inkjet is the only noncontact technology that can print on curved, recessed, or rough-textured surfaces. There are many different inkjet technologies in use today and the technology is poised to explode within the next decade. Compared to xerography, the principal limitations are low process speeds and the cost of the inks.

Thermography

Thermography can be classified into several categories.
- thermal direct
- direct thermal transfer
- dye diffusion thermal transfer
- resistive thermal transfer

Thermal direct uses heat-sensitive paper. The process is very similar to the old electrofax process. Thermal direct is wide spread in barcode printing applications such as airline tickets. Direct thermal transfer can print any surface that can be coated with an imaging layer and can be brought into contact with a print head. The surface must be very smooth when coating takes place in order to gain the best results. In dye diffusion transfer, a thermal print head causes subtractive dyes to transfer from a donor ribbon to a receiver. This process can create images that appear just like photographs. Resistive thermal transfer uses a self-heating ribbon carrying a thermoplastic ink that is held against a receiver with high pressure.

How does xerography work?

Xerography is a complex process. When Chester Carlson invented this process he started out with five steps:
- charging, using Selenium as a photoconductor
- exposure, bleeding certain areas away by light and lenses
- development, allowing the charged toner particles to come in contact with the photoconductor
- transfer, moving the toner to the paper
- fusing, making the toner adhere to the paper via a melting-cooling process

Subsequently, two more steps were added to the process:
- Photoreceptor cleaning
- Photoreceptor erase

In order to get a fair picture of how xerography works it is necessary to describe every step of the process and what their respective purposes are.

1. Photoconductor charging

   The first step in the xerographic process is the deposition of a uniform electrical charge on the photoconductor surface. This can be accomplished by a roller charging device or a corona discharge device. Corona discharge devices have the advantages of higher charging rates and more uniform charging but they have the disadvantage of emitting a lot of ozone which is a major environmental concern. The advantage of the roller charging devices are compactness and a significant reduction of chemical emissions and ultraviolet radiation. Most high-volume engines use corona discharge devices while low-volume engines more commonly use roller charging devices.

2. Latent image formation (exposure)

   The absorption of an image exposure by the photoconductor creates electron-hole pairs. Under influence of a field, a fraction of the pairs separate and are displaced to the free surface and the substrate electrode. The surface charge is thus dissipated in the exposed regions and an electrostatic charge pattern is created. For optical copiers, the image exposure is reflected from a document, then imaged onto the photereceptor through a lens. The source of radiation is usually a Xenon-filled lamp for flash exposures or a Halogen lamp for scan or continuous exposures. These lamps require that the photoreceptor have sensitivity throughout the visible light spectrum (400-700 nm). For digital xerography, the exposures are usually derived from a semiconductor laser or an array of light-emitting diodes. For digital xerography it is only necessary that the photoreceptor be receptive at the emission wavelength of the laser. Lasers operate in the infrared spectrum of light.

3. Image development

   In image development, charged toner particles are deposited on the photoreceptor surface. There are two main techniques used today. One is called charged-area-development (CAD) and the other is called discharged-area-development (DAD).

In CAD, toner particles are attracted to the charged areas of the photoreceptor. This requires that the polarity be the same as the photoreceptor surface. CAD processes are used in most optical copiers.

In DAD, the toner polarity is the same as the photoreceptor surface. As a result the toner particles are repelled from the charged areas of the photoreceptor (non-image area) and deposited in the discharged regions (image area). This requires the use of a development electrode with the same polarity as the photoreceptor surface potential. DAD is widely used in digital xerography. For these applications, it is preferable to expose the photoreceptor in regions that correspond to areas that will be toned in the final image, rather than expose the background areas, as in optical copiers.

Toner-based printing can be accomplished either by black-and-white or by colorant concentrations. For the black-and-white carbon black is used. In order to flow correctly, the toners are designed to have glass transition temperatures between 50° and 70° C. If the transition temperature is above this range, the energy required for fusing becomes excessive. Transition temperatures below this range result in keeping problems. In order to prevent adhesion to the fusing roller, low molecular weight waxes are frequently added. Toner particles are between 8 and 12 mm in diameter and produced by grinding or milling.

4. Toner transfer

In this step, toner particles are transferred from the photoreceptor to a receiver. The receiver or substrate is usually paper. The transfer is accomplished electrostatically. In electrostatic transfer, a receiver is placed in contact with the toned image. The free surface of the paper is then charged by a corona discharge with a polarity opposite to the toner particles. The paper is then separated from the photoreceptor. For efficient transfer, there must be intimate contact between the toned image and the paper. There is a limit to the extent to which this can be done. The maximum toner transfer efficiency rate is between 80 and 95%. The density of the transferred image will not be as high as the original. Toner transfer occurs when the forces on the toner due to the fields from the charge on the paper exceed the adhesion forces between the toner and the photoreceptor.

5. Image fusing

If image fusing is not done properly, the toner will eventually fall off. In order to render the image permanent it has to be fused. This can be accomplished by pressure, heat, radiation, or solvent fusing. Solvent fusing generally does not work well with a wide range of receivers and requires complex solvent entrapment equipment to avoid solvent emissions to the atmosphere. Cold-pressure processes are limited to low-volume applications and give lower image quality than hot-pressure processes. In radiant fusing, heat generated from a quartz lamp or heated coil is used to melt the toner into the paper. The basic limitation of radiant fusing is that the time required to heat the toner to the required temperature is such that the process is not amenable to high-process speeds.

Processes that involve combinations of heat and pressure are the most widely used. This is normally accomplished by hot-roll pressure devices in which at least one roll is heated with a quartz lamp. Offset of the toner to the fuser roll can be avoided by the use of special oils wicked onto the surface of the roll. Most roller fusing devices use heated rolls coated with silicone or fluorocarbon elastomers.

6. Photoreceptor cleaning

When toner particles are transferred from the photoreceptor to the receiver, some particles invariably remain and must be removed before the next image forming cycle. Adhesion of toner to the photoreceptor results from electrostatic and dispersion forces which must be overcome to separate the toner particles from the photoreceptor. Cleaning is one of the major factors that determines the photoreceptor process lifetime.

7. Photoreceptor erase

The purpose of the erase exposure is to remove any residual surface charges so that prior to the next process cycle the photoreceptor charge density is near zero, yet not in such a way that space charges are created.

Dry toner/liquid toner

When xerography started it used dry toner as charging material. Later on another technology was invented, called liquid toner electrophotography. It is very similar to xerography but the toner particles are dispersed in kerosene or a kerosene derivative such as isopar. The advantage of liquid toner is that the particles are very fine. Some of them are as small as 2 mm. By comparison, dry toner particles have a typical size of 10-12 mm. This affects the printer's ability to reproduce fine details.

The Xeikon digital press and Indigo E-Print 1000

The Xeikon digital press is a dry toner machine. It is based on the xerographic technology and uses laser diodes; the technology is called electrography. Electrography means writing with electricity. The Xeikon uses the paper as an insulator. The whole web of paper will be charged. The toner, which is charged too, will carry the same charge as the non-image areas (white) and the toner is then repelled (+ to +).

The laser's work is to repel the charge where the image area will be (+ to -). Doing it this way, the laser will only have to be on (DAD technology) when the image is "painted" and this prolongs the laser life. The particles of the toner are so fine that it seems to be liquid when shaking the toner bottle but it is not. This is one of the reasons that the Xeikon-quality is considered to be fairly close to traditional offset. Another reason for the quality is that the Xeikon is able to modulate the levels of the toner within one pixel (64 different levels in 1 pixel).

This press came on the market in 1993 and was revolutionary because it did not involve imagesetters and films, platemaking or assembly. It appeals to a different kind of print buyer that the graphic arts industry didn't have before. The quality of the Xeikon output is not quite as good as offset and it is based on short runs which was exactly what the "new" print-buyers were looking for. It supports variable data printing. You can personalize as much as your imagination is capable of.

Xeikon is web-fed; Indigo is sheet-fed. The Xeikon uses dry toner and the Indigo uses liquid toner. What this basically means is that the Xeikon is not able to print as many particles per inch/pixel as the Indigo. The Xeikon runs with a maximum of 600 dpi, while the Indigo has a maximum of 800 dpi. Some would say that 800 dpi is closer to offset, thus better quality.

Problems of digital machines

The technological challenge for all toner-based digital machines is keeping the toner on the sheet. The marketplace forces the manufacturers to produce faster machines producing better and better quality. The fusing of the toners on the paper (step 5) is the biggest issue because it is a give-and-take situation. At one point the speed of the toner-based machine must be fast but the toner also has to stick to the paper.

Limits of toner-based technology

With the technology we have today one would think that the maximum speed of paper reproduction is limitless. The fact is that there is a natural limit to how fast a piece of paper can be imaged. Within a laser printer there is a recording laser scanner, usually with a rotating polygon-shaped mirror and a laser. This is one of the areas that controls the speed of imaging because, unlike a printing press with a fixed image carrier, toner-based systems must re-image the page for every copy. This is good because it allows variable data printing and books on demand. It is bad because it essentially slows down reproduction.

The polygon

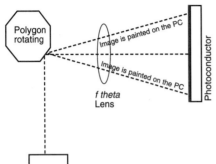

The laser can be turned off and on very rapidly and the rotating polygon mirror rotates very fast. The polygon has 8 facets or more and each facet paints one scanline horizontially. The polygon in modern printers rotates about 187.5 times per second or 11250 rpm. Rotating it any faster would distort the shape.

The laser can be switched on and off 7.2 million times per second in a 600 dpi printer. These numbers could potentially be altered but there is still the particle size to consider. There is a limit on how many pages you can print a minute. While speaking about pages a minute, it is worth mentioning that when the manufacturers say that their printer can produce 12 pages a minute, they mean 12 identical pages a minute from only one RIPped file. Its main purpose is to print out different pages every time, RIPping every page.

Toner-based laserwriting will be very hard to improve, because it will be hard making the polygon go any faster without distortion and it will be hard to turn the laser on and off any faster. One solution to more pages out per minute could be more facets on the polygon. Holograms are also used in laser writers today. A hologram is the same you see on your Visa card, for instance, but more focused.

The hologram has a bit more development to it and costs more than the polygon. Regarding advantages, the hologram does not tear itself apart in terms of speed. The technology still uses a laser and the photoconductor. The photoconductor in the Apple Laserwriter is located in the cartridge-box with the toner. This is why recycled cartridges might not be such a good idea because the photoconductor is used and may be scratched.

Chapter 13

TYPOGRAPHY & DESIGN

All pages and documents begin with basic design. No matter what reproduction technology is used, you must create and produce a cohesive layout that meets the needs of the product. Here are some simple rules:

1. Be consistent

Set up your document pages to the trim size of the final product. Use the same margins throughout the publication. Keep a consistent look to heads and subheads. Do not change typeface or size too much. Handle the various elements of graphic design within each page and within a publication consistently, especially in regard to placement of running headers and footers, folios, and rule lines.

2. Avoid dullness

Too much balance and symmetry can lead to boredom. Interrupted eye movement occurs when the reader's eyes are faced with too many equal-sized elements. Asymmetry adds interest to a page. Unequal left/right or top bottom balance helps provide movement— but don't make every page different.

3. Each page should have a dominant visual element

Provide a focal point for the reader's eyes as they travel through the page. This is not possible in book work or directories, but there are many types of publication, like catalogs, magazines, etc., that lend themselves to innovative layout.

4. Design facing pages

Concentrate your design efforts on two-page spreads so that pages work together. We view two pages at a time when we read. This is why many display-based systems have not been well accepted.

5. Create a grid

A grid consists of nonprinting horizontal and vertical lines which define the placement of graphic elements which make up a page. They form the basis of a publication's overall visual organization and consistency.

6. Standardize margins

Indent copy, headlines, titles, and page numbers the same distance from margins on all pages.

7. Use borders as frames

Frame your pages with appropriate white space. Use borders where appropriate. Use simple borders.

8. Organize text into columns

Select column widths appropriate to the size of type. Use wide columns for large type sizes and narrow columns for small type sizes.

9. Organize the page with horizonal or vertical rules

Rule weight should depend on how the rule relates to the copy and white space. Vertical rules separated columns in the old days; white space does it today. Use horizontal rules sparingly at half point weight.

10. Post sign posts

Running heads refer to information contained at the top of each page. Page numbers can be placed in the header or the footer (bottom of the page). Tell me where I am in the document.

11. Use type with personality—sparingly

Each typeface evokes a different feeling, speaks in a different tone of voice. The typeface you select for headlines, subheads, body copy, and captions affect the way readers experience your ideas. Use only a few but make them count.

12. Provide a strong flag or identifier

The flag is your publication's title set in a unique way. The flag is usually the dominant visual element on the first page of a publication.

13. Use dominant, descriptive headlines

Headlines determine the overall appearance by strengthening the message you want to communicate. Headlines must be large enough but must not overwhelm other page elements.

14. Let subheads provide transition

Subheads lead readers into the body copy. Subheads also break up long blocks of copy. Subheads make it easy to locate information.

15. Use captions to describe photographs and artwork

Captions should be set in smaller type, so they do not compete with the body copy. A little contrast goes a long way.

16. Use color to set elements apart

Use color to highlight borders, rules, or headlines. Color gains impact when it is used selectively.

17. Use big type to emphasize big ideas

Type size should reflect importance. Headlines should be larger than subheads. Subheads should be larger than body copy and body copy should be larger than caption and footnote size or weight.

18. Use type styles for emphasis

Add emphasis to copy by setting headlines, subheads, and body copy with different type styles.

19. Use white space as an element

White space emphasizes whatever it surrounds, so frame pages with white space.

20. Use tints and reverses for attention

Screen tints and reverses can be used to add interest to page elements without photographs or illustrations.

21. Focus ideas with graphics

Use photographs, illustrations, charts, and graphs to communicate ideas at a glance, and add visual variety. Graphics and images are now easier to use and therefore more common in documents.

22. Check text and layout

Always check your work. Make sure that nothing has been left out. Check names, addresses, and phone numbers. Check any word that begins with a capital letter. Check for graphic consistency and accuracy. And, never, ever, trust the spelling checker, but run it anyway.

Design elements

A critical design element involves fonts. Most graphic designers use PostScript fonts, which number over 100,000, or, in a few cases, they use TrueType fonts. What typefaces are right for the job? It depends on the job, your typographic sense, what you have available, and then what you do with those fonts. You must decide the fonts and point sizes for heads, subheads, text, page numbers, captions, footnotes, etc. Typeface choices must be balanced with decisions on point sizes, leading values, tracking, and line lengths.

Letterspacing is the amount of spacing between letters and it makes your job look professional as well as aiding readability. Negative or positive letterspacing between two letters is called kerning, and negative or positive letterspacing between more than two letters is called tracking. Your page layout application can handle letterspacing automatically, and most allow you to edit kerning pairs or tracking values by point size for a font.

PostScript and TrueType Fonts. The PostScript language defines the shapes of letterforms using a set of PostScript instructions that draws a series of straight lines and Bézier curves defining the outline of a character's shape—and then fills the area in black or a color. Each character is a PostScript program and a font is a collection of these programs.

Even with electronic technology there is still the need (especially with this book) to proofread and markup copy. Basic symbols are:

⊙	Period or full point
⋏ ⋌	Comma
⊨ /-/	Hyphen
ⵌ	Semicolon
⋎	Apostrophe
!/	Exclamation Mark
/en/ /N/	En Dash
/em/ /M/	Em Dash
(|)	Parentheses
⋎⋎ | ⋎⋎	Quotation Marks (Double)
⋎ | ⋎	Quotation Marks (Single)
≡	Align Horizontally
‖	Align Vertically
⊏	Move To The Left
⊐	Move To The Right
⌐	Move Matter Up
⌊⌋	Move Matter Down
✗ ⊠	Broken Letter
℟	Set In Lowercase
lc	Lowercase (In Margin)
∼∼∼	Set In Boldface Type
Bf	Boldface Type (In Margin)
≡	Capitalize Material
cap	Capitalization (In Margin)
___	Set In Italic Type
ital	Italics (In Margin)
∧ ∨	Caret
#	Insert Space
hr#	Insert Hair Space
☐	Indent One Em Space
σ	Delete Or Take Out
σ̄	Delete And Close Up Space
⌣	Close Up
⟨?⟩	Query To Author
.....	Let Indicated Material Remain As It Is
stet	Let It Stand (In Margin)
⊔ ∩	Transpose Material
tr	Transpose (In Margin)

When a PostScript interpreter processes a Type 1 font, it reads these instructions and renders the type font bitmap according to the resolution of the output device. Thus one page with its fonts can be output at the resolution of the output device, whatever it might be.

TrueType is the font method developed by Microsoft and Apple as an alternative to PostScript fonts, back when both companies were worried about the dominance of Adobe Systems in the font arena. Microsoft adopted TrueType for use starting with Windows 3.1. You can use PostScript or TrueType fonts in your jobs on either PC or Mac platforms, but it is not recommended that you mix them in the same job. PostScript uses complex rasterization and simple hints; TrueType uses simple rasterization and complex hints.

Font issues

Most graphic designers have at least 300 fonts. Some prepress operations and service bureaus have 3,000 or more fonts. When you have more than 50 fonts, including the standard 35 that come with every Mac and PC, you need some way of managing those fonts. For every PostScript font you purchase, you need:

- a screen version of the font
- a printer version of the font

TrueType combines both versions into one file. The computer and the printer use different methods for displaying and printing the font, respectively. The computer monitor uses individual pixels to represent each character, so it requires a bitmap version of the font to display. This screen font contains outlines that have been rasterized for the resolution of the computer screen. Printer fonts, whether PostScript or TrueType format, contain outline descriptions of the characters. The characters in printer fonts can be scaled to any size. Screen fonts do not scale easily. Once, font manufacturers created screen fonts using the most commonly used point sizes: 8, 9, 10, 12, 14, 18, and 24 point. If you needed a different size, the computer used the closest size and tried to scale it. Scaling a bitmap doesn't work as well as scaling an outline (as the printer does). Scaled bitmap screen fonts are almost impossible to read.

Chapter 14

THE FUTURE OF COMMUNICATIONS

The never-ending cycle of change

First you make semiconductor chips that can calculate faster and faster. New techniques bring the cost of manufacture down and thus everything that can use computerization does.

You then increase clock speed to keep the chip humming along. You now have a very fast computer that can process picture or color data with blazing speed.

All that data needs a place to go so storage technology advances, letting you store more and more data in smaller and smaller areas. This goes for internal magnetic disks as well as new kinds of removable disk storage.

Since you can process and store all this information very quickly you will want to see it in all its glory. This leads to bigger and more color-accurate screens. It even means flatter, lighter, cheaper screens as well. This not only affects computer displays but TVs.

But you still need to get data or deliver data so modem speeds accelerate. Modems are only the tip of the telecommunications iceberg and this leads to new network capabilities and new data communications approaches, especially for connection to the Internet.

Then you want hardcopy at some point. This leads to new lasers for laser printers and other approaches to print, all communicating with your computer through high-speed links.

Software advances to take advantage of all this computing power, developing new functions that test the limits of the hardware.

Which is why new chips are developed to keep up with new software and new systems. And the cycle starts all over again.

Technology is running rampant

It all started with the transistor and Moore's Law. In 1965, Intel cofounder Gordon Moore predicted transistor density on microprocessors would double every 12 months. This prediction, so far, has proven amazingly accurate with minor revisions to the number of months. Whether densities double every 12, 18 or 24 months, their progression is still remarkable by any standard. The advancement from 2,300 transistors with 20-micron features to chips with 10 million transistors at .18-micron features is the stuff of technological legend. But things are changing.

Every day sees announcements of new technological wonders. They clearly demonstrate that the tools of information technology will become more ubiquitous, more powerful, and, above all, more cost-effective.

The seven pillars of new technology

1. New semiconductor technology

Chips are packing more transistors that run at higher speed, at lower cost. These are the building blocks of the computer age.

2. New display technology

Displays are getting bigger—with more color accuracy—thinner, and lighter. This will affect your computer display and your home television. High definition digital TV is coming fast.

3. New storage technology

Disks are packing more data in less space at less cost. We have moved from kilobytes (thousands) to megabytes (millions) to gigabytes (billions) and terabytes (trillions) are on the horizon.

4. New modem technology

Telecommunications is getting easier. Modems have broken the 56 Kbps speed limit. However, new approaches to connection, such as ASDL, may obviate the need for a modem altogether.

5. New Internet capability

The net is getting more bandwidth to support more data at higher speed and more users. There is already a second Internet for high-level research academics and the next generation Internet is being specified right now.

6. New laser technology

New lasers will enable other areas of technology, such as data storage and toner-based printing. Smaller spots mean higher density of data and higher resolution of output.

7. New network technology

New network technology is accelerating data transfers among linked computers. Private networks are evolving in the quest for ultra high-speed interconnection.

All of these technologies are inter-related and are evolving into a new world for information technology.

World's tiniest transistor, or "nanotransistor"

An experimental "nanotransistor" is four times smaller, five times faster, and draws 60 to 160 times less power than today's transistors. The achievement paves the way for powerful new integrated circuits that pack many billions of transistors on a single silicon chip, as opposed to the millions on today's chips. In microelectronics, chip features are measured in microns, or millionths of a meter; in nanoelectronics, chip features will be measured in nanometers, or billionths of a meter. Such a transistor could mean additional capabilities, longer battery life because of less power consumption for consumer electronics, and less weight for products like portable computers.

Clock outputs up to 160 MHz

A new clock multiplier Integrated Circuit (IC) designed to replace crystal oscillators in electronic system designs, called the Low Cost Oscillator, or LOCO, generates high-accuracy clock outputs up to 160 MHz from a lower frequency crystal input, at a cost below $1. It enables electronics designers to say goodbye to can-type oscillators.

Superfast "wonder chips"

IBM will begin manufacturing semiconductor chips that are smaller and up to 40% more powerful than advanced chips currently produced. A new manufacturing process is 20% to 30% less expensive than current methods. For 30 years, chip makers etched aluminum circuits on silicon wafers. Most semiconductor chips available today contain transistors that are 0.35 micron wide but the advanced ones have circuits with a width of 0.25 micron. At 0.20 micron, or about one five-hundredth the width of a human hair, aluminum begins to slow the chips down and can't conduct enough electricity to make these circuits fast enough.

Copper is a much better conductor, but up to now, when chip makers used it, the metal bled into the silicon, contaminating the chip. Intel, which has been trying to develop copper chips, does not expect to market them until 2002. IBM's new copper chips will appear as mainframe computer chips and PowerPC chips for IBM computers as well as the Macintosh. These new chips will run at speeds as fast as one gigahertz, compared to the fastest microprocessors, now way beyond 300 megahertz. Eventually, all semiconductors will go to copper.

1000 MHz microprocessor

An experimental microprocessor that can run at 1000 megahertz (MHz) is about double the speed of today's fastest commercial chips. The design and circuits will eventually be applied to chips using "copper chip" technology. The first use of copper technology on a product-level design is in a 750 MHz chip in a PowerPC line of processors.

IBM disk drive technology

IBM has made a major step forward for data storage. Most disk drive improvements involve shrinking the area needed to store individual bits of data. But as those areas become smaller, more sensitive devices are needed to read the data. New heads, called Giant Magnetoresistive (GMR) heads, which boost storage density on drive platters to over 10 billion bits per square inch, are based on a scientific effect discovered in 1988. The first drive to deploy the new technology will set a density record with about 2.7 billion bits per square inch.

New drives will hold 16.8 gigabytes of data, or 8 hours of full-motion video. Other drives offer 14.4 Gb of high-speed storage at pricing from $275 for a 3.2 Gb drive to $895 for 16.8 Gb. Intel and Hewlett-Packard have even faster chips.

Intel and Hewlett-Packard have a project to design a new chip—codenamed Merced. Set for release within the next two years, it would mark the most significant shift in the history of the popular Intel microprocessor family, which began in 1979 with the Intel 8088 chip that powered the first IBM PC and has continued through Intel's latest, the Pentium II. The Merced would use an "instruction set" radically different from the one in Intel microprocessors.

The instruction set, etched into the chip's circuitry, comprises hundreds of basic operations, like adding, subtracting, multiplying and moving, which all other components and software in the computer depend upon.

Changing the instruction set for personal computing is creating a new alphabet—with all the potential for spelling errors and communication breakdowns. That change, on top of the perhaps seven-fold increase in the number of transistors packed onto the surface of the chip, portends a greater transformation in the computer industry in the next five years than in the preceding 25 years.

The first Intel personal computer chip in 1979 had 30,000 transistors; the most recent Pentium II has more than 7 million. When it arrives, the Merced is expected to contain 20 million to 50 million transistors. And the chip will probably have a basic clock speed of almost 1,000 megahertz—more than twice the performance of today's fastest chips. The Merced will be a 64-bit microprocessor—compared with the 32-bit limit of the current Intel Pentium. It will process twice as much information at once, for faster and complex searches of databases and more realistic audio and video multimedia capabilities.

The PC chip that represents an alternative to the Intel standard—the PowerPC used in the Apple Macintosh—has an uncertain future. Work on the next-generation PowerPC by a team of developers from Apple Computer, IBM, and Motorola has stalled. The Merced's designers must figure out how to insure that the chip's new instruction set will be able to read and run the thousands of existing MS-DOS and Windows software programs written for Intel's older family of chips—or risk having 80% of the world's existing PCs rendered obsolete. Computer designers expect the new Merced to be something of a silicon chameleon—able to adapt to and handle many different types of software written for other computer-chip instruction sets, whether for older Intel chips or competing hardware.

Paper-thin LCD

The Japanese electronics firms Sharp and the Semiconductor Energy Laboratory have developed liquid crystal display (LCD) technology that will make possible the development of literally paper-thin displays. The technology, called continuous grain silicon (CGS), would allow the development of a large glass panel that incorporates LCD drivers and thin-film-transistor LCD displays. It also allows LCD displays and chips to be manufactured by the same process. This would enable the development of high-speed multimedia terminals, including personal computers and credit-card-sized communications tools, formed on a single glass sheet of any size. The CGS panel can also produce high-resolution images because of high electron mobility, where electrons travel through semiconductors in LCDs about 600 times faster than they do in amorphous silicon. Thin Film Transistor (TFT) LCDs are widely used. Sharp used the technology to develop a 60-inch video projector, incorporating LCD drivers with a speed of 13.8 MHz, the industry's fastest.

High-resolution color flat panel display

A spinoff off from Xerox Corporation called dpiX has developed a 19-inch diagonal, high-resolution color flat-panel display it says will compete with bulky 20- and 21-inch professional computer screens. dpiX said its new display is the largest active-matrix liquid crystal display made in North America and provides sharper, clearer distortion-free images than existing monitors while using less power and space. The liquid crystal display will be initially targeted for use in professional markets such as high-end graphics and pre-press printing. The displays are now available in sample units for less than $10,000. The worldwide market for cathode ray tube (CRT) monitors is some 80 million a year, while workstation displays of the large 19–21 inch format are about two million a year. 21% of monitors on the desktop will be liquid crystal display monitors by the year 2003, up from the present less than 1%. The latest screen provides a two-page viewing area and can support full-frame video at 30 frames per second. Xerox spun off the company as part of its New Enterprise program.

New TVs

Mitsubishi Consumer Electronics America Inc. will stop marketing tube-based television sets in the US to concentrate on projection, digital, and flat-panel units. They will become the first major manufacturer to devote all resources to advanced sets and abandon the screen technology that has been standard since the invention of TV in the 1920s. Mitsubishi is a top seller of projection units, the most lucrative and fastest-growing niche of the TV business, representing 917,000 of the 24.5 million sets sold in the US last year. The ultra-clear digital transmissions just beginning from broadcasters are best experienced on larger screens. The company will begin selling a 73-inch rear-projection TV that displays high-definition digital signals at a price between $8,000 and $11,000. Its 80-inch rear-projection analog TV costs $9,000. Mitsubishi is betting that plasma-technology-based flat TVs, just a few inches thick, will succeed small direct-view TVs when costs fall. They just started selling a $10,000, 40-inch flat TV.

Plastic TV

Cambridge Display Technology unveiled the world's first plastic TV display which could eventually see the demise of the standard television set. The Cambridge, England-based company in which Intel has a minority stake has developed light-emitting polymer (LEP) technology, which it calls "plastic that glows." CDT hopes this thin, flexible LEP technology will lead to the production of flat panel display screens and ultimately be an alternative to the cathode ray tube.

New 8-bit column driver expands color depth

Vivid Semiconductor Inc. introduced the first commercially available 8-bit column driver to provide true-color depth to notebook computers. The new integrated circuit is designed with an innovative combination of the company's patented extended voltage range architecture and charge conservation technology to produce more than 16 million colors while actually reducing liquid crystal display (LCD) power consumption. It is optimized to support full motion display video for active-matrix resolutions.

The 8-bit driver employs a patented extended voltage range architecture that enables the integrated circuit to accommodate higher voltages than are normally associated with standard digital processing. Using this technology allows the combination of 9.6V dynamic range and 8-bit resolution that gives TFT LCD displays the best viewing characteristics. The IC enables 256 distinct voltages per output to provide more than 16 million colors on a TFT display. The new IC is designed for direct-drive

LCDs using pixel inversion. By applying the new charge conservation technology, power consumption drops to 37 milliwatts per driver and 296 milliwatts per XGA panel. This enables the highest available image quality while reducing power consumption.

New blue laser technique

A new short wave blue laser technique will revolutionize many electronic products. The color of laser light corresponds to the size of its wavelength, from blues at the shorter end of the spectrum to red at the long end. Different laser devices require different wavelengths. Disc players currently use infrared lasers but would work better with wavelengths as blue as possible, as would other electronic products.

Light at the blue end of the spectrum allows for denser data storage. The new laser is a gallium nitride blue light semiconductor laser that operates at room temperature. The laser lasts for up to 3,000 hours, with a potential of 10,000 hours. This now reaches the realm of commercial application, where lifetimes of 10,000 to 20,000 hours are required.

Scientists at the Xerox Palo Alto Research Center (PARC) have generated a blue diode laser beam for a new generation of high-speed, and high-quality laser printers. Scientists have been working to create light-emitting diodes (LEDs) and laser diodes that operate in the blue to green region of the visible spectrum, where the shorter wavelength of the beam results in a two-fold increase in printing resolution. The spot diameter of a blue laser is half that of an infrared laser—critical for color laser printing, where accurate spot placement and size control are necessary.

Modems that handle up to 56,000 bits of data per second

You may find free 56K modems inside Crackerjack boxes because of ADSL, or Asymmetric Digital Subscriber Line. ADSL modems can download millions of data bits per second over a standard phone line. There's no need for a second line, because you can download and talk at the same time. ADSL had been too expensive and complicated, but soon an ADSL modem will sell for about $300 and let you receive data from the Net at up to 1.5 million bits per second. Sending is slower at 512,000 bits per second. Major computer and telephone companies will announce a plan to make ADSL an international standard. Look for built-in G.Lite modems in PCs, and expect telephone companies to offer ADSL Internet access for $40 a month. Microsoft, Intel, and Compaq are spearheading the effort.

ADSL is not new, but it's taken years to prepare it for the mass market. Telephone companies don't want a repeat of the fiasco with ISDN, a hot prospect in digital communications that tops out at 128,000 bps. The Internet boom spurred high demand for ISDN lines but many phone companies couldn't keep up, and consumers suffered through problems and delays. Traditional ADSL systems require a "splitter" device to separate voice and data signals. Before deploying ADSL, somebody had to lick the installation problem and make new ADSL devices work like a standard modem—just plug it in the phone outlet. ADSL will make all of us rethink the way we communicate.

There'll be no more busy signals, because ADSL sidesteps the traditional phone switch. You'll never disconnect an ADSL modem—it stays on line all the time. There'll be less reason to copy files from the Net—just bookmark the data, and return to the site at blazing speed whenever you want. A 1.5 megabit T1 line costs about $1,000 a month. The phone companies will lose that market when ADSL rolls out. ADSL devices that run at 8 megabits per second are next. Several local telephone companies have already deployed ADSL in limited areas with an installation fee of about $200 and a monthly fee of abut $40 and will deliver higher speeds than 1.5 million bits a second. Modems cost about $150, while access to the Internet costs $20 a month.

1Mbps digital modem technology goes beyond K56flex modems

A new technology for modems can be priced, sold and installed much like popular V.34 and K56flex modems, yet offer data transfer speeds that are 10 to 20 times faster. Rockwell's Consumer Digital Subscriber Line (CDSL) modem technology offers 1Mbps. Consumer DSL may represent the next logical step after K56flex modems. Internet users are starving for more bandwidth so they are working on the next Internet connectivity breakthrough even as K56flex modems are establishing their place in the market. We will see a seamless transition from 56 Kbps PCM modems to this next higher-speed technology.

Once telephone companies adopt the new technology they will offer the next performance progression after K56flex modems, although these will remain ubiquitous for a number of years. Rockwell will deliver CDSL modems which incorporate all existing modem modulations, such as K56flex and V.34, to provide broad global interoperability. Although similar to industry-standard Discrete Multitone (DMT) ADSL technology, CDSL can be implemented more easily because it operates at a lower 1Mbps data rate. CDSL eliminates the ADSL "splitter" equipment and associated wiring that phone companies previously had to install to separate POTS (Plain Old Telephone Service) and ADSL frequencies. CDSL modems are simply plugged into telephone outlets just as conventional modems are.

	To CPU Kbps	From CPU Kbps	Cost per month
ADSL Lite /CDSL	384–1500	384–512	$40–100
ADSL	144–1500	128–1100	$40–200
Cable modem	800–3000	33.6	$30–60
T1	1544	1544	$1200
Satellite dishes	200–400	33.6	$20–130

Faster Internet

Personal computer makers have joined with local telephone companies to enable consumers to receive Internet data over regular telephone lines at speeds much higher than currently possible. The formation of the new group is a significant early move in what promises to be a years-long battle between telephone and cable television companies for control of how consumers get high-speed access to the Internet and its successors. The companies have teamed with GTE and with four of the five Bell telephone companies to set technical standards for the next generation of access to cyberspace at speeds up to 30 times faster than today's fastest modems.

Pages that now take minutes to load would appear on a computer's screen almost instantly. The products envisioned by the consortium would essentially be new modems. They would plug into normal telephone lines but would remain connected at all times without the need to dial a service and without interfering with voice conversations over the same line. Such access has traditionally been possible only in offices or over cable modems, which are available in few parts of the US. The technology, known as digital subscriber line, or DSL, has been under development for years but has been held back by a lack of agreement on technical standards.

Bell Atlantic is leaning toward a non-standard sort of DSL. As computer users have become more sophisticated and as the Internet has become loaded with graphics, traditional modems have not kept pace. The result is often long delays. The cable television industry is pinning some of its hopes on cable modems, which access the Internet using the cable network. Only about 100,000 people have signed up for cable modems and the service is available to only about 10% of the nation's homes. People with a need for speed online today can often order high-speed data lines from their local telephone company. But many of those options are cumbersome and expensive.

Some engineers think that standard copper telephone wires can carry as many as 8 million bits of information a second, though the consortium is initially developing standards for modems that can carry only 1.5 million bits a second. A bit is the smallest amount of information a computer can process, either a zero or a one. Today's fastest standard modems are rated at 56,000 bits per second but are actually limited to 52,000 bps.

The Next Generation Internet (NGI) will transform today's slow and sometimes unreliable Internet into a multimedia superhighway from its present one-lane highway with unlimited access. The members of Internet 2, who are working on NGI, hope the NGI will solve this and related problems of handling huge volumes of information at speeds 100 to 1,000 times faster than the current Internet can handle. In development since 1996 but formally organized in late 1997, the Internet 2 consortium is now laying the foundation. They will begin testing new applications, most focused on educational needs. This means developing more complex routing and switching systems and expanding their inherent capacity. NGI will push the state of the art to deal with hundreds of billions, then trillions of bits per second.

Private networks

Major corporations—like Microsoft and Apple Computer, whose publicly tout the we-are-one-world web philosophy—are increasingly relying on their own, private network entryways, called Private Network Access Points (PNAPs), for on-line access. Maintaining private network access points—which cost thousands of dollars per month—lets companies avoid the most congested public Internet trafficways. Where there once was one Internet, there are now two: one for the classes, and another for the masses.

The technical performance of the web has "degraded" by 4.5% since last spring. Meanwhile, traffic at Internet access points like MAE East and MAE West—like cloverleaf ramps that link different highways—is frequently snarled. To maintain acceptable performance, Internet backbone providers continually monitor the traffic of the Net and change their routing assignments through new peering agreements. The average speed that content traveled on the Internet was just 5,000 characters per second, or only 40 kbps.

If the U.S. had just one Internet network, the system would work without a hitch. But it doesn't: What we know as the Internet is made up of networks from more than 47 different Internet-backbone providers located in the U.S. alone, and some 4,300 Internet-service providers connect users to those networks. The result is the average Internet transaction—from server to user—ends up crossing at least three transit points between networks. Most backbone providers are very good at running their own networks, but they don't make routing decisions based on the performance that end-users will receive. The result can be Internet clogged arteries as information bogs down.

That's where the PNAPs come into play. Corporate customers can't tolerate delays. So they're working with companies which are creating dozens of private network access nodes all over the world. These private networks link—or in Internet lingo, peer—directly with backbones run by the likes of MCI, AT&T and Sprint, without having to link to the public MAE points. With the new PNAPs, experts claim, switching of Internet traffic will be much more efficient, virtually eliminating the congestion that often delays message delivery.

The PNAPs are being designed to effectively and optimally broker the connectivity between all things local and all things global. They are extensively multi-homed, not just into two or three upstream backbones, like a local Internet service provider would do, but actually to the eight major backbones simultaneously. That gives users the ability to connect to the networks that comprise 90% of the global routes on the network. Last year, Apple switched all of its networking operations at its Austin, Texas, site over to a PNAP; this spring, the company plans a similar switch for Internet operations at its Cupertino, CA headquarters. The percentage of corporate customers that demand improved broadband services will increase in the coming year to 60% from 15%.

Just adding routers and modems isn't going to do it. A fleet of venture-capital firms including Hambrecht & Quist, Vulcan Ventures, PS Capital and Kirlan Venture Capital recently underwrote a $20 million investment in InterNAP, which plans to roll out new routing technologies it is patenting to 35 to 40 major metro markets internationally within the next few years.

The other Internet

A new Internet is available, although access is still strictly limited and its users tend to be astrophysicists, engineers, medical researchers and other specialists. It is the second-generation Internet, which about 100 U.S. computer scientists are using in preference to the old network they invented just decades ago.

The new network, called the Very-High-Performance Backbone Network Service, is sponsored by the National Science Foundation and built by MCI using some of its existing fiber-optic networks. It is a giant, 14,000-mile figure 8 that links the nation's five academic supercomputer centers.

The CPU advances

With the introduction around the millennium of Intel's next generation P7 microprocessor, with about 10 million transistors, the company will have fallen hopelessly behind even the 18-month cycle, which predicts nearly 170 million components in 2000, much less the 2.2 trillion predicted by Moore's original equation. One of the surest signs of the law's demise is the revisionism of Moore's Law to maintain its illusion of truth. On an Intel Web page celebrating the company's 25th anniversary, Moore's Law changed from a 12-month cycle to a 24-month cycle.

There are barriers now that are so difficult to surmount that advancement from this point on will only come at an enormous price. The end point of the great rush towards the frontier is still decades away. One of the main hurdles looming years into the future is trying to strike the .10 micron point in microprocessor design. Smaller etchings mean that you can pack more components into a tighter space, and these higher densities result in greater speed.

The problem is that getting below .10 microns will require a shift to exotic light sources with extremely high frequencies, like X-rays. It can be done, but every advancement comes at an exponential increase in the equipment costs. Intel's latest fabrication plant in Arizona for .25 micron chips cost $1.5 billion. Moore's Law has been replaced by Rock's Law, named after an Intel board member, Arthur Rock, who observed that the cost of semiconductor fabrication equipment doubles every four years.

The future of visual communications is based on the way we capture, store, display, process and communicate information. The underlying technology infrastructure is changing rapidly.

You can see that computer chips, storage technology, display technology, and information delivery technology are all advancing. The very nature of the publishing industry will change as a result of these advancements. This will also impact printing as we know it as more people have more access to electronic technology for creating and delivering information.

Index

A

AAP. *See* Association of American Publishers
Ablation technology. *See also* Laser printer
  for flexographic plate, 147
  for proofs, 59
Ablative recording, 222
Absorption. *See also* Paper; Substrate
  by substrate, 153
Academic Licensing Service (ALS), 467
Additives. *See also* Ink; Toner
  in ink, 115
Addressability, image quality and, 84-85
Adhesives. *See also* Bindery; Books
  for binding books, 351, 352, 353, 354
  solvent migration affecting, 353
Adobe Acrobat. *See also* Portable Document Format
  for on-demand publishing, 135, 563, 564-568
Adobe Acrobat Distiller, 237, 422-423, 424, 568
  "addPS" plug-in, 424
  Text Touchup add-on, 566
Adobe Acrobat Reader, 237
Adobe Extreme, 396, 437
Adobe Framemaker, 42, 382
Adobe Illustrator, 32, 198, 250, 254, 257, 382
  trapping tools in, 42, 156, 424
Adobe PageMaker, 42, 43, 256, 257, 396, 419, 573-574
Adobe PhotoShop, 32, 37, 39, 161, 198, 240, 247, 250, 254, 257, 294, 310, 311, 314, 335, 482
Adobe PostScript. *See* PostScript
ADSL/SDSL. *See* Asymmetric/Symmetric Digital Subscriber Line
Advertisements
  commercial impact of, 497, 592
  digital standards for, 421-422
  first known printing of, 11
  formatting for, 41
  in magazines, 480
  paper requirements, 372
Advertising agency, production role of, 187-188
Agfa Apogee, 437
Agfa Calibrator, 161
Agfa Chromapress, 27, 133, 415
Agfa Total Film Scanning technology, 308
Alphabet, 3
ALS. *See* Academic Licensing Service
Aluminum, lithography plates of, 13, 98
AM. *See* Amplitude Modulation
AM Varityper, 23
Amazon.com, 493
American National Standards Institute (ANSI), 516
American Standard Code for Information Interchange (ASCII),
  character sets, 181, 517, 562, 565
Amplitude Modulation (AM), compared to Frequency Modulation
  (FM), 77, 78, 79
Anilox roller. *See also* Flexography
  in flexographic printing, 116, 141, 164
  characteristics of, 142-143
ANSI. *See* American National Standards Institute
Apple computer. *See also* Macintosh
  LaserWriter printer for, 21
  origins of, 19, 306
AppleTalk, 409-410, 429, 430
APR. *See* Automatic Picture Replacement
Art. *See also* Computer-ready art; Design; Graphics
  characteristics of, 2, 15-16
  digital conversion of, 34-25
  scanners for, 322
Art creation
  analog, 32
  by illustrator, 190-191
  digital, 32-33
  recommendations for, 249-252
Artists. *See also* Creative professionals
  knowledge requirements for, 30
ASCII. *See* American Standard Code for Information Interchange
Association of American Publishers (AAP), 470, 473
  PUBNET, 474-475
Asymmetric/Symmetric Digital Subscriber Line (ADSL/SDSL),
  described, 404, 615-616, 617
Asynchronous Transfer Mode (ATM), described, 405

ATM. *See* Asynchronous Transfer Mode
.AU file format, 525-526, 553
Authoring tools
  for multimedia, 501-503
  for variable input document, 575
Authors, role in publishing, 456, 457
Autologic, 23
Automatic Picture Replacement (APR), 454

B

Babylon, 4
Back-edge curl, 378
Backup. *See also* Storage
  recommendations for, 80, 217-224
Badger, Robert, 471
Bag
  caliper of, 154
  printing on, 138
Baghdad (Iraq), 2
Banding, 587
Bar code printing, 111. *See also* Label printing
  recommendations for, 164
Basis weight. *See also* Paper
  of paper, 172, 344
BCM. *See* Billion Cubic Microns
Bearer bars, 164
Bergman, Folke, 5
Billboard printing, 113. *See also* Wide-format printing
Billion Cubic Microns (BCM), cell volume measurement with,
  142-143
Binary data, 51, 180
Bindery. *See also* Books; Finishing; Magazines
  cover stock concerns, 173, 351, 352
  creep and lap considerations, 355
  hardcover
    building-in, 358
    casemaking, 357
    casing-in, 358
    channel binding, 361
    hole drilling, 360
  in-line
    and off-line finishing, 359
    perfect binding, 361
    saddle stitching, 361
    stapling, 359
  inserting, 357
  lay-flat capability, 352, 353, 355
  layout considerations for, 256
  mechanical
    channel binding, 361
    comb binding, 360
    tape binding, 360-361
    wire coil binding, 360
  on-demand digital, 358-359
  Otabind process, 353
  paper characteristics affecting, 174
  perfect binding, 174, 351, 352
    allowances for, 354
    in-line, 361
    vs. saddle stitching, 355-356
  RepKover process, 353
  role in publishing, 457
  saddle stitching, 354-355, 363, 365
    in-line, 361
    vs. perfect binding, 355-356
  sewing
    side sewing, 350
    Smyth sewing, 351
  side stitching, 359
  solvent migration affecting, 353-354
  tipping, 357
Bit, described, 60, 61, 75, 180, 297, 580
Bit depth, defined, 62, 63, 75, 315
Bitmap, 577, 579, 580
  bi-level, 577, 579-580
  compared to bytemap, 62
  described, 182
  file extensions for, 182
  RIP generation of, 44, 45, 48, 51, 606
Bitmap files

  described, 228-229, 577
  file formats for, 243
Bitmapped images, 62
  creation of, 319
Black bodies, relation to viewing conditions, 295-296
Black ink, 115, 273, 288, 380. *See also* Ink; Toner
Black pigment, 4
Bleed, causes, 586
Bleeds, recommendations for, 165, 354
Blends. *See* Vignettes
Blocking, 178, 378
Blue line, imposition proof as, 38
.BMP file extension, 182
Books. *See also* Bindery; Finishing; Intellectual property; Paper
  cover stock for, 173, 351, 352, 372
  distribution of, 457-458, 461-462
  educational, 473-475
  finishing and bindery concerns, 174
  illustrations in, 15
  Internet marketing of, 493-494
  origins of, 6-7
  paper requirements, 372
  qualities of, 455-459, 462-463, 496
Bridge, in network, 431
Bruce, David, 17
Bubble forming recording, 223
Bubble-jet printer, 114
Buddhist prints, 6, 7
Burt, W.A., 16
Business, multimedia applications for, 504
Business forms. *See also* Forms
  paper requirements, 373
Byte, described, 62, 180, 297
Bytemap, compared to bitmap, 62

C

Cables for network computers, 415-416
Cache memory, relation to performance, 208
CalComp Crystal Jet, 584
Calendaring, effect on opacity, 176
Caliper. *See* Paper; Substrate
  of substrate, 154, 173
Callout file, 427
Camera-ready art, 23
Canon CLC-1000, 133
Canvas, 3-4
Carli, Don, 278
Carlson, Chester F., 125, 128-129, 582, 592-593, 594
Cast removal, procedures for, 40, 301
Catalogs
  inks for, 120
  paper requirements, 373
  printing processes for, 138
Cathode ray tube (CRT). *See also* Monitor
  in film recorder, 114
  in monitor, 225-226
Catholicon, 10
Cave drawings, 2
Caxton, William, 11
CCC. *See* Copyright Clearance Center
CCD. *See* Charge-coupled device
CD-E, 220-221
CD-ROM. *See also* Digital video disk
  for audio, 312
  discussed, 485, 486, 487, 489-490, 505-506, 514-516
  for magazines, 484
  on-line publishing and, marketplace considerations, 488-490
  for storage and backup, 82-83, 217, 220-221, 514
.CDR file format, 243
CDSL. *See* Consumer Digital Subscriber Line
Cells Per Inch (CPI), in anilox roller, 142
CEPS. *See* Color Electronic Prepress System
CERN. *See* European Council for Nuclear Research
CGATS. *See* Committee for Graphics Arts Technologies
.CGM file format, 243
Chalking, 179, 378
Charge-coupled device (CCD). *See also* Digital photography;
  Scanners
  in digital camera, 180, 339-340
  in scanner, 36, 307, 309, 311, 314, 317-319, 322, 323-324, 325

Checks, paper requirements, 373
China, printing origins in, 5, 6-7, 8
Choke plate. *See also* Trapping
   application of, 145
Chroma, defined, 269
CIELAB color, discussed, 273-274, 276, 303
CIP3. *See* International Cooperation for Integration of Prepress, Press, and Postpress
Cities, publishing in, 2
ClarisDraw, 32
Cleanliness
   for flexographic process, 149-150
   for photographic processes, 53
   print defects and, 119, 294-295
   for printing paper, 175
CMS. *See* Color management system
CMYK image. *See also* Color printing; RGB image
   Big Gamut CMYK, 278-279
   characteristics of, 180, 254, 256, 257, 264, 276, 303, 311
   discussed, 272-273
Color. *See also* Hue
   control fields, 447
   design considerations for, 193, 603
   in digital workflow, 439
   in general, 259-262, 299
Color bars, for registration, 367
Color casts, affecting highlights, 330
Color correction. *See also* Tone correction
   fine-field, 335
   general, 334
   issues in, 298
   procedure for, 282-284, 332-333
   scanner controls for, 334
   selective, 334-335
   steps in, 286-287, 301-302
   3-6-9 rule for, 301
Color depth, of monitors, 213
Color Electronic Prepress System (CEPS), file formats, 227, 232, 382
Color management, discussed, 385
Color management system (CMS), discussed, 428-429
Color matching systems, 274-276
Color printing. *See also* CMYK image; Four-color process; Halftone dots; RGB image
   bitmaps for, 45
   in desktop publishing, 56
   flexographic, 144-145
   high-fidelity, 162
   with laser printer, 59
   origins of, 14
Color reproduction theory. *See also* CMYK image; RGB image
   additive and subtractive color, 263-265, 272, 283
   color imaging systems, 266-268
   color viewing requirements, 276, 277
   gamuts, 268
   Munsell system, 268-271
Color separation. *See also* Desktop Color Separation; Four-color process
   black plate selections and, 299
   dot gain compensation and, 161
   golden rules for, 298
   memory colors affecting, 285-287
   procedures for, 23, 337
   proofs for, 44
   role in prepress, 43, 304, 310-311, 335
   screen angles for, 71-73
   Total Area Coverage (TAC) value selection, 337
Color separators, desktop publishers and, 25-26
Color space, discussed, 268-271
Color viewing requirements
   effect on print quality, 295-296
   human factor affecting, 296-297
   influence of artwork borders, 297
   light source adjustment, 297, 303
   light source for, 277, 296, 303
   theory for, 276, 277
Color-Atlas, 278
Colorants. *See also* Ink
   in ink, 115
Colorimeters, 87
Columns, halftone dots in, 75

Committee for Graphics Arts Technologies (CGATS), SC6 digital standard, 421
Communication history, 1-2
Communications
   confluence in, 555-556
   expanding opportunities in, 487
   future of, 607-622
   networks and, 429-432
   on paper, 563
Compact discs. *See* CD-ROM
Company reports, paper requirements, 373-374
Component files, 382
Comprehensive, description and purpose, 38
Compression. *See* File compression; Tone compression
Compugraphic, 23
Computer science, 195
Computer-ready art, designing, 253-254
Computer-To-Plate (CTP). *See also* Digital printing; Direct to press; Direct-to-plate
   description and use, 53-54
   imposetter use in, 27
   RIP and, 48, 49, 307, 392
   stochastic screening and, 79
Computers. *See also* Digital printing; Monitors; Networks; Software; Storage
   business applications, 496
   hardware, 195, 199
      bus, 201
      clock speeds, 200, 610
      CPU, 199-200, 610-611, 621
      expansion slots, 201
      memory chips, 201-202
      random access memory (RAM), 202
   input/output devices, 215-216
      digitizing tablets, 225
      pen-based systems, 225
   operating environment/Graphical User Interface (GUI), 210-211
   operating systems, 208-209, 212
      proprietary/portable, 211, 245
   platforms
      Macintosh, 196
      UNIX, 196, 198
      Windows/PC, 196, 197, 211, 212
   role in digital printing, 30
   in scanner, 316, 317, 319
   software, 209-210
      multitasking, 209-210, 413
   storage technologies, 216-224, 611-612
   viruses affecting, 410-411
Consortium for University Printing and Information Distribution (CUPID), 472
Consumer Digital Subscriber Line (CDSL), 616-617, 618
Continuous tone. *See also* Contone files; Photography; Tone reproduction
   conversion to halftone, 68, 69, 76-77
   described, 577-578
   examples of, 62-63, 295
   for proofs, 56, 57
Contone files (CT), 577-578, 580
   in PostScript, 395
   in TIFF/IT, 231, 233
Contone raster data, defined, 580
Contrast. *See also* Density range; Highlights; Shadows
   keyness and, 332
   tone reproduction and, 281, 331
CONTU. *See* National Commission on New Technological Uses of Copyrighted Works
Copyright, intellectual property and, 464-465
Copyright Clearance Center (CCC), goals and procedures, 465-469
Copywriters. *See also* Creative professionals
   creative productions of, 192
Corel Photo-Paint, 32
Corel Ventura, 42, 382
Corel WordPerfect, 34, 523
CorelDraw, 32
Corona Powdered Electrostatic Transfer, 582
Corona treatment, with screen printing, 107
Corrugated. *See also* Paper; Substrate
   design considerations for, 156
   typical flexographic plate thickness, 159
Costs
   of book returns, 473

   of CD-ROM, 489
   of digital photography, 190
   of DVD, 511
   of ink, 287
   of paper, 171
   of publishing, 460
Counterfeiting, 5
Covalent Systems Job Monitor Protocol, 396
CPI. *See* Cells Per Inch
CPSI, RIPs and, 45
Creation, digital printing and, 31
Creative professionals
   categories of, 188
      color separators, 25-26
      copywriters, 192
      designers, 192-195
      illustrators, 190-191
      multimedia, 556
      photographers, 189-190
   described, 187-188
Cropping
   crop and fold marks, 367
   of images, 39
   recommendations for, 80-81
CRT. *See* Cathode ray tube
CT. *See* Contone files
CTP. *See* Computer-to-plate
CUPID. *See* Consortium for University Printing and Information Distribution
Customer
   in digital workflow, 440
   identifying on press sheet, 368
Customized printing. *See* Digital printing; On-demand printing; Variable printing
Cut areas, recommendations for, 165
Cutting. *See also* Bindery; Folding
   data transfer for, 447
CyberChrome Inc., 239

D

D5000/D50 lighting. *See also* Color viewing requirements
   for viewing color, 277, 296, 303
Daguerreotype, 14
Dalim software, 198
Darwin, discussed, 572-575
Darwin (Scitex), 132
DAT. *See* Digital audio tape
Data cartridges, for storage and backup, 222
Databases. *See also* Storage
   in digital publishing, 486, 505
   for magazines, 482
   PDF document as, 566
   role in variable printing, 132, 390-391
   servers for, 411
Davis HiFi Project, 278
Davis, Mills, 278
DCS. *See* Desktop Color Separation
DDAP. *See* Digital Distribution of Advertising for Publications
DDES. *See* Digital Date Exchange Standards
Demand printing. *See* On-demand printing
Deneba Canvas, 32
Densitometer, 40
Densitometry, discussed, 85-87
Density, 298
Density bars, for registration, 367
Density range, tone compression and, 40, 282
Densmore, James, 16
Design
   for multimedia, 501-502
   of pages, 37-38
   recommendations for, 249-252, 601-604
   workflow and, 438
Design services, 26
Designers. *See also* Creative professionals
   creative productions of, 192-195
Desktop Color Separation (DCS). *See also* Color separation
   EPS and, 419, 428
   OPI and, 419-420, 428
   procedures for using, 239-240, 247, 321, 450
Desktop publishing, 187-188
   flexographic printing and, 138
   origins of, 21, 24, 25

Detail, 335
DFE. *See* Digital Front End
.DFX file format, 243
DI. *See* Direct Imaging
Diamond Sutra, 7
Dictes or Sayengis of the Philosophers (Caxton), 11
Die cutting and converting. *See also* Folding carton
　discussed, 164-165, 170
Digital audio tape (DAT), for storage and backup, 221-222
Digital cameras. *See also* Digital photography
　described, 36
　Kodak PhotoCD, 25, 37
Digital Data Exchange Standards (DDES), 230-231, 234
Digital Distribution of Advertising for Publications (DDAP), stan-
　dards, 421, 564
Digital Front End (DFE), 102
Digital images. *See also* Digital photography; Scanners
　production of, 180, 249-250
Digital libraries, discussed, 487-488
Digital Linear Tape (DLT), 221
Digital Object Identifier (DOI), discussed, 470-471
Digital photography. *See also* Digital cameras; Photography
　digital camera technology, 309-310, 341
　photo memory for, 340-341
　resolution in, 340
　role in printing industry, 25, 180
　scanners and, 341-342
　technology of, 189-190, 251, 309-310, 338-339
Digital presses
　compared to inkjet devices, 134
　packaging applications, 137-138
　variable data, 132-134
　variable printing, 134-136
Digital printing, 30-31, 133, 134, 485, 559
　bindery concerns for, 358-359
　for book printing, 461
　compared to on-demand printing, 134
　direct-to-plate, 183-184
　direct-to-print, 184-185
　distribute and print, 186
　document management for, 420-421
　fast turnaround, 186
　features of, 132-133, 180-186
　graphical data, 182-183
　image transfer process, 97
　inking system, 97, 128-129
　on-demand printing, 185
　Open Prepress Interface (OPI) servers for, 417-418
　organizational trends in, 469-475
　personalization in, 186
　processes for, 27-28, 108-114
　　dot matrix, 109
　　electrostatic, 109
　　laser, 109-110
　proofs in, 56
Digital publishing. *See* Desktop publishing; On-demand publishing
Digital recorders, 47-48
Digital television (DTV), 496
Digital type, 181
Digital video, discussed, 487
Digital video disk (DVD), 312, 484. *See also* CD-ROM
　codes for, 512
　described, 224, 488, 505, 506-507, 508-513
　DIVX, 507
　DVD+RW, 508
　DVD-R/W, 507
　DVD-RAM, 508
　DVD-ROM, 507, 509
　rewritable DVD-R, 507
Digits. *See also* Bit; Byte
　described, 30, 60, 75, 180
DIMMs. *See* Dual Inline Memory Modules
Direct Imaging (DI)
　digital front end (DFE), 102
　technologies for, 54-55, 101-103, 183-184
Direct to press, technologies for, 54-55
Direct-to-plate printing, 183-184
Direct-to-print technology, 184-185
Display list, creation of, 387
Dissemination, digital printing and, 31
Distribute and print, discussed, 186
Distributed demand printing, 135

Dithering, 228
DK&A Trapper, 43
DKA Island Trapper, 155
DLT. *See* Digital Linear Tape
Doctor blade, in flexographic printing, 104, 140, 141, 142
Document management, for digital printing, 420-421, 438-439
Document transfer, discussed, 80
Document Type Definition (DTD), 518
DOI. *See* Digital Object Identifier
Dot area density, 69-71
Dot etching, 65
Dot gain. *See also* Dot gain compensation; Halftone dots
　causes, 85-86, 160-161
　discussed, 66, 85-86
　effect on registration, 70-71
　in flexographic printing, 146, 149, 160-161, 169-170
　ink properties effect on, 116, 287
　percentages for, 71
　physical/optical, 71
　stochastic screening and, 79
　tone reproduction and, 281-282
　in waterless process, 78
Dot gain compensation, 70-71, 161
　proof process and, 167
Dot matrix printer, 20, 109
Dots per inch (dpi), measurement of, 74, 315, 335
Dots. *See* Halftone dots; Pixels; Spots
Doubling, 378
Downloading, compared to printing, 45
dpi. *See* Dots per inch
Drawing programs, vector-based, 32, 229-230
.DRWG file format, 243
DTD. *See* Document Type Definition
DTV. *See* Digital television
Dual Inline Memory Modules (DIMMs), 203
DuPont Chromalin, 167, 293
Durometer, of flexographic plates, 146, 170
DVD. *See* Digital video disk
Dye diffusion printers, described, 111
Dye polymer recording, 223
Dye-sublimation printer, 290
　described, 58, 127

E

E. Remington & Sons, 16
e-mail, 407, 495, 522
Eastman, George, 14
Edge enhancement, 335
Editing. *See also* Image editing procedures
　files, 83, 383
　images, 39
　　recommendations for, 80-81, 255
　portable documents, 562, 566
　PostScript files, 397
Education, multimedia applications for, 503, 555
Educational texts, on-demand production of, 473-475
EFI Fiery/CLC, 290
ElectroInk process, 125, 127
Electronic printing. *See* Digital printing; On-demand publishing
Electrophotography, 128, 129
Electrostatic printer, 107, 109. *See also* Laser printer
　direct, 125, 126
　paper requirements, 371
　processes for, 125, 584-585, 592-593
　for wide-format printing, 582-583
Embossing, 90, 378
Employment, in publishing, 21, 25
Encapsulated PostScript (EPS) files. *See also* PostScript
　DCS and, 419, 428
　described, 238, 239
　file storage and transfer with, 182, 227, 246-247, 398, 449, 564
Engraving, 12, 22
　lithographic, 22
　photoengraving, 22, 23
Envelopes, paper requirements, 374
Environmental concerns
　for fountain solution, 120
　for ink and toner, 128, 131
EOCOM Company, 54
EPS. *See* Encapsulated PostScript
.EPS file format, 182, 243, 244
Equivalent neutral density (END). *See* Gray balance

Errors. *See also* Ink defects
　correcting, 388
　file size and, 81
　in PostScript files, 234
　in proofs, 292-293
Ethernet, 409-410, 416, 591. *See also* Networks
　topology for, 429-430
European Council for Nuclear Research (CERN), 518, 519
eXtensible Markup Language (XML), 491, 522

F

Fabric printing, 111
Farallon Computing Replica, 563
Fax machine, 110
Feathering, 172, 586
File
　editing, 83
　printing to, 45, 393
　transmission of, 194
File compression
　file transfer and, 83
　for images, 240-242, 487, 529, 548
　methods for, 241-242
　　JPEG, 242
　　lossy/lossless, 242, 245, 548
　　LZW, 241-242
　　run-length, 241, 242
File extensions
　for bitmaps, 182
　discussed, 243-244
File formats, discussed, 227, 245-248
File management
　discussed, 80
　file size considerations, 80-81, 233, 400
　hot folders, 436
　for WWW pages, 521, 553
File transfer. *See also* Telecommunications
　for digital photography, 341
　recommendations for, 83, 387-388
Film
　for color separations and plates, 23, 258
　description and use, 52
　development and processing, 52, 53
　digital printing elimination of, 27
　dry processed, 52
　halftone production on, 68
　for photopolymer plates, 163
　proofs from, 57, 168
　role in prepress market, 23
Film recorder, 114
Fingerprint. *See also* Preflight check
　recommendations for, 161, 169-170, 331-332
　for stochastic screening, 163
Finishing. *See also* Bindery; Books; Imposition
　discussed, 174
　in-line and off-line, 359
　methods for, 343
　wrinkles, 174
Fixed disks. *See also* Computers; Storage
　RAID technology for, 219
　for storage and backup, 218
Flexographic press
　CIC, 144
　corrugated, 144
　in-line, 144
　multicolor capabilities, 144-145
　stack press, 144, 169
Flexography
　characteristics of, compared to gravure and lithography, 136
　design considerations
　　die-cutting and converting, 164-165
　　dot gain, 160-161
　　halftones and screening, 159
　　highlights, 161
　　packaging conclusions, 168-170
　　plate distortion and elongation, 157-159
　　prepress output, 165-166
　　proofing, 166-168
　　screen angles, 162
　　screen ruling and substrate, 162
　　step and repeat, 163-164
　　stochastic screening, 162-163

trapping, 154-155
typography, 155-157
vignettes, 161
discussed, 90-92, 140
image transfer process, 97
anilox roller, 116, 141, 142-143, 162, 170
doctor blade, 104, 140, 141, 142
inking system, 97, 116, 117, 138, 145, 153
for packaging printing, 91, 137-138, 140-142
paper requirements, 371
plate
characteristics, 145-146
distortion and elongation, 157-159
laser-ablated, 147
molded rubber, 146-147
mounting systems, 148-149
mounting tape, 149
photopolymer, 148
plate cylinders
preparation, 149-150
and repeat length, 143-144
print quality, 98
reverse-side printing, 145
substrate influence on, 150-151
Floppy disks, for storage and backup, 82, 499
Fluorescing, 586
Flush, 115
FM. *See* Frequency Modulation
Focoltone, 167, 274
Folding. *See also* Bindery; Signatures
crop and fold marks, 367
digital data for, 446-447
folder types, 349
buckle folders, 350
illustrated, 368-369
tape/knife folders, 350
layout for, 348-349
paper grain effect on, 349
procedures for, 363-364
Folding carton. *See also* Die cutting and converting
paper requirements, 373
printing, 138
typical flexographic plate thickness, 159
Fonts. *See also* Text; Type; Typography
design considerations for, 604-606
for flexographic printing, 157
including in file, 81, 565-566
TrueType compared to PostScript, 181, 252
TrueType fonts, 181, 252, 604-606
Food containers. *See also* Packaging
inks for, 128
printing on, 119, 373, 374
Formatting. *See also* File formats; Information formatting
errors occurring in, 83
of information, 37-38
for page assembly, 41
for text, 33-34
Forms
paper requirements, 373
personalization of, 568-569, 571-572, 576
Fountain solution, 95. *See also* Offset lithography
alcohol-free, 120
print problems related to, 171
Four-color process. *See also* Color printing; Color separation; Halftone screen
customized printing in, 134, 365
dot gain considerations for, 161
origins of, 14
proofs for, 294
Fractal Design Painter, 32
Frequency Modulation (FM). *See also* Stochastic screening
compared to Amplitude Modulation (AM), 77, 78, 79

G

Gamuts, 268. *See also* Color reproduction theory
Gateway, in network, 431
GCR. *See* Gray component replacement
.GEM file format, 243
Generalized Markup Language (GML), 516
Ghosting, 119, 377
GIF. *See* Graphic Interchange Format
.GIF file format, 243, 547
Glass, printing on, 119

Gloss, of substrate, 153-154
GML. *See* Generalized Markup Language
Goldfarb, Charles, 516
Graphic Interchange Format (GIF) images
compared to JPEG images, 529, 548
in HTML documents, 524-525, 547
Graphical data, for digital printing, 182-183
Graphical User Interface (GUI)
in Apple computer, 19, 20
discussed, 210-211
Graphics, 33
design considerations for, 604
flexographic printing for, 137
in HTML document, 546-547
importing into page layout, 42
for Web pages, 521
Graphics tablet, 216
Gravure
characteristics of, compared to offset lithography and flexography, 136
described, 139-140
doctor blade, 104
image transfer process, 97
print rollers, 116
inking system, 97, 116
paper requirements, 171, 370-371
press construction, 104
print quality, 98
proofs for, 293
Gray balance, description and application, 279-280
Gray component, color correction and, 334
Gray component replacement (GCR), procedures for, 40, 287-288, 299, 317, 337-338
Gray levels
described, 61-62
production of, 63-65
Grayscale image
described, 62-63, 180
storing photograph as, 234
Greeting cards, paper requirements, 374
GUI. *See* Graphical User Interface
Gutenberg Bible, 9-10
Gutenberg, Johann, 6, 8-11

H

Halftone, 68-71
Halftone cells, 68, 75
Halftone dots. *See also* Dot gain; Pixels
discussed, 63-65, 75
dot area density, 69-71
errors in, 378
imagesetter grid and, 76-77
in printing, 30, 33
in proofs, 56, 59, 289, 290, 292-293
shape, 65-69, 77, 86, 160-161
size, 65, 69, 77, 86, 160
Halftone screen, 64. *See also* Screen printing
Amplitude Modulation vs. Frequency Modulation, 77, 78, 79
flexographic, design considerations for, 159, 162
origin and procedure for use, 15-16
resolution of, 74
screen angle recommendations, 71-73, 162, 170, 290
screen frequency, 73-74, 76
screen ruling, 162
in proofs, 292-293
stochastic screening recommendations, 79, 162-163
Haloid Corporation, 593
Hard drive. *See* Fixed disks
Harris Intertype Fotosetter, 18
Heidelberg, Direct Imaging technology, 54-55, 101-102, 184
Heligraphs, 305
Hell, Dr. Rudolph, 338
Hewlett-Packard
HP DeskJet printer, ink characteristics, 121
PCL, 48, 392
Hickeys, 119
High fidelity (HiFi) color, described, 278
Highlights. *See also* Density range; Tone compression; Whiteness/brightness
color casts effecting, 330
design considerations for, 161
dot shape effect in, 67
identifying, 328

selection of, 300, 317, 328
specular, 329
step wedge use with, 328-329
Histograms, 301-302
Holograms, 600
Hot folders, description and use, 436
.HPG file format, 243
HSV color model, characteristics of, 276
HTML. *See* Hypertext Markup Language
.html file format, 531
http. *See* Hypertext Transport Protocol
Hue, 161, 269
Hue error. *See also* Color correction
compensating for, 332-333
formula for determining, 333
printing inks and, 333
Hypertext, discussed, 490-491
Hypertext Markup Language (HTML)
described, 491, 498, 516-518, 519, 520
document creation, 531
block quote, 539
character emphasis, 535-538
formatting tags, 538
graphics, 546-547
headings, 532
horizontal rule, 534
images, 524-525, 529, 546-547, 548-553
line break/paragraph tags, 533
links, 543-544, 545-546, 552
lists, 540-542
preformatted text, 538
video and sound, 525-526, 552-553
document structure, 530-531
inline vs. external images, 524-525
programming with, 523-524
Hypertext Transport Protocol (http), 491, 519, 527-528

I

IBM Corporation, 306, 495, 516
ICC. *See* International Color Consortium
Ice Age art, 3
Icon, in Apple computer, 20
ICR. *See* Integrated color removal
IIC. *See* Information Identifier Committee
Illustration, 22
Illustration programs, discussed, 254
Illustrators, creative productions by, 190-191
Image capture. *See also* Digital photography; Scanners
in general, 305-311
resolution and, 85
vision and, 266-267
Image editing procedures, 39-41. *See also* Editing
cast removal, 40
digital retouching, 41
resampling, 39
sizing and cropping, 39
tone compression, 40
UCR/GCR, 40
unsharp masking, 41
Image quality, printer maintenance and, 294-295
Image recorder. *See* Digital recorders; Imagesetter
Image sharpness, discussed, 284
Image transfer systems, described, 97
Images
Automatic Picture Replacement (APR), 454
categories of complexity for, 587
compression for, 240-242, 487, 529, 548
continuous tone, 62-63
copyright for, 468
creating, 250-251
digital conversion of, 34-25
editing, 39, 80-81, 255
in HTML documents, 524-525, 529, 546-547, 548-553
resolution of, 81, 84-85, 427, 578, 590
rotating, 81
thumbnails for, 37-38, 525, 529
Imagesetter
accuracy and calibration, 85, 166
capstan type, 46, 52
compared to image recorder, 46
description and procedures for use, 46-47, 76-77, 292
development of, 23-24
digital, 47-48

Imagesetter, *continued*
  drum type, 46-47, 52
  exposure value adjustment, 86-87
  for flexography, 165-166
  halftone production with, 68-69
  as imposetter, 26-27
  laser intensity concerns, 85
  repeatability concerns, 85
  typesetter use of, 25
Imagesetter grid, halftone dots and, 76-77
Imaging issues
  for digital press, 132
  quality concerns for, 84-85
Imaging programs, examples of, 32
Imation Matchprint, 167
Imation Rainbow, 290
Imation SuperDisk, 218
.IMG file format, 243
Imposetter, imagesetter as, 26-27
Imposition. *See also* Finishing; Signature imposition
  collate-and-cut, 366
  described, 43, 343, 362, 386
  ganged image, 348
  nomenclature for, 344
  procedures for, 43, 234, 439
  sheetwise (work-and-back), 345-348
  signature, 347
  types of, 364-365
  work-and-tumble, 346-347, 365, 366
  work-and-turn, 346, 366
Imposition marks, 367
Indigo E-Print 1000, discussed, 598-599
Indigo ElectroInk, 127, 128, 133
Induction charging, 126
Information, for digital publishing, 486
Information formatting, 37-38
Information Identifier Committee (IIC), 469-470
Information technology, 195
Ink. *See also* Toner
  black ink, 115, 273, 288, 380
  body and viscosity, 116, 117, 585, 586
  compared to toner, 130
  comparisons of, 136
  components, 115-117, 120
  control fields, 447
  in digital printing, 30
  drying characteristics, 115, 117, 118-120, 287
  in general, 115-117
  gloss, 115, 118
  historic preparations, 4
  hot melt/phase-change, 121-122
  hue error and, 333
  length, 117
  lithographic, 13
  radiation, 118
  relation to substrate, 119-120, 151
  rheology, 116
  solvent migration effects on bindings, 353-354
  surface tension, 585, 586
  tack, 115, 117
  thermoplastic, 123
Ink defects. *See also* Paper reproduction issues
  banding, 587
  bleed, 586
  blistering, 179
  blocking, 178, 378
  chalking, 179, 378
  contamination, 283-284, 379
  feathering, 586
  fluorescing, 586
  ghosting, 119, 377
  halftone dots and, 70
  hickeys, 119
  misregister, 378
  mottle, 177, 378, 379-380, 586
  picking, 116, 117, 119, 153, 378
  piling, 119, 171, 377
  pooling, 586
  process ink error, 283-284
  repelling, 587
  scumming, 119
  set-off, 178-179, 378

show-through, 378
strike-through, 176, 586-587
tack, 115, 117, 171, 174, 287, 378
tinting, 119, 378
wet-on-wet, 287
wicking, 121
Ink hu, compensating for, 161
Ink mileage
  paper holdout and, 178
  runnability and, 380
Ink painting, 4
Ink use, reducing, 40
Inking systems, described, 96-97
Inkjet printer
  bubble-jet, 114, 121, 124
  color, 121, 123, 124
  compared to digital press, 134
  compared to offset lithography, 128
  compared to xerography, 593
  continuous, 112-113, 121, 122, 123, 124, 125
  described, 112-113, 120-125
  digital recorder use of, 47
  drop-on-demand, 113, 121-123, 124-125
    piezo (PZT), 583-584
  ink characteristics, 121-122
  liquid/solid inkjet, 124-125, 289
  paper requirements, 372
  phase-change, 113-114, 584-585
  proofs from, 56, 289, 290
  pulsed/thermal inkjet, 124
  quality and speed developments, 591-592
  substrate choices, 586-590
  technologies for, 59, 560
  thermal, 584
  for wide-format printing, 583-593
Intaglio. *See* Gravure
Integrated color removal (ICR), 337
Integrated Services Digital Network (ISDN) lines, 402-404, 616
Intellectual property. *See also* Books
  copyright and, 464-465
  discussed, 463-465
  fee charges for, 474
Interactivity. *See also* Multimedia
  digital video and, 506-507
  discussed, 497
International Association of Scientific, Technical & Medical Publishers (STM), 469
International Color Consortium (ICC), goals and members, 429
International Cooperation for Integration of Prepress, Press, and Postpress (CIP3), discussed, 445-454
Internet. *See also* World Wide Web
  access to, 416-417, 431, 617-619
  advantages of, 493-494
  commercial applications, 492-493, 495, 497
  disadvantages of, 494
  discussed, 485
  impact on publishing, 492
  Next Generation Internet (NGI), 618-619
  on-line publishing for, 490
  trends of, 495
  Very-High-Performance Backbone Network Service, 621
Interoperability, 211
Interpretation, in RIP, 387
Iomega drives, 218
ISDN. *See* Integrated Services Digital Network
Isenberg, Diether von, 11

J

Jaz drives, for storage and backup, 82, 218
Job information, press sheet identification of, 368
Jobs, Steven, 19, 20
Joint Photographic Experts Group (JPEG). *See also* Images
  compared to GIF format, 529, 548
  described, 240-241
JPEG. *See* Joint Photographic Experts Group

K

Keyboard, 215-216
Keyness, 332
Kodak Approval, 291
Kodak PhotoCD, 25, 37, 489
Korea, printing origins in, 6-7, 8
Kornei, Otto, 125, 128

KPG Approval, 57, 289, 290
Kruppers, Harold, 278

L

Label printing, 111, 119, 138, 170
  imposition for, 347
  paper requirements, 372, 374
  trapping considerations, 155
  typical flexographic plate thickness, 159
LAN. *See* Local Area Network
Language, 3
Lanston, Tolbert, 17
Large-format printing. *See* Wide-format printing
Lascaux (France), 3
Laser printer
  described, 59, 109-110
  development of, 20-21
  halftone production with, 68-69
  toner characteristics, 125-131, 599-600
Lasergraph, 54
Lasers, 609
  blue lasers, 615
LaserWriter printer, 21
Layout. *See* Page layout
Le Blond, Jacques, 14
Leeds *Mercury*, 17
Legal forms, paper requirements, 373
Letterpress, historic, 12
Light. *See also* Ultraviolet light
  for color viewing, 277
  relation to color, 260-261, 265, 297
Light Valve Technology (LVT), in slide recorder, 114
Limestone
  for coating/filling, 171, 176
  use in lithography, 13
Line art, defined, 577
Linearization, discussed, 85-86
Linecaster, 22-23
Linen paper, 6
Lines per inch (lpi), screen measurement in, 73-74, 75, 327, 335
Linework files (LW)
  PostScript and, 395
  in TIFF/IT, 395
Linofilm, 18
Linotype machine, 17
Liquor labels, printing, 119
Lisa (computer), 19, 20, 210
Lithography. *See also* Offset lithography
  invention of, 12-14
  plate, blanket, impression cylinders, 93-94, 95
  principles of, 92-93
Live Picture, 32, 39
Local Area Network (LAN), 405, 406-407, 411, 430
LocalTalk, 409-410
lpi. *See* Lines per inch
Luminous TrapWise, 43
LVT. *See* Light Valve Technology
LW. *See* Linework files

M

MacDraw, 32
Macintosh computer. *See also* Apple computer
  described, 196
  networks with, 409-410
  origins of, 19, 20, 306
  platform, 196, 212, 612
Mackie, Alexander, 18
Macromedia Freehand, 32, 250, 254, 382
  trapping tools in, 42, 156
Macromedia xRes, 32
Magazines
  advertising revenue, 480
  association/custom publishing for, 480-481
  industry overview, 478-479
  inks for, 120
  on-demand publishing by, 135, 476-477, 481-483
  paper requirements, 376
  plate use by, 52
  printing processes for, 138-139, 140
  proofs for, 294
  subscriptions and newsstands, 480
  types of, 477-478
Magneto optical (MOs) disks, 82, 218, 219-220

Mainz, 11
Maps, paper requirements, 373
Marks. *See also* Imposition marks
    Imagesetter generation of, 46, 84-85
    registration marks, 368, 447
Mazarin Bible, 10
Memory, 201-202
    for digital photography, 340-341
Memory colors, 285-287, 297
Menus, paper requirements for, 373
Merced chip, 611
Mergenthaler Linotype, 23
Mergenthaler, Ottmar, 17
Metafiles, 182
Metameric colors, relation to viewing conditions, 295
Metamerism patch, for viewing color, 277
Micrografx Picture Publisher, 32
Microsoft Word, 34, 523, 573-574
Midtones. *See also* Density range; Highlights; Shadows
    dot shape effect in, 67
    identification of, 331-332
Milking, causes of, 171
Mill, Henry, 16
Misregister, 378. *See also* Registration
Modems, discussed, 401-402, 607, 609, 615-617, 618
Moiré pattern
    cell angles and, 143
    observing in proof, 289
    screen angles and, 71
    stochastic screening and, 79
Moisture content relative humidity (RH), of paper, 174
Money, on paper, 5
Monitors. *See also* Computer; Pixels; Video RAM (VRAM)
    characteristics of, 212-213, 225-226, 263-264, 271, 608
    color depth, 213
    display accelerators, 215
    flat panel display/LCD, 226, 612-615
    high-definition (HDTV), 226
    for multimedia, 500-501
    pixel brightness and, 61
    plastic/LEP, 614
    projection, 613-614
    refresh rates, 214
    resolution, 212
    screen size, 215
    24-bit/36-bit, 62, 214, 271
Monophoto, 18
Monotype machine, 17-18
Moore, Gordon, 608, 621
Moss, Franklin, 148
Mosstype Corporation, 148
Motion Picture Experts Group (MPEG), 510, 526
Mottle, 177, 378-380, 586. *See also* Ink defects
Movable type, historic origins of, 4, 8
.MOV file format, 526, 553
MPC. *See* Multimedia Personal Computer
MPEG. *See* Motion Picture Experts Group
.MPEG file format, 553
.MPNT file format, 243
Multi-color press, 94. *See also* Offset lithography
Multilayer/laminations. *See also* Substrate
    absorption by, 153
    caliper, 154
    examples of, 150
    gloss, 153-154
    opacity determination, 152
    smoothness, 153
    whiteness/brightness, 152
Multimedia, 498-505, 554-555
    professionals for, 556
    21 rules for, 557-558
Multimedia Personal Computer (MPC) specifications, 499-500
Munsell, Albert H., 269
Munsell color model system, 268-271
Music
    paper requirements, 376
    printing of, 12-13

N

NACS. *See* National Association of College Stores
Nanotransistor, 610
Nassau, Adolph von, 11

National Association of College Stores (NACS), 473
National Commission on New Technological Uses of Copyrighted
    Works (CONTU), 466
Native files, transfer of, 83
Nesting, 163-164
NetPaper, 472, 473-474
Networks, 406-407
    communications and, 429-432, 609
    implementation of, 416-417
    infrastructure, 415-416
    with Macintosh computers, 409-410
    printer queues, 413-415
    private, 619-620
    security for, 410-411
    servers, 411
        choosing, 411-412
        dedicated, 412
        evolution and integration, 432-435
        file, 426
        Open Prepress Interface (OPI), 417-420, 427, 435
        print, 411, 413, 426-427, 432
        proprietary, 412-413
        for WWW applications, 527
    topology for, 407-408
    with Windows PCs, 410
Neutrality test. *See* Gray balance
New York Daily Graphic, 15
New York Times, 54
Newcastle *Chronicle,* 17
Newsletters, 478
Newspapers
    flexographic halftone printing, 162
    image processes for, 51
    image resolution for, 326
    paper requirements, 373-374
    printing processes for, 138, 139, 140
    proofs for, 294
    typical flexographic plate thickness, 159
Newsprint. *See also* Paper
    halftones for, 66
    ink for, 118, 120
    screen frequency for, 76
Newton, Sir Isaac, 261, 263
Next Generation Internet (NGI), 618-619
NGI. *See* Next Generation Internet
Nicolaus V, Pope, 9
Niepce, Joseph N., 14, 305
No Hands Software Common Ground, 563

O

Object-oriented file, file formats for, 243-244
Object-oriented graphic, compared to bitmap, 229-230
O'Brien effect, described, 336
Obsolescence, of printed material, 133, 462, 559
Offset lithography, 138-139
    characteristics of, compared to gravure and flexography, 136
    compared to inkjet printer, 128
    dampening system, 95
    density range of, 40
    development of, 22-23
    image transfer process, 94, 97
    inking system, 96-97, 116, 117, 139, 171
    paper requirements, 171, 344, 370
    perfecting press, 94, 96
    plate, blanket, impression cylinders, 93-94, 95, 97-98
    press types, 94, 96
    print defects in, 70
    print quality, 98
    printing unit, 95
    registration system, 148-149
    screen frequency for, 74
    waterless process, 98-101
Omni-Adast, 54
On-demand printing, 133, 185, 561
    discussed, 559, 561
    for magazines, 476-483
    requirements of, 133
On-demand publishing, 135
    approaches to, 475-476
    for educational texts, 473-475
    organizational trends in, 469-475
Opacity, of substrates, 152, 176

Open Prepress Interface (OPI) servers, 417-419, 427, 435, 453
    DCS and, 419-420, 428
OPI. *See* Open Prepress Interface
Output, processes for, 44
Output media
    film, 52
    resin-coated (RC) paper, 51
Oversampling, discussed, 81
Oxidation, of ink, 118
Oxillography. *See also* Inkjet printer described, 122

P

Packaging. *See also* Food containers; Substrate
    flexography printing for, 91, 137-138, 140-142, 159, 168-170
    gravure printing for, 140
    imposition for, 347
    lithographic printing for, 138
    paper requirements, 374
    step and repeat printing, 163-164
    trapping considerations for, 155, 168-169
    typical flexographic plate thickness, 159
Page assembly, procedures for, 41-42
Page design, layout and production, 37-38
Page layout. *See also* Design
    file management for, 80
    page assembly and, 41-42
    page design and production, 37-38
    recommendations for, 256-258, 601-604
Page layout programs
    compared to word processors, 34, 253
    examples of, 42
PageMaker, 34, 253, 382
Pages, imposition of, 43
Painter, 250, 254
Palo Alto Research Center (PARC), 19
Panel printing, 139
Pantone Hexachrome process, 278-279
Pantone Matching System (PMS), 167, 253, 256, 257, 274-275
Paper. *See also* Newsprint; Stock; Substrate
    absorption by, 153
    alignment of, 344-345
    caliper, 154, 173
    coated, 171, 176
    coated and uncoated, compared, 172
    cover stock, 172, 351, 352
    examples of, 150
    gloss, 153-154
    grades, 377
    grain
        effect on binding, 352, 356
        effect on folding, 349
        long fibers in, 6
    introduction of, 3-7
    opacity, 152, 176
    press requirements
        electrostatic, 371
        flexography, 371
        gravure, 370-371
        inkjet, 372
        letterpress, 371
        offset lithography, 370
        screen printing, 371
        sheet sizes, 362
    print defects and, 377-378
    recycled, 116, 151
    screen frequency and, 76
    smoothness, 152-153, 177
    weight, effect on signature, 349
    whiteness/brightness, 151-152, 176, 265
Paper reproduction issues. *See also* Ink defects
    basis weight, 172, 344
    cleanlineas, 175
    conditioning and trimming, 175
    dimensional stability, 174
    finishing and bindery concerns, 174
    formation, 177-178
        absorbency and holdout, 177-178
        two-sidedness, 177
    grain direction, 173
    gripper edge, 344-345
    ink mileage, 178
    moisture content relative humidity (RH), 174

Paper reproduction, *continued*
  paper size, 172-173
  print quality, 175-176
  racking/traying, 179
  runnability, 171-172, 378
    cleanliness concerns, 379
    milking, 379
    whitening, 379
  smoothness, 152-153, 177
  strength/stretch/distortion, 175
  substance weight, 172-173
  wild edge, 345
Papyrus, 4, 6
Parchment, 4
.PCT file format, 244
.PCX file format, 182, 243
PDF. *See* Portable Document Format; Printer Description File
Perfecting press, 94, 96. *See also* Offset lithography
Periodicals. *See* Magazines
Persistent Internal Polarization, 593
Personalization, in variable printing, 568-569, 572
Phase change recording, 222
Phone books, paper requirements, 376
Photediting applications, for image editing, 39-41
Photo, 23
Photocopying, 109
Photoengraving, height-to-paper number, 22
Photographers, creative processes of, 189-190
Photography. *See also* Digital photography; Film
  copyright for, 468
  design considerations for, 603
  halftone reproduction of, 68, 69, 76-77
  illustrations and, 15
  origins of, 14, 189-190, 305
  processing procedures, 53
  technical aspects of, 305-306
Photomedia, development and processing, 52
Photomultiplier tube (PMT). *See also* Scanners
  in scanner, 36, 309, 311, 314, 316, 319, 321-322, 323-325
Photon-Lumitype, 18
Photopolymer plate
  film for, 163-164
  for flexographic printing, 148
Phototypesetting, 18, 23
  commercial success of, 18-19
Pi Sheng, 8
Picking, factors affecting, 116, 117, 119, 378
.PIC file format, 244
PICT, 235, 244, 246
  DCS and, 419
Pictographs, pre-historic, 2
Pictorial information, for digital publishing, 486
.PICT file extension, 182
Pigments. *See also* Ink
  in ink, 115, 145
  in toner, 131
Piling, causes of, 119, 171, 377
Pinholes, causes of, 149
Pius II, Pope, 10
Pixels, 61-62, 69, 297
  as picture elements, 74-75, 228-229, 233, 315, 501
  role in printing, 30, 33, 51, 64-65
Pixels per inch (ppi), resolution measurement, 307, 335
Planographic process. *See* Lithography; Offset Lithography
Plastic film, printing on, 119
Plate bounce, 164
Plate elongation. *See also* Flexography
  calculation and compensation for, 157-159
  design considerations for, 169
Plate mounting systems, compared, 54
Platemaking services, 25
Plates
  description and use, 52
  in digital workflow, 440
  in direct imaging press, 54-55
  in flexography, 90-91
  in offset lithography, 13, 94, 98
  preparation of, 23
  waterless, 99
Platesetter, contemporary use of, 27, 54, 388
Playing cards, 5

PMS. *See* Pantone Matching System
PMT. *See* Photomultiplier tube
PNAPs. *See* Private Network Access Points
Polaroid Polaproof, 57
Polyautography. *See* Lithography
Polyester, for film, 52
Polyethylene, printing on, 155, 156, 169
Polymer film. *See also* Packaging; Substrate
  absorption by, 153
  caliper, 154
  examples of, 150
  gloss, 153-154
  opacity, 152
  smoothness, 153
  whiteness/brightness, 152
Polypropylene, printing on, 169
Pooling, 586
Portable document, described, 561-562
Portable Document Format (PDF)
  characteristics of, 240, 382, 396, 563-566
  compared to PostScript, 422-423
  in digital workflow, 440
  file creation, 423
  file storage and transfer with, 81, 83, 240, 246, 386, 389, 421, 437, 564-566, 567-568
  for on-demand publishing, 135
  prepress issues, 424
  repurposability of, 567-568
Porzholt, E., 18
Post-press issues, in digital workflow, 441
Postcards, paper requirements, 376
Poster printing, 113. *See also* Wide-format printing
  compared to PDF, 422-423
PostScript. *See also* Adobe; Encapsulated PostScript files
  development of, 24, 181, 251
  digital fonts in, 181, 182-183
  file formats, 236-237, 386
  file transfer, 81, 83
  outputting, 397-398
  platforms for, 196
  PPF and, 446, 451
  printer description files, 50-51
  RIPs with, 44-45, 49, 392-394
  spot function, 67
  using, 396-399
PostScript clones, RIPs and, 48, 49, 392
PostScript Printer Description (PPD) files, 393-394
  printer information in, 50-51
PostScript 3, described, 394-395
Powder-cloud development, 127
PPD. *See* PostScript Printer Description
PPF. *See* Print production format
ppi. *See* Pixels per inch
Precipitation, of ink, 118
Preflight check, 385, 442. *See also* Fingerprint
  concepts of, 84
  for file management, 81
  for magazines, 483
  workflow issues, 443, 444
Prekissing, 378
Preparation, digital printing and, 31
Prepress, 29-30
  digital printing and, 31, 442-444
Prepress processes, 31, 41
  color separation, 43
  output, 44
  page assembly, 41-42
  trapping, 42-43
Pressroom issues, in digital workflow, 441, 442
Presstek, Direct Imaging technology, 54-55, 102, 184
Primis system, 475
Print defects, halftone dots and, 70
Print production format (PPF), 445-454
Print Shop Mail, 132
Printer. *See also* specific printers
  effect on image quality, 294-295
  queue management, 413-415
  role in publisher, 457
  servers for, 411, 413, 426-427, 432
Printer Description File (PDF), drivers for, 50-51, 394
Printer's spread, 348

Printing. *See also* Digital printing
  in PostScript, 44-45
  traditional, 496-497, 569
Printing industry, contemporary, 21-28
Private Network Access Points (PNAPs), discussed, 619-620
Process camera, 313, 335
Process colors, matching, 274-275
Productivity
  of digital press, 132
  paper grain effect on, 173
Progin, X., 16
Proofing, 291
Proofreading, symbols for, 605
Proofs
  blueline, 388-389
  color, 38, 44
  for color separations, 44, 332-333
  comp, 26
  continuous tone, 56, 57
  contract, 38, 55, 57, 167
    digital, 293-294, 388
  digital, 31, 57, 190, 308, 388, 439, 481-482
    contract, 293-294
    disadvantages of, 292-293
    discussed, 58-59, 288-289, 290-291
  dot gain in, 86
  dummy, 26, 167
  flexographic, 166-168
  imposition, 38, 57
  issues in, 57
  for position only (FPO), 290, 418, 427
  pre-proofs, 38, 290
  procedures for, 55-57
  registration concerns for, 291-292
  remote proofing, 387-388
Publisher, duties of, 456-457, 459-460
Publishing, 2, 455-463
  Internet impact on, 492
  Standard Industrial Classifications for, 24-25
PUBNET, 474-475
PubWeb, Inc., 472, 473

Q

QMS ColorScript 230, 127
QMS Magicolor, 290
.QT file format, 526, 553
Quality. *See also* Image quality; Paper reproduction issues
  dot gain and, 85-86
  dot shape effect on, 66-67
  of images, 294-295
  imaging issues for, 84-85
  ink properties effect on, 116, 120
  paper affecting, 175-176
  for proofs, 293-294
  relation to screen frequency, 74
  visual, 62
QuarkXPress, 34, 37, 42-43, 252-257, 275, 310, 382, 394, 396, 450, 482
QuarkXPress Datamerge, 132
Quick printers, digital printing and, 27
QuickMaster-DI, 54-55, 102
QuickTime, video standard, 526-527

R

Racking/traying, 179
RAID technology, for fixed disks, 219
RAM Doubler, 208
RAM. *See* Random access memory
Random access memory (RAM). *See also* Memory
  characteristics and requirements for, 202, 203-207
  RAM extenders, 208
Raster, 23-24
  in inkjet printer, 122
Raster files
  compared to bitmapped files, 229, 245
  interchangeability of, 234
Raster image, 577-579
  compared to vector image, 231, 233
Raster Image Processing (RIP), 23-24
  in direct imaging, 54-55, 102, 319, 391, 392-394, 432-435
  file size affecting, 80-81
  hardware and software, 394

Index

hot folders for, 436
internal functions, 387
PostScript standards for, 44-45, 48, 49, 51, 181
in prepress operations, 44, 48-49, 307, 387, 563
RC paper. *See* Resin-coated paper
RCA Electrofax, 593
Registration. *See also* Trapping
with color bars, 367
in direct imaging technology, 103
dot gain effect on, 70-71
in flexography, 138, 147, 166-167
with imposition marks, 367
misregistration causes, 154-155
paper quality affecting, 174, 344
pin register and micro-dot, 148-149
in proofs, 291-292
registration marks, 368, 447
in signatures, 354
Relief printing/letterpress, 89-90
image transfer process, 97
inking system, 97, 116
paper requirements, 371
print quality, 98
Removable disks, for storage and backup, 218
Repeat length, in flexographic printing, 143-144
Repeater, in network, 431
Repelling, 587
Resampling, of images, 39
Resin-coated (RC) paper, described, 51
Resolution, 335
of bitmaps, 228
of digital camera, 340
in direct imaging technology, 103
in electronic imaging, 307, 308
of halftone screens, 74
of images, 81, 84-85, 427, 578, 590
of monitors, 213
of scanners, 307, 308, 314, 322, 326-327
Resolution grid, 64
Retouching, digital, 41
RGB image, 271-272
characteristics of, 180, 256, 264, 276, 303, 311
RH. *See* Moisture content relative humidity
Rich Text Format (RTF), 565
RIP. *See* Raster Image Processing
Rivers, Earl, 11
Rosette, screen angles and, 72-73
Roto-gravure. *See* Gravure
Rotophoto, 18
Router, in network, 431
Rows, halftone dots in, 75
RTF. *See* Rich Text Format
.RTF file extension, 182
Runnability, 171-172

S

Salt print, imposition proof as, 38
Samples per inch (spi), 315
Saturation, defined, 269
SC6 standard. *See* Committee for Graphics Arts Technologies
Scanners. *See also* Digital photography; Image capture
CCD use in, 36, 307, 309, 311, 314, 317-319, 322-325
density range of, 40
desktop, 26, 313-314, 317-321
development of, 23, 25, 306-308
for digital cameras, 36
digital photography and, 341-342
hot folders and, 437
image capture technology, 36
image sharpness effected by, 284
prices for, 25, 307
recommendations for using, 326-327
resolution of, 307, 308, 314, 322, 326-327
text origination with, 33
types and technologies of, 35-36, 180, 190, 251, 307-309, 312-317, 319-321, 323-325
drum, 35-36, 309, 316-317, 319-320, 321-323
enlargement ratio, 327
flatbed, 35-36, 323
handheld, 320
sampling ratio, 327

transparency, 35-36, 320, 322-323
Scholes, Christopher Latham, 16
Scitex, 133
Scitex CT, 139, 244, 450, 580
Scitex Iris, 57, 291
Scitex VPS, 572-576
Scitex/KBA, 54, 103
Screen, 54
Screen angle, color separations and, 71-73, 162, 170
Screen capture programs, 235
Screen frequency, measurement of, 73-74
Screen printing, 4, 106-108
image transfer process, 97
inking system, 97
paper requirements, 371
print quality, 98, 139
printing capability, 107
Scrolls, and books, 6-7
Scumming, 119
Searchability. *See* Editing
Senefelder, Alois, 12-13, 92
Servers. *See* Networks
Service bureau, role in printing industry, 21, 24, 25
Set-off, 178-179, 378
74 Karat, 103
SGML. *See* Standard Generalized Markup Language
Shadows. *See also* Density range; Midtones; Tone compression
dot shape effect in, 67, 287
selection of, 300, 317, 330-331
Sheet fed press, 94. *See also* Offset lithography
paper requirements, 175, 362, 370
waterless process for, 100-101
Shoeffer, Peter, 10
Short-run printing, 560
for book printing, 461
characteristics of, 134-135, 185, 186, 358-359
Show-through, 378
SIC. *See* Standard Industrial Classification
Signature imposition, 347, 362, 364
Signatures, 362
creep and lap affecting, 355
crop and fold marks for, 367
in magazines, 361
paper weight effecting, 349
registration concerns in, 354
SIMMs. *See* Single Inline Memory Modules
Single Inline Memory Modules (SIMMs), 203
Sizing, of images, 39
.SLD file format, 244
Slide recorder, 114
Slurring, 378
Smoothness, of substrate, 152-153, 177
Software. *See also* Computer; Networks
application, 209-210
for calculating plate elongation, 158-159
categories of, 248
pirating of, 476
for pre-flight check, 84
role in digital printing, 60
for scanners, 35-36, 308, 314
Solidification, of ink, 118
Solvent migration, affecting binding, 353
Sound. *See also* Multimedia
in digital publishing, 486
in HTML document, 525-526, 552-553
Specifications for Web Offset Printing (SWOP), 287
Spectrophotometer, 87
Spectrophotometry, 303
Speedmaster 74-DI, 103
spi. *See* Samples per inch; Spots per inch
Spot color
matching in proof, 167-168, 294
matching in swatch book, 274
Spot size, image quality and, 85
Spots, 85
bitmap locations for, 48, 51
role in printing, 30, 33, 74
Spots per inch (spi), measurement of, 335
Spray powder, for preventing set-off, 178-179
Staggering, 164

Standard Generalized Markup Language (SGML), 491, 498, 516-518, 523
Standard Industrial Classification (SIC), for typesetter, 24-25
Star, 23
Stationery, paper requirements, 376
Stein, Sir Aurel, 7
Stencil printing. *See* Screen printing
Step and repeat printing, discussed, 163-164, 170
Step tablet/step wedge, procedure for using, 328-329
Stochastic screening, 79, 162-163, 170
proofs for, 292
Stock. *See also* Paper; Substrate
ink properties effect on, 116
relation to quality, 99
screen relation to, 73-74
Storage. *See also* Memory
of digital data, 389, 611-612
of PostScript files, 238
recommendations for, 80, 82-83
Storage technologies
CD-ROM, 217, 220-221, 514
recommendations for, 216-224, 607, 609
digital video disk (DVD), 224
magneto-optical disks, 218, 219-220
WORM, 223-224
Strike-through, 176, 586-587
Stripping process, 23
Style sheets, formatting and, 41
Substrate. *See also* Paper; Stock
absorption by, 153
caliper, 154
comparisons of, 136
effect on proofs, 167
gloss, 153-154
influence on flexographic printing, 150-151
opacity determination, 152
relationship to
dot gain, 150
ink, 119-120, 151, 294
screen ruling, 162
smoothness, 152-153
whiteness/brightness determination, 151-152
for wide-format printing, 587-590
SWOP. *See* Specifications for Web Offset Printing
Symbols, pre-historic, 2
SyQuest cartridges, 218, 220

T

Tack, characteristics of, 115, 117, 171, 174, 287, 378
Tagged Image File Format for Image Technology (TIFF/IT) files
contone image (CT) component, 231, 233
described, 230-231, 243, 246, 382
digital standards and, 421-422
file storage and transfer with, 449, 579-580
final page (FP) component, 232
high resolution Contone image (HC), 231
linework image (LW) component, 231, 232, 233, 579
monochrome components, 232
Tagged Image File Format (TIFF) files, 230-234
file storage and transfer with, 83, 244, 246, 428, 448, 579-580
Tags and tickets, paper requirements, 377
Tail-end hook, causes, 174, 378
Talbot, Fox, 14
TAPPI. *See* Technical Association for Paper and Pulp
TARGA file format, 227, 243, 244
TCP/IP protocol, 490
Technical Association for Paper and Pulp (TAPPI), whiteness/brightness specification, 176
Technology, seven pillars of, 608-609
Tektronix Phaser, 290
Telecommunications. *See also* File transfer; Networks
ADSL/SDSL, 404
analog/digital data signals, 401
ATM lines, 404
ISDN lines, 402-404
LAN installations, 405
modems, 401-402
recommendations for, 400
WAN installations, 404
wireless communications and, 405-406

629

Professional Prepress, Printing, and Publishing

Templates. *See also* Page layout
for page assembly, 41
Text. *See also* Fonts; Typography
creating and importing, 252
design considerations for, 602
digital conversion of, 34-25
origination processes for, 33-34
on WWW pages, 522
Textiles, relation to printing, 4
Textual information, for digital publishing, 486
.TGA file format, 182, 243
Thermal printers, discussed, 110-111
Thermal wax printer, 289, 290
described, 58-59, 111-112, 127
Thermography, described, 594
3M, dryographic process, 98
Three-dimensional printing, with screen printing, 107
Thumbnails. *See also* Images
description and purpose, 37-38, 525, 529
TIFF. *See* Tagged Image File Format files
TIFF/IT. *See* Tagged Image File Format for Image Technology files
Time Warner, 479
Tinting, 119, 378
TIR. *See* Total Indicated Runout
Tone compression. *See also* Density range
density range and, 40, 282
Tone correction. *See also* Color correction
recommendations for, 301
Tone reproduction. *See also* Continuous tone
procedures for, 280-282, 301
Tone reproduction and neutral density (TRAND). *See* Gray balance
Toner. *See also* Electrostatic printer; Laser printer
compared to ink, 130
discussed, 125-131, 582-583, 596, 598-600
dry, 130
dual-component, 125-126
liquid, 127, 130-131
monocomponent, 126
relation to image quality, 295
Toning, ink properties effect on, 116
Total Indicated Runout (TIR), tolerances for, 150
Toy containers. *See also* Packaging
inks for, 128
Training, multimedia applications for, 504, 555
Transparencies, 29. *See also* Slide recorder
printing, 112
scanners for, 35-36, 307-308, 320, 322-323
Trapping. *See also* Registration
chokes, 42, 43, 156, 451
described, 42, 234
discussed, 42-43, 154-155, 386, 451-453
halftone dots and, 73
object based, 452
for packaging printing, 168-169
problems with, 40
programs for, 43, 198, 257, 452-453
spreads, 42, 43, 156, 451
zone based, 452
TrapWise, 155
Triboelectrification, 125-126
TrueType fonts, 181, 252, 604-606. *See also* Fonts
Tulle, described, 15
Turkencalendar, 9
Type. *See also* Fonts
hot metal, 16-17
Typecasting machine, development of, 17
Typefaces, unofficial standards for, 157
Typesetter, 22, 23
Standard Industrial Classification for, 24-25
Typewriter, origin of, 16
Typography. *See also* Digital type; Fonts
design considerations for, 155-157, 169, 193, 256
recommendations for, 601-604

U

UCA. *See* Under color addition
UCC. *See* Universal Copyright Convention
UCR. *See* Under color removal
Ultraviolet (UV) light. *See also* Light
fluorescent agents and, 176
for ink drying, 117, 119

for plate exposure, 99
Under color addition (UCA), procedure for, 287-288
Under color removal (UCR), procedures for, 40, 287-288, 299, 317, 337
Uniform Resource Locator (URL), 519, 543. *See also* World Wide Web
absolute vs. relative, 544-545
Universal Copyright Convention (UCC), 466
UNIX platform, discussed, 196, 198
Unsharp masking
described, 335, 336
procedures for, 41, 302
URL. *See* Uniform Resource Locator
UV. *See* Ultraviolet light

V

Variable data printing. *See* Variable printing
Variable printing. *See also* Digital printing; On-demand printing
characteristics of, 132-134
Common and Unique Building Blocks (CUBB), 573
discussed, 134-136, 390-391, 560, 568-569
forms printing, 568-569, 571-572, 576
master-page/variable-fields implementation, 570-571
page-to-page variability, 569-570
Scitex VPS approach, 572-576
variable input (VI) document, 573-575
Vector files. *See also* PostScript; Raster files
described, 579
storage and transfer, 382
Vector graphics. *See also* Graphics
discussed, 229-230, 245, 254
Vector image, compared to raster image, 231, 233
Vector-based drawing programs
compared to pixel-based images, 33
examples of, 32
Vehicles. *See also* Ink
in ink, 115, 116
Vellum, 4, 7
Ventura Publisher, 42
Versioning. *See* Variable printing
Very-High-Performance Backbone Network Service, 621
Video RAM (VRAM). *See also* Monitors
described, 203, 207, 214
Vignettes, design considerations for, 161
Vinyl printing, 105, 139
Virtual office, 482-483
Viruses, 411
Vision
color experience and, 261-262, 263, 266, 275-276
color viewing and, 276-277
Vivid Semiconductor, 614
Vogelherd (Germany), 3
VRAM. *See* Video RAM

W

Waffling, 378
Wall Street Journal, 54, 488
Wallpaper, 92, 105
WAN. *See* Wide Area Network
Waterless process
in direct imaging, 102, 103
dot gain and, 78
for offset lithography, 98-101
Web fed press, 94. *See also* Offset lithography
gravure, 105
ink for, 118
paper requirements, 362, 370
waterless process for, 101
Web pages. *See also* World Wide Web
creation of, 29, 395, 521-522
Wescott, Charles, 17
Westover, George, 18
.WGM file extension, 182
Whiteness/brightness. *See also* Highlights
of substrates, 152, 176
Whitening, 377
Wide Area Network (WAN). *See also* Networks
discussed, 406-407
installing, 404, 431
Wide-format printing
electrostatic, 582-583
in general, 581-600

inkjet, 583-585
quality and speed considerations, 591-592
substrate options for, 587-590
superwide inkjet, 592
Windows 95/98, characteristics of, 197
Windows/PC platform
discussed, 196, 197, 211, 212
networks with, 410
Wireless communications. *See also* Communications; Telecommunications
discussed, 405-406
.WMF file format, 244
Wood block printing, 5, 7
Word processing programs
compared to page layout programs, 34, 42
text origination with, 33-34, 252, 253
Workflow
color management, 385
component files, 382
consolidated files, 382
corrections, 388
embedded elements, 382, 383
in general, 381-385
imposition, 386
islands of automation, 383-385
PDF file creation, 386
plate output, 388
PostScript file creation, 386, 394-399
preflighting, 385
printing, 389
proofing, 387-389
RIPping, 387, 392-396
storage, 389
telecommunications, 400
trapping, 386
variable printing, 390-391
Workflow models. *See also* Networks
described, 425-428
print production, 438-444
World Wide Web (WWW). *See also* Internet; Web pages
access speeds, 401-402
browsers, 498, 522, 528
commercial aspects of, 416, 458, 461, 462, 463, 469, 470-471, 483-484, 522
discussed, 497, 519, 520
image compression standards for, 245
image resolution for, 326
WORM. *See* Write-Once-Read-Many
Wozniak, Steven, 19
Wrapping paper, 92
Write-Once-Read-Many (WORM), described, 223-224

X

Xeikon, 126, 128, 133, 415, 570
discussed, 570-571, 598-599
Xerography. *See also* Electrostatic printer
color, 125, 126
discussed, 594-598
invention of, 582, 592-593
Xerox, electrostatic process, 125
Xerox Docucolor, 133, 415
Xerox Docutech, 110, 126, 133, 361, 475
XML. *See* eXtensible Markup Language

Y

YCC color system, 37

Z

Zines, 478
Zip disks, for storage and backup, 82, 218